A SILENT PATRIARCH

Kyrillos VI (1902–1971)

Life and Legacy

A Silent Patriarch

Kyrillos VI (1902–1971)
Life and Legacy

REV. DR DANIEL FANOUS

ST VLADIMIR'S SEMINARY PRESS

YONKERS, NEW YORK

2019

Library of Congress Control No: 2019943673

COPYRIGHT © 2019
ST VLADIMIR'S SEMINARY PRESS
575 Scarsdale Road, Yonkers, NY 10707
1-800-204-2665
www.svspress.com

ISBN 978–088141–649–7 (paper)
ISBN 978–088141–650–3 (electronic)

PRINTED IN THE UNITED STATES OF AMERICA

To my children, Chloe, Luke, and Mia:
May you see beyond the icons on the wall.

Table of Contents

Abbreviations

BBG   Monir Atteya Shehata. *Biography of Bishop Gregorious* [in Arabic]. 3 vols. Cairo: Association of Anba Gregorious, 2005.

BDC   *Between Desert and City: The Coptic Orthodox Church Today.* Edited by Nelly van Doorn-Harder and Kari Vogt. Eugene, OR: Wipf & Stock, 2012.

CE   *The Coptic Encyclopedia.* Edited by Aziz Suryal Atiya. 8 volumes with continuous numeration. New York: Macmillan, 1991.

FRC-1 and FRC-2   Father Raphael Collection, Part 1 and Father Raphael Collection, Part 2. Archives of Patriarch Kyrillos' correspondence; see "Note on Sources" at the beginning of the Bibliography.

HS   *Harbor of Salvation*, periodical written and edited by Patriarch Kyrillos when he was Monk Mina el-Baramousy.

NPNF²   Nicene and Post-Nicene Fathers, Second Series. Edited by Philip Schaff and Henry Wace. Reprint, Peabody, MA: Hendrickson Publishers, 1995.

RC-1 and RC-2   Reda Collection, Part 1 (2015) and Reda Collection, Part 2 (2016). Archive of Patriarch Kyrillos' correspondence; see "Note on Sources" at the beginning of the Bibliography.

SSC   Saint Samuel Collection. Archive of Patriarch Kyrillos' correspondence from the Monastery of Saint Samuel; see "Note on Sources" at the beginning of the Bibliography.

Preface

". . . for you died, and your life is hidden with Christ in God."
—Colossians 3.3

"**Y**OUANNIS OF GIZA HAS—" yelled the men as they frantically knocked on the doors of the patriarchate, "Bishop Youannis . . . has been shredded to pieces on the train tracks of Cairo!" Dawood, the doorkeeper, flung the doors open—only to find himself set upon. The men bound the nearby guards and silenced the servants. Confusion embraced the patriarchate. Awakened by the commotion, the patriarch, Yusab II, emerged from his quarters. Torn between astonishment and disbelief, he stared at his would-be abductors. Yusab was forced to sign his abdication before being violently bundled into a waiting taxi, only narrowly escaping gunshots—according to one mildly sensational report—from security forces in pursuit. On that night, July 24, 1954, the elderly patriarch was abducted, as strange as it is to say.

When he was eventually found by the police at a monastery in Old Cairo, the Synod seemed to react with ambiguity. A year later they "relieved" Yusab of his duties and exiled him to a desert monastery. For almost four years there would be no patriarch upon the throne. The exile was a deeply tragic moment in the history of the Coptic Church—and yet, at the same time, an apt summation and embodiment of the previous half-century. So painful was that moment that it has, for the most part, been willfully ignored, rarely spoken of, and (somewhat inevitably) piously forgotten.

This is, regrettably, where this story must begin. To deny, forget, or ignore this mournful period—which might well have otherwise brought Coptic Christianity to its knees—is to do an injustice to the seismic shift in the Church before and after Pope Kyrillos VI (1902–1971). Kyrillos inherited a broken, weeping, and profusely bleeding Church from his abducted and later exiled predecessor. Yet, just twelve short years later, Kyrillos stood at the head of a nearly impossible spiritual revolution. What began in a cave deep within the desert continued in a small and unassuming house in Old Cairo, and ended in the transformation of an entire Church. It is, to my knowledge, one of the most profound, beautiful, pervasive, and overwhelmingly spiritual revolutions in the history of Christianity since the Apostolic Age. This is the story of Kyrillos VI, a most unlikely patriarch, a silent urban recluse.

* * *

I am utterly convinced that no one, not even his closest disciples, knew anything of Kyrillos' inner life. How well could anyone know a man who was virtually silent, lived quietly, and was perpetually consumed by prayer and liturgy? Even those who knew him best insist they knew him not at all. Other than his confessor, Kyrillos confided in no man; he sought refuge and consolation in only one place, the eucharistic altar. For a half-century, it was there, daily, even when he was an elderly patriarch, that he remained hidden, silent, known only to his God.

This is both the principal difficulty in writing this critical biography, and the absolute necessity behind writing it. The years of silence have meant that only that which was public, manifest, and observable—the tens of thousands of mesmerizing and inexplicable miracles at his hands—have formed the image of Kyrillos VI. On June 20, 2013, forty-two years after his death, Kyrillos was canonized. Some eighteen volumes of miracle accounts have emerged, yet until now, only a few of his writings and letters have been known, appreciated, and studied. The story of this unique man—his asceticism, virtue, wisdom, and profound capacity to disciple, along with the intriguing story of the Church's transformation during his patriarchate—has slowly faded into a mass of the extraordinary, supernatural, and mystical miracles. Moreover, those who personally knew him—as much as he could really be known—unfortunately, will soon not be with us. And so Kyrillos, for the next generation, like mine, will inevitably be known only as an icon on the wall—for many, perhaps, he already is.

It is no exaggeration to say that there is no figure so loved by Copts (and by not a few Muslims) as Kyrillos. His photographs adorn almost every Coptic home; almost every family counts at least one Kyrillos (after his patriarchal name) or a Mina (after his monastic name); and most, if not all, count the saint among their intercessors, too. Still, he remains hidden. To give some sense of this, in my research, not one of his closest disciples, friends, or even family members could recall the name of Kyrillos' mother—his blind nephew was my saving grace in this respect—and many were shocked to discover that Kyrillos had sisters. This is, of course, indicative of just how silent and hidden this man was—despite being patriarch. What, then, of his inner life, his vision, his method of reform? Until now, they have remained enshrouded in mystery.

I have lived for the last four years with this yoke tied to my neck—a yoke that was at once sweet, light, and excruciating. I knew the difficulty of the task ahead and its importance for the next generation, and I felt, with some trepidation, that it would be the "revealing" of a man who is undoubtedly closer to the hearts of Copts than any other. In this respect, at times, this story has been painful to write. Kyrillos, unknown to most, suffered from the day he entered the monastery until the day he died. He was persecuted, rejected, ridiculed, and mocked for the greater part of his life at the hands of other monks, clergy, and bishops. For many of my readers, I am sure, a whitewashing of history would have sufficed, the painful days should have been forgotten, the scandalous episodes should have been ignored, and those who plotted against him should have been rehabilitated to preserve their pious memory. But I can think of no greater injustice to Kyrillos than this. He was born, formed, ordained, and consecrated in a most bleak period of the Church. To attempt to unwrinkle the sheets of history is to remain ignorant of the life of Kyrillos—a life lived in suffering, self-emptying, and crucifixion. To those who would object and prefer a more subdued telling of his life—forgetting for the moment that it would be ahistorical and disingenuous—I can only gently ask what is more profound, edifying, and transformative: that Kyrillos was a holy patriarch in a healthy, robust, and immaculate Church, or that he was a holy patriarch who healed and transformed a suffering and feverish Church? Or, to put it somewhat differently, can one dare contemplate the Resurrection without the Crucifixion?

I am persuaded that theology is most convincing, palpable, and best told in the *lives* of those who lived theology in the truest sense of that word, as an encounter with God. Biography is, in my estimation, the greatest theology, for it is incarnational theology. It is for a similar reason, no doubt, that saints, for the everyday believer, hold such an inestimable place in the life of the Church. And so, for a life to be theology, it must be true in every respect. But there are other reasons.

Recent studies (as we shall see in chapter 9) on the nature of ecclesial reform—for instance, that of Ladner or Congar—have identified that the earliest Christian idea of reform, whether in the New Testament or patristic eras, is that of *personal* ascetic reform, rather than institutional reform. If authentic and intrinsically Christian senses of reform are ultimately *personal*, in the pursuit of the realization of the image of God that is Christ, then any explication of that remarkable transformation that took place in mid-twentieth century Egypt must itself be intensely personal—in a word, *biographical.*

This narrative will take the following structure. Part I describes the prepatriarchal life of Kyrillos as the basis of his method of reform. Chapter 1 details his childhood, early influences, and path to the monastery. Chapters 2 and 3 employ newly discovered correspondence and autobiographical fragments to describe some of the earliest "turning points" during his first years as a monk and hermit. At this point, we encounter two influences that would never leave Kyrillos: the notion of solitude in the thought of Isaac the Syrian, and the Eucharist. Chapter 4 follows him to a deserted windmill on the outskirts of Cairo, where his gift of miracles first became well known. Chapter 5 analyzes the intersection of several movements in the unassuming Church of St Menas in Old Cairo, where Fr Mina the Recluse (as he was then known) became the confessor of a most illustrious group of university students.

A somewhat melancholic interlude in chapter 6—the unfortunate history of the aforementioned abduction of Yusab—precedes Part II, Kyrillos' years as patriarch. Chapter 7 narrates his consecration as patriarch and his first moves toward reform, as well as his confrontation—which would mark his patriarchate—with dissension and corruption. Chapter 8 examines Kyrillos' approach to "extraecclesial" forces: his unexpected "method" of reform in granting autocephaly to the Ethiopian Church; befriending a Muslim president in the face of the emergence of the Muslim Brotherhood; and the "mummy's curse" of the *waqf* (monastic endowments), which saw the previous patriarchs tragically contend with the *maglis al-melli* (Community Council). Chapter 9 is the climax of the narrative. It carefully explores the *kenotic* ("self-emptying") ecclesiology of Kyrillos, which underlies his method of reform in the persons of his closest disciples. This method drew upon the earliest (and now somewhat forgotten) Christian idea of reform—that of *personal* ascetic reform—which Kyrillos adapted as a unique means of reaching out beyond the traditional sphere of ascetic influence. This chapter is intensely personal, as it follows Kyrillos' interactions with his illustrious disciples. The biography concludes with chapter 10, which details the unprecedented apparitions of the Theotokos at Zeitoun and their meaning to both Kyrillos and the Egyptian nation, and the text ends with the final moments of Kyrillos' remarkable life and his unceasing care for the Church.

* * *

Despite being a Coptic Orthodox priest and having in hand a letter from the current patriarch, Tawadros II—who was most encouraging of my research—I still found Egypt to be an impenetrable place. This cannot be overstated. Truth, falsity, imaginings, and fantasy all seem to merge indiscernibly (and comically). In pursuit of the few original letters and writings from Kyrillos' hand, and in the hope of other almost legendary primary sources, my journey took me from the Monastery of St Menas in the Western Desert, to Kyrillos' family home in bustling Alexandria, to the cryptic patriarchal archives in Cairo, to the Monastery of St Samuel some two hundred kilometers (124 miles) farther south, as well as through countless other monasteries, parishes, villages, and homes.

In Egypt I discovered a methodology of sorts. It may be best described as the "seven ways." Each discovery was somewhat of a miracle. For example, I once encouraged a dear relative of Kyrillos' to part with a beloved collection of letters with repeated assurances, despite persistent denials of their existence, only to hear his wife hours later, after seven different lines of reasoning, unexpectedly divulge their contents and whereabouts. On another occasion, though this account really cannot do the reality any justice, I interviewed a blessed and elderly monk in the desert west of Alexandria, and I gently questioned him about the possibility of other letters. The monk, unsurprisingly, insisted they had been destroyed. Seven "ways" later, he dug up hundreds of letters, as well as an intact copy of Kyrillos' original autobiography, quite literally from the ground. One shudders at the thought of their eventual fate had they not been discovered—an inestimable treasure of documents left to rot, or, worse still, simply to be forgotten. On another morning—and again, without overstating the drama—I sat in Kyrillos' old monastic cell at the Monastery of St Samuel, sipping coffee while negotiating access via a satellite phone that only had reception an hour away on some mountaintop; reassuring that breaking a lock to the cell for which the key had been misplaced was not sacrilege; pleading, begging (and occasionally demanding) in seven different ways, in several languages, before noticing a momentary glance, despite anxious protests, to the corner of an unassuming room where lay a pile of documents, at the bottom of which were a hundred or so letters of Kyrillos never before seen. Yet again, this is a mere intimation of the intensity, prolongation, and desperation of those moments. In between were adventures in the desert, frequently misleading trails, walls of silence, monks of obstruction, encounters with genuine holy men and women, mesmerizing interviews with those who had lived with Kyrillos, and an evolving joy that will never leave my heart.

From the moment I began that journey, a monk by the name of Fr Philemon el-Antony stood, drove, suffered, translated, and begged by my side. No words can describe my love for him and my thanks to him. Our adventures, conversations, discoveries, and frequent bouts of uncontrollable and hysterical laughter will never be forgotten. This work would have been impossible without him. For much of that journey, we were joined by another monk, Fr Anthony St Shenouda, who was the first, many years ago, to suggest to me this current study, and so I began gathering invaluable sources well before I had even committed to the project. Countless others, such as Terry Lovat, Nelly van Doorn-Harder, Kathleen McPhillips, Fr Chad Hatfield, Fr Benedict Churchill, Fr Ignatius Green, Nabih Fanous, Mona Fanous, Samuel Kaldas, Elizabeth Oliver, Fr Paul Fanous, Fr Antonios Kaldas, Fr Raphael Ava Mina, "Reda" Marcos Atta, and Fr Tadros Yacoub Malaty, assisted me morally, financially, academically, and spiritually. Others, such as my spiritual father, Fr Jacob Magdy, who has always seen in me what I could not, forever encouraged my unconventional ways. I am, as always, indebted to my beautiful wife, Sherry, who, I am certain, still does not regret marrying me. Finally (and the last will be first), I would like to make mention of a delightful and indefatigable lady who came to me in most unexpected circumstances. She forbade me to make mention of her name. For several years, she meticulously translated, without fee, thousands of pages of documents to assist my research. My only consolation for the sorrow of not being able to name her is that I witnessed her irrepressible joy at being the first person in half a century to read the letters of her beloved patron saint.

As I close, I should mention two final concerns. Those letters, documents, records, ledgers, memoirs, and accounts, few of which have ever been seen (in any language), hidden for half a century, represent our only window into the hidden life of Kyrillos.[1] They provide an exceedingly rare disclosure of his inner life, vision, thought, and struggles. The first concern of many, consequently, will be whether there is any tension between the image of Kyrillos that emerges from the (*unknown*) primary sources and the (*known*) secondary literature. Do the letters agree, for instance, with the biography written by his brother? Or does a "different" Kyrillos emerge?

It appears that for the most part they do in fact agree.[2] This is not surprising. Both Kyrillos' brother, Hanna Youssef Atta, and his later disciple, Fr Raphael Ava Mina, had access to many of these letters (indeed, they were their sole custodians), and no doubt they made use of them as they prepared their respective biographies. But, importantly, they each had access to *certain* groups of letters—

not *all* the extant (or at least discovered) primary sources.[3] This biography will, therefore, seek to bring together these various and mostly unknown sources in giving voice to Kyrillos—an account that I hope is both faintly familiar and at once refreshing, if not curiously unexpected.

A second and perhaps more immediate fear of those who were "encouraged" to part with these exquisite documents was that hidden within them would be found some event, reference, issue, or mention that would tarnish the reputation of Kyrillos. To that concern, I can only reply, after poring over every word written in the letters, memoirs, and documents, and interviewing dozens of eyewitnesses with various agendas, that—and I have no reason to lie—I found not one such issue. According to the evidence before me, the man was a saint in every sense of the word.

* * *

I had seven ways into his world, but Kyrillos, it appears, had only one way: *prayer*. And so, even though I was granted this gift of seeing something of his inner life, it seems to me, no doubt as a vanishing endpoint, that there remains a certain transcendence, ultimately a hiddenness, to Kyrillos. And this is due not simply to his unceasing preference for silence, nor to his perpetual escape to solitude even while living in the city. No, I feel—and this is perhaps the most genuine thing I can say—that the man might only be known, studied, and properly appreciated by those who have followed his path. Not, I might add, necessarily the path of a monastic recluse, but the path of living singularly, purposefully, and absolutely for God—a path of hiddenness, stillness, smallness, of being unknown to all but God. If there is one fault of this study (other than any errors, which are of course mine), it is this: a personal incapacity and weakness in following that path, and for this, I ask for prayer and forgiveness.

Notes

[1] I hope to publish these as a second volume, an edited collection of letters and works.

[2] These tensions or disagreements between the primary and secondary literature—as well as the overwhelming points of consensus—will be dealt with implicitly (and at times explicitly) throughout this study, on occasion within the text, though predominantly as footnotes. Most often, it should be noted, there are not actually tensions, but rather differences in detail, perspective, or purpose.

[3] For a brief discussion of sources, see the final appendix: "A Note on Sources."

PART I

A Life Hidden in God:
Monastic Formation (1902–1959)

He Is One of Our Stock:
Early Years (1902–1927)

The Young Azer: Early Childhood, 1902–1912

> "Fathers and mothers:
> Go and lead your child by the hand into the church."
> —*St John Chrysostom*

"SCORNED AS I AM, I was born in August 1902. My parents raised me in the fear of God."[1] It was in the sweltering heat of Damanhur that Azer Youssef Atta was born. He was cast into a world that only years earlier had been deeply scarred by the "temporary" British occupation in Egypt, and he was baptized into an acutely fractured Church in the wake of decades of internal dissent. It was a landscape that was seething with nationalist and ecclesial discontent. The words *revival, reformation,* and *revolution* were resonating throughout the Egyptian landscape, from street to church to mosque. Every established institution and echelon—political and religious—was under threat.

* * *

Azer's family members claim to have hailed originally from the village of Zouk in the governorate of Souhag, before being displaced during the latter era of the Mamluk Sultanate in Cairo (1251–1571). They eventually migrated to Tukh al-Nasara (literally the "region of the Christians") in the governorate of Menoufia.[2] It was here that they became known as the Ziki family, in reference to their original village. Although most accounts claim with peculiar certainty that it was here in Tukh al-Nasara that Azer was born, the evidence suggests otherwise.[3] Towards the end of the nineteenth century, before his birth on August 2, 1902, the family moved and settled further north at Damanhur in the governorate of Beheira. Azer's birth certificate not only places the town of his birth registry in Beheira (and not Menoufia) but also records his father's governorate of residence as the very same Beheira.[4] Perhaps this almost unanimous misconception betrays some mild reimagining in that his supposed birthplace, Tukh al-Nasara, was a "Christian village" because of its name and because two previous patriarchs had also been born there, namely Matthew III (1631–1646) and John XVI (1676–1718).

Damanhur, the birthplace of the future patriarch, a city of Lower Egypt, was originally dedicated to the ancient Egyptian god Horus. It lies some 160 kilometers (100 miles) northwest of Cairo and 70 kilometers (44 miles) southeast of Alexandria, at the center of the western Nile Delta. Now a boisterous hub of agricultural industry and transportation, at the turn of the twentieth century it was home to wealthy landowners endowed with burgeoning and richly cultivated lands. Azer's father, Youssef Atta (1859–1941), was a general manager for one such landowner. He directed his agricultural and commercial trade along the lines of three bordering provinces in Gharbeya, Menoufia, and Beheira.[5] This accounts for the numerous familial relocations during Azer's early childhood, which were somewhat uncharacteristic of the age.

Youssef Atta was born in or around 1859.[6] In the memoirs of his son Hanna, as well as in the recollections of his grandson Marcos, he is remembered as a pious deacon of "exemplary behavior, excellent voice, and outstanding calligraphy."[7] He was a traditional man; diligently observed the Church rites; was adept in Church chant; and hallowed the art of penmanship, by scribing many Arabic and Coptic books in fine calligraphy.[8] His work and success as a general manager, perhaps a reflection of his love of mathematics, ensured a comfortable middle-class upbringing for his growing family.

Azer's mother, Esther Atta (1870–1912), was warmly remembered in her son's memoirs as an "ideal parent with respect to raising her children."[9] She carefully and painstakingly planted the seeds of love between her children and scarcely had to resort to punishing them. In the evenings the family would gather to read Scripture and reflect upon the lives of the saints and martyrs. Icons filled every corner of their house, and the lives of these saints permeated every nook of the imagination of her children. The family lived, as it were, from the feast of one saint to another.[10]

A few years into his parents' marriage, Hanna Youssef Atta (1895–1976), the first of three brothers (and the primary biographer of the future patriarch), was born. Following his father's love of mathematics, he was a successful accountant by trade. Being seven years older than Azer, he was in many ways more a beloved father figure than a brother, and later he would provide perhaps the only credible insight into Azer's childhood.[11] Unknown to all extant biographical accounts, the next-born was a girl by the name of Mariam (1900–1963), and not Azer, as is generally assumed. Youssef and Esther had, in fact, three sons and three daughters. Oddly, these three daughters are not mentioned in any of the Arabic or English biographical accounts, including Hanna's memoirs, a fact that undoubtedly reflects what was then a strictly patriarchal society. Azer (1902–1971) was, accordingly, the third-born child and was baptized at St Mary's Church in Mahmoudeya, Beheira.[12] He was followed by two further sisters, Martha (1903–1955) and Makhtoura (1905–1987), and a final brother, Mikhail (1906–1975), who would go on to become a much-loved priest.[13]

After the premature death of his wife, Youssef remarried and had two more daughters, Aziza and Shafia.[14] Azer was therefore reared in a house of six (and then eight) siblings, teeming with life and noise. One thing may be said for certain of his childhood, from his own handwritten autobiographical comment: "My parents raised me in the fear of God."[15] His childhood in a bustling household may also in some small part explain Azer's quiet and yet embryonic desire for an eventual life of solitude.

* * *

We have a first glimpse of the young boy just before his fourth birthday. That day, the Atta family received a visitor who would irrevocably change—or as the accounts themselves claim, prophetically announce—the path of Azer's life. Almost simultaneously, perhaps in the very same month, Egypt (as we shall soon see) would be shocked and convulsed by the infamous Denshawai Incident.

Hanna, Azer's brother, recalls that the family home was always open to monks from the nearby Baramous Monastery as they traveled the country to collect donations.[16] Before Azer had celebrated his fourth birthday, in 1906, an elderly monk by the name Fr Tadros el-Baramousy knocked on the family door. The monk was accompanied by a certain Saweros, who assisted him because of his failing vision. The boy Azer was mesmerized. He gazed in innocent curiosity at the monk's long white beard. After a brief period of restrained observation, as is characteristic of children, Azer found immense joy in climbing up and smothering the elderly monk. The sweltering desert night, though tempered by the coastal breezes typical of the region, drew long. Oblivious to the mundane conversation of adults that often persists long into the night, the child fell asleep on the monk's lap. Esther, rather embarrassed, quietly mumbled an apology and immediately made to carry away the sleeping Azer. Fr Tadros serenely protested and looked her in the eyes. His words would never be forgotten: "Let him sleep here because he is from our stock. *He is one of us*."[17] Esther, startled, with tears welling in her eyes as she looked at her sleeping son, retreated. She, unfortunately, would not live to see the words fulfilled.

Hanna, though only eleven years old at the time, noticed that his brother began to change. "From that day on," he wrote in his memoirs, "Azer truly was one of them."[18] The young boy began to act in a manner that his family initially found to be confronting, if not disturbing. Whenever they would buy him new clothes, he would refuse to wear them unless he could cover the clothing with a black *galabeya*, an Egyptian cloak that resembled the black monastic cassock. Though over time his parents would eventually come to terms with his changed demeanor, they "felt sadness for his insistence and stubbornness."[19] By the time Azer was tonsured as an *epsaltos* (chanter) at Archangel Michael's Church in Damanhur, his parents had reluctantly accepted these changes in their little boy. Azer's own autobiographical remarks (written decades later) similarly suggest a very early change or "turning point," one that is remarkably consistent with the biographical accounts. "Since my early youth," he wrote, "I was inclined to quietness, seclusion, and I would wear black clothing."[20]

A year later, in 1907, following Youssef's work as a general manager, the family relocated southeast, back to Tukh al-Nasara in the governorate of Menoufia, eighty kilometers (50 miles) north of Cairo. They would live there for the next few years, and there the young Azer completed most of his primary schooling.[21] It was also there that the interior revolution that was taking place in the boy began to convict his family deeply. Hanna preserves one such incident that expresses his family's initial irritation and eventual contrition on account of Azer.

As is customary in many Egyptian households, the day before Great Lent is an occasion of great feasting, whereby the very last remains of all non-fasting foods are consumed in a joyous celebration. On one such eve of Great Lent, Azer arrived home from primary school and walked into the dining room to behold a lavish and exorbitant feast.[22] "Why should we have an abundance of food," questioned Azer, "while others have plain bread?" His family hardly expected such a reaction from a ravenous schoolboy. Azer turned to his mother in disappointment and added, "How can we eat this luxurious food while a poor Kurdish family lives next to us?" Their neighbors were an elderly Turkish Muslim family that had no source of income and survived on the bare necessities. Encouraged, conceivably by his mother's silent dismay, and with delight returning to his face, he continued, "It would be good for us to offer them this food for Christ's sake. Tomorrow we will fast and be satisfied with a modest meal." According to the memoir, though surprised and famished by this point, his family members could not withstand Azer's integrity and fervor. His parents immediately gathered their feast and brought it to their Kurdish neighbors, whose only response to the act of generosity was to kiss and bless the young Azer.[23]

This rather ordinary and yet moving incident is revealing as it is telling. In one sense it discloses and makes palpable the interior ascesis and transformation that was taking place in the boy Azer. But in another sense, it prefigures the kenotic (self-emptying) selflessness of the future patriarch, as well as laying bare his exceedingly generous charity for all, Christian or Muslim. Here, already, we find a remarkable and organic continuity with his eventual ecclesial vision.

Some time later, while Azer was still a schoolboy in Tukh al-Nasara, a local Muslim sheikh, Ahmed Ghalloush, visited the family house and suggested that Azer attend the local *kuttab* during his school holidays.[24] This was a form of elementary school often attached to either a church or a mosque, one that relied heavily on rote memorization, penmanship, and arithmetic. By the twentieth century the *kuttab* existed in a modified form, often attended outside of the more mainstream "primary school" hours.

Youssef and Esther consented to the sheikh's request. Azer attended every day and befriended the sheikh, who quietly observed the young schoolboy's unusual fascination with the Scriptures. Hanna recalls that the sheikh (one may assume for the mere novelty and challenge of memorizing something unfamiliar) suggested to Azer that he should locate a copy of the Gospel of John. To his parents' amazement, by the end of the holidays, not only had Azer memorized the entire Gospel of John, but so had the sheikh.[25] The skill of memorization that this honorable Muslim taught Azer would serve him for the rest of his life. The experience and friendship of both Azer's Muslim neighbors and teacher would mark his ecclesial attitude of love and openness, which would prove necessary in a world confronted by the birth of the Muslim Brotherhood.

* * *

These formative experiences, at once unassuming and yet arresting, depict a family with a sense of evolving greatness among them. In a few years, the young child Azer had changed. There was a sense that he was different, almost fated. But how or why was still entirely unforeseeable.

His mother, Esther, nurtured and cultivated a loving formative environment for this young boy who would one day become patriarch. Her love would be short-lived but long-treasured. On an untimely day in 1912, when Azer was only ten years old, Esther passed away prematurely. The unspeakable agony of his mother's death is lost in history. We have no record, document, or memoir of how Azer or any of his siblings dealt with or reacted to that tragic day. That the loss would indelibly mark the young boy is certain, but it is impossible to say how. What may be said with some certitude is that Esther perceived and pondered the interior transformation in her child that would one day be made manifest in the revival and transformation of her beloved Church. She would not see that day, but she had no need. She had already seen its beginnings in her little boy.

St Menas: A Surprising Patron

> "I have seen sin and corruption. . . . I have left it and flee far away.
> I will abide in the desert and I shall see my God."
> —*St Menas the Martyr*

BEFORE HER UNTIMELY DEATH, Esther offered her young son an unusual and rarely noticed gift. It was a courtesy that would be of immeasurable significance in the life of her son. She introduced him to a once illustrious saint who at the turn of the century was largely forgotten.

It was merely an introduction, for in the Christian tradition a patron saint is not always chosen—the saint often chooses. Despite the name a child is given, the icons that surround the cradle, and the intercessors through whom the parents pray, in the end, it may be the saint who determines and adopts. At least, this is true in the life of Azer. For reasons unclear, the relatively unknown St Menas fascinated the young boy, and within a brief period became *his* saint.

* * *

Though much has been written of Azer's relationship to St Menas, little has been said of its beginnings and implications. As will become clear, the relationship was rather unconventional. Seldom does the affinity to one's patron saint take on such an intense and exceptional character. St Menas functions in the life of Azer, as witnessed by his biographers as well as in Azer's own words and thought, as a present, tangible, and living friend. Whether in the apparent and abundant miraculous healings, or in the almost obsessive concern for constructing a monastery for the saint, or in the numerous pleadings for intercession, the figure of Menas is ever present in Azer's life. The relationship moves well beyond the ordinary bounds of an intercessory relationship (if one may ever call it ordinary). It was somehow more real; strangely palpable; and, for most witnesses, mesmerizing, if not convicting. It was, in a word, unusual.

Most sources mark the beginnings of Azer's affinity to St Menas at the moment of his tonsure as a monk in February 1928, when he was given the name of Fr Mina.[26] But it began far earlier and may be traced to an annual pilgrimage of Azer's family. In Hanna's memoirs, he recalls that their mother, Esther, engendered a love of the saints in the hearts of her children and that the family would live earnestly from feast day to feast day of these beloved saints. Each year, in particular, they would travel to Ibyar, twenty-eight kilometers (17 miles) northeast in Kafr al-Zayat, Beheira, to celebrate the feast of a largely unknown saint.[27]

We can with some certainty date the annual pilgrimage to the years that the family lived at Tukh al-Nasara (1907–1910).[28] It was during these week-long expeditions that the young boy Azer, from the ages of five to eight, would become infatuated with St Menas. In the memoirs of his brother, these were festal experiences that "left a deep impression on Azer's heart."[29] In late November each year, Youssef and Esther, with their six children trailing behind, would walk to Ibyar, a journey of five and a half hours. There, they would celebrate the *maulid* ("birthday") of St Menas. The Coptic Church, like other Orthodox churches, "saw in the martyrdom of one of her saints his [or her] birthday."[30] It was the "sacred birth" into life everlasting.

The *maulid* was marked by a period of open-air festivity, liturgical celebration, and an air of expectation. It was far more inclusive than other religious events. Families, Christian and Muslim alike, would bring an oblation or donation to the church of the saint as a token of their devotion and prayerful hopes.[31] St Menas' *maulid* would take place in and around his church in Ibyar (meaning "several wells"), which was situated in the midst of multiple farming properties.[32] Azer's family, along with other pilgrims, took advantage of the vast surrounding fields to make camp for the festival week that would culminate in the celebration of the saint's feast day on November 24.[33] It was a festival in every sense. While there were mandatory liturgical celebrations inside the two-domed church, outside could be found live music, theater, primitive fireworks, much-loved delicacies, and all manner of amusements. Children (and, one may imagine, their parents in tow) would have delighted and basked in the assorted sounds, sights, and aromas. Yet, Azer was not to be found among them.

Apparently oblivious to the outside festivities, the young boy is remembered by his family as remaining decidedly within the church.[34] What happened inside this church during these week-long pilgrimages is impossible to determine. It may well have been rather ordinary and uninteresting, or perhaps something more. But the effects upon the young boy were clearly recognizable in at least two measures: his brother discerned that the experience "left a deep impression" on Azer; and second, from then on, a most unusual relationship proceeds that touches every fabric of his history and existence. Quite understandably, St Menas warrants an extended introduction.

* * *

When Azer became "acquainted" with St Menas—possibly to the surprise of many today—the saint was little-known. Other than the annual *maulid* celebrated in Ibyar, he did not figure greatly in the Coptic imagination. Why, then, Azer's infatuation with this largely unknown saint?

Things had not always been so. St Menas had once practically been the "patron saint of Lower Egypt."[35] An entire city essentially grew, evolved, and flourished around his shrine. In earlier times, his shrine at Mariout, just outside Alexandria, was counted as one of only two martyrs' shrines of international reputation, and that of "Saint Menas was undoubtedly the more celebrated one."[36] Over the centuries, in variously unfortunate circumstances, Menas' shrine, along with the popularity of its saint, faded into ruins hidden deep within the desert. Only in 1906, oddly the same year as Fr Tadros-el-Baramousy's apparent monastic prophecy, did a German team headed by C. M. Kaufmann discover and explore the ruins at the site of Abu Mena.[37]

Excavating, as it were, the *vita* ("life") of Menas is similarly daunting. Extensive accounts exist in the Greek, Coptic, Arabic, Old Nubian, Ethiopian, Latin, Syrian, and Armenian languages.[38] Azer, evidently, would have been familiar with only the Arabic *Synaxarion*, Coptic *Martyrdom*, and quite possibly the Coptic *Encomium*.[39] The historicity or hagiographic analysis of these texts is, at least for our present concern, less important than the tradition that Azer would have received growing up in early-twentieth-century Egypt.

Menas (285–309) was born at the end of the third century of the Christian era in Nikiou, twenty kilometers (12 miles) south of modern-day Cairo. His parents, Eudoxius and Euphemia, were without children. Euphemia, barren and distraught, went before the icon of the Theotokos on her feast day and besought her in tears. A voice was heard from the icon, uttering a single word: "Amen." Euphemia ran to her husband and, elated, told him what she had heard. In the expected time her prayers were answered, and she delivered a boy. They had hoped to give him the name of his grandfather, but Euphemia recalled the word she had heard from the icon and called him "Menas," a play on the word she had heard ("Amen").⁴⁰ The family would eventually move to Phrygia, where Menas mastered the Scriptures and was reared in the mysteries of Christianity. When he was only eleven years old, his father passed away; three years later his mother shared the same fate. Following in the footsteps of his father, Menas entered the military, serving under a certain Firmilianus. The Greek accounts add that he "possessed considerable mental ability and was of a fine and commanding stature."⁴¹

According to the Coptic *Martyrdom*, in AD 303, when Emperor Diocletian began to persecute the Christians, Menas felt drawn to the desert:

> And they were compelling everyone, entering their houses and dragging them all to offer sacrifices to the vile gods. And the holy Abba Menas was a God-fearing man. When he saw the deception of the evil one, he could not bear [to] endure to witness these abominations, but he withdrew from his regiment to a solitary retreat where he remained in tranquillity, worshipping God with his whole heart, since he did not wish to be a spectator to their polluted worship.⁴²

The Coptic *Encomium* notes that before he left for the desert, he distributed all his wealth and properties to those in need.⁴³ In another account, he is heard to cry out as he leaves, "I have seen sin and corruption. . . . I have left it and flee far away. I will abide in the desert and *I shall see my God*."⁴⁴ These are words that resonate when taken in the context of the epiphany that Menas receives while he is in the desert. Here the Coptic *Encomium* and Ethiopian *Martyrdom* accounts converge:

> And he dwelt there for many days in great privation. . . . And after a time the grace of God *lighted upon him*, and he saw heaven open, and the interior

thereof was filled with angels of light who were carrying crowns of light and laying them upon the heads of those who had consummated their martyrdom. . . . And St Menas longed to become a martyr for the name of our Lord Jesus Christ. And he heard: "Blessed art thou Menas . . . thou shalt receive crowns incorruptible, like [those of] the Holy Trinity . . . one for thy virginity, and one for thy patient endurance, and for thy martyrdom."[45]

The revelation continues that Menas' name shall be honored by people from around the world. Many will come and take "refuge in thy church which shall be built in the land of Egypt, and *works of power shall be made manifest*, and wonderful things, and signs, and healings shall take place through thy holy body."[46]

Menas, without delay, departs his solitude for the city and dramatically interrupts the occasion of games and festival at Cotinaeum in Asia Minor, announcing, "I have come to those who have sought me. . . . I am Menas, a holy man, a servant of my Lord Jesus Christ."[47] The governor, rather disconcerted, asked what manner of person this was. Some began to recognize Menas and told the governor. After the perturbed governor interrogates Menas, he attempts to force him to sacrifice to the pagan gods. The saint is staunch in his refusal. The governor has him flogged and bound upside down, and his flesh torn at by instruments of torture. Menas is immovable. He is then tortured with fire, dragged over iron stakes, and flogged a second time, severely.

Finally, the governor is informed by one of his servants that Menas is of the Christians, who are known to "never turn backward," and as such the governor's efforts to force the saint to apostasy are futile. Now furious, the governor calls for the execution of the saint. Menas looks up to heaven, stretches out his hands, and cries out to his God,

> I give thanks unto thee, O God of heaven, Jesus Christ, because thou hast neither forsaken me, nor removed thyself far from me . . . and because thou hast given me the power not to deny thy holy name. And now keep thou me in this hour, and grant me strength to endure to my end.[48]

Moments later, in the fateful year AD 309, "with his face shining with light," Menas is beheaded.

* * *

The story of St Menas, as may be expected, hardly ends there—neither in the history of the Menas shrine nor in the life of the young Azer.

It would not be an exaggeration to claim that Menas—admittedly, more than one and a half millennia removed—was the most important figure in the life of Azer. Their lives intersect in ways that are rarely noticed, if ever properly explored. Perhaps for willful fear of the unknown, or for inadvertent ignorance, most biographical sources shy away from anything more than a superficial treatment of this unique relationship. Assessing the claim of how a patron saint may interact with the physical world is somewhat of a non-issue in this setting. What is important is Azer's conscious and rational awareness of the irrevocable bond that he shared with Menas. In that vein, a few brief and pertinent claims may now be sketched.

In an icon of St Menas, based upon the ampullae (water flasks) and manuscript folios that bear his image, he is depicted in a tunic, wearing a belt over a cloak, parts of which are braided. In his hand, he bears a long spear pointed to the ground, and above his head are three crowns, one each for his *virginity*, *solitude*, and *martyrdom*.

Two of these crowns are rarely, at least not sufficiently, appreciated. A first hint may be found here of why Azer felt an irresistible affinity to the little-known saint. Celibacy and solitude, it seems, were two movements that Azer's heart had been beating since childhood. In his own words: "Since my early youth I was inclined to quietness, seclusion, and would wear black clothing [i.e., the monastic cassock]."[49] Whether these sentiments within the young boy were in imitation or rather in similitude with Menas cannot be reasonably resolved. Beyond this, Menas was the only military saint (all of whom are cherished by Copts) explicitly said to be of Egyptian birth. Moreover—and this is vital to see—he was the only military saint to live as a *solitary* in the desert before martyrdom.[50] The points of similarity reach even further into their lives. Menas lost his father at eleven years of age and mother three years later; Azer would suffer the loss of his mother at ten years of age. Menas, and eventually Azer, would leave their careers in pursuit of solitude, and both would reportedly have a dramatic epiphany of "light" after a similar period of ascetic struggle in the desert. Both suffered inestimably in their respective ministries: Menas in martyrdom, Azer in what may be termed an "episcopal martyrdom." And finally, both would become renowned for the same singular reason: they were perceived to be *thaumaturges* (miracle workers) shortly after returning from solitude.

It can only be proposed that there was more to this relationship than is generally presumed. What precisely happened during Azer's annual pilgrimage remains indeterminable. Its consequences are discernible, but its figure is obscure. Did Azer draw near to St Menas and pattern his life in imitation? Or was the relationship founded upon a common vision, kinship, and similar inclination? Or perhaps it was a mold into which Azer hoped to be cast and refashioned? Whatever the answer may be, this would be the beginning of a relationship that was at once mystical and paradigmatic. *This* would be the final abiding gift that Esther would bestow upon her son.

The Crescent and the Cross: Early-Twentieth-Century Egypt, 1912–1919

> "The enemy of mine enemy is my friend."
> —*Sanskrit proverb*

I N 1910, A FEW YEARS BEFORE the death of his wife, Youssef moved with his six children to Alexandria, a city along the coast of the Mediterranean Sea.[51] It was a time of radical social transformation. The literal exodus of Egyptians from the rural countryside to Cairo and Alexandria had far-reaching socioeconomic and ecclesial consequences. A century earlier, at the time of the French occupation, Alexandria had a population of some six thousand residing in what was then a modest and sleepy fishing village. By the time Azer would leave Alexandria for the monastery in 1927, it was a thriving seaport harboring a population of half a million.[52]

* * *

The passing of their mother meant that the six children were often left to their own devices. As the boy Azer became a young man, his family found his demeanor trending in a singular direction. His elder brother, Hanna, reminisces that Azer would grow increasingly uncomfortable whenever the conversation was spent in empty jest and idle laughter. They would often find him quietly retreating to his room, only to return a short while later with a generous smile, gently coaxing them to a more productive and edifying conversation.[53]

But he was not always so tame. On one occasion, Hanna recalls that he returned home to a rather odd sight. As he neared the house, he heard the wild screams of his little sisters, only to enter and find the young girls ascending various pieces of antique furniture, frantically trying to escape their now-pubescent brother. There Azer was, at the base of a provincial cupboard, twirling a damp- ened towel and snapping the towel at his hysterical and petrified sisters. When Hanna managed to calm them all down (and negotiate the towel's release from Azer's hands), he asked the reason for the theatrical scuffle. Azer's response was not unusual: "Because they are annoying me!" "Yes," Hanna pressed further, "but *how* are they annoying you?" "Because," Azer quickly retorted, "I can't seem to find a Bible in their midst, and they refuse to read it." Hanna could only shake his head and chuckle while quickly putting the house to order before their father returned from work.[54]

Youssef, in the meantime, had found employment as a general manager for a successful cotton trader by the name of Ahmad Yahya Pasha.[55] Ahmad had accumulated vast agricultural properties and businesses, and was, significantly, a founding father of the Wafd political party. His son, Abdel Fattah Yahya Pasha (1876–1951), would eventually go on to become the prime minister of Egypt from 1933 to 1934. And it was there at the Pasha residence that the patriotic Wafd Party would meet in its early days; there the first illicit mentions of revo- lution were uttered. In his memoirs, Hanna notes that these influences found their way into the home of Youssef Atta, thereby forging a robust patriotism in the maturing Azer.[56]

Words of revolution were slowly seeping from the marketplace to the pal- ace, from the mosque to the church. But in the family home, Azer was fond of repeating with slight irritation, "You fill the air with talk. . . ."[57] One thing was certain: revolution was in the air.

* * *

Decades earlier, in 1882, the British had quelled the Urabi revolt against the Khedival regime of Egypt. Their initial intention had been to establish political stability in the face of a looming Egyptian economic crisis, as well as to insulate British foreign investment. Whatever genuine hopes and benign promises of a "temporary" occupation the British may have held, it promptly became evident that a swift withdrawal was nearly impossible. Financial collapse was imminent, and the Egyptian regime, weakened by the Urabi revolt, was left impotent and helpless. Meanwhile, a rebellion at the southern border in Sudan threatened the very stability of the entire British Empire.[58]

The burden of establishing financial and political stability rested upon the shoulders of Sir Evelyn Baring (1841–1917), commonly known as Lord Cromer, agent and consul-general from 1883 to 1907. Little can be said against his masterful economic and political success. Within years, debt was halved, government revenue doubled, imports strengthened, and the Sudan was "reconquered."[59] Other policies, however, were not so well received. And it was these that would channel deeper currents of nationalist discontent.

Cromer's view of his subjects was prejudiced and demeaning. He held to a "frankly racist ideology" of European rule that dismissed higher education as at once irrelevant and precarious for an ultimately unintelligent and incapable people.[60] Cromer's was a tenure that sought *only* to secure and bolster foreign interests. There was little concern for the "primitive" subjects, who at any moment, supposedly with a little education, could stir up nationalist discontent against the British. That had been the mistake of British colonialism in India—a mistake Cromer cared not to repeat.[61]

Coptic Christians fared little better in Cromer's estimation. The only distinguishing feature between Copts and Muslims, in his mind, was that one worshiped in a mosque and the other in a church.[62] Cromer's own memoirs are telling: "The modern Copt has become from head to toe, in manners, language and spirit, a Moslem, however unwilling he may be to recognise the fact."[63]

This has in part led to claims that the Christian population was an insignificant minority of little concern to the British.[64] Vivian Ibrahim has convincingly shown this to be a fallacy. Cromer's theoretical indifference toward the Copts in his memoirs (and imagination) bears little on actual history. Particularly in the lead-up to World War I, the British followed a two-tiered policy regarding the Copts, that of "divide and rule." First, they sought to weaken the Church by exploiting the already deepening rifts between the clerical establishment and laypeople. And second, Copts were given preferential treatment in the allocation of highly-sought-after bureaucratic employment.[65] Though subtle in method, the clandestine policy would slowly induce fractures in an increasingly agitated nation.

By June 1906, within months of Azer's "prophetic" call to monasticism, things would come to a head.[66] On June 13, some seventy kilometers (44 miles) from Azer's home, five British officers sought recreation in a pigeon shooting expedition near the village of Denshawai—unaware that the pigeons were the source of livelihood for the locals. A scuffle ensued. The wife of the local *imam* (leader of Muslim prayers) was inadvertently shot and wounded. Excitement arose, and the villagers descended upon the officers. A wounded officer managed to escape, only to collapse and die from apparent heatstroke en route back to camp. An unfortunate innocent villager, oblivious to the day's events, tended to the collapsed officer. When fellow officers found him by the side of the wounded soldier, he was shot and killed.

The reaction was unprecedented. Fifty-two Egyptians were arrested. They were brought before a court in Shibin al-Kom presided over by the minister of justice, Boutros Ghali Pasha, and three British officials.[67] After a hasty trial, on June 27, the British hand fell heavily in the hope of warding off any future uprising. The punishment was disproportionate and unnecessarily brutal. Four of the Egyptians were sentenced to death, and one of them was allegedly hanged in front of his own house the very next day. At least six others were severely flogged in front of fellow villagers, who were forced to watch.[68] Many others were sentenced to terms of imprisonment with hard labor.

What should have been dealt with as a routine matter, as a minor disturbance of spontaneous self-defense in which there were only two casualties, became immortalized. The Denshawai Incident embodied the humiliation and barbarity of British rule.[69] Rather than heading off an imagined insurgency, it baptized a revolution.

It would, unfortunately, be the Church that would suffer most. From this explosive incident we can accurately date the "reactivation of the Islamic versus Christian dimension of the Egyptian question."[70] One simple explanation for this is that the judgment and sentencing were presided over by a Copt. British preferential treatment (part of the "divide and rule" policy) meant many Copts had been allocated senior bureaucratic positions within the government; one of those was Boutros Ghali Pasha (1846–1910)—the Copt in question.[71] A few years later, on November 8, 1908, Ghali was appointed prime minister. Within a brief time, he had further succeeded in infuriating public opinion.[72] The identification of a leading Copt with the unpopular British administration, heightened by his involvement with the Sudan Condominium and his support for the Suez Canal concessions, did little to appease the simmering sectarianism.[73]

Before long a "press war" was raging, with rapidly developing hate propaganda, reflective of the currents of intracommunal tension.[74] It began in June 1908 when an article surfaced in a Coptic newspaper, *al-Watani*, that was critical of Islamic history. Sheikh Abdel Aziz Gawish retaliated tactlessly in the National Party's newspaper *al-Liwa*:

> [Copts] should be kicked to death. They still have faces and bodies similar to those of demons and monkeys, which is proof they hide poisonous spirits within their evil soul. . . . You sons of adulterous women, have you become so foolhardy that you should start and abuse the Muslim faith. The curse of

Allah on you! . . . you tails of camels, with your monkey faces! You bones of bodies! You poor, dreaming fools! You sons of mean rogues![75]

A heightened state of anxiety ensued. On February 29, 1910, as he left the Ministry of Foreign Affairs, the Coptic prime minister, Boutros Ghali Pasha, was shot by a twenty-three-year-old Muslim, Ibrahim el-Wardani. Ghali died from his wounds the next day. Though the alleged motive was political and not religious, it was not popularly celebrated as such. One could hear the Cairo mobs chanting, "El-Wardani killed el-Nossrani [the Nazarene, i.e., Christian]."[76] The Christian populace was understandably unnerved. A Coptic Congress was convened to air grievances on March 6, 1911, in Asyut, Upper Egypt.[77] Muslim Egyptians responded in kind with a General Egyptian Congress a month later. Sectarian conflict seemed imminent, and violence certain. Christians feared the worst. But just as suddenly, the tide turned. The archduke of Austria was assassinated on June 18, 1914, and the world, with Egypt enmeshed, abruptly spiraled into the First World War.

* * *

Despite British guarantees that the empire would shoulder the entire burden of the war, its millstone fell upon the neck of more than a million Egyptian conscripted men, and its scourge upon the widowed and fatherless. Masses of imperial troops landed in Egypt, inflation soared, the peasantry suffered labor exactions, property was requisitioned, and unemployment was endemic. On November 5, 1914, Britain declared war on the Ottoman Empire. Fearful of any "pan-Islamic sentiments" among the Egyptians, the British established a formal protectorate over Egypt.[78] Rather than preparing for withdrawal from their "temporary occupation," the pro-Ottoman Khedive was deposed and replaced with a pro-British puppet. By war's end, all Egyptians—Christian and Muslim, wealthy landowners and *fellahin* (peasants)—were seething with disgust and indignation. When would the oppression of the British come to an end?

As the war neared its end in 1918, the dissolution of the Ottoman Empire meant pan-Islamism was fading. Common enmity toward the British, the distraction of war, and a more secular intellectual climate all aligned to reverse the fortunes and fates of the Copts dramatically.[79] As it was once said, "the enemy of mine enemy is my friend."[80] The fears of a sectarian religious conflict were displaced by the zeal of revolution.

Two days after the armistice of World War I, on November 13, 1918, Saad Zaghloul (1859–1927), along with an Egyptian delegation (*wafd*), sought a meeting in London to demand political independence. His demands were rejected. Simultaneously, a grassroots movement of civil disobedience was simmering. By early March 1919, Zaghloul, who by now had enamored the Egyptian people, was arrested and exiled to Malta.[81] Egypt erupted in protest and riot. Cairo and Alexandria were set alight with anarchy. Azer, now a young man of sixteen years, would have hidden in his home and watched in frightful awe from a boarded window. In just a few weeks, villages were reduced to ashes; martial law, enforced; landed properties, plundered; railways, ravaged; and British officers, murdered.[82] It was the eruption of revolution! The religious tensions of the prewar years were swept away by a tide of nationalist fervor.

Archpriest (Hegumen, or *Qommos*) Sergius recalls the moment. In early March, he had been visiting a Coptic family near the al-Fagallah church in Cairo when he heard chanting in support of Zaghloul: "I felt a strange shaking and my blood was boiling in my veins. I left the family and found my feet taking me straight to al-Azhar!"[83] He quite literally marched in his cassock to the al-Azhar Mosque and became the first ever Christian priest to stand and preach from its pulpit.[84] Between March and April 1919, he preached for fifty-nine consecutive days in al-Azhar against the British. Zaghloul named him the "Orator of Egypt." On one occasion, Sergius was standing in Ramses Square and enraptured the crowds with a teasing question: "Guess what I did today?" All eyes were transfixed on him, as he continued, "I chanted a Christian wedding for a Muslim girl!" Eyes grew wider, as he added, "I joined Egypt in Holy Matrimony to Independence." The applause was deafening.[85] Slogans could be heard: "Long live the Crescent and the Cross"; "Religion is for God, and the nation for all."[86] It was the first time in the nation's history that the Crescent and Cross were seen on one and the same flag.[87] Though the next two years were to be painfully scarred by acrimony and anarchy, priests and sheikhs walked arm in arm against a common enemy. Copts, it would seem, had finally found a political home in Zaghloul's Wafd Party.[88]

In November 1919, the Milner Commission investigated the emergent revolution and reported that the state of the protectorate was, quite simply, unsatisfactory. By February 22, 1922, the British government abolished the protectorate and unilaterally declared Egypt an independent sovereign state.[89] Egyptians were justifiably infatuated with Zaghloul, and in 1924 he was elected the prime minister of the first Wafdist government. In that very moment, "the Crescent and the Cross" were united—albeit ever so briefly.

* * *

Unfortunately, we have no record of Azer's life for most of this period. His brother, Hanna, briefly mentions that their father, Youssef, was the general manager for Ahmad Yahya Pasha, in whose home the Wafdist movement would find its roots. The memoirs are altogether succinct: "Azer's exposure to this environment helped him develop a strong patriotism."[90]

But it is important to discern at least two points within this "exposure." From 1906 to 1914, sectarianism was rife, and the gathering forces of conflict between Christian and Muslim would have been burned deep into the memory of the primary-school-aged boy. This conflict would have been at odds with the love that Azer felt toward his Muslim neighbors and the sheikh who had tutored him in Tukh al-Nasara. It was a mournful and acute awakening to the realities of religious prejudice. Yet from 1914 to 1922, Azer, now a young man, would have been exposed to just the opposite. He would have become aware of the capacity for religious dialogue and the brilliance of standing patriotically under one united flag.

So, before he had reached his twenties, Azer had seen both irrational hate and the vigor of solidarity. One would serve as an impending warning; the other, an all-too-fleeting ideal.

The Path to the Monastery, 1920–1927

> "Saints by their nature are as disturbing as they are inspiring."
> —*Susan Ashbrook Harvey*

A ZER WAS NOT BORN A SAINT. It was a path he chose. Not in the sense that one can seriously or consciously elect to be a saint; rather, in the sense that he yearned absolutely for a solitary life with God. To say this desire was met with disapproval would be an understatement. His family was devastated.

* * *

Only a year after the revolution, in 1920, Azer completed his schooling. While Egypt awaited independence with increasing impatience, he anxiously sat his final secondary exams and received his baccalaureate. Intermittent martial law, scattered violence, and the occasional uprising formed the backdrop to his graduation into uncertain times. But the anxiety was short-lived. The unilateral declaration of independence in 1922 granted some measure of stability to the nation. Within a brief period, Azer was able to secure employment managing the accounts for an English company by the name of Thomas Cook and Son.[91] The firm had been founded in 1841 by its namesake, Thomas Cook, as a travel company. Oddly enough, it was originally established with a religious purpose—transporting parishioners to temperance and Sunday School meetings in and around central England. By the 1880s the firm was involved in military transport and postal services for the British in Egypt, as well as the odd travel tour.

A rare photograph of Azer from the period, found on a national ID card, reveals a tall, handsome, and almost athletic young man in a single-breasted suit, with a dapper mustache and a typical Egyptian nose. His eyes are deep, deliberate, and penetrating—almost as though one were laid bare before him. He is wearing a conical, flat-topped, brimless red hat with a tassel, commonly known as a *fez* or *tarboosh*—a symbol of social status and "badge" of a white-collar worker in the Ottoman Empire.[92] Other than his discerning and somewhat riveting eyes, Azer looks, at first glance, an ordinary young Egyptian man.

During these years, Hanna notes, Azer would pray each morning at St Mark's Cathedral in Mahatet al-Ramleh, Alexandria, before walking to work.[93] The general manager at Thomas Cook, an Australian man, was known to be a tenacious (and perhaps stubborn) man who would often keep watch at the entrance of the building, carefully noting what time his employees arrived. He was all too aware that he was feared, and that many would often plan their arrival at work to avoid him. One morning, his brother recollects, Azer arrived at work after morning prayers at the church and purposefully made to greet the general manager at the entrance directly. "Why are you so late?" the manager asked. Azer calmly looked at his watch and firmly replied that it was exactly nine o'clock, and therefore he was not late. The general manager walked away silently and found Azer's immediate manager, commenting that he was "proud of this young man who respected himself and did not avoid him, as many others did."[94] Though an everyday—even ordinary—event, it indicates a fundamental disposition, at once noble and firm, that would play out time and time again throughout Azer's ecclesiastical career.

* * *

During the year 1922, when Azer was twenty years old, he experienced what would be a decisive and irresistible turning point. Though the change in

demeanor had been progressive since his childhood, the movement now accel-
erated. This turning point or epiphany has never been properly appreciated in
the literature. Yet all three of the most credible sources agree that *something* happened.[95] In Hanna's memoirs, the account of Fr Raphael Ava Mina (his future
disciple), and an anecdote of Archdeacon Iskander (his mentor), the moment
of change is given as 1922, five years before Azer entered the monastery.[96] But
what specifically took place is unfortunately lost to us. We may only look in, ever
so cautiously, from the outside.

"Since my early youth," Azer reflected decades later in a handwritten
fragment,

> I was inclined to quietness, seclusion, and would wear black clothing. When I
> reached the *age of maturity*, I heard much of the monasteries and the monks,
> and *my heart became alight*; I longed so much to join a monastery.[97]

We may suggest that it was this suddenly expansive and overwhelming desire
for the monastic life that was at the epicenter of the change. "[Azer's] love for
God," his brother notes, "was very evident in his behavior at this stage of his
life."[98] While other young men were accumulating wealth, searching for appropriate partners, and reveling in momentary pleasures, Azer spent the entirety of
his spare time absorbed in liturgy and prayer. His family soon noticed dramatic
changes. He spent every evening locked in his room in prayer and reading the
Scriptures.[99] Even his own brother had little idea as to what was happening; in
keeping with monastic practice, Azer carefully guarded his room and absolutely
denied his family entry.[100] They were privy only to the outward manifestations
of what was happening interiorly in Azer. It is therefore unsurprising that the
details of this "turning point" are lost to history. Fr Raphael, in turn, claims (we
may assume from what was told to him in confidence) that it was during these
five years that Azer began to practice the life of solitude in his room, unknown to
his family. He ate very little and abandoned his comfortable bed for the austerity
of the ground.[101] Monasticism and the yearning for a life of solitude had well
and truly embraced the young man.

A decade later, Azer (then a monk) wrote a letter to his brother that grants
us a glimpse into his carefully guarded life of those five years:

> Commit yourself to go straight from home to work and vice versa, likewise
> to church and spiritual meetings. Do not hurry in walking except when nec-
> essary. Do not turn right and left when walking in the street. Look straight
> ahead while walking, praying in your heart, "Lord take care of me; hide me

under the shadow of your wings. Oh, my Lord Jesus Christ deliver me from any offences. . . ." When you come back from work, take off your clothes, wash your face and rest for a little. If you want to have some recreation, you can go outside far from noise, and ponder the works of the Creator and the beauty of nature. . . . Do not reflect too much on the affairs of life. Do not worry about anything. Cast your burdens on the Lord, and he shall sustain you. Do not stay too late outside; it is better not to be out after eight o'clock.[102]

We may infer that the advice was founded upon his own practice when he longed for the monastic life. The letter continues,

Go to bed early and awake early . . . when you awake, do not remain in bed. . . . Start your day worshipping God in prostration twenty or thirty times or as many times as possible, for, among all other virtues undertaken by people, there is none better than this. . . . After that go and wash your face and stand before God and thank him for watching over you this night and keeping you alive until the morning. . . . Read the Holy Bible with care. Give it time, as you do with the newspapers, for the word of God is sweeter than honey.[103]

And so those five years passed, with Azer living as a monastic within his bedroom, and his family looking on bewildered, somewhere between inspired and disturbed. Quietly, without fuss, Azer was preparing for another life. He lived as an "urban monastic," a precursor for the mode of much of his monasticism. Though the imminent decision was glaringly obvious in retrospect, his brother noted in his memoirs that his family members still were in the dark. Azer had not divulged anything to them. And when Azer finally made his decision known, it would "surprise everyone."[104]

* * *

On an unassuming morning in early June 1927, Hanna received an unsettling phone call. Azer's general manager, the same Australian, asked very sharply to meet with him immediately. Little was given away. As Hanna made his way to Thomas Cook & Son, he recalls that his heart became heavy. He knew too well that Azer was responsible for the company's accounts and expenses, and, playing out the possible scenarios in his mind, Hanna feared the worst.[105] When Hanna sat with the general manager, he was met with impossible news. Azer had apparently, earlier in the morning, suddenly tendered his resignation with a cryptic explanation: "As I have a very important task to fulfil, please accept my resignation as of the end of June 1927."[106] The manager then asked, what could possibly be a higher priority than Azer's vital role in the company? Hanna, still in the dark, pled ignorance and promised to investigate promptly.

In the evening, when the family had customarily gathered, with his father sitting expectantly, Hanna demanded to know what exactly was going through his younger brother's mind. "Which is preferable," Azer meekly challenged, "a holy life and real internal happiness, or the suffering and painful life one must live in the secular world?"[107] These words, in Hanna's memoirs, reveal Azer's inner turmoil and disclose what had been consuming him day and night these past five years. He wished solely, undividedly, to be alone with God. Life in the world, for Azer, was unbearable. The resignation, though seemingly impetuous and abrupt, came as a dramatic, overpowering, and impassioned climax to what was a sustained, burgeoning, and thoroughly sober aspiration. Long immersed in his "urban monasticism," Azer's desire to leave and be with God enthralled and engrossed him. He could no longer wait. He had waited long enough. He yearned for solitude; every moment until then was nothing short of intolerable.

In his own memoirs, a decade later, Azer writes teasingly that the moment of his resignation was not random or impulsive, but that the "day came that God had appointed."[108] What those words mean, like the five years that preceded them, remains concealed, locked away in his room, hidden from history. But Azer certainly remembered the tense conversation that evening, albeit in considerably calmer words, he recalls:

> I longed so much to join a monastery. . . . When the day came that God had appointed, I discussed my intentions with my father and brothers. At first, *they objected strongly*, but this did not make me change my mind. I constantly prayed to God that they would permit me to go the monastery.[109]

That was putting it lightly. His family and friends (only frantic phone calls away) gathered to force a change of mind.[110] How could he, a twenty-five-year-old man, just throw away a successful life for something worse than a peasant's existence? In all ages, those who live in security have found it difficult to appreciate how someone could turn from comfort to a monastic alternative that "appears to them at best incomprehensible, at worst downright perverse."[111] The situation in early-twentieth-century Egypt was far more dramatic. Monasteries were effectively in ruins, without electricity, running water, or any of the basics of contemporary urban society. For the most part, they were spiritually and physically derelict, in a state of neglect and abandon. No one educated or from a decent family would even contemplate such a life. Monasticism was for the uneducated, unsuccessful, and unmarriageable. Azer's family's dismay was therefore understandable, if not perfectly reasonable. In the end, the exchange remained intense and unresolved. Hanna's memoirs confess the family's lament: "All their petitions and advice were in vain. He could not be convinced to change his mind."[112]

Without their consent, and no doubt frustrated, Azer met with Youannis, the metropolitan of Beheira and Menoufia, who was also responsible for the Baramous Monastery.[113] Youannis (1855–1942) learned that the young man was the son of Youssef Atta, whom he knew well. Sensing that something was amiss, the metropolitan sensitively asked as to why his father and brother had not accompanied him. Azer replied that he was prepared, with or without their consent, to embark on this path. Youannis, for his part, could do no such thing. Without the family's prior permission, the matter, sadly, could proceed no further.[114]

Azer returned home dejected. His hopes and dreams of the previous five years lay in tatters. Seeing that he was distressed, the family seized upon what they thought was the perfect opportunity to relay the apparently tempting news. Azer's general manager had called again to offer an "exceptional raise" if only he would change his mind. The words fell on decidedly deaf ears.[115]

At this point, according to Hanna's account, their father, Youssef Atta, surprisingly relented. Perceiving his son's spiritual strength and will, he advised Azer to attend Liturgy, receive the Eucharist, and then make his decision. The family, Youssef professed, would accept and support the outcome, no matter how painful that might be.[116]

It is, however, unlikely that the resolution came about so swiftly and smoothly, especially given the preceding controversy and tension. A step, it seems, is missing from his brother's memoirs.[117] Archdeacon Iskander Hanna (1880–1944), a famous and influential preacher of the period, recounts an event that came just before—and certainly explains—Youssef Atta's rather sudden change of heart. The Arabic written account is for the most part unknown, and to my knowledge has never been reproduced in any study.[118] According to the anecdote, Azer had long attended the archdeacon's lectures at St Mark's Cathedral, as well as at the "Society for Spiritual Renaissance" that met at Moharam Bek in Alexandria. Iskander recalls well the family's reaction to Azer's decision for monastic life: "They became furious and ridiculed his idea and tried to make him change his mind, sometimes with rational dialogue, and at other times by frightening him concerning his uncertain future. Meanwhile, Azer was steadfast and determined. The most agitated and furious of them was Azer's older brother Hanna."[119]

Azer, after the heated exchange with his family and the rejection by the metropolitan, sought advice from Iskander. "Your family, my son," Iskander reassured, "do not know anything about you and speak the language of the flesh."[120] Azer, vindicated, returned home and relayed these words. In disbelief, Hanna went the very next morning to the society's office and awaited an opportunity for a private meeting with the archdeacon. "Hanna, leave your brother alone and do not block his road!" Iskander declared before Hanna could even say a word. "Azer," he continued,

> has been coming to me after work nearly every day for the *past five years*, asking questions of the difficult verses of Scripture. He already has a diary organized in alphabetical order, in which he writes the verses along with whatever explanation I have given him. He has read the entire Scriptures and knows their every meaning. . . . He conducts his life in accordance with the biblical demands. Hanna, leave him alone, for he has a bright and joyful future.[121]

Iskander makes clear Azer had not made an erratic or fanciful decision; it was five years in the making. There is no reason to doubt the authenticity of the account. It is remarkably consistent with the image of Azer that is developing in the other sources. And when asked in an interview in 1959, after his enthronement, as to his greatest mentors before monasticism, Azer (then Kyrillos VI) replied with a few words: "Archdeacon Iskander Hanna and the great Hegumen Youhanna Girguis of Alexandria [Azer's spiritual father/confessor]."[122] We might, therefore, suggest that Iskander's influence on Azer, at least in some part, was related to the pivotal role the archdeacon played at that crucial moment.

Only *after* this decisive meeting did Hanna return and convince his father of Azer's path. Their father, it seems, took the advice of the authoritative archdeacon to heart, and at that point advised his son to attend the Liturgy to discern the will of God. Azer obeyed. At next opportunity, Azer and his father earnestly prayed and received the Eucharist. By the liturgy's end, there was no need for further debate; Youssef Atta reluctantly surrendered. Azer's (and Youssef's) spiritual father, a popular and wise priest by the name of Youhanna Girguis, was resolute; this path was God's will for the young man.[123]

* * *

Azer returned (no doubt grinning) with his father and brother to Metropolitan Youannis. Hanna's memoirs reveal, however, that the matter was still far from settled. Youannis was forthright and direct. He held significant reservations: monasticism was a treacherous path; every step was filled with anguish, insult, and diverse temptation; and Azer would not have a single day of peace.[124]

Hanna notes that Azer was equally adamant. For the past five years, Azer insisted, he had already traveled this road alone in his room, and so, "what [he] would face would not be new to him."[125] "Son," Youannis, skeptical, in turn replied, "I have seen through my experience that the young men coming from major cities seldom proceed with life in the monastery."[126] Monasticism at the time was not approached except by the poor, peasants, or illiterate. Azer, on the other hand, was educated relative to his peers (and had even mastered English); came from a relatively wealthy family; and was, most significantly, a city dweller. The objection was, as far as Azer was concerned, trivial and irrelevant.[127] "My hope and trust in God are very strong," managed Azer, "I believe that if you bless and ask the Lord to grant me strength and success, I will succeed. The Lord Jesus Christ is fair and will not forget those who love him."[128] Youannis, perceiving the strength and tenacity of the young man, could not resist and conceded, blessing him saying, "I will prepare your path towards monasticism."[129]

According to Hanna's account, Azer could hardly contain his ecstasy and prostrated himself before the metropolitan many times. But, in Azer's own autobiographical fragments, the resolution ultimately came about by divine intervention: "I constantly prayed to God that they would permit me to go the monastery. God heard my plea."[130] Azer's words to his family were but a faint reflection of his inestimable joy:

> Who am I, the wretched one? What is my situation compared to the sons of the kings, Maximus and Domadius, who abandoned the kingdom of the world to gain the everlasting kingdom, giving up kingdoms and wealth for the sake of the love of the King of the heavens? . . . I wish I could be the dust under their feet.[131]

As they left the metropolitan and arrived home, emotions began to settle, and reality acutely set in. That evening they knew Azer's decision was necessary; inescapable; and, in the end, the will of God. Still, it meant the agonizing loss of a beloved brother and cherished son. "Truly," said Hanna, "it was a very hard night for all of us."[132]

Notes

[1]Hegumen Mina the Recluse [Kyrillos VI], "Autobiographical Fragments" [in Arabic], in FRC-1: Letter 1 (Old Cairo, n.d., probably between 1945 and 1949). The autobiographical fragments have previously been published in pieces. I was fortunate to discover them in their entirety. Although no addressee or date is given, this work was possibly written from 1945 to 1949 to the monks of the Monastery of St Samuel, given it is signed as "Hegumen Mina el-Baramousy the Recluse." Unfortunately, he appears to have left it unfinished, for he stopped writing half way down the page—with the words: "I will explain them in later details." Fr Raphael Ava Mina states the account was discovered in the patriarch's personal drawers, indicating perhaps that he changed his mind and never sent the autobiography to the intended addressee(s).

[2]I. H. al-Masri, *The Story of the Coptic Church: 1956–1971* [in Arabic], vol. 7 (Cairo: Maktabat al-Mahabba, 1988), 17; Nashaat Zaklama, *The Spiritual Life and Pastoral Message of Pope Kyrillos VI* [in Arabic], vol. 1 (Cairo: Sons of the Evangelist, 2007), 20.

[3]Most accounts in Arabic, and all in English, place Azer's birth in Tukh al-Nasara, Menoufia. This apparently is secondary to the ambiguity of the Arabic sources in placing his birth, for instance in Hanna's memoirs Azer's birth is described, and *then* the relocation from Tukh al-Nasara to Damanhur is mentioned. However, the impression is that the author begins with the birth and then recounts the history of the family. There is thus a degree of ambiguity concerning the birthplace, and thus it is likely the earliest accounts in English have become confused on account of this; see Hanna Youssef Atta and Father Raphael Ava Mina, *The Life of Pope Kyrillos the Sixth* (Cairo: Sons of Pope Kyrillos VI, 2002), 1. In English, biographical accounts have all followed Wakin (who wrote in 1963) and Meinardus (in 1970): see Edward Wakin, *A Lonely Minority: The Modern Story of Egypt's Copts* (New York: William Morrow & Company, 1963), 110; Otto Meinardus, *Christian Egypt: Faith and Life* (Cairo: The American University in Cairo Press, 1970), 43. See also Otto Meinardus, *Coptic Saints and Pilgrimages* (Cairo: The American University in Cairo Press, 2002), 73.

[4]The birth certificate gives a date of August 8, 1902, whereas the actual birth was on August 2, 1902. The discrepancy is accounted for by the well-attested delay in birth registrations. The place of birth is given as Abu Hummus, which was the administrative center for birth registrations in the governorate of Beheira. Interestingly, a later ID card as he entered adulthood also gives the birthplace as Abu Hummus. If Azer had been born in Tukh al-Nasara, the birth registration would have taken place in the governorate of Menoufia. In personal correspondence with Marcos Hanna Youssef Atta, also known as Reda Marcos (the nephew of Pope Kyrillos VI and the son of his primary biographer), I was able to confirm this. Marcos Hanna Youssef Atta, "Personal Correspondence, January 28, 2015," ed. Daniel Fanous (2015). Marcos' memory is rather impeccable in that he was made blind in rather unfortunate circumstances as a child and accordingly bears an almost photographic memory of circumstances and dates.

[5]Zaklama, *Pope Kyrillos VI*, 1:20.

[6]The biographical details of Pope Kyrillos' family and his early childhood are scarce and exceedingly difficult to verify. The dates of Pope Kyrillos' parents' births and deaths have been identified from correspondence with Marcos Hanna Youssef Atta, and have been confirmed from correspondence of other family members.

[7]Atta and Raphael Ava Mina, *Life of Pope Kyrillos*, 1.

[8]Ibid.

[9]Ibid. Esther's biographical details are nearly impossible to come by. Her name in fact was lost to history, never once being mentioned in any biographical account. As I approached her grandchildren and great-grandchildren, not one was able to recollect even her name, let alone her date of death. I was, however, able to discover several biographical details in correspondence with her grandson, the aforementioned Marcos Hanna Youssef Atta. I suspect the reason for her disappearance in history is threefold: her husband remarried after her death; women were often only remembered fleetingly relative to men in what was then a somewhat patriarchal society; and finally, she died more than a century ago, in 1912, when her children were extremely young. Her early death accounts for her brief appearances

in her son Hanna's memoirs. Also, we should note that on Azer's birth certificate, the mother's details are not given.

[10]Ibid.

[11]Ibid.

[12]Despite many oral accounts suggesting Azer was baptized at St George's Church in Tukh al-Nasara in the governorate of Menoufia, it is unlikely given the above evidence for his birthplace in the governorate of Beheira and not Menoufia. Pope Kyrillos' nephew mentioned in personal correspondence, "I really have no idea why people have confused his birth and baptism place; perhaps it is because the family moved to Tukh al-Nasara when Azer was about five years old." Atta, "Personal Correspondence, January 28, 2015."

[13]Interestingly, one Arabic historian states that his closest advisers were Hanna and Mikhail. The latter was ordained on December 8, 1962. Mikhail died on November 13, 1975, and Hanna on February 8, 1976. See Fr Samuel Tawadros el-Syriany, *The History of the Popes of the Chair of Alexandria, 1809–1971* [in Arabic] (Cairo: Hijazi Press, 1977), 200.

[14]I am immensely indebted to the grandchildren of Youssef Atta and their families for providing these almost lost biographical details.

[15]Mina the Recluse [Kyrillos VI], "Autobiographical Fragments."

[16]Atta and Raphael Ava Mina, *Life of Pope Kyrillos*, 1. The Baramous Monastery, also known as "Parameos Monastery" and the "Monastery of the Romans," was founded by Macarius the Great and is located in the Wadi al-Natrun desert in the governorate of Beheira, some 110 km (68 mi) from Damanhur.

[17]Ibid. Of interest, I. H. al-Masri notes that the visit of Fr Tadros took place in Damanhur, further granting weight to the claim that Azer lived in Damanhur from 1902 to 1907; see al-Masri, *Story of the Coptic Church*, 7:17.

[18]Atta and Raphael Ava Mina, *Life of Pope Kyrillos*, 1.

[19]Ibid.

[20]Mina the Recluse [Kyrillos VI], "Autobiographical Fragments."

[21]Atta, "Personal Correspondence, January 28, 2015." This is contrary to most English accounts, which claim that Azer attended primary school in Damanhur and high school in Alexandria; Meinardus, *Christian Egypt: Faith and Life*, 43.

[22]It is impossible to date this incident, but according to Hanna's account it occurred after the prophetic visit of Fr Tadros, and Azer's mother, Esther, was still alive at the time. This places the incident between 1906 and 1912. Given the family moved to Tukh al-Nasara in 1907, and left for Alexandria in 1910, it is likely that it occurred there. Accordingly, Azer was between five and eight years of age.

[23]Atta and Raphael Ava Mina, *Life of Pope Kyrillos*, 1–2.

[24]Hanna's account omits the name of the Sheikh, whereas other Arabic sources and popular accounts provide it. For instance see, al-Masri, *Story of the Coptic Church*, 7:18.

[25]Atta and Raphael Ava Mina, *Life of Pope Kyrillos*, 2.

[26]The claim of Watson is representative: "Having once taken the saint's name [Menas] as his own name in religion, Kyrillos was always determined to emulate Abu Mina in every way possible." See John H. Watson, "Abba Kyrillos: Patriarch and Solitary," *Coptic Church Review* 17, nos. 1–2 (1996): 20.

[27]Atta and Raphael Ava Mina, *Life of Pope Kyrillos*, 1.

[28]This may be claimed on the basis of three facts: in Hanna's memoirs Esther plays a primary role in these celebrations of the feast days; Esther died in 1912; and Tukh al-Nasara (28 km / 17 mi from Ibyar), where the family lived from 1907 to 1910, was significantly closer to Ibyar than Damanhur (50 km/31 mi). This places the annual pilgrimage during this period, though it certainly may have continued when the family moved to Alexandria (albeit at a greater distance).

[29]Atta and Raphael Ava Mina, *Life of Pope Kyrillos*, 1.

[30]Meinardus, *Christian Egypt: Faith and Life*, 216.

[31]Ibid., 218–19.

[32]The Church of St Menas had been there since at least the twelfth century, and one may presume the festivals dated to then. According to the Arabic version of the saint's life, Menas was born in Ibyar, though this is unlikely given the other sources.

[33]Hatour 15, in the Coptic Calendar.

[34]Atta, "Personal Correspondence, January 28, 2015."

[35]De Lacy O'Leary, *The Saints of Egypt* (New York: Macmillan, 1937), 196.

[36]Otto Meinardus, *Two Thousand Years of Coptic Christianity* (Cairo: The American University Press in Cairo, 1999), 151.

[37]Otto Meinardus, *Monks and Monasteries of the Egyptian Deserts (1989)*, rev. ed. (Cairo: The American University Press in Cairo, 1999), 170–78.

[38]We have the histories of no fewer than ten different saints named Menas, eight of which are in the Coptic *Synaxarion*. Drescher suggests four different options for the historicity of St Menas: he was either (1) an Egyptian martyr; (2) a Phrygian martyr; (3) two different martyrs; or (4) a confusion of a Phrygian god. Drescher himself suggests the third option as most likely but warns "a lack of evidence precludes anything like certainty." See James Drescher, *Apa Mena: A Selection of Coptic Texts Relating to St. Menas* (Cairo: Publications de la Société d'Archéologie Copte, 1946), IV. The sources may be further divided into genres of martyrdom, synaxarion (collection of saints' biographies), encomium (speech praising a figure), and miracle collections.

[39]The Arabic *Synaxarion* is in part derived from the Coptic *Encomium*. The *Encomium* was authored by John the Archbishop of Alexandria, about whom Drescher suggests three different options, as there were in fact three different archbishops by the name of John. This would place the manuscript anywhere from AD 640 to 893 (ibid., 129). Where consistent, the other sources will be reasonably considered, especially when the material converges.

[40]Ibid., 132.

[41]E. A. Wallis Budge, *Texts Relating to Saint Mena of Egypt and Canons of Nicaea: In a Nubian Dialect* (London: Trustees of the British Museum, 1909), 23.

[42]Drescher, *Apa Mena*, 102.

[43]Ibid., 135.

[44]The Ethiopian *Martyrdom of St Menas*; see Budge, *Texts Relating to Saint Mena*, 46.

[45]Ibid., 46–47. The Coptic *Martyrdom* states that it was only after a "long time" in solitude that Menas received the revelation and the call to martyrdom. See Drescher, *Apa Mena*, 102. Notably, all sources agree to the first and third crowns. The second crown is variously given as "asceticism," "patient endurance," and "solitude."

[46]Budge, *Texts Relating to Saint Mena*, 47.

[47]Ibid.

[48]Ibid., 53–54.

[49]Mina the Recluse [Kyrillos VI], "Autobiographical Fragments."

[50]Voile is the only scholar who has seen beyond the superficial in the relationship of Azer to Menas, but even she stops short, tracing the affinity to "his family's special devotion as well as certain features that may have attracted him." See Brigitte Voile, *Les Coptes d'Égypte sous Nasser: Sainteté, Miracles, Apparitions* (Paris: CNRS Éditions, 2004), 192–95.

[51]This is dated on the basis of Azer's (Kyrillos VI) stating in a 1968 interview that the family was living in Alexandria from 1910—and, fascinatingly, at that time St Mary "healed a sick person in that house." One can only suggest that it was his mother, Esther, who would die a few years later in 1912. See Michael Khalil, "Interview with Pope Kyrillos" [in Arabic], *al-Akhbar*, May 11, 1968; Atta, "Personal Correspondence, January 28, 2015."

[52]Robert L. Tignor, *Egypt: A Short History* (Princeton, NJ: Princeton University Press, 2010), 248.

[53]Atta and Raphael Ava Mina, *Life of Pope Kyrillos*, 3.

[54]This account was told to me by Hanna's son, Marcos, who was in near hysterics telling me the story. He mentioned that the story stuck clearly in his memory because every time his father told it, they would all break out in uncontainable laughter. Atta, "Personal Correspondence, January 28, 2015."

[55]See al-Masri, *Story of the Coptic Church*, 7:18; Zaklama, *Pope Kyrillos VI*, 1, 25; Atta and Raphael Ava Mina, *Life of Pope Kyrillos*, 3.

[56]See Atta and Raphael Ava Mina, *Life of Pope Kyrillos*, 2.

[57]Al-Masri, *Story of the Coptic Church*, 7:19.

[58]M. W. Daly, "The British Occupation, 1882–1922," in *The Cambridge History of Egypt: Modern Egypt, from 1517 to the End of the Twentieth Century*, ed. M. W. Daly (Cambridge: Cambridge University Press, 1998), 239.

[59]Ibid., 242.

[60]Ibid.

[61]Tignor, *Egypt: A Short History*, 231. For a fair and succinct assessment of Lord Cromer's rule, see P. J. Vatikiotis, *The History of Egypt: From Muhammad Ali to Mubarak*, 3rd ed. (Baltimore: The Johns Hopkins University Press, 1985), 172–77.

[62]Evelyn Baring, Earl of Cromer, *Modern Egypt*, vol. 2 (New York: Macmillan, 1908), 206.

[63]Despite the fact that this quote is often attributed to him, Cromer was in fact quoting from Klunzinger's work *Upper Egypt* (ibid., 203). That said, Cromer cites in complete agreement. He was willing to at least concede that Copts had "developed certain mediocre aptitudes" that made them somewhat more useful in the sphere of economics (ibid., 207–8). Vatikiotis further cites Sir John Bowring's *Report on Egypt*: "[Copts] are the surveyors, the scribes, the arithmeticians, the measurers, the clerks, in a word, the learned men of the land. They are to the counting house and the pen what the fellah is to the field and the plough." See Vatikiotis, *The History of Egypt*, 206–7.

[64]S. S. Hasan, *Christians versus Muslims in Modern Egypt: The Century-Long Struggle for Coptic Equality* (New York: Oxford University Press, 2003), 35. Intriguingly, a survey of scholarship on the modern history of Egypt reveals very little indeed as to the role of the Coptic Church. In the words of Gorman: "There is a tendency in academia to marginalize Coptic history as peripheral or irrelevant to the national narrative" (Anthony Gorman, *Historians, State, and Politics in Twentieth Century Egypt: Contesting the Nation* [New York: RoutledgeCurzon, 2003], 153). The words of Ghali Shukri are especially poignant: "It is astonishing that we do not recognize a Coptic Egypt, that is, a Christian Egypt, an Egyptian Egypt. This is even more astonishing in light of the fact that . . . what has survived [from] Coptic Egypt . . . *are people who live among us like an authentic scarlet thread in the weave of the Egyptian nation*. . . . As if the Islamic conquest was the beginning of the history of Egypt, and the non-Muslims are the uninvited guests of this history" (ibid.). There is consequently, for instance, great difficulty in assessing the reign of Kyrillos VI historically *vis-à-vis* the Nasser government, given that most of secular scholarship of the period marginalizes the impact of Coptic history on the fabric of Egypt in the '60s and '70s.

[65]Vivian Ibrahim, *The Copts of Egypt: Challenges of Modernisation and Identity* (New York: Tauris Academic Studies, 2011), 42.

[66]Daly has called it the "most important milestone in Anglo-Egyptian relations between 1882 and 1914." See Daly, "The British Occupation," 243.

[67]Vatikiotis, *The History of Egypt*, 205.

[68]Tignor, *Egypt: A Short History*, 238.

[69]Daly, "The British Occupation," 243.

[70]Tignor, *Egypt: A Short History*, 205.

[71]Mohamed Heikal claims the choice of Boutros Ghali Pasha "more than anything else compromised the position of the Copts." See Mohamed Heikal, *Autumn of Fury: The Assassination of Sadat* (London: Corgi, 1984), 157.

[72]Ibrahim, *The Copts of Egypt*, 55. For a discussion of the controversy in the appointment of Boutros Ghali, see Samuel Tadros, *Motherland Lost: The Egyptian and Coptic Quest for Modernity* (Stanford: Hoover Institution Press, 2013), 121–22.

[73]Boutros' signing of the Sudan Condominium effectively gave complete control of the Sudan to the British Empire and thereby clearly identified Ghali with the British administration.

[74]Vatikiotis, *The History of Egypt*, 208.

[75]*Egyptian Gazette*, August 27, 1908, cited in Douglas Sladen, *Egypt and the English* (London: Hurst and Blacket Limited, 1908), xxi–xxii. For an analysis of the "press war," see B. L. Carter, *The Copts in Egyptian Politics* (London: Croom Helm, 1986), 10–11.

[76]Carter comments: "The Muslim and nationalist press naturally described the crime as a political act; the Copts, just as naturally, saw it as a religious one. Wardani was, in fact, celebrated publicly not only as a nationalist but as a Muslim who had rid his people of an intolerably arrogant Christian. Storrs, the Oriental Secretary, reported that groups of Muslims roamed the street singing about "Wardani who killed the Nazarene," and he noted that the assassin "had become a national hero." See Carter, *The Copts in Egyptian Politics*, 12–13. Interestingly, Mohamed Heikal, an advisor to Nasser and Sadat, remembered Wardani as a "Moslem fundamentalist." See Heikal, *Autumn of Fury*, 157.

[77]Meinardus, *Christian Egypt: Faith and Life*, 39–40. Their main concerns were the calling for Sunday to be a day off, the removal of any discrimination in employment or government funding, equal access to education, and their representation in parliament. Only one demand seems to have been met. In 1913, Kitchener became the British consul-general of Egypt and increased political representation of the Copts.

[78]Tignor, *Egypt: A Short History*, 240.

[79]J. D. Pennington, "The Copts in Modern Egypt," *Middle Eastern Studies* 18, no. 2 (1982): 161.

[80]Ancient Sanskrit proverb.

[81]Vatikiotis, *The History of Egypt*, 264.

[82]Ibid., 264–65.

[83]Cited from Ibrahim, *The Copts of Egypt*, 64.

[84]Ibid.

[85]I. H. al-Masri, *The Story of the Copts: The True Story of Christianity in Egypt*, vol. 2 (California: St Anthony Coptic Orthodox Monastery, 1982), 375.

[86]Gorman, *Historians, State, and Politics*, 156.

[87]Meinardus, *Christian Egypt: Faith and Life*, 41.

[88]Gorman writes, "The spirit of this unanimity of purpose and basis for collective identity among Egyptians was institutionalized in the Wafd, whose leadership included prominent Copts, the so-called 'Coptic pillars' of the party, such as Makram Ubayd, Wasif Ghali, and Wisa Wasif. . . . In short, the Wafd was the 'political home of the Copts' (*bayt al-aqbat al-siyasi*)." See Gorman, *Historians, State, and Politics*, 156. Cf. Anthony O'Mahony, "Coptic Christianity in Modern Egypt," in *The Cambridge History of Christianity: Eastern Christianity*, ed. Michael Angold (Cambridge: Cambridge University Press, 2006), 497.

[89]There were, however, four "Reserved Points" as they came to be called. The British Empire retained the rights to the security of imperial communications within Egypt, defense of Egypt against foreign aggression, protection of foreign interests and *minorities*, and the Sudan. See Vatikiotis, *The History of Egypt*, 270. Severe limitations to the independence were inevitable, and Anglo-Egyptian relations would be embittered for another thirty years. See Daly, "The British Occupation," 250.

[90]Atta and Raphael Ava Mina, *Life of Pope Kyrillos*, 2.

[91]Ibid., 4; al-Masri, *Story of the Coptic Church*, 7:18. There is an occasional reference in the secondary literature that before joining Thomas Cook & Son, Azer first found employment at a Dutch firm with his brother (Voile claims he remained there until 1924). For instance, see Wakin, *A Lonely Minority*, 110; Voile, *Les Coptes d'Égypte*, 190. Unfortunately, the source of this claim remains elusive and impossible to confirm.

[92]See Figures 1 and 4. The photograph, perhaps the earliest extant, comes from a family portrait and is in keeping with a national ID card in 1925, when he was twenty-three years old. Oddly, it lists his place of residence as *Bab al-Sharia*, which is in Cairo, even though it is signed three various times giving the location of signature as Alexandria. His nephew, Morcos Youssef Atta, likewise finds it odd that that place was listed as his place of residence, as the family never left Alexandria once they moved there in 1910; see Marcos Hanna Youssef Atta, "Personal Correspondence, March 5, 2015," ed. Daniel Fanous (2015). The ID card also makes mention of a tattoo on his wrist (the classic sign of a Coptic Orthodox Christian in Egypt), as well as bilateral facial mark identifiers. The ID card gives his height at 175 cm (5'9"), though other photographs reveal a considerably taller man. Nelly van Doorn-Harder came to

a similar, and humorous, conclusion: "This man was a towering personality, not only in charisma but, judging by the size of his house shoes . . . in physical size as well." See Nelly van Doorn-Harder, "Kyrillos VI (1902–1971): Planner, Patriarch and Saint," in *BDC,* 223–24.

[93]Watson has claimed that Azer attended a "daily Liturgy" before work; see John H. Watson, *Among the Copts* (Brighton: Sussex Academic Press, 2000), 49. It is actually very unlikely that he did so, as the practice of daily Liturgies was incredibly rare if not nonexistent at the time. Liturgy was generally celebrated only on Friday (the official day off) and Sunday. The practice of daily Liturgies was only introduced in widespread practice by Kyrillos VI himself, first as a monk-priest and later as patriarch. See Rudolph Yanney, "Pope Cyril (Kyrillos) VI and the Liturgical Revival in the Coptic Church," *Coptic Church Review* 4, no. 1 (1983): 32 (hereafter "Liturgical Revival").

[94]Atta and Raphael Ava Mina, *Life of Pope Kyrillos,* 4.

[95]The accounts of Hanna Youssef Atta, Father Raphael Ava Mina, and the autobiographical fragments.

[96]Atta and Raphael Ava Mina, *Life of Pope Kyrillos,* 4; Father Raphael Ava Mina, *Pope Kyrillos VI and the Spiritual Leadership* (Cairo: Sons of Pope Kyrillos VI, 1977), 7. In his own autobiographical account a specific period of years is not given. But it should be noted that his brother, Hanna, places the revelation that he had been preparing for the monastic life for five years in a quotation at the mouth of Azer.

[97]Mina the Recluse [Kyrillos VI], "Autobiographical Fragments."

[98]Atta and Raphael Ava Mina, *Life of Pope Kyrillos,* 4. Interestingly, Meinardus (and Watson who seems to follow him) suggests that it was "during his days in Alexandria, while working for Thomas Cook and Sons, that he began reading *The Lives of the Desert Fathers,* an experience that determined the course of his life." See Meinardus, *Two Thousand Years,* 78; Watson, "Abba Kyrillos," 8. While altogether likely, given it is a seminal work and familiar literature for any monastic (or seeker of monasticism), there is no reference to this in the Arabic sources. I suspect it is a mistaken reference to an interview in which the patriarch recalls the events of July 1927 when he was awaiting his departure to the monastery and had access to the library of the Theological College for Monks in Alexandria. For a transcript of the interview, see Ramzy Wadie Girguis, *Pope Kyrillos: The Heavenly Harp,* trans. Safwat Youssef (Cairo: Sons of Pope Kyrillos VI, 2003), 12.

[99]Atta and Raphael Ava Mina, *Life of Pope Kyrillos,* 4.

[100]Ibid.

[101]Raphael Ava Mina, *Spiritual Leadership,* 7.

[102]Monk Mina el-Baramousy [Kyrillos VI], "Letter to Hanna Youssef Atta, undated, ?1930" [in Arabic], in FRC-1: Letter 489 (Cairo: undated; ?1930). It is similar in content to another letter, and therefore is indicative of his own teaching and behavior; see Father Mina el-Baramousy [Kyrillos VI], "Letter to Attia Labib, March 1933" [in Arabic], in FRC-2: Letter 19 (Cairo: 1933). These letters have been amalgamated in Father Raphael Ava Mina, *Christian Behaviour: According to the Saint Pope Kyrillos the Sixth* (Cairo: Sons of Pope Kyrillos VI, 2000), 9–12. These letters are suggestive of his familiarity with the "Jesus Prayer," albeit in varying forms.

[103]Mina el-Baramousy [Kyrillos VI], "Letter to Hanna Youssef Atta, undated, ?1930."

[104]Atta and Raphael Ava Mina, *Life of Pope Kyrillos,* 4.

[105]Ibid.

[106]Ibid.

[107]Ibid., 5.

[108]Mina the Recluse [Kyrillos VI], "Autobiographical Fragments."

[109]Ibid.

[110]Atta and Raphael Ava Mina, *Life of Pope Kyrillos,* 5.

[111]S. P. Brock, "Early Syrian Asceticism," *Numen* 20, no. 1 (1973): 1–2.

[112]Atta and Raphael Ava Mina, *Life of Pope Kyrillos,* 5. The fact that he approached Metropolitan Youannis without his father or brother itself speaks volumes to the contention that followed the conversation the night Azer announced his intentions.

[113]Metropolitan Youannis was also the vicar of the diocese of Alexandria because the incumbent (Cyril V, referred to as "Cyril" to avoid any possible confusion with Kyrillos VI, though in the original

the form of the name is the same for both) was elderly and needed assistance, and in fact would die only a month or so later, on August 7, 1927.

[114]Atta and Raphael Ava Mina, *Life of Pope Kyrillos*, 5.

[115]Ibid.

[116]Ibid.

[117]This is likely for the sake of brevity rather than any ulterior motive.

[118]Anonymous, *Archdeacon Iskander Hanna (1880–1944)* [in Arabic] (Nasr, Cairo: Sons of Pope Kyrillos VI, n.d.). Archdeacon Iskander Hanna became famous when preaching in St Mark's Cathedral in Alexandria; for a brief biography see Wolfram Reiss, *Erneuerung in der Koptisch-Orthodoxen Kirche: Die Geschichte der Koptisch-Orthodoxen Sonntagsschulbewegung und die Aufnahme ihrer Reformansätze in den Erneuerungsbewegunen der Koptisch-Orthodoxen Kirche der Gegenwart* (Hamburg: Lit Verlag, 1998), 152, n. 317. Reiss briefly mentions Iskander's relationship with Azer but does not give the above-mentioned details.

[119]Anonymous, *Iskander Hanna*, 23.

[120]Ibid.

[121]Ibid.

[122]Interview from *Saint George's Magazine*, April/May 1959, reproduced in Girguis, *The Heavenly Harp*, 13.

[123]Atta and Raphael Ava Mina, *Life of Pope Kyrillos*, 5. I. H. al-Masri claims that Father Youhanna told Youssef Atta: "I see that he [Azer] has planned the straight way, as God has called him for monastic life." See al-Masri, *Story of the Coptic Church*, 7:19. This seems to be a quote placed in the mouth of Father Youhanna that was in a sense created by I. H. al-Masri from Hanna's account: "After the Divine Liturgy, the priest advised Youssef to help Azer fulfil his plans and that Azer clearly knew what he was doing. He personally felt that this was God's choice for Azer." See Atta and Raphael Ava Mina, *Life of Pope Kyrillos*, 5. Also it should be noted that Father Youhanna was the confessor of the whole family, including Youssef himself—hence the efficacy of his words; see Atta, "Personal Correspondence, March 5, 2015."

[124]Atta and Raphael Ava Mina, *Life of Pope Kyrillos*, 5.

[125]Ibid.

[126]Fr Raphael Ava Mina recalls Metropolitan Youannis' words: "My son, the people who get used to urban life are incapable of pursuing the severe route of monasticism." See Raphael Ava Mina, *Spiritual Leadership*, 7.

[127]Ibid.

[128]Atta and Raphael Ava Mina, *Life of Pope Kyrillos*, 5.

[129]Ibid.

[130]Mina the Recluse [Kyrillos VI], "Autobiographical Fragments."

[131]Hanna Youssef Atta and Father Raphael Ava Mina, *My Memories about the Life of Pope Kyrillos VI* [in Arabic] (Cairo: Sons of Pope Kyrillos VI, 1981), 12. The English translation of this book, while generally good, at certain points misses details, or in this case, the entire quotation; see Atta and Raphael Ava Mina, *Life of Pope Kyrillos*, 5.

[132]Atta and Raphael Ava Mina, *Memories about the Life of Pope Kyrillos*, 12. The English translation again misses this.

2

Monk Mina: The Beginnings of Prayer (1927–1933)

The Call to the Monastery of the Romans, 1927

"That day on which I forsook the world was the happiest day of my life."
—*Pope Kyrillos VI*

WHEN AZER AWOKE the next morning, he knew his life had changed—inescapably so. From that day on, circumstances pending, he was a monk, albeit still in the world. While awaiting his departure to the monastery, he spent the Apostles' Fast (June 13 to July 12 that year) absorbed day and night in prayer.[1] During this period, Azer was fortunate to accompany monks who had traveled from their respective monasteries to study at the Monastic Theological College in Alexandria. "I was given a great opportunity," he recalls in a later interview,

> . . . to meet many of the monks; I sat with them and listened to the stories of their lives, as well as the lives of the saints, so I loved them. From the Church I began to borrow books and the histories of the saints, and I aspired to attain this life of dedication to the Church.[2]

It was a time of profound preparation, Azer's first sustained exposure to authentic monasticism. Pilgrimages or retreats to monasteries at the time were all too rare, most often impossible. Yet here, amid monks in Alexandria, Azer tasted patristic and monastic works, foremost of which was *The Paradise of the Desert Fathers*.[3] Not only would this experience determine the course of Azer's life, as one scholar notes, but it would also place "many questions against the life of the Church as he saw it."[4] What he read of the saints and monastic fathers was, to some degree, tragically removed from the Church of his day.

By the fast's end, the young man's elation had grown considerably. On the Apostles' Feast, July 12, his family brought him a large basket of oily pastries (*feteer*) to distribute to parishioners for the Feast of the Archangel Michael—which happened to fall a few days later.[5] Incapable of restraining his joy at the prospect of monasticism, Azer arrived grinning at St Mark's Church dressed in his finest suit, with a peasant's oil-soaked basket on his shoulder. The sight was unusual, bordering on scandalous for the middle class. Azer was unbothered and remarked, "If the Lord's disciples each carried a basket of the remaining leftovers after the miracle of feeding the multitudes, am I better than they?"[6] Carried away by excitement, Azer went so far as preparing a *curriculum vitae*—which, of course, was hardly necessary.[7]

At the end of the semester at the Theological College, the monks began preparing to return to their monasteries. Azer waited, nervous and expectant. Finally, Metropolitan Youannis called—the date was set. Within a few weeks, Azer would depart with a recently ordained monk-priest, Fr Bishara el-Bara-mousy (1906–1980).[8] Youannis gave Fr Bishara a letter of recommendation for the abbot concerning the young postulant. The metropolitan, Hanna recalls, also quietly whispered to the accompanying monk, "Be careful to hold on to the young man's clothes and belongings."[9] He reasonably anticipated that perhaps Azer would not last long in the austere and unrelenting desert.

* * *

In the early hours of Wednesday, July 27, 1927, Azer awoke (if he slept at all) and packed to anticipate his immediate needs.[10] His father, brothers, and sisters slowly walked with him to the Mahattat Misr Railway Station in Alexandria, a kilometer (0.6 mi) away.[11] There, his family and friends gathered to see him off. We can only imagine the tearful embraces, painful kisses, and last words. His direct manager from Thomas Cook & Son, Alfred Fadel, was also present. He had come to communicate the well-wishes of the general manager and, notably, to remind Azer that his job would indefinitely be waiting for him should he change his mind. Azer quietly smiled, Hanna notes, and thanked him for his generous words. All presumed or at least hoped that this was an impetuous and short-lived foray into the world of monasticism. But they had only the faintest idea of the unquenchable desire for solitude burning deep within the heart of the young man. "They took me to the train station and gave me their blessing," wrote Azer in a revealing autobiographical fragment, "[and] that day, on which I forsook the world, was the *happiest day of my life*."[12]

Little else was previously known of his journey to the monastery and his first days there. Yet at the end of the first two issues of the periodical *Harbor of Salvation*—which Azer would write in early 1928—there are autobiographical depictions of the journey. These priceless comments have never been studied, reproduced (in any language), or even acknowledged. They were seemingly glossed over, given their rather abrupt place in the "narrative section" of the periodicals.[13] They *were* lost to history—until now. Azer, according to the account, along with Fr Bishara and the monks who had been studying in Alexandria, left the world. "The train departed from Alexandria station and was going so fast," Azer writes,

> . . . then it stopped at Damanhur Station, so we met the honorable Awad and Hanna Effendi, who were waiting for us; we exchanged greetings, and then they bade us farewell, wishing us success. Then the train went forth and stopped at Itay al-Baroud Station, so we changed to the train going to al-Khatatba, where we had a break at the rest house. There we ate with the fathers—fried fish and watermelon.[14]

At four in the afternoon, they boarded an old train of the Salt & Soda Company to al-Hokaria (Bir Hokir).[15] "I was amazed," Azer recalls, "at the look of the train, as it was extremely ancient, as if from the days of the Prophet Noah."[16] They arrived at al-Hokaria at ten o'clock at night.[17] As he left the train, according to the account of Fr Raphael (his later disciple), Azer asked the conductor why he was not wearing the customary *tarboosh* (or *fez*). The conductor replied that he did not have the funds to purchase one. Azer promptly took off his *tarboosh* and gleefully handed it to the conductor. Moments later, he gave his suit jacket to another, an impoverished train driver. He promised to also send his shirt and trousers the moment he arrived at the monastery (and he actually did so).[18] Fr Bishara never had a chance to honor the metropolitan's request to preserve Azer's clothes should he change his mind. The metropolitan may have had reservations, but the young man was absolute in his renunciation and consecration. He had no intention of ever returning to the world.

There at the station, one of the monks awaited them, to begin the final journey on foot:

> We walked through this magnificent endless mountain. While walking, I was looking around for the monastery, and after an hour and fifteen minutes, we saw from afar a glimpse of light coming from the top of the mountain. I was so peaceful, and God knows that I had *never* felt that comfort before![19]

Azer and the monks approached the monastery in the stillness and silence of the desert. As they drew closer, its obscure form became clearer.[20] Finally, they reached the place Azer had long dreamed of, the home of his enduring hopes. He stood before the monastery's remarkable wall, some ten meters (33 feet) high and two meters (7 feet) thick, covered in an ancient plaster long weathered by the golden sands of the Wadi al-Natrun. Atop the walls, a walkway spanned its entire length, so that monks could stand guard against raiding Berbers and Bedouins.

"I was so astounded," Azer writes as he neared the whitewashed tower,

> ... and was looking for the door; then the father pointed to a door that was very small compared to this huge building. It was a very solid iron door, two meters high and one meter wide [7 feet by 3.3 feet], at the top end of the door there was a bell. [This was] so that whoever arrived at the monastery would ring it, [and] then the priest responsible for the door would come and, through a window overlooking the door, could see the visitor. . . . We rang the bell, [and] they opened.[21]

* * *

The Baramous Monastery, the earliest-known monastic settlement in the desert of Scetis, was founded in or around AD 340. In Abba Serapion's *vita* of St Macarius of Egypt (300–391), Maximus and Domadius, two Roman princes and sons of the Emperor Valentinian, arrived in Scetis after a pilgrimage in Palestine. There they met Macarius, the priest of the desert. After witnessing the profound lives and deaths of these two "little strangers," Macarius consecrated their cells, declaring, "Call this place the Cells of the Romans." The monastic community that gathered around Macarius dwelt near these Roman cells, hence the name Baramous (Coptic: *Paromeos*, "that of the Romans").[22]

Foreign visitors to the monastery, contemporary with Azer, paint an intriguing picture of the time. The reality is likely to be found somewhere in the middle of these accounts. Konstantin von Tischendorf, who discovered one of the earliest extant biblical manuscripts (the *Codex Sinaïticus*), visited the monastery in 1844, and noted that there were twenty monks: "Here the cells were the blackest of all . . . they live carelessly from day to day. To such an existence, what is the past and what is the future?"[23] In October 1913, Johann Georg noted the refectory looked more like a prison than a dining hall.[24] A decade later, in 1923, Doctor William Hatch was rather impressed by the state of the library and monastery, counting some thirty monks.[25] And Prince Omar Toson, who visited in 1931, claimed from his studies that the monastery was the wealthiest of the Wadi al-Natrun.[26] One visitor even shared Azer's awe in approaching the monastery. H. V. Morton, a renowned travel writer, was intrigued by the monastery's wall and the vast archway that stood in stark contrast to the unusually small gate:

> The archway was made for giants, but the gate for dwarfs. There was no need to ask the reason for this narrow postern; it spoke eloquently enough of desert raids. . . . I spent some moments examining the door. Never have I seen one so loaded with chains, bolts, locks, and wooden cross-bars.[27]

* * *

"When I entered I felt as though I had walked into Paradise, and the monks were like angels," Azer recalls.[28] Once through the disproportionately small door, there was a six-meter corridor with a barrel-vaulted roof leading to another fortified-iron door that opened into the heart of the monastery. As Azer passed through the gates, he was euphoric. The previously undiscovered autobiographical account describes the scene:

> All the monks came out from their cells. . . . They greeted us and then led us to the palace prepared for guests. It was a two-story luxury palace; the ground floor contained four rooms, and [there were] another four on the top floor, which were very well furnished. We waited in a room on the ground floor ready for dinner, then they brought some water, and everyone participated in washing our feet, the younger monks and the elders. We were *ashamed*, but they informed us that it was a very old custom since the early fathers. We were served dinner and thanked God. After a little while they took us to the top floor to sleep, so we slept calmly and peacefully.[29]

Azer awoke early Thursday morning, to the bell of prayer, with uncharacteristic energy after only a few hours of sleep. He thought little of the fact that this monastery *seemed* a world away from Metropolitan Youannis' austere and onerous description, and he immediately made for the church, where he "enjoyed its beauty which no one could describe."[30] "We attended the Divine Liturgy," Azer recalls, "and by chance, the priest who served was an honorable pious elder praying with the spirit . . . we left so happy and thanked God."[31] In another autobiographical account, he is all too brief: "I went to the church, attended the Divine Liturgy, and received abundant grace."[32]

After the Liturgy, Fr Bishara presented the abbot, Hegumen Shenouda, with the metropolitan's letter. The abbot's face suddenly contorted. Azer had spent the night in the guest palace, but he was no guest. The "guest palace," a nineteenth-century Levantine villa, had been built by Metropolitan Youannis himself in 1911.[33] It was hardly a residence for monks, let alone beginning novices. In Hanna's memoirs, Azer's treatment was a mistake in the confusion of night. Fr Bishara had inadvertently introduced the young man as a "visitor" from Alexandria, a spiritual son of Metropolitan Youannis.[34] For this reason, he was treated to relative luxury: he was served dinner, and the generator was even switched on to provide lighting.

Nevertheless, it was still a momentous, albeit curious, arrival. Novices were few and far between, and rarely, if ever, were they educated city dwellers. The abbot ordered the bell rung and informed the gathered monks that their young "guest" had, in fact, come to join them. Many of the monks cautiously whispered and murmured, wondering what manner of monk this would be.[35] It was the first time a novice had spent the night in opulence.

"We ate breakfast," Azer reminisces,

> . . . then Father Shenouda, the Abbot, showed me the room I would stay in, that is, until they found a cell for me. It was a beautiful room next to the altar and was previously customized for the Pope, but now it was used by visitors. I stayed there for a week and rejoiced in abundance.[36]

The room in question was once the accommodation for Pope Cyril V (1831–1927)—in altogether unpleasant and unfortunate circumstances. As the week went on, Azer would have certainly reflected upon the infamous incident. In 1892, Cyril had been exiled to the Baramous Monastery following a prolonged contention with the Community Council (*maglis al-melli*).[37] The six months of his exile were catastrophic. A puppet replacement, Athanasius, was excommunicated. Churches throughout Egypt were desolate, sacraments went unadministered, and the once-faithful became disillusioned. Though Cyril V would return shortly after, the episode would be burned into the monastery's desert memory and would stand as a future word of warning concerning the *maglis* for all who dared to enter (and later exit as bishops) the monastery's unusually small gates.

As the week came to an end, the abbot at last found a permanent cell for Azer. The abbot proceeded to show him where the bread was kept and then left without another word.[38] "I went to have a look," Azer remembers:

> It was a cell in a one-hundred-fifty-year-old building. It had two rooms: an outer room, and an inner one called the "hermitage." I cleaned and organized

it, hanging some icons and the *kandil* [lamp] that I had brought with me, and it became so beautiful.[39]

The cell had previously been inhabited by a blind and saintly monk, presumably Awad el-Barhemey (d. 1878).[40] Since then, it had been left in a state of neglect and disrepair. Hanna notes that the cell was "old and deserted," initially uninhabitable. Azer painstakingly scrubbed the ground, sprinkled crushed gypsum, and resealed the floors. He placed his suitcase at the center of the outer room, and this became his makeshift table.[41] The young man donned his cherished black cassock, placed a black covering over his head, and, according to Hanna's memoirs, "looked like he had been a monk for many years."[42] Azer's irrepressible dreams and hopes of the last five years had finally been realized. For the next few days, he lived in prayer. When the bell rang for the midnight psalmody (*tasbeha*), he would rush to the church. When the service concluded at seven in the morning, Hanna is careful to note, he would silently return to his cell "*without mingling* with the other monks."[43]

The accounts here, we should note, are unanimous. Other than the brief and moderately mistaken welcome, Azer was apparently isolated. No one had helped him, and he had not asked for help. He had neither spoken to the others, nor they to him. Already, it would seem, he was very much alone.

Novitiate under Fr Abdel Messih el-Masudi, 1927–1928

> "An elder is one who takes your soul and your will, into his soul and his will."
> —*Fyodor Dostoyevsky*

THE YOUNG AND INEXPERIENCED novice was not left to fend for himself without purpose. Fr Bishara (who accompanied Azer to the monastery) had earlier approached the abbot and expressed his dismay that at least some form of guidance or help had not been offered. But the abbot, in Hanna's account, was emphatic; Azer was to be left alone.[44] If he could survive the week in relative solitude with invariable discomfort and hardship, then perhaps he could be considered. The abbot, it would appear, held misgivings similar to those of the metropolitan.

Having heard nothing—neither complaint nor plea for help—the abbot, on Saturday evening, took with him four elders (Fr Bishara and Hegumens Bishay, Basilious, and Abdel Messih el-Masudi) in order to examine the case of this aspiring monk.[45] Surprisingly, they found the cell to be carefully restored, with few to no furnishings, but nonetheless beautifully arranged.[46] In a previously undiscovered autobiographical fragment, Azer recalls that one of the fathers christened the cell "the Temple of Jerusalem." Afterward the name became widely known, and visiting monks would merrily bow before an icon of the Theotokos in the outer room while declaring, "I want to worship in the Temple of Jerusalem."[47]

As the party of now-satisfied elders made to leave the cell, Azer prostrated himself before them. Without any reason or warning, almost abruptly, Fr Abdel Messih el-Masudi took the hand of the novice, looked him ever so intently in the eyes, and blessed him. Hanna, fortunately, preserves the words in their entirety. "My son," the elder said,

> . . . the blessing of monasticism is to give your heart to God. This is a great treasure, more valuable than all the world's treasures. The monk, who voluntarily selects poverty and has prepared himself to be an honest soldier of Jesus Christ, is greater than all the world's kings and rulers in both strength and position. *My heart is totally opened to you.* I ask the Lord Jesus Christ to guide you and to open the door of grace for you. I ask him to fill your heart with peace to live in this sojourn peacefully, so do not fear any evil, God be with you, his rod and his staff will comfort you.[48]

Azer could only manage to prostrate himself again before the elderly monk, kissing his hand. "From this hour," Masudi said while embracing the young novice, "you are a *gift from God,* and you will be a son to me."[49] With little explanation, Masudi became the spiritual father of the future patriarch.

The elder's only disclosure was that his "heart [was] totally opened" to Azer. Intriguingly, the character of the discipleship was atypical. The young novice was, in Masudi's own words, the "gift from God," and not the reverse. What the elder saw in Azer beyond these few curious and remarkable words is not known. Be that as it may, the profound influence of this extraordinary elder—though rarely appreciated—is unmistakable.

* * *

The figure of this elderly monk, Abdel Messih el-Masudi, is shrouded in confusion. Most scholars of the period struggle to determine his history precisely.[50]
The simple reason for this is that there was more than one Masudi, many being
related and having partially overlapping names—three of whom, at least, entered
the Baramous Monastery in the nineteenth century.

The first was known as Fr Abdel Messih Girguis el-Masudi el-Muharraqi
el-Kabir (1818–1906). He was born in el-Shaikh Masoud, west of Tahta, deep
in the Souhag governorate some 550 kilometers (342 miles) from the Baramous
Monastery. From that town the family would take the name Masudi.[51] Girguis
el-Masudi, known as *el-Kabir* ("the Great") to differentiate him from his future
nephew, began his monasticism in 1835, closer to home at the Muharraq Monastery. Though young, only seventeen years of age, he was quickly ordained a
priest and was noted for his intelligence. His sister, Aziza (d. 1870), became a
nun at St George's Convent in Zuwayla. Another brother, Salib, also attempted
to enter the Muharraq Monastery, but his father had him forcibly removed and
conveniently married.[52]

Girguis el-Masudi spent twenty-two years at Muharraq Monastery and was,
by all accounts, an esteemed scholar. There, he came under the tutelage of Fr
Paul el-Muharraqi (1829–1914), the future bishop and saint, Abraam of Faiyum
and Giza.[53] We should also be careful to note that there was, in fact, another
"Masudi" at the Muharraq Monastery, by the name of Fr Abdel Messih ibn
Abdelmalek el-Masudi el-Muharraqi; he was apparently a distant relative, and
was acclaimed for his studies on the liturgical canon and the psalmody.[54]

After some contention within the monastery, Girguis el-Masudi settled further north at the Baramous Monastery, where he became the confessor of the
monks, and eventually abbot.[55] In 1870, after the death of Pope Demetrius II,
Girguis was one of the papal candidates, and on a number of later occasions
refused the episcopacy.[56] He spent most of the last fifteen years of his life in
varying degrees of solitude, dwelling in a number of caves that he carved out
himself.[57] Girguis was renowned for his rare capacity of marrying an ascetic
life with prolific scholarship—he scribed (and memorized) many of the Syriac
writings of Sts Isaac and Ephraim, and wrote widely, from expositions on the
Orthodox faith to numerous polemical works, as well as an invaluable biography of St Pachomius the Great (292–348).[58] In September 1906 he died at
eighty-eight years of age.

Salib, his brother, though unable to become a monk himself, would go on
to father seven children, four of whom became monastics. Two daughters took

vows at the Abu Sefein Convent; Justina (d. 1928) became the abbess, and the other, Sefina (d. 1919), was remembered as an able scribe and scholar.[59] That the family produced literate daughters, let alone scholars, in late nineteenth-century Egypt should not be passed over lightly. Two sons entered the same monastery as their uncle, Girguis el-Masudi. The birth name of one (to make matters ever so confusing) was Girguis Salib Girguis. He entered the Baramous monastery in 1884 and was, from then on, known as Fr Yacoub el-Masudi el-Baramousy, or the "silent monk," from his vow of silence.[60] The other son, Fr Abdel Messih ibn Salib el-Masudi el-Baramousy (1848–1935), was incomparably the more illustrious of the two—and the eventual spiritual father of Azer.

Abdel Messih ibn Salib el-Masudi was born in the same village as his father and uncle. In 1873 he followed his uncle to the Baramous Monastery, where he was tonsured a monk a year later and ordained a priest in 1875.[61] He was an industrious scholar and was responsible for the renaissance of the Baramous Monastery. Within years he had catalogued the monastery's library, and he often left the monastery to study at the Patriarchal Library in Cairo.[62] From 1887 to 1932, his writing was prolific. He mastered English, French, Hebrew, Arabic, Coptic, Greek, Syriac, and the Ethiopic languages, and his works reveal he was a polymath. He wrote widely and profusely, from historical studies of the monasteries of the Wadi al-Natrun to evaluations of psychological methods; he was often consulted by the patriarchs Cyril V and Youannis XIX; and he wrote a number of theological works in response. His work on Arabic grammar in 1888, *The Apostrophe*, was long used by the al-Azhar sheikhs.[63] As keeper of the Patriarchal Library, he contributed the lives of Cyril IV to Youannis XIX in the monumental *History of the Patriarchs*.[64] He became most renowned for his study on the *Interpretation of the Epact* (1925), that is, the methodology for determining the ecclesial calendar, a work that was written over twenty years.[65] Perhaps his most important work, though certainly not most celebrated, was his penetrating study of the liturgical texts that appeared in 1903. This was the first time all three Liturgies of the Coptic Orthodox Church appeared in one volume, with scholarly translations, commentaries, and appendices.[66]

Fr Abdel Messih el-Masudi was remembered as erudite, ascetic, mostly silent, and enduringly humble.[67] That Azer should come under his discipleship—learning from the leading light of scholarship (and authentic monasticism) in early twentieth-century Egypt—is altogether peculiar and rare. The extraordinary heritage of the Masudi family, in the person of his spiritual father, was passed on to the unsuspecting novice. In a later interview, Azer recalled that this scholar-monk had the "deepest influence on my soul."[68] A later comment in the same interview is telling: "He was a very humble man, who appeared to people *as though he were illiterate*, while in reality, he was one of the greatest minds of the Church during his time."[69] Azer's words, it may be suggested, were both paradigmatic and subtly autobiographical.

In old age Abdel Messih el-Masudi could be seen traveling by third-class carriage to Cairo, and quietly praying at St Stephen's, a small and modest church adjacent to the cathedral.[70] Standing next to him, few would suspect the exceptional genius of the hunched-over and elderly man. On March 15, 1935, he died at the age of eighty-seven.[71] Masudi's legacy and the depths of his family's heritage would live on through the young novice whom he esteemed as a "gift from God."

* * *

Under the guidance of Masudi, Azer quickly proved himself to be an exemplary novice in both meekness and humility. He often gave himself to the most unpleasant of tasks and found gratification in serving the elderly monks, washing their clothes, cleaning their cells, and preparing their meals. They, in return, never forgot him in their prayers. "But," Hanna is careful to note, in keeping with Azer's characteristic self-imposed seclusion, "he *never* visited anyone *except* to offer him service."[72]

Each month the abbot would distribute the tasks of the monks. Azer, as might be expected for a novice, was allocated the dreaded kitchen duty. This was no mean feat in early-twentieth-century Egypt, and in the desert, of all places. But he set about his work with diligence, cleaning copper pots and repairing wood stoves. Water tanks had to be cleaned, and pitchers filled for the elderly monks. Grain had to be ground, and the holy eucharistic bread (*qorban*) had to be baked. Each task, according to his brother's memoirs, was performed with care, unflinching obedience, and deep concern for his elders.[73] Never once would his spiritual father, Masudi, respond with praise. Humility was a virtue to be forged in the depths of a broken will, shattered by toil, and reformed by obedience. Flattery had no place. All the while, undeterred by the slaving schedule, his life of prayer, study of Scripture, and liturgy continued uninterrupted.[74]

In early September 1927, as the summer months passed, several monks began preparing to resume their studies at the Monastic Theological College in Alexandria. The abbot called for the young novice to see whether he would like to return to the world. "Please allow me to continue on the road I have started,"

Azer begged the abbot. "I am confident that the Lord would never leave those who call upon him."[75] The abbot happily consented. Before leaving, Fr Bishara asked whether he would at least like to send a letter to his family. Azer's words, in his brother's memoirs, disclose his determined sentiments:

> Joseph didn't send a letter to his father when he called him to come to Egypt, but said to his brothers, "Tell my father what your eyes have seen, and what your ears have heard." And I, the meek, do similar to what Joseph did. I ask the traveling fathers to tell my family of the blessings God has given me through the prayers of the fathers.[76]

* * *

Toward the end of 1927, we have a glimpse of a first apparent, albeit implicit, "miracle" at the hands of Azer.[77] According to Hanna's account, a monk by the name of Armanious (who would be the future bishop of the monastery), was given the task of delivering the monastery's mail to the post office via a "stubborn, hard-to-control mule." After unknown struggles with the unruly animal, Armanious was thrown to the ground, and the mule escaped into the endless desert. Following a grueling search for the beast in the wilderness, Armanious returned exhausted, late at night, to the monastery, where the monks had gathered fearing the worst.

One monk, who had something of a reputation for "being too obsessed with the monastery's property," was less concerned for Armanious' safety than for the loss of the mule.[78] He angrily confronted Armanious, shouting that in no way would he be allowed back into the monastery without the mule in hand. Given the deadness of night, a scene of sorts ensued. Azer, at the time still a young novice, dared, in turn, to reprimand the fuming monk. "Father," Azer uttered, "let him in and allow him to rest. . . . One of the Bedouins will find [the mule] and bring it here." Should the animal not be found, Azer offered to compensate the monastery the full price of the mule. The enraged monk had little time for the novice. Even his fellow monks were incapable of appeasing him despite their protests that Azer "spoke with wisdom." Moments later, the bell of the monastery rang. A flurry of dark cassocks rushed down the corridor, through the door, to the moonlit desert. There, before the disproportionate gate of the monastery, stood an unwitting Bedouin, with the unhappy mule restrained. The monks handsomely tipped the finder, with, Hanna recalls, the largest amount coming from Azer.[79]

Unsurprisingly, the next morning Armanious refused to ride the disorderly beast. The novice curiously stepped forward. The abbot, of course, tried to advise against it quietly; this was no job for a novice or a city dweller. But Azer at some earlier point had apparently learned to ride horses, and buck as it may, he was able to tame the animal—with, we may imagine, some occasional setbacks if not incidental bruising.

Armanious may never have ridden that animal again, but he was eventually made abbot of the Baramous Monastery in 1948, and a year later was ordained its bishop, thence known as Anba Macarius (d. 1965).[80] This well-known episode, like any oral or written tradition, would, therefore, have been rejected had it been an embellishment, especially given its potential embarrassment for the future bishop. It also depicts a personality of the young novice that is consistent with the portrait emerging from other sources. Within only a few months as a novice, he had earned the respect of his fellow monks, though *some*, we need to add, would harbor jealousy and ill intentions toward him. These mixed sentiments would mark his life from this point forward.[81]

Despite his relative spiritual infancy, Azer was not afraid to voice his concerns—speaking the truth in love—even at a cost to himself; in this case he was willing to bear the brunt of his superior's indignation, potentially becoming liable for the monetary loss and, in the end, taking upon himself, willingly, the arduous task of taming the mutinous mule. If this is, as Hanna implicitly suggests, the first miracle, then it materializes only (and inherently) within Azer's "vocation of loss" as a movement of kenotic self-giving.[82] Fittingly, the phenomenon occurs ever so naturally, in a few simple words, without drama or flair—suiting rather well the unpretentious young novice.

The Birth of a Monastic Recluse, 1928–1930

"Love all men but keep distant from all men."
—*St Isaac the Syrian*

I N EARLY MARCH 1928, six workers from the Suez Canal Company in Northern Egypt met with a young "firebrand" schoolteacher by the name of Hassan el-Banna (1906–1949). It was the beginning of the infamous "Muslim Brotherhood."[83] Almost simultaneously, only days earlier, a young novice's profession instituted a very different movement. Both would become deeply entrenched and enduring, both in contention for the heart of the nation.

* * *

"After my novitiate of about nine months," Azer warmly recalls,

> God *wished* that I become a monk. The reverend fathers unanimously agreed to nominate me, and the abbot was in agreement. I was tonsured in the Old Church that contained all the relics of the saints.[84]

And so, it was on Friday night, the eve of February 25, 1928, that the twenty-five-year-old Azer entered the ancient Church of the Holy Virgin—as "God wished"—to be tonsured a monk.[85] The basilica, near the eastern wall of the monastery, the oldest of the Wadi al-Natrun, was originally built in the late sixth century. Its lengthy history would not have been lost on the novice as he made his way into the nave of the candlelit church, surrounded by thirty or so other monks, gazing at the ethereal iconography clothing the walls. As he stood there, at the threshold of certain consecration, his tears could not be restrained.

The abbot, in accordance with the Rite of Tonsure, devoutly drew the curtains in front of the main sanctuary for the beginning of Vespers, placing the new monastic clothes (cassock, head covering, and leather girdle) upon the intricately hand-carved wooden altar.[86] Azer was asked to stand in front of the sanctuary's door, while the abbot asked, "Does anyone object?"[87] The church remained silent. Azer prostrated himself in front of the sanctuary, between the relics of St Moses the Black and St Isidore, then in the direction of the monastery's door (a symbol of obedience), and finally before his fathers, begging for absolution and forgiveness. After conferring with the other monks as to the choice of monastic name (apparently a cause of some debate), the abbot thrice made the sign of the Cross over the garments while pronouncing the new name.

"The fathers had been arguing," Azer reminisces,

> . . . as to what name to give me, and finally they decided to name me after the saint of the day in the *Synaxarion* and that would be the will of the Lord; it happened that it was the commemoration of the departure of Menas [Mina] the monk, and so I was named by the blessed name of Menas. . . .[88]

We have no record of Azer's reaction to hearing the words "Fr Mina"—the uttering of the name of his revered saint. But we can well imagine. Once more, it would appear, St Menas had chosen the young novice.

The significance of the name—personal and ecclesial—should not be overlooked. Although certainly mistaken in claiming that Azer chose the monastic name of Mina himself, a few scholars have at least perceived the ramifications.[89] Following the discovery of the Menas shrine in Mariout in 1906, the saint was quietly rediscovered. Decades later, in August 1929, a Muslim lawyer by the name of Ahmad Hussein famously denounced the ongoing British presence, citing St Menas, surprisingly, as a national hero who had resisted foreign oppression, and in doing so, suddenly catapulted the saint into the national consciousness.[90] In receiving the name, therefore, Azer was inescapably entwined with one whom Voile has called a "complete figure," a saint of profound sanctity, beyond reproach; an authentically Coptic figure who was revered also by Muslims, practically being "erected as a national symbol."[91] Whether prescience, mere coincidence, or divine intervention, the name would bear within it the hopes of the nation.

The night continued in solemn prayer and psalmody. Early in the morning, as the later rite maintains, Azer lay on his back on the ground before the relics of the saints, crossing his hands on his chest, as though he were dead in a coffin. It was his funeral. According to the rite, the Scripture readings and hymns were chanted in the "mournful" tone, and over the body of the reposed young novice, the Litany of the Departed was prayed. Having died to his old self, the novice now arose as a monk in Christ. After cutting his hair five times in a cruciform pattern, the abbot clothed Azer in his monastic cassock, head covering, and leather girdle. Azer was no more. Henceforth he was Fr Mina el-Baramousy.

Immediately after the Divine Liturgy, according to Hanna's account, the monks gathered. Fr Yacoub el-Masudi el-Baramousy, the brother of Abdel Messih el-Masudi, casually entered their midst. All eyes turned to him, first curiously, and then expectantly. Yacoub, known as the "silent monk," had not spoken in many years. Yet now he slowly began to open his mouth. The monks (and Fr Mina with them) stared on in disbelief. "Dear son," Yacoub whispered,

> . . . may God's blessing be with you and may he grant you his grace, and pave your path so that you will be successful in all you do. May he fill you with his Holy Spirit so that you will be honest to your last breath with the talents the Lord Jesus Christ will give you, to invest them and make them grow.[92]

The monks, new and old, were speechless: Why had the silent monk finally chosen to speak now?

* * *

"From that day forward," Fr Mina writes in an autobiographical fragment,

> I began to learn the rules of monasticism from the fathers and started study-
> ing the books of the saints, especially those written by the great St Isaac
> [the Syrian]. I felt the grace of God *growing* within me day by day. . . . I was
> obedient to all, and thus, took their blessings. I was very keen on serving the
> elders, so I spent one year serving the learned Fr Abdel-Messih el-Masudi.
> I was taught the psalmody by Hegumen Pakhoum, who was my father in
> confession. I also served Fr Anthony for one year.[93]

Day by day, the grace of God was "growing within" the young monk. In his
brother's memoirs, Fr Mina's meticulous care for the elderly fathers never fal-
tered even though he was now their equal. He refused to relinquish the blessing
of baking the *qorban* (eucharistic bread), painstakingly sifting the flour in the
early hours of the morning. Not yet a priest, it was the beginning of his almost
organic union to the Eucharist that would remain until his last breath.[94] He was
meek, his brother recounts, tolerating all manner of discomfort; was invariably
forgiving, habitually calm, forever avoiding anger, and he "never expected nor
looked for praise or glory."[95]

This period was marked most by the influence of Abdel Messih el-Masudi.
A few weeks before his monastic tonsure, Masudi had requested Fr Mina (then
Azer) to publish a theological periodical.[96] On February 9, 1928, the first volume of the *Harbor of Salvation* (*Mina al-khalas*) appeared.[97] While searching
through a number of patristic and monastic works in preparation for the periodical, he came across a description of the monastery as an "earthly harbor
of salvation," and hence the name.[98] Each handwritten volume was divided
into three sections: a personal theological discourse; excerpts from patristic or
monastic fathers; and a narrative section that at times was autobiographical,
though mostly it contained excerpts from contemporary spiritual writings.[99]

The theological periodical was published monthly from February 1928 to
January 1930, with at least seventeen volumes still extant. Ranging from seven
to thirteen pages, each volume was laboriously scribed into some fifty copies by
Fr Mina.[100] Fragments have only occasionally appeared, with the majority of the
exquisite writings remaining unknown until now.[101] Needless to say, these once-
hidden periodicals shed revealing light on the intellectual world of the young
monk, exposing a penetrating mind that was immersed in patristic and monastic thought—a mind absorbed in (especially eucharistic) theology, scriptural
exegesis, the lives of the saints, and occasional philosophical thought. Mina's

writings forcefully challenge the popular and oft-repeated notion that he was merely an unlearned ascetic. As Fr Raphael Ava Mina (his future disciple) once noted, a preference for silence is not necessarily synonymous with "inaptitude or deficiency."[102] The future patriarch, lest we forget, came under the tutelage of some of the greatest scholars of his day and spent years immersed in patristic literature.[103] "[He] himself told me," Raphael recalls, "that what he gained from silence greatly exceeded what he would have achieved by any other means."[104] Silence hardly warrants nearsighted and premature judgment.

Much of Mina's time during these years was spent in the monastery's library under the guidance of the inexhaustible Masudi. The southern sanctuary of the Church of St John the Baptist had been transformed into a well-appointed library through the efforts of Masudi, who classified thousands of manuscripts, as well as translating and scribing many himself. There, Fr Mina shared in his spiritual father's labors, restoring and transcribing manuscripts; and there, Hanna recounts, the "doors of knowledge were opened to him."[105]

But of all the works in the library, there was one that would indelibly mark his innermost soul: the *Ascetical Homilies* of St Isaac the Syrian.[106] In this, he followed in the hallowed footsteps of Abdel Messih el-Masudi, and Girguis el-Masudi before him. Quite possibly, it was the most prodigious and sublime gift he would inherit from them; practically, it was the most instrumental and, evidently, the most influential too. Fr Mina was so taken by the *Ascetical Homilies* that he scribed the work into five volumes, devouring and memorizing them.[107] All the more infatuated, he studiously scribed the work a further four times, making them readily available to his brethren.[108] Each reading, transcription, and memorization was a vigorous, determined, and consummate immersion in the thought-world of the Syrian.

How, and to what extent, this shaped the worldview of the young monk has rarely been appreciated. For now, we should at least note that early in his study of the *Ascetical Homilies* he came across a saying that would become a lifelong maxim. His brother recalls that it was a law unto him for the rest of his days, and his future disciple notes that it was even written above the door of his patriarchal cell.[109] Yet none have noticed—then or now—that it was an aphorism borrowed and memorized from the writings of St Isaac the Syrian: *"Love all men, but keep distant from all men."*[110]

* * *

For Fr Mina, these words were a paradigm. On January 17, 1929, he somewhat characteristically replied to a concerned letter written to him by his brother Hanna. On a recent visit to the monastery, Hanna could not help but notice that Fr Mina rarely left his cell, and looked to be at enmity with his fellow monks. The letter in reply, perhaps the earliest extant (and hence quoted in full), substantiates the emerging portrait of an early recluse yearning for what may be termed "solitude within solitude."[111]

"My beloved, I received your kind letter," Fr Mina writes in response,

> . . . and I thank you for your warm feelings and valuable advice. As for me, God knows, I am quite content with my life. I live as peacefully as I can with everyone, refusing to side with anyone. *I live in solitude* in my cell, welcoming all who come to see me, doing my utmost and respecting all, young and old. I do not interfere with what does not concern me. I go back and forth straight from the church to my cell, as well as attending to whatever task is entrusted to me. In this, I am the *same man before and after monasticism*. Do not be concerned about me, as I am depending on God. Have you ever known anyone that trusted in God and was disappointed? Never!

Mina does not deny the charge: he lives in solitude, even within the borders of the cloister, just as he had in his private room before monasticism—as his brother undoubtedly recalls. "Be assured," the young monk continues,

> . . . I am not biased toward anyone. Nor do I avoid some and socialize with others; rather, *I remain in seclusion from all*—even if some of the fathers feel this is a sign of bias. You should know, my beloved, that I have taken the advice of respected fathers such as Hegumen Mansour and Hegumen Boctor, and remained in seclusion in my cell, refusing to interfere in that which does not concern me. I have found complete peace in heeding their advice. Our fathers, the saints, said, "The one who sits in his cell reciting the psalms is like a man that beholds the king; and he who sits in solitude weeping over his sins, is like a man in conversation with the king." There is nothing greater than for a man to *remain alone* in his cell, constantly begging God to grant him a fountain of tears to weep over his sins, that God may forgive him.
>
> When Hegumen Phillip, the monastery's superintendent, read your letter, he was very surprised and said, "My son, from the day you came to the monastery, I have never seen you biased against anyone nor avoiding anyone. You do not mingle with anyone, but have always been happier alone, in your cell."[112]

Though he does not deny the charge, his solitude was not out of bias, nor enmity, nor avoiding any specific monk; rather he sought to avoid them *all*. Mina is explicit: his primary concern is to "remain alone" with God. But to avoid any place for self-deceit, he first sought the advice of his superiors and went so far as to show his brother's letter to the monastery's superintendent. Though he genuinely perceived his brethren to be as angels and carefully served all who were in need, he was something of a realist. "My beloved," Mina concludes,

> . . . from the first day I did not always keep to myself, but after I dealt with all, I found that not all were suitable for conversing with; some are of good character, and others, not so much. The monastery is but a net that has caught various kinds. The almighty God has directed me to this path of seclusion. We thank him that he has always directed our steps to the road of peace.[113]

Solitude was hardly a personal choice, nor was it merely a reaction to his occasionally distracting monastic brethren. Even at this early stage he sincerely felt that the call to solitude was above all a call from God. More than a maxim or aphorism, Fr Mina would deeply breathe, inhabit, incarnate, and exhale the words of Isaac the Syrian all the days of his life: "*Love all men, but keep distant from all men.*"

Helwan Theological College: Earliest Eucharistic Reform, 1931–1933

> "I am convinced that the genuine revival of the Church
> begins with Eucharistic revival."
> —*Fr Alexander Schmemann*

S INCE HIS MONASTIC TONSURE three years earlier, Fr Mina's heart had ached for solitude. It would be a solitude endured, nourished, and revived at the liturgical altar.

On Saturday, July 18, 1931, he was ordained to the priesthood by Bishop Demetrius of Menoufia (d. 1950).[114] Fr Mina, now twenty-eight years of age, wept uncontrollably for the duration of the ordination, and in his brother's recollection, provoked all present to tears.[115] Upon the specific request of Pope Youannis XIX (1858–1942)—Youannis had since become patriarch—Fr Mina was called to St Mark's Cathedral to "receive the oblation." After ordination, a new priest undertakes an immersion into the rites of the Church for forty days, at the end of which he officiates at the Liturgy of the Eucharist, holding the body of Christ (the "oblation") for the first time. Curiously—and it is no small matter—this instruction apparently took place at the hands of the patriarch himself.[116]

Discovering that Fr Mina was in Alexandria, only a short walk from the family home in Moharem Bek, his father, Youssef Atta, requested that the patriarch permit his son a short visit. Despite the patriarchal concession, in Fr Raphael's memoirs, Mina initially refused, though eventually (and reluctantly) he complied. Awaiting the much-loved and sorely missed son and brother was an imposing banquet. But—to perhaps no little surprise—the monk-priest refused to eat, and was "content with only a cup of coffee."[117] Immediately after the visit, with (we may imagine) some impatience, Fr Mina returned to the cathedral, much to the patriarch's admiration. "The asceticism was not paraded," an English scholar notes, "but it was there."[118]

* * *

Sometime in 1931, most likely after his ordination, Fr Mina was chosen to study at the prestigious and newly founded Monastic Theological College in Helwan.[119] The new priest was neither impressed nor remotely flattered. "Just to be obedient to [Youannis] . . . I studied at the Theological School for two years," Fr Mina recounts in an autobiographical fragment, "but I had always *longed* for the path of solitude."[120] Though the study was something of a distraction, Mina reluctantly obeyed.

Youannis, at the outset of his papacy, had perceived the dramatic potential of theological education for monastics—especially for those eventually called to the episcopacy—and he knew, just as dramatically, the tragic aftermath of inexperienced and theologically illiterate bishops. With this vision as background, the institution was officially opened on March 4, 1929, to much celebration.[121] In his inaugural address, Youannis pronounced, in elation, that for fifty years he had dreamed of reforming monastic formation. He exhorted his future monastic candidates to give themselves diligently to their theological studies, cognizant that they might one day be called upon to serve the Church.[122] Youannis' intentions were hardly veiled; he sought to transform monastic learning, and in doing so, to lay the foundation for future episcopal candidates. He also promised to visit the College regularly—as we shall soon see.

The college was founded at the complex of St Mary's Church in Helwan, 140 kilometers (87 miles) from the Baramous Monastery, just south of Cairo. Among the generous and resplendent gardens of the compound stood several large houses, four of which were transformed into residences for the monastic students, while the fifth served as a lecture hall. The first cohort was of thirty hand-selected monks from various monasteries around Egypt. Students were engaged in a rigorous five-year degree, involving an unusually advanced and thorough curriculum of twelve subjects: theology; New Testament; Old Testament; Church chant; homiletics; canon law; languages, including Coptic, Arabic, English, French, Biblical Greek, and Hebrew; biblical geography; history, both Church and modern; philosophy; rhetoric; and finally, psychology.[123] It made for grueling study. But by the same token, it stood to cultivate and forge bishops who were competent, dynamic, and capable.

At the helm stood the dean, Mikhail Mina (1883–1956), who was, by all accounts, something of a genius and one of the most eminent theologians of his time—which in part explained the progressive and ambitious curriculum. Mikhail, the son of a learned priest, was born in Nag Hammadi.[124] In 1897, Bishop Morcos of Esna and Luxor (1848–1934) was celebrating the Liturgy at the local church, and after chanting the gospel in Coptic he was unable to locate an Arabic *Katameros* (daily lectionary). Mikhail, aged fourteen at the time, stood up before the Coptic lectionary and proceeded, in the sight of the visibly shocked bishop, to translate the Gospel "on the fly" from Coptic, chanting it in Arabic. Without the need for further inquiry, the bishop immediately sent the young boy to be admitted directly to the Theological College in Cairo.

There, under the tutelage of Youssef Manqarius (d. 1918) and the recently appointed Habib Girgis (1876–1951), he studied for five years and continued to surprise his colleagues with his unusual aptitude.[125] That Mikhail, Youssef Manqarius, and Habib Girgis all shared various classrooms in varying capacities in the same institution is fascinating, to say the least.[126]

After graduating, Mikhail was appointed dean of a small monastic college in Bush, where St Antony's Monastery had a dependency.[127] During this time he was apparently forced into marriage by his father, but his wife sadly died only eight years later. In 1929, he was finally named the dean of the Helwan Theological College for Monks. Little known to most, after his wife's death, he was tonsured a monk and ordained a priest (a rare occurrence) on the same day (even rarer) in July 1932 at the Baramous Monastery.[128] Later in life, he wrote a three-volume compendium on systematic theology, as well as several exegetical and pastoral works.

Hegumen Mikhail served as dean for twenty-seven years, until his death on August 7, 1956. During that time Youannis' blueprint of episcopal reform was evidently fruitful. A plethora of bishops studied and graduated at the hands of Mikhail, including the future Pope Kyrillos VI and future Bishops Morcos of Abu Tig, Abraam of Giza, Demetrios of Menoufia, Antony of Souhag, Makarios of Qena, Mina of Gerga, and Thomas of Gharbeya—to mention but a few.

* * *

Though Fr Mina had been reluctant to leave the monastery for theological study at Helwan, his time there was of inestimable significance. Regarding his aca-demic experience, his brother is all too concise: "[Mina] was very successful."[129] However distinguished he may have been, it was not this that was of primary interest.

One of the first things that Fr Mina did at Helwan was to strike a up friendship with a like-minded monk by the name of Fr Kyrillos—the future Metropolitan of Beliana (d. 1970)—who had come from St Paul the Anchorite's Monastery near the Red Sea.[130] Each evening they would pray Vespers, and in the early morning before classes, they celebrated Matins and the Divine Liturgy. Fr Mina would have had to rise even earlier to bake the *qorban* (eucharistic bread). The two young monks continued in this practice for several months.[131]

Just before three o'clock one morning, still in the trance of slumber, Fr Mina went to knead the *qorban* only to find that the oven had been deliberately destroyed. Apparently, according to Hanna's account, their daily liturgical habit had become the cause of some contention.[132] We may also reasonably suggest that at the time, in early-twentieth-century Egypt, the very notion of a daily Liturgy was unheard of; and, therefore, their practice may have understand-ably provoked some jealousy, or at the least, disturbance, given the unavoidable noise in the quiet of the night. Had anyone else been in that helpless situation, the matter would have been concluded at a more reasonable hour. Not so for Fr Mina. He rushed to Fr Kyrillos, awakening him with some panic and explained the disaster: without the *qorban,* it would be impossible to celebrate the Divine Liturgy. But Mina had an ingenious idea. Recalling that the bakery across the street opened in the early hours of the morning, he asked the owner whether he could bake the *qorban* in its oven. And so, undeterred by the momentary delay, the Liturgy was "celebrated as usual."[133] Perhaps it was on that occasion that Fr

Mina minted his famous adage: "If the priest is present, flour is handy, and the altar is available," he would repeat with conviction, "[then] if we don't pray, what shall we say to God?"[134]

It is vital to discern here the beginnings of a eucharistic devotion, or even more, a *modus vivendi* ("way of living").[135] It should again be noted that at that time the practice of celebrating the Liturgy *daily*, which could take some two to three hours, was unknown.[136] The single exception was the Muharraq Monastery, which offered a daily Eucharist on an altar above a stone that, in tradition, had been the cradle for the infant Jesus during his family's sojourn in Egypt. Though, to be precise, it was not a single specific monk, but rather a roster of monks that celebrated the Eucharist sequentially.[137] Never before, at least for several centuries, had any one monk or priest been the sole celebrant of a daily Eucharist. It would be the one constant of Mina's life, as a monk, hermit, and somewhat sleepless patriarch. Even to the reach of old age, no matter whether he was enfeebled or exhausted, his practice persisted, uninterrupted and unceasing.

A glimpse into his eucharistic devotion, something of a godly obsession, may be caught in a volume of the theological periodical, *Harbor of Salvation*, which he wrote in August 1928. Though this was written in his first years of monasticism, and hence before priesthood, it is at least revealing of his thought. The Eucharist is, for Fr Mina, above all, kenotic. The "self-emptying" of Christ, he writes,

[who] abandoned his lofty glory and most-honorable status to release his servants from the bondage of death, and who, through the shedding of his blood as a propitiation on their behalf, and the offering of his body on the Cross as a remission for their sins, brought them unto himself. And *then* he chose, out of his inexpressible generosity, to delight believers under the visible form of bread and wine, with the very same body and blood he sacrificed on the Cross.[138]

Just as the Cross reveals the self-emptying of Christ, the Eucharist is the counterintuitive revelation of Christ under a visible form. If there is, Mina continues, a "healing medicine" or "renewal of the covenant" or "forgiveness" or "sustenance," it is only because of the self-giving and self-emptying of Christ.[139] Christ's unwillingness to negotiate the terms of his declaration—"He who eats my flesh and drinks my blood abides in me, and I in him"—is simply an affirmation of this. "In essence," Fr Mina writes, "he legally sealed and declared that

should even his disciples abandon him . . . the words he spoke were immutable
. . . he was about to offer himself as a sacrifice."[140] Citing from John Chrysostom
and Cyril of Alexandria, Mina is resolute: we may partake in the life of God only
because he was sacrificed and emptied himself for our sakes.[141]

It would be hard to exaggerate the meaning of these words not only in his
eucharistic life but also in his entire way of living, in his personal ascesis and as
manifest in his future ecclesial reform. Self-emptying love was the one necessary means of healing the tensions of human existence, personal, ecclesial, and
national. If the "genuine revival of the Church begins with Eucharistic revival,"[142]
as Fr Alexander Schmemann once aptly noted, then the revival of the Church,
at least in twentieth-century Egypt, first began in the eucharistic life of Fr Mina.
His life was essentially fixated upon the place where heaven and earth met, the
Eucharist; and consequently, heaven and earth would meet in unfathomable
ways in the personal, ecclesial, and national life of the future patriarch.[143]

Here we should follow Schmemann in drawing a subtle and yet imperative
distinction that is of infinite value in exploring Fr Mina's eucharistic vision:

> For the early Christians, the Body of Christ is on the altar because *he is
> among them*. For the contemporary Christians, Christ is here because *his
> body is on the altar*. It seems to be analogous, but in fact, there is an essen-
> tial difference between the early Christians and us. For them, everything
> is in knowing Christ, loving him. For us, everything is in the desire to be
> enlightened.[144]

In his disciple's reckoning, Fr Mina, like the earliest Christians, was "moti-
vated by his instinctive eagerness to stand within the hands of the Lord."[145]

* * *

Seeking a more permanent solution, and conceivably wishing to avoid any further unexpected "attacks" upon their beloved eucharistic oven, Fathers Mina
and Kyrillos sought a meeting with the dean, Mikhail Mina. They suggested
that their "out of bounds" daily Liturgy be officially incorporated into the theological program, and as such the daily schedule would begin with Matins and
the Liturgy of the Eucharist in the morning and conclude with Vespers in the
evening. Each monk would serve according to a rotating roster and give a sermon when officiating at Vespers.[146] Mikhail was very much in agreement. This
reform—mild, limited, and modest in scale that it was—needs to be staunchly
emphasized. For the first time, at least in many centuries, theological education

formally and intelligibly pivoted around, and was contingent upon, Liturgy—not a mere performance, but in a mystical communion in the self-emptying, self-giving life of God. Any recitation, instruction, or tutelage in theology otherwise, in the mind of Fr Mina, was but a parody. The Eucharist was once more at the creative center.

Meanwhile, this humble and yet urgent reform would play out in a personally unexpected way in early 1933.[147] Pope Youannis had made good on his promise to regularly visit the College. As fate or otherwise would have it, Fr Mina was praying Matins and Vespers that day, and thereupon was forced to deliver his evening homily in the intimidating presence of the patriarch. The sermon apparently lasted a full hour, his brother recalls, and drew from patristic works, especially the thought of St Isaac the Syrian.[148] Youannis was mesmerized, afterward blessing Fr Mina and praying that "he would be a pillar of the Church of God."[149] Still unsatisfied, however, Youannis approached the dean and told him of his plans to ordain Fr Mina as a bishop over his previous diocese.[150] That a single sermon could so move Youannis makes Fr Mina's future preference for silence all the more shocking and, at the least, argues strongly against any claim of inability or intellectual simplicity.

Mikhail, ecstatic that another of his students was on the cusp of the episcopal rank, relayed what he thought was joyous news. But Fr Mina returned to his room heavy-hearted and despondent. His dear friend, Fr Kyrillos, tried as best he might, until the early hours of the morning, to console the grieving monk. "Leave it in God's hands," Kyrillos encouraged, "and accept God's blessing."[151] It was a futile effort. Fr Mina refused to be comforted. The night drew long, with sleep eventually overcoming them both. Fr Kyrillos awoke, as was his habit, at daybreak to prepare for Matins and the Liturgy. As he entered the church, he looked, as he had for the last two years, for the heartening face of Fr Mina. But he was not to be found. He had simply vanished.

Notes

[1]Atta and Raphael Ava Mina, *Life of Pope Kyrillos*, 5. The fast is variable in length, from the Monday after Pentecost to the Apostles' Feast.

[2]Interview from *Saint George's Magazine*, April/May 1959, reproduced in Girguis, *The Heavenly Harp*, 12.

[3]Meinardus (and Watson, who seems to follow him), suggests that Azer began reading monastic literature while working for Thomas Cook & Son. According to the *Saint George's Magazine* interview in 1959, the reading likely took place while he was awaiting his departure to the monastery. That said, Watson's conclusion that it would have opened his eyes about the true calling of the Church is quite accurate. See Meinardus, *Two Thousand Years*, 78; Watson, "Abba Kyrillos," 8. This may well have also been the period of another influence. Nasr makes a brief and unreferenced claim that Azer was inspired

by the life of Anba Abraam (1829–1914), bishop of Faiyum and Giza; see Amir Nasr, *Readings in the Life of Abouna Mina el-Baramousy the Recluse* [in Arabic] (Cairo: Al-Nesr Press, 1996), 13. Though Nasr does not substantiate his claim, there may be something to it. First, the fame of the bishop, especially his love for the poor, was widespread throughout Egypt. Second, Anba Abraam, then a monk, actually spent a period of exile at Baramous Monastery from 1861 to 1881. Third, after the death of Abraam in 1914, Fr Abdel Messih el-Masudi (the future spiritual father of Azer) wrote a biography of the bishop. And fourth, interestingly, Azer's first issue of the *Harbor of Salvation* periodical, in February 1928, features a biography of Anba Abraam; see *HS* [in Arabic], vol. 1 (Wadi al-Natrun: Baramous Monastery, Amsheer 1644; February 1928). Finally, on June 10, 1964, Azer (then Pope Kyrillos VI) canonized Anba Abraam.

[4]Watson, "Abba Kyrillos," 8.

[5]This particular delicacy, *feteer*, is classically distributed on the commemoration of Archangel Michael, which falls on the twelfth of each Coptic month. Though Hanna claims it fell on the same day as the Apostles' Feast, here is a difficulty in that July 12, 1927, was in fact the fifth of Coptic month. The two events seem to have merged in the mind of Hanna, his brother.

[6]Atta and Raphael Ava Mina, *Life of Pope Kyrillos*, 5.

[7]Ibid.

[8]In Coptic monasticism, the last name of a monk is derived from his monastery. In this case the last name is "Baramousy," given the monk is from the Baramous Monastery. Fr Bishara entered the Baramous Monastery in 1921; was ordained a priest on May 8, 1927; was ordained a bishop (Anba Morcos of Abu Tig, Tama, and Tahta) in 1934; and died in 1980. Given he was only twenty-one at the time, and returned to the College in September 1927, it is very likely he was a student there. See Father Augustinos el-Baramousy, *The Baramous Monastery: Past to Present* [in Arabic] (Cairo: Baramous Monastery, 1993), 177–78.

[9]Atta and Raphael Ava Mina, *Life of Pope Kyrillos*, 6.

[10]Ibid.

[11]Though the specific railway station is not given, the family lived *in Moharrem Bek*, which was only 1 km (0.6 mi) away (a thirteen-minute walk). The only other railway station in Alexandria (which would also have to be passed through to go to Damanhur) was Sidi Gaber Railway Station, which was about 4 km (2.5 mi) away.

[12]Mina the Recluse [Kyrillos VI], "Autobiographical Fragments."

[13]Each periodical is concluded with a narrative or story section. The first two issues had details of his journey to the monastery in this "narrative" section with little explanation, and thus they may have been ignored previously as mere stories. Also, the periodicals have been held tightly in the possession of Father Raphael Ava Mina (who kindly shared them), and in consequence much of what they contain has been hidden for decades. Unfortunately, after the first two issues, the autobiographical comments were abandoned in favor of excerpts from John Bunyan's *The Holy War*. This was much to my dismay especially given that the second issue teasingly concluded with the words "to be continued." See Monk Mina el-Baramousy [Kyrillos VI], *HS* [in Arabic], vol. 2 (Wadi al-Natrun: Baramous Monastery, Baramhat 1644; March 1928), 8.

[14]Mina el-Baramousy [Kyrillos VI], *HS*, 1:8. Alexandria to Damanhur is some 60 km (37 mi); Damanhur to Itay al-Baroud is 27 km (16.8 mi); and Itay al-Baroud to al-Khatatba is another 68 km (42 mi).

[15]Zaklama, *Pope Kyrillos VI*, 1, 43. It was apparently a common route; see, for another visitor's account, Meinardus, *Monks and Monasteries (1989)*, 66.

[16]Mina el-Baramousy [Kyrillos VI], *HS*, 1:8.

[17]Mina the Recluse [Kyrillos VI], "Autobiographical Fragments."

[18]Raphael Ava Mina, *Spiritual Leadership*, 8.

[19]Mina el-Baramousy [Kyrillos VI], *HS*, 2:7–8. They arrived at the monastery between 12 and 2 AM. The walk from *el-Hokaria* station (Bir Hokir) to the monastery is some 10 km (6 mi) and takes approximately two hours.

[20]Around the same time, in 1931, a British woman by the name of Mary Rowlatt wrote as she neared the monastery on foot after their cars had broken down, "We did the last bit on foot, as both cars had

stuck, so we approached the first monastery in absolute silence. And the silence of the desert can be absolute. The only live things in view were a few swallows which circled round our heads, swooping forth and back again in great curiosity. On arrival we clanged the great bell in a whitewashed tower above us and waited. Eventually a young bearded monk opened a postern gate and welcomed us." See Meinardus, *Monks and Monasteries (1989)*, 66.

[21] Mina el-Baramousy [Kyrillos VI], *HS*, 2:7–8.

[22] Meinardus, *Monks and Monasteries (1989)*, 52–53.

[23] Constantin von Tischendorf, *Travels in the East* (Cambridge: Cambridge University Press, 2010), 53.

[24] Cited in Meinardus, *Monks and Monasteries (1989)*, 66.

[25] William Henry Hatch, "A Visit to the Coptic Convents in Nitria," *American School of Oriental Research Annual*, no. 6 (1924): 100.

[26] Cited in Meinardus, *Monks and Monasteries (1989)*, 67.

[27] H. V. Morton, *Through Lands of the Bible* (London: Dodd, Mead & Company, 1938), 234.

[28] Mina the Recluse [Kyrillos VI], "Autobiographical Fragments."

[29] Mina el-Baramousy [Kyrillos VI], *HS*, 2:7–8.

[30] Ibid., 8.

[31] Ibid. This refers to the Liturgy of St Gregory the Theologian, one of three eucharistic Anaphoras still used by the Coptic Orthodox Church.

[32] Mina the Recluse [Kyrillos VI], "Autobiographical Fragments."

[33] Meinardus, *Monks and Monasteries (1989)*, 69; Augustinos el-Baramousy, *The Baramous Monastery*, 175. Youannis, having begun his monasticism at the Baramous Monastery, was known to visit the monastery at least annually, and continued this practice first as metropolitan and then eventually as patriarch.

[34] Atta and Raphael Ava Mina, *Life of Pope Kyrillos*, 6.

[35] Ibid.

[36] Mina el-Baramousy [Kyrillos VI], *HS*, 2:8.

[37] For a lay perspective for the reasons of the exile, see al-Masri, *True Story of Christianity in Egypt*, 2:352–53.

[38] Atta and Raphael Ava Mina, *Memories about the Life of Pope Kyrillos*, 13. This detail is missed from the English translation.

[39] Mina el-Baramousy [Kyrillos VI], *HS*, 2:8.

[40] The autobiographical account in the *Harbor of Salvation* concludes with the story of the previous anonymous occupier of the cell. The account may be found in the appendices. I suspect—given the monk was blind in Azer's account and that the cell had been deserted for some time—that this refers to a blind monk by the name of Awad el-Barhemey (d. 1878) who at one stage was the only monk in the monastery for three years. He was remembered as having a very keen intelligence and a clear mind, being tall with a long beard, and being fond of saying, "The monk is a monk from his father's house; good in his father's house, good in the monastery. . . ." See Augustinos el-Baramousy, *The Baramous Monastery*, 232.

[41] Atta and Raphael Ava Mina, *Life of Pope Kyrillos*, 6.

[42] Ibid.

[43] Ibid. The attitude is confirmed in a letter Azer (then Father Mina) wrote to his brother in 1929; see Monk Mina el-Baramousy [Kyrillos VI], "Letter to Hanna Youssef Atta, January 17, 1929" [in Arabic], in RC-2: Letter 57 (Baramous Monastery, 1929).

[44] Atta and Raphael Ava Mina, *Life of Pope Kyrillos*, 6. This certainly makes sense of the delay in the allocation of his cell.

[45] Atta and Raphael Ava Mina, *Memories about the Life of Pope Kyrillos*, 13. The English translation does not give mention of the names, which are present in the Arabic.

[46] Atta and Raphael Ava Mina, *Life of Pope Kyrillos*, 6, and their *Memories about the Life of Pope Kyrillos*, 13. Masudi, while exploring the cell, commented, "He has sown and is waiting for the rain." This is missing from the English translation. The Arabic also adds the following explanation: "which means he has prepared himself and is waiting for the rain of the grace of God."

[47] Mina el-Baramousy [Kyrillos VI], *HS*, 2:8.

[48] Atta and Raphael Ava Mina, *Life of Pope Kyrillos*, 6. The final sentence was mistranslated in the printed edition, but it is corrected above. See Atta and Raphael Ava Mina, *Memories about the Life of Pope Kyrillos*, 13.

[49] Atta and Raphael Ava Mina, *Life of Pope Kyrillos*, 6.

[50] For instance, Watson, among many others, somewhat forgivably, suggests that Azer was a spiritual son to Abdel Messih ibn Abdelmalek el-Masudi, and that he became an assistant to the librarian, Abdel Messih ibn Salib el-Masudi; see Watson, "Abba Kyrillos," 9. This, of course, was impossible given that ibn Abdelmalek was at Muharraq Monastery, and likely reposed before the time of Fr Mina's monasticism.

[51] Augustinos el-Baramousy, *The Baramous Monastery*, 234.

[52] Ibid. His wife's name is given as Mary.

[53] I. H. al-Masri, *The Story of the Coptic Church: 1870–1927* [in Arabic], vol. 5 (Cairo: Maktabat al-Mahabba, 1986), 107.

[54] He was the son of Abdelmalek, according to his name. Little else is known of the figure, other than that throughout the literature he has been confused with Girguis el-Masudi, who spent twenty-two years at the same monastery. See Bishop Gregorious, *Muharraq Monastery: History, Description, Content* [in Arabic] (Al-Qusiya: Muharraq Monastery, 1992), 329; al-Masri, *Story of the Coptic Church*, 5:109.

[55] Augustinos el-Baramousy, *The Baramous Monastery*, 234. Note that he came to Baramous at the time of Awad and Hanna the Scribe (the future Pope Cyril V).

[56] Gregorious, *Muharraq Monastery*, 325.

[57] Augustinos el-Baramousy, *The Baramous Monastery*, 235.

[58] See ibid., 236; Gregorious, *Muharraq Monastery*, 327; al-Masri, *Story of the Coptic Church*, 5:108. It should be noted that Baramous Monastery was also the home (at least for a brief period) of a Syrian monk, Naoum, at the turn of the twentieth century—a monk who, despite being temporarily excommunicated for "insubordination," was also a well-accomplished scholar; see Meinardus, *Monks and Monasteries (1989)*, 64. That such scholars converged at the Baramous Monastery just before the arrival of Azer is fascinating.

[59] Sisters of Abu Sefein, *Abu Sefein: Biography and History of the Convent* [in Arabic] (Old Cairo: Abu Sefein Convent, 1989), 319.

[60] One record of breaking this vow of silence is at Azer's monastic tonsure. See Atta and Raphael Ava Mina, *Life of Pope Kyrillos*, 8. Little else is known of his life, other than that he entered the monastery just after his brother, Fr Abdel Messih ibn Salib el-Masudi; see Augustinos el-Baramousy, *The Baramous Monastery*, 236.

[61] Augustinos el-Baramousy, *The Baramous Monastery*, 236.

[62] Many of the following intimate insights into the life and movements of Abdel Messih el-Masudi are from a letter written in January 1969 by another disciple of Masudi, Fr Daoud el-Baramousy. The letter was reprinted in Youssef Habib, *Goodbye Pope Kyrillos: Among the Fathers and Leaders* [in Arabic] (place and publisher unknown, 1971), 20.

[63] For references of his works, see Aziz Suryal Atiya, "'Abd al-Masih Salib al-Masu'di," in *CE*, 7b; al-Masri, *Story of the Coptic Church*, 5:108.

[64] Atiya, "'Abd al-Masih Salib al-Masu'di," 7b; Johannes Den Heijer, "History of the Patriarchs of Alexandria," ibid., 1241a.

[65] Habib, *Among the Fathers*, 20; Atiya, "'Abd al-Masih Salib al-Masu'di," 7b.

[66] Atiya, "'Abd al-Masih Salib al-Masu'di," 7b.

[67] Habib, *Among the Fathers*, 20.

[68] Girguis, *The Heavenly Harp*, 13.

[69] Ibid., 12.

[70] Habib, *Among the Fathers*, 21–22.

[71] Augustinos el-Baramousy, *The Baramous Monastery*, 238.

[72] Atta and Raphael Ava Mina, *Life of Pope Kyrillos*, 6.

[73] Ibid., 8.

[74] Ibid.

[75] Ibid.

[76] Ibid.

[77] Ibid. According to the account, Azer was still a novice, and the episode followed the departure of his fellow monks to Alexandria in September 1927. This places the event sometime between October 1927 and January 1928.

[78] Ibid.

[79] Ibid.

[80] He was made abbot of the monastery after the resignation of Fr Barnaba el-Baramousy on March 9, 1948; was ordained as its first bishop on January 23, 1949; and died on January 5, 1965. See Augustinos el-Baramousy, *The Baramous Monastery*, 226.

[81] Anonymous bishop, "Interview about the Life of Pope Kyrillos," audio recording, ed. Daniel Fanous (2016). From his very earliest days as a novice—though it is a surprise to many—he reportedly fell victim to abuse and ridicule from some of his fellow monks.

[82] The expression "vocation of loss" is borrowed from a letter Fr Lev Gillet wrote on March 9, 1928, to his bishop, Metropolitan Andrei Szeptycky: "The more I examine myself. . . . What attracts me is a *vocation of loss*—a life which would give itself freely without any apparent positive result, for the result would be known to God alone. . . ." It is a phrase that speaks eloquently to the life of the subject of this study. See Elisabeth Behr-Sigel, *Lev Gillet: A Monk of the Eastern Church*, trans. Helen Wright (Oxford: Fellowship of St Alban and St Sergius, 1999), 9.

[83] For an analysis of the period, and contributing factors see Vatikiotis, *The History of Egypt*, 317–28.

[84] Mina the Recluse [Kyrillos VI], "Autobiographical Fragments."

[85] Some discrepancy has appeared in the literature as to the date of his monastic tonsure. This may be traced to a mistranslation in Hanna Youssef Atta's account. In Arabic the date is given as "February 25, 1928 at the beginning of Lent," whereas the English translation has—for some unknown reason (perhaps from some confusion as to which St Menas was intended; 17 Amshir, Menas the monk, versus 15 Hatour, Menas the Miracle Worker)—mistakenly translated it as "November 25, 1928, at the beginning of the Christmas fast." The date was mistranslated and hence the Fast was changed to make sense of this (given the Nativity fast began on November 25, 1928). See Atta and Raphael Ava Mina, *Memories about the Life of Pope Kyrillos*, 15, and their *Life of Pope Kyrillos*, 8. In any event, the autobiographical fragments place the tonsure at "nine months" after he entered the monastery in July 1927, thereby confirming the date of tonsure as February 1928; see Mina the Recluse [Kyrillos VI], "Autobiographical Fragments."

[86] For a description of the church and its altars, see Augustinos el-Baramousy, *The Baramous Monastery*, 62–65.

[87] The Rite of Tonsure is described in great detail in Bishop Mettaous, *The Sublime Life of Monasticism* (Putty, Egypt: Saint Shenouda Monastery Press, 2005), 89–98, and this coheres extremely well with the description given in Hanna's account: see Atta and Raphael Ava Mina, *Life of Pope Kyrillos*, 7.

[88] Mina the Recluse [Kyrillos VI], "Autobiographical Fragments." It should be noted that the saint commemorated on that day (17th of Amshir) was Menas the monk, and not Azer's patron saint, Menas the Miracle-worker (commemorated on 15th of Hatour).

[89] It would appear, from the autobiographical fragments, that there had been some contention as to the new name of the novice, before final agreement upon the saint commemorated on that day. This is an important corrective to a number of sources that have suggested that Azer himself chose the name; for instance, see Voile, *Les Coptes d'Égypte*, 196; van Doorn-Harder, "Planner, Patriarch and Saint," 230; Watson, "Abba Kyrillos," 20.

[90] Cited from Voile, *Les Coptes d'Égypte*, 195. Voile notes that this may be at first glance quite odd, but the union of sorts between Copts and Muslims in the 1920s and 1930s against the British, as well as the original reverence given to Menas by Muslims in the seventh to tenth centuries (especially the Bedouins), account for Ahmad Hussein's reference.

[91] Ibid., 196.

[92] Atta and Raphael Ava Mina, *Life of Pope Kyrillos*, 7.

[93] Mina the Recluse [Kyrillos VI], "Autobiographical Fragments."

[94] Atta and Raphael Ava Mina, *Life of Pope Kyrillos*, 8.

[95] Ibid.

[96] Another reason, likely in combination with the request of Masudi, is given in the preface of the first volume: "After I had noticed that many people would like to know the characteristics and rules of the monastery, especially M. Michael, who has asked relentlessly concerning this issue, I decided—with the grace of God—to write something about this subject. Though I cannot describe the beauty of the monastery, I will do my best. . . ." See Mina el-Baramousy [Kyrillos VI], *HS*, 1. In a later volume, December 1929, a further reason is given: "The only aim of publishing this magazine is related to my *repeated reading of the sayings of the saintly fathers, and the benefits and comfort which fill the soul.* As I found myself being filled with these teachings I thought that I would share them with my brethren." See Monk Mina el-Baramousy [Kyrillos VI], *HS* [in Arabic], vol. 16 (Wadi al-Natrun: Baramous Monastery, Kiahk 1646; December 1929). It also appears Hanna may have played a role in determining the length and structure; see Monk Mina el-Baramousy [Kyrillos VI], "Letter to Hanna Youssef Atta, November 21, 1930" [in Arabic], in RC-1: Letter 11 (Baramous Monastery: 1930).

[97] Mina el-Baramousy [Kyrillos VI], *HS*, 1.

[98] Ibid., 1.

[99] Fr Mina had originally planned to write according to three divisions: "a *spiritual section*, a *historical section,* and an *administrative section*; in this last section I will write about the rules and characteristics of the monastery." See ibid. But it appears the periodical evolved otherwise.

[100] Atta and Raphael Ava Mina, *Life of Pope Kyrillos*, 7.

[101] All seventeen volumes have been kindly passed on to me by Fr Raphael Ava Mina, who holds the originals in his possession. The contents will be consulted when relevant throughout this work.

[102] Raphael Ava Mina, *Spiritual Leadership*, 21.

[103] Archdeacon Iskander Hanna and Hegumen Abdel Messih el-Masudi.

[104] Raphael Ava Mina, *Spiritual Leadership*, 21–22.

[105] Atta and Raphael Ava Mina, *Life of Pope Kyrillos*, 8. Other than the work of St Isaac the Syrian, Hanna states that he also gave himself to a study of the monastic fathers, such as Sts Anthony, Macarius the Great, and Shenouda the Archimandrite.

[106] In a later interview, a month before his enthronement as patriarch, when asked as to his favorite book, he replied: "The works of Mar Isaac the Syrian which examine the life of solitude and silence"; see Galal el-Gowaily, "Interview with the Monk That Will Become Patriarch" [in Arabic], *al-Ahram*, April 25, 1959.

[107] The English translation misses that he learned to bind the books from an elderly monk whom he was serving, named Pakhoum, who in an autobiographical fragment is identified as his confession father. See Atta and Raphael Ava Mina, *Memories about the Life of Pope Kyrillos*, 17, and their *Life of Pope Kyrillos*, 8; Mina the Recluse [Kyrillos VI], "Autobiographical Fragments."

[108] One copy eventually found its way into the possession of Fr Matta el-Meskeen, who referenced the work as: " 'The Four Books of St Isaac the Syrian, Bishop of Nineveh,' copied from a manuscript in the possession of Father Mina el-Baramousy." See Fr Matta el-Meskeen, *Orthodox Prayer Life: The Interior Way* (Crestwood, NY: St Vladimir's Seminary Press, 2003), 292. We should note that the classification of Part I and Part II (and III) of the *Ascetical Homilies* was somewhat unknown to the Arabic world. Rather, there are "Four Books" in the Arabic version—the version that Fr Mina would have been familiar with. These four books primarily consist of Part I, but also contain sections from Part II and III, as well as other Syriac Fathers under the name of Isaac. This makes it often difficult to appreciate which "part" Fr Mina is referring to—though as mentioned, Part I primarily dominates the Arabic "Four Books." See Sabino Chiala, "The Arabic Version of Saint Isaac the Syrian: A Channel of Transmission of Syriac Literature," in *St Isaac the Syrian and His Spiritual Legacy*, ed. Hilarion Alfeyev (Yonkers, NY: St Vladimir's Seminary Press, 2015). Also, for a discussion of Eastern and Western recensions, see Hilarion Alfeyev, *The Spiritual World of Isaac the Syrian* (Kalamazoo, MI: Cistercian Publications, 2000), 29–31.

[109] Atta and Raphael Ava Mina, *Life of Pope Kyrillos*, 8; Father Raphael Ava Mina, "Interview about the Life of Pope Kyrillos VI," audio recording, ed. Daniel Fanous (2016).

[110]St Isaac the Syrian, *The Ascetical Homilies of Saint the Syrian* (Boston: Holy Transfiguration Monastery, 2011), 64. 457 [the citations to this this publication will give the homily number first, then, after a period, the page number]. The maxim is more revealing in context: "Instead of an avenger, be a deliverer. Instead of a faultfinder, be a soother. . . . Beseech God on behalf of sinners. . . . Conquer evil men by your gentle kindness. . . . Love all men, but keep distant from all men."

[111]Mina el-Baramousy [Kyrillos VI], "Letter to Hanna Youssef Atta, January 17, 1929."

[112]Ibid.

[113]Ibid. It should also be noted that a letter he writes in 1933 further develops his reasoning, whereby he seeks solitude out of weakness, not out of thinking he is better than others; see Father Mina el-Baramousy [Kyrillos VI], "Letter to Hanna Youssef Atta, December 3, 1933" [in Arabic], in RC-2: Letter 8 (Baramous Monastery: 1933).

[114]Atta and Raphael Ava Mina, *Life of Pope Kyrillos*, 8. In attendance were his brothers, Hanna and (Hegumen) Mikhail, Youssef Girguis (the future patriarchal secretary), and another Mikhail (the head cantor of the patriarchate). The English translation misses these details: see Atta and Raphael Ava Mina, *Memories about the Life of Pope Kyrillos*, 17. There appears to be some confusion in the sources as to the location of the ordination, but it is likely it took place in the monastery before Father Mina was summoned to Alexandria. The opposing view seems to have stemmed from the account of his future disciple; see Raphael Ava Mina, *Spiritual Leadership*, 8.

[115]Atta and Raphael Ava Mina, *Life of Pope Kyrillos*, 8.

[116]His "reception of the oblation" in Alexandria is recounted by his future disciple, Fr Raphael Ava Mina, and though not specifically mentioned by his brother, Hanna, it certainly is in keeping with his account where Hanna obviously was in close communication with Pope Youannis after the ordination. Raphael Ava Mina, *Spiritual Leadership*, 8; Atta and Raphael Ava Mina, *Life of Pope Kyrillos*, 8, and their *Memories about the Life of Pope Kyrillos*, 17.

[117]Raphael Ava Mina, *Spiritual Leadership*, 8.

[118]Watson, "Abba Kyrillos," 9.

[119]Few, if any, scholars have noticed several contradictions here. It is exceedingly difficult to date when precisely he began at Helwan: (1) Fr Mina claims, in the autobiographical fragments, to have studied there for two years after four years in the monastery, which is unanimously supported by all accounts; (2) Hanna suggests this began after priesthood (July 1931) and that he sought solitude soon after when he was thirty (at least after August 1932); (3) Hanna later on mentions that Bishop Thomas of Gharbeya studied with Fr Mina at Helwan, and yet he was ordained a bishop in October 1930—suggesting that Fr Mina studied at Helwan before then; (4) there is also the discrepancy about the diocese for which he was to be ordained. While at least one scholar (Zaklama, *Pope Kyrillos VI*, 1:69–72) has noticed these discrepancies and has attempted to maneuver through these somewhat conflicting details by suggesting that Fr Mina began studying at Helwan before October 1930, this is unnecessary. One possibility is that Bishop Thomas may have reasonably continued at Helwan after his ordination. That Fr Mina was not in Helwan from at least December 1930 is certain, given that letters to his brother, Hanna, in the period October to December, were written from the Baramous Monastery—one of these specifically states that Mina felt he would *soon* be asked to study and wished it would not happen. See Mina el-Baramousy [Kyrillos VI], "Letter to Hanna Youssef Atta, November 21, 1930." Interestingly, we have in our possession no letters from his hand from December 10, 1930, to December 3, 1933, suggesting a period away from his monastery. A likely chronology for these years is as follows: July 1927–July 1931 at Baramous Monastery; July 1931 to early 1933 at Helwan; period at the Monastery of St Shenouda in Souhag; and in late 1933, Fr Mina enters solitude at Baramous Monastery. The latter two periods will be examined as we progress.

[120]Mina the Recluse [Kyrillos VI], "Autobiographical Fragments."

[121]Many metropolitans and all heads of monasteries were present, as well as Archdeacon Habib Girgis, the esteemed (and recently canonized) dean of the Theological College in Cairo; see I. H. al-Masri, *The Story of the Coptic Church: 1928–1946* [in Arabic], vol. 6 (Cairo: Maktabat al-Mahabba, 1988), 40–42; Nasr, *Readings in the Life of Abouna Mina*, 45.

[122]Al-Masri, *Story of the Coptic Church*, 6:41; van Doorn-Harder, "Planner, Patriarch and Saint," 232.

[123]Al-Masri, *Story of the Coptic Church*, 6:42–43.

[124]Some otherwise reliable sources claim he was born in 1880, but most suggest 1883, which is consistent with the anecdote that he was fourteen in 1897 when "spotted" by Bishop Morcos; for instance, see Augustinos el-Baramousy, *The Baramous Monastery*, 237–38.

[125]For a brief biography of Manqarius, see al-Masri, *Story of the Coptic Church*, 5:8.

[126]Of note, Nazir Gayed, the future Pope Shenouda III, was appointed a full-time lecturer at the Helwan Theological College in 1953; see Meinardus, *Two Thousand Years*, 4.

[127]Before long he managed to open another, significantly overcrowded, elementary school, for the poverty-stricken children; see Augustinos el-Baramousy, *The Baramous Monastery*, 238.

[128]Ibid. He was elevated to hegumen the next month.

[129]Atta and Raphael Ava Mina, *Life of Pope Kyrillos*, 8.

[130]Kyrillos was the metropolitan of Beliana from 1948 to 1970; thus he died the year before his friend.

[131]Atta and Raphael Ava Mina, *Life of Pope Kyrillos*, 8.

[132]Ibid.; Fr Raphael Ava Mina, *My Memories about the Life of Pope Kyrillos VI: Part II* [in Arabic] (Shoubra: Sons of Pope Kyrillos VI, 1985).

[133]Atta and Raphael Ava Mina, *Life of Pope Kyrillos*, 8.

[134]Raphael Ava Mina, *Spiritual Leadership*, 11.

[135]Fr Mina's eucharistic vision may even be carefully traced to his daily practice in baking the *qorban* even before priesthood, and hence before he had personally officiated at a Liturgy. Conceivably, it may have been further deepened by Fr Abdel Messih el-Masudi's pioneering translation and study of the Coptic Liturgies. We should also note that Fr Mina had attended his local church daily (though not for Liturgy, as the practice was then unheard of) to pray, before becoming a monastic.

[136]His daily practice would lead to unfounded accusations, including even heresy, in his later time as a public monastic. Importantly, Fr Mina would pray the Liturgy more quickly than the classical rite—often taking only one to two hours.

[137]Yanney, "Liturgical Revival," 32.

[138]Monk Mina el-Baramousy [Kyrillos VI], *HS* [in Arabic], vol. 7 (Wadi al-Natrun: Baramous Monastery, Misra 1644; August 1928), 1.

[139]Ibid.

[140]Ibid., 2–3.

[141]Ibid., 3–4.

[142]Fr Alexander Schmemann, *The Eucharist: Sacrament of the Kingdom* (Crestwood, NY: St Vladimir's Seminary Press, 1988), 242.

[143]One question that has intrigued me for years, and that has been asked of me on more than one occasion, is whether Isaac the Syrian's eucharistic theology had any influence on Fr Mina—given his pervasive discipleship. It is almost impossible to say, given that, first, the extant writings of Isaac rarely discuss the Eucharist and, second, Fr Mina rarely cites Isaac in connection with the Eucharist. The exception, as far as I am aware, is a letter Mina wrote to Fr Antonious el-Syriany (the future Pope Shenouda III) congratulating him on the occasion of his ordination to the priesthood. Mina instructs Antonious in a beautiful eucharistic teaching of Isaac the Syrian; namely, that celebrating the Eucharist unites the solitary to the world; see Hegumen Mina the Recluse [Kyrillos VI], "Letter to Father Antonious el-Syriany, September 6, 1958" [in Arabic], in FRC-1: Letter 443 (Old Cairo: 1958). Fr Mina seems to be following (or perhaps citing) his version of Isaac the Syrian; see *Ascetical Homilies*, Part II, 5, 26–30; cited in Alfeyev, *World of Isaac the Syrian*, 205.

[144]Father Alexander Schmemann, *The Journals of Father Alexander Schmemann, 1973–1983* (Crestwood, NY: St Vladimir's Seminary Press, 2000), 31.

[145]Raphael Ava Mina, *Spiritual Leadership*, 11.

[146]Though the English translation claims that a "council of monks" made this suggestion, the original account in Arabic specifies that it was Frs Mina and Kyrillos who made the suggestion; see Atta and Raphael Ava Mina, *Life of Pope Kyrillos*, 8, and their *Memories about the Life of Pope Kyrillos*, 18.

[147]It is impossible to date precisely when Fr Mina left Helwan. But given that he evidently began there after priesthood in July 1931 and his autographical writings clearly state he was there for two years, we may suggest early 1933. He then spent some months at the Monastery of St Shenouda in Souhag, before returning to the Baramous Monastery before his thirty-first birthday (in August 1933), which we can gather from Hanna's account; see Atta and Raphael Ava Mina, *Life of Pope Kyrillos*, 9. Also, a letter written in December 1933 to his brother indicates that there was contention in the monastery as Fr Mina intended to leave for solitude at that point; see Mina el-Baramousy [Kyrillos VI], "Letter to Hanna Youssef Atta, December 3, 1933."

[148]Atta and Raphael Ava Mina, *Life of Pope Kyrillos*, 8.

[149]Ibid.

[150]Ibid., 9. Hanna claims that Pope Youannis wanted to ordain Fr Mina a bishop for the diocese that he vacated in ascending to the papacy, which was Gharbeya and Beheira (Menoufia was added after its bishop reposed). This is problematic in that Bishop Thomas was ordained for Gharbeya (October 1930 to March 1956) and Bishop Demetrius for Menoufia (March 1931 to October 1950). Yet Fr Mina left Helwan the day after Youannis attempted to ordain him, which must have been at least after his ordination to priesthood in July 1931, since he officiated at Vespers that evening. Therefore, the attempted ordination of Fr Mina to episcopacy could not have been for the dioceses of Gharbeya or Menoufia, since they had been occupied from October 1930 and March 1931, respectively. It is entirely feasible, however, that Pope Youannis may have considered annexing Beheira into its own diocese—as was done decades later.

[151]Ibid.

3

The Making of a Hermit (1933–1936)

Escape from the Episcopal Ranks, 1933

> "A monk ought by all means to fly from women and bishops."
> —*St John Cassian*

THAT MORNING IN EARLY 1933—just hours after hearing the call to the episcopacy—Fr Mina quickly and silently gathered his possessions. He boarded the first train for Souhag in Upper Egypt, and from there he went to the White Monastery of St Shenouda. It was a journey to a remote location, 430 kilometers (267 miles) south. Mina's intention could hardly be mistaken: he sought to disappear permanently.

In this, he was in good company. Late in the fourth century, a monk by the name of Ammonius also refused the episcopacy. Before the eyes of his pursuers, he took a pair of scissors and cut off his left ear at the base, declaring he was now deformed and therefore disqualified from ordination. The patriarch, Timothy of Alexandria (381–384), was anything but convinced, that is, until Ammonius threatened to cut off his tongue next.[1] Another, Nilammon, only a few years later, begged Theophilus, the next patriarch of Alexandria (384–412), for one day of prayer before his episcopal ordination. In Sozomen's account, he indeed prayed—for nothing less than his death—and "thus died Nilammon . . . rather than accept a bishopric of which, with extraordinary modesty, he considered himself unworthy."[2] Others took a far less drastic, though still altogether effective, approach: Pachomius simply hid from Athanasius.[3] A vestige of this not so uncommon reaction to the call is still found within the Coptic Rite of Patriarchal Ordination: the monk to be consecrated enters the cathedral bound in iron fetters, with bishops escorting him at both arms.

Seen within this context, Fr Mina's action was rather mild and modest in comparison. In the words of Claudia Rapp, however, it does give a sense of "paradoxical inversion."[4] The rejection of ordination out of humility at once paradoxically established and authenticated his worthiness of the episcopal office.

* * *

"One day," Fr Mina recalls of his unexpected departure,

> I decided to leave the school [Helwan Theological School for Monks] and walk the path of solitude. I had heard about the Monastery of St Shenouda, the father of hermits. So . . . I went to Souhag and to the monastery, which is a short distance from the town.[5]

Notably, he does not even mention the small detail of his impending ordination. But was this omission only out of humility? Or did he perhaps view his action not as an escape, but rather as a God-ordained opportunity to pursue that which he had always desired? Whatever the case, his sudden disappearance caused quite a storm. Several authorities from the Theological School contacted his brother, Hanna—who was "greatly surprised"—and asked him to look for Fr Mina "so as not to upset the Pope."[6] Hanna recalls begging the tight-lipped and reticent Fr Kyrillos (the friend of Fr Mina) with tears to explain his brother's behavior. Finally, plagued by Hanna's incessant pleas, he confessed: Fr Mina had escaped to Souhag.[7]

Following a considerable effort from a Christian merchant in Souhag, Hanna was eventually able to communicate with his brother, who had, by his own account, settled in quite well.[8] Fr Mina's dream was, however, short-lived. "The place was indeed suitable for what I had desired," he recounts in an autobiographical fragment, "but the Pope [Youannis XIX] became extremely angry and refused to allow me to dwell there. He sent me a telegram to meet with him. I obeyed and came into his presence, and he was *infuriated*."[9]

Though he had purposefully omitted that he had escaped ordination, Mina certainly records the patriarch's indignant reaction. Timidly, Fr Mina made clear to Youannis that he had little care for the episcopacy. In fact, that was hardly the problem; he simply yearned with all his being for solitude. With overwhelming urgency, he felt he had no choice but to escape. He felt that his entire life, even as a youth, was unbearably torn from solitude. It was the one thing he had desired. Family life, the Theological College, and remarkably even the monastery were, in a word, *distractions*. "I had always longed for the path of solitude," Fr Mina writes, "the path so many fathers have pondered, especially St Isaac [the Syr-ian], who commands all monks, saying that every monk who has left the world and joined monasticism should not stay with the main assembly for *too* long."[10] Time and time again, his immersion in and embodiment of St Isaac's thought comes out in inviting glimpses. "Monasticism," writes Fr Raphael definitively, "did not satisfy his thirst."[11]

The pope's anger dissipated as the young monk spoke of his desire to be alone and hidden within God.[12] "I was given two choices," Fr Mina continues,

> I was either to continue at the Theological School or I was to return to my original monastery. I asked to return to my monastery and received his bless-ing. But I kept yearning for the life of the solitary, until I could see *no other way* except to pursue it. . . . Indeed, on my way to the monastery, the Lord Christ, directed me to a cave in the mountain. . . .[13]

Fr Mina was allowed, according to Hanna's account, to return to his original monastery to "rest" before taking the guidance of his spiritual father, Abdel Messih el-Masudi.[14] We have no indication of how long precisely he remained in Souhag (we may assume a few months), but we do know that he returned to the Baramous Monastery before his thirty-first birthday in August 1933.[15] Though the autobiographical fragments (at least implicitly) and his brother's account (more explicitly) suggest that he almost immediately departed to soli-tude once returning to the Baramous Monastery, a letter that Fr Mina wrote in December 1933 indicates it was *at least* several months later.[16] The inter-lude may be explained rather simply: his solitude was very much—at one stage almost forcefully—discouraged.

* * *

On his return from Souhag, prompted by the discovery of (or possibly divine "direction" to) a suitable cave near the Baramous Monastery, Fr Mina immedi-ately declared the desire for solitude. A monastic council gathered. Hegumen Basilious (the superintendent) was present along with Hegumens Shenouda, Pakhoum, Gregorious, and Luke.[17] They were, to his frustration, unanimous in their disagreement. Hegumen Abdel Messih el-Masudi was also present, yet for the time being remained silent. Hanna, fortunately, preserves the entire conten-tion—and with reasonable credibility, given a heated letter of the period, reveals he also opposed the idea of solitude.[18]

"You are only thirty years old," said the monks,

... and have only been a monk for five years. Do you want to live the life of solitude in which monks with thirty or forty years of experience have failed? Or is it that you wish to escape responsibility, either at the Faculty [Theological College] or in the monastery? Also, there is the physical danger of living alone in a cave in the desert. . . . That is why we absolutely do not agree. . . .[19]

Fr Mina patiently endured their resistance. "My fathers and brothers," he quietly responded,

I appreciate your love and care for me. I appeal to you as an obedient son asking for the opinion of his fathers who have spent many years worshipping God. You know more about the mysteries of the solitary life than I. But I also trust that the Lord Jesus Christ will prepare the narrow road that I will travel. . . . I will be the obedient son and will not walk in any way without the guidance of my *spiritual father*.[20]

He purposefully drew their attention to his spiritual father in accordance with the patriarch's directive. All eyes intently turned toward Fr Abdel Messih el-Masudi who stated that potential danger is an irrelevant obstacle for one who places his trust in God, adding, "I see with a clear eye that Fr Mina will succeed, as he was chosen from his mother's womb for this grace. Do not stand in his way."[21] "Father," another of the council retorted,

. . . have *you* ever considered the solitary life? Have the [other] elders thought of going this way? Please advise this young monk to go back to the Faculty of Theology to obtain his degree, and then return to serve the monastery. And, when God wills, he will receive a higher rank as the fathers who preceded him.[22]

"Do not let your pity or your love," Masudi gently reprimanded, "prevent the grace of God from entering him." "Why didn't you travel that path?" rebuked the now increasingly vocal monk, "How can you push someone else to take that road?" Aware that little was now being achieved (and no doubt wishing to avoid a tangential confrontation), Masudi humbly deferred to the monastic council, maintaining that he and Fr Mina would abide by their decision. Silence, we are told, prevailed for some time. After due deliberation, the council quite surprisingly declared that Fr Mina could enter solitude under the spiritual direction of Masudi.[23]

There is, however, good reason to distrust that the unusual controversy came to an end so swiftly and painlessly. A first suggestion of this is that another monk, Fr Abdel Messih el-Habashy (the "Ethiopian"), only a few years later, had his desire for solitude forcibly obstructed and was placed under literal house arrest.[24] This is not unremarkable, especially given that solitude at that time was exceedingly rare. A second reason to suspect the immediate resolution is that it was a seemingly erratic and insecure approval: when Fr Mina eventually entered solitude, not a single day had passed before the monks descended upon the cave in an attempt to return him to the monastery.[25] A third reason, unknown to all scholars, is that in December (and therefore at least four months after the monastic council gathered), Fr Mina wrote an intriguing letter—and his single lament was that he was *not* yet in solitude!

* * *

The letter in question was written to his brother on December 3, 1933.[26] It is a rather heated reply to an obviously far more heated rebuke from Hanna. It also gives a sense of the oft-overlooked scale of controversy surrounding Fr Mina's movement to solitude. Moreover, the letter also provides an important chronological corrective to all biographical sources in dating his actual departure into the desert.[27]

"Do you want to sit alone in a cave to seek fame, the praise of people, and high esteem?" Hanna sarcastically quips. "What are you saying?" Fr Mina questions in shock,

> If I were seeking glory, I would have continued in the Monastic Theological School to gain fame in knowledge and studies, which in time would have been followed by higher ranks. You said, "You are full of envy and cannot bear to see others in a higher rank than you!" It is better and more desirable that a man escape far away so as not to envy his brother. You asked, "Is this a way to escape working in the monastery?" You are right, I want to eat the bread of laziness! *You made several other comments that I am unable to repeat.* And in conclusion, you say that the grief and distress, God forbid, have revisited you! Why? Who do you think I am better than? Am I better than the sons of the kings who dwelt in caves, or the early fathers of even the dust of whose feet I am not worthy? Certainly not! I am less than the least of the monks, the most insignificant, the most despised monk of all the monasteries, and permit me to say, that I am not even worthy to be compared to a wild donkey.[28]

These replies are to accusations that presumably represent the "nicer" of the comments heaved at him; some Fr Mina could not even bring himself to repeat. The accusation is threefold: the desire for solitude is a ploy to achieve higher rank, that is, the episcopacy; it is founded upon envy (implying that another had recently been ordained); and finally, it is an escape from the requisite monastic duty. Fr Mina is, however, resolute; if he sought ecclesiastical ranks, he would have remained at the Theological College that inherently prepared for the episcopacy; solitude is, on the contrary, an escape from envy; and as to laziness, he cynically dismisses the suggestion.

"Do you know why I want to live in a cave?" Fr Mina inquires,

> No, you do not. You judge according to appearances, for what man knows the thoughts of another, save the spirit that dwells within him? Do you really think I want to live in a cave because I am better or more holy than others? No, I desired this path because, as one of the fathers said, a monk who finds himself faced with struggle and wars, should have tranquility in his cave to conquer his evil thoughts. If you experienced the wars that face me, you would agree with what this father said about his own experiences.[29]

Here he gives Hanna (and us) a fleeting yet penetrating insight into his desire for solitude. He does not seek solitude out of spiritual strength, but rather out of weakness. It is something of a counterintuitive, though altogether experiential, monastic paradox, and this would not be the last time he would make note of it.[30]

"Do you know how long I have had this idea?" Fr Mina again counters:

> . . . for three years; you probably will not believe that, but what I tell you is the truth. Whenever I thought about it, my heart palpitated, and my entire body trembled with fear. These thoughts haunted me over and over, leaving me in unbelievable dejection and despair because I lacked the courage to take such a step. Do you know the reason why I celebrate so many Divine Liturgies? I was pleading with God day and night to guide me on this path according to his will. Do you know why I traveled to Souhag? It was this idea, to live in a cave and not the monastery. Do you know why I left the school [Helwan Monastic Theological School] after the pope gave me two choices? It was for the same reason; I wanted to live in solitude in the cave. This information is for you so that you are no longer disturbed concerning this matter.[31]

Should there be any doubt, he makes clear that this was not a decision made in haste; it had plagued him for at least three years and caused him untold trepidation and agony. Solitude was the one underlying meaning of his existence and behavior over the last three years. It explained not only his seclusion in his monastic cell and escape from the episcopacy and Theological College, but unspeakably coerced and forcefully compelled him daily to the eucharistic altar. Only there could he make sense of his need to be alone with God.

"At any rate," he concludes,

> and for your sake, I will continue to live in the monastery, beseeching the Lord Jesus Christ to look upon me with his mercy and prepare the path for me. I will continue to reveal my thoughts to the faithful fathers and seek their advice; I will study the monastic fathers and saints; I will celebrate Liturgies; all in the hope that if this is from God, then may it continue; otherwise, if it is from the Enemy, then may it fail.[32]

But though he was not yet in solitude, it appears he could sense its immediacy. "So be comforted, do not think too much," he calmly pacifies. "Leave the matter in the hands of God, for man *cannot* obstruct what God has ordained."[33]

First Solitude at the Cave: "I Saw the Light," 1934–1936

> "Whosoever is delighted in solitude is either a wild beast or a god."
> —*Aristotle*

O N A FATEFUL MORNING in or around the new year of 1934, after several painful months of disharmonious debate (which he quietly glosses over in the autobiographical fragments), Fr Mina finally left the monastery destined for solitude.[34] The monastic council had eventually acceded to his request. The fathers bade him farewell, some we may imagine, with tears. Fr Mina promised in accordance with Masudi's instruction to return each week for the communal Sunday Liturgy.[35] Mina also secured their assurance that no one would visit, let alone be concerned on his account. With a single laborer, a few essentials, meagre belongings, some beans, and a little flour, he disappeared into the endless horizon of the desert, destined for a primitive cave. "He did not take bread," his brother Hanna claims, "so that he would *not* have more than his one day's food."[36]

Fr Mina had previously discovered—or in his words, been divinely "directed to"—the cave in mid-1933 on his way back to the Baramous Monastery from Souhag. "I kept yearning," he writes,

> for the life of the solitary, until I could see no other way except to pursue it. Indeed, on my way to the monastery, the Lord Christ, *directed* me to a cave in the mountain that had been carved out by the late Hegumen Sarabamoun.[37]

The cave was two and a half kilometers (1.6 miles) northwest, about an hour's walk away from the monastery, and it had previously been occupied by a certain Sarabamoun (d. 1934).[38] On the day of his engagement to a local girl in 1905, Sarabamoun escaped from his hometown of Menoufia to the Baramous Monastery.[39] After his family made several attempts to remove him forcibly, he fled further into the desert and occupied a cave that from then on was known as the "Rock of Sarabamoun."[40] Some decades later he was appointed "head" of the monastery from 1925 to 1930, before resigning on account of illness and moving north of Cairo, where he died on December 7, 1934.[41]

The cave—last occupied in 1925—measuring six by eight meters (20 by 26 feet), carved three meters (10 feet) deep into rock—was in an extreme state of disrepair, and so Fr Mina, with the help of a laborer, set about sealing the walls and floors with gypsum.[42] He fashioned a timber door that lifted upward, before moving his meager belongings and cooking vessels into his new "cell."[43] As he entered and settled into the underground cave of his solitude—the solitude that he had feverishly dreamt of from the very first moment of entering the monastery—he enacted a movement. "The move can *now* be seen," an English scholar reflects, "as a part of a major revival of anchorite asceticism in Egypt."[44] But in the mind of Fr Mina, he was simply and finally alone with God.

* * *

We have a rare and tantalizing glimpse into the spiritual struggle of Fr Mina at the outset of his solitude in an autobiographical fragment. "It is difficult for me to describe my first night in that cave," he recalls,

> I felt that the Enemy gathered all his forces and might to battle against my weak self. The Enemy, through terrible sounds and forceful earthquakes, terrified me. This was due to the weakness of my human nature. But with God's

amazing care, and as if with invisible power, I was encouraged, saying: "Do not fear, for those who are with us are more than those who are with them." . . . These verses and similar verses encouraged me, and thus fear departed from me.[45]

What he experienced is beyond us, but, at the least, this almost paralyzing disclosure reveals the depths of his ascetic struggle. It also gives us a sobering sense of his formative years. Solitude was for him "bright sadness."[46] Each day was lived in piercing and torturous affliction, but each day brought Fr Mina closer into the embraces of his God. And though these struggles may confront and shock us, this shock should not lead us, as the historian Peter Brown notes, "to miss the deep social significance of asceticism as a long drawn out, solemn ritual of *dissociation*—of becoming the total stranger."[47] And it was this "dissociation"—the absolute renunciation of the world, the transformation into a stranger, unknown to all but God—that provoked, at least in the reckoning of Fr Mina, the violent and unstable reaction of the "Enemy."

Even old wars erupted. Not a day had passed before the monastic council recanted its permission. "The following day some monks came," writes Fr Mina,

> and wanted to take me back against my wishes, but they failed. So, they sent a telegram to His Holiness and another to the abbot. But after endless opposition and resistance from all, the patriarch agreed that I could continue in my solitary life. I thanked the Lord for his mercies.[48]

After this unfortunate hindrance, Fr Mina belatedly settled into solitude. The week passed in prostrations, continual prayer, and scribing patristic works. According to his brother's account, this became his routine for "twenty hours per day."[49] This at first glance seems to be hagiographical inflation, except that it was his well-attested and unanimously recorded life habit, both as a public monastic and as an elderly patriarch.[50] "I persisted on this path," Mina continues,

> through the grace of God, and would return to the monastery weekly to partake of the divine mysteries and obtain my monastic ration. In this path, I met severe wars, opposition, and persecution that I will later write about in detail.[51]

At the end of the first week, he returned to the monastery to attend Vespers on Saturday evening. Afterward, he met with Fr Abdel Messih el-Masudi and revealed the strange happenings. The other fathers (many of whom had opposed and attempted to obstruct his solitude) clamored around him, and, we are told, questioned him as to "what he had seen" and the "amount of suffering" that had assailed him in the desert.[52] This again confirms that the controversy concerning his solitude was out of genuine concern for his safety—and given the first night that Fr Mina chronicles, they seem well justified. Undeterred by his steadfast silence, the monks pressed him further. His only response was transparent, alarming, and altogether unnerving. "Don't worry," he modestly replied, "I didn't struggle to the death."[53]

* * *

Watching Fr Mina reenter the desert after the Sunday Liturgy would have been an inspiring and thoroughly humbling sight for his brethren. Cloaked in a coarse cassock, carrying water in one arm, and a stick in the other, he faded into the blinding heat haze of the desert. With each passing week, his brother recalls, the fathers began to relax. Each time Fr Mina returned, his face radiated with solace and quiet satisfaction. Soon Saturday evening became something of an event; the monks would gather around to be comforted by the hermit.[54]

Other than these few details, we have very little record concerning these years of solitude (which may be expected given the inherent nature of the activity). As far as one can tell, and for reasons unknown, Fr Mina's autobiography was never continued beyond this point and was destined to languish unfinished in a drawer of his desk.[55] There are, however, two particular visits that are preserved in Hanna's memoirs; one, we may suggest, on account of the young hermit's future movements, and the other, for no apparent reason other than that it was simply memorable.

The first occurred after some months, perhaps in mid-1934, when Fr Mina heard a knock on the makeshift door securing the cave.[56] There stood a Bedouin with two visitors in tow. One was an Egyptian, Dr Hassan Fouad, the director of the Ministry of Arabic Antiquities, and the other an American, an unnamed dean of a theological school in New York.[57] Fr Mina cordially greeted them and welcomed them into his cell. They carefully descended into the cave and sat on a blanket set out on the floor. The American, Hassan translated, had come to visit the monasteries of the Wadi al-Natrun Desert in research for a book on early monasticism.[58] They had unexpectedly come upon this Bedouin, he said, who led them to the hermit's cave.

Fr Mina happily spoke to them of the history of monasticism, the early desert fathers, as well as reading to them a few excerpts from the *Ascetical Homilies* of Isaac the Syrian. Having met a rare hermit who happened to be unusually well versed, the American took profuse notes before affably declaring that the previous two months in the Patriarchal Library paled in comparison with the last few hours.[59] As they made to leave, he attempted to hand Fr Mina some money as a symbolic gift. The hermit absolutely refused. "Why do I need this money?" he asked, "The love of money is the source of all evil . . . an obstacle in the way of solitude."[60] Mina thanked the American and promptly returned the gift. As to a photograph for the cover of the book, the hermit again graciously declined. Overcome with admiration, Hassan Fouad embraced the hermit. "My father, you have crowned the monks with pride and honored the Egyptians," he proclaimed, before adding, "I hope someday I can show my respect."[61] That day would eventually come.

History records only one other visitor during these years—the pope. Youannis XIX (1858–1942), according to the all too brief account, sought to visit Fr Mina in his solitude and take the "blessing from the cave that had become holy through the spiritual struggle of this hermit."[62] Upon hearing that the elderly patriarch was en route and on foot, Mina rushed to meet and escort him for the rest of the journey to the cave. After seeing his way of life, sharing a meal, and blessing the young hermit, Youannis made the difficult journey back to the monastery.

The account is obviously important in that the patriarch (at eighty years of age) walked for an hour in the unbearable heat of the desert to take the "blessing" of a relatively unknown and insignificant monk. But though an obviously memorable episode in the life of the Baramous Monastery, it was more than this; time after time we see the curious and evolving concern of the pope for the young monk. Was Youannis checking up on the tenacious young monk who had escaped the clutches of the episcopacy while at the Helwan Theological College? Or was he possibly looking for reassurance concerning his decision to allow Fr Mina to remain in solitude? Perhaps, as the account states, the patriarch simply came to be blessed.

* * *

In 1936, toward the end of his solitude at the Baramous Monastery, Fr Mina experienced an unprecedented epiphany that would fundamentally alter the course of his life. After years of indescribably severe ascetic struggles in the desert—physical, mental, and spiritual—something unexpectedly changed. The decisive and abrupt moment was quietly disclosed in a letter that he wrote to his brother and that provides an invaluable insight into his eremitic life.[63]

"Dear brother, as I promised," begins Fr Mina,

> I will write to you regarding the path of solitude which by the grace of God I have taken. Before I begin, I confess privately and publicly, that all this is a result of the blessing of my fathers and brothers in the monastery. For, in fact, I am the least of them all. I say this from my heart and not out of false humility. No, indeed this is the honest truth. I am living this path because I am a *wild dog* and lest I should bite someone, I fled to solitude.[64]

Modestly, he ascribes his progress in the path of solitude to the blessing of his brethren and again repeats the paradoxical rationale for his solitude: he fled to solitude not out of strength but from weakness—perceiving himself to be a threatening "wild dog."[65]

"You know there is nothing that takes place," he continues,

> in the world without God's will and plan. God knows that my yearning for this path did *not* come from knowledge or experience of this path, because I certainly did not know it. Indeed, the saintly fathers gave us some signposts, and those who seek the life of solitude must earnestly beg God to prepare someone to direct this path for them. *Three years* ago, I begged him to guide me on this path, but because of a lack of knowledge, I lost the way. I was repeatedly attacked by the Enemy; in distress and despair I became overwhelmed with depression and lost hope. My body was weakened and emaciated in consequence of the frightening thoughts that attacked me during this prolonged period.[66]

The years of ascetic struggle had taken their toll. He paints an exceedingly divergent picture to the utopian desert paradise of serene psalmody and tranquil worship that we may imagine. Lost, distressed, and despairing, Mina was mentally and physically "emaciated." Other than the autobiographical description of his first night in solitude, we have no idea as to the exact nature of these afflictions—that is, aside from their severity. "But," he reminisces,

> the merciful God, who does not desire for any man to fall into such tribulations, helped me with his mighty hand, and directed me into the way and opened the door for me. I sighed deeply in relief of all the suffering that befell me because of the Enemy. *He illuminated my eyes, and I saw the light.* I realized the depth to which I was in darkness and despair. My heart rejoiced,

and my soul was made glad. I kept chanting with David the Prophet: "If I say, 'My foot slips,' your mercy, O Lord, will hold me up. In the multitude of my anxieties within me, your comforts delight my soul."[67]

Though the timing is inexact, the suggestion is that after three years (1934–1936) of agony, God "illuminated" his eyes and he "saw the light." But what did he mean by such words? Was Fr Mina merely describing his relief from demonic affliction? Did he experience a vision of God? Or was it the elusive "uncreated light" of union with God that is often described in the Orthodox tradition?

If we read the letter in the wider context of monastic experience, and solitude in particular, many Fathers describe a period of intense struggle or "purification" that is followed by a state of *theoria*, or "illumination," culminating in "perfection."[68] These three stages are well attested in the monastic and patristic literature and become intensely relevant when we consider the life of his much-loved St Menas. After years of ascetic struggle in the desert, St Menas had a remarkably similar epiphany: "He dwelt there for many days in great *privation* . . . and after a time the grace of God *lighted upon him*, and he saw heaven open."[69]

Of course, it is unwise to rest a case that Fr Mina had attained to a state of "illumination" (in the patristic sense) upon a single sentence that he wrote in an informal letter. But taken in context, the words, at the least, were *not* a mere expression of relief. Whatever one's conclusion as to the precise nature of the event, after years of acute and harrowing spiritual warfare, Fr Mina claimed to have experienced an abrupt act of infinite mercy, comfort, and mystical joy; a direct, vivid, and powerful intervention of God in his ascetic struggle and demonic affliction. Following an antecedent state of intense crisis and inner turmoil, this sudden "turning point" fundamentally touched and transformed every fabric of his life.[70] And though the epiphany was momentary, the transformation and illumination were, as far as one can tell, enduring.[71] Fr Mina's eyes were opened—"I saw the light"—and from that unique, unforgettable, and mystifying moment, everything stood to change.[72]

St Isaac the Syrian:
Patristic Discipleship and an Urgent Corrective

> "Wait for me, Father," a monk once said. "I am running after you for God's sake."
> But the other replied, "And I, for God's sake, am fleeing from you."
> —St Arsenius the Great

IN AN UNDATED LETTER that Fr Mina wrote to his disciples, likely a decade after his own experience of solitude, he instructs them concerning the three essential requisites for a life of solitude.[73] The first is "blameless intent": not even the faintest desire for charismatic gifts, flattery, ecclesial rank, or even virtue is tolerable; the only legitimate incentive for solitude is "stillness of heart." The second condition, Fr Mina continues, is the observance of the "canonical prayers," and the third, a "spiritual guide." Prayer, he notes, may be lacking from a matter of weakness, and a guide may be inaccessible (or nonexistent) because of circumstances. But the first requisite is absolutely indispensable.[74] There can be no substitute nor surrogate, in Fr Mina's thought and experience, for "blameless intent." Solitude founded upon anything else is delusional at best, and demonic at worst.

This advice, it would seem, was modeled upon his own solitude. Certainly, the previously discussed letters written to his brother are suggestive of the purity of his intent and prayerful existence. But who was his guide in the solitude of the desert? Or perhaps his advice was borrowed from experience, and a guide was not to be found?

* * *

"In the desert, miles away from civilisation," wrote a famed and leading Coptologist in 1961, "the desert saint [Fr Mina] met the desert prophet, Abuna Abdel Messih the Ethiopian [el-Habashy]."[75] The author, Otto Meinardus, a prolific scholar, made this claim on the back of his pioneering study of Egyptian monasticism, in which he established an assured fact of scholarship: this same Abdel Messih el-Habashy was the inspiration for Fr Mina's solitude and profoundly influenced it.[76] A few years later, Edward Wakin (seemingly in consequence) repeated the claim suggesting that el-Habashy was Mina's "spiritual father."[77] And since then, Western scholars have followed suit—fascinatingly, without exception.[78] That el-Habashy was his spiritual father has, in short, become authorized history.

The claim is certainly hagiographically soothing in that two celebrated desert saints are portrayed as partnering in the revival of anchorite monasticism, but it is, unfortunately, also deeply problematic. To begin with, not a single extant primary source (such as an autobiographical fragment or letter) even mentions el-Habashy. In a later interview from 1959, Fr Mina cites Abdel Messih el-Masudi as his greatest monastic influence—again without reference to el-Habashy.[79] Moreover, not even a faint mention of el-Habashy is to be found in any of the original Arabic secondary sources (Hanna Youssef Atta or Fr Raphael Ava Mina). The absence is suggestive of an inadvertent scholarly misstep.

This confusion is, to be fair, not that surprising, as Fr Abdel Messih el-Habashy (1898–1973), otherwise known as the "Ethiopian," is something of an elusive saintly figure. He was born in Ethiopia, where he took the monastic name Abba Gabra Krestos ("Servant of Christ"). The only Western scholarly study of his life begins with an intriguing admission: "Sadly, many fascinating sources for the early life of Abuna Abdel Messih . . . are contradictory. . . . At the beginning of the twenty-first century, no definitive primary sources have been unearthed."[80] With that said, Watson—who follows Meinardus in claiming that el-Habashy was Fr Mina's spiritual father—suggests that el-Habashy lived from circa "1935–1937" to "1970–1974" as a solitary at the Baramous Monastery in Egypt.[81] Strangely, despite dating the earliest point of his solitude as 1935 (at least a year after Fr Mina entered solitude), Watson still blindly makes the claim of el-Habashy's spiritual fatherhood.

According to a biography of el-Habashy published in 1996 by the Baramous Monastery, Bishop Macarius suggests a more reliable chronology based upon the monastery's records:[82] after living a number of years as a hermit, el-Habashy left Ethiopia on January 7, 1934, and walked for some three months to Sudan, crossed the border to Egypt, and arrived at the monastery on March 30, 1934.[83] To suggest that el-Habashy became the spiritual father of Fr Mina would require that the former entered solitude immediately—though Mina still would have been a hermit in the desert for at least a few months prior.

But even this is stretching the fabric of history. Monastery records indicate that el-Habashy first attempted to enter solitude *after* he became aware that Fr Mina had forsaken his cave in the desert on April 4, 1936. That is to say, Fr Mina had left the monastery well before el-Habashy even considered solitude! Only at that point did el-Habashy seek to inhabit the now-unoccupied cave. "The Abbot [Fr Basilious]," Bishop Macarius notes, "totally refused his proposal, and did not even allow further discussion about the matter."[84] History preserves that a defiant el-Habashy attempted to escape into solitude on at least three occasions, once even attempting to scale and descend the monastery's towering walls by rope.[85] Apparently—as was the case with Fr Mina's experience—the elders feared solitude.[86] After his third attempt to escape, the patriarch person-ally intervened, and el-Habashy was left to his own devices.[87] Interestingly, the records reveal that he first entered solitude in June 1936—two months after Fr Mina had left the monastery.[88] A few months after inhabiting Fr Mina's cave, el-Habashy carved out his own cave some three kilometers (1.9 miles) from the monastery.[89] It would be his home for the next three decades.

We should happily admit, however, that there is some evidence that the two monks were briefly acquainted. Fr Mina entered solitude in very early 1934 at the latest, and el-Habashy arrived at the monastery at the end of March 1934; thus it is reasonable to infer that they may have occasionally met, as Mina returned to the monastery each week for Liturgy. Decades later, Mina (then the patriarch) feared the anger of el-Habashy, who "wanted to reprimand the Pope bitterly for leaving his rite of solitude."[90] And on another occasion Mina (as patriarch), after hearing el-Habashy's complaint concerning the multitude of visitors that disturbed his silence, banned pilgrims from approaching the hermit, declaring, "Leave him, so that God may lift his wrath away from the world for his sake."[91] It is also evident that Fr Mina and el-Habashy shared a common affinity for St Isaac the Syrian.[92] But we should, nonetheless, bear in mind that el-Habashy was mostly silent, and when he did choose to speak, it was often in broken Arabic, and in riddles at that—all of which argues against anything more than a friend-ship built upon fleeting and occasional encounters.[93]

Beyond this, there is nothing to suggest that Fr Mina was a disciple of, nor influenced by, nor even inspired to live in solitude by el-Habashy. In fact, the evidence is perhaps suggestive of the reverse. When Fr Mina returned from solitude for the Sunday Liturgy, we may imagine that el-Habashy (who had been a hermit in Ethiopia) would have longed to share his solitude; and when Fr Mina left his cave in 1936, it was el-Habashy who sought to occupy that very *same* cave.

With some heaviness, despite the assurances of unanimous scholarship founded upon the mistaken claim of a leading Coptologist, we must conclude that the solitude of these two extraordinary hermits was in every sense inde-pendent, with only an insecure and somewhat precarious suggestion that el-Habashy was in some very partial (and perhaps insignificant) way influenced by Fr Mina—but in any event, not the reverse. This rather urgent corrective is necessary, as Mina's solitude was formative not only in his own personal ascesis but also in his ecclesial reform. To claim that he was "deeply influenced" by el-Habashy is to misconstrue history—as heartwarming as that claim would be.[94]

*   *   *

Who, then, was Fr Mina's spiritual guide? A first thought suggests that it may have been Fr Abdel Messih el-Masudi, who had been his "father in monasticism." But Masudi passed away in early March 1935 and spent the better part of his final few years in Cairo at the Patriarchal Library. It is thus exceedingly unlikely that he played an active (or present) role during these first years of solitude. Furthermore, there is no record of any other monk who was in solitude at the same time as Fr Mina, nor does the latter mention any guide.[95]

Though he taught his disciples to carefully maintain "blameless intent" in solitude should a spiritual father be lacking in solitude, it seems that in his own experience he sought out a most unlikely guide—someone who had long been reposed.[96] He evidently turned to his beloved St Isaac the Syrian.[97] In the voluminous *Ascetical Homilies*, he unearthed the most profound of directors in the life of solitude and began what may only be termed a "patristic discipleship."

If, then, we seek to enter the mind of Fr Mina, we must first inhabit the thought world of Isaac the Syrian. Mina cannot be properly understood otherwise. And though Isaac is an oft-recognized influence in the life of Fr Mina, the recognition is always superficial.[98] No one has genuinely, properly, or thoroughly perceived the extent of the impact and influence St Isaac had on Fr Mina, or the degree to which the thought of the Syrian permeates and suffuses his life and takes charge in it. I suspect the reason for this is simply a lack of familiarity with the Syrian's thought. Indeed, any examination of Fr Mina's letters and autobiographical fragments reveals copious and penetrating citations from the *Ascetical Homilies*. But more than this, Mina's entire thought and behavior resonates, emanates, and radically incarnates their energy. In short, Isaac became to him a spiritual father.[99]

Reading Isaac, one gets the uncanny awareness that he is reading about Mina; the father is distinctly and unnervingly recognizable in his son. And just as discipleship entirely redefines and remakes, Mina was radically and irrevocably transformed by Isaac. In an *al-Ahram* interview just before his patriarchal ordination, on April 25, 1959, he was asked which was his favorite book apart from Scripture. "The book of Abba Isaac the Syrian," Mina responded, "which discusses the life of *solitude* and *silence*. The Saint was nominated to be the bishop of Iraq, but he *escaped* that office and became a hermit."[100] These few words—solitude, silence, escape—betray his "patristic discipleship."

In other words, Isaac the Syrian (613–700) was to Fr Mina an example in life *before* thought. After five years as the bishop of Nineveh, Isaac "abdicated his episcopacy for a reason which God knows, and he departed . . . and he dwelt in stillness together with the anchorites who dwelt thereabouts."[101] He was remembered as "exceedingly well versed in the divine writings, even to the point that he lost his eye-sight by reason of his reading and asceticism."[102] An East Syrian account attempts to provide a rationale for his escape: two men came to him disputing the terms of a loan, one threatening to take the other to court. "Since the Holy Gospel," intervened Isaac, "teaches us not take back what has been given away, you should at least grant this man a day to make his repayment." "Leave aside for the moment the teachings of the Gospel," the man interrupted. "If the Gospel is not to be present," Isaac questioned, "what have I come here to do?" And with those words, he departed into solitude.[103] Even the life of Isaac, in his flight from the episcopacy, was paradigmatic for Fr Mina.

* * *

A first move in discerning St Isaac the Syrian's influence upon Fr Mina is to recognize the "hero" in Isaac's writing: the *ihidaya*—the "solitary," literally the "single one." The original meaning, a distinguished Syriac scholar notes, points to one who is unified, to a "unity of the human person within himself and to his unity with God."[104] There is perhaps a no more apt description of Fr Mina.

Solitude for the *ihidaya* is founded upon a profoundly experiential union with God: "No one can draw nigh to God save the man who has separated himself from the world."[105] "The soul that loves God," Isaac reiterates, "finds rest only in God. First, loose yourself from all external bonds, and then you will be able to bind your heart to God, because the being bound to God is preceded by the being loosed from matter."[106]

But how can this be reconciled with the commandment to love one's neighbor?[107] "The commandment," Isaac replies,

> which says, "Thou shalt love the Lord thy God . . ." is fulfilled when you patiently endure in your stillness. And the commandment that speaks of the love of neighbor is included in the former. Do you wish to acquire in your soul the love of your neighbor . . . ? Separate yourself from him, and the heat and flame of love for him will burn in you.[108]

Solitude paradoxically draws the hermit closer to his neighbor. And, Isaac is cautious to note, this is no mere theoretical position; he personally knows it to be so: "Truly, experience is the teacher of all."[109] Solitude not only unites one with God but, as an irresistible consequence, with all humanity.

Here we should see that Isaac is dreadfully clear: coming out of solitude for the sake of bringing healing to the world is fraught with danger, at dire cost of one's own union with God.[110] "Love the idleness of stillness," he teaches, "above providing for the world's starving and the conversion of a multitude of heathen to the worship of God. It is better for you to free yourself from the shackle of sin than to free slaves from their slavery."[111] Needless to say, the advice is given specifically to solitaries—and to them alone—but it in no small part explains Fr Mina's future reluctance to depart from solitude. It also sheds light on his unusual cleaving to solitude even "within the world": first as a public monastic, and later as patriarch.

But what if the solitary is involuntarily met by one who is afflicted? "I do not mean," Isaac clarifies in the *Sixty-Fourth Homily* (which was much loved by Fr Mina),[112]

> that if the affair is far removed from you, you should go and cast yourself into works of this sort [merciful acts], for deeds of this kind do not belong to your way of life. If, however, the affair is placed directly into your hands and is within your power . . . then take heed to yourself, lest you become a partaker of the blood of the iniquitous man by not taking pains to deliver him.[113]

Should the one suffering come to the solitary, the solitary must relieve the affliction with all his capacity. But while a solitary should not seek to heal the world, Isaac is at pains to say that union with God in solitude allows one to partake in the "mercy which God has *for* the world."[114] Isaac calls this "mercy" the *hubba sapya* ("luminous love").[115] Such divine love for humanity cannot be attained by a mere act of will or ascetic struggle but only through an "inebriation in God" from which the divine love overflows onto humanity.[116] The solitary who tastes this "divine love" draws near to the "luminous love of humanity," which is nondiscerning and unconditional.[117]

Hilarion Alfeyev has accurately noted that a schema of sorts thus emerges within Isaac's thought. Withdrawal from the world (and even the monastery) to seek stillness beckons the solitary to God; there, in union with his or her Maker, the solitary acquires a genuine love for God, and in turn, God's love impregnates him or her with the overflowing "luminous love" of humanity. We may add to this a fourth part of the schema: sharing in God's mercy—his luminous or divine love for humanity—directly and forcefully feeds into the first; it simultaneously draws the monastic into further solitude, chasing away his or her passions, enacting a deeper union with God, and therefore vivifying and catalyzing a God-like love for his or her fellow human beings.

Fr Mina's solitude, and therefore the very basis of his ministry, emerges from these eternal Syrian springs. *Solitude* beckoned the love of God into his soul, overflowing, as Isaac reveals, upon all humanity. This became, almost exclusively, the counterintuitive method of his ecclesial reform. In pursuit of his unusual choice of spiritual father, Fr Mina loved humanity in ways that are barely fathomable, ways that were perhaps divine. Unlike the seventh-century Syrian, however, Fr Mina would henceforth be involuntarily and persistently torn away from solitude and stillness.

The Intriguing Story of the Seven Monks, 1936

"Antony, as from a shrine, *came forth* initiated
in the mysteries and filled with the Spirit of God."
—*St Athanasius,* Life of Antony

TOWARD THE BEGINNING of the fourth century, Antony the Great barricaded himself in an old, isolated, and abandoned Roman fort deep in the Egyptian desert. Two decades of solitude continued in this manner until the many monks and crowds that had now gathered around his fort could no longer bear the separation and, in a state of unrest, suddenly wrenched the door off the fort. After years of unseen and relentless spiritual warfare, Antony was *forced* from solitude. He emerged "as from a shrine . . . initiated in the mysteries and filled with the Spirit of God."[118] "His soul was free from blemish," Athanasius writes,

> for it was neither contracted as if by grief, nor relaxed by pleasure, nor possessed by laughter or dejection, for he was not troubled when he beheld the crowd, nor overjoyed at being saluted by so many. But he was altogether even as being guided by reason, and abiding in a natural state.[119]

Those words might just as easily have been spoken of Fr Mina.

* * *

The following events of a fateful day in early April 1936 are preserved in Hanna's memoirs.[120] The relevant text is reproduced here in full, given that the episode marks a dramatic turn in the life of Fr Mina. There is no other detailed source for the episode. Hanna was not actually present for most of the contention (though he certainly played a part), so presumably he gathered the details and dialogue from those involved—undoubtedly along with their interpretations of the event.[121] But there is little reason to suspect the account, given that Hanna was intimately involved and that it was originally published together with the recollections of Mina's future disciple, Fr Raphael Ava Mina, who would have questioned the historicity had it been unsound. The episode also explains Fr Mina's subsequent movements—no other explanation for his departure from the Baramous Monastery has ever been given—and it accounts as well for the subtle intimations of (at least perceived) animosity from the Baramous leadership, to which he was apparently subjected later in life.[122]

* * *

On Lazarus Saturday, April 4, 1936, Fr Mina returned to the monastery from his cave to attend Vespers on the eve of Palm Sunday. Unknown to him, it would be his last day at the Baramous Monastery.

Fr Mina arrived to unusual commotion. Putting down his staff and meager belongings, he asked what had caused the disturbance. Seven elderly monks, he was told, were to be expelled from the monastery within the hour. No reason or offense, we should note, is stated in the account other than that the seven elderly monks had disobeyed the unnamed abbot.[123]

During my research, the monks of the Baramous Monastery refused to discuss the episode. They stated that they had only heard rumors and therefore declined to discuss the 1936 incident, nor would they confirm the name of the abbot at the time. But a letter (previously unknown to scholarship) written two decades later by Macarius, the later bishop of the Baramous Monastery—whom we met previously as the monk Armanious, who fell off the mule when Fr Mina was still a novice—claims that the seven monks had challenged Hegumen Basilious (the superintendent), and that this challenge then developed into a "rebellion" against Hegumen Barnaba (the abbot).[124] Fr Basilious was well known (and feared) as something of a "hard man"—he objected to el-Habashy's solitude, and he headed the monastic council that initially opposed Fr Mina's solitude in 1933.[125] But it was, in fact, Fr Barnaba who stood at the center of the contention and ordered the expulsion of the seven monks.[126] Whether their expulsion was warranted or even justified is not known.

Hurriedly, and with little thought given to such things, Fr Mina made his way to the monastery's hall to find the abbot present, with the governor, a policeman, and a handful of sergeants intervening amid several agitated monks. Fr Mina knelt in front of the abbot. "Father, I came to welcome you back," he said after customarily kissing the hand of the abbot, "and to ask about your health, and about the truth regarding the dismissal of the seven monks?"

"My son, these are Pope Youannis' orders, and I am simply here to execute them," shrugged the abbot, hardly taking notice of the protest.

Mina, for a moment forgetting himself—or perhaps not—looked up at the abbot. "It would surely be mournful for the pope if these monks were expelled on the eve of Palm Sunday. He would never accept"—said Mina while standing up—"that these fathers should lose their hope in Christ. You are our head and shepherd, the father of monks; responsible in front of God of the sick, confused, and lost. In your hands is the monastic authority to guide and restore the lost." Mina paused for an awkward moment. "I plead before you, in the name of the Lord and these holy days, postpone this order until the elderly fathers at least have a chance to appeal to His Holiness, and allow them to be judged inside (and not outside) the monastery. Please," Fr Mina said, now growing emboldened and carefully looking the abbot in the eyes, "do not expel them during the week of Pascha."[127]

The abbot was taken aback. His face contorted and, Hanna recalls, could barely restrain his hurt pride. How could a young monk dare, in front of a crowd no less, to object while senior monks sat silent? "Listen, my son," he said, pointing a solemn finger at Fr Mina, "do not stand in my path; otherwise, you will be disobeying the patriarch himself. Besides"—he looked around at those present—"you are a hermit, and this is none of your concern!"

Though only a monk for eight years, Fr Mina would not submit. "In the name of Christ," he persisted, "who sacrificed himself for our sake, I ask you, my father, to proceed slowly and in a manner that would please our monastic predecessors . . . they taught us to intercede for the wrongdoers and lawbreakers, and to give each one his punishment *without* causing him to lose his hope."

The abbot, according to Hanna, became enraged. He commanded the soldiers to expel the seven monks, before sternly warning Fr Mina to remain in the monastery and forbidding him any return to solitude until he personally brought the young hermit's disobedience to the attention of the pope. Mina said nothing for a few moments. "My father," he finally said, entirely unconcerned about provoking a further reaction, "I will devote myself to serving these fathers who are to be expelled without mercy. I will be their *slave* until they return to the monastery." Suddenly aware of the escalation, and cognizant of Fr Mina's relationship with Pope Youannis, the abbot's face paled.

And so, on the eve of Palm Sunday, 1936, Fr Mina, in defense of a matter that hardly concerned him, left with the seven elderly monks for Cairo.[128] The young hermit—like the first monk, Antony the Great—was forced from solitude.

* * *

As the events unfolded, it immediately became obvious that the pope would have to intervene. Pope Youannis XIX (1858–1942) hailed from Asyut and had entered the Baramous Monastery at the age of seventeen, in 1875.[129] He was tonsured at the hands of a blind, saintly monk by the name of Awad el-Barhemey (d. 1878), who would have presumably told him of an unfortunate incident two decades prior: in or around 1850, an altercation took place after which the head of the monastery had five monks expelled—allegedly *unjustly*—leaving Awad as the sole remaining monk for several years.[130] It would, perhaps, be a veiled warning for Youannis' future patriarchate.

Youannis went on, in 1878, to become head of the Baramous Monastery. A decade later, on Sunday, March 3, 1887, he was ordained metropolitan of Beheira and Gharbeya.[131] After the death of Cyril V in 1927, Youannis became the patriarchal deputy (locum tenens) and on December 16, 1928, took the unprecedented step of becoming patriarch. Needless to say, the decision of overturning ancient custom—a diocesan bishop, according to Coptic Orthodox canon law, could not be nominated for the papacy—was met with protest and indignant demonstration.[132] Many in the community, one scholar notes, were, however, more concerned with his "arch-conservatism and persistent rumors that he had bribed his way into the papal position."[133] And though he would go on to enact a number of important and far-reaching reforms, these rumors would hound him until his death.

* * *

Fr Mina and the seven monks found temporary refuge for the night at the Monastery of Archangel Michael in Old Cairo. One of the expelled monks, Fr Shenouda, was a relative of the monastery's vicar, a well-respected priest by the name of Fr Marcos Dawood (1892–1970)—who, we should mention, only narrowly escaped excommunication for daring to house the exiled monks.[134] There, they would be visited by a host of influential figures and renowned priests, including the famed musicologist Ragheb Moftah (1898–2001) and the commissioner of the Giza governorate, Marcos Fahmy.[135] Seeing that their situation was unreasonable, the visitors, according to Hanna, rented a two-story house for the monks, with Fr Mina acquiring the essentials for their needs.[136]

Meanwhile, fearing Fr Mina would have the ear of the pope, the abbot immediately left for Alexandria, going so far, we are told, as to rent a car despite the expense. Having found Pope Youannis, he slandered Fr Mina, accusing him of breaking the monastic laws; the abbot even, to the pope's shock, claimed the hermit had lunged at him with a large rod, only to be stopped by the intervening sergeants. "I cannot believe what you are saying," gasped Youannis. "His behavior has always been disciplined and wise. Why," he asked, "are you the first to complain about him in this way?"

Rather than merely defending the expelled, Fr Mina, it would seem, had taken upon himself the state of the expelled. Youannis immediately called Hanna (in part explaining his intimate knowledge of the episode), who was well known to him. "Your brother deserves punishment," he yelled, "why did he interfere in the monastery's business, disobey, and verbally assault the abbot, almost striking him on the head with a rod?"

Hanna was in the dark. He was not aware that Fr Mina had left solitude, let alone that he was in Old Cairo. "I know nothing about this matter," replied Hanna, "but my heart tells me something is not right, and as you investigate the matter, the truth will be revealed." At this point, Youannis made clear that it was *his* order that monks be expelled. "I hope the final judgment is yours *alone*," said Hanna. This suggests that Hanna felt the papal order might have been based upon misinformation.

Upon hanging up the phone, Hanna immediately left for Cairo and met with his brother, explaining that Youannis was on his way to Cairo to personally investigate the controversy. Fr Mina insisted on first meeting with the patriarch alone.[137] We should not pass over this detail lightly. The hermit, according to the account, had now entirely taken the place of the expelled monks; he stood in their stead. This may have been a simple appeal to his history with the pope, but it is suggestive of something more. Fr Mina, to all appearances, sought to shoulder the entire burden *alone*; the expelled monks were kept well away from the patriarch, and he insisted that Hanna (an able mediator) should return to Alexandria.[138]

After entering the patriarchate, Fr Mina first, almost routinely, went to pray at the altar before meeting Youannis. There was little cordial welcome or familiarity.[139] Youannis was irate. "You are still at the first steps of worshiping," reprimanded the patriarch, and thinking deluded pride was at play, he added, "Perhaps you have been deceived by the devil?"

Fr Mina's response was, in a word, odd. There was no apology, no explanation of his actions, and no defense of the other expelled monks. "My Lord Jesus Christ is honest and just," he replied. "He does not leave those who seek him. He shelters them with his angels." Mina implicitly appealed to the nature of Christ as the simple explanation of his behavior.

"And . . ." Youannis retorted, lingering with frustration, "do the teachings of Christ allow you to interfere in matters that do not concern you?"

"Yes," Fr Mina replied, "Christ taught us to struggle for honesty even if it means shedding one's blood. One who does not defend the truth is like the devil. I am the son of the monastery. How can I see things that are not according to the monastic laws and yet remain silent? I did not," he said now in exasperation, "resist or hurt my father, the abbot. Instead, with all respect and reverence, I pleaded for the sake of Christ, to whose service he devoted himself, not to leave those fathers to despair. . . . I begged him not to keep them away from the shelter of hope during those days of Christ's entry into Jerusalem; to postpone their expulsion from the monastery until the end of the Holy Week, after which he could request Your Holiness' mercy."

"But why did you interfere in this matter, since you are a hermit away from the monastery?"

"I would deserve your anger if I had not interfered," interrupted Fr Mina, "if I neglected defending the reputation of the great Baramous Monastery, the monastery of Your Holiness, and if I had left seven reverend elders to be expelled in such a shameful way. They would collapse and lose hope of God's mercy during Pascha."

"Didn't you revolt against the abbot?" repeated Youannis, still in disbelief. "You wanted to crush his head with a rod!"

"God forbid," the hermit said with tears welling in his eyes, "that I would even think of doing such a thing. I asked only that he look with compassion at the monks as their shepherd and judge them according to the Church canons." Fr Mina quietly wept.

Youannis was moved by the tears of a hermit that he had known for years to be beyond reproach. Recalling Mina's escape from the episcopacy and his care for nothing but solitude, the patriarch could not hold back his own tears. Clearly, he had been misinformed. Fr Mina's presence was enough for Youannis to be persuaded to forgive the elderly monks. Even if they had genuinely disobeyed the abbot, mercy was greater than sin. Youannis pardoned the elderly monks and granted them permission to return to their monastery.

When the young hermit returned to the rented house in Old Cairo, the monks were stunned.[140] The seven elderly monks made their way, speechless, to the patriarchate to ask Youannis for absolution before returning to their monastery. But, Hanna is careful to note, Fr Mina waited behind. There was something *else* to be discussed. He had a request of sorts.[141]

* * *

This lengthy and fascinating dialogue is valuable not only as an explanation of Fr Mina's departure from solitude but more significantly as an insight into his personal ascesis and method of reform. We may accordingly suggest that it is a primitive nucleus of what might be termed his "kenotic ecclesiology." By this I mean the notion of *kenōsis*—"self-emptying" or "self-humbling"—that originates in the Christological hymn of Philippians 2:

> Although being [*hyparchōn*] in the form of God, [Christ] did not consider it robbery [*or* exploitation] to be equal with God, but made himself of no reputation [*enkenōsen*], taking the form of a *slave*. . . . He humbled himself and became obedient to the point of death, even the death of the cross.[142]

One New Testament scholar has suggested that a participative and transformative paradigm—*although [status], not [selfishness], but [selflessness]*—emerges from these verses, a pattern that the Apostle Paul himself "inhabits."[143] Here the participle "being" (*hyparchōn*) may be translated in a concessive sense as "although being," but also in a causative sense as "because being."[144] Thus, it is not simply "although" Jesus was God that he emptied himself and became a slave to the point of violent death, but also "because" he is God. This is, in short, *who* God is. On the cross, divinity is most perfectly revealed. Kenosis is, therefore, the "counterintuitive 'truth about God.'"[145] Christ was not acting out of character on the Cross, but rather in character, by manifesting the piercing reality of who he is as the *cruciform* God. It is this paradigm that the Apostle Paul himself inhabits, and he begs the Philippians to do the same: "Let this mind be in you which was also in Christ Jesus . . ."[146]

That pattern or "mind," when extended to the life of Fr Mina, is altogether revealing: although he was an innocent hermit, he did not exercise or exploit that status, but rather he emptied himself of his rights and became the "expelled." At every turn of the above dialogue, his rationale (and the very necessity) for his actions are secondary to this cruciform kenosis. Christ empties himself *because* he is God, and it is this truth which Fr Mina lives. How could he possibly remain silent? The mind of Christ left him no choice. When the abbot became furious, Mina declared, echoing the words of Philippians: "I will be their *slave* until they return to the monastery."[147] In other words, it was not merely *although* he was a solitary hermit that he sacrificed himself for others; it was *because* he was a solitary. In his estimation, this was who a solitary was called to be and how, evidently, a solitary should act.

Fr Mina was not simply forgoing his monastic status. Rather, as we have seen, he had spent years yearning, contending, indeed begging, for *solitude*; and yet in a moment, he voluntarily and knowingly forsook that *same* solitude and "emptied" himself without so much as a thought. He became the "expelled," the "lawbreaker"; he became the elderly monks' "slave," caring for their every need in Old Cairo; and, standing in their stead, pleading their cause, he met the Patriarch *alone*—all at the preciously kenotic loss of his solitude.

Though he was enduringly humble, we should not miss that he was at once fearless in his pursuit of this truth.[148] These two features—humility and irre-provable courage—would forever mark his ecclesial method of kenosis. It is here, therefore, that we find a primitive nucleus of his cruciform and kenotic ecclesiology that would play out (as we shall see) throughout his life. Like Christ, this was his counterintuitive truth. It would be a truth at a deep personal cost. Years later, he would disclose to one of his disciples that he had been acutely distraught over the loss of his desert cave where he had hoped to live out his days. "Whenever," wrote Fr Mina,

> . . . I remember those sweet days that I spent in the wilderness, tears fill my eyes. I never have forgotten, and will never forget, that day when I left the wilderness. I can remember quite well that I kept crying bitterly for three days over departing that place. . . .[149]

Notes

[1]W. K. Lowther Clarke, *The Lausiac History of Palladius* (New York: The Macmillan Company, 1918), 64. The account is worth reproducing: " 'Well, be convinced now that it is impossible for me to be ordained, since the law forbids a man with ear cut off to be raised to the priesthood.' So then they left him

and departed and went and told the bishop [Timothy of Alexandria (381–384)]. And he said to them: 'Let the Jews observe this law. For my part, if you bring a man with his nose cut off worthy in character, I'll ordain him.' So they went off again and implored Ammonius. And he swore to them: 'If you use force on me, I'll cut off my tongue.' So then they left him and went their way."

[2]Sozomen, *Ecclesiastical History* 8.19, in NPNF² 2:411.

[3]Armand Veilleux, *Pachomian Koinonia*, vol. 1, *The Life of Saint Pachomius and His Disciples* (Kalamazoo, MI: Cistercian Publications, 1980), 51.

[4]Claudia Rapp, *Holy Bishops in Late Antiquity* (Berkeley, CA: University of California Press, 2005), 144. It should be noted that Fr Mina (then Pope Kyrillos) seemed at several points to recognize this, too, as a paramount quality in potential candidates; for instance, Bishops Shenouda, Samuel, and Gregorious were forced against their wills to be ordained.

[5]Mina the Recluse [Kyrillos VI], "Autobiographical Fragments."

[6]Atta and Raphael Ava Mina, *Life of Pope Kyrillos*, 9.

[7]Ibid.

[8]Ibid. Hanna also writes, "Fr Mina received a lot of blame and rebuke, which he accepted patiently." Fr Mina's own account records this episode with the same (if not more) intensity, again indicating that the documentary evidence is in harmony with the primary biographical sources.

[9]Mina the Recluse [Kyrillos VI], "Autobiographical Fragments." In the autobiographical account, Fr Mina states that he, in fact, had requested from Youannis to leave for Souhag and that the pope agreed, but when Mina asked to stay there permanently, Youannis became angry and sent the telegram requesting his return. It is conceivable that Youannis had granted the permission for a "visit" at an earlier occasion, but had not expected an escape when he sought to ordain him. This would also explain why in Hanna's account Youannis was unware of Mina's whereabouts.

[10]Ibid.

[11]Raphael Ava Mina, *Spiritual Leadership*, 8.

[12]Atta and Raphael Ava Mina, *Life of Pope Kyrillos*, 9.

[13]Mina the Recluse [Kyrillos VI], "Autobiographical Fragments."

[14]Atta and Raphael Ava Mina, *Life of Pope Kyrillos*, 9. A simple question at this point emerges: why would Youannis XIX allow Fr Mina to pursue potential solitude at Baramous Monastery and not at Souhag? It is conceivable that at the Baramous Monastery, Fr Mina would still be, in a sense, within reach, especially given the patriarch's manifest relationship with the Baramous Monastery, and therefore all hope would not be lost for a future ordination.

[15]Ibid.

[16]Ibid. Hanna's apparent disapproval of solitude comes out in a letter he wrote to Fr Mina; see Mina el-Baramousy [Kyrillos VI], "Letter to Hanna Youssef Atta, December 3, 1933." For another account of the dispute at the monastic council, see Fr Raphael's brief account (though it seems to follow Hanna's); Raphael Ava Mina, *Spiritual Leadership*, 9.

[17]Atta and Raphael Ava Mina, *Life of Pope Kyrillos*, 9. Zaklama also adds the last names of two of the monks, Basilious Saad and Pakhoum Matta; see Zaklama, *Pope Kyrillos VI*, 1:76.

[18]Mina el-Baramousy [Kyrillos VI], "Letter to Hanna Youssef Atta, December 3, 1933."

[19]Atta and Raphael Ava Mina, *Life of Pope Kyrillos*, 9. These very same concerns are brought up in Fr Mina's defensive letter that he wrote to Hanna in December 1933; see Mina el-Baramousy [Kyrillos VI], "Letter to Hanna Youssef Atta, December 3, 1933."

[20]Atta and Raphael Ava Mina, *Life of Pope Kyrillos*, 9.

[21]Ibid.

[22]Ibid.

[23]Ibid.

[24]See the following chapter for an important corrective on Fr Abdel Messih el-Habashy.

[25]Mina the Recluse [Kyrillos VI], "Autobiographical Fragments."

[26]Mina el-Baramousy [Kyrillos VI], "Letter to Hanna Youssef Atta, December 3, 1933."

[27]The entirety of scholarship claims that he entered solitude in 1933. This obviously is secondary to the assumption (which, to be sure, is not explicit in the biographical accounts) that he immediately went

into solitude after returning to the Baramous Monastery—an impossibility given that he returned before his thirty-first birthday (in August), and left for solitude after December 1933.

[28]Mina el-Baramousy [Kyrillos VI], "Letter to Hanna Youssef Atta, December 3, 1933."

[29]Ibid.

[30]See Father Mina el-Baramousy [Kyrillos VI], "Letter to Hanna Youssef Atta, undated, ?1936" [in Arabic], in FRC-1: Letter 529 (Baramous Monastery, undated). This crystallizes in the thought of St Isaac the Syrian, which inevitably was at least a partial influence; see Isaac the Syrian, *Ascetical Homilies*, 73.507–8. See also the following monastic aphorism: "It is not through virtue," an early desert Father genuinely exclaimed, "that I live in solitude but through weakness. Those who live in the midst of men are the strong ones." Abba Matoes 13, in Bendicta Ward, *The Sayings of the Desert Fathers: The Alphabetical Collection* (Michigan: Cistercian Publications, 1984), 145.

[31]Mina el-Baramousy [Kyrillos VI], "Letter to Hanna Youssef Atta, December 3, 1933."

[32]Ibid.

[33]Ibid. The letter concludes, "I do appreciate your love and kindness, and I am unable to express myself towards them; but remember who it is that I serve, and into whose hands you have submitted me. Am I a servant to a cruel or harsh master? No, I serve a merciful master and a great God; nothing can stand against him. He is the one who made me a monk and is capable of completing my path in life well. What shall I say but: 'Cast your burden on the Lord, and he shall sustain you' (Ps 55.22) and 'Blessed are those who trust in God.'" In a letter a few weeks later, Fr Mina requests forgiveness from his brother for the tone of his prior letter, and reveals he was still *not* in solitude; see Fr Mina el-Baramousy [Kyrillos VI], "Letter to Hanna Youssef Atta, December 24, 1933" [in Arabic], in RC-2: Letter 10 (Baramous Monastery: 1933).

[34]Given the previously mentioned two letters written to his brother in December 1933, in which he states that he was not yet in solitude, we can assume he entered solitude at the very end of 1933 (after December 24), or at the latest, very early 1934.

[35]Strangely, Masudi also asked him when he returned each week to "wash his [own] clothes and the clothes of the elderly and sick fathers who could not help themselves." It appears Masudi sought to show Fr Mina that his solitude would forever be intertwined with service; see Atta and Raphael Ava Mina, *Life of Pope Kyrillos*, 10.

[36]Ibid.

[37]Mina the Recluse [Kyrillos VI], "Autobiographical Fragments."

[38]For a brief and fascinating biography of Sarabamoun, see Samuel Tawadros el-Syriany, *The History of the Popes*, 172–73.

[39]Augustinos el-Baramousy, *The Baramous Monastery*, 224.

[40]Ibid.

[41]Ibid. He built a house as well as St Mary's Church in el-Qanater, Egypt, where he would stay until his death. Meinardus mistakenly claims that Fr Mina occupied the cave shortly after Sarabamoun's "death"; it seems he confused Sarabamoun's stepping down as abbot with his actual death. See Meinardus, *Christian Egypt: Faith and Life*, 43. Also, it should be noted that there is some overlap in the sources between the "head" of the monastery and the "abbot." Whereas nowadays most heads of monasteries in Egypt are bishops and abbots are generally monks, that was not always the arrangement. Around the time of Fr Mina's monasticism at the Baramous Monastery, the "head" was a senior monk who would often not reside in the monastery, but rather would visit every few months. The abbot was a monk who resided in the monastery and was responsible for the daily operation of the monastery, reporting to the "head." This explains how a "head" of the monastery could live in solitude, as well as the names of the abbots mentioned by Fr Mina in his autobiographical fragments and letters that seem to conflict with the historical heads of the monastery (these are often mistakenly called abbots in the sources).

[42]Mina the Recluse [Kyrillos VI], "Autobiographical Fragments."

[43]Atta and Raphael Ava Mina, *Life of Pope Kyrillos*, 10.

[44]Watson, *Among the Copts*, 51.

[45]Mina the Recluse [Kyrillos VI], "Autobiographical Fragments." The biblical reference is to 2 Kgs 6.16.

[46]The distinctively Orthodox term comes from the Greek *charmolype*, which may be translated "bitter joy" or "joyful mourning," and is often used to describe the inexpressible experience of Great Lent leading to Holy Pascha.

[47]Peter Brown, "The Rise and Function of the Holy Man in Late Antiquity," *The Journal of Roman Studies* 61 (1971): 91. Brown further develops this in his rather sobering revolution of thought in a later article: "Asceticism was not a consolation for the absence of opportunities for the martyr's experience of pain . . . it was passing on, in a manner appropriate to the times, the mighty image of the presence of Christ among men." See Peter Brown, "The Saint as Exemplar in Late Antiquity," *Representations* 1, no. 2 (1983): 16.

[48]Mina the Recluse [Kyrillos VI], "Autobiographical Fragments."

[49]Atta and Raphael Ava Mina, *Life of Pope Kyrillos*, 10.

[50]The various accounts witnessing this will be referred to at appropriate places within this work.

[51]Mina the Recluse [Kyrillos VI], "Autobiographical Fragments."

[52]Atta and Raphael Ava Mina, *Life of Pope Kyrillos*, 10.

[53]Ibid. Cf. Heb 12.4.

[54]Ibid.

[55]It concluded, "In this path I met severe wars, opposition, and persecution that *I will later write about in detail.*" This likely formed the last fragment of the autobiography, as we have not discovered any further fragments, as well as the fact that the writing stopped halfway down the page, suggesting it was not completed. Fr Raphael Ava Mina states the account was discovered in Kyrillos' personal drawers, indicating perhaps that he changed his mind and never sent the autobiography to the intended addressee(s).

[56]Atta and Raphael Ava Mina, *Life of Pope Kyrillos*, 10. It should be noted that Hanna dates this visit to 1933. This is likely a simple mistake given that Fr Mina wrote letters in December 1933 complaining that he was not yet in solitude. Therefore, we have suggested a date, assuming the visit occurred early on in his solitude, of early 1934. I. H. al-Masri, on the other hand, suggests (without reference) that the visit took place seven months after Fr Mina entered solitude; al-Masri, *True Story of Christianity in Egypt*, 2:434.

[57]I devoted some effort to attempting to determine who this American visitor was. After chasing down several suspicions, unfortunately, I was still unable to arrive at a conclusion. Out of all the Coptologists, Egyptologists, and theologians who have written on monasticism during the 1930s, not one seems to have been the scholar in question.

[58]Noticing that Fr Mina understood much of the conversation, the American tried to directly converse with him. But the hermit apologized, as although he had once been proficient English during his time at Thomas Cook & Son, he was no longer fluent; see Atta and Raphael Ava Mina, *Life of Pope Kyrillos*, 10.

[59]Though it is natural to approach this episode with some skepticism, it should be noted first, that Hassan Fouad would later be deeply indebted to Fr Mina, and second, that the *Harbor of Salvation* periodical testifies to Mina's encyclopedic knowledge of the monastic literature, and third, this knowledge was unquestionably experiential in character and thus would have been deeply moving for the American.

[60]Atta and Raphael Ava Mina, *Life of Pope Kyrillos*, 11.

[61]Ibid.

[62]Ibid.

[63]See Mina el-Baramousy [Kyrillos VI], "Letter to Hanna Youssef Atta, undated ?1936." Though there is no date given to this letter, there are two possibilities. The first is that the "demonic" attacks for three years refers to the years prior to solitude, and the relief was his permission to enter solitude, thus dating the letter at early 1934. The second possibility is that it refers to the attacks during solitude (1934–1936), and the relief as a divine intervention sometime in 1936 before April 4, when he left the Baramous Monastery. Given that the final autobiographical fragment specifies the severe wars that he encountered, in remarkably similar language, the latter seems to be the more likely.

[64]Ibid.

[65]The same is to be seen in another letter; see Mina el-Baramousy [Kyrillos VI], "Letter to Hanna Youssef Atta, December 3, 1933."

[66]Mina el-Baramousy [Kyrillos VI], "Letter to Hanna Youssef Atta, undated, ?1936."

[67]Ibid. The reference is to Ps 94.18–19.

[68]For instance see Hierotheos Vlachos, *Orthodox Psychotherapy: The Science of the Fathers*, trans. Esther Williams (Levadia, Greece: Birth of the Theotokos Monastery, 1994), 38–42, 70–77. In regard to Isaac the Syrian, he speaks of illumination as an inward experience of God's light, interestingly, in the context of ascetic struggle, solitude, and *theoria*; see Isaac the Syrian, *Ascetical Homilies* 4.149–53. Isaac also speaks of three degrees of knowledge of God that roughly correspond; ibid., 52.390–401. It should be noted, as Alfeyev accurately indicates, that "illumination" in Isaac the Syrian differs in some respects from the "divine light" of the later Hesychast literature; see Alfeyev, *World of Isaac the Syrian*, 239–40.

[69]Budge, *Texts Relating to Saint Mena*, 46–47.

[70]It was, to borrow a phrase from a renowned sociologist, nothing short of a "major epiphany." Norman K. Denzin, *Interpretive Biography* (London: Sage Publications, 1989), 71. Denzin identifies four loose types of epiphany: a *major epiphany*, which touches the fabric of a person's life; a *cumulative epiphany*, which signifies eruptions or reactions to ongoing or chronic experiences; a *minor epiphany*, which is symbolically representative of a major problematic event; and a *relived epiphany*, whereby a past epiphany is relived and reappropriated in the present. Anselm Strauss has also noted that these "turning points" often take place in the context of "critical incidents"; for instance, see Anselm Strauss, *Mirrors and Masks: The Search for Identity* (Cambridge: Cambridge University Press, 1959), 93; Denzin, *Interpretive Biography*, 70–71.

[71]McDonald has discerned a number of "stages" to any such epiphany, foremost of which is the enduring permanence of such moments; see Matthew McDonald, "The Nature of Epiphanic Experience," *Journal of Humanistic Psychology* 48, no. 1 (2008): 93.

[72]The letter concludes, "Thanks, praise, glory, honor, worship, and reverence to our great Redeemer. He is faithful and true to his promises, and always takes care of us. He is the greatest leader; he provides us with full armor, to enable us to stand before the enemies. Without him we can do nothing. We ask for his goodness to crown our struggles with success, and give us strength to complete the course, and at the end receive what he prepared for us, not that we are worthy of it, but only through his grace. Glory be to God forever and ever. Amen."

[73]See Hegumen Mina the Recluse [Kyrillos VI], "Letter to Monks at the Monastery of Saint Samuel, undated" [in Arabic] (Old Cairo, undated). The letter was likely written to the monks at St Samuel Monastery in the mid-1940s when he was their abbot.

[74]Ibid.

[75]Otto Meinardus, *Monks and Monasteries of the Egyptian Deserts (1961)* (Cairo: The American University Press in Cairo, 1961), 156; cf. Meinardus, *Christian Egypt: Faith and Life*, 43.

[76]Meinardus, *Monks and Monasteries (1961)*, 156–57. Though he claims that el-Habashy influenced Mina, he later suggests, "It is difficult to ascertain the influence which the prophet [el-Habashy] may have had on the mystic [Mina]." Yet by 1970, he seems to have become far more confident: rather than an uncertain influence, el-Habashy was the "inspiration" for Fr Mina's solitude—a claim repeated in his 1989 revision of *Monks and Monasteries*; see Meinardus, *Christian Egypt: Faith and Life*, 435; Meinardus, *Monks and Monasteries (1989)*, 71.

[77]Wakin, *A Lonely Minority*, 110. It is very evident that Wakin is directly following Meinardus given the context of the passage. That said, his claim is rather ambiguous: "A famous monk at the monastery had been his spiritual father. A monk known as Abuna Abd el-Masih the Ethiopian and renowned as a prophet influenced Abuna Mina greatly as he lived his solitary life. . . ." It is ambiguous in that it is impossible to determine if the first sentence refers to Masudi, or that it points to the following sentence. It should be noted that the passage comes chronologically after Fr Mina enters solitude in Wakin's account and thus is suggestive that Wakin meant el-Habashy was his spiritual father. In any event, Western scholarship has followed suit.

[78]For instance, see Watson, "Abba Kyrillos," 10–11; John H. Watson, "The Ethiopian Servant of Christ: Abuna Abdel Mesih el-Habashy," *Coptic Church Review* 27, no. 2 (2006): 47; Nelly van Doorn-Harder, *The Emergence of the Modern Coptic Papacy: The Egyptian Church and Its Leadership from the Ottoman Period to the Present* (Cairo: The American University Press in Cairo, 2011), 131; Voile, *Les*

Coptes d'Égypte, 191; O'Mahony, "Coptic Christianity," 505; Mark Francis Gruber, "Sacrifice in the Desert: An Ethnography of the Coptic Monastery" (Ph.D. diss., State University of New York at Stony Brook, 1990), 147.

[79]Interview in April/May 1959, reprinted in Girguis, *The Heavenly Harp,* 12–13.

[80]Watson, "The Ethiopian Servant," 51–52, also see 34.

[81]Ibid., 42.

[82]Macarius goes on to say, "All the information in this book is documented in either voice recordings or written accounts of metropolitans, bishops, priests, monks or lay people." Macarius was cognizant of the numerous contradictory (and hagiographical) materials that had been circulating since el-Habashy's repose; see Bishop Macarius, *The Ethiopian Servant of Christ: The Life of Father Abdel Mesih el-Habashy,* trans. Michael Cosman (Sydney: St Shenouda's Monastery Press, 2009), 10.

[83]Ibid., 20–24. Apparently there was an established custom for Ethiopian monks to travel to the desert of Scetis, Egypt, to take the blessing of the early desert fathers of monasticism; see Augustinos el-Baramousy, *The Baramous Monastery,* 240. This certainly accounts for the number of Ethiopian monks recorded at the monasteries of the Wadi al-Natrun Desert in Egypt at that time and earlier.

[84]Macarius, *Ethiopian Servant of Christ,* 27.

[85]Ibid., 27–28. Also for another account of the history of the monastery that makes a similar claim, see Augustinos el-Baramousy, *The Baramous Monastery,* 240.

[86]Macarius, *Ethiopian Servant of Christ,* 29. But also, we are told, given the imminence of World War II, there were some very reasonable fears given el-Habashy's status as an Ethiopian citizen (not that he could provide paperwork to prove it) that he might well be harmed outside the monastery's care.

[87]Interestingly, the patriarch, Youannis XIX, also personally intervened to allow Fr Mina to go into solitude; see Mina the Recluse [Kyrillos VI], "Autobiographical Fragments." Again, that the matter required escalation to Youannis (who, we should recall, had a great love for the Baramous Monastery) is indicative of the genuine distaste for solitude at that time.

[88]Macarius, *Ethiopian Servant of Christ,* 29.

[89]Ibid., 32.

[90]Ibid., 64. According to the anecdote, el-Habashy had miraculously left his solitude and returned to the monastery to see the patriarch, without anyone advising him of the visit. In the presence of the assembled bishops and dignitaries, the patriarch took water and sprinkled some of it on el-Habashy as he entered to reprimand him, and made the sign of the cross, at which point el-Habashy calmed down.

[91]Ibid., 65; Atta and Raphael Ava Mina, *Life of Pope Kyrillos.* According to most sources, el-Habashy left the Baramous Monastery in 1972, stayed in the cathedral in Cairo until July 1973, before leaving for Jerusalem. This was in keeping with another Ethiopian custom for monks to spend their final years in pilgrimage in Jerusalem. Beyond this there is much speculation, with many claiming he never arrived in Jerusalem and that he died in a Syrian Orthodox monastery in 1978; for a number of variously contradicting accounts of his final days, see Augustinos el-Baramousy, *The Baramous Monastery,* 240; Macarius, *Ethiopian Servant of Christ,* 109–14; Watson, "The Ethiopian Servant," 53–55.

[92]A number of sources confirm that el-Habashy was influenced by Isaac the Syrian, and that he would often quote from him, as well as base his behavior around his thought; see Watson, "The Ethiopian Servant," 48–49; Macarius, *Ethiopian Servant of Christ,* 76.

[93]Of note, Pope Shenouda III is recorded as saying concerning el-Habashy's silence: "Even though I lived in the cell next door to his [presumably he meant "cave" by "cell"], I realized it was very hard for any monk to become his disciple." See Macarius, *Ethiopian Servant of Christ,* 69.

[94]Interestingly, the English translation of Hanna and Raphael Ava Mina's biography misses a paragraph in the original Arabic, in which Raphael recalls that when Habashy, a few decades later, visited Kyrillos VI (Fr Mina had since become patriarch), Kyrillos did not know him well at all, and asked him about his basic biographical details as they got to know each other. This clearly indicates the two were only very briefly acquainted. See Atta and Raphael Ava Mina, *Life of Pope Kyrillos,* 41, and their *Memories about the Life of Pope Kyrillos,* 112.

[95] A letter he wrote three years after entering into solitude (thus we may assume 1936) suggests that he was without a spiritual guide in solitude, and suffered some tribulations accordingly. See Mina el-Baramousy [Kyrillos VI], "Letter to Hanna Youssef Atta, undated, ?1936."

[96] This is well attested in the Orthodox tradition; see Kallistos Ware, *The Orthodox Way* (Crestwood, NY: St Vladimir's Seminary Press, 2003), 98.

[97] For a fair discussion of Isaac's Christology and whether he was "Nestorian"—which evidently he was not in the theological sense, nor was the early East Syrian tradition—see Alfeyev, *World of Isaac the Syrian*, 15–25.

[98] Often the influence is noted without taking stock of just how radical the influence was. The one exception is Voile. Though she notes, "His reference in monasticism is not Macarius or Shenouda, but rather Isaac the Syrian," she too does not bring out how this permeates and transforms his life, though she does briefly mention how Isaac would have influenced Fr Mina in his behavior; see Voile, *Les Coptes d'Égypte*, 191–92.

[99] Though not elaborating, Pope Shenouda III (himself a spiritual son of Fr Mina) clearly perceived the role of Isaac the Syrian: "He [Fr Mina] chose the life of solitude because of his love of prayer, so he lived as a recluse for a long time, *he was the disciple* of the greatest teacher who wrote about solitude in the history of monasticism; that is St Isaac. . . . I have read hundreds of ascetic books and could find none greater than those of St Isaac written about the life of serenity and solitude." See Pope Shenouda III, "Speech at the First Year Commemoration of Kyrillos VI" [in Arabic] (Cairo, 1972).

[100] El-Gowaily, "Interview with the Monk."

[101] The account comes from a ninth-century East Syrian writing by Isho'denah, *The Book of Chastity*; cited in Isaac the Syrian, *Ascetical Homilies*, pp. 52–53.

[102] Isho'denah, *The Book of Chastity*, ibid. The account goes on to say, "He entered deeply into the divine mysteries and composed books on the divine discipline of solitude." A West Syrian source also recalls, "He was quiet, kind, and humble, and his word was gentle. He ate only three loaves a week with some vegetables, and he did not taste any food that was cooked"; ibid.

[103] Cited from Alfeyev, *World of Isaac the Syrian*, 27. Alfeyev goes on to question the historicity of the account.

[104] Ibid., 62. At the time it was used to designate a solitary monk as opposed to a monk in community (cenobitic).

[105] Isaac the Syrian, *Ascetical Homilies* 1.113.

[106] Ibid., 4.141.

[107] I follow Hilarion Alfeyev in asking this question of Isaac; see Alfeyev, *World of Isaac the Syrian*, 67.

[108] Isaac the Syrian, *Ascetical Homilies* 44.353–54.

[109] Ibid.

[110] "If a man perceives in himself," he writes, "that through such a way of life and continual communion with men his conscience is weakened . . . and that while he seeks to heal others he loses his own health . . . then let him . . . turn back, lest he hear from the Lord the words of the proverb, 'Physician, heal thyself' "; cf. 6.174.

[111] Ibid., 4.144–45. Isaac goes on to say that many have healed, and done mighty acts in the world, only to fall in "vile and abominable passions . . . for they were still sickly in soul."

[112] This *Sixty-Fourth Homily* seems to be much loved by Fr Mina, as he drew his maxim—"Love all men, but keep distant from all men"—from it, and repeatedly and frequently referred to this homily and cited it in his letters.

[113] Isaac the Syrian, *Ascetical Homilies* 64.456.

[114] Ibid.

[115] Alfeyev notes that the term *hubba sapya* ("luminous love") is borrowed from the *Macarian Homilies*, as well as other Syrian fathers, and is developed in Part II of Isaac. The *Ascetical Homilies* fall into what is known as Part I of Isaac's writings, with the recently discovered manuscript (found in 1983 by Sebastian Brock) forming Part II.

[116]Part II/10, cited in Alfeyev, *World of Isaac the Syrian*, 74–75. It should be duly noted that Fr Mina was primarily acquainted with Part I (though as mentioned previously, the Arabic *Four Books* also contain sections of Part II and III), but with that said, the notion of God's "divine love" filling the solitary and then overflowing onto the world is abundantly present at least in concept throughout Part I, and thus Mina would have been very well acquainted with the idea, if not with the specific term. See, for instance, Isaac the Syrian, *Ascetical Homilies* 64.456.

[117]Part II/10, cited in Alfeyev, *World of Isaac the Syrian*, 74–75.

[118]Twice a year Antony would accept those who came to see him to lower some bread and water through the rooftop. He never went out, nor did he even see those who came to him. But deafening voices and unbearable violence could be heard. Looking in through some burrowed holes, his visitors saw no one. Becoming exceedingly afraid, realizing the voices and violence were demonic in nature, they called out to Antony in feeble cries, who, in Athanasius' account, calmly comforted them. This gives us some sense of his daily struggles. See St Athanasius, *Life of Antony* 12–13 (NPNF² 4:199).

[119]Ibid., 14 (NPNF² 4:200).

[120]The account is found in Atta and Raphael Ava Mina, *Life of Pope Kyrillos*, 11–13. Given the length of the account and its nature as a string of dialogues, the quotations will be paraphrased while their meaning will be maintained.

[121]While Hanna reproduces "exact conversations" in this episode, we must of course keep in mind that he was not actually present during many of these conversations. Consequently, this account (written decades later) was likely dependent on Fr Mina's memory (and therefore interpretation) of the event. Though in this particular case, given Hanna's friendship with Youannis XIX, he may have confirmed many of these details to create a credible account. Similar comments may be made for other events that Hanna (or Fr Raphael Ava Mina for that matter) did not physically attend and yet report in detail.

[122]Fr Raphael Ava Mina writes that at one point certain hierarchs sought to annex St Menas' Church in Old Cairo to place it under the authority of the Baramous Monastery; see Atta and Raphael Ava Mina, *Memories about the Life of Pope Kyrillos*, 47.

[123]Atta and Raphael Ava Mina, *Life of Pope Kyrillos*, 13. There is some confusion in the Arabic sources as to the number of the expelled monks; Hanna, for instance, states that there were seven (*excluding* Fr Mina), whereas Fr Samuel Tawadros el-Syriani (*The History of the Popes*, 171), states that there were seven, *including* Fr Mina.

[124]Bishop Macarius, "Letter to Hegumen Youssef el-Baramousy, August 20, 1956" [in Arabic], in SSC: Letter 14 (Baramous Monastery: 1956). This letter was discovered among others in the monastery's records and was addressed to one of the seven exiled monks. The reasons for the monks' challenge are not given. The only other account I am aware is that of Fr Samuel Tawadros el-Syriany, which also gives the abbot's name as Fr Barnaba, as well as indicating the names of the expelled monks. See Samuel Tawadros el-Syriany, *The History of the Popes*, 171.

[125]Atta and Raphael Ava Mina, *Life of Pope Kyrillos*, 9; Macarius, *Ethiopian Servant of Christ*, 27–28.

[126]Barnaba (1874–1963) entered the monastery in 1897 and was made vicar of the diocese of Menoufia for eight years, was treasurer of the Patriarchate for sixteen years, and then was appointed "head" of the Baramous Monastery from 1930 to 1948. He was noted to have visited the monastery every three months, before resigning in 1948 and becoming a patriarchal vicar where (as we shall see) he would cross paths with Fr Mina once more. He served in various capacities outside the monastery before his death in March 1963. For a brief biography, see Augustinos el-Baramousy, *The Baramous Monastery*, 225–26.

[127]This concern is repeated at several points in the dialogue. It seems Fr Mina was not particularly disturbed that elderly monks were to be punished on account of their disobedience, but rather feared they "would lose hope" and grow despondent.

[128]There are echoes here of Isaac the Syrian's advice (in Mina's favorite *Sixty-Fourth Homily*) that one should never leave solitude to "heal the world," but one should nevertheless be at pains to heal anyone who is "placed directly into your hands." Isaac the Syrian, *Ascetical Homilies* 64.456.

[129]Augustinos el-Baramousy, *The Baramous Monastery*, 173–75. For an account of his papacy, see also van Doorn-Harder, *Modern Coptic Papacy*, 112–20; Mounir Shoukry, "John XIX," in *CE*, 1351a; al-Masri, *Story of the Coptic Church*, 6:11–103.

[130]See Augustinos el-Baramousy, *The Baramous Monastery*, 232–34. The account suggests they were unjustly expelled. Awad el-Barhemey (d. 1878) lived alone in the monastery for three years. Awad was left to fend for himself as the only remaining monk for three years until he was joined by one of the expelled monks: Hanna the Scribe, the future Pope Cyril V (1824–1927). Fr Girguis el-Masudi the Great (1818–1906), the uncle of Abdel Messih el-Masudi, also joined them in 1857, after unrelated contention plagued the Muharraq Monastery.

[131]Later, Menoufia was also added to his jurisdiction.

[132]Van Doorn-Harder, *Modern Coptic Papacy*, 112; Carter, *The Copts in Egyptian Politics*, 30–31.

[133]Van Doorn-Harder, *Modern Coptic Papacy*, 112.

[134]I. H. al-Masri claims that Youannis threatened to excommunicate Fr Marcos Dawood but eventually backed down when Fr Marcos explained giving shelter is not grounds for such an action. She also suggests that this was the reason for Fr Mina's lifelong friendship with Fr Marcos. For a discussion of their relationship and the biography of Fr Marcos Dawood, see al-Masri, *Story of the Coptic Church*, 7:85–91; Zaklama, *Pope Kyrillos VI*, 1:95. Also note Dawood's first impression of Fr Mina: "I was touched by the presence of that monk who fascinated me with his desire for solitude and praying the Liturgy"; see Nabil Adly, *Fr Mikhail Dawood's Memoirs with Pope Kyrillos VI* [in Arabic] (Cairo: Egyptian Brothers Press, 1993), 9.

[135]Atta and Raphael Ava Mina, *Life of Pope Kyrillos*, 12. One of the priests mentioned was the renowned Fr Youhanna Shenouda.

[136]Ibid. Strangely, though he was an isolated hermit, he had become well known—perhaps through his theological periodical.

[137]Ibid.

[138]Ibid. Hanna notes that at this point Fr Mina asked him to return to Alexandria and "to leave him in God's hands."

[139]Ibid. Apparently some clergy in the Patriarchate spoke rudely to him, after hearing that he had disobeyed the abbot.

[140]Hanna claims that Pope Youannis sent Metropolitan Thomas of Gharbeya (1899–1956) to meet with the monks after they were forgiven. It is not clear why. The memoirs suggest that Thomas had been sent to give the monks monetary aid so that they could make their way back the Baramous Monastery. But at the same time, the monks, *after* meeting with Thomas, visit Youannis to ask for absolution before making their way. That aside, the anecdote is consistent with the main dialogue: Thomas surprisingly begins to attack the monks for their disobedience. Fr Mina once more defends them reminding the metropolitan that he remembered him as a "modest and poor monk" back when they studied at Helwan together—Thomas was also a monk at the Baramous Monastery from 1924 to 1930—whereas now Thomas's preference for a certain degree of luxury was "unacceptable to God." Needless to say, Thomas was apologetic. The dialogue is given in ibid., 13.

[141]Ibid.

[142]Phil 2.6–8.

[143]Michael J. Gorman, *Inhabiting the Cruciform God: Kenosis, Justification, and Theosis in Paul's Narrative Soteriology* (Grand Rapids, MI: Eerdmans, 2009), 16–17.

[144]A number of New Testament scholars have suggested this, including Moule, N. T. Wright, Bockmuehl, and Fowl, among others. For a discussion see ibid., 22–29.

[145]Ibid., 28–29. Gorman aptly describes it as the "constitutive characteristic of the divine identity."

[146]Phil 2.5. For instance, in 1 Cor 9.1–23, Paul states that "although" as an apostle he had the right take along a wife, he did not exploit that right, but rather enslaved himself to the needs of the Corinthians. In other words, he is participating in Christ's kenosis.

[147]Atta and Raphael Ava Mina, *Life of Pope Kyrillos*, 12.

[148]See van Doorn-Harder, *Modern Coptic Papacy*, 132. Also Hanna writes of Mina—betraying his biased (though perhaps understandable) admiration: "An accurate picture of this kind, shy, quiet monk,

who was filled with God's grace, can now be seen. His appearance showed modesty and weakness, but he was brave and defended the truth relentlessly." See Atta and Raphael Ava Mina, *Life of Pope Kyrillos*, 12.

[149]Hegumen Mina the Recluse [Kyrillos VI], "Letter to Fr Makary el-Samuely, October 27, 1950" [in Arabic], in FRC-1: Letter 246/210 (Old Cairo, 1950).

4

The Windmill of Moqattam: An Unsuspected Thaumaturge (1936–1941)

An Odd Choice of Residence: The Fated Windmill, 1936

> "Be simple, hidden, quiet, and small."
> —Fr Thomas Hopko

A S THE SEVEN ELDERLY MONKS prepared to depart Cairo for the Baramous Monastery in the sweltering heatwave of June 1936, they took note of Fr Mina's peculiar absence. He would not be returning with them.

Once he had resolved the matter of their expulsion, Mina had instead approached Pope Youannis with an odd request. "I intend," he said, declaring more than asking, "with the help of God, to stay at the Eastern Mountain . . . in one of the windmills. It is as isolated as a cell. . . ."[1] Youannis knew that stretch of the desert well; though desolate, it had become infamous as a backwater for underworld sorts. But Youannis was not merely concerned for the monk; he would have been positively confused. Since his earliest years, Fr Mina had been obsessed with solitude; why now, then, had he chosen not to return to his cave at the Baramous Monastery? It is a question that, fascinatingly, has not been asked in any of the literature.

A first hint at a response is given in Hanna's recollection of Fr Mina's disclosure to the patriarch: "my *heart* tells me that I will receive God's comforting grace in this place."[2] Again he claims to have felt some "divine direction" to this site, just as he had previously with the cave. Another suggestion is that he may have reasonably sought to escape the wrath of the infuriated and deeply embarrassed abbot, who, apparently, would not so soon forget the interfering young monk.[3] Both explanations seem plausible. The scandal of the expelled monks would invariably place both Fr Mina's solitude under scrutiny, and, at the least, his anonymity in question. A remote and nameless windmill on the outskirts of Old Cairo would, therefore, provide greater solitude than even a cave in the desert. Fr Mina's elementary concern, it would seem, was to be "simple, hidden, quiet, and small"[4]—unknown to all but God.

Curiously, we should note here that most Western sources (following Meinardus) claim that the option of the windmill only surfaced after Youannis rejected Fr Mina's original petition to inhabit and rebuild the Monastery of St Menas at Mariout.[5] But the only reference to that particular request in the secondary Arabic literature comes more than six months later.[6] In January 1937, a solicitor, Maher Morgan, published an article in which he lamented the destruction of the site at Mariout.[7] Barely a month later, Morgan received a letter from Fr Mina beseeching the association to mediate with the patriarch on his behalf concerning rebuilding the monastery. Their pleas fell on deaf ears. Maher and his son then traveled to the windmill to personally relay Youannis' decision. Despite the attempted intervention of powerful individuals, the patriarch categorically refused with unfortunate sarcasm: "Have we finished rebuilding the cities to begin rebuilding the desert?"[8]

* * *

A windmill is, no doubt, an odd choice of residence. Fr Mina had chosen the place before meeting with the Patriarch in mid-1936, when he was still serving the elderly exiled monks in Old Cairo in a rented house near the Monastery of Archangel Michael.[9] Each day, according to Hanna's memoirs, Mina would escape the noise of the city and climb the mountain on which the monastery was built. On one occasion during his wanderings through the remnants of the Napoleonic windmills, he came across a guard of the area. That stretch of desert southeast of Cairo, he was told, was a protected site under the Ministry of Arabic Antiquities; accordingly, it was illegal to inhabit the windmills without the express permission of the director himself. No one, the guard added, had ever been granted such a permit (though we may imagine very few would have applied).[10]

At this point, the two most credible sources diverge. The more widely known account is found in Hanna's memoirs.[11] After the guard mentioned the name of the director of the Ministry of Arabic Antiquities, Fr Mina immediately recognized that it was this Hassan Fouad who had once visited him (along with an American theologian) in the cave at the Baramous Monastery in 1934.[12] No doubt encouraged by this apparent coincidence, he visited the office of the director, who, after hearing the name of the hermit, rushed to embrace Fr Mina. A lease was hurriedly prepared for the windmill at a nominal rent, with the director himself paying the lease for an "extended period" and instructing his staff to attend to the monk's needs personally.[13]

The original lease is still extant and is reproduced here in full as documentary evidence of this fortuitous episode:

> I, the undersigned, monk-priest Mina el-Baramousy, declare that I will take one of the windmills next to "The Seven Girls' Domes" in Hosh Abu Ali Mountain as a residence, living alone for worship, after having the permission of the Acting Director of the Arabic Antiquities Organization, paying half a piaster monthly as rent for this place, which will always be possessed by the government; it has the right to take it back at any time without notice.
>
> Signed on *June 23, 1936,* by Acting Director of the Arabic Antiquities Organization, *Hussein Rashed*; Witnessed by: Zaki Abdo, Engineer at Tram Terminal Station in Old Cairo.[14]

It is here, with the introduction of a certain "Acting Director" Hussein Rashed—not Hassan Fouad, as Hanna claimed—that confusion enters the episode. Another earlier source, found in an article of the *al-Watani* newspaper on May 10, 1959 (the day of Mina's patriarchal ordination), follows the lease in giving the name of the acting director as Hussein Rashed.[15] The article is quite exacting with dates and claims to have been written after consulting the records of the Ministry of Arabic Antiquities.[16]

According to this account, on June 21, 1936, Zaki Abdo met with the acting director to seek permission for "a friend of his, an ascetic monk who wished to live in solitude in one of the mills." Rashed, though a Muslim, was enamored by the history of monasticism and granted permission for the monk, who, the article makes clear, was "unknown to him." The very next day, the article continues, Rashed nominated a windmill. This was mildly displeasing to Fr Mina, given that he sought total isolation. The selected windmill, though still nearly impossible to find without a guide, was only two hundred meters (656 feet) away from the nearest security outpost.[17] It would seem the acting director, like the patriarch, had concerns for the monk's safety among underworld elements in the area. Pointedly, this stands against I. H. al-Masri's embellishment that Fr Mina selected the most debilitated windmill "out of asceticism," to the acceptance and "amazement" of Rashed.[18] On the following day, June 23, 1936, the lease was signed in Rashed's office for half a piaster per month.[19]

The discrepancies of the accounts are not so easily explained. One later (and rather credible) account claims that the full name of the acting director was "Hussein Fouad Rashed."[20] But even then, Hussein and Hassan are distinct names in Arabic. It can only be suggested, therefore, that Hanna mistakenly recalled the name (some forty years later) as Hassan, when it was in fact Hussein.[21] This may also explain the director's rather convenient interest in Coptic monasticism in the *al-Watani* article—which betrays the possibility of a prior meeting (unknown to the author of the *al-Watani* article) with Fr Mina at the Wadi al-Natrun desert in 1934.[22]

On at least one detail, however, there is unanimous agreement in the sources: the young monk's move to the windmill was inconspicuous, without display, and concealed even from his closest friends.

* * *

Living unknown in an abandoned windmill, Fr Mina would only reenter the "world" each Sunday, almost silently, at the nearby Monastery of Archangel Michael for Divine Liturgy. Immediately after, he would disappear just as suddenly. Fr Marcos Dawood (1892–1970), who had previously given shelter to the seven expelled monks on their first night in Old Cairo, noticed this rather unusual behavior; Fr Mina had obviously *not* returned to the Baramous Monastery.[23]

Eventually, after several weeks, Fr Marcos was approached by a parishioner, Marcos Bey Fahmy (one of Fr Mina's benefactors during his exile the month earlier), who also began noticing the fleeting appearances of the young hermit.[24] "That is what he always does," Fr Marcos commented.[25] Intrigued, the following Sunday they sent a youth to secretly follow the monk and determine his manner of living. The young boy found the monk living in a decrepit windmill and immediately reported it to Fr Marcos. Hurriedly gathering a few parishioners and a fellow priest, Fr Marcos went to the reported address at the southeastern corner of the Moqattam Mountain.[26] Before them stood, at the top of a deep valley, a haggard and crumbling windmill, exposed to the elements, without a roof, let alone a door.[27] With nothing to knock on, they simply entered. They found the poor monk sitting on the floor, his back to the wall, reading the letters of the eighth-century John of Dalyatha ("the Elder"). Not a single piece of furniture was in sight.[28] They were speechless. "What am I?" Fr Mina offered according to Hanna's memoirs. "I am only a worm, not a human being."[29]

The windmill, known popularly in Arabic as the *tahuna*, was one of fifty windmills in the desert southeast of Cairo—previously known as the "hill of the mills." They were constructed during Napoleon Bonaparte's campaign in the Orient in 1798–1799 before the French were forced to evacuate by the British in 1801.[30] Eventually, the windmills fell into disuse. Their upper portions collapsed inward, and opportunistic scavengers stripped the timber doors, windows, and even staircases. Fr Mina's windmill was some six meters high and two and a half meters wide (20 by 8 feet); the remains of a two-story stone, mud, and concrete cylindrical structure.

The situation was clearly unsatisfactory. Fr Mina had been at the mercy of the elements, sleeping on the ground in sackcloth, and living off occasional gifts of food and a ration of water organized by the Ministry of Arabic Antiquities.[31] Builders and laborers were dispatched as a matter of urgency. Over the next few weeks, a roof was built, structural works undertaken, a staircase fashioned, and a door installed. A fascinating diagrammatic image of the period (likely from Fr Mina's own hand) details the layout of the windmill.[32] The *lower level* contained a single round table with chairs, shelves for some basic food items, a kerosene oven for cooking and baking the *qorban*, a porcelain water pot, and a small bathroom under the stairs. Fashioned from stone and timber, the stairs lead to an *upper level* with a small window. At the eastern end, there was an altar that was handmade by Fr Mina, a lectern for readings, and a primitive iconostasis surrounded by a multitude of oil lamps that seemingly were continually lit—which, several visitors claimed, helped mark out the windmill from others at night.[33] Alarmingly, though perhaps by now predictably, the diagram makes *no* mention of a bed![34]

* * *

Shortly after the reconstruction of the windmill, an inaugural Liturgy was celebrated—which may well mark the beginning of Fr Mina's "public monasticism."[35] Fr Youhanna Shenouda provided the altar needs, and Fr Marcos Dawood brought the *qorban*. Also in attendance were two well-known laymen, Marcos Bey Fahmy and Yacoub Bey Makary, an elderly deacon by the name of Maleka (whom we shall meet shortly), and finally, a seventeen-year-old boy.[36]

It is unclear why that teenager, Ramzy Kaldas (1919–1989), was present at the Liturgy, but his fate would be intertwined with Fr Mina's from that day on.[37] The next year, in 1937, he would join Fr Mina in the windmill before being tonsured a monk a few years later, henceforth known as Mina "the Younger" to distinguish him from Fr Mina "the Recluse."[38] Eventually he would become the bishop of St Samuel's Monastery in Faiyum. It is from the hand of this Ramzy

Kaldas that we have a rare and incredibly valuable insight into the life of Fr Mina during these years—indeed, it is perhaps the only extant credible source for his interior life in the late 1930s. "[He] used to wake up," Ramzy recollects,

> . . . at two a.m., start the midnight *agpeya* [canonical] prayers, sing the *tasbeha* [psalmody], bake the *qorban*, raise incense [that is, Matins], and then serve the Holy Liturgy which would end at around eight a.m. This meant spending six continuous hours in prayer. Afterwards, he would meet with those who were hungry and thirsty for God's mercy. Here is a sick person looking for a cure which he attains through the prayers of Father Mina. There is another facing a major decision in need of God's guidance. . . . A third is tormented by demons and is healed. . . . Having satisfied the needs of those who sought him, Father Mina, who used to fast until three p.m., carries on with his prayers and readings. In the evening, he raises the Vespers incense. . . . Whoever sat with Fr Mina obtained a divine relief . . . a heavenly relief . . . so one would leave knowing that the ship had found a true haven and filled the soul with peace.[39]

This exhausting schedule (which as we have seen was his habit since his time in the cave) would remain fixed for the rest of his life, even to his last moments. At the end of each day he would dismiss his visitors with the characteristic words, "We have work [to do]."[40] By this he manifestly meant prayer. As to his diet, the sources are unanimous in their description of Fr Mina's extreme asceticism. "[He] was never concerned," Ramzy continues,

> about his own physical needs. Whether or not he ate did not matter to him. He would eat bread with any ground seeds such as cumin or salt, and comment on how tasty it was. He was always thankful to God for everything.[41]

The years of asceticism would leave indelible marks, both spiritual and physical. A rare photograph of the now thirty-four-year-old recluse at the windmill (the earliest as a monk) is revealing of the dramatic transformation from his portrait in a national ID card a decade earlier. The dapper moustache is replaced with a thick black beard; the single-breasted suit, with a black cassock covered by an outer flowing cassock ("faragia," or *exorason*); and the *fez*, with a long black shawl. In his right hand he holds a characteristic wooden cross; in his left, a small Bible. He is thinner, the sequelae of a decade of ascetic struggle; his face athletic, perhaps slightly emaciated. His eyes have changed: still somewhat riveting and reserved, and yet they are more serious, more penetrating, even piercing. They provoke a sense of awe bordering on fear; they at once betray overwhelming strength and conceal it.[42]

* * *

The young disciple recalled one other memorable conversation with the recluse.[43] At one point during these early years at the windmill, Mina the Younger grew audacious as he witnessed Fr Mina's grueling daily liturgical canon. In jest, though perhaps not unaware of the potential of his spiritual father, Mina the Younger teased, "If the Lord chose you to become the patriarch, what would you do?" The conversation, as all hypothetical wanderings, was mere banter, and yet it disclosed the foundation of these years at the windmill, revealing the very essence of Fr Mina's being. The recluse thoughtfully looked into the eyes of his disciple and for a moment was willing to indulge him: "I would make all churches celebrate a *daily* Liturgy."

"But you know priests have families and many other responsibilities?" his disciple questioned. "Well . . . at least on Wednesdays and Fridays," Fr Mina conceded. "And suppose," the disciple, now emboldened, further speculated, "there is a poor church, and it can't afford to hire a person to bake the *qorban* [oblation]?" "I would make the *qorban* in the patriarchate," Fr Mina soberly replied, with a gleam in his eye, "and deliver it by cars to the churches."[44]

Parrhesia and Miracles, 1936–1940

<blockquote>
"There is nothing of which prayer is incapable . . ."

"Let prayer be the mirror by which you see yourself each day;
let it be your scale upon which you weigh your heart . . ."
—*Pope Kyrillos VI*
</blockquote>

"WHEN DID [FR MINA] become a *saint*?" inquires the French historian Brigitte Voile. "All sources agree on this point," she answers.[45] It was at the windmill. Within months Fr Mina's reputation, despite his steadfast desire for solitude, blazed throughout Old Cairo. A myriad of healings, prophecies, visions, and unusual divine happenings surround the period.[46] It was there that the abundant miracles began (or at least became widely known), and, therefore, it was there at the windmill in the late 1930s that he reluctantly became a "public monastic," or in the words of some, a "saint."

At the very center of these miracles was prayer. In the early Christian literature, this "prayer" is often referred to as *parrhesia*—a Greek term meaning "freedom to say anything" or "boldness of speech"—whereby a "holy man" is capable of interceding on behalf of the faithful because of his boldness before God.[47] And it is this that most marked these six years (the most formative of his life) at the windmill.[48] Pilgrims would climb the arid desert hills en masse in the hope of taking the *baraka* ("blessing") of the holy man.[49] Some hoped for healing, others direction. "Innumerable miracles," writes one scholar, "are believed to have happened during this period."[50] In Hanna's memoirs, crowds from all around Egypt, seeing that "God accepted his prayers," sought Fr Mina's intercessions.[51] And thus at some early point in these years, he was forced to set an "opening time" for the windmill, adjusting even the hours of his daily eucharistic Liturgy for public attendance.[52] He was held in such great adulation that a business card of sorts—not a mysterious "talisman" written in Coptic, as Hasan mistakenly imagines—became a necessity.[53]

But—and we should make this sufficiently clear—this should not beckon the assumption that mid-twentieth-century Egypt was especially superstitious or ignorant. "No other period in the recorded history of the Coptic Church," a prolific German Coptologist notes, witnesses "so many reports of unfamiliar and extraordinary events."[54] Few miracles in the literature, if any, are attributed to the patriarchs prior to Fr Mina; nor are they claimed of his immediate successor Shenouda III (1923–2012), a patriarch who was greatly esteemed in the Coptic imagination; nor to his contemporary Habib Girgis (1876–1951), who, we might add, was canonized along with Fr Mina. In other words—and again it should be reiterated—the recluse living in the windmill was very much an anomaly. And so appeared Fr Mina: a "holy man" in twentieth-century Egypt, a man who could speak with boldness before God.

* * *

One of the earliest miracles at the windmill is reported by Fr Raphael Ava Mina (his future disciple).[55] In late 1936, the acting director of the Ministry of Arabic Antiquities tasked the nearby guard outpost (some two hundred meters [656 feet] from the windmill) to supply a provision of drinking and washing water for the monk as well as basic food items.[56] One morning the guard, by the name of Am el-Sayed, grew lethargic and, considering the arduous climb up the hill with a weighty bucket in hand, resolved not to deliver any water to Fr Mina. As the hours passed in the heat of the day, the previous water ration was exhausted. Now, as darkness descended, it would be nearly impossible to acquire water, thereby precluding the possibility of preparing the *qorban* for the Liturgy in the early hours of the next morning. Suddenly, at midnight, Fr Mina awoke to a frantic knock at the door of the windmill. He arose from the ground to find the visibly distressed guard, drenched in sweat, shakily carrying a large bucket of water. He hysterically relayed that just moments before he had a "vision" of a man, similar in appearance to Fr Mina, rebuking him: "Take the water and deliver it, lest you receive severe punishment." Curiously unperturbed, and as though he almost expected it, the recluse had but one correction: he had not appeared to the guard—it had been, in fact, St Menas.[57]

Later versions of the account betray various hagiographic garnishes; one memorable retelling, for instance, has St Menas riding upon a horse and terrifying the guard.[58] But what is of concern, at least for now, is the presence from the very beginning of the peculiar act of "double intercession" of the monk and St Menas.[59] This virtually paradigmatic miracle would be the first of many.

Of the myriads of miracles attributed to Fr Mina, it is the proliferation of *healing* miracles that most marks the literature of this period. Two of the earliest healings concern those closest to Fr Mina. The first account—the healing of a deacon by the name of Maleka—is nearly impossible to verify historically, given that no early or reliable source for the miracle can be found.[60] Nevertheless, it frequently recurs in the literature and is a much loved and much told memory of the first healing miracle.

Near the windmill, in late 1936, lived an elderly deacon who had fallen ill with influenza and a bout of pneumonia.[61] Medical care, the account claims, had been of no avail (widely available antibiotics were still a decade away), and soon he developed congestive cardiac failure and began going in and out of consciousness. Preparations, we are told, were made for his funeral. A certain Azmi Farid Girgis, a medical student who happened to share the house with the elderly man, had left that morning to complete some task at the university, before returning to assist the family in expectation of Maleka's imminent death. But to his shock—so much so that he nearly fainted—he found the elderly deacon comfortably reclining and peeling an orange, having just consumed his dinner. A few hours prior, Maleka explained to the disbelieving medical student, the recluse from the windmill had come to visit (we may assume, by request of the family), sat next to him, prayed, and then proceeded to anoint him with oil ("unction of the sick"). Before he left, Fr Mina told Maleka to come daily to the windmill to share with him in the Divine Liturgy. Within a few hours, the elderly man's strength completely returned. Each day he made good on his promise, serving as Fr Mina's deacon for the next six years in the windmill (from the very first Liturgy) and later at St Menas' Church in Old Cairo. From the day of his healing, he would live another fifteen years.[62]

A few years later, a far more high-profile healing would take place. It is the earliest specific healing miracle documented in Hanna's memoirs, though he mentions that many previous miracles had occurred.[63] In or around 1940, Hegumen Ibrahim Luka (1897–1950), the parish priest of St Mark's Church in Heliopolis, sent to Fr Mina begging for a visitation and prayer. Rather embarrassed and genuinely confused as to why someone of such standing would ask for him, Fr Mina sent in reply: "Who am I, the lowly, to be asked to pray for him?"[64] The hesitation was somewhat justified. Fr Ibrahim was a graduate of the Theological School under Habib Girgis in 1918 and had become one of the most beloved (and scholarly) priests of the period, later being appointed the vicar of the Patriarchate.[65] This gives us an early insight into the burgeoning reputation of Fr Mina not only among the uneducated faithful but even among the high-ranking clergy. It was a far cry from his desire of anonymity on the outskirts of Cairo; evidently, news of his sanctity (and miracles) was irrepressible.

After some persistence and pleading, Fr Mina consented, though, we should note, he refused to have a car escort him, preferring to make his own way on foot. Arriving at the house, staff in hand, with a flowing black shawl covering his head and cassock, he would have made for an unusual sight in urban Cairo. "My father," the recluse said to Ibrahim, who had long been bed-bound, "I have come to receive your blessing." Fr Ibrahim begged him to anoint him with oil and pray for him. Fr Mina complied, praying simply with little airs, and afterward left just as suddenly—and again "politely declined" transport back to the windmill. Soon Fr Ibrahim was completely healed. He would never forget the episode, often fondly retelling the "miracle" of Fr Mina, one day hoping to repay the kindness with good measure (which he shortly would).[66]

Numerous other healing miracles abound in the literature; in fact, there are at least eighteen "official" volumes of miracles.[67] For now, it suffices to say that most of the credible healing miracles follow a similar pattern: a supplicant in need, an act of *parrhesia* in prayer, anointing with oil (or a piece of cotton in oil for the sick if they were not physically present), and resultant healing. These prayers were almost always (and unusually) an act of "double intercession" whereby Fr Mina would entreat the help of St Menas, and "both would pray to God."[68] Occasionally, though, rather fascinatingly, the miracle was in the "negative"—that is to say, the miracle paradoxically was in the *absence* of the healing. I. H. al-Masri, a well-known Church historian, for instance, recalls that her own uncle, Lamehe el-Masri, was unwell and called for Fr Mina. But while the recluse prayed over a cup of water, the glass broke. Fr Mina left quietly, saying, "The will of God is for Lamehe to depart to paradise." Two days later, the historian notes, he died.[69]

Looking at the voluminous literature, the most apparent characteristic of the miracles is that they were marked by *simplicity* (albeit with seemingly spectacular results). Fr Mina did not seek to heal on a public stage, nor did he act with drama, artistry, or flair; miracles simply happened, "as if they were to be expected."[70] "Nothing was strange," Metropolitan Athanasius of Beni Suef (1923–2000) recalls, "about his appearance, about his speech. But what he said conveyed meaning; the man was simple and deep but all *natural*."[71] Miracles were for Fr Mina a feature of ordinary life.

* * *

How, then, did Fr Mina understand this *parrhesia*, or boldness in prayer, that so clearly underlies his miracles?

We have in our possession two writings on prayer from his hand: one from the *Harbor of Salvation* periodical written on May 9, 1928, and the other in an undated, though more sustained, reflection on the theological nature of prayer.[72] Both are remarkably consistent with his pastoral letters over the next few decades, providing fascinating insights into his life of prayer, and so we should not miss the deeply experiential nature of these discourses. His earliest disciples tell us that this life of prayer spanned the entire day: from six hours of "formal" prayer (psalmody, Matins, and Divine Liturgy) in the early hours of the morning, as well as evening Vespers, to the unseen hours of "informal" prayer when he would disappear, declaring enigmatically, "We have work."

These discourses, unpublished and therefore unknown to scholarship, confirm another previously mentioned matter: Fr Mina was formed in a "patristic discipleship" to St Isaac the Syrian.

"Every good care of the mind," Isaac claims,

> directed towards God, and every meditation upon spiritual things is delimited by prayer, and is called by the name of prayer ... whether you speak of various readings, or the cries of a mouth glorifying God, or sorrowing

reflection on the Lord, or making bows with the body, or psalmody in verses, or all other things from which the teaching of genuine prayer ensues.[73]

Prayer is for Isaac the "refuge of help, source of salvation, a treasury of assurance, a haven that rescues from the tempest . . . a staff of the infirm, a shelter in times of temptation, a medicine at the height of sickness, a shield of deliverance in war, an arrow sharpened against the face of his enemies. . . ."[74] But whereas for Isaac prayer is anything that brings one into converse with God, for Fr Mina "converse" can only mean union. "Prayer," Fr Mina begins in the undated article,

> . . . is a *conjoining* of man and God in unity. It means actual reconciliation with God, the mother of tears and also their daughter, the forgiveness of sins, the bridge to pass over tribulations and a support to our weaknesses. It puts away devilish wars, it is the work of angels, the food for those who need charity, happiness, the work that is beneficial, the core of virtues, and the giver of other gifts. It is nourishment for our souls, light to our minds, filling for our days, proof of our hope, our grace, the treasure of monks, and the repository of the silent in serenity.[75]

Immediately the similarity of style becomes evident. Mina seems not only to be deeply influenced by the thought of Isaac but even by his linguistic manner, stringing multiple phrases in definition. We also begin to perceive that for Fr Mina prayer is both the beginning and the end of the spiritual life, its nourishment and its treasure, the means and the goal; the "support," "core," and "giver" of virtues.

In the 1928 *Harbor of Salvation* article, prayer is again the "communion with God; a relationship between the slave and his Lord."[76] "Prayer is," he continues,

> the mother of virtues and every religious instinct, the hedgerow of every virtue and its protector. It is the store of graces, the metal of blessings, guard of satisfaction, controller of anger, and the calming of the haughty spirit. It is the victory of the warrior, the banner of the fighter, the seal of chastity and the rein of virginity, the sentry of the travelers and guard of the sleepers. It is power for the weak, wealth for the poor, a resort to the afflicted, a comfort to the grieving, and an intercessor for the sinners.[77]

This is no mere poetic discourse, but rather a thoroughly experiential understanding of prayer as "*everything*."[78] "Prayer is the power of everything," Mina writes. "Without it, we lose everything."[79] It is little wonder that it became the one thing needful in his life.

With this prayer now defined, both Isaac and Mina make clear that there are certain "requirements" for prayer. "When standing before your Lord," Fr Mina teaches, "the attire of your soul should be woven with threads of non-hatred . . . without envy and grudge"; prayer must be offered with pure intention and requires fierce resistance.[80] "If you have to go out of your cell," he continues, "protect what you have gathered," and if you are "happy" when a visitor arrives, "know that you have prepared yourself for boredom and not God."[81] Isaac the Syrian echoes many of these sentiments.[82] One must pray with "humility," Isaac counsels, "deep affection," "patience," and "love."[83] Isaac also attaches great value to prostrations: "More than the practice of psalmody, love prostrations during prayer;"[84] and in another place, he says, "Nothing more excites envy in the demons than if a man prostrates himself before the Cross."[85] Mina categorically agrees, "Among all other virtues undertaken by people, there is none better than [making prostrations],"[86] which "terrifies the demons."[87]

But, perhaps most importantly, both fathers make clear the necessity of preparing for "night prayer." "Spend the most of your night," Mina suggests, "in prayers and praise; as much as you can prepare for them during the day."[88] Though certainly an unusual concept, night vigil is for the solitary the front-line of ascetical struggle.[89] Again Mina's words (interestingly, from the *Sixty-Fourth Homily* that is quickly emerging as his favorite) betray Isaac's direct influence: "Let every prayer that you offer in the night become more precious than all your activities of the day."[90] "Why, O man," Isaac laments, "do you govern your life with such a lack of discernment? You stand the whole night through and suffer travail in psalmody . . . and does a little heedfulness during the day seem to you to be so great and arduous a task?"[91]

* * *

There are, of course, many more aspects of their teachings that are in unison—as in any discipleship—but there is one aspect that requires sustained attention: reading as a means of mystical *insight*.

"Persist in reading and honor it," Fr Mina wrote to one of his own disciples, "if possible more than prayer. Reading is the *wellspring* of intelligent prayer."[92] He said as much in his undated article on prayer.[93] These words seem to flow from Isaac—again, we quietly note, from the *Sixty-Fourth Homily*—almost effortlessly: "Give more honor to reading, if possible, than standing, for it is the *source* of pure prayer."[94] "Its importance cannot be exaggerated," Isaac the Syrian instructs,

> . . . for it serves as the gate by which the intellect enters into the divine mysteries and takes strength for attaining luminosity in prayer . . . from these acts prayer is illumined and strengthened—whether it be that they are taken from the spiritual Scriptures, or from among things written by the great teachers in the Church . . . without reading the intellect has no means of drawing near to God.[95]

Here it is vital to note that both Isaac and Mina were all too aware that not all reading was profitable for the solitary. Reading, for Isaac, should be "parallel" to life,[96] for reading otherwise may cause "him loss and darken his mind, obscuring its goal, which lies with God."[97] As Hilarion Alfeyev notes, a solitary was never meant to be especially learned or well read, only "pure in mind."[98]

This is to say, the purpose of such prayer and reading is solely "mystical insight," what Isaac calls *sukkale*. "Discern," he teaches,

> the purport of all the passages you come upon in the sacred writings, that you might immerse yourself deeply in them, and might fathom the profound insights [*sukkale*] . . . those who in their way of life are led by divine grace to be enlightened are always aware of something like a noetic ray running between the written lines.[99]

Isaac (and Mina who follows him) indicates that these "insights," through reading in prayer, are the points at which the solitary takes departure from the activity of the mind, to the direct communion with God.[100] But these "insights," Isaac continues elsewhere, are not merely personal; they in a sense "[belong] to the community."[101] In prayer the "insight" revealed to a solitary can serve, by means of personal revelation, to integrate the experience of the whole Church into his own experience.[102] Insights may, therefore, be of far-reaching ecclesial significance and, we may suggest, be the means and *method* of authentic reform; not mere structural or institutional reform, but more so radical healing, restoration, and transfiguration. Could this be how Fr Mina's personal ascesis would directly lead into his method of ecclesial reform?

Whatever our response to that may be, we do well to heed Isaac's warning that those who have reached such a state of pure prayer are all too rare. "Only one man," Isaac laments, among thousands will be found who . . . has been accounted worthy to attain to pure prayer. . . . But as to that mystery which is after pure prayer and lies beyond it, there is scarcely to be found a single man from generation to generation who by God's grace has attained thereto.[103]

Was—we dare to inquire—Fr Mina one such man?

Eviction from the Mountain, 1941

> "The beginning of freedom from anger is silence of the lips
> when the heart is agitated."
> —*St John Climacus*

O NE THING THAT EMERGES when reading the lives of the early Christian martyrs is that they commonly had foreboding visions of the exact circumstances of their deaths. Ascetics are privy to the same. On occasion, certain ascetics are even said to have experienced "premonitory visions" of a different type of "death"—that of ordination.

Porphyry of Gaza and Rabbula of Edessa, for instance, "dreamt" that they would one day be "married" to the Church.[104] Often the vision may be indirectly communicated through a holy man. Zeno had a premonition that Peter the Iberian would be ordained a bishop, and Paphnutius in Egypt foretold Epiphanius' episcopacy in Cyprus.[105] In addition, Claudia Rapp notes in her insightful study, certain childhood episodes may be—"with the advantage of hindsight"— imbued with "premonitory significance."[106] Athanasius, we are told, first came to the attention of Patriarch Alexander when he was a child, after being reprimanded for playing at the seashore pretending to be a bishop and baptizing his pagan childhood friends.[107] Ambrose, in turn, was remembered as playing at bishop, even teasing his friends by holding out his hand so that they would kiss it, and Eutychius of Constantinople reportedly wrote "patriarch" as his career aspiration on the schoolyard wall.[108] Such visions or events assert and confirm that the ordination of these bishops "was, in effect, divinely preordained."[109]

To return then to Fr Mina, we have already seen the first premonition when he was four years old at the mouth of a traveling monk: "He is one of our stock." Yet it is a second "premonitory vision" that is far more intriguing, in that it presents an enduring, penetrating, and unifying *insight*—one that has been consistently missed.

* * *

On June 21, 1942, at the age of eighty-seven, Pope Youannis XIX reposed. Regardless of how his legacy will be remembered in history, the patriarch was much loved by Fr Mina—a feeling that was certainly mutual. Youannis had been instrumental in Mina's entrance into monastic life, overcame the almost unanimous opposition against his desire for solitude, and wept with him during the scandal of the expelled monks. At each stage of Fr Mina's monastic journey, Youannis was present, quietly empowering, encouraging, and all the while—as Hanna once noted—"taking the blessing" of the intriguing young monk.[110]

It is little wonder then that Fr Mina was grieved by the death of the elderly Patriarch. As is customary, Mina would commemorate Youannis daily during the Divine Liturgy.[111] On the fortieth day (July 31, 1942), after the Liturgy, Fr Mina was overcome by sleep. Hanna's account does not explicitly reveal the exact circumstance of the vision, but only states that Fr Mina "saw Pope Youannis come to him." Far more important, obviously, is the vision itself.

Fr Mina, according to the memoir, was "surprised" that the pope had made such a strenuous effort at his age to climb the "mountain." "I am saddened," Youannis unexpectedly said,

> ". . . that the papal staff *broke* while I was climbing the mountain." Father Mina said, "I wish the Pope would leave it with me for a while." The Pope gave it to him. Father Mina *fixed* it and returned it. The Pope rejoiced, examined it carefully, and said, "Take it Father Mina; *I am giving it to you*." He took it happily from his hand. He woke up thinking about this vision regarding the staff and his conversation with the Pope.[112]

This account was written by his brother, Hanna Youssef Atta, in the early 1970s.[113] One immediate concern with this "premonitory vision" is the dating. Forty days after Youannis death in mid-1942 would have been after Fr Mina had left the windmill (late 1941)—and so the question must be asked: how could Fr Mina have had such a vision while still at the mill?

There is, however, another source to be found within the literature. Writing in 1961, Otto Meinardus, a celebrated Coptologist, states that in or around 1939 (while Youannis was still alive), Fr Mina was visited by the patriarch at the windmill.[114] In other words, for Meinardus the account was history and not a vision. Unsurprisingly, all English sources follow Meinardus in squarely situating this episode within history in the late 1930s.[115] The details of the accounts are otherwise identical. Youannis' patriarchal staff—in Meinardus' words the "symbol of his calling"—was broken on account of the arduous journey and was repaired by Fr Mina. But while Hanna was satisfied to leave the conclusion tantalizingly implicit, Meinardus asked the glaring question: "Was this gesture a prophecy that his anchorite host would become his successor some twenty years later?"[116] "The Copts relish such anecdotes," Wakin echoed in 1963; "the divine origin of choice is reinforced."[117]

Can these two accounts of vision and history be taken together? If it is a vision as Hanna claims, then the issue of dating may be resolved by suggesting either that his memoirs confused the place of the vision (it was not at the windmill) or that he confused the timing of the vision (it was not forty days after Youannis' death). Both seem unlikely given that he specifically and explicitly states that it was a "vision" that took place following Youannis' death on July 31, 1942. We should also recall the memoirs were copublished with Fr Raphael Ava Mina (the future disciple of Fr Mina), who has never taken issue with the account throughout its numerous printings. A far simpler explanation—and one that is certainly more perceptive to the nature of visions—may be that the vision was of the "windmill" *after* Fr Mina had in fact left the windmill. Just as one may dream of a place where one once lived, likewise—especially given that Mina had lived there for six years—could this vision have occurred in mid-1942 and been an experience at the windmill, though he had since left it. The happenings, we may suggest, of a vision need not relate to one's exact physical circumstances. It is possible, therefore, that the vision occurred after he had left the windmill and was staying at either the Monastery of Archangel Michael or the Church of St Mary at Babylon in Old Cairo.

Nevertheless, the specificity of Hanna and the insistence of Meinardus on historicity are impossible to reconcile. But—and this needs to be emphasized—that which is of importance in this context is not the "how" but rather the "why." Both sources agree perfectly on the actual substance of the episode, and it is these details that are of profound significance.

In both cases, whether a prophetic historical act or an inexplicable vision, the account reveals an *insight*. As we have seen, under the "patristic discipleship" of Isaac the Syrian, Fr Mina would have been all too aware of the nature of "mystical insights" (*sukkale*); and, most especially, of their communal and ecclesial dimensions. In this tradition, the solitary in prayer could receive "insights" directly impacting the Church. Perhaps, then, Fr Mina's "premonitory vision" of his future calling as patriarch was one such insight, not simply in that it prophesied this calling, but rather in that it indicated the very *nature* of the calling.

No one has paid sufficient attention, either in Arabic or in English, to the details of this fascinating account. Youannis presented to Fr Mina a "broken" patriarchal staff. Fr Mina then took the staff for "a while," "fixed" it, and returned it to Youannis. Seeing it restored, the pope gave it back to Mina, who, we are told, took it "happily." If this acts as "premonitory vision" in a similar vein to the experience of the early ascetics of the Church, then each of these words is of premonitory significance. Scholars have routinely noticed the symbolism of the staff (the "patriarchal calling") but curiously have neglected its state at the time, namely, its brokenness. The staff was "broken," for truly Fr Mina was presented with a "broken" Church—a Church that was bleeding profusely and severely fractured, and that, to many, seemed irreparable. Fr Mina then took that acute brokenness for "a while," mended it, reformed it, healed it, and presented it to Youannis, only to receive it once more as *his* Church. Theologically this "insight"—whether it be vision, prophecy, or history—is important. The premonition was not *only* that he would be a patriarch; it was that he would be a patriarch who would heal a deeply divided and fractured Church.

But such a calling was still many years (and two patriarchs) away. And Fr Mina would soon be faced with a far more immediate crisis.

* * *

Toward the end of the decade, the underworld elements at play in and around the Moqattam Mountain intensified. Two bands of criminals, one from northern Cairo and the other from Giza, would apparently meet regularly (for untoward arrangements) at an abandoned stretch of desert near Fr Mina's windmill.[118] It seems that at some point they became concerned for the privacy of their dealings, and feared the presence of the solitary monk.

Late at night, possibly toward the end of 1939, three of those men approached the mill.[119] Fr Mina opened the door and was asked for some of his drinking water. As he turned his back to get the water, one of the men struck him sharply on the head. When he regained consciousness sometime later, he noted he was bleeding heavily. Crawling, still recoiling from the shock, he managed to grasp an icon of St Menas—interestingly, his first concern—and placed it upon the wound. "And so," Fr Raphael writes as a matter of fact, "the bleeding stopped."[120] The recluse then made his way to the Hermal hospital (6 km/3.7mi away) where he sought the necessary treatment.[121] (Decades later, Mina showed the scar on his head to Fr Raphael; the wound, we may imagine, must have been rather deep.[122]) After he left the hospital, the account continues, a young man came to Fr Mina weeping and begging for forgiveness, confessing that it was he who had struck the monk. The other two, the criminal said, had suffered strange happenings: one was struck by a train at Helwan, and the second was convicted of an unrelated crime.[123]

After the failed attempt at murdering Fr Mina, others of a similar persuasion sought a more diplomatic route. According to documentary evidence, numerous objections and complaints were lodged with the Department of Arabic Antiquities from February to September 1940, calling for Mina's immediate eviction.[124] The accusations stated in no uncertain terms that the monk was conjuring up curses, dabbling in black magic and Satanism, as well as the milder complaint that he was smuggling illicit goods.[125] Receiving these complaints in disbelief, the acting director of the Arabic Antiquities, Hassan (or "Hussein") Fouad, met with the governor of Cairo to explain their context.[126] Wishing to see for himself, the governor traveled with Hassan to the windmill, only to find the residence (of sorts) in good order, and the poor recluse upstairs quietly and calmly praying. The governor immediately declared that the harmless monk should be left alone.

It would not, however, be the end of his troubles at the windmill. And yet, from what we can tell—at least from a letter of the period in response to the concerns of his disciples—Fr Mina was not worried in the least:

> Be very comforted that the martyr St Menas sleeps here every night— although he does not sleep but constantly gives praise—as you know well, and along with him comes the martyr St George. . . . Some have heard that they have undertaken to protect this place.[127]

* * *

Before long, his now-rare peace at the windmill would be disturbed again. Because of the eruption of World War II in late 1939, many of the details of this period in Fr Mina's life are marked by confusion, obscurity, and imprecision.[128] Nevertheless, a convincing reconstruction is possible.

A dramatic depiction of an attempted second eviction is preserved by Fr Raphael Ava Mina.[129] A new director of Arabic Antiquities was appointed in late 1940 and was evidently not as understanding of Fr Mina's occupation of an abandoned windmill.[130] An eviction order was swiftly dispatched. One of the guards from the nearby outpost (presumably fearing the renowned monk) refused to comply, only to hear the words: "I'll go myself and evict him."[131] Fr Mina was told rather bluntly by the director that his lease was "terminated" and that he should leave immediately. The monk asked for an extension until the end of the year, but the director was immovable. "I am not leaving this place," Fr Mina declared as he closed the mill's door. "Do what you want. . . . The Lord exists [*rabenna mawgood*]."[132]

Furious, the director returned home vowing to use force to evict the recluse. Around midnight, according to the account, his wife awoke in a state of hysteria. A man, she managed to say, with a long beard was strangling her, saying, "I have to strangle you because your husband wants to evict me although I have done him no harm."[133] That morning the director and his wife rushed to the windmill to beg for forgiveness. As Fr Mina opened the door and welcomed them, the woman, visibly distressed, mumbled, "This is the man who came to me at night." "No," Fr Mina quietly answered after listening to the agitated woman, "it was St Menas."[134]

Other renderings of the incident, though less violent, were not so forgiving, with the inspector being mysteriously dispatched to another city.[135] This may be telling of the capacity of the literature to downplay (as well as embellish) certain events over time.[136]

The sources from here diverge even further, with three different accounts of Fr Mina's eventual eviction from the mountain: some claim that he left directly to become the abbot of the Monastery of St Samuel;[137] others that he was evicted by the British, who were securing the area during World War II and thought him to be a spy;[138] and others still, that his eviction was for the sake of an archaeological excavation.[139] The first suggestion is made in apparent ignorance of the letters that indicate he would only be appointed abbot two years later,[140] and the second, though historically accurate, mistakenly concerns a future eviction in 1945.[141] It is, in fact, the last suggestion—an archaeological excavation—that accounts for *this* particular departure from the windmill. It would be the first of *two* eventual evictions from the mountain.

* * *

Fr Mina, try as he might, could not escape the attention of the civil authorities. By late 1941, the Ministry of Arabic Antiquities came under increasing pressure to resolve the highly unusual matter of a Christian monk living in an abandoned heritage site. The next director—who conceivably replaced the aforementioned terrified man—coming across the modestly refurbished windmill of Fr Mina, sought to designate it a "public rest house," thereby seeking a cancellation of the lease. A significant debate erupted, with many of Fr Mina's (now-growing) supporters opposing the director's plans.

In the end, according to the ministry's records, government officials determined to cancel the lease for the express need of an archaeological excavation that happened to be precisely under Fr Mina's windmill—which, we should note, never happened.[142] Two weeks later, on October 28, 1941, several police officers arrived to evict the recluse amid his clamoring supporters. Quietly, despite the protests of his spiritual children, he gathered his inconsiderable possessions and left his beloved windmill. Looking around at their tears and despair, with a small bag in arm, Fr Mina comforted them:

> Do not cry my children. The Lord's will must be done. His plans are sublime. The Lord will not abandon me. He who provides his feeding to the weakest bird will give me shelter and bread. Do not be anxious for me.[143]

Notes

[1] Atta and Raphael Ava Mina, *Life of Pope Kyrillos*, 13.

[2] Ibid.

[3] There is some suggestion of this in later dealings with the Baramous Monastery. Fr Raphael Ava Mina suggests Masudi, his spiritual father, had died in 1935, and therefore, if the abbot was his sole director—a relationship which was somewhat irreparable at that stage—it would lead to further contention; see Fr Raphael Ava Mina, "Pope Kyrillos VI—Some Misconceptions," audio recording, in *Liturgy in the Coptic Orthodox Church* (Alexandria, 2015).

[4] Fr Thomas Hopko, "Fifty-Five Maxims for Christian Living" (unpublished, 2008), Maxim 31.

[5] Meinardus, *Monks and Monasteries (1961)*, 157; Meinardus, *Christian Egypt: Faith and Life*, 43; Meinardus, *Two Thousand Years*, 78; Wakin, *A Lonely Minority*, 111. We should note that Wakin follows Meinardus' claim; whereas van Doorn-Harder and Voile appear to follow I. H. al-Masri's ambiguous claim that Fr Mina's request was in fact accepted by Yoannis but was rejected by the British; Voile has correctly seen that Masri may have meant the original request occurred in 1942, as she did not date her claim; see Voile, *Les Coptes d'Égypte*, 196, n. 20; van Doorn-Harder, *Modern Coptic Papacy*, 132. Also note that in I. H. al-Masri's English abbreviated history, she indicates this was immediately after the exile from the Baramous monastery, whereas the Arabic is ambiguous; see al-Masri, *True Story of Christianity in Egypt*, 2:434; al-Masri, *Story of the Coptic Church*, 7:24.

[6] It also should be noted that such a claim makes little sense of the original Arabic sources that state that Fr Mina's request to Youannis concerning the windmill was not haphazard or an afterthought, but instead followed his premeditated securing of a permit for the windmill site.

[7] Atta and Raphael Ava Mina, *Memories about the Life of Pope Kyrillos*, 41–42. Maher Mahrous Morgan, the son of that solicitor, who was a member of the board of the "Friends of the Holy Bible Association," recalls the episode in a letter to Fr Raphael Ava Mina, who published it as part of his memoirs.

[8] Ibid., 42.

[9] It seems then—especially given he had already secured permission from the Ministry of Arabic Antiquities—Fr Mina had decided upon moving to the windmill before meeting with the patriarch,

and thus was intending on doing so irrespective of the outcome of the judgment of the expelled monks (himself included).

[10] Atta and Raphael Ava Mina, *Life of Pope Kyrillos*, 13.

[11] Ibid., 13–14; Atta and Raphael Ava Mina, *Memories about the Life of Pope Kyrillos*, 27.

[12] I. H. al-Masri somewhat exaggerates when she claims that Fr Mina passed on a "card" to the secretary of the director, saying: "Please tell the director that the one who received this card from you, wishes to meet you." It is certainly unlikely that Mina held onto a business card for two years in solitude, though perhaps not impossible. See al-Masri, *Story of the Coptic Church*, 7:22.

[13] Atta and Raphael Ava Mina, *Life of Pope Kyrillos*, 14.

[14] See Figure 5.

[15] Anonymous, "From the Deserted Windmill of Bonaparte to the Throne of Saint Mark" [in Arabic], *al-Watani*, May 10, 1959. Though a source is not given for the article other than the archives of the Ministry of Arabic Antiquities, many of the articles written in and around the date of enthronement were based upon interviews with those colleagues of Fr Mina. It is the earliest written account of his time at the windmill.

[16] The article goes on to claim that the lease was "made legal" and properly redrafted on August 23, 1938, and that the lease is "still kept there" and continues to be source of confusion in the office given its unique and unusual nature. See ibid.

[17] Ibid.; cf Zaklama, *Pope Kyrillos VI*, 1:110. The guard station was a timber hut that archaeologists could use to secure their tools and discovered artifacts. It was, according to the article, protected by two armed guards in the day, and four at night. The article also suggests that the guard station was instructed to supply water for the monk, as well as to supply food items from the nearby food market (some two kilometers [1.24 mi] away)—which, the article's author notes, was meager given the monk's diet of "dry bread, rocket [arugula], and some vegetables."

[18] Al-Masri, *Story of the Coptic Church*, 7:22. As has already been hinted at throughout many prior footnotes (and will become increasingly obvious going forward), I. H. al-Masri's studies in Coptic history are not always strictly "historical" (though certainly admirable) and, consequently, cannot always be entirely trusted. This is identified where relevant throughout.

[19] Anonymous, "The Deserted Windmill."

[20] Adly, *Father Mikhail Dawood's Memories*, 12; cf. Zaklama, *Pope Kyrillos VI*, 1:110. It is a widespread practice for Egyptians to have multiple names; for instance, the name of the father, grandfather, and so on. Therefore, his name could be given as Hussein Fouad Rashed, Hussein Rashed, or Hussein Fouad.

[21] Accordingly, the name of the director that Fr Mina met in 1934 should be corrected to *Hussein Fouad Rashed*. Of course, there is also the possibility—though I find it unlikely—that there were two different directors: *Hassan Fouad*, whom Fr Mina met in the Wadi al-Natrun Desert; and *Hussein Rashed*, who granted the lease for the windmill. But this would necessitate that we dismiss Hanna's entire account of the director recognizing Fr Mina. Also, it would require dismissing the account of Fr Mikhail Dawood (son of Marcos Dawood) in which Mikhail states that he personally met "Hussein Fouad Rashed," who told of his surprise on seeing Fr Mina walk into the Department of Arabic Antiquities and recognized him from two years prior in the desert. See Adly, *Fr Mikhail Dawood's Memoirs*, 12.

[22] It may be reasonably suggested that the author of the *al-Watani* article (given that it was written while Fr Mina was relatively unknown) was unaware of the 1934 meeting and had simply written the account based upon the documentary evidence in the Arabic Antiquities records.

[23] Atta and Raphael Ava Mina, *Life of Pope Kyrillos*, 14; Adly, *Fr Mikhail Dawood's Memoirs*, 11. This is rather fascinating given Fr Marcos was a close friend of Fr Mina's and eventually became his "confession father." It is indicative of the lengths to which Mina went to achieve solitude and anonymity.

[24] Marcos Bey Fahmy was a well-respected member of the Cairo *maglis* (Community Council). He would be forever indebted to Fr Mina. Marcos' daughter was paralyzed after giving birth, until Fr Mina left the windmill and traveled to their family home in Shoubra and healed her. See Fr Raphael Ava Mina, *The Miracles of Pope Kyrillos VI*, vol. 3 (Sydney: Coptic Orthodox Publication and Translation, 1992), 5.

[25]Atta and Raphael Ava Mina, *Memories about the Life of Pope Kyrillos*, 27; and their *Life of Pope Kyrillos*, 14. The English translation misses this comment attributed to Fr Marcos Dawood.

[26]This is the same Moqattam (meaning "cut or broken off") that was made famous by the events during the time of Patriarch Abraham (975–978) in which the mountain "moved" in response to the prayers of the entire Coptic community after the Muslim Ibn Killis threatened: move the mountain with "faith of a mustard seed," or the entire Christian community would be put to the sword. For a lucid discussion of this dramatic and fascinating event, see Mark N. Swanson, *The Coptic Papacy in Islamic Egypt* (Cairo: The American University Press in Cairo, 2010), 48–52.

[27]Atta and Raphael Ava Mina, *Life of Pope Kyrillos*, 14.

[28]Fr Raphael Ava Mina comments, "He lived in it in the same condition as he found it, without a door or a bed. Why? Because he found real comfort in his God. . . ." See Raphael Ava Mina, *Spiritual Leadership*, 10.

[29]Atta and Raphael Ava Mina, *Life of Pope Kyrillos*, 14; Adly, *Fr Mikhail Dawood's Memoirs*, 11–12. Cf. Ps 22.6. Fr Mina's words continue: "I wish that the Lord would help me become like those righteous who fled into desert and mountains because of their love for the name of Christ."

[30]They were built as part of the French campaign in 1798–1801 in a bid to protect French interests and undermine British access.

[31]Zaklama, *Pope Kyrillos VI*, 1:106.

[32]See Figure 6.

[33]Zaklama, *Pope Kyrillos VI*, 1:113.

[34]Fr Raphael suggests that Mina developed an odd sleep posture for the rest of his life (on his side with his legs stretched perfectly straight) from sleeping on a pew; see Raphael Ava Mina, "Interview about the Life of Pope Kyrillos VI."

[35]Atta and Raphael Ava Mina, *Life of Pope Kyrillos*, 14. Hanna suggests that this Liturgy marked the beginning of his public life. Interestingly, we should also add, these few months may have been the first time since priesthood that he had been deprived of daily Liturgy.

[36]Ibid.; Atta and Raphael Ava Mina, *Memories about the Life of Pope Kyrillos*, 28. The English translation misses the name of the two prominent laymen mentioned in the Arabic original. Fr Youhanna was priest of the "Hanging Church" of St Mary, and Fr Marcos was the priest of the Monastery of Archangel Michael. Marcos Bey Fahmy was a member of the Cairo *maglis*, and Yacoub Bey Makary was an inspector for the Ministry of Education. See al-Masri, *Story of the Coptic Church*, 7:22–23.

[37]Ramzy was born in Akhmim in the Souhag governorate in Upper Egypt, and lived with Fr Mina from 1937, before being tonsured a monk in 1939 at St Barbara's Church in Old Cairo at the hands of Bishop Basilios (1894–1947) of Luxor and Esna. He would go on to be ordained a priest in 1945; in 1952 he would be elevated to Hegumen, and two years later became the head of the monastery. On June 2, 1985, he was ordained Bishop of the monastery before his death in April 1989. For a brief biography, see Nasr, *Readings in the Life of Abouna Mina*, 51.

[38]His name in Arabic was Mina *al-Saghir*; this may be translated as Mina "Junior" or "the Younger"— though it should be noted that it could also have meant "the Small" given his physically small stature.

[39]Fr Raphael Ava Mina, *Service and Humility in the Life of Pope Kyrillos VI* (Cairo: Sons of Pope Kyrillos VI, 1999), 12–13. Another similar account is given in Zaklama, *Pope Kyrillos VI*, 1:116–17.

[40]Zaklama, *Pope Kyrillos VI*, 1:117.

[41]Raphael Ava Mina, *Service and Humility*, 25. One particular woman, the account continues, recalled that Fr Mina would always remind her mother to avoid adding sesame to the *dukkah* (ground seeds mixture) as an "extra measure of austerity."

[42]See Figures 7 and 8.

[43]Raphael Ava Mina, *Service and Humility*, 18.

[44]Ibid.

[45]Voile, *Les Coptes d'Égypte*, 201.

[46]One rather unusual account is of Fr Mina and a neighboring wolf; see al-Masri, *Story of the Coptic Church*, 7:23.

[47]Rapp, *Holy Bishops*, 67. Also see James Skedros, "Hagiography and Devotion to the Saints," in *The Orthodox Christian World*, ed. Augustine Casiday (Abingdon, UK: Routledge, 2012), 450.

[48]Van Doorn-Harder, "Planner, Patriarch and Saint," 232; Watson, *Among the Copts*, 51.

[49]For a fascinating discussion of the notion of "taking *baraka*," see Anthony Shenoda, "Cultivating a Mystery: Miracles and a Coptic Moral Imaginary" (dissertation, Harvard University, 2010), 41–45.

[50]Van Doorn-Harder, "Planner, Patriarch and Saint," 232.

[51]Atta and Raphael Ava Mina, *Life of Pope Kyrillos*, 14.

[52]Ibid. It should be noted that though Hanna seemingly suggests that at this point Fr Mina had to begin a daily Liturgy, it seems that he meant a "public" daily Liturgy that could be attended by his visitors. This certainly is consistent with Hanna's earlier claim that Maleka, his deacon, attended Liturgy every day with Fr Mina.

[53]Hasan, *Christians versus Muslims*, 86. Some of these "business" cards are still extent; on them is written a biblical verse in Arabic (for instance, "What would a man benefit if he gains the entire world but loses himself," Mk 8.36), and at the bottom is written in Coptic his name, "Hegumen Mina the Recluse" (not a magical talisman as Hasan mistakenly suggests).

[54]Meinardus, *Coptic Saints and Pilgrimages*, 93.

[55]Fr Raphael Ava Mina, *The Miracles of Pope Kyrillos VI: Volume 1* (Cairo: Sons of Pope Kyrillos VI, 1983), 7–8. Though a multitude of volumes would eventually appear detailing thousands of miracles, it is in this first work that most credibility may be reasonably grasped given that these first "miracles" were written by Fr Raphael himself, and that he repeats the accounts in his other work: Raphael Ava Mina, *Spiritual Leadership*, 10–11. We should also note that these miracle volumes (at present numbering eighteen), though anonymous, are in fact edited and compiled by Fr Raphael. The original Arabic volume 1 appeared first in 1973 with this interesting preface: "This book, we expect, is *not* going to be the last word in the miracles of Pope Kyrillos VI, as while the book is in press, letters are continually being received"; see Raphael Ava Mina, *Miracles of Pope Kyrillos VI*, 1:6.

[56]Anonymous, "The Deserted Windmill."

[57]Raphael Ava Mina, *Miracles of Pope Kyrillos VI*, 1:10; Raphael Ava Mina, *Spiritual Leadership*, 7.

[58]Zaklama, *Pope Kyrillos VI*, 1:118.

[59]Voile, *Les Coptes d'Égypte*, 204; Nelly van Doorn-Harder, "Practical and Mystical: Patriarch Kyrillos VI (1959–1971)," *Currents in Theology and Mission* 33, no. 3 (2006): 229.

[60]The fullest written account is given in Zaklama, *Pope Kyrillos VI*, 1, 114.

[61]Given that the account pre-dated the inaugural Liturgy at the windmill in late 1936, and that Hanna states Maleka was present at that Liturgy, we may assume it occurred prior to this Liturgy, thereby indicating that it is the earliest healing miracle claimed for Fr Mina.

[62]Another miracle concerning this Maleka is recorded in Fr Raphael Ava Mina's first miracle volume, Raphael Ava Mina, *Miracles of Pope Kyrillos VI*, 1:9.

[63]Atta and Raphael Ava Mina, *Life of Pope Kyrillos*, 14–15.

[64]Ibid., 14.

[65]For a biography see Boulos Ayad, "Fr Ibrahim Luka: His Deeds, Program, Struggle for the Renaissance of the Coptic Church and the Christian Unity," *Coptic Church Review* 27, nos. 3 and 4 (2006). Also see Ibrahim, *The Copts of Egypt*, 108.

[66]The English translation notes that Fr Ibrahim planned to personally visit the windmill to thank Fr Mina, but it misses the Arabic ending: "But this visit was postponed for a while." This implicitly suggests that the next visit would be when Fr Ibrahim came to repay the favor; see Atta and Raphael Ava Mina, *Life of Pope Kyrillos*, 15. and their *Memories about the Life of Pope Kyrillos*, 29.

[67]The volumes (originally in Arabic) date from 1973 to the present day, and reproduce those miracles which the editor felt were credible—for instance, any anonymous miracles that were not verifiable by follow-up correspondence were rejected. Of course, as any traveler to Egypt will quite quickly note, even this does not do justice to the sheer number of alleged miracles.

[68]Van Doorn-Harder, "Practical and Mystical," 229; Voile, *Les Coptes d'Égypte*, 204.

[69]Al-Masri, *Story of the Coptic Church*, 7:25.

[70]Van Doorn-Harder, "Practical and Mystical," 229.

[71]Bishop Athanasius of Beni Suef in a 1998 interview; ibid.

[72]Monk Mina el-Baramousy [Kyrillos VI], *HS* [in Arabic], vol. 4 (Wadi al-Natrun: Baramous Monastery, Pashans 1644; May 1928), 1–3; Pope Kyrillos VI, "Article Twenty-Nine on Prayer" [in Arabic] (unpublished, undated). The latter was seemingly unpublished and was found, written in his hand, among other articles from Fr Raphael Ava Mina—unfortunately, though, it is undated. Interestingly it is "article twenty-nine," though it is the only handwritten document examined by the author to have such a numerical title.

[73]Isaac the Syrian, *Ascetical Homilies* 63.445.

[74]Ibid., 8.186.

[75]Kyrillos VI, "On Prayer," 1. This immediately brings to mind Isaac's notion of the solitary as the *ihidaya*—the one united with God, others, and himself.

[76]Mina el-Baramousy [Kyrillos VI], *HS*, 4:1.

[77]Ibid.

[78]For Fr Mina there is even value in a fall with prayer: "Let them be sure, those who fell in sin because of their desires and weaknesses, those who are humiliated as a result . . . that after their recovery, they will be a source of light. . . ." See Kyrillos VI, "On Prayer," 4.

[79]Mina el-Baramousy [Kyrillos VI], *HS*, 4:2.

[80]Kyrillos VI, "On Prayer," 1.

[81]Ibid., 2.

[82]For instance: Isaac the Syrian, *Ascetical Homilies* 21.229–30. "I tell you in very truth, that if I go out to pass water, I am shaken from my mind and its order. . . ."

[83]For an analysis of Isaac's "requirements for prayer," see Alfeyev, *World of Isaac the Syrian*, 146–48.

[84]Isaac the Syrian, *Ascetical Homilies* 64.151. Interestingly, as we have indicated, Fr Mina seems to have had great affinity for the *Sixty-Fourth Homily*.

[85]Ibid., 4.51.

[86]Mina el-Baramousy [Kyrillos VI], "Letter to Hanna Youssef Atta, undated, ?1930." See also his "Letter to Attia Labib, March 1933." These letters have been combined in Raphael Ava Mina, *Christian Behaviour*, 9–12.

[87]Hegumen Mina the Recluse [Kyrillos VI], "Letter to Fr Makary el-Syriany, undated, ?1948–1951" [in Arabic], in FRC-1: Letter 427 (Old Cairo, undated). See also Raphael Ava Mina, *Christian Behavior*, 37.

[88]Kyrillos VI, "On Prayer," 2.

[89]For instance, see Isaac the Syrian, *Ascetical Homilies* 75.515–527 (i.e., the entire homily).

[90]Ibid., 64.450.

[91]Ibid., 20.223.

[92]Hegumen Mina the Recluse [Kyrillos VI], "Letter to Fr Makary el-Syriany, 1951" [in Arabic], in FRC-1: Letter 522 (Old Cairo, 1951). Also see Raphael Ava Mina, *Christian Behaviour*, 40.

[93]Kyrillos VI, "On Prayer," 2.

[94]Isaac the Syrian, *Ascetical Homilies* 64.450.

[95]Part II/21, cited in Alfeyev, *World of Isaac the Syrian*, 175.

[96]Isaac the Syrian, *Ascetical Homilies* 64.450.

[97]Part II/21, cited in Alfeyev, *World of Isaac the Syrian*, 176. In a 1959 interview prior to his patriarchal ordination, Fr Mina was asked, "What is the best book you have read . . . a non-religious book?" His response echoed Isaac: "Monasticism and seclusion provide a unique philosophy on life, a philosophy that takes a very deep interest in all that binds man to God. The way to this is to read only spiritual books. Reading any other books hurts the monk more than it benefits him, or at the very least, will make his mind go astray." See el-Gowaily, "Interview with the Monk."

[98]Alfeyev, *World of Isaac the Syrian*, 177.

[99]Isaac the Syrian, *Ascetical Homilies* 1.116–17.

[100]Alfeyev, *World of Isaac the Syrian*, 184.

[101]Part II/15, cited in ibid., 215.

[102]Ibid.

[103]Isaac the Syrian, *Ascetical Homilies* 23.240.

[104]Mark the Deacon, *The Life of Porphyry, Bishop of Gaza*, trans. G. F. Hill (Oxford: Clarendon Press, 1913), 19; "Life of Rabbula" cited in Rapp, *Holy Bishops*, 296.

[105]John Rufus, *The Lives of Peter the Iberian, Theodosius of Jerusalem, and the Monk Romanus*, trans. Cornelia B. Horn and Robert R. Phenix (Atlanta: Society of Biblical Literature, 2008), 105–7; "Life of Epiphanius" cited in Rapp, *Holy Bishops*, 296.

[106]Rapp, *Holy Bishops*, 296.

[107]Rufinus of Aquileia, *The Church History of Rufinus of Aquileia: Books 10 and 11*, trans. Philip R. Amidon (Oxford: Oxford University Press, 1997), 26. Interestingly, the baptism was considered legitimate, only needing confirmation.

[108]Paulinus, *Life of St Ambrose, Bishop of Milan*, trans. R. J. Deferrari, pp. 33–38 in *Early Christian Biography*, Fathers of the Church Series, vol. 15 (Washington, DC: Catholic University of America Press, 1952), 4; *Life of Eutychius*, cited in Rapp, *Holy Bishops*, 296.

[109]Rapp, *Holy Bishops*, 296.

[110]Atta and Raphael Ava Mina, *Life of Pope Kyrillos*, 11.

[111]Ibid., 15.

[112]Ibid.

[113]Though it was published with Fr Raphael's postpatriarchal life appended in 1981, it was written before Hanna died in 1976.

[114]Meinardus, *Monks and Monasteries (1961)*, 157–58.

[115]Wakin, *A Lonely Minority*, 110; Watson, "Abba Kyrillos," 17. The one Arabic exception is Youssef Habib, who reproduces the account as history, with the (perhaps unintended) ambiguous suggestion that it occurred during Youannis' visit to the Baramous Monastery; see Habib, *Among the Fathers*, 6. To my mind, there seem to be two possibilities of a historical occurrence: it was a visit at the Baramous Monastery during which the staff may have been broken during the journey, or a 1939 visit at the windmill, as Meinardus indicates. The former is highly unlikely given the absence of any supporting evidence of such an occurrence in the literature. The latter, while historical as opposed to a vision, is neither more nor less viable than Atta's position simply because it does *not* necessitate a "miracle."

[116]Meinardus, *Monks and Monasteries (1961)*, 157–58.

[117]Wakin, *A Lonely Minority*, 110.

[118]Anonymous, "The Deserted Windmill."

[119]Given that the letters of objection began in early 1940, and that the *al-Watani* account suggests the objections followed the beating of Fr Mina, we may suggest the episode occurred in late 1939. This is confirmed by Fr Samuel Tawadros el-Syriany's account, which suggests it was in 1939, and that he visited Fr Mina in hospital on that occasion. See Samuel Tawadros el-Syriany, *The History of the Popes*, 174.

[120]Raphael Ava Mina, *Spiritual Leadership*, 10–11.

[121]Ibid., 11. An early account in 1966 states that after the healing there was no need for further medical attention; see N. Fanus, "Man of Prayer and Goodness" [in Arabic], *Nahdat al-Kanais* 3 (1966): 85. The episode is also recorded as early as 1959; see anonymous, "The Deserted Windmill."

[122]Fr Raphael Ava Mina, "Lecture on the Virtues of Pope Kyrillos," audio recording (Alexandria: Monastery of St Menas, undated).

[123]One Arabic author gives slightly different fates to these men: one died in a car accident as he was fleeing, another had a "nervous breakdown" and disappeared, and the third returned for forgiveness. See Zaklama, *Pope Kyrillos VI*, 1:119. Another unrelated account of other troubles with these criminals is documented in the same work, p. 120.

[124]Anonymous, "The Deserted Windmill." The dates of the letters of complaint were February 22, March 25, April 25, June 3, July 4, and September 1940.

[125]Ibid. Also see Zaklama, *Pope Kyrillos VI*, 1:126.

[126]See the earlier chapter, "An Odd Choice of Residence: The Fated Windmill, 1936."

[127]The letter is reproduced in Zaklama, *Pope Kyrillos VI*, 1:125.

[128]We do know that Fr Mina left the windmill at one point in 1939 for forty days to comfort his confession father, Marcos Dawood, after the death of his wife. Adly, *Fr Mikhail Dawood's Memoirs*, 4.

[129]Raphael Ava Mina, *Miracles of Pope Kyrillos VI*, 1:10.

[130]Given that Hassan was acting as late as September 1940 (which we know given his intervention concerning the objections previously detailed), we may assume that this event occurred in late 1940, or very early 1941.

[131]Raphael Ava Mina, *Miracles of Pope Kyrillos VI*, 1:10.

[132]This phrase "the Lord exists" (*rabenna mawgood*) was made famous by Pope Shenouda III (1923–2012) as a characteristic response to tribulation, but it may have originated with Fr Mina.

[133]Raphael Ava Mina, *Miracles of Pope Kyrillos VI*, 1:10.

[134]Ibid.

[135]Fanus, "Man of Prayer," 85. In this account, the director's refusal of an extension saw Fr Mina travel to the police station in Old Cairo, where the police commissioner granted his request. But the very next day, before Fr Mina could make plans for alternate accommodation, the director was dispatched to the "Delta."

[136]In Fr Raphael's later account in 1975, he notes that the woman was certainly terrified after her dream, though the details of the violent dream are interestingly omitted; see Raphael Ava Mina, *Spiritual Leadership*, 10. Other later accounts likewise omit the details of the dream; for instance see Zaklama, *Pope Kyrillos VI*, 1:127–28.

[137]Atta and Raphael Ava Mina, *Life of Pope Kyrillos*, 15. Hanna suggests that Fr Mina left the windmill directly to become Abbot of the Monastery of St Samuel, only returning a few years later to be evicted by the British, on account of "his safety" during WWII. Other Arabic scholars follow him; for example, see al-Masri, *Story of the Coptic Church*, 7:23; Zaklama, *Pope Kyrillos VI*, 1:140.

[138]Meinardus, *Monks and Monasteries (1961)*, 158; Meinardus, *Christian Egypt: Faith and Life*, 44. Most English scholars follow Meinardus' claim that Fr Mina was evicted in 1942—he makes clear this was *before* Mina became the abbot of St Samuel Monastery—by the British "believing him to be a spy." For other scholars who follow Meinardus, see van Doorn-Harder, *Modern Coptic Papacy*, 133; Watson, "Abba Kyrillos," 11. Interestingly, Wakin, writing in 1963, was already aware of the two theories for his eviction; namely that he was evicted by the British or that his lease was ended for "archeological reasons"; see Wakin, *A Lonely Minority*, 111.

[139]Anonymous, "The Deserted Windmill." Another Arabic account suggests he was evicted by the Department of Arabic Antiquities in 1942 because of "fear for his life in a military zone"; see Samuel Tawadros el-Syriany, *The History of the Popes*, 174.

[140]This suggestion is rather unlikely given the documentary evidence in Fr Mina's letters (which were unknown to scholars) indicates he was not made abbot of St Samuel's till December 1943. Hanna was not explicit with his dates for this particular period, and it would seem that he simply omitted the years from 1941 to 1943. He does, however, mention the affair that Mina "did not want to leave his cell at the windmill" to go to St Samuel's—thus, in his account, suggesting Mina left directly to that monastery.

[141]It seems to me that Meinardus' explanation of his eviction is a mistaken "retrojection" of an event that occurred in 1945, when Fr Mina was indeed evicted by the British when he had returned to the windmill after completing some work at the Monastery of St Samuel.

[142]This occurred, according to the records, on October 11, 1941.

[143]Wakin, *A Lonely Minority*, 111. Cf. Mt 6.26. The exact words are also recorded in the 1959 *al-Watani* article; see anonymous, "The Deserted Windmill." This suggests that this article was Wakin's source for the eviction.

5

Urban Monasticism:
A Public Holy Man (1941–1959)

Unwilling Abbot at the Monastery of St Samuel, 1941–1945

> "Faith requires obedience, and not curiosity;
> and when God commands, one ought to be obedient, not curious."
> —*St John Chrysostom*

THOUGH FR MINA'S WORDS on the day of his eviction from the windmill were certainly valiant, we should not overlook his pain at the loss of solitude. In that same year Mina's father, Youssef Atta, would also die. Though we have no record of a reaction nor any mention of the death in Fr Mina's letters or memoirs, we can only imagine the agony of this twofold loss.

The pain would foreshadow that of the entire nation only a few months later. Ever since Egyptian "independence" in 1922, the British, Wafd Party, and the Palace had been engaged in a constant wrestle for power. With the international crisis of the Italian invasion of Ethiopia in 1936, the "Anglo-Egyptian Treaty" became something of a necessity, though it was not popularly perceived as such.[1] The limited and almost insignificant concessions of the treaty—essentially a continued and confused state of perpetual British occupation—saw the Wafd Party lose legitimacy.[2] And with the eruption of World War II, especially when German forces crossed the Libyan-Egyptian Border en route to population centers, the British were forced to disappoint even such "concessions." Talk of several young Egyptian officers (allegedly including Sadat) approaching the German command to rid Egypt of the "dreaded British military presence" provoked a British incursion.[3] On February 4, 1942, British forces surrounded

King Farouk's palace in Cairo. The "boy" (as the king was known) was ordered to either appoint a Wafd cabinet or abdicate. That day would be remembered as "the Great Humiliation"; the once-loved Wafd had been reelected by the "strength of British bayonets."[4]

Though the nation wept that day because of its searing humiliation, members of the Young Officers Corps of the Egyptian Army watched on with quiet indignation for both king and party. Their moment was still to come.

* * *

Little was previously known of the "interval" years following Fr Mina's eviction from the windmill in October 1941—one scholar even grumbled that "most sources are unreliable at this point."[5] This undoubtedly reflects the confusion and chaos of World War II. We are, however, able to trace his movements through an examination of his letters during this period, many of which have been previously unknown to scholars.[6]

A first insight into these years is that Fr Mina did not, contrary to most sources, immediately depart from the windmill to the Monastery of St Samuel.[7] According to multiple letters he left to become Abbot of St Samuel's in very late 1943, thus leaving two years (1941–1943) after his eviction unaccounted for. What we do know about the period is that it was awfully difficult for Fr Mina. He would spend these two years without a monastery, let alone a cell. Perhaps for this reason he sought (once more) to rebuild and inhabit the Monastery of St Menas at Mariout.[8] On this attempt, he was granted patriarchal consent, but it was the British who denied him access to the area.[9] The compounded rejection must have caused him considerable grief. At one melancholic point, we are told, he was forced for lack of accommodation to spend the night on the uncomfortable pavement in front of a locked church in Cairo.[10]

For these two years Fr Mina would live as something of an itinerant prophet, with nowhere to lay his head, traveling from parish to parish, followed by crowds whose needs displaced his own for a permanent abode. For the most part, he sought out the churches of Old Cairo, living between the tenth-century Monastery of the Archangel Michael and the Church of St Mary at Babylon (both only a thirty-minute walk from his beloved windmill).[11] He was in good "company"— several patriarchs once resided at St Mary's, with at least seven patriarchs from the eleventh to fifteenth centuries having also reposed in that place.[12] There, at the mercy and kindness of two dear friends, Fr Marcos Dawood (1892–1970) and Fr Ekladios Youssef (1897–1980), he found some measure of comfort and stability.[13] Other than the lack of a fixed monastic cell, his life of prayer, Liturgy, and (often miraculous) care for the afflicted continued uninterrupted. But soon he would be moved once more.

* * *

Toward the end of 1943, Fr Mina, now forty-one years of age, received word that he was to be immediately relocated to an isolated and collapsing monastery. Metropolitan Athanasius of Beni Suef and Bahnasa (1883–1962) had requested of the locum tenens, Metropolitan Yusab of Girga (1876–1956), that Mina be appointed the abbot of the Monastery of St Samuel—a monastery that, Hanna tells us rather mildly, "was not doing well financially."[14] The news was not especially well received. "I met His Grace Metropolitan Athanasius," wrote Fr Mina to his brother on December 24, 1943,

> . . . he assigned to me the responsibility of the monastery . . . so I accepted, *although I did not want to*, but the Lord is capable of helping us to serve Anba Samuel and his monastery. Be very comforted concerning us. From here Monk Mina "the Younger" el-Samuely is fine and sends you his greetings. . . .
> The wretched Fr Mina el-Baramousy the Recluse.[15]

Other than documentary evidence of his movements, the letter also gives us, unexpectedly, some sense of his monastic progression. Examining the "signing" of his letters (and ignoring the adjective "wretched") we can quite easily piece together his monastic career, as Fr Mina seems to have been quite strict and consistent in his self-titling. The earliest extant letters in 1929 are signed "*Monk Mina el-Baramousy*,"[16] whereas after his ordination in 1931, it is "*Fr Mina el-Baramousy*."[17] Similarly, the letters after late March 1945 are signed "*Hegumen Mina el-Baramousy the Recluse*," confirming that he was indeed elevated to the rank of "hegumen" ("archpriest") by early 1945. Many have suggested this, but the exact date has remained a mystery until now. Previously unseen letters from the period clearly indicate that his elevation to hegumen (and the ordination of the other Mina—known as Mina "the Younger"—to the priesthood) was at the hands of Metropolitan Athanasius on March 16, 1945.[18] This did not, however, take place during the consecration of the church at the Monastery of St Samuel, as is unanimously claimed, but rather at the bishopric in Beni Suef.[19]

The final—and perhaps the most significant—word, "recluse" or "solitary" (*el-mutawahid*), a nickname of sorts, is the name by which he would be most popularly known. This indicates that by 1943, whether he coined the moniker (which I suspect) or merely embraced it, Fr Mina was content to be known as "the Recluse."[20] It was a determining epithet in honor of the hero of Isaac the Syrian's monastic writings—*ihidaya*, "the solitary" or "recluse."

* * *

Of all the early medieval monasteries of the Faiyum oasis, the Monastery of St Samuel—one hundred and sixty kilometers (99 miles) southwest of Cairo—was the only one presently inhabited (though in a state of extreme disrepair). It was located at the Qalamoun (Greek for "reed-bed") Mountain, so called for the salt marshes of the area, which also made for barely drinkable water.[21] Though it had been home to anchorites from as early as the third century, the namesake of the monastery, Samuel the Confessor, was born centuries later in 598, entering the monastery as a teenager.[22] After an apparently brief discipleship under Abba Agathon at Wadi al-Natrun, Samuel became a confessor during the persecutions of the seventh century before living out his final days in peace. He was not, as we may imagine, the founder of the monastery, but rather, as Meinardus notes, "the rebuilder of an old settlement" that had been abandoned during the Persian persecution a few decades earlier.[23] By the time of his death in 695, the monks who had gathered around him numbered 120. Two centuries later it would again be destroyed by the Arabs, before being rebuilt, only to be abandoned once more from the seventeenth to the nineteenth centuries.

In 1896 a certain Fr Ishaq el-Baramousy (d. 1938) settled at the abandoned site with ten fellow monks from the Baramous Monastery. They had allegedly been excommunicated by Pope Cyril V (1831–1927), before being pardoned a few years later, after which event only five or six remained.[24] Johan Georg noted during his visit in 1930 that there were seven monks under Fr Ishaq; Georg claimed they were the "poorest" he had ever encountered.[25] A decade later, an archaeologist, Ahmad Fakhry, noted during his visits in 1942 and 1944 that there were only four monks: an Ethiopian abbot by the name of Hegumen Raphael; Fr Tawadrus, who had lived there for fourteen years; and two monks, Frs Athanasius and Mikhail, who were present in 1944 but not in 1942, suggesting they were perhaps newcomers.[26] It would thus appear that there were only four (or possibly five) monks at the monastery when Fr Mina was appointed abbot—and one of them would be the cause of not a little dissent.[27]

On December 29, 1943, just after his arrival with Mina "the Younger," Fr Mina received a letter from Metropolitan Athanasius (who, we should note, was the bishop of the diocese to which the monastery belonged). "To the honorable and blessed son," wrote the Metropolitan,

> Fr Mina, abbot of St Samuel's Monastery, the blessed by God. . . . I have received your letter that you have arrived safely at the monastery. Also, I have heard that Fr [no name is given] has come to the monastery and given you the monastery possessions that he had kept, except the pistol, which we can do without; it is evil, and we should stay away from it. I also heard that *he went away*. I ask the Almighty God to support you with his Holy Spirit, aid you, and assist you in this blessed service. . . . Keep on praying the Liturgies so that God may have mercy on us and grant all his people mercy from all temptations and tribulations, and *select for us a shepherd* to guide us in righteousness and rid his Church of those troublemakers.[28]

This rather intriguing letter alludes to the previous (and possibly continuing) contentions at the monastery. Besides the dramatic reference to a weapon and a leading monk who evidently was displeased by the Metropolitan's appointment of Fr Mina, the letter also hints at certain hierarchical maneuverings. Pope Youannis XIX had died in June 1942, leaving the Church in the hands of the locum tenens, Yusab, until a suitable candidate could be identified. The next patriarch (Macarius III) would, amid great controversy, be enthroned two months after this letter—hence Athanasius' allusion to "troublemakers."[29]

But, we might ask, did Metropolitan Athanasius mean more than simply "pray" Liturgies so that God might select a shepherd? Was his eye already on Fr Mina? Had he hoped that Mina would be *that* shepherd to follow Youannis? Certainly nothing in the literature (Arabic or English) makes mention of this letter, but if we look to the future at Athanasius' persistent nomination of Fr Mina to the patriarchate, a faint and yet discernible glimmer emerges.[30]

* * *

In late December, when Fr Mina arrived at the monastery's administrative center in al-Zora near Maghagha in the governorate of Minya, he was faced with a paradoxical sight. The center was in a beautiful and lush setting along the Nile River but was itself composed of "soft bricks," in a state of unacceptable poverty and disrepair, almost unlivable. The church was apparently structurally "unsafe," even for prayer.[31] From there Fr Mina turned his attention to the actual monastery at the Qalamoun Mountain, which was some fifty kilometers (31 miles) northwest. When the villagers heard that he planned to visit the monastery, Hanna recalls, they sent with him a seven-camel convoy loaded with gifts including "wheat, honey, and cheese."[32] Despite his initial reluctance to become abbot, as well as his dismay on observing the decrepit state of the monastery, Fr Mina was overwhelmed by its beauty. "My dear," he wrote to his brother on January 20, 1944,

> I headed to Anba Samuel's Monastery, this great monastery; I cannot describe how beautiful it is, or express the blessings and grace inside it, especially that the body of Anba Samuel the great man is there. We stayed for four days and prayed the Holy Liturgy; it was pouring blessing, then we went back to al-Zora. . . . [33]

"I wonder about his words," notes Fr Raphael Ava Mina (his future disciple), "what beauty did he see, how could he say these words and yet we all know that this Monastery was in desperate need of overhauling. . . . [He] saw a different kind of beauty, which no eye could see."[34] Be that as it may—beautiful or not—urgent renovations were necessary.

Fr Mina immediately returned to Cairo and enlisted the help of a contractor (and friend), Hanna Nessim, and he also drew on his considerable supporters for financial aid.[35] Two tugboats full of steel, cement, and clay were transported down the Nile, provoking a wave of enthusiasm among the villagers of Maghagha. Extensive structural works and renovations were undertaken at the monastery's center at al-Zora; the church was completely rebuilt (and was covered with a new roof), and a new two-story residence was built for the monks.[36] Subsequent works over the next year were also undertaken at the monastery in the Qalamoun Mountain. Arrangements were made for supplies to be brought from al-Zora twice a month, making the monastery once more "inhabitable" and encouraging several monks who had left over the previous years to return.[37]

Having "revived" the monastery, Fr Mina appointed Mina the Younger—who had recently been ordained a priest by Metropolitan Athanasius—to oversee the daily affairs of the monks.[38] Mina the Younger would remain at the Monastery of St Samuel for the rest of his life, eventually becoming its bishop.

Now that the monastery was in good order, in mid-1945, Fr Mina made his way, quite unexpectedly, back to his beloved windmill, this time without any legal permission.

* * *

For the next decade, until Mina the Younger became abbot in 1954, Fr Mina would care for the monastery from afar in Old Cairo, visiting only occasionally.[39] Much of this care took the form of correspondence.[40] For this reason, many of his letters (other than those to his brother) are addressed to the monks of St Samuel. There is even some suggestion that the rare autobiographical fragments from his hand were originally written for the edification of these same monks.

Though the monastery may have been renovated, a cursory look at these letters indicates that the contentions among the monks would not be dealt with so easily. "I am pleading," Fr Mina writes to the monks in one letter, "to make peace, assurance, love, and companionship dwell among you, so that you become of one heart and of one opinion, being humble with each other because you are brothers in Christ."[41] The entire letter, written strangely on the occasion of the Nativity, begs the monks to "reconcile with each other in gentleness and love," "be humble toward each other," and "do not annoy your brothers with a harsh word."[42] Almost every letter to these monks bears the same call for peace.[43] Eventually, these divisions would come to a head (as we shall see) when Fr Mina began sending his disciples in Old Cairo to St Samuel's for monastic tonsure.[44] Two of these young disciples, the so-called "Sunday School monks," would go on to play pivotal roles in the reform of the Church.

It is here that we begin to discern the gravity of the move—although he would not stay there long—to St Samuel's. Fr Mina's newfound capacity as abbot to "tonsure" monks provided him with the vehicle with which to change the Church, and it was this (through the wisdom of Metropolitan Athanasius) that was the lasting significance of his abbacy at St Samuel's.[45]

But for all this—renovated, remodeled, and revived—the monastery lacked official ecclesial status as a "monastery"—a recognition that would have to wait until the first Synod meeting of Fr Mina's patriarchate in 1959, when he would bestow the recognition himself.[46]

Habib Girgis and the Sunday School "Movement"

> "Despair never penetrated my soul even for one day. . . .
> There is no honey without the bee sting, and he who abandons
> the positive work for the sake of the murmurings of people
> resembles the horse that bolts when it sees its own shadow."
> —*Archdeacon Habib Girgis*

I N MID-1945 Fr Mina quietly returned to the windmill just outside Old Cairo. Hoping to escape the peering eyes of the authorities (civil and ecclesial), he resumed his life of solitude. On occasion, as mentioned above, he would correspond with the Monastery of St Samuel from afar. But it would not last long. A few months later, Fr Mina was evicted once more. As World War II came to an end, the British grew uncomfortable with the Recluse residing so near their desert operations and, fearing him to be a "spy"—or in other accounts, fearing for his safety—asked him to leave.[47]

One relative recalls that during 1945, for lack of accommodation, Fr Mina spent some forty days in Alexandria with his family.[48] Later that year he returned to Old Cairo, living, as he had previously, between the Monastery of Archangel Michael and the Church of St Mary at Babylon.[49] Correspondence from the period suggests that for the most part, he resided in one room at the former.[50] During this same year, he was also appointed (by force) the confessor of the St Mercurius Convent in Old Cairo. "I tried on several occasions," wrote Fr Mina to his brother on February 25, 1945,

> not to accept the position, but I had no say in the matter. As you may remember when [Pope] Youannis, God rest his soul, gave an order and it was disobeyed, he became angry. It is the same thing with His Holiness. . . .[51]

It was somewhat of a tolerable annoyance, though the relationship with the convent would eventually be crucial in the movement of monastic reform, and Fr Mina reluctantly obeyed. The next time he received a telegram from the patriarchate he would *not*. In mid–1946, shortly after the enthronement of Yusab II (1876–1956), a papal decree was issued ordering all monks to return to their original monasteries.[52] Having no recourse except to appeal, Mina wrote to the Vicar of the patriarchate, Hegumen Ibrahim Luka (1897–1950), stating that as the abbot of the Monastery of St Samuel he could not possibly return to his original Baramous Monastery.[53]

Years earlier (as we previously noted) that *same* vicar had been bedridden, having been healed in the late 1930s by Fr Mina, who at the time was still living at the windmill. Luka promised one day to repay the kindness, and that he did. In October 1946 Fr Mina received word from the patriarch. "I have received your letter," wrote Yusab II,

> in which you mentioned that you need to spend periods of time in Cairo for the monastery's benefit and that you are seeking permission to pray at the church of the Monastery of the Archangel in Old Cairo, which you have renovated while in Old Cairo. I find no objection for you to do so on a temporary basis as this will be beneficial to St Samuel's Monastery.[54]

Fr Mina went—and this is vital to see—from an occasionally public recluse at the windmill, to an accessible urban monastic in the churches of Old Cairo.[55] He finally had found some hope of stability. In the meantime, almost simultaneously, both Church and nation were edging upon revolution.

* * *

After the "Great Humiliation" of 1942 and the subsequent spurious reelection of the Wafd Party, the people of Egypt lost hope in their traditional leaders. The Muslim Brotherhood, meanwhile, had increasingly gained a foothold among the lower and middle classes. Its oppositional, factional, and reactionary nature took on a violent accent in these years; and, with the partition of Palestine in September 1947, the Brotherhood's real face emerged.[56] Mass demonstrations, anti-Semitism, political violence, and even the occasional assassination became commonplace. In December 1948, fearing a "radical threat to domestic politics," el-Nuqrashi, the Egyptian prime minister, dissolved the Brotherhood.[57] Less than three weeks later, he was assassinated. Though Hassan el-Banna, the founder and supreme guide of the Brotherhood, allegedly distanced himself (and his movement) from the act, the reaction would be swift.[58] On February 12, 1949, Banna was murdered as he awaited a taxi.[59] And, with his death, the newly emerged Brotherhood decidedly moved underground.

Weaving in between the Palace, Wafd, and Brotherhood, were the Communist and Young Egypt movements. These nonparliamentary movements, though incapable of disseminating their ideas widely, contributed to the "destabilisation of the constitutional monarchy in Egypt";[60] allowing and indeed forging an "ideological climate" in which Gamal Abdel Nasser's future revolution could thrive.[61] Experimentation with liberal democracy in Egypt was failing—and with the fall of democracy came the rise of Islamism.

A persisting identification of Copts with the despised British overlords,[62] together with a weakening Coptic presence in an already disabled Wafd Party,[63] saw the tide—headed by the Brotherhood and Young Egypt—turn once more against the Church. Already, by the end of the 1940s, Coptic anxiety was palpable. Fr Sergius (who had once championed the "Crescent and the Cross" at the pulpit of al-Azhar) began to write furiously and uncompromisingly in *al-Manarah* of the "Muslim persecution of Copts,"[64] suggesting in an increasingly inflammatory manner that Banna had been a British puppet, a "clown for rent," and, among other things, an idiot—a *himar* ("donkey").[65] The words were hardly unilateral. Both the Coptic and Muslim press frequently descended into arguments that involved "mothers, wives, and sisters."[66] Only a few years earlier, words had given way to violent action, with churches torched, Coptic businesses destroyed, and priests beaten.[67]

Witnessing this cultural and political destabilization, the reaction of many young Copts was not that of a visceral or reactionary outward-looking activism. Disillusioned by the political upheaval and burned by the searing heat of rising sectarianism, they looked to the Church—a deeply fractured, impoverished, and debilitated Church. Theirs would be a revolution—a revolution of inward healing.

* * *

"Spiritual life is weak," wrote Fr Ibrahim Luka in October 1943,

> [and] our national unity is broken. . . . Our churches have become empty, and the lambs have run away. The authority of the Church has weakened. . . . The Church has lost its glory and honor in every direction. Our issues are now subject to the scrutiny of others. Once we were a head, we have now become a tail.[68]

Another, the dean of the Theological College, was far more forthright in his analysis of the Church during the period. "If it is permissible," he lamented, "for us to describe that age, then we would call it the age of darkness, stagnation, and backwardness."[69] That dean was Habib Girgis (1876–1951).

When looking at the revival of the Coptic Church in the twentieth century, many scholars have sought to situate the inception of reform in either Fr Mina or Habib Girgis, though the reality (as we shall see) is far more intricate and complex.[70]

Born in Cairo, Girgis was reared in the Great Coptic School that was established by Cyril IV.[71] After completing his secondary education, he was one of
the first cohort to join the Theological College under the direction of Yousef
Manqarius.[72] During his final year in 1898, he was chosen to teach at the college—indicating both his academic excellence, as well as the paucity of staff—
and was formally appointed a lecturer the year after.[73] In 1918 he was eventually
made dean, a position he would hold until his death in 1951.[74]

At some point before 1912, he was ordained an archdeacon—he remained
celibate his entire life.[75] Though he is often portrayed as the model *lay*-scholar,
Wahib Attallah (the future Bishop Gregorious) recalls that Girgis hardly saw
himself as such. "After a ministry of thirty-five years in my Church, one lesson
I did not yet discern," related Girgis, ". . . I did not know that until now I was
not considered among the men of the cloth."[76] On several occasions he was in
fact nominated to the episcopacy, once even to the papacy, and, oddly, was the
only nonepiscopal member at the convening of the Holy Synod.[77] Girgis thus
held a highly unusual role in the life of the Church. "Invite our beloved [Habib
Girgis]," Cyril V was remembered as saying, "as he is a monk like us."[78] Despite
such esteem, Girgis had little time or interest for clerical rank; he was pained
by what he saw, the Church was but a shadow of her former glory. And though
reform was precariously urgent, Girgis was resolute: true reform could only be
from *within* the Church.[79]

In 1900, Girgis began gathering the children of *al-Fagallah* in central Cairo
for a simple and modest catechism, otherwise known as "Sunday School."[80]
The initial results were not promising. But it did convince him of the desperate
need for theological education and like-minded teachers.[81] He would spend
the next few decades laboring in the acquisition of funds, property, and an able
faculty, all in the hope of securing the theological education of a future generation of priests who would take the place of illiterate (and often spiritually suspect) clerical dynasties.[82] He published a theological periodical, *The Vine*, and
wrote profusely in his almost single-handed quest to "educate" a Church. Taking
the mission well beyond the borders of the college, Girgis traveled throughout
Egypt, lecturing in defense of Orthodox theology—perhaps partly in reaction to
Protestant missionaries—and always concluded with an urgent call to establish
religious instruction for youth at a grass-roots level.[83]

Girgis' movement—as it eventually became—was, to be sure, not well
received either at the parish or hierarchical levels. It was perceived as an impetuous and immature encroachment upon the authority of the established (and

almost universally uneducated) clergy, and, for the most part, was ridiculed as a waste of expenditure.[84] Despite this, by 1938 there were eighty-five branches in Cairo alone, rapidly spreading to Damanhur and Alexandria in the late 1940s.[85] A powerful movement was born after decades of lethargic progress. The Church would never be the same. "Our teacher, Archdeacon Habib Girgis," wrote one of his students (the late Pope Shenouda III),

> . . . started his life in an age which was almost void of religious education and knowledge . . . The earth was without form, and void, and darkness was on the face of the deep, as the Book of Genesis describes. Then, God said, "Let there be light," and there was light. And the light was Habib Girgis.[86]

Reform begins with light: the capacity to see things as they truly are.

* * *

As this "light" spread like fire throughout Cairo and Giza, the movement took shape. The words "Sunday School"—often mistakenly understood to be mere children's classes held after Liturgy on Sunday—hardly capture the resolve, tenacity, and almost fanatical intrepidity of this deeply countercultural movement. The mere mention of the words to the few living members of the original reformers brings a certain insurgent blaze to their eyes; education was their means of inciting grassroots ecclesial reform. It was, to be clear, an all-embracing movement. "We were very angry with the way things were in the Church," a leader of the movement recalls. "We wanted to study the old Church in order to revive the modern Church. The priests weren't preaching, they didn't visit people. . . ."[87]

Within this early Sunday School Movement (SSM), several "centers" or "schools" of thought may be discerned. Wolfram Reiss, a German scholar, has carefully noted that four distinct "baselines of reform" grew out of the dissemination of the movement: the centers of Giza, St Antony's in Shoubra, Geziret Bedran, and Archangel Michael's (also near Shoubra).[88] Certainly, it must be said, their differences were far less than their similarities, but the delineation is helpful in examining elements within the movement. We might suggest, though, that there were, in fact, two essential schools of thought—St Antony's and Giza—with the other "centers" appearing to be hybrid; Geziret Bedran, for instance, was closely aligned to the philosophy of Giza and appears to have simply adapted it to an urban setting.[89] Even then, as Tadros notes, the "lines were not always sharply drawn," with many members falling into both camps.[90]

The first center, St Antony's Church, grew out of the neighborhood of Shoubra behind the well-known "Kitchener Hospital." For various reasons an unusually high concentration of Copts was found there, one of whom was a student by the name of Zarif Abdullah Iskander who had recently arrived from Asyut in 1934.[91] In between engineering lectures at Cairo University, Zarif would hurriedly gather the neighboring young children and excite them with the stories of the saints, subtly introducing them to the beauty of their faith. A few years later—and thus after the inception of Sunday School in the area—a church was built and a priest, Fr Boutros el-Gawhary, ordained.[92] But Fr Boutros, bearing a rather ascetical worldview (especially regarding Church rites), was not so understanding of Zarif's methods.[93] A falling out in October 1936 would see Zarif leave for Giza.

Fr Boutros, harsh and brusque as he may have been, was interested in theological education and intensely fixated on pastoral care, and as such became remarkably popular.[94] Many students who accepted Boutros' "ascetic strictness" aligned themselves with him, thus giving a characteristic ascetic quality to the St Antony's movement.[95] They looked, therefore, to Antony, their patron saint, as a model par excellence. As they looked to the earliest monastic mindset, these young men quickly realized that the Church could only be reformed "from the inside out"—not by "politics, social, or sociocultural commitment, and not through a critique of the current problems of the Church, but in embracing its ancient traditions."[96] Antony's solitude, asceticism, and individual struggle for perfection—that is to say, his individual transformation—beckoned others (and the Church) to that same transformation.[97] As one of the St Antony's movement noted, this regressive orientation was the only means of arriving at an authentic vision of the Church.[98] It is no exaggeration, then, to say that this ascetic concern led to an almost "military spirit" among those in the movement.[99] Students were immersed in an atmosphere of prayer, discipline, and asceticism. Teaching, likewise, was not didactic but rather by example, founded upon a monastic model of discipleship. Only those who had been prepared for one to two years were permitted to become "servants" (youth leaders) in the SSM.[100] One illustrious student claimed that it was especially this that differentiated St Antony's from the Giza movement.[101]

Focusing on the positive transformative aspects of the Church rather than on a criticism of its current weakness was refreshing and alluring. As a result, St Antony's youth meeting eventually became the largest in Cairo.[102] One seventeen-year-old in attendance in 1940 was Nazir Gayed (the future Pope Shenouda

III), who by 1945 would be intimately involved in the St Antony's leadership. Sitting next to him were several wide-eyed youths—the future bishops Athanasius of Beni Suef (the second), Youannis of Gharbeya, Pachomious of Damanhur and Beheira, and Arsenius of Menya—as well as a host of eventual monks, nuns, and priests. It would not be amiss to follow Ragheb Abdel-Nour's suggestion: St Antony's was very much a "second seminary."[103]

* * *

The other formative center of the SSM was in Giza, at the border of Upper and Lower Egypt. There—within the diverse diocese of Giza, Qaloubiya, and Quesna—urban Egypt met the poorer, and largely illiterate, agricultural Egypt. Giza was also the location of the Fouad University, where higher education could be sought without fear of the Islamic influences as at al-Azhar in Cairo. And it is this, Reiss suggests, that gave most shape to the Giza movement: acting as something of a gateway and a hotbed of university youth—students would travel back and forth between Giza and Upper Egypt, bearing a "time-limit" of three to four years of study before heading elsewhere, creating an unusually rapid turnover of the movement.[104]

Unlike the St Antony's movement, the SSM in Giza was not influenced or shaped by existing clergy, except perhaps as a reaction. It was, Reiss claims, "barely tolerated by the local church in the early days and certainly not encouraged."[105] Beginning in 1930 with small classes on Sunday afternoons, the movement subsequently struggled.[106] Things changed, however, with the arrival of Zarif Abdullah from St Antony's in Shoubra—after the abovementioned conflict with Fr Boutros—who immediately befriended Waheeb Zaky (the future Fr Salib Suryal), and later Saad Aziz (the future Bishop Samuel).[107] In contrast to the discipline and rigor of St Antony's, Zarif's service was characterized by "a certain playful freedom."[108] He initiated Bible quizzes, played the oud ('ūd, Arabic lute) at meetings, and called not only for personal spirituality but also "communal and social cohesion."[109] It was this call that most moved the young lawyer, Saad Aziz.

The eyes, hearts, and minds of Giza, with Saad at their head, gazed outward. Rather than working on an individual as a "spiritual nucleus" within a local parish, they strove for a "total ecclesial renewal"—looking to the "unreached."[110] But as the SSM servants arrived in the villages that formed part of the "gateway" diocese to which Giza belonged, it immediately became obvious that "service" could not be confined to religious instruction. The villagers were poverty-stricken, illiterate, and in many cases totally oblivious to their faith. "Only old men attended," recalled one servant, "and it was not unusual to find a twelve-year-old child that had not even been baptized."[111] Little support, unfortunately, was to be found among the local clergy.[112] So here it remained a decidedly lay movement. Many of these university and working youth gave up to half of their salaries for the service; one (the future Fr Matta el-Meskeen) went so far as allowing servants to reach into his pharmacy's cash register should the Sunday School service require it.[113] A self-funded and rather elaborate network eventually developed. By the early 1940s there were some three hundred branches in contact with Giza, serving the majority of Upper Egypt.[114] This very same network would, shortly, be vital for *disseminating* reform.

In the villages, the traditional "backbone" of Egypt, was to be found fertile soil for renewal. And so was born the "rural *diakonia*" of Giza.[115] Whereas the St Antony movement's method was to return to the Fathers and the early Church, Giza turned to the very meaning of the Gospel itself. Rather than the intense environment of ascetic preparation, Giza sought out a more collaborative approach that was experimental and innovative, because, at least in rural Egypt, life was the "best school."[116]

* * *

A parched and desiccated Church awaited and yearned for the waters of reform. As time would eventually tell, St Antony's and Giza's philosophies—the ascetic transformation of the individual and the embrace of a total ecclesial renewal—were both necessary. During the formative years of the movements, however, these Sunday School centers had little contact or exchange and, other than certain points of individual acquaintances, were very much independently developing orientations under the watchful eye of Habib Girgis.[117] But by the late 1940s the combined force of the SSM became irrepressible. "[The SSM] is our only hope," wrote Pope Yusab II in March 1948 to the priests of Cairo, "on which we can build a new generation which is firm and steadfast in the Orthodox faith. . . ."[118] Whether or not this was a genuine sentiment—some suggested it was a means of reining in and controlling a formidable force—is secondary to the importance of the official recognition of the movement.[119] Although the declaration would mean little to the contemporary priests and bishops, it paved the way for a new wave of clergy (and even a patriarch) reared in the movement.[120]

On August 21, 1951, Habib Girgis, the founder of the Sunday School Movement, reposed. In his final days, he was still pained by what he saw: a Church still deeply divided, a theological college perpetually obstructed (on the edge of forced closure), and a body of clergy with no visible signs of reform.[121] But though the Church had not visibly changed, the ground most certainly had. When he closed his eyes, Girgis was not to know that a radical, even seismic, transformation was a mere decade away—a transformation that fed organically on the movement he founded half a century earlier. "The great teacher has failed in his reform," wrote one of his disciples in an obituary, "but he failed where shortcoming and failure are considered an honor. It was the *failure of a martyr*."[122]

St Menas' Church: The Intersection of a Movement, 1946–1950

> "When Abba Macarius received all the brethren in simplicity,
> some of them asked him why he mixed with them like this.
> He replied, 'For twelve years I served the Lord, so that he might
> grant me this *gift*, and do you all advise me to give it up?'"
>
> —St Macarius the Great

SEVERAL YEARS PASSED, and still Fr Mina was without a permanent cell; a solitary without a monastery, a wandering recluse. For the most part, he continued to occupy a small room at the Monastery of the Archangel Michael in Old Cairo.[123] There his life of urban solitude would captivate the hearts and minds of the nearby towns—and, we might add, provoke the intrigue (and resentment) of not a few hierarchs.[124]

On one memorable occasion in early 1947, between his prayers, Fr Mina took an engineer, Youssef Soryal, up to the roof of the monastery. "St Menas wants this land to build a church," he declared looking out at a neighboring property, "the owner is traveling and wants to sell it for three pounds a metre . . . expensive!"[125] Youssef recalls that he quietly mumbled to himself that Fr Mina did not have the funds to purchase even a single meter, let alone the whole 150-square-meter property (1615 square feet). A week later Youssef came to visit again. "Once he realized it was for St Menas, the owner said he would sell it for two pounds a meter," casually noted Fr Mina, and, without blinking an eye, added, ". . . one lady was there who had the money, and she paid it on the spot."[126] And so was conceived St Menas' Monastery in Old Cairo.[127]

A year later an adjoining piece of land was purchased, increasing the property to some six hundred square meters (6,458 square feet).[128] Those who had been healed (or who had loved ones healed) over the years had not forgotten the kindness of the quiet recluse.[129] Generous donations were promptly secured, and an old friend, Hanna Nessim (who had rebuilt St Samuel's), began construction.[130] The monastery was a two-story building, twenty by eight meters (65 by 26 feet), and housed a large church on the ground level that had three sanctuaries along with a few rooms for baking the *qorban* and for a caretaker to live.[131] A cell was built for Fr Mina on the top floor directly over the central sanctuary, with four other rooms on the southern side. Shortly afterwards, on the additional land, an annexed residence was built in the courtyard for boarding university students.[132]

In late 1947, St Menas' Monastery was consecrated at the hands of Metropolitans Athanasius of Beni Suef and Abraam of Giza.[133] "On this blessed day," wrote Fr Mina to his brother, Hanna, barely containing his joy,

> God looked down from the highest heaven and answered our prayers. . . . I cannot express to you the great joy that was felt by everyone. I am not exaggerating when I say that the great St Menas, St George, Abba Samuel, and foremost St Mary *participated with us*, and the angels rejoice.[134]

What did he mean by "participated with us"? And "I am not exaggerating"? Was this a guarded allusion to an apparition? It certainly was not the first time Fr Mina had made such intimations, nor would it be the last. Whatever he may have meant, the forty-five-year-old recluse was finally able to pursue that which was needful: a life of prayer in solitude—albeit in the middle of Cairo.

Each midnight, Fr Raphael Ava Mina recalls of the period, the recluse would prepare the *qorban*, chant the psalmody, celebrate Matins and the Liturgy until the early hours of morning, and then attend to the needs of the many students who had gathered around him, eventually breaking his fast at two-thirty in the afternoon, before working and cleaning until Vespers in the evening.[135] Remarkably—and this certainly must be reiterated—each and every recollection of his daily "spiritual canon" by numerous disciples, beginning from his time at the cave in the Baramous Monastery until his death, is precisely the same. Though he lived at the center of bustling Cairo, it was as though he were alone in the desert.

In fact, only *once* in over a decade is he said to have ventured outside the gates of St Menas' in Old Cairo. "I cannot remember," noted a disciple (the future Pope Shenouda III), "that he ever left that place at all, except to have surgery."[136] The reference was to an evening in which, during the psalmody, Fr Mina had fallen violently ill.[137] Recovering from the anaesthetic, having just had his appendix removed, several accounts recall the shock of the medical staff at Hermal Hospital—though in and out of consciousness, the recluse was chanting the Liturgy.[138] His canon seemingly continued uninterrupted, whether in desert or city, in church or hospital, indeed whether he was conscious or not.

* * *

Though solitude was evidently his principal concern, it appears that almost immediately Fr Mina discerned the potential of his small monastery in Old Cairo. In his mind, from what we may gather from his letters, the monastery was the "Harbor of Salvation Institute."[139] Borrowing the name from his theological periodical two decades earlier, Mina sought to create a safe harbor amid the turbulence of Cairo.

The purpose of the monastery (or institute) was fourfold: a primary level Coptic school; theological education; studies by correspondence; and a reference library.[140] Each evening he gathered the local children for Vespers, teaching them Church chant and the Coptic language, promising—with some success—a full *qorban* to those who attended Liturgy from the beginning of the service.[141] Many who prayed with him reported their delight in seeing the recluse—who, we should note, was a renowned miracle worker by this time—put a "cassock over his cassock," tuck his beard into his clothes, and roll up his sleeves so that he could properly knead the *qorban*.[142] Lectures were also held for young adults (one series being compiled into a biblical commentary), and an entire wing of the residence adjoining the monastery was devoted to vocational training— once more rousing the concerned eyes of the patriarchate.[143] But it was another of his ventures that would be far more significant and provocative.

Students had begun to flock from the provinces to Cairo (Fouad) University in the late 1940s. Fr Mina, seeing this mass exodus, established a small boarding house in the annexed residence at a near pittance. He had, one disciple claims, a single intention: to create "a shelter for their faith and chastity."[144] "As much as he was merciful and loving," notes Hanna in his memoirs, "he was firm."[145] Three conditions were placed on those students wishing to live at the monastery: a reference from their parish priest, adherence to the monastery's rules, and regular attendance at the Divine Liturgy.[146] Word spread and soon the small "monastery" was overrun. "But [Fr Mina] was never angry," recalls Abdelmessih Bishara (the future Bishop Athanasius of Beni Suef),

> or made anyone feel that there wasn't enough room for them. We used to sit in a room, writing, discussing Sunday School issues, preparing curriculums, chanting. . . . He had a large heart, fitting in the pashas, the very poor people, the sick—a large heart fitting everyone in. Those who knew him observed that he was very simple, there was nothing unusual about his lifestyle; praying, chanting the psalmody, making *qorban*, lighting the candles, talking to whoever met him. . . . A spiritual giant yet so simple. Everyone received comfort there. . . .[147]

At St Menas', the students lived as quasi-monks, sharing in the duties of the monastery, studying, receiving guidance, and witnessing, according to their accounts, almost daily supernatural occurrences. Miracles were allegedly commonplace, and exorcisms, peculiarly frequent.[148] Fr Mina lived day and night at the bidding of these students, happily being interrupted by them, relieving their burdens, and becoming to them a father.[149] "Although one of them was responsible for the kitchen duties," recalled a relative of the recluse, "Fr Mina took charge of watching out for everyone, especially that they were all fed."[150]

* * *

A distant relative of Fr Mina's was a young man from Giza by the name of Waheeb Zaky (1916–1994).[151] Since 1936, he had sought the advice of the recluse at the windmill. World War II brought about an "intensification of their relationship" when Fr Mina was forced to move to Old Cairo.[152] There, with the proximity to Giza, Waheeb could regularly visit, unknowingly setting in motion one of the most significant movements of reform the Church would ever know.

Waheeb graduated as lawyer from Cairo University, and with the arrival of Zareef Abdullah in the late 1930s, he became one of the founders of the Sunday School Movement in Giza.[153] Through Waheeb, the Sunday School leaders of Giza were introduced to Fr Mina, many of them eventually taking him as their confessor.[154] Word quickly spread, one recalled, that here was a monk "with whom one could speak openly and receive solid advice. . . . From Shoubra [i.e., St Antony's movement] many came, and his fame spread more and more, as well as from Cairo and Alexandria."[155] In all problems, personal and ecclesial, these youths turned to Fr Mina, forging a powerful spiritual connection between the recluse and the Sunday School Movement. Many lived with him, confessed with him, and in him, came to know a holy man who was *also* a member of the clergy—in their eyes, at least, something of a rarity.

In 1948, one of Fr Mina's earliest disciples, Zareef Abdullah, became the first of the movement to be nominated a priest.[156] The only issue was that he was unmarried. A suitable bride was eventually found; they were engaged on a Wednesday, married on a Thursday, and three days later, on March 7, 1948, Zareef was ordained a priest (Fr Boulos Boulos) for St George's Church in Daman-hur.[157] It was a momentous moment in the history of the movement—reform, in a sense, became "clericalized."

The bishop of Giza had initially hoped to make of it a "double-ordination" with Waheeb, but out of respect to his fiancée's family, delayed his ordination until May 30, 1948.[158] Her family did not take the ordination well; Waheeb's father-in-law refused to speak to him well into the 1980s.[159] Priesthood, it would appear, was very much frowned upon. But this meant little to Waheeb (now Fr Salib Suryal) for the movement was now part of the Church, and it was this that mattered.[160] This did not necessarily mean, however, that the hierarchy was in complete support. Fr Salib was required before ordination to sign a contract that strictly denied him any financial aid or salary from the diocese.[161] The consecration of reform entailed nothing less than radical renunciation; and uncertainty—that is, other than certain poverty.

In mid-July 1948, immediately after Fr Salib's "forty days" (a time of preparation after priesthood), a "possessed" young boy was brought to him. The episode is recounted by Salib himself and, given his standing as one of the most respected priests of the twentieth century, it has a certain enduring credibility.[162] "I tried to pray for him," recalls Fr Salib, aware that he was a new priest without the gift of exorcism. "I prayed over some water in a clay pot . . . but he broke it. . . . I tried a number of other things." "You think you're a priest," said the demon-possessed boy, "you, a priest who were only ordained yesterday—you're useless—you're trying to take me out and send me away, shush, be quiet and mind your own business!" Shocked, the new priest called a taxi, hoping to take the boy to Fr Mina in Old Cairo. As they were driving, the possessed boy shrieked, "You are going to take me to that man who will kill me. . . . [*taab he*] take this!" And with that final word, claims Fr Salib, all four tires blew at the same moment. The taxi driver could only manage to say—translated roughly—"Burn your houses! Four tires! Not one, two, or three, but four!" "We gave him money and caught another taxi," continues Salib, "and I said to the possessed boy: if you make another move"—showing him a cross—"I'll burn you with this." Arriving at St Menas' in Old Cairo, the exhausted and very much terrified Salib relayed to Fr Mina the day's events. "Don't worry, my son," Fr Mina said. At which point he began to pray for some thirty minutes.[163] Quietly, and very naturally, the boy's voice changed, and he returned to himself. Salib recalls he was petrified and began walking the boy in laps around the monastery, fearful of leaving Fr Mina in case the boy was still possessed. "Don't worry," calmly reassured Fr Mina, perhaps with the beginning of a smile, "Go home . . . nothing else will happen."[164]

A close friend of Salib, whom he also introduced to Fr Mina, was Saad Aziz (1920–1981). Joining the Giza movement in the late 1930s while completing his law degree at Cairo University, Saad became the father of the "rural *diakonia*" initiative, in which he saw the "key to the revival of the Church."[165] A selfless man, he was remembered as always seeking out the most difficult villages for his rural service.[166] After his graduation in 1941, he was denied a license to practice law (as he was younger than twenty-one), and so began a degree in social work while working at a bank. Later that year he shocked his family and friends by declaring he would become a "full-time servant"—the first of what would later be known as the "*takrees* [consecrated] movement"—and began studying theology with Waheeb (Fr Salib) under Habib Girgis.[167] During these years Saad became very close with his confessor, Fr Mina, and before long would take the second momentous step of the Sunday School Movement.

One night in early 1948, Saad told his friends—the movement in Giza would often gather at his house—that he was intent on becoming a monk.[168] His friends, shocked, decided to take him to Fr Mina, certain that he would counsel against monastic tonsure. At that time, Waheeb (still a layman) recalls, "Most of the Sunday School movement in Giza were confessing with [Fr Mina]."[169] They arrived at Old Cairo at five in the morning and caught Mina just before the Liturgy. "You know Saad wants to become a monk," bluntly started Waheeb, "and you know well how difficult this path is for an educated man." Fr Mina suddenly left them, Waheeb claims, and went into the sanctuary, kneeling before the altar. An hour later he emerged from the iconostasis: "We will tonsure him as God wills." "*We* will tonsure him?" replied a perplexed Waheeb. "Tonsure him where?" "Here, my son," Fr Mina calmly replied. "*Here*? How, Father . . . is this a monastery?" "Don't you know, my son," said the recluse, laughing, "that I am an abbot of a monastery and can tonsure monks?" And indeed, on April 14, 1948, Saad was tonsured Monk Makary by Fr Mina.[170] Makary, the first of the "Sunday School monks," would go on to become Bishop Samuel of Ecumenical and Social Services.

Waheeb's concern was, however, well placed. At that time Fr Mina was being hounded by the patriarchate as his "St Menas' Monastery," though not an officially recognized monastery, had become increasingly popular, much to the displeasure of some hierarchs.[171] Once word emerged that the recluse was tonsuring monks in the city, the highly unusual situation would come under certain scrutiny. A few months later, another young man knocked on his door also seeking monasticism, further infuriating the patriarchate.

* * *

Youssef Iskander (1919–2006) had become connected to the Giza movement while studying pharmacy at Cairo University in the early 1940s, and there, like most of those in the movement, he came under the guidance of Fr Mina. Upon graduation, he returned to Damanhur, where he operated successful pharmacies and played an instrumental role in the ordination of Zareef Abdullah (Fr Boulos Boulos). Against most scholarly claims, however, he was not, properly speaking, "part" of the Sunday School Movement. "In my youth, I did not serve at Sunday School," Iskander wrote in his autobiography, "in spite of my friendship with all those who served there, because I felt that it was sterile and artificial to teach religion in the same manner as that of civil education. This I refuse up to this day."[172] But though he may have disagreed with the movement's methods, there can be no doubt that he shared in its sense of reform and revival—and, we might add, certainly opened his cash registers to their cause.[173]

In mid-1948—the same time Zareef, Saad, and Waheeb entered their respective vocations—Iskander arrived from Damanhur at St Menas' in Old Cairo.[174] He had not come for a retreat. He relayed that he had just sold his pharmacies and brought the proceeds as a donation to aid Fr Mina in his projects. "If you want to follow Christ," Fr Mina replied, "leave everything and come and follow him. Distribute your money as you want. *Come poor*; owe nothing. Taste the sweetness of the voluntary poverty so you can feel the richness of Christ."[175] Iskander obeyed; "he returned poor, having nothing."[176] Fr Mina's concern was not to build, nor even to accomplish social work, but rather spiritual formation. It was also a lesson for the young novice to relinquish control—a struggle that would remain for some time.

"I was confronted," wrote Iskander in his autobiography,

> since the beginning of my entry, during the monastic test, by the head of the monastery [i.e., Fr Mina], in his attempt to keep me in Cairo. He frequently summoned me for people from all classes and nationalities to meet me

desiring that I should stay with him to serve with him, while our departure
to the monastery [of St Samuel] was only for the blessing. I strongly refused,
saying that I wanted to be tonsured in the monastery [of St Samuel], for the
monastery, and not leave it. It was the beginning of a conflict that increased
and became ramified later.[177]

For three months he kept asking the recluse when he would send him off to the
desert. Eventually, Fr Mina gave in, and Iskander was tonsured Monk Matta
el-Samuely—eventually known as the famed Fr Matta el-Meskeen.[178] Matta
would defy Fr Mina time and time again over the next three decades. It appears,
however, from this and other accounts that Fr Mina held genuine concerns
for the young man among the illiterate (and perhaps contentious) monks of
St Samuel.[179] With these two monastic disciples—even though one was rather
unruly—Fr Mina laid the foundations of monastic reform, and therein, episcopal reform.

A few years later he would ask those two disciples (Makary and Matta) to
move to the Syrian Monastery in Wadi al-Natrun.[180] During the next decade, he
would send many to join them. The abbot and bishop of the monastery, Theophilus (1908–1989), was something of a trickster, and though only having completed secondary education, was "exceptionally broad-minded."[181] Ordained
a bishop in July 1948, he was the first to esteem education and wholeheart-
edly opened his monastery's gates to the new generation of educated monks
and in doing so was "instrumental to monastic reform."[182] By 1956, at least ten
other members of the Sunday School Movement would be directed to the Syrian Monastery.[183] But even there in the desert, they would look to the recluse,
at one low point even leaving their monastic enclosure to seek shelter with him
in Old Cairo.[184]

"We considered ourselves as his children," said one of these monks. "We
would go and seek his guidance during challenging times."[185] These words were
spoken by the foremost among them, Nazir Gayed (1923–2012), who entered
the Syrian Monastery in July 1954. Years earlier, after graduating with degrees
in history and theology, he too had been a disciple of Fr Mina.[186] Many at St
Antony's in Shoubra had followed those of Giza in taking the recluse as their
confessor. "I knew [him]," recalls Gayed, "in 1948 when I used to attend the
church in Old Cairo. I ended up living with him to enjoy his Liturgies, prayers,
care, and guidance in that beautiful environment at St Menas." "He had a strong
personality," continues Gayed. "Everyone revered him; his awe and love overwhelmed whoever met him."[187] From 1950 to 1951, Gayed lived at St Menas' in

Old Cairo after resigning from secular employment and taking up a full-time lecturing position at the Theological College.[188] He would go on to become Fr Mina's most illustrious disciple, living for several years as a hermit in solitude, before eventually becoming, himself, a future patriarch (Shenouda III).

These were some of the many young men who came under the discipleship of Fr Mina at St Menas' Monastery in Old Cairo. Numbered among them stood not a few bishops: Waheeb Atallah, the future Bishop Gregorious (1919–2001), who, as a teenager, climbed the mountain to Fr Mina's windmill to "sit at his feet";[189] Abdelmessih Bishara, the future Bishop Athanasius of Beni Suef (1923–2000); Michael Khalil, the future Bishop Domadius of Giza (1925–2011); and Soliman Rizk, the future Bishop Mina (1923–1996) who would be entrusted with St Menas' Monastery at Mariout—to name a handful.[190] Another, and by no means less influential, was a police clerk who, after spending three years with Fr Mina, was ordained a priest at the age of fifty-two: Fr Mikhail Ibrahim (1899–1975). In later years, a line of bishops would often be seen at Ibrahim's door, sitting nervously, while they waited for the elderly priest to hear their confession.[191]

* * *

Within a single decade under that peculiar roof of St Menas' Monastery in Old Cairo was to be found—almost without exception—*every* reforming voice of the Coptic Church in the twentieth century. It was, and this is no exaggeration, the embryo of reform, a "model for the new era."[192]

In that unassuming church, Fr Mina modeled a rare and radical monastic ideal, an ascetic lifestyle that was just as radically open to the intellectual aspirations of the present age.[193] He was, in the words of Shenouda III, an "intermediary between the old generation and the new,"[194] exemplifying the reconciliation between a progressive laity and conservative clergy. He had found a place for fervent youth, "for whom there was no place yet in the existing monasteries,"[195] carving out a "harbor of salvation" in a Church that at the time saw no need for them and had not the faintest desire to accommodate them. At no point, it must be said, did the quiet recluse actively seek out candidates for the consecrated life (nor, presumably, did he have any intention of reform); rather, these young men came to him. "Young intellectuals surrounded him," comments a French historian. "They recognized themselves in him."[196]

Fr Mina's life of solitude, transformative ascesis, and, in the words of Samuel Rubenson, "utter lack of compromise" would leave a profound mark upon clerical life.[197] The significance can hardly be overstated. In a matter of only a few years St Menas' in Old Cairo, through Fr Mina (the confessor of so many of its members), had inspired the Sunday School Movement to enter the clerical ranks. Here at St Menas', a host of lay servants, priests, monks, abbots, bishops, metropolitans, and two patriarchs, no less, were to be found. The seeds once planted by Habib Girgis, and now nourished, directed, and empowered by Fr Mina, would literally, in the space of a decade, take Egypt by storm. Here, the Giza and Shoubra movements would converge. Here, in a very real sense—both literally and figuratively—Fr Mina became the confessor of the Sunday School Movement. Here, under that one very peculiar roof, he became the *confessor of reform* itself.

Desert as a State of Mind: An Urban Monastic, 1950–1959

> "Indeed," said the monks to the patriarch of Alexandria,
> "when we look at you, it is as if we look upon Christ. . . ."
> —*Life of Pachomius*

EGYPT IN THE EARLY 1950s was at the capricious threshold of revolution. A king would be overthrown, constitutional monarchy abolished, and the British finally evicted. A revolution is not, however, always a re-*formation*. "Violent, sudden, and calamitous revolutions," warns the eloquent David Bentley Hart,

> are the ones that accomplish the least. While they may succeed at radically reordering societies, they usually cannot transform cultures. They may excel at destroying the past, but they are generally impotent to create a future. The revolutions that genuinely alter human reality at the deepest levels—the only real revolutions, that is to say—are those that first convert minds and wills, that reshape the imagination and reorient desire, that *overthrow tyrannies within the soul*.[198]

At play in the quaint Monastery of St Menas in Old Cairo was a revolution of the latter sort: "gradual, subtle, exceedingly small and somewhat inchoate at first"—like the revolution of Christianity in its first centuries—"slowly introducing its vision of divine, cosmic, and human reality into the culture around it, often by *deeds* rather than words. . . ."[199] There is perhaps no more apt description (albeit written of a far more momentous though intimately related revolution) of these years at St Menas'. Surprisingly, nothing especially significant is recorded of the period other than the miracles which by now had become somewhat "normative" for those dwelling in and around the monastery. Indeed, most sources appear to follow the voluntary silence of Fr Mina during this decade, and pointedly pass over these years with few words, if any at all.[200] It may be suggested, however, that if the years at the windmill were, as many contend, the most formative of his life, then these years at St Menas' were the most formative in the life of the *Church*.

* * *

What happens in the desert does not stay in the desert. The revolution quietly taking hold in Old Cairo first began as a life of *ascesis* in a cave of the Baramous Monastery two decades earlier. But can such ascesis, solitude, and monasticism be lived authentically *outside* the desert?

It appears so. "Do not be in a hurry to multiply monks," wrote St Tikhon of Zadonsk to the Russian ecclesial authorities. "The black habit does not save. The one who wears a white habit, the clothing of an ordinary person, and has the spirit of obedience, humility and purity, that one is an untonsured monk, one of *interiorized monasticism*."[201] "Let us seek after the desert," urges John Chrysostom, "not only that of the place but also that of the *disposition*."[202] For Clement of Alexandria the true seeker of knowledge (*gnōstikos*) "lives in the city as in a desert,"[203] whereas for the Cappadocian Fathers monastic withdrawal (*anachōresis*) meant the liberation of the soul; an internal disposition of detachment irrespective of the landscape.[204] "It is possible," concludes a perceptive desert mother, Amma Syncletica, "to be a solitary in one's mind while living in a crowd, and it is possible for one who is a solitary to live in the crowd of his own thoughts."[205] Solitude, in other words, necessitates withdrawal from society—the cultivation of the desert as a state of mind.

Though classically this has meant physical withdrawal into a desolate place, it may also take the shape of "social withdrawal"—for instance, in feigning madness,[206] or more commonly, in an "interior withdrawal," an inner solitude, whereby one is physically and socially present, and yet is interiorly alone. It is the latter that makes sense of Fr Mina. As an urban monastic, he revealed to the young men that gathered around him a "pattern": that of interiorized monasticism, inhabiting the desert as a state of mind.[207] And these young men in "white habits"—to adopt the words of St Tikhon once more—would one day become the "black habits" of ecclesial reform.

One of these university students was Abdelmessih Bishara (1923–2000), who would go on to become the future Bishop Athanasius of Beni Suef. He grants us a rare glimpse of these years that have for the most part been forgotten. At that time many of these young men came to Fr Mina disenchanted and hurt, but he characteristically refused to hear their criticisms of other priests. "If anyone of us complained," Abdelmessih recalls, "[Fr Mina] used to say, 'You want to pray at a church, here is a church, pray.'"[208] He had little time to dwell on negatives. It was this attitude that most marked Fr Mina's capacity as a confessor. "I personally remember," continues Abdelmessih,

> that I could go to him any time . . . whenever I felt worn out I ran to him; he was my confession father. He never let one leave depressed but rather only having hope. [In confession], he would look to the ground and quote sayings of the saints, mingling them with familiar words of wisdom and the Scriptures. . . . He encouraged us to develop our gifts; each according to our strengths, not developing one style and obliterating another, but rather encouraging each person according to his personal inclination. He had a remarkable capacity to encourage. . . . He embraced and uplifted people. We used to go to him burdened and threw everything on him; and he carried us with a smile, peace, and power.[209]

As a confessor to these university students—many of whom would become leading lights in the Church—Fr Mina sought to cultivate spiritual freedom. Never did he create in his own image. Though he was certainly excruciatingly strict on himself, his only concern for these young men was that they would live for God, whatever direction that path would take. "In our confessions," Abdelmessih reminisces,

> he was never overbearing with the canon; all his spiritual canons were moderate. . . . He gave freedom; for one he would instruct him in short prayers, "O my Lord Jesus Christ have mercy upon me," for another who liked to pray the *agpeya* [canonical] prayers he would instruct him to do so. [Fr Mina] would remove conceit and complexes from a person, by showing him how to live in simplicity. He didn't overburden people with more than what the Church recommends. . . . He who loved hymns would be with him day and night chanting, he who loved the Holy Bible would study it day and night, he who

loved psalmody would praise day and night, he encouraged those who loved
to serve . . . supporting them with supplies and money. He used to give us
money for the Sunday School service and for the area of Old Cairo. . . .[210]

For the young men who lived at St Menas', this was something unlike anything
they had ever seen. It was in a very real sense the incarnation of something lost.
Fr Mina was a famed miracle-worker and holy man, and yet here he was caring
for each one of them.

The once glorious figures of holiness that leapt from the pages of the early
monastic literature (which the Sunday School Movement had discovered but
thought to be no more) was here before them in the person of Fr Mina. It was—
and this is no mild suggestion—the rediscovery not only of a "pattern" of holiness, but even more of their identity. It has been said that the Sunday School
Movement was an awakening and reaction to the loss of the historical roots of
the Coptic identity.[211] If that is true, then here, in Old Cairo, was that identity
in flesh and blood.

* * *

In the desert literature—for instance, the life of Antony—when the "holy man"
emerged from solitude, he was clothed with definitive "otherness."[212] Surrounding the "holy man" was an aura; one that instilled fear, and yet, at once, attracted
with "a power greater than any eros, any desire, or passion of human knowing."[213] This otherness also had the piercing capacity to challenge traditional
structures of authority and privilege. It was, in short, "socially, theologically, and
politically, subversive."[214] Whether intentional or not, premeditated or not, Fr
Mina would be perceived as such by the established clergy, hierarchy, and even
the patriarchate.

Various accounts indicate that the recluse was met during these years in
Old Cairo with "many hardships and excessive persecution."[215] Though the
fact is largely unknown to the faithful today, Fr Mina had powerful detractors.
Working among the young students with programs in vocational training and
education—"tasks that the hierarchy should have undertaken"—he provoked
many of the established clergy.[216]

Again, as in Helwan during his days at the Theological College, Fr Mina's
celebration of a daily Liturgy of the Eucharist became divisive. Soon a charge
of "heresy" was leveled at him by some who were fundamentally (and theologically) mistaken, because he celebrated the Liturgy on a Saturday. "What is
Saturday?" a renowned hegumen by the name of Youssef Asaad, recalls being

asked by Fr Mina. "A holiday [i.e., 'day of rest']," Asaad replied. "And where do we find our rest?" Asaad was silent. "Of course, in our Lord," continued Mina, "so if we pray a Liturgy are we being heretics?"[217]

Most irritating to the patriarchate was Fr Mina's practice of tonsuring monks—*outside* the monastery. Fr Salib Suryal well remembers his fear when Saad Aziz (the future Bishop Samuel) was tonsured at St Menas' in Old Cairo. "Look, we didn't come here to inflame the issues," Salib recalls saying, "we know there are problems between you and the patriarchate."[218] The patriarchate had, in fact, become enraged on hearing that Fr Mina was tonsuring in the city and attempted to instigate his eviction from Cairo.[219] Interestingly, Salib goes on to situate the blame on a certain Melek—the right-hand man of the patriarch and a dark figure we shall soon meet—who had been agitating against Fr Mina ever since he began construction of St Menas' in 1947.[220]

Words soon gave way to action. As Fr Mina's popularity increased, Hanna claims, so too did their envy.[221] At some point in 1949, a move was made by the patriarchate to seize St Menas' Church in Old Cairo and make it a dependency of the Baramous Monastery.[222] "When we issued our decree," wrote Pope Yusab II to Bishop Athanasius of Beni Suef and Bishop Macarius of the Baramous Monastery on January 26, 1949,

> to appoint Fr Mina el-Baramousy as an Abbot for St Samuel's Monastery . . . the decree of appointment was restricted to supervising the affairs of this monastery, caring for our sons the monks who visit it, and working towards maintaining its buildings and church. But unfortunately, this monk *exceeded* these boundaries . . . and he has tonsured monks [outside the monastery] . . . although he was warned. We have received letters from our brothers the abbots and heads of the monasteries objecting to the behavior of that monk. . . .[223]

Though Fr Mina had later attempted to tonsure at the Monastery of St Samuel (where he was still abbot) instead of St Menas' in Old Cairo, Yusab decreed that it *too* was not an officially recognized monastery, nor would the Synod recognize the monasticism of anyone tonsured outside of the "canonical" monasteries. Finally, the letter concluded with a command for the bishops to remove Fr Mina:

> Please take the necessary measures to let Fr Mina el-Baramousy and whoever is in St Samuel's Monastery know. . . . We ask Fr Mina to return to his monastery (Baramous) as before, and our beloved spiritual brother Bishop

Athanasius . . . to take the necessary measures to protect the monastery, which is part of his diocese.[224]

Metropolitan Athanasius of Beni Suef was livid when he received the letter. "Just leave [Fr Mina] alone," Athanasius is remembered as replying to the patriarchate. "The man is minding his own business—you mind your own, and let him mind his own. . . . Why are you giving him grief?"[225] Fortunately, some rather influential friends, Kamal Rizq and Helmy Yacoub Makari, were able to intervene and prevent the execution of the decree.[226]

Things would escalate further on a later occasion, with an attempt to kidnap Fr Mina—allegedly the work of some *within* the patriarchate—only just being foiled.[227] Years later, in his bid to rebuild the monastery at Mariout, Mina wrote a carefully worded letter making a specific request that all of the monastery's assets be registered under the monastery's name itself (and, implicitly, not under the patriarchate), "since the ambitious greed of *other directions* has been so clear."[228] For Fr Raphael Ava Mina, the intent of this pestering harassment was all but clear: "to stop his activities . . . and restrain his movements."[229]

* * *

"The saint is a medicine because he is an antidote," wrote G. K. Chesterton,

> . . . indeed, that is why the saint is often a martyr, he is *mistaken for a poison* because he is an antidote. He will generally be found restoring the world to sanity by exaggerating whatever the world neglects, which is by no means always the same element in every age.[230]

"It is the paradox of history," Chesterton continues, "that each generation is converted by the saint who contradicts it most."[231] Fr Mina's urban monasticism stands at the very center of this conversion in modern-day Egypt. The Church and society that was clamoring for modernism by way of revolution were healed by the one who most contradicted it—a monk providentially forced into the public eye; a monk who sought to be small, quiet, hidden, and unknown.

Amid this decade of ecclesial and national turbulence, his life of solitude in an "internalized desert" persisted without interruption. Notwithstanding the patriarchate's tiresome persecution, these years were formative in the life of the Church: the way of interiorized urban monasticism infiltrated the clerical ranks. Whatever he may have suffered, Fr Mina's words (spoken in later years as patriarch) betray his consummate joy during this decade: "I write to you from

St Menas' in Old Cairo . . . my soul longs for the cell in which we spent many years; *they were the best years*."[232]

Notes

[1]The 1936 treaty continued that of 1922 but added three concessions to Egypt: the treaty would continue for twenty years; the British would be limited to ten thousand men stationed away from population centers; and Egypt would obtain membership in the League of Nations. For a history and analysis of the treaty, see Vatikiotis, *The History of Egypt*, 291–92.

[2]Tignor, *Egypt: A Short History*, 251.

[3]Ibid.

[4]Selma Botman, "The Liberal Age, 1923–1952," in *The Cambridge History of Egypt: Modern Egypt, from 1517 to the End of the Twentieth Century*, ed. M. W. Daly (Cambridge: Cambridge University Press, 1998), 300. Also see Vatikiotis, *The History of Egypt*, 347–49.

[5]Watson, "Abba Kyrillos," 14, n. 15.

[6]On the value of *epistolography*, see Claudia Rapp, " 'For Next to God, You Are My Salvation': Reflections on the Rise of the Holy Man in Late Antiquity," in *The Cult of Saints in Late Antiquity and the Middle Ages: Essays on the Contribution of Peter Brown*, ed. James Howard-Johnston and Paul Antony Hayward (New York: Oxford University Press, 1999), 67.

[7]For instance, see Atta and Raphael Ava Mina, *Life of Pope Kyrillos*, 15; Nasr, *Readings in the Life of Abouna Mina*, 51; Zaklama, *Pope Kyrillos VI*, 1:138; al-Masri, *Story of the Coptic Church*, 7:23. Atta claims that "Fr Mina was obliged to obey [the appointment to St Samuel's], even though he did not want to leave his cell at the windmill"; whereas Nasr (like most English sources) suggests that he spent a short period at the churches in Old Cairo before leaving for St Samuel's in 1942.

[8]This occurred in 1943; see Fr Mina the Recluse [Kyrillos VI], "Letter to Habib Pasha el-Masri, June 28, 1943" [in Arabic], in FRC-1: Letter 327 (Alexandria, 1943). Also see Mina's letter to Mounir Shoukry: "You have to know, my dear son, that in 1943 I came to Alexandria and met the late Banoub Habashy and presented to him the idea of praying the Liturgies and living at St Menas' Monastery. He was exceedingly glad and approached the manager of the Antiquities . . . but *God's will did not permit it* to happen at that time . . ." Hegumen Mina the Recluse [Kyrillos VI], "Letter to Mounir Shoukry, March 5, 1958" [in Arabic] (Old Cairo: 1958). The letter is cited in Raphael Ava Mina, *Memories: Part 2*, 44–45. Also see Hegumen Mina the Recluse [Kyrillos VI], "Letter to Hanna Youssef Atta, March 5, 1958" [in Arabic], in FRC-1: Letter 511 (Old Cairo, 1958).

[9]Al-Masri, *Story of the Coptic Church*, 7:24. I. H. al-Masri suggests that her father even wrote a letter in support of Fr Mina's petition to rebuild St Menas' Monastery, but the British denied access on account of their military operations in the area.

[10]Anonymous, *Pope Kyrillos VI: School of Virtue* (Cairo: Sons of Pope Kyrillos VI, undated), 46. It is difficult to tell whether this occurred after the first or second eviction from the windmill. Many surrounding priests were displeased with his presence and popularity; perhaps this accounted for his sleeping on the pavement outside a parish as they closed doors to him; Samuel Tawadros el-Syriany, *The History of the Popes*, 172.

[11]Meinardus, *Two Thousand Years*, 192–93; Samuel Tawadros el-Syriany, *The History of the Popes*, 172.

[12]Meinardus, *Two Thousand Years*, 192.

[13]Al-Masri, *Story of the Coptic Church*, 7:85–91, 94–98.

[14]Atta and Raphael Ava Mina, *Life of Pope Kyrillos*, 15.

[15]Fr Mina the Recluse [Kyrillos VI], "Letter to Hanna Youssef Atta, December 24, 1943" [in Arabic], in RC-2: Letter 70 (Old Cairo, 1943). There is a Gregorian date written on the letter in another pen (and perhaps handwriting), which is 1944, but the Coptic date in Fr Mina's handwriting (and pen) corresponds to 1943 in the Gregorian calendar. Also 1943, we should add, is in keeping with Metropolitan Athanasius' letter concerning the appointment that same month; see Metropolitan Athanasius, "Letter

to Hanna Youssef Atta, December 17, 1943" [in Arabic], in RC-2: Letter 1 (1943). This is a constant issue throughout his early letters to his brother Hanna (a Coptic date in Mina's handwriting, and an overlying Gregorian date in possibly another hand), which means many of the letters have two dates that often differ by a year—no doubt because of the confusion in Fr Mina's use of the Coptic calendar.

[16]Mina el-Baramousy [Kyrillos VI], "Letter to Hanna Youssef Atta, January 17, 1929."

[17]For instance, see Mina el-Baramousy [Kyrillos VI], "Letter to Hanna Youssef Atta, December 24, 1933."

[18]Letters from Metropolitan Athanasius to Fr Mina, and Fr Mina to Hanna are here revealing. Fr Mina had written to Athanasius requesting the priesthood ordination of Mina "the Younger"; Athanasius in turn stated he would do so on the following Friday (March 16, 1945) but would *also* elevate Fr Mina the Recluse as hegumen on the same occasion—as well as indicating the ordination took place at the "bishopric in Beni-Suef" and not at the Monastery of St Samuel as is routinely claimed. See Metropolitan Athanasius, "Letter to Fr Mina el-Baramousy, March 12, 1945" [in Arabic], in SSC: Letter 7 (Beni Suef, 1945); Hegumen Mina the Recluse [Kyrillos VI], "Letter to Hanna Youssef Atta, undated, March ?1945" [in Arabic], in RC-2: Letter 30 (St Samuel's Monastery, undated). We should note that both letters have unclear writing as to the year, but it may be suggested to be 1945, given the letters all bear the appellation "Hegumen Mina" rather than "Fr Mina" *only* after late March 1945.

[19]Atta and Raphael Ava Mina, *Life of Pope Kyrillos*, 15; Nasr, *Readings in the Life of Abouna Mina*, 52; al-Masri, *Story of the Coptic Church*, 7:23. All sources mistakenly follow Hanna on this, with I. H. al-Masri adding that the elevation to Hegumen took place at the consecration of the Church of St Mary at al-Zora circa 1945.

[20]The earliest mention or use of that title was in fact a few months earlier; Mina the Recluse [Kyrillos VI], "Letter to Habib Pasha el-Masri, June 28, 1943."

[21]Rene-Georges Coquin, Maurice Martin, and Peter Grossmann, "Dayr Anba Samu'il of Qalamun," in *CE*, 758a.

[22]For a brief biography, see Meinardus, *Monks and Monasteries (1989)*, 144–46.

[23]Ibid., 146.

[24]Beadmell states that in his 1899 visit there were "five or six persons" inhabiting the monastery; see H. J. L. Beadnell, *The Topography and Geology of the Fayum Province of Egypt* (Cairo: National Printing Department, 1905). Meinardus writes of what he learned from the monks: "I was told that after many years of desolation, the monastery was reinhabited in 1896 by Abuna Ishaq el-Baramusi and ten other monks who had come from the Wadi al-Natrun monasteries. In 1882, Abuna Ishaq al-Baramusi had entered the Monastery of al-Baramus. Dissatisfied with certain matters concerning the ascetic discipline in the Wadi al-Natrun, he gathered around himself several monks with whom he went to the mountain of al-Qalamun, where he and his disciples reinhabited the ruined Monastery of St. Samuel." See Meinardus, *Monks and Monasteries (1989)*, 151.

[25]Johann Georg cited in Meinardus, *Monks and Monasteries (1989)*, 150.

[26]Ahmed Fakhry, "The Monastery of Kalamoun," *Annales du Service des Antiquités de l'Égypte* 46 (1947): 72.

[27]It is unclear which monk is referred to in Metropolitan Athanasius' letter of December 29, 1943; but it may be presumed the monk had some role in the leadership of the monastery. According to the monastery's records, Fr Awad Mikhail served as abbot from 1938 to 1942. Interestingly there is no mention of him by Ahmed Fakhry—though perhaps he is the "Fr Mikhail" that Fakhry names. There was in fact another abbot between 1942 and 1943, a certain Ibrahim. It is conceivable he is the monk in question, as there were severe issues with his leadership—indeed, his name has been all but wiped from the memory of the monastery, according to several monks from St Samuel's who preferred anonymity.

[28]Metropolitan Athanasius, "Letter to Fr Mina el-Baramousy, December 29, 1943" [in Arabic] (1943).

[29]Also Fr Mina the Recluse [Kyrillos VI], "Letter to Fr Mina el-Samuely [the Younger], February 5, 1944" [in Arabic], in FRC-2: Letter 13 (Qalamoun Mountain: 1944). Fr Mina writes, "Move Anba Samuel, tell him, 'You are the one responsible for the issue of electing the patriarch, because the date is due, February 4, the situation is very bad, may the Lord have mercy upon us, that's all.'"

[30]This, it seems to me, makes far more sense of Athanasius' appointment of Fr Mina as abbot than another theory suggested by some scholars. Mark Gruber, for instance, hazards that his appointment to an isolated monastery was a "means of placating the charismatic monk, while distancing him from the public." See Gruber, "Sacrifice in the Desert," 149. This seems exceedingly unlikely for a number of reasons: the appointment came from Athanasius himself, who was keen on rebuilding and reviving a monastery in his diocese; Athanasius would later nominate Fr Mina to the papacy; and finally, Fr Mina was yet to cause any contention in Cairo (though he would some years later). It appears this mistaken claim has retrojected later contentions onto an earlier event. Furthermore, the claim ignores the important relationship of the Baramous Monastery to St Samuel's. In 1896 the monastery was reinhabited by a group of disaffected monks from the Baramous monastery. For this see Meinardus, *Monks and Monasteries (1989)*, 151. Furthermore, a number of monks from the Baramous, including for instance Fr Matias el-Barmousy, had spent part of their monastic sojourn at St Samuel's; see Habib, *Among the Fathers*, 26–28. It was therefore natural and in line with this history for Metropolitan Athanasius to appoint Fr Mina, a monk from the Baramous Monastery, as the abbot.

[31]Atta and Raphael Ava Mina, *Life of Pope Kyrillos*, 15.

[32]Ibid.

[33]Fr Mina the Recluse [Kyrillos VI], "Letter to Hanna Youssef Atta, January 20, 1944" [in Arabic], in RC-2: Letter 42 (1944).

[34]Raphael Ava Mina, *Memories: Part 2*, 69.

[35]Atta and Raphael Ava Mina, *Life of Pope Kyrillos*, 15; van Doorn-Harder, *Modern Coptic Papacy*, 133; Zaklama, *Pope Kyrillos VI*, 1:138–39.

[36]Atta and Raphael Ava Mina, *Life of Pope Kyrillos*, 15.

[37]Ibid. Also see Hegumen Mina the Recluse [Kyrillos VI], "Letter to Hanna Youssef Atta, August 7, 1945" [in Arabic], in RC-2: Letter 69 (1945).

[38]Atta and Raphael Ava Mina, *Life of Pope Kyrillos*, 15.

[39]Though Voile suggests that Fr Mina stayed at St Samuel's for only a few weeks in total, this is in fact inaccurate, for he stayed at least a few weeks initially, and at least twenty-nine days (he had already been there for fifteen days and would stay until the end of the fast of St Mary) at Qalamoun in August 1944, and he visited regularly. See Voile, *Les Coptes d'Égypte*, 200. In the Coptic tradition the fast of St Mary runs from August 7 to August 21 and precedes the Feast of the Dormition on August 22.

[40]Nasr, *Readings in the Life of Abouna Mina*, 52.

[41]Hegumen Mina the Recluse [Kyrillos VI], "Letter to the Monks at the Monastery of Saint Samuel, January 7, 1950" [in Arabic], in FRC-1: Letter 429 (Old Cairo: 1950).

[42]Ibid.

[43]For instance, see Hegumen Mina the Recluse [Kyrillos VI], "Letter to Monk Makary el-Samuely, January 11, 1950" [in Arabic], in FRC-1: Letter 438 (Old Cairo, 1950).

[44]For instance, see Fr Matta el-Samuely, "Letter to Hegumen Mina el-Baramousy, undated, ?1950" [in Arabic], in SSC: Letter 17 (St Samuel Monastery: 1950).

[45]Year by year, the monastery under his leadership grew in vocations and holiness. By 1955, a visiting Franciscan theologian, Fr Gabriele Giamberardini, noted that were at least thirteen monks; his account is cited in Meinardus, *Monks and Monasteries (1989)*, 150. Interestingly, Hegumen Raphael was still there and remarked to the visitor that he had been living at the Qalamoun Mountain for thirty-three years. Giamberardini noted that upon entering the gates of the monastery, he was welcomed by a singing "blind old monk" (the saintly Fr Andrawes el-Samuely).

[46]Nasr, *Readings in the Life of Abouna Mina*, 52.

[47]See notes 137 and 138 on p. 149.

[48]Atta, "Personal Correspondence, March 5, 2015." Fr Mina wrote to his brother in June 1945 that he was planning to travel to Alexandria "soon." See Hegumen Mina the Recluse [Kyrillos VI], "Letter to Hanna Youssef Atta, June 18, 1945" [in Arabic], in RC-2: Letter 54 (1945).

[49]Atta and Raphael Ava Mina, *Life of Pope Kyrillos*, 16. By November 1945 he would write to his brother from the Monastery of Archangel Michael in Old Cairo; Hegumen Mina the Recluse [Kyrillos VI], "Letter to Hanna Youssef Atta, November 1, 1945" [in Arabic], in RC-2: Letter 55 (Old Cairo, 1945).

In that intriguing letter, Fr Mina writes that he heard Hanna's wife was in the hospital for an operation, and so he sat in front of icons of St Menas and St Samuel until they "assured him of their intercession."

[50]Pope Yusab II, "Letter to Hegumen Mina el-Baramousy, October 18, 1946" [in Arabic], in FRC-1: Letter 199 (Cairo: 1946). Also see al-Masri, *True Story of Christianity in Egypt*, 2:435. Meinardus (and Wakin) suggest that he stayed in a room nearby the churches of Archangel Michael and St Theodore the Eastern; see Meinardus, *Monks and Monasteries (1961)*, 158; Wakin, *A Lonely Minority*, 111.

[51]Fr Mina the Recluse [Kyrillos VI], "Letter to Hanna Youssef Atta, February 25, 1945" [in Arabic], in RC-2: Letter 61 (Old Cairo, 1945). Later in the letter he writes that it was not yet official and that he would still try to escape. Another letter, a week later, suggests that he eventually accepted: "I could not convince the patriarch and he insisted that I should go to Abu Sefein Monastery, and that whenever I am in Cairo I should go once a week, and when I am at the monastery I should come once a month. Anyway, the peace of the Lord be on the great martyr Abu Sefein, perhaps he wants to join the faction of St Menas." See Fr Mina the Recluse [Kyrillos VI], "Letter to Hanna Youssef Atta, March 2, 1945" [in Arabic], in RC-2: Letter 68 (Old Cairo: 1945). The letter has an unclear numeral after "194[. . .]," but most likely is 1945. To confuse matters further it also has another date written by another hand stating "1942," yet refers to him residing at both the "monastery" and at "Cairo," and is signed as "Father" not "Hegumen." The mix of details is in keeping with others in 1945.

[52]Fr Samuel Tawadros el-Syriany dates the decree as May 26, 1946. In his account, Yusab sought to "force" his opponent Fr Dawood el-Makary to leave Cairo; see Samuel Tawadros el-Syriany, *The History of the Popes*, 180. This appears to have been a remedy to an unusual dilemma; recent graduates from the Theological College were unable to be ordained as priests, as monks (outside of their monasteries) had filled many of the vacancies in urban Egypt. Though Atta does not date the decree he places it before the consecration of St Menas' Church in Old Cairo in 1948, see Atta and Raphael Ava Mina, *Life of Pope Kyrillos*, 16.

[53]Atta and Raphael Ava Mina, *Life of Pope Kyrillos*, 16. We should note that this appeal was necessary given that the Monastery of St Samuel was yet to become a recognized monastery. In July 1946, he requested official permission to pray in Old Cairo at the Monastery of Archangel Michael; see Hegumen Mina the Recluse [Kyrillos VI], "Letter to Hanna Youssef Atta, July 6, 1946" [in Arabic], in RC-2: Letter 4 (St Samuel's Monastery: 1946).

[54]Yusab II, "Letter to Hegumen Mina el-Baramousy, October 18, 1946."

[55]A fascinating letter of December 1946, states that some were criticizing Fr Mina for using the title, "the Recluse," whereas now he was in Old Cairo as a "remote abbot" and confessor of the Abu Sefein convent; as such he requested his brother to publish in *al-Ahram* a short tract stating he would use the name "Hegumen Mina Youssef" to placate his critics, "*until* he goes back to the life of solitude after finishing his existing service." See Hegumen Mina the Recluse [Kyrillos VI], "Letter to Hanna Youssef Atta, December, 1946" [in Arabic], in RC-2: Letter 11 (Old Cairo, 1946).

[56]Botman, "The Liberal Age," 301.

[57]Ibid., 305.

[58]Richard P. Mitchell, *The Society of the Muslim Brothers* (Oxford: Oxford University Press, 1993), 68–69.

[59]Ibid., 71.

[60]Botman, "The Liberal Age," 302.

[61]Ibid.

[62]Carter suggests that paradoxically "the British presence in Egypt was both a restraint and an encouragement of Muslim hostility to Copts." But the British "disinclination to act after 1936," merely left the British presence as a constant source of provocation—especially for the Muslim identification of Copts with the British. See Carter, *The Copts in Egyptian Politics*, 79.

[63]Pennington, "The Copts in Modern Egypt," 161. Embroiled in the rapid weakening of the Wafd was the party's secretary-general, Makram Ebeid. Though remembered by such slogans as an "uninterested spectator in Coptic affairs," and a "Copt by religion, a Muslim by fatherland," and certainly never seeing himself as a "Coptic voice," his fall from power was seen popularly (by Copts and Muslims) as the end of a Coptic political presence. For a brief biography and analysis see Ibrahim, *The Copts of Egypt*, 80–85.

[64]Pennington, "The Copts in Modern Egypt," 161.

[65]Ibrahim, *The Copts of Egypt*, 93. On a slight tangent, Ibrahim details a fascinating "intense personal rivalry" that resulted in an ideological "cold-war" between Fr Sergius and Fr Ibrahim Luka—especially as to the role of the Church in Egypt. Both, we should note, were fiercely concerned for their Church. See also p. 108.

[66]This was the conclusion of a journalist, Mustafa Amin, who was writing for political and religious papers of the period; cited in Ami Ayalon, *The Press in the Arab Middle East: A History* (Oxford: Oxford University Press, 1995), 79.

[67]For an examination of the rising sectarianism in the 1930s to the 1940s, see Tadros, *Motherland Lost*, 148–51. Also see Pennington, "The Copts in Modern Egypt," 16; Ibrahim, *The Copts of Egypt*, 88–89.

[68]Ibrahim Luka, *al-Yaqazah* (October, 1943), cited in Ibrahim, *The Copts of Egypt*, 130.

[69]Habib Girgis, *The Coptic Orthodox Theological College: Past and Present 1893–1938* [in Arabic], 5, cited in Bishop Suriel, "Habib Girgis: Coptic Orthodox Educator and a Light in the Darkness" (Ph.D. diss., Fordham University, 2010), 137. Suriel does, however, caution with great insight that we should be careful not to overstate nor generalize the darkness of the period on the basis of Western accounts of that time, which, in significant part, sought to "demonize" the state of the clergy to secure funds for their proselytization efforts; see Bishop Suriel, *Habib Girgis: Coptic Orthodox Educator and a Light in the Darkness* (Yonkers, NY: St Vladimir's Seminary Press, 2017), 43–44.

[70]Both would be canonized on the same date—June 20, 2013.

[71]For an English biography and analysis of his work in Sunday School and the Theological College, see Suriel, *Habib Girgis*. Also see Rudolph Yanney, "Light in the Darkness: The Life of Habib Girgis (1876–1951)," *Coptic Church Review* 5, no. 2 (1984): 44–58; Reiss, *Erneuerung in der Koptisch-Orthodoxen Kirche*.

[72]The college was reopened for the second time by Cyril V on November 29, 1893, and its location was varied until 1912 when it moved to Mahmasha. See Reiss, *Erneuerung in der Koptisch-Orthodoxen Kirche*, 45.

[73]Ibid. Girgis taught in 1898 before his graduation, and on May 8, 1899, was officially appointed a "Lecturer of Christian Religion."

[74]Ibid. Reiss goes on to accurately claim that Girgis was responsible for the entirety of the curriculum and structure, and as such "must be regarded as the real founder of the theological seminary."

[75]Suriel, "Habib Girgis," 73.

[76]Cited in Suriel, *Habib Girgis*, 26. Having been the personal deacon of Cyril V, he also worked closely with Youannis XIX, Macarius III, and Yusab II.

[77]Girgis was a member of the Sunday School Committee, had been elected multiple times to the *maglis al-melli*, and was nominated to the papacy in 1928 after the death of Cyril V. The most controversial nomination was after the death of the Bishop of Giza in 1948—which will be examined in the following chapters. But such nominations were rejected because of his lack of formal monastic tonsure.

[78]The recollection of Sulayman Nasim, cited in Suriel, "Habib Girgis," 78. See also Sulayman Nasim, "Habib Jirjis," in *CE*, 1189a–89b. It is important to note that Cyril V was a great supporter of Girgis and issued a number of decrees and letters encouraging the religious education of children.

[79]In 1923 Girgis wrote, "Those who sought reformation differed in their paths. Some thought that it was in education alone. Others asked for it in the Council of Laymen [i.e. Community Council, *maglis al-melli*]. Others restricted it to something else. All of them forgot that these are crooked paths which have a long way to go, and that *the only short and straight way to proper reformation is the Church*." Cited in Yanney, "Light in the Darkness," 48. Also see Hasan, *Christians versus Muslims*, 75. Hasan notes "the initiative of the SSM actually came from *outside* the Church. It was essentially a lay movement." This is not entirely accurate—as laypersons are an essential *part* of the Church.

[80]Many have sought to trace the Sunday School Movement to 1918 with its official establishment, though Reiss and Suriel correctly note it was born at least eighteen years earlier; see Reiss, *Erneuerung in der Koptisch-Orthodoxen Kirche*, 53; Suriel, "Habib Girgis," 75.

[81]Reiss, *Erneuerung in der Koptisch-Orthodoxen Kirche*, 53–54.

[82]For an analysis of his work in the Theological College see Suriel, "Habib Girgis," 136–245.

[83]Reiss, *Erneuerung in der Koptisch-Orthodoxen Kirche*, 54. Suriel notes that Girgis had a "mixed relationship with the west. He was very Orthodox in his life and teachings and at times appeared to criticize Western doctrines and practices, and at the same time he envied the organizational structure and intellect of the West." See Suriel, "Habib Girgis," 87. Also see Hasan, *Christians versus Muslims*, 71. Hasan suggests the movement began as reaction to Protestant missionaries. I would suggest, rather, that the movement was reflective of many intellectual awakenings throughout Orthodoxy; that is to say, Western education in the East lead to intellectualization, which forced a reflection upon core Eastern values and constructs, and thus provoked a reaction in the call for reform.

[84]Reiss, *Erneuerung in der Koptisch-Orthodoxen Kirche*, 58–59; Tadros, *Motherland Lost*, 171.

[85]Suriel, "Habib Girgis," 89. Cf. Hasan, *Christians versus Muslims*, 58–59.

[86]Pope Shenouda III, "Our Teacher Archdeacon Habib Girgis: Pioneer of Religious Education in Modern Times" [in Arabic], *al-Watani*, 18 August 1991.

[87]Wakin, *A Lonely Minority*, 142. Also see Hasan, *Christians versus Muslims*, 59–61. Hasan makes the argument that the rise of the SSM was via an ascent "through the ranks of deacons," and that these "diaconal corps" welcomed them, allowing a "third pole" which provided a "synthesis between two competing community structures." This is somewhat unclear. There is, to begin, a significant difference between *epsaltos* ("chanters") which most of the SSM were, and the actual tonsured *diaconate* (which is actually a rank of priesthood) which most of the SSM were *not*—and yet Hasan seems to have merged the two. The mere fact that *epsaltos* are laity undermines her argument.

[88]Reiss, *Erneuerung in der Koptisch-Orthodoxen Kirche*, 79–80. Reiss is right to suggest that his work was the "first time" such centers were described in detail, though it should be said, that many in the centers were aware of the distinctions.

[89]Ibid., 120–21.

[90]Tadros, *Motherland Lost*, 171–72. Tadros suggests that Nazir Gayed (Pope Shenouda III) had an "all-encompassing view" of the Church; Youssef Iskander (Matta el-Meskeen) was ecumenical; Abdelmessih Bishara (Bishop Athanasius) though from al-Fagallah aligned himself with Saad Aziz (Bishop Samuel); and Waheeb Atallah (Bishop Gregorious) spent time in multiple Sunday School centers.

[91]For an explanation, see Reiss, *Erneuerung in der Koptisch-Orthodoxen Kirche*, 80.

[92]Ibid., 82.

[93]Ibid., 83–84.

[94]Ibid., 85.

[95]A few prominent names include: Ragheb Abdel Nour, Labib Ragheb (Fr Antonios Ragheb), Awad Farag (Fr Antonios Farag), Mikhail Wahba (Fr Mikhail Wahba), and Malak Mikhail (Fr Angelos Mikhail). Ibid., 84.

[96]Ibid., 87.

[97]This did not mean that the SSM at St Antony's originally aspired to monasticism. At that time there was no place for such students until 1948; rather, these young men sought out St Antony's monastic spirituality independent of actual tonsure.

[98]Ragheb Abdel Nour notes, "If they concentrated on the problems of the child himself and the young man himself, they could gain something. But if they were busy with general problems [of the Church] they could not do anything. . . ." Cited in Reiss, *Erneuerung in der Koptisch-Orthodoxen Kirche*, 87, n. 55.

[99]One of the young men notes, "We considered ourselves as soldiers in an army. There was no say. There were just commands issued [and followed], as is done in the military service. . . . I remember once the instructor Labib Ragheb assigned the new classes . . . but no one answered on something or resisted. Everyone heard his name and knew where he was going or what grade he had to serve. I remember that once one of the servants rejected his class. It so happened that the lecturer Labib Ragheb took the class away from him and he remained for a whole year without a service. . . ."; ibid., 91, n. 71.

[100]Ibid., 90.

[101]Shenouda III, ibid., 92, n. 77.

[102]Ibid., 93.

[103]Ibid., 93, n. 82.

[104]Ibid., 98–99.

[105]Ibid., 101.

[106]It began initially in 1930 with Khella Tawfik and Kamel Yanna holding small classes.

[107]We should note that the high turnover meant the movement was less tied to individuals than in Shoubra, but that said, the formative influence of a few young men, especially Zarif, is undeniable. Also see Reiss, *Erneuerung in der Koptisch-Orthodoxen Kirche*, 113. The rapid turnover, Reiss argues, made the "transfer of experience necessary," thus leading to the rapid development of high-quality, readily available material for perusal, printing, and distribution.

[108]Ibid., 101.

[109]Ibid., 101–2.

[110]Ibid., 106.

[111]Youhanna el-Raheb cited in Hasan, *Christians versus Muslims*, 79.

[112]See Yassa Hanna's comment cited in ibid.

[113]Ibid., 83.

[114]Reiss, *Erneuerung in der Koptisch-Orthodoxen Kirche*, 112–13.

[115]Hasan, *Christians versus Muslims*, 79. Hasan correctly notes that these ad hoc trips, which brought spiritual, material, and medical aid, "soon became institutionalised in the form of permanent departments in the provinces." Also see Reiss, *Erneuerung in der Koptisch-Orthodoxen Kirche*, 114.

[116]Reiss, *Erneuerung in der Koptisch-Orthodoxen Kirche*, 109–11.

[117]Ibid., 139.

[118]"Letter of Yusab II to the Priests of Cairo, March 18, 1948"; ibid., 153–54.

[119]Ibid., 152–54.

[120]Yanney notes, "Until his death the seminary was a dead end for many students; most bishops did not accept them as priests, they were not accepted to teach religion in schools, nor could they become members of the Lay Council [*maglis al-melli*]. During the last sickness of Habib Girgis, the Lay Council ordered the closure of the graduate Theological School." See Yanney, "Light in the Darkness," 51.

[121]In 1942, Girgis wrote, "I envisioned how great and glorious my Church was in previous eras. How the Coptic people were strong in their faith, determination and knowledge. Then I encountered where we were, and what we had become. So, I became sad, in pain, and my hurt increased, since I spent all of my past life in suffering, and struggled as much as I was capable of, to do what was required for the good of my people." See Habib Girgis, *Practical Means toward Coptic Reform: Hopes and Dreams*, 1, cited in Suriel, "Habib Girgis," 101–2.

[122]Morad Wahba cited in Yanney, "Light in the Darkness," 51.

[123]For a history of the churches in Old Cairo, see Meinardus, *Two Thousand Years*, 182–94.

[124]Many surrounding priests were displeased with his presence and popularity; see Samuel Tawadros el-Syriany, *The History of the Popes*, 175.

[125]Anonymous, *The Path of Virtue* [in Arabic] (Cairo: Sons of Pope Kyrillos VI, undated), 47.

[126]Ibid.

[127]This should be differentiated from the ancient Church of St Menas in Fum al-Khalig in Old Cairo; see Meinardus, *Two Thousand Years*, 191. Voile adds, "Mina the solitary was at the head of a current which promotes the figure of Menas and in doing so promotes him"; see Voile, *Les Coptes d'Égypte*, 198.

[128]This was on September 2, 1948. Atta and Raphael Ava Mina, *Life of Pope Kyrillos*, 16; Zaklama, *Pope Kyrillos VI*, 1, 202.

[129]For a representative account see al-Masri, *True Story of Christianity in Egypt*, 2:435.

[130]Atta and Raphael Ava Mina, *Life of Pope Kyrillos*, 16; al-Masri, *Story of the Coptic Church*, 7:24. Throughout construction a number of unusual divine happenings are said to have taken place; for instance, a certain Habib recalls (though it is impossible to verify the authenticity) Fr Mina's words during the inaugural Liturgy: "My beloved, my children, I asked Anba Yusab to pray with us today, but he was on retreat in Helwan. I tried to ask Anba Ephraim . . . but he had another appointment. I did not want to delay the prayers, but I would like to tell you that when they lifted up this marble pillar, the church was full of incense. And when they were building the dome of the sanctuary, there was a lamp of light. Those

who told me had no reason to lie; may God's wonders show in his saints . . . let us pray. . . ." See Raphael Ava Mina, *Miracles of Pope Kyrillos VI*, 1:128.

[131]The sanctuaries were in the names of Sts Menas, Samuel the Confessor, and George. Zaklama, *Pope Kyrillos VI*, 1:202–4. Zaklama states there were three rooms, one of which was occupied by a monk named Farag. Little to nothing is known of this monk, though the fact is corroborated by Fr Raphael Ava Mina. See Fr Raphael Ava Mina, "My Memories of the Life of Pope Kyrillos VI," audio recording (St Menas' Monastery, Mareotis: St Menas' Monastery, undated).

[132]Zaklama, *Pope Kyrillos VI*, 1:202; Atta and Raphael Ava Mina, *Life of Pope Kyrillos*, 16; al-Masri, *Story of the Coptic Church*, 7:24.

[133]Atta and Raphael Ava Mina, *Life of Pope Kyrillos*, 16. Metropolitan Athanasius of Beni Suef was a great supporter of Fr Mina, and Abraam of Giza was a dear friend from the years at Helwan Theological College.

[134]Hegumen Mina the Recluse [Kyrillos VI], "Letter to Hanna Youssef Atta, September, 1947" [in Arabic], in RC-2: Letter 12 (Old Cairo, 1947).

[135]Raphael Ava Mina, "My Memories," audio recording. In a 1959 *al-Ahram* interview, just before his ordination, a newspaper reports, "He has never answered a phone-call, sleeps three hours out of twenty-four. In those twenty-one hours he meets his God and meets people . . . he shuts himself in his cell from 9:00 PM to 2:00 AM, till 11 AM after which he has breakfast . . . his disciples say he is sensitive, firm, and patient." See el-Gowaily, "Interview with the Monk."

[136]Pope Shenouda III, "Speech at the Funeral of Kyrillos VI" [in Arabic] (Cairo: 1971). Also see Mahmud Fawzi, *Pope Kyrillos and Abdel Nasser* [in Arabic] (Cairo: Al Watan Publishing, 1993), 15. Another account also claims this, as well as interestingly claiming that as of August 18, 1947, Fr Mina was still living at Archangel Michael's; see Raphael Ava Mina, *Miracles of Pope Kyrillos VI*, 1:127.

[137]The surgery was, according to one account, on October 30, 1955; Samuel Tawadros el-Syriany, *The History of the Popes*, 197.

[138]Raphael Ava Mina, "My Memories," audio recording; Raphael Ava Mina, *Spiritual Leadership*, 12.

[139]The letterhead bearing the title is found on each letter of the period.

[140]This fourfold purpose is listed as part of the official letterhead of St Menas', which Fr Mina writes is the "Harbor of Salvation Institute."

[141]Anonymous, *School of Virtue*, 50; Raphael Ava Mina, *Service and Humility*, 18.

[142]Atta, "Personal Correspondence, January 28, 2015."

[143]Raphael Ava Mina, *Spiritual Leadership*, 19. This vocational training encompassed textiles, electrics, mechanics, welding, and metal works. Fr Raphael claims he was forced to stop by the patriarchate; cf. al-Masri, *True Story of Christianity in Egypt*, 2:435.

[144]Raphael Ava Mina, *Spiritual Leadership*, 19. Wakin makes an ambiguous comment that after being forced to stop tonsuring monks, Fr Mina then began to rent out the rooms; see Wakin, *A Lonely Minority*, 111.

[145]Atta and Raphael Ava Mina, *Life of Pope Kyrillos*, 16.

[146]Ibid.

[147]Bishop Athanasius, "Interview about Pope Kyrillos VI," audio recording (1990).

[148]Atta and Raphael Ava Mina, *Life of Pope Kyrillos*, 16.

[149]Raphael Ava Mina, *My Memories*, audio recording. Fr Raphael recalls Fr Mina's joy at being disturbed in the late hours of night for the sake of serving a struggling youth. Also see Raphael Ava Mina, *Miracles of Pope Kyrillos VI*, 3:22–23.

[150]Raphael Ava Mina, *Service and Humility*, 25. The author claims that Fr Mina did all the cleaning himself "without letting anyone notice it"; see ibid., 33–34.

[151]Reiss, *Erneuerung in der Koptisch-Orthodoxen Kirche*, 210, n. 31. El-Raheb states that Fr Mina and Waheeb (Fr Salib) were second cousins.

[152]Ibid., 105, n. 39.

[153]For a brief biography see ibid., 104. As a lawyer he was (somewhat unusually for the Giza school of thought) more interested in the Church on an ecclesial level. Studying theology (along with Saad Aziz

and Yassa Hanna) during his evenings under Habib Girgis from 1941 to 1944, he became intrigued by canon law, and was appointed a lecturer in the field at the Theological College in 1944—a post he would hold until his death in 1994.

[154]Ibid., 105, n. 139. It would appear their relationship with the local priest in Giza remained tense.

[155]Youhanna el-Raheb cited in ibid., 210.

[156]For a brief biography see Wakin, *A Lonely Minority*, 143–45. Writing in 1963, Wakin says of Fr Boulos Boulos (formerly Zareef Abdullah), "This priest with his jolly holiness helped to break the ancient mould in the Egyptian church. He is neither self-seeking nor indifferent but constantly concerned about his flock. . . . When last seen, he was saying for the fifth or sixth time that he wanted a movie camera in order to make religious films in the little theatre attached to his church. He talked with childish delight at the prospect of being a movie producer in that one-horse Delta town. But he was serious about it; he knows his Copts well"; ibid., 145.

[157]For Yassa Hanna's recollection, see Hasan, *Christians versus Muslims*, 80.

[158]Reiss, *Erneuerung in der Koptisch-Orthodoxen Kirche*, 178–79.

[159]Fr Salib Suryal, "On the 'Takrees' Movement: Part 1," audio recording, in *Lectures on the History of the Modern Church* (Cairo, 1988).

[160]Fr Matta el-Meskeen (then Youssef Iskander) sent a concise telegram to Waheeb when he heard that the fiancée's family were against the idea of ordination: "No wedding other than for the reason of priesthood." See Fr Matta el-Meskeen, *Autobiography of Fr Matta el-Meskeen* [in English] (Wadi al-Natrun: St Macarius Monastery, 2015), 45, n. 8.

[161]Reiss, *Erneuerung in der Koptisch-Orthodoxen Kirche*, 179. Fr Salib recalls that he chose to distribute even his savings before ordination as a sign of radical renunciation, and went so far as attempting to prevent a collection plate during the Liturgy. Salib claims this was in imitation of Fr Mina's practice at St Menas' in Old Cairo; though Habib Girgis prevented Salib by reminding him that such a practice was in fact apostolic. For the account see Suryal, "On the 'Takrees' Movement: Part 1," and "On the 'Takrees' Movement: Part 2."

[162]Suryal, "Pope Kyrillos VI."

[163]It becomes apparent, here and in later exorcisms, that Fr Mina's "method" (if it may be called that) of exorcism radically differs from that of the "holy man" described by Brown which "tends to have a stylized, articulated quality of an operetta." See Brown, "The Rise and Function of the Holy Man," 88. Most of Mina's exorcisms lack drama, verging upon the mundane if not for the subject matter.

[164]A similar account is found at the mouth of Fr Matta el-Meskeen. He claims that in or around 1951, after spending three years at St Samuel's Monastery, he returned to St Menas' in Old Cairo. An eighteen-year-old boy who was allegedly possessed was presented to Fr Mina, who asked those accompanying him to take him to the church. Fr Mina then went upstairs and told Fr Matta to pray for the boy. "I do not understand these things," replied Matta, "and I don't even know what to do." "Don't worry, just do it for my sake," said Fr Mina while giving Matta his own wooden hand-cross. Matta recalls that he prayed for some four hours, after which the boy calmed down. Matta still had his reservations, and gave the boy some water that he prayed on (hidden away from the boy) with Fr Mina's cross. But the boy threw the water away, screaming, "It's bitter!" This was repeated a second time with the same result. The third time Fr Matta gave him water that he hadn't secretly prayed on—and the boy drank it happily, remarking how beautiful it was. "My God," exhales Fr Matta as he recollects the episode, "my God . . . the power of the cross!" For the account see Fr Matta el-Meskeen, "On Pope Kyrillos: Part II," audio recording, in *Recollections* (Wadi al-Natrun, undated).

[165]Fr Salib Suryal cited in Reiss, *Erneuerung in der Koptisch-Orthodoxen Kirche*, 103, n. 132.

[166]Suryal, "On the 'Takrees' Movement: Part 1"; Reiss, *Erneuerung in der Koptisch-Orthodoxen Kirche*, 103.

[167]Reiss, *Erneuerung in der Koptisch-Orthodoxen Kirche*, 175–76.

[168]Fr Matta el-Meskeen says of that house, "His home was the pasture of our youth with a group of the holiest young men this generation has known. Spiritual evenings and prayers were held until morning. In his home the spirit of consecration overflowed on all of us, and the Lord invited us to serve him.

Every one of us consequently departed rushing to his call." Oratory on the occasion of Bishop Samuel's death published in *St Mark's Magazine* in October 1981, cited in Matta el-Meskeen, *Autobiography of Fr Matta el-Meskeen*, 7.

[169]Suryal, "On the 'Takrees' Movement: Part 1."

[170]Saad entered St Menas' in Old Cairo on March 18, 1948, where he lived in a room next to the dome of the church. Thus, he lived as a novice for a month before tonsure.

[171]Suryal, "On the 'Takrees' Movement: Part 1."

[172]Matta el-Meskeen, *Autobiography of Fr Matta el-Meskeen*, 15. [We have made a slight emendation to the unpublished English translation.] This is against Reiss's claim that he founded the Sunday School Movement in Damanhur and played a key role in it; see Reiss, *Erneuerung in der Koptisch-Orthodoxen Kirche*, 181.

[173]Hasan, *Christians versus Muslims*, 80. Iskander (Fr Matta) also lobbied for Zareef's ordination in Damanhur; see Reiss, *Erneuerung in der Koptisch-Orthodoxen Kirche*, 181, n. 97.

[174]This year, marking the consecration of St Menas' in Old Cairo, thus saw the ordination of the first two Sunday School priests and the tonsure of the first Sunday School monks. That all four came under the fatherhood of Fr Mina is a matter of great significance.

[175]Atta and Raphael Ava Mina, *Life of Pope Kyrillos*, 16.

[176]Ibid.

[177]Matta el-Meskeen, *Autobiography of Fr Matta el-Meskeen*, 20.

[178]Matta el-Meskeen, "On Pope Kyrillos: Part I." Fr Matta el-Meskeen lived for three months with Fr Mina before his tonsure at St Samuel's, while Fr Makary returned to Cairo shortly after. Both would later head to the Syrian Monastery. Their story will be picked up in detail in later chapters. See Fr Mina el-Samuely [the Younger], "Letter to Hegumen Mina the Recluse, August 10, 1948" [in Arabic], in FRC-1: Letter 256 (Qalamoun Mountain: 1948). Another, later letter indicates that Fr Makary had returned to Cairo by December, 1948; Fr Makary el-Samuely, "Letter to Fr Matta, December 14, 1948" [in Arabic], in FRC-1: Letter 213 (Qalamoun Mountain, 1948).

[179]Makary el-Samuely, "Letter to Fr Matta, December 14, 1948."

[180]Gruber claims that by sending monks to the Syrian Monastery, he "gained acceptance in the Wadi al-Natrun, where formerly he was not highly regarded since he left Deir el-Baramous." Gruber, "Sacrifice in the Desert," 149. This seems to me to overstate the animosity as well as his apparent "acceptance." For the letter in which he recommends the two monks to the Syrian Monastery, see Hegumen Mina the Recluse [Kyrillos VI], "Letter to Syrian Monastery Superintendent, October 7, 1950" [in Arabic], in FRC-1: Letter 89 (Old Cairo, 1950).

[181]Hasan, *Christians versus Muslims*, 61; Reiss, *Erneuerung in der Koptisch-Orthodoxen Kirche*, 83, n. 104. Theophilus, while esteeming education, also took the step of rebuilding monastic cells and installing water pumps, thus naturally creating a more practical environment for recently educated graduates; see Gruber, "Sacrifice in the Desert," 149.

[182]Reiss, *Erneuerung in der Koptisch-Orthodoxen Kirche*, 104. For a few well-known illustrations of his trickster nature see Hasan, *Christians versus Muslims*, 65, 69.

[183]Most of these monks hailed from the St Antony center in Shoubra, given the ascetic spirit of the movement there. Reiss, *Erneuerung in der Koptisch-Orthodoxen Kirche*, 187. Reiss also suggests that the Sunday School monastic pioneers (especially Fr Matta) were the predominant cause of clerical renewal. This fails to discern clearly the effect of Fr Mina on these young men, though Reiss does note a few sentences later that these monks were introduced to monasticism by Fr Mina. See ibid., 179–80, 212.

[184]Ibid., 188.

[185]Shenouda III, "Speech at the First Year Commemoration of Kyrillos VI."

[186]For a brief biography see van Doorn-Harder, *Modern Coptic Papacy*, 157–58; John H. Watson, "Signposts to Biography—Pope Shenouda III," in *BDC* 243–53.

[187]Pope Shenouda III, "Speech at the First Year Commemoration of Kyrillos VI."

[188]Pope Shenouda III, "Speech at the Tenth Year Commemoration of Kyrillos VI" [in Arabic] (Cairo: 1981).

[189]Hasan, *Christians versus Muslims*, 86.

[190]Nasr, *Readings in the Life of Abouna Mina*, 80.

[191]Mikhail was a police clerk for the Ministry of the Interior, and as such was forced to move all around Egypt. His last tour of civil service in 1948–1951, during which he came into contact with Fr Mina, was in Old Cairo, where he was remembered by many of the Sunday School Movement for his piety. In 1951, at the age of fifty-two, he became a priest in his hometown, Kafr Abdo in Quesna. Later he nominated a younger priest to assist him, who unfortunately turned the congregation against him. Rather than defending himself, he left for Old Cairo once more, where Fr Marcos Dawood needed a priest to fill in at St Mark's Shoubra, and then he went on to become a renowned priest, well known especially for the power of his spiritual guidance. See especially Pope Shenouda III, *A Model of Service: The Life of Hegumen Mikhail Ibrahim* [in Arabic] (Cairo: Patriarchate, 1977), 44, 83.

[192]Reiss, *Erneuerung in der Koptisch-Orthodoxen Kirche*, 210.

[193]Voile, *Les Coptes d'Égypte*, 200. Also see Van Doorn-Harder, *Modern Coptic Papacy*, 133–34.

[194]Atef Kamal, "An Interview with Pope Shenouda III" (video recording) (CYC, undated), Part 2.

[195]Van Doorn-Harder, "Planner, Patriarch and Saint," 233; van Doorn-Harder, "Practical and Mystical," 226.

[196]Voile, *Les Coptes d'Égypte*, 200.

[197]Samuel Rubenson, "Matta el-Meskeen," in *Key Theological Thinkers: From Modern to Postmodern*, ed. Staale Johannes Kristiansen and Svein Rise (Surrey: Ashgate, 2013), 416.

[198]David Bentley Hart, *Atheist Delusions: The Christian Revolution and Its Fashionable Enemies* (New Haven, CT: Yale University Press, 2009), 183.

[199]Ibid. Hart is describing the singularly unique revolution of Christianity.

[200]For instance see al-Masri, *Story of the Coptic Church*, 7:24.

[201]Nadejda Gorodetzky, *Saint Tikhon of Zadonsk: Inspirer of Dostoevsky* (Crestwood, NY: St Vladimir's Seminary Press, 1976), 48. For a fascinating discussion of "interiorized monasticism," see Paul Evdokimov, *The Struggle with God* (Glen Rock, NJ: Paulist Press, 1966), 111–30.

[202]John Chrysostom, *De compunctione ad Stelechium* 2.3, cited in Rapp, *Holy Bishops*, 119.

[203]Clement of Alexandria, *Stromata* 7.12, in Ante-Nicene Fathers, ed. Philip Schaff (repr., Peabody, MA: Hendrickson Publishers, 1999), 2:545. In his writing he refers to the "true *gnostikos*." Also, Theodoret of Cyrrhus counseled that "inhabited land . . . does not offer the least hindrance to the attainment of virtue," nor is virtue "circumscribed in place"; "see also his *Historia religiosa* 4:1, cited in Rapp, *Holy Bishops*, 120.

[204]For instance see Basil the Great, *Letter to Gregory* 2 (NPNF² 8:110–11).

[205]Amma Syncletica, 19, in Ward, *Sayings of the Desert Fathers*, 234. Local geography, it appears, merely "provides a scene but does not dictate the role"; see Han J. W. Drijvers, "Hellenistic and Oriental Origins," in *The Byzantine Saint*, ed. Sergei Hackel (Crestwood, NY: St Vladimir's Seminary Press, 2001), 16.

[206]Robert Browning, "The 'Low Level' Saint's Life in the Early Byzantine World," ibid., 124.

[207]"He was a master of the monastic symbol," Nelly van Doorn-Harder comments, "convincingly exhibiting it under public scrutiny for years on end." See her "Planner, Patriarch, and Saint," 233. See also Abba Poemen's insightful words: A monk once told Abba Poemen, "Some brethren have come to live with me; do you want me to give them orders?" "No," said the old man. "But Father," the monk persisted, "they themselves want me to give them orders." "No," repeated Poemen, "*be to them a pattern*, not their legislator." See Abba Poemen, 174, in Ward, *Sayings of the Desert Fathers*, 191.

[208]Athanasius, "Interview about Pope Kyrillos VI."

[209]Ibid.

[210]Ibid. This letter, along with those quoted earlier, suggests Fr Mina's familiarity and frequent use of the "Jesus Prayer"—albeit in varying forms.

[211]Paul Sedra, "Class Cleavages and Ethnic Conflict: Coptic Christian Communities in Modern Egyptian Politics," *Islam and Christian-Muslim Relations* 10, no. 2 (July 1999): 224.

[212]Michel de Certeau, *The Mystic Fable*, vol. 1, *The Sixteenth and Seventeenth Centuries* (Chicago: University of Chicago Press, 1992), 40–45.

[213]Michael Plekon, *Hidden Holiness* (Notre Dame, IN: Notre Dame University Press, 2009), 11.

[214]Philip Sheldrake, "Christian Spirituality as a Way of Living Publicly: A Dialectic of Mystical and Prophetic," *Spiritus* 3, no. 1 (2003): 25.

[215]Anonymous, *School of Virtue*, 46. In October 1949, Fr Mina reassured his brother concerning circulating rumors; Hegumen Mina the Recluse [Kyrillos VI], "Letter to Hanna Youssef Atta, October 11, 1949" [in Arabic], in RC-2: Letter 14 (Old Cairo, 1949).

[216]Van Doorn-Harder, "Planner, Patriarch and Saint," 233.

[217]Hegumen Yousef Asaad cited in Raphael Ava Mina, *Memories: Part II*, 32.

[218]Suryal, "On the 'Takrees' Movement: Part 1."

[219]Ibid. This may well relate to the same event that Atta describes, in which the patriarchate attempted to remove Fr Mina from Cairo. Also see Matta el-Meskeen, *Autobiography of Fr Matta el-Meskeen*, 33, n. 3. Also see Suryal, "On the 'Takrees' Movement: Part 2."

[220]Suryal, "Pope Kyrillos VI."

[221]Atta and Raphael Ava Mina, *Life of Pope Kyrillos*, 17. Fr Salib Suryal repeats this claim in his "On the 'Takrees' Movement: Part 1."

[222]Raphael Ava Mina, *Memories: Part II*, 47. I have an inkling this may have also been related to the events of three days earlier, when the Sunday School Movement protested Yusab's consecration of Youannis as bishop of Giza. Given that many of these young men were disciples of Fr Mina, it is quite possible that Yusab (and/or Melek) sought to silence Fr Mina.

[223]Pope Yusab II, "Letter to Bishop Athanasius and Bishop Macarius, January 26, 1949" [in Arabic], in FRC-1: Letter 259 (Patriarchate, Cairo: 1949). The letter was addressed from the "Office of the Pope's Secretary" suggesting once more that the hand of Melek (the manservant of Yusab) was at play. It is unclear what these false statements concerned—other than his tonsuring activities in the city—though rumors of black magic and incantation were often offered as explanations of Fr Mina's capacity to heal. Also, note that this was written to Bishop Athanasius the former (d. 1962).

[224]Ibid.

[225]Suryal, "On the 'Takrees' Movement: Part 1." We should note this was Athanasius' response to the patriarchate's attempt to remove Fr Mina; it is assumed to have also been his response to the letter.

[226]Atta and Raphael Ava Mina, *Memories about the Life of Pope Kyrillos*, 33. This is missed in the English translation; see Atta and Raphael Ava Mina, *Life of Pope Kyrillos*, 17.

[227]Fr Raphael Ava Mina, *The Miracles of Pope Kyrillos VI* [in Arabic], vol. 9 (Cairo: Sons of Pope Kyrillos VI, 1989), 39. Fr Mina apparently had a premonition of the attempt and refused to leave the church despite a request that a sick man was lying in a nearby car. A novice secretly followed the "friends" of the sick man, only to find that no one was in fact sick. The anonymous disciple (now a monk) concluded this recollection with the following: "Years later Fr Mina was ordained as a patriarch, and one day a person came to him weeping and complaining of poverty and seeking support, he confessed to him that he was one of the men who headed to St Menas' Church to kidnap him, incited by a person who was working at the patriarchate, who, unfortunately, had great power and authority." We can only assume that the person at the patriarchate was none other than the infamous Melek (whom we shall soon meet).

[228]Mina the Recluse [Kyrillos VI], "Letter to Hanna Youssef Atta, March 5, 1958."

[229]Raphael Ava Mina, *Memories: Part II*, 47.

[230]G. K. Chesterton, *St. Thomas Aquinas and St. Francis of Assisi* (San Francisco: Ignatius Press, 2002), 22.

[231]Ibid., 23.

[232]Pope Kyrillos VI, "Letter to Hanna Youssef Atta, undated, ?1959–1962" [in Arabic], in FRC-1: Letter 280 (Old Cairo, undated). The letter is not dated, but was likely written between 1959 and 1962, given he visited Old Cairo as a patriarch and his brother Mikhail was not yet ordained.

Figure 1
Azer Youssef Atta

Figure 2
Youssef Atta

Figure 3
Hanna Youssef Atta

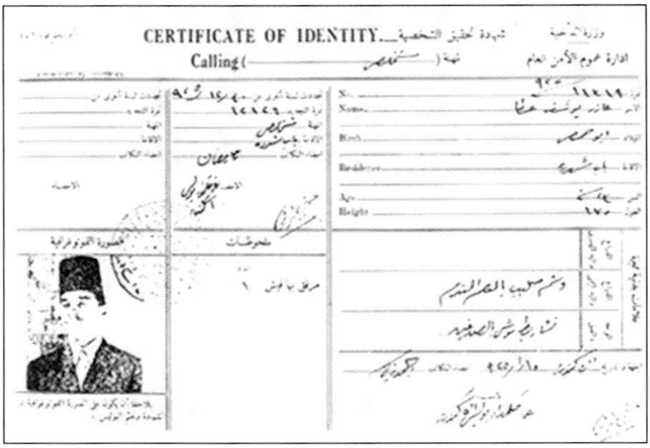

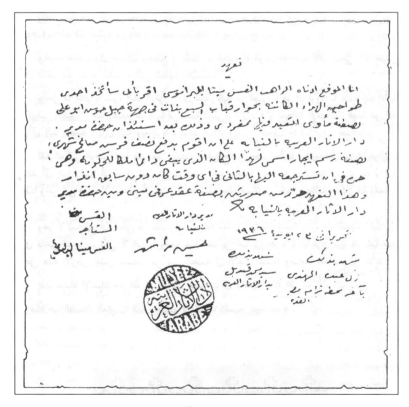

Figure 4
National ID Card, 1925

تعهد

انا الموقع ادناه الراهب القس مينا البراموسى اقر بأنى سأتخذ احدى
طواحين الهواء الكائنة بجوار قباب السبع بنات فى جهة جبل موسى ابو على
بصفة مأوى للتعبد وذلك بمفردى وذلك بعد استئذان حضرة مدير
دار الآثار العربية بالنيابة على ان اقوم بدفع نصف قرش صاغ شهرى
بصفة رسم ايجار اسمى لهذا المكان الذى يبقى دائماً ملكاً للحكومة وهى
حرة فى ان تسترجعه البلد بالثانى فى اى وقت كان دون سابق انذار
وهذا التعهد حرر منه صورتين بصفة عقد عرفى بينى وبين حضرة مدير
دار الآثار العربية بالنيابة

تحريراً فى ٢٣ يونيه ١٩٣٦

Figure 5
Lease of the Windmill, June 23, 1936

Figure 6
Windmill Diagram

Figure 7
Father Mina at the Windmill, 1936

Figure 8
Father Mina as an Urban Monastic

Figure 9
The Windmill on the outskirts of Old Cairo

Figure 10
The Ruins of the Windmills

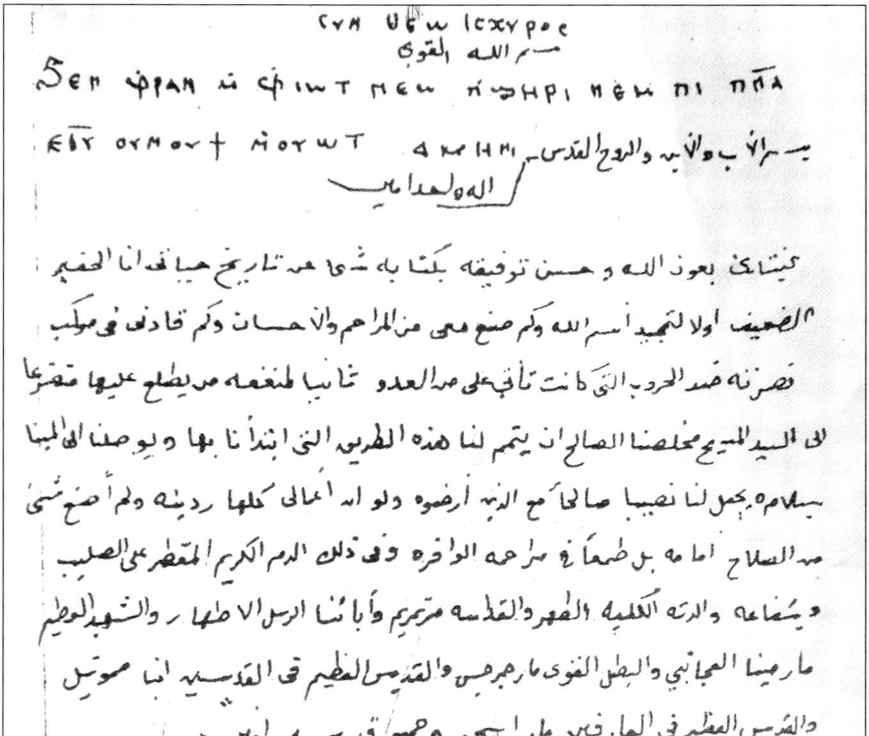

ⲥⲩⲛ ⲑⲉⲱ ⲓⲥⲭⲩⲣⲟⲥ
بسم الله القوي
Ϧⲉⲛ ⲫ̀ⲣⲁⲛ ⲙ̀ⲫⲓⲱⲧ ⲛⲉⲙ ⲡ̀ϣⲏⲣⲓ ⲛⲉⲙ ⲡⲓⲡ̅ⲛ̅ⲁ̅
ⲉⲑ̅ⲩ̅ ⲟⲩⲛⲟⲩϯ ⲛ̀ⲟⲩⲱⲧ ⲁ̀ⲙⲏⲛ
بسم الآب والابن والروح القدس
الاله الواحد آمين

نبتدئ بعون الله وحسن توفيقه بكتابة شيء عن تاريخ حياتي انا الحقير
الضعيف اولا لتمجيد اسم الله وكم صنع معي من المراحم والاحسانات وكم قادني في موكب
نصرته ضد الحروب التي كانت تأتي علي من العدو ثانيا لمنفعة من يطلع عليها متضرعا
الى السيد المسيح مخلصنا الصالح ان يتمم لنا هذه الطريق التي ابتدأنا بها ويوصلنا الى الميناء
بسلام ويجعل لنا نصيبا صالحا مع الذين ارضوه ولو ان اعمالي كلها رديئة ولم اصنع شيء
من الصلاح امامه بل طمعا في مراحمه الوافرة وفي ذلك الدم الكريم المقطر على الصليب
وبشفاعة والدة الاله الكلية الطهر والقداسة مريم وابائنا الرسل الاطهار والشهيد العظيم
مارمينا العجايبي والبطل القوي مارجرجس والقديس العظيم في القديسين انبا صموئيل
والقديس العظيم في العارفين مار [illegible] وجميع قديسيه امين
حضرتي المدعو بالاسم الرهباني مينا البراموسي المتوحد الذي كان اسمي قبلا عازر
يوسف عطا عائلتي من طوخ النصارى منوفية ترك والدي البلد وجاء الى البحيرة
وقطن في بلدة تدعى بسنتاواي مركز ابوحمص بوظيفة ناظر زراعة ورزقه الله ابناء
كثيرين منهم حضرتي ولدت في شهر اغسطس سنة ١٩٠٢ ميلادية فرباني والدي وعلمني
السلوك بمخافة الله ولكنني اتعلم بالكتاب ومن صغر سني كنت اميل الى الهدوء
والوحدة ولبس الملابس السوداء ولما بلغت سن الرشد وكنت اسمع كثيرا عن
الاديرة والرهبان فكان يلتهب قلبي نارا واشتاق للذهاب الى الدير
الى ان جاء اليوم المعين من قبل الله وعرضت الفكرة على والدي واخوتي

Figure 11
First Page of Father Mina's Unfinished Autobiography

Figure 12
Father Mina in Old Cairo on hearing the news of the Altar Ballot

Figure 13
After the Altar Ballot

Figure 14
Ordination: Fr Mina being lead into the Cathedral next to his brother, Hanna

Figure 15
Ordination

Figure 16
Ordination

Figure 17a
Ordination: during the Liturgy he returned to his simple vestments

Figure 17b
Ordination

Figure 18
Ordination: Kyrillos VI weeping during the consecration

Figure 19
A rare photograph, as Patriarch, without his shawl

Figure 20
Visit to Abu Mena, Mariout, in 1959 to consecrate
the site for St Menas' Monastery

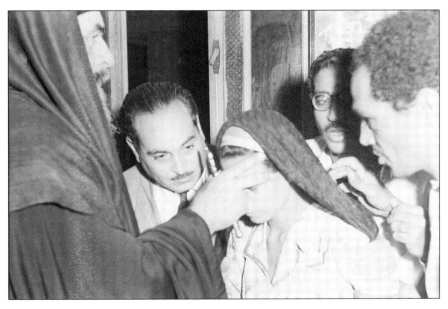

Figure 21
Praying for the sick; October 5, 1959

Figure 22
With Mother (Tamav) Irini

Figure 23
Returning to pray in his Church in Old Cairo

Figure 24
Returning to pray in his Church in Old Cairo

Figure 25
With Eastern Orthodox Hierarchs

Figure 26
Kyrillos in his characteristic posture
when not celebrating the Liturgy of the Eucharist

Figure 27
Kyrillos praying Matins

Figure 28
Kyrillos in Ethiopia

Figure 29
With Eastern Orthodox Bishops

Figure 30
Ordination of Bishop Shenouda and Bishop Samuel, September 30, 1962

Figure 31
Kyrillos Visiting President Gamal Abdel Nasser in his home

Figure 32
Kyrillos with Anwar Sadat (future President of Egypt)

Figure 33
Kyrillos with Sheikh Hassan Mamoun of al-Azhar

Figure 34
Preparing the Holy Myron (Chrism) 1967

Figure 35
Kyrillos with Roman Catholic clergy

Figure 36
Bishop Shenouda (Left); Bishop Gregorious (Center);
Bishop Domadius (Right)

~ 24 ~

Figure 37
Receiving Relics of Saint Mark from the Vatican, June 25, 1968

Figure 38
Inaugural Liturgy at the New Cathedral, June 25, 1968

Figure 39
Return of Bishop Shenouda from suspension, June 25, 1968

Figure 40
Kyrillos being surprised by the photographer

Figure 41
Kyrillos in his rare patriarchal vestments

Figure 42
Opening the cathedral June 25, 1968

Figure 43
Kyrillos (Right) with Father Matta el-Meskeen (Center)
and Salib Suryal (Left) during their reconciliation, May 9, 1969

Figure 44
The Coptic delegation at Gamal Abdel Nasser's Funeral; Bishops Gregorious,
Shenouda and Samuel at front centre; September 28, 1970

Figure 45
Kyrillos in his final years

Figure 46
Repose of Kyrillos VI, March 9, 1971

A Melancholic Interlude (1954–1959)

The Unfortunate Case of Pope Yusab II
(1954–1959)

Short History of a Long Conflict:
The Maglis al-Melli Council

> "No matter how thin you slice it, there will always be two sides."
> —*Baruch Spinoza*

"I WISH," SAID THE grayed and broken man, "I listened to you and stayed in my diocese." After a few moments of uneasy silence, with his tears tracing his face and disappearing into his beard, he added, "When I was metropolitan, God answered each of my prayers immediately through people or words sent to me. But now as patriarch"—his hands began to shake visibly—"God has turned his back on me."[1]

Those tormented words of Pope Macarius III (1872–1945) might have been spoken just as well by the patriarchs before *and* after him. For a little less than a century, whoever dared to ascend that precarious throne of the patriarchate (legitimately or not) would be thrown against the unrelenting rocks of the infamous Community Council, the *maglis al-melli*. Unfortunately, such words are how this melancholic interlude must begin.

* * *

After the death of Demetrius II in 1870, Bishop Marcos of Beheira, as locum tenens, took the fateful step of selecting several lay notables to "assist" him, especially in the matter of financial affairs. Thus was formed the nucleus of the Community Council (*maglis al-melli*).[2] Eventually, the arrangement was formalized, and a Khedival decree on February 5, 1874, approved the formation of a council of twenty-four lay members under the patriarch.[3] Meinardus suggests that three streams of lay reform merged at this point: one group calling for the Church's increased support of the poor; another insisting on the broader education of clergy; and another still—this would be by far the most significant and problematic—insisting that the clergy should concern themselves *only* with "spiritual matters," leaving all other affairs—financial, legal, and educational—to "capable laymen."[4] The move echoed many of the calls for reform that were resounding throughout the nation and Ottoman Empire. But it had its own internal dynamic: the cardinal concern was the legitimization of lay representation within the Church.[5]

It was very much a pressing concern. Lay leaders at the time were far more educated than most clergy, and they had crucial monetary experience. Moreover, I. H. al-Masri notes, the problems of Personal Status Laws (marriage, divorce, and inheritance) were quite reasonably considered to be the "domains of fathers of families" and not that of celibate bishops.[6] In other words, as Carter discerns, the *maglis* was the "chief mechanism by which [the lay reformers] sought to gain control of the community."[7] Masri's and Carter's comments, though accurate, are far more revealing than perhaps intended, and they, along with most scholarship, fall short of explicitly articulating what is obvious. The concerns of the *maglis al-melli* and its condensation of lay reform was not simply the legitimization of laymen, but rather their legitimization over and against—so they claimed—incapable, incompetent, and relatively illiterate clergy. It could never have been received as anything else. Indeed, when Cyril V was ordained patriarch in late 1874, only months after the formation of the *maglis*, his reaction was in a sense understandable, if not expected. The first council under his chairmanship was dissolved and the second never held a meeting. Whenever they tried to assemble at the patriarchate, they found the doors locked.[8]

* * *

The saga of the *maglis* under the patriarchs of the late nineteenth and early twentieth centuries is hardly edifying. Cyril V (1874–1925), to begin, rejected the council almost from its inception, refused to chair its meetings for nearly a decade, decried its very existence, and dreamt feverishly of its dissolution. His lay opponents, however, were formidable. They counted among their number well-educated and wealthy landowners; a few governors; and the first-ever Copt to become a "pasha," Boutros Ghali.[9] On March 22, 1883, they forcefully

"requested" Cyril V to reconvene a new *maglis.* "There is no need for the Council," wrote Cyril V in a letter that he delivered by hand to the Prime Minister,

> which some members of the congregation seek to create.... When we
> assumed the patriarchy, our experience with the Council led us to the con-
> clusion that it is useless and can serve no purpose whatsoever and we, there-
> fore, dispensed with it.[10]

The Khedive had little interest in the protests of the patriarch and instead
looked favorably upon the reforming laymen. An apparent compromise was
struck with the *maglis'* constitution of May 14, 1883. It granted the *maglis,* in
cooperation with four clergy, authority over all personal status issues, monastic
endowments (*waqf*), Coptic schools, theological institutions, and benevolent
societies; it also directed the *maglis* to audit and keep records of all parishes,
monasteries, and convents; and finally, it empowered the *maglis* to work for
the education and spiritual development of clergy.[11] This "compromise" was
expansive, and would clearly step on clerical toes.

One of these directives would become the acute point of contention between
the patriarch and the *maglis,* forging deep factionalism within the community
that would last well into the twentieth century. This was the *waqf.*[12]

For centuries monasteries had "reclaimed" their surrounding deserts
for agricultural use, which, given the enormous land holdings, had become
extremely lucrative for the Church. These monastic endowments, along with
other less significant patriarchal and charitable lands, collectively known as the
waqf, had by the late nineteenth century eclipsed all other sources of income
for the Church.[13] And, as the *maglis* soon discovered, reform was expensive.
The *maglis* saw the *waqf* as the means of establishing, rebuilding, and reinvigo-
rating clerical education, parishes, schools, and the service of the poor.[14] But
beyond this, they felt that the sheer disparity between these monastic endowments and the current state of the Church was the inevitable result of the misappropriation of such funds. This, they alleged, was certainly in dire violation of
the "vow of poverty" that these ascetic monks had apparently taken—especially
since these same monks lived in squalor and poverty.[15] The *maglis* cried out for
accountability, urged transparency, demanded integrity, and above all, sought
control.[16] In many ways then, the *waqf* became the symbolic battlefield and flag
for reform and, therefore, the singular wedge of enmity between the patriarch
and the laymen.

Needless to say, a failure to agree on the 1883 constitution—primarily around the supervision of the *waqf*—lead to a fragile standoff.[17] By 1891 the conflict erupted into popular demonstration. Societies (both pro-*maglis* and pro-patriarch) were formed with varying slogans and a mass of propaganda. Numerous appeals from both sides were made to the Khedive.[18] A year later, Cyril V was forced by the government to concede, and monasteries were commanded to present their accounts to the *maglis* for audit (though the monasteries were, pointedly, allowed to keep the profits). Cyril then reacted with his own petition. The *maglis* countered, leading to a "historically unprecedented dismissal" of the patriarch.[19] On September 1, 1892, a Khedival decree saw Cyril V withdraw to the Baramous Monastery.[20] "The vast majority of the Coptic people," wrote Leeder, a British observer,

> . . . whatever the reformers might think, were desolated by the removal of a man who was still their head. And then too, Cyril's parting thunders of excommunication had brought the whole Church to a standstill, drying up the comforting wells of absolution and benediction. . . .[21]

The six months of his exile were catastrophic. A new puppet-patriarch, Bishop Athanasius of Sanabu, was appointed by the government and, just as promptly, was excommunicated by Cyril.[22] Parishes became desolate, sacraments were not administered, and the once-faithful became disillusioned. The government grew restless and, along with the now embarrassed Community Council, called for Cyril's return. On February 4, 1893, Cyril V (and his government envoy) was received with a triumphant procession through the streets of Cairo.

As far as history reveals, the action of the *maglis* in this awkward episode was a serious misstep. Exiling the patriarch was evidence, Ibrahim claims, of what "many in the community could not accept, the infringement of laymen in the spiritual duties of the Church."[23] Reform may have been welcomed and warranted, indeed even necessitated, but the exile of the patriarch undermined their very credibility. It also revealed just how divisive the *waqf* could be as the focal point for competing visions of the Church. There is also a suggestion, as Seikaly argues, that the Khedive played a far more significant part in the exile than most sources recognize; with another scholar claiming that the Khedival intervention politicized the conflict between clergy and laity "on several levels."[24] The unfortunate episode not only saw lay intrusion in the spiritual authority of the Church, but it also gave an unfortunate precedent for government intervention.

The hostility between patriarch and *maglis* would wax and wane for the next three decades.[25] Various modifications to the constitution of the *maglis* were made, for the most part in favor of the patriarchate.[26] On July 22, 1927, things would take another dramatic turn. After a great deal of political maneuvering and filing suits against each head of monastery, the *maglis* successfully petitioned the government once more. Its constitution was reverted, granting the *maglis* their full rights secured in 1883.[27] Two weeks after hearing the news, Cyril V died at 103 years of age. Though his patriarchate saw a great deal of controversy, it would appear, ironically, that many of his efforts were in line with the reformers. Schools were supported, a theological college opened, churches renovated, and women's education championed.[28] And, we should take care to note, he was remembered by *all* as a man of "purity, great simplicity, and self-denial, with his personal expenditure not exceeding more than LE 60 a year."[29]

* * *

The following patriarch, Youannis XIX (1928–1942), fared little better. Initially there were some promising signs, in part explained by his sobering exile (while still a metropolitan) with Cyril V in 1892. Before his elevation to patriarch, as locum tenens in 1927, he issued an effective system—essentially a supervisory committee of three laymen and two bishops—for the management of the *waqf*. For a short while, it even satisfied both clergy and laity.[30] It was not, however, the *waqf* that were of concern during his reign—but rather his very right to become patriarch at all.

After the death of Cyril V in 1927 the Synod and *maglis* agreed to overturn more than a millennium of custom (and canon) of selecting the patriarch from among the monks. They allowed a bishop to become patriarch "if no monks were deemed suitable for the position."[31] Youannis' patriarchate would, unfortunately, from then on be marred by persistent rumors, inefficacy, and communal strife.[32] "I wish," he was once heard to have exclaimed, "that the day was doomed when I sought the papacy."[33] Many scholars have argued that Youannis' patriarchate was the principal reason for the descent of the Church into darkness for the next three decades; he would be the first of three patriarchs elevated from among the bishops to patriarch. Sadly, and yet fairly, one eminent Coptic historian has gone so far as to entitle her volume of the period, "how the mighty have fallen."[34]

With the death of Youannis in 1942, the debate erupted once more. Here, however, the lines were not so neatly drawn between clergy and laity. Many bishops called for the ordination of the patriarch from among the monks; while some laymen (including the *maglis*) suggested that reform could only ever be achieved by an experienced bishop.[35] But even then, many disagreed and the opinions were diverse.[36] The ensuing months saw unseemly election campaigns for candidates that had "increasingly political overtones."[37] A few, however, cared little for such maneuvering, preferring instead to look to the principles of ancient tradition. "You know, holy father, my love and reverence for you," Habib el-Masri, a member of the *maglis*, recalls warning one of the metropolitans, "but my loyalty to the principle takes precedence even over my loyalty to you."[38] The metropolitan's answer, "The people want me," did little to pacify him.[39] That metropolitan was the future Pope Macarius III (1872–1945).

As metropolitan of Asyut for forty-seven years, Macarius had a significant reform legacy and was quite apt at delegating non-spiritual affairs.[40] Thanks to some enthusiastic supporters, he also had the vote of the populace. The newspapers of the period abound with pro-Macarius pieces written by Hegumen Sergius (an activist priest we have already met more than once), as well as the publicized support of the *maglis* through their self-proclaimed spokesman Ibrahim el-Minyawi (1887–1958).[41] On the day of the election, February 13, 1944, Macarius III was very much the people's choice—the result not of corruption but of electioneering, lobbying, and enamoring the press; more representative perhaps of a parliamentary election than of a patriarchal ordination. And, true to his legacy, Macarius did not shy away from his early reforming tendencies. "Why are we so concerned with *waqf*?" he asked his fellow bishops in a resounding attack, just before his ordination,

> . . . We are all monks and being that we have given our lawful inheritance to the Church, is it right for any person to give up his share and then demand it back thereafter? It is no longer ours.[42]

Within eleven days of his elevation as patriarch, Macarius had seemingly resolved a conflict that had been burning for more than half a century. He came to an agreement with the *maglis* that monastic endowments (*waqf*) would be put exclusively to the use of the community to initiate and sustain revival.[43] All endowments, previously administered by heads of monasteries, would now be directed by a central office at the patriarchate in Cairo under Macarius' direct supervision with the aid of five members of the *maglis*. Pointedly, the endowments would be for the express use of edifying the Church. The decision unsurprisingly "provoked outcry."[44] Abbots and bishops categorically refused. It must be cautioned, however, that this was not simply self-preservation or archcon-servatism on the part of such bishops. Much of the clerical opposition, as Ibra-him notes, actually stemmed from the *maglis'* own "misconduct and failings."[45] They too had mishandled non-monastic *waqf*; and since their governance of the Great Coptic Schools of Cairo in 1928 there had been a marked and rapid dete-rioration in education standards, not to mention the gross mismanagement of the patriarchal *diwan* (rent from properties).[46] This challenges the view of many Western and Coptic historiographers that the *maglis* was an impeccable, mod-ern, and transparent reformer of a "reactionary" Church—a matter we do well to remember in the later *maglis*-patriarch conflicts of our present subject.[47]

* * *

Standing in between the powerful bishops and the *maglis*, it was inevitable that Macarius would fall foul of both. Both—perhaps unfairly—felt he was attempt-ing to wrest power away from both the monasteries *and* the *maglis*; that is, to himself.[48] Minyawi and the *maglis* claimed they only backed Macarius' nomi-nation as there were "no other suitable candidates."[49] Once more the newspa-pers became alight with communal strife, protests were made to government, and the *waqf* tore deeper into the fabric of the Church. Chancing upon Habib el-Masri at a wedding on August 1, 1944, Macarius embraced him with tears flowing down his long, gray beard: "You were right; I should have remained in my bishopric; I should not have allowed the tide to carry me away."[50] A few days later, seeing no way through, Macarius retreated to the Monastery of St Antony at the Red Sea in a self-imposed exile. Upon arriving at the monastery, he insisted on walking to its gates, prostrating himself until he arrived at the church, crying out, "I sinned when I became patriarch. I never want to return to the cathedral, may I become lame or blind. . . . I regret it my Lord, is there any repentance for such a sin?"[51] The previous months had worn heavily upon the old man. "While I have only been a patriarch for half a year, it feels like half a century," wrote Macarius from the monastery to Prime Minister Ahmed Mahir on November 19, 1944,

> . . . I remonstrated with Minyawi and his fellow *maglis al-melli* members, with a broken heart and tears I begged Minyawi. I asked him to have mercy on me and to be kind to me and to accept my plea in such hard times. [I told him that] I cannot breathe, and my stomach was burning and much more of the similar sayings. But he never responded or cared about my pain, crying,

and remonstration and had no mercy on me and did not return my requests. I, therefore, decided to go away to the monastery.[52]

Several months later he returned. In mid-1945 the Synod passed a resolution reasserting clerical authority. Factionalism once more erupted. By the time of Macarius' death on August 31, 1945, nothing had changed.[53] Those who were left in the Church lost hope—and whatever hope still faintly survived would soon be dashed in a wretched decade that many have chosen to forget.

Ecclesial Chaos: The Unseemly Events of July 25, 1954

> "Lying is a delightful thing for it leads to the truth."
> —*Fyodor Dostoyevsky*

S OME MIGHT FEEL uncomfortable or prefer a more subdued telling of the following account in the life of Yusab II (1880–1956). But to avoid the episode is not only a disservice to history and the quest for truth, it also betrays the undeniably seismic shift in the Church before and after Fr Mina.

"It was as if the weaknesses of the father," wrote a Western journalist, "showed up the weaknesses of his family to the embarrassment of all the children—who, meanwhile, were fighting among themselves."[54] The previous decades of cumulative calamity evidently materialized in the person of Yusab II, and more so, in his odious manservant. Thus, as humiliating and scandalous as it may be, the unfortunate episode must be examined without prejudice. Anything else is ahistorical, disingenuous, and, though superficially pious, it misses the transformative significance of the healing that Fr Mina brought to a festering wound.

* * *

The death of Macarius III in August 1945 did little to alleviate the confusion and dissension within the Church.[55] Stepping in as locum tenens, Metropolitan Yusab of Girga set about organizing an election campaign that, oddly, was for himself. That such a campaign was even permitted testifies to the amnesia that repeatedly descended upon the populace. Once more the ancient canons calling for the ordination of a monk (or layman) to the patriarchate were willfully ignored. A few dissenting voices, such as that of Bishop Athanasius of Beni-

Suef (1883–1962), were immediately silenced, with at least one priest being later excommunicated.[56] In the end, though, it would make little difference. The election was seemingly preordained. Earlier on, the electoral rolls had been manipulated to exclude certain eligible voters; and on the day of the election, May 12, 1946, a coincidental transport strike (likely orchestrated) prevented those who *were* eligible from casting their votes. That is, other than Yusab's supporters who were, fortunately, able to procure an army convoy to the voting hall in the heart of Cairo.[57] One historian was hardly able to contain her shock: "He won with only one hundred and eighty votes!"[58] Two weeks later Metropolitan Yusab was enthroned as patriarch.

Yusab II (1880–1956), to be fair, was considered by many to be exceptionally well prepared for the patriarchate.[59] Born in a village of the city of Girga in Upper Egypt, he entered the Monastery of St Antony at seventeen years old and was made hegumen a few years later. Between 1902 and 1905 he studied theology in Athens, became fluent in Greek and French, and later returned to become the abbot of several monasteries. Eventually, he was ordained the Metropolitan of Girga in 1920, serving, we should note, on no fewer than three occasions as locum tenens of the patriarchate.[60] Such experience and formation were, sadly, of trivial consequence. Almost immediately after becoming patriarch, Yusab reneged on his promises to the *maglis*—by which he had secured their unanimous support in the election—to transfer the *waqf* to the (predominantly lay) council. "The bishop of Girga signed it, not the patriarch," he reportedly replied when faced with the signed agreement.[61] Yusab instead entrusted the *waqf* to the abbots of the monasteries whom he had ordained as bishops for good measure.[62] But even this contention with the formidable *maglis*, the despoiler of not a few patriarchs, would be eclipsed by the rapidly mounting discontent with Yusab's initially insignificant manservant, a certain Melek Kamel Girgis.

Exhausted by the election, Yusab brought with him to the patriarchate his "fellah," a valet of sorts, who had served him while he was metropolitan of Girga. Yusab made the unfortunate mistake of entrusting him with inordinate and excessive authority.[63] Described variously, but most aptly as a "grey eminence," Melek first acted quietly then overtly as the enfeebled patriarch's go-between.[64] Some sources suggest he began as an honorable servant but was seduced by power and wealth and, enabled by the "weak and malleable personality" of Yusab, promptly set about corrupting the patriarchate.[65] (Melek, we should note, was the same dark figure that previously sought to banish Fr Mina from his church in Old Cairo, apparently even attempting to kidnap him.[66]) Distribution of property, patriarchal administration, promotions of priesthood, and even episcopal ordinations were all subject to the approval of Melek. Power could not but corrupt the illiterate and infamous "fellah."

No fewer than sixteen of the nineteen episcopal ordinations during the time of Yusab were allegedly "sold," many fetching as much as LE 5000 with Melek "perhaps collecting this fee at some later date from endowment revenues."[67] Melek, a peasant whose salary could hardly exceed LE 10, had amassed in a few short years at least four buildings in Cairo and three in Alexandria, and, much to the lament and dismay of the populace, had gone so far as to file a lawsuit against the bishop of Souhag over a failed IOU (promise of payment).[68] "I witnessed an event," wrote an eminent priest, Ibrahim Luka, in 1947,

> that confirmed this [simony] to me. An overly ambitious man personally offered me, or to my church projects in Heliopolis, LE 5,000 in return for a Bishopric in a diocese. . . . I also discovered the [Papal] courtiers had hands in transferring the priests of Cairo, in spite of the fact that this was within the scope of my job as *wakil* [vicar]. This, however, was being manipulated by someone else. . . .[69]

Before long it became nearly impossible to approach Yusab without passing through Melek. The windows to the patriarchate were fitted with iron bars, and the doors securely bolted in what may be termed a "closed-door policy." Yusab—forever wearing his peculiar (for a patriarch) "tea-shade" sunglasses—was to be seen less and less, having been "warned" by Melek that many were conspiring to assassinate him.[70] This would eventually become a very real concern.

* * *

An incident in late 1948 is most revealing. It is fortunately documented in detail by Nazir Gayed (the future Shenouda III) as editor-in-chief of the Sunday School Movement periodical.[71] On December 12, Metropolitan Abraam of Giza, who had allowed some "openness" to the Sunday School Movement (SSM), reposed. Just three days later, lay notables and clergy met to determine his successor.[72] The patriarchate had suggested Fr Metias el-Antony. This came as something of a shock to the wife of one of the leading Copts of Giza, Aziza Mashriqi, who had known him well during the monk's service in Jerusalem. She stated in no uncertain terms that the monk had a "bad reputation."[73] A short while later, her husband abruptly expressed the very opposite concerning the monk and agitated for his nomination. "We suspected," one of those present claimed, "that the sudden change of the family of el-Mashriqi was bought with money."[74]

Fr Salib Suryal, who had been recently ordained, along with the SSM, categorically rejected the proposal, instead calling for a man who was beyond reproach, Archdeacon Habib Girgis. On December 20, a meeting of the priests of Giza, to which Salib was *not* invited, was held. Surprisingly they were "unanimous" in confirming the candidacy of Fr Metias. It was later discovered, Fr Salib claims, that the board of priests was bought by Melek and that the ordination was, in fact, preordained—purchased at some unfortunate price of simony.[75] "One of those around the pope," wrote Nazir Gayed in the SSM periodical, "has misused his privilege to ordain a metropolitan. . . . We cannot stand silent, we have learned bitter and painful lessons. . . . We cannot bear the *recurrences* of these tragedies."[76] Despite the protests of virtually the entire diocese, begging at least to delay until a more suitable and worthy candidate could be found, their petitions fell on deaf ears. "What do these things have to do with the youth?" retorted Yusab. "Let them concentrate on their studies and leave us to handle the Church's affairs."[77]

When news broke of Fr Metias' ordination, the youth of Giza (and a great deal of the SSM in Cairo) descended upon the patriarchate. Instead of being greeted by the pope, they were greeted by a barricade of armed police. Unable to meet Yusab, they returned a few days later, only this time to be met by "laborers" armed with weapons. "We tell the truth," writes Gayed, "and Jesus is our witness that we were absolutely stunned. . . . What is this? What age are we living in? To be humiliated to such a degree in our father's house!"[78] To their disbelief, the ordination date had already been set for January 23, 1949. The SSM saw no other choice. They would prevent the ordination "even if it meant our death."[79] "We arrived on the ordination day," wrote the fiery Gayed (evidently being present himself),

> . . . and when they entered the church, and the patriarch began to lay his hand on him [Metias], we all screamed with one voice: "The *Didascalia* and the canons forbid you . . . the ordination of Fr Metias is against the will of the people!" We were expecting what would happen. The police entered with large sticks and began to beat us mercilessly at the direction of the patriarchal personnel [one may suggest Melek], in the presence of the patriarch . . . kicking us out of the church. . . . It is amazing that after all this commotion they could assemble at the altar and begin singing *eporo* ("O King of Peace").[80]

The doors were bolted shut, and a large barricade was—quite symbolically—erected between the patriarch and the congregation. And so was ordained Metropolitan Youannis of Giza (1949–1963), against the canons and against the will of the people. These young men, and with them the hopes of the greater Church, were left totally despondent in the face of a patriarch under the sway of the unscrupulous and profiteering Melek.

By the early 1950s few could tolerate such a state of affairs. Ibrahim suggests that the Free Officer's 1952 revolution in Egypt saw the emergence of the *harakat al-tathir*, a "purification or cleansing movement."[81] Originally a notion that sought the "purge" of political corruption and the inauguration of reform, modernization, and progression of the nation, it would only be a few months before the Coptic press (*Misr*) adopted such language, provoking a flood of telegrams to the new government: "As you have purged the country, purge our patriarchate."[82] The SSM (as we have just seen) was no less vocal in decrying the actions of the patriarch and especially the simony of Melek.[83] In the Synod, however, a dilemma of sorts emerged; on the one hand, the humiliation and exploitation of the patriarchate could not go unpunished, and on the other, many of its members had benefited in varying degrees from the very same underhanded dealings.[84]

Soon it became clear to all—even to the many bishops who had a share in simony—that Melek had gone too far. With the support of the newly formed *Revolutionary Command Council* (RCC), in September, 1952, the minister of the interior was finally persuaded to remove Melek to his hometown Girga, along with five others.[85] Yusab was inconsolable. When asked a few months later by the newly appointed Prime Minister Naguib as to what he could do for the Church, he is reported to have asked, only, as a matter of urgent priority, for the return of his indispensable manservant.[86] And so, four months later, on December 31, 1952, Melek returned, to the disgust and embarrassment of all.[87]

Provoked by Yusab's incomprehensible actions, Fr Mina could no longer hold his silence. He had looked on quietly from St Menas' in Old Cairo; he had seen his beloved Church torn apart, he had heard of demoralizing rumors that gave way to indisputable and outright corruption and extortion, and he now tended to his disciples who were beaten and traumatized in the presence of the patriarch.[88] Now he had to speak. An unpublished letter from Fr Mina written to Yusab II in the early 1950s—one may suggest in the year of 1953—is the only record of his stance during these difficult years:

To the holy and honored Anba Yusab, Metropolitan of the Chair of Girga, and *not* the patriarch of St Mark's throne, God keep your life. . . . Now the peace of the Church and all the congregation has been lost, so I beseech you in the name of the beloved Jesus that you assemble the Holy Synod and declare the error that the fathers, the metropolitans, committed who set their eyes on the chair of the patriarch. After that you should select a committee to search the monasteries for three righteous monks who are beyond reproach according to all; call for a fast for three days and an altar ballot, and whosoever is chosen by the Lord will be your vicar. After you have enjoyed a long and peaceful life, he will take over from you as patriarch. If you do this, you will please heaven and earth, and history will write of you with golden ink. . . .[89]

Such words should be read slowly and carefully. They could not have been written nor received lightly. We have no record of Yusab's reaction, nor of his reply. But we can well imagine it. Even if we could somehow ignore Fr Mina's reference to Yusab's errors and death, the very first sentence borders upon the scandalous: no metropolitan can ever, without "error," be elevated to patriarch.[90] Consequently, Yusab, in the mind of Fr Mina was "*not* the patriarch." These highly inflammatory words were precarious for a monk—especially one living outside his monastery—and suggest forcefully that Mina's only concern was the Church, irrespective of the personal cost. Whether others in the Church shared his views or not, one thing was clear to all. Something had to be done.

* * *

Just before midnight on July 24, 1954, thirty-three young men, led by a young lawyer by the name of Ibrahim Hilal, knocked frantically on the door of the patriarchate.[91] Dawood, the door-keeper, startled from his sleep, inquired as to the panic. "Youannis of Giza has . . . ," yelled the men, ". . . Youannis . . . has been shredded in a train accident!" Dawood flung the doors open, only to find himself apprehended, along with the two soldiers guarding the doors. As the men approached the patriarch's quarters, two elderly Ethiopian servants chanced upon them and were also captured. Hearing the commotion, Yusab unwittingly opened the door to his abductors. The patriarch was, Hilal commented in an interview a number of years later, "torn between astonishment and disbelief, staring at us for over five minutes before uttering a word."[92] Standing before him, in a seeming parallel to the overthrow of King Farouk two years earlier, were men with documents demanding Yusab sign his abdication in favor of

Saweros, bishop of Menia.[93] The aged patriarch was then hurriedly forced into a waiting taxi—according to one sensational report, narrowly escaping gunshots from security forces in hot pursuit—before being bundled out at St George's Monastery in Old Cairo.[94]

The patriarch had been abducted. Those remaining at the patriarchate, under siege by numerous security forces, demanded the immediate recognition of Yusab's abdication by the Synod. Within a few hours, the press and major parishes had received signed copies of the abdication and the group's demands. But by evening on July 26, 1954, the patriarch had been rescued, and the would-be kidnappers arrested.

Those young men—all members of the JUQ (*Jamaat al-Umma al-Qibtaya*), "Coptic Nation Society"—were part of a youth movement established by Ibrahim Hilal on September 11, 1952. Historians have differed in their rationale for the emergence of the JUQ; some claiming it was an answer to and therefore imitation of the Muslim Brotherhood, others suggesting it was "middle-class reaction" to a "political void" of Coptic representation after the downfall of the Wafd Party.[95] But it appears that neither of these, nor even the call for *tathir*, or "purging," was the primary motivation for the abduction. In a little-known 2003 interview, Hilal disclosed what some had suspected: the abduction was, in fact, a reaction to Yusab's dissolution (with the support of Gamal Abdel Nasser) of the JUQ in April 1954, and, therefore, a response to a personal slight. Notwithstanding, Hilal also dubiously claimed he acted on the direct request of the Synod itself.[96]

While the exact details of the abduction vary, the reaction of the wider Church was unanimous.[97] The issue of the SSM periodical published immediately after the abduction strangely makes no mention of the event, but instead, tellingly, calls for the election of the next patriarch from among the monks.[98] The perpetrators, Vivian Ibrahim notes, received "very little admonishment" from the community and the government; and, while they were reproached by the clergy, the Synod was "careful not to condemn them."[99] In fact, the Synod went so far as to secure their freedom and acquittal. "We should not play down," declared Mikhail, Bishop of Asyut, at the meeting of the Synod,

> the actions of the JUQ by arguing that they were either unemployed or workers. If the patriarchal chair continues in this method, then the Church will continually shake. . . . I declare that the Church issues and matters are now in the hands of the servant Melek.[100]

Though few would or could condone the actions of the JUQ, all appreciated that there were legitimate grievances. On September 25, 1954, the Synod convened with its final decision, signed by some sixteen bishops: Yusab would withdraw his charges and officially forgive the JUQ for their abduction; Melek and his associated patriarchal servants would be expelled immediately; and a triumvirate of metropolitans would assist Yusab in managing the Church.[101] Yusab accepted only the first decision, though even then it was apparently coerced, but categorically declined the latter two conditions.[102] Youannis of Giza (ordained, as seen above, at the hands of Yusab and Melek) "personally" requested Yusab once more to heed the decisions of the Synod.[103] Yusab furiously refused, declaring: "I said there was a conspiracy in the Holy Synod."[104] Eventually, after a "voluntary withdrawal" of the majority of the Synod to St Antony's Monastery, Yusab relented.[105]

It would not be long, to the utter disbelief of the Synod (and community), before Yusab once more returned Melek "on the excuse that he was irreplaceable."[106] Within days Melek had resumed his deplorable trade. Somehow blind to history—in a fatal fit of greed or amnesia—Melek set his sights upon the valuable and perilous *waqf*. In mid-1955, he suggested that Yusab dismiss several bishops from their monasteries and appoint others to benefit from the *waqf* directly. And so, in obedience to his avaricious valet, Yusab, on August 14, 1955, dismissed Bishop Gabriel of St Antony's Monastery.[107] Gabriel, in turn, summoned the Synod.[108] On September 20, the perplexed members of the Holy Synod were unceremoniously locked out of the patriarchal residence of Yusab who, once more, refused to hear them.[109] It would be the last straw. There could be no other recourse. The Synod, in their words, were unwilling to leave the "Church in disgrace," and summarily decreed Yusab's permanent removal from office. The *maglis* was in rare accord.[110] "The government has agreed," announced the Coptic politician, Gindi Abdel Malik,

> to relieve the patriarch of his powers in response to the wishes of the Coptic people and the leaders of the Church, after all agreed that His Eminence is not fit to carry out his duties.[111]

Two days later, Patriarch Yusab II was dethroned by the Synod. He was exiled outside Cairo and Alexandria, with the care of the Church once more returning to a triumvirate of bishops.[112] On September 27, 1955, he left for Muharraq Monastery—his monastery of choice—with the blinds of his car pulled down, and some thirteen bags in tow.[113] For the first time in more than half a century, the *maglis* and Synod, clergy and lay, finally acted in unison—that is, to *dethrone* the patriarch.

*   *   *

A last-ditch effort by some to negotiate the return of Yusab (without Melek) unsurprisingly failed.[114] The defiant patriarch was undeterred. But the Church, both clergy and lay, could bear no more. When Yusab arrived—against the will and decrees of the Synod—at the patriarchate on June 21, 1956, the gates were locked, and he instead found himself escorted to the Coptic Hospital in downtown Cairo. He would never leave it. A few months later, in late September, grief-stricken and broken, he began to deteriorate, eventually becoming comatose for the last week of his life. Unwilling to neglect the dignity of his office, the Synod allowed the unconscious patriarch to be transferred to the cathedral for the last twenty-four hours.[115] On November 13, 1956, Yusab II, still wearing his darkened "tea-shade" sunglasses, reposed.

To what degree Yusab was complicit or manipulated remains unknown. Likewise, we have no record of his ever disciplining, reproaching, or even apologizing for Melek's unseemly conduct.[116] Yusab's reluctance to part with such an individual at first, and later his pleas for Melek's return at the cost of all else, suggests a deeply misguided and deluded dependence at best.

Only weeks later the Synod would declare a "state of mourning." Nasser, in what appeared to be an opportunistic conspiracy against a hemorrhagic and despondent Church, abolished the religious courts and blatantly intruded in the "Personal Status Laws" of the Copts.[117] The Synod, in a dramatic "gesture of passive resistance," called for bells to be rung, celebrations canceled, functions boycotted, and parishes closed; the patriarchate and dioceses would deny any exchange of greetings with the Muslim government on the imminent feast of Nativity—and should that fail, each and every bishop would retire to his monastery in protest.[118] It was, beyond its immediate context and history, a most unfortunate and yet apt summation of the previous decades—the Church was in an inconsolable state of mourning.

Notes

[1] Al-Masri, *Story of the Coptic Church*, 6:161.
[2] Meinardus, *Christian Egypt: Faith and Life*, 22. For a useful summary of the history of the *maglis*, see Zaklama, *Pope Kyrillos VI*, 1:387–411.

[3]Ibrahim notes that the move had historical precedence with Ibn al-Assal, a thirteenth-century jurist, justifying the formation of a body consisting of "specialized laity" to "assist" the clergy; see Ibrahim, *The Copts of Egypt*, 34.

[4]Meinardus, *Christian Egypt: Faith and Life*, 23. Accordingly, the original constitution stipulates the Council's management of the monastic endowments (*waqf*), schools, benevolent societies, and personal status issues; see Ibrahim, *The Copts of Egypt*, 35–36. For a discussion of the PSL issues, see John Khalil, "A Brief History of Coptic Personal Status Law," *Berkeley Journal of Middle Eastern & Islamic Law* 3, no. 1/2 (2010): 81–139.

[5]Van Doorn-Harder, *Modern Coptic Papacy*, 88; Donald Reid, *Whose Pharaohs? Archaeology, Museums, and Egyptian National Identity from Napoleon to World War I* (Berkeley: University of California Press, 2002), 261. Nelly van Doorn-Harder suggests that similar reform was taking place at the al-Azhar with likewise similar reactions from the traditional Islamic legal scholars.

[6]Al-Masri, *True Story of Christianity in Egypt*, 2:352; van Doorn-Harder, *Modern Coptic Papacy*, 89; Samir Seikaly, "Coptic Communal Reform: 1860–1914," *Middle Eastern Studies* 6, no. 3 (1970): 262.

[7]Carter, *The Copts in Egyptian Politics*, 28.

[8]Adel Azer Bestawros, "Community Council, Coptic," in *CE*, 580b–82b; Ibrahim, *The Copts of Egypt*, 37; Meinardus, *Christian Egypt: Faith and Life*, 23.

[9]Van Doorn-Harder, *Modern Coptic Papacy*, 90. *Pasha*, in prerepublican Egypt, was one of the highest ranks in the Ottoman Empire's political system.

[10]Ibid.

[11]Meinardus, *Christian Egypt: Faith and Life*, 23–24.

[12]To limit confusion, and given the audience, I will refer to the "monastic endowments" by its popular singular usage ("*waqf*"), rather than differentiating between singular (*waqf*) and plural (*awqaf* or *waqfs*).

[13]Seikaly, "Coptic Communal Reform," 260–61. For a sense of the enormity of the figure, see: Carter, *The Copts in Egyptian Politics*, 42; Ibrahim, *The Copts of Egypt*, 126–27. Nelly van Doorn-Harder suggests that in 1926 there were 100 monks inhabiting seven monasteries who had access to 300,000 Egyptian pounds (hereafter abbreviated as LE) in revenues from 5–9000 feddans of land, an astronomical figure at the time; see van Doorn-Harder, *Modern Coptic Papacy*, 92–93. [One Egyptian pound converted to US $0.20 in 1926, or just over $2.81 in 2019 terms (dollartimes.com). One feddan is equal to 1.038 acres (or 4200 m²; justintools.com and other sites).]

[14]Carter, *The Copts in Egyptian Politics*, 29.

[15]Van Doorn-Harder, *Modern Coptic Papacy*, 92; Ibrahim, *The Copts of Egypt*, 117. Ibrahim also notes that the married priests lived in a state of poverty: the average salary was 3 LE a month, which in fact was only given as a charitable contribution 3–4 times per year, with most living off gifts of food from their congregation. This further suggested a drastic misappropriation of funds; see ibid., 124–25.

[16]Van Doorn-Harder, *Modern Coptic Papacy*, 92. Watson suggests many saw the *maglis* as a brake on patriarchal excess; Watson, *Among the Copts*, 47.

[17]Ibrahim, *The Copts of Egypt*, 117.

[18]Ibid., 118.

[19]Meinardus, *Christian Egypt: Faith and Life*, 25; Ibrahim, *The Copts of Egypt*, 119; al-Masri, *Story of the Coptic Church*, 5:42.

[20]For a lay perspective for the reasons of the exile see al-Masri, *True Story of Christianity in Egypt*, 2:352–53. Also see Meinardus, *Monks and Monasteries (1989)*, 41. Youannis XIX (the patriarch after Cyril V, and the secretary of the Synod at the time) was also exiled, in his case to Anba Paula Monastery.

[21]S. H. Leeder, *Modern Sons of the Pharaohs* (London: Hodder and Stoughton, 1918), 260.

[22]For a discussion of the period see Seikaly, "Coptic Communal Reform," 251–60.

[23]Ibrahim, *The Copts of Egypt*, 120. For various interpretations of the event, see ibid., 121.

[24]For a discussion of the khedival intervention see Seikaly, "Coptic Communal Reform," 251–60; van Doorn-Harder, *Modern Coptic Papacy*, 91.

[25]For a summary see Meinardus, *Christian Egypt: Faith and Life*, 24–25; Ibrahim, *The Copts of Egypt*, 118–24.

[26]For details of the changes, see Meinardus, *Christian Egypt: Faith and Life*, 24. Two significant modifications in the favor of the patriarch were those of December 31, 1908, and February 12, 1912. In the former, the patriarch was given the right to appoint an acting president of the *maglis* in his absence and the supervision of the *waqf* was given to the patriarch along with four members of the clergy. The latter specified that four members of the *maglis* would be elected by the patriarch and eight by the people, whereas the monastic *waqf* would be supervised by the patriarch and four bishops.

[27]Ibid., 24–25.

[28]Ibrahim, *The Copts of Egypt*, 123–24. Also see Seikaly, "Coptic Communal Reform," 261. "For centuries the Church had survived," Seikaly writes, "despite the vicissitudes of politics and political conditions, by withdrawal, by catering silently to its adherents, and by leading a discreet existence. . . . To accept a programme of reform was to drag the Church and community away from its safe obscurity, to advertise its existence and, by forcefully seeking social and economic advancement, to risk retribution from a suspicious government and an envious populace. Both Patriarch and laity were dedicated; they were, however, *dedicated to different things*." Seikaly goes on to add that the claim that Cyril V was obstructive to reform or opposed to the laity "is an easy one, but manifestly wrong." History bears out the possibility that Cyril V's intention was not to obstruct reform, but rather he had simply learned from the past—namely, that Cyril IV's sudden death was rumored to be related to Sa'ad Pasha's displeasure. El-Khawaga and Carter suggest that the *maglis* and Synod actually had the same aims at heart, however different their means; see Dina el-Khawaga, "The Laity at the Heart of the Coptic Clerical Reform," in *BDC*, 144–45; Carter, *The Copts in Egyptian Politics*, 28.

[29]Leeder, *Modern Sons of the Pharaohs*, 248.

[30]Meinardus, *Christian Egypt: Faith and Life*, 26. By 1932 the committee had been abandoned.

[31]"Declaration of Patriarchal Election Law, July 18, 1928," reprinted in *al-Yaqazah*, August 1928; cited in Ibrahim, *The Copts of Egypt*, 132.

[32]Van Doorn-Harder, *Modern Coptic Papacy*, 122; Ibrahim, *The Copts of Egypt*, 131.

[33]Yassa Abdel-Messih, "Letter to Mr. Kamel, August 20, 1942" [in Arabic], in FRC-1: Letter 357 (1942). Also see Tadros, *Motherland Lost*, 156.

[34]Al-Masri, *Story of the Coptic Church*, 6. For a fascinating discussion—scholarly and historically accurate—see a letter by the (then) Curator of the Coptic Museum: Abdel-Messih, "Letter to Mr. Kamel, August 20, 1942."

[35]Ibrahim, *The Copts of Egypt*, 132.

[36]Sergius suggests history had also effected apathy: "The Copts have very little interest towards the Pope or the role he plays, which has resulted in a lack of responsibility when it comes to his election. The Patriarch's image is one of an old man with rosary beads and no action. People do not get involved as they have no reason to choose [a new patriarch]. People have become spiritually disheartened and the Church as a result has been weakened. Every Pope that has died has been unable to achieve reform. The result is that people are waiting for the following one [new patriarch] to achieve what the previous could not. This has resulted in the departure of tens of thousands of people from the religion and Church." Sergius, *al-Manarah al-Misriyyah*, January 22, 1944 (ibid., 130).

[37]Ibid., 133.

[38]Al-Masri, *True Story of Christianity in Egypt*, 2:409.

[39]Al-Masri, *Story of the Coptic Church*, 6:126; van Doorn-Harder, *Modern Coptic Papacy*, 121.

[40]Van Doorn-Harder, *Modern Coptic Papacy*, 120–22. She also notes he had, for instance, hosted the Coptic congress, opened schools in his diocese, encouraged education, lay servants, and, interestingly, had sided in the past with lay reformers.

[41]Ibrahim, *The Copts of Egypt*, 135–37.

[42]Transcript of speech given by Macarius, January 29, 1944, in *al-Manarah al-Misriyyah*, February 1, 1944; cited in ibid., 144.

[43]Ibid., 145.

[44]Ibid., 146.

[45]Ibid., 148.

[46]Ibid., 148–49.

[47] For instance, see Watson, *Among the Copts*, 47; Seikaly, "Coptic Communal Reform." It is important to note though, as O'Mahony suggests, that many of the *maglis'* suggested reforms seem to have been modeled upon democratic American Presbyterian methods: "It was an odd model to choose for a Church whose very survival says something about the aptness of its ways"; see O'Mahony, "Coptic Christianity," 495–96.

[48] Meinardus, *Christian Egypt: Faith and Life*, 26.

[49] Ibrahim Minyawi, *Misr*, June 19, 1944.

[50] Al-Masri, *True Story of Christianity in Egypt*, 2:410.

[51] Al-Masri, *Story of the Coptic Church*, 6:165.

[52] Macarius to Prime Minister Ahmad Mahir, November 19, 1944, reprinted in *al-Manarah al-Misriyyah*,
April 21, 1945; cited in Ibrahim, *The Copts of Egypt*, 153. This was a reply and explanation to Mahir who was inquiring as to when Macarius planned on returning, in some regard pledging implicit support.

[53] Ibrahim Minyawi was reported by the local newspapers to have walked behind the funeral procession for Macarius III, wearing a *white suit and red tie*—needless to say, a sign of incredible disrespect; *al-Watani*, October 3, 1945, cited in ibid., 155.

[54] Wakin, *A Lonely Minority*, 94.

[55] Al-Masri, *True Story of Christianity in Egypt*, 2:417.

[56] Carter, *The Copts in Egyptian Politics*, 36; al-Masri, *Story of the Coptic Church*, 6:13; Mounir Shoukry, "Yusab II," in *CE*, 2363. The latter claims that the controversial Hegumen Sergius was excommunicated in response to his opposing Yusab in the preelection.

[57] Tadros, *Motherland Lost*, 156. For the rigging of the election see al-Masri, *Story of the Coptic Church*, 6:14–15; Carter, *The Copts in Egyptian Politics*, 37.

[58] Al-Masri, *Story of the Coptic Church*, 6:15.

[59] Wakin, *A Lonely Minority*, 93; van Doorn-Harder, *Modern Coptic Papacy*, 123. Van Doorn-Harder adds, "And he was neither too young nor too old to hold the office." For issues from the beginning of his reign until his abduction, see al-Masri, *Story of the Coptic Church*, 6:37–38.

[60] For biographical details, see van Doorn-Harder , *Modern Coptic Papacy*, 123; Shoukry, "Yusab II." He served as locum tenens (patriarchal deputy) once when Youannis XIX traveled to Europe and also after his death in 1942, and finally after the death of Macarius III in 1945.

[61] Wakin, *A Lonely Minority*, 150.

[62] Meinardus, *Christian Egypt: Faith and Life*, 26; van Doorn-Harder, *Modern Coptic Papacy*, 125. In 1947 Yusab attempted to replace the *maglis* with new members, the *maglis* ceased their work in protest—in turn, "Yusab left Cairo in frustration." For a discussion of the lead-up to the confrontation of Yusab with the *maglis,* see Carter, *The Copts in Egyptian Politics*, 37.

[63] Al-Masri, *True Story of Christianity in Egypt*, 2:418.

[64] Wakin, *A Lonely Minority*, 94; Meinardus, *Christian Egypt: Faith and Life*, 42.

[65] Pennington, "The Copts in Modern Egypt," 163; al-Masri, *Story of the Coptic Church*, 6:37–38.

[66] Raphael Ava Mina, *Miracles of Pope Kyrillos VI*, 9:39.

[67] Carter, *The Copts in Egyptian Politics*, 38. Carter's reference for these claims is the *French Embassy Archives*, Box 144, File 31/2, the Ambassador to the Minister of Foreign Affairs, March 7, 1953; also see Wakin, *A Lonely Minority*, 94; Meinardus, *Christian Egypt: Faith and Life*, 42. That this was no exaggeration is seen in Kyrillos VI's original move (as we shall see) at an early Synod of his patriarchate to investigate the bishops whose episcopates were an act of simony—before being told, by the secretary of the Synod, this could in fact mean the majority of the Synod. For the account see Samuel Tawadros el-Syriany, *The History of the Popes*, 198. We should also point out that Yusab had in fact ordained twenty-four bishops, but it appears that in the sources the five Ethiopian bishops were not included in this figure of nineteen bishops. The unusual support of the Ethiopians in the face of the events of 1954 even brings this into question. For the bishops at the time of Yusab, as well as the alleged bishop of Souhag mentioned in the lawsuit, one may draw conclusions from the register provided in Nasr, *Readings in the Life of Abouna Mina*, 221–22. I have, however, personally refrained from providing the names, given

that they—unlike those that I have named—are not public knowledge and were accused (in hearsay) without actual trial. It should, perhaps, also be briefly noted (though this is certainly not a justification of simony) that this was the "reality" of the ordinations under Yusab—even of those that may have been worthy; and so, to speculate, many worthy candidates (or diocesan committees) might have had no other choice but to pay Melek's fees.

[68]Wakin, A Lonely Minority, 94. He cites "responsible Coptic sources"; also see Ibrahim, The Copts of Egypt, 61.

[69]Ibrahim Luka, al-Yaqazah, November 1947; cited in Ibrahim, The Copts of Egypt, 61. Fr Ibrahim's wife had since died and thus theoretically he could be ordained to the episcopacy.

[70]Suryal, "Pope Kyrillos VI."

[71]Nazir Gayed, "Why We Interfered" [in Arabic], Sunday School Magazine 2, no. 9 (1949). The articles were written by the "Editor." Nazir Gayed (the future Pope Shenouda III) was editor-in-chief from 1947 to 1954, after which he left to become a monk.

[72]Ibid., 5. The Sunday School Movement (SSM) expressed their shock that this discussion occurred so quickly given the previous customs prevented the discussion of a successor until forty days after the bishop's repose.

[73]Reiss, Erneuerung in der Koptisch-Orthodoxen Kirche, 155; Suryal, "Pope Kyrillos VI." It is of note that the SSM in their lengthy article refuse to name the nature of their complaints against the monk except to say that the reasons were well known, and that the patriarchate should have been aware of this had they investigated. See Gayed, "Why We Interfered," 10.

[74]Cited in Reiss, Erneuerung in der Koptisch-Orthodoxen Kirche, 155.

[75]Suryal, "Pope Kyrillos VI."

[76]Gayed, "Why We Interfered," 2. Interestingly, Gayed, writing in February 1949, refrains from naming Melek, perhaps knowing all too well the tragic power that the manservant held over the patriarch.

[77]Ibid., 7.

[78]Ibid., 8.

[79]Ibid.

[80]Ibid., 9.

[81]Ibrahim, The Copts of Egypt, 157.

[82]Lambeth Palace Archives LEC 87: Crisis in the Coptic Patriarchate, September 1952; cited in ibid., 160.

[83]Reiss, Erneuerung in der Koptisch-Orthodoxen Kirche, 167–68.

[84]Meinardus, Christian Egypt: Faith and Life, 42.

[85]Misr, August 31, 1952, cited in Ibrahim, The Copts of Egypt, 161. Prior to this, Hegumen Sergius declared in front of General Naguib that Yusab had fifteen days to enact administrative reform before he would personally lead a march against the patriarchate—a threat that in part eventually resulted in his excommunication. Lambeth Palace Archives LEC 87: Crisis in the Coptic Patriarchate, September 1952, in ibid.

[86]Bishop Serapion, "Choosing the Patriarch: Lessons from the History of Our Glorious Church" (Los Angeles, 2012), 26. Also see al-Masri, True Story of Christianity in Egypt, 2:419.

[87]Misr, January 3, 1953, cited in Ibrahim, The Copts of Egypt, 168.

[88]In this respect, Wakin's assessment of the period is fair: "Internally, the Copts bickered and feuded over the issue. Community leaders were at odds with bishops; clergy conspired with laity. Reports were widespread about corruption in the religious courts; price tags were placed on bishops' appointments as defamatory stories about the Patriarch embarrassed the Coptic minority." See Wakin, A Lonely Minority, 95.

[89]Hegumen Mina the Recluse [Kyrillos VI], "Letter to Pope Yusab II, 195_" [in Arabic], (Old Cairo, 195_). The letter is on a St Samuel's Monastery letterhead with the date only given as "195_" as the letterheads would be photocopied many times, and the author would then fill in the date. That the year was not filled in is not unusual for his letters. Given the turmoil of 1952–53, it would appear that the letter was written during this time. Admittedly, I had some suspicions about this letter (given its content and lack of signature) and nearly decided against including it, until I had expert handwriting analysis performed

to determine whether it was indeed from the hand of Kyrillos. Only one Arabic translator suggested it was possibly not Kyrillos' hand, whereas four others argued that it was genuine.

[90]The principal concern, stemming from the earliest centuries of the Church, was that a bishop was in fact "wed" to his diocese and as such could not leave a diocese to become patriarch. The Coptic Church observed this canon from its beginning until well into the twentieth century.

[91]Ibrahim suggests, based on other accounts, there were in fact eighty-seven, whereas Hilal in his 2003 interview suggests thirty-three. See Ibrahim, *The Copts of Egypt*, 168; anonymous, "Confrontation with the Man Who Deposed the Pope Fifty Years Ago" [in Arabic], *al-Musawwar*, July 4, 2003.

[92]Ibrahim, *The Copts of Egypt*, 169.

[93]Hilal suggests Bishop Saweros was willing; see anonymous, "Confrontation with the Man." I. H. al-Masri states that they threatened to shoot Yusab should he not sign (though Hilal categorically denies even knowing how to use a weapon); al-Masri, *Story of the Coptic Church*, 6:80.

[94]*Misr,* July 31, 1954, cited in Ibrahim, *The Copts of Egypt*, 171.

[95]Carter, *The Copts in Egyptian Politics*, 280–81; Ibrahim, *The Copts of Egypt*, 165; Gorman, *Historians, State, and Politics*, 169–73. Though the JUQ's "ten-point manifesto" of late 1953 certainly resembles the Muslim Brotherhood's "ten commandments," it undoubtedly also was a bid to fill the Coptic political void.

[96]Anonymous, "Confrontation with the Man." Also see Carter, *The Copts in Egyptian Politics*, 281. Quite reasonably, Hilal's interviewer makes a number of editorial comments about whether his account can be entirely trusted, especially since it is given over half a century later.

[97]There are three main accounts of the incident: (1) *Misr*, July 31, 1954, newspaper account, entitled "The Whole Story" that was contemporary with the event and was based upon "police investigative sources" including statements by eyewitnesses (even that of Hilal himself). But then again, note must be made of *Misr's* pro-RCC and pro-*maglis* agenda. (2) Hilal's interview with Malak Luqa in 1970, which was subject to less political sensitivity. (3) Hilal's 2003 interview. For a discussion of the first two sources see Ibrahim, *The Copts of Egypt*, 168–71. For the latter, see anonymous, "Confrontation with the Man."

[98]Reiss, *Erneuerung in der Koptisch-Orthodoxen Kirche*, 167–68.

[99]Ibrahim, *The Copts of Egypt*, 172.

[100]"Report of Holy Synod Meeting," *Misr,* October 1, 1954, cited in ibid.

[101]For the entire decree see al-Masri, *Story of the Coptic Church*, 6:83–84.

[102]Ibid., 84. For the letter forgiving his abductors see ibid., 82.

[103]Ibrahim, *The Copts of Egypt*, 173.

[104]Ibid.

[105]Al-Masri, *Story of the Coptic Church*, 6:89.

[106]Ibid.

[107]Bishop Gabriel was the head of Yusab's original monastery where he had previously voluntarily retreated.

[108]Al-Masri, *Story of the Coptic Church*, 6:90.

[109]The details of the incident are given in the Synod's decree; for the entire decree see ibid., 90–94. There are some reports of a failed assassination attempt by Abdelmessih Bishara—one of those arrested for the original abduction; Meinardus, *Christian Egypt: Faith and Life*, 27.

[110]The Synod's decree stated how the bishops had since 1954 labored to meet and correct Yusab, who closed the "gates in their faces," and hence subsequently called for: (1) Yusab's removal, (2) his exile from Cairo, (3) establishing a triumvirate of bishops to administer the Church, (4) informing the government and Yusab himself of this ruling, and (5) informing the *maglis* for their endorsement. Al-Masri, *Story of the Coptic Church*, 6:90–94.

[111]Wakin, *A Lonely Minority*, 98.

[112]Ibid., 98–99.

[113]Al-Masri, *Story of the Coptic Church*, 6:93–94.

[114]Ibid., 95–97. I. H. al-Masri details the complexity of this attempt, including the role played by the Ethiopian Church.

[115]Ibid., 92.

[116]Van Doorn-Harder does, however, suggest that Yusab's reign was not without some positives; for instance, he was the first pope to accept the Sunday School Movement (though perhaps reluctantly), and there were significant advances in ecumenical activities under his papacy. Van Doorn-Harder, *Modern Coptic Papacy*, 123. See also al-Masri, *True Story of Christianity in Egypt*, 2:148.

[117]Wakin, *A Lonely Minority*, 99.

[118]Ibid.

PART II

The Reluctant Patriarch:
Reign of Pope Kyrillos VI (1959–1971)

7

The Consecration of Reform (1959)

Nomination and Ordination, 1959

> "I wished to live a stranger and die a stranger.
> But let it be the will of God. . . ."
> —*Pope Kyrillos VI*

YUSAB'S BANISHMENT—what one Western observer described as a "painful and slow amputation"—did little to remedy the endemic infirmity of the Church.[1] The lamentable patriarch's death in late November 1956 saw the eruption of chaotic and frantic feuding, internal dissent, and warnings of imminent upheaval. The amputation, as far as one could tell, had maimed, not healed. It would take close to four years for another patriarch to be enthroned.

* * *

One week after Yusab's death the triumvirate of bishops governing the Church was replaced by the locum tenens, Athanasius, metropolitan of Beni-Suef (1883–1962). He would need broad shoulders. Electing a patriarch in the face of a deeply fractured community that was grappling with what "kind" of leader it wanted (or needed), in the wake of three predecessors who were all elected in questionable circumstances with arguably regrettable reigns, was nearly impossible.

On the streets and in the Synod one question was repeatedly asked: who *could* become patriarch?[2] History, at least for the Copts, was fairly consistent; the patriarch was to be elected from among the monks.[3] The earliest manuscripts of the "Rite of the Consecration of the Patriarch of Alexandria," for instance, simply assume the patriarch-elect is a monk. One Coptologist, Burmester, observes that there are in fact two "rites" within the rite; first the consecration and ordination of the elect as bishop, and then his enthronement as patriarch.[4] Fascinatingly, though, the rite permits one (a layman) who is not a monk or a priest to become patriarch—but never could a bishop become patriarch.[5] In 1862, for instance, when a bishop dared nominate himself, nine bishops of the Synod signed a "deed of excommunication" against all who dared vote for a candidate that was already of the episcopal rank.[6] Only with Youannis XIX in 1928, along with Macarius III and Yusab II who both followed him, do we hear of the elevation of bishops to the rank of patriarch.[7]

With Yusab's death in November 1956, this concern became most divisive. The Synod had learned an all-too-painful lesson and largely (though not unanimously) called for the election of an "unsullied" monk. But, strangely, almost blind to the last three decades, the *maglis* favored an experienced bishop, one who was a proven administrator.[8] Metropolitan Athanasius as locum tenens— who had been ignored a decade earlier when he begged the Synod not to elevate a bishop—vehemently rebuked the Synod for even daring to consider the possibility of another bishop.[9]

The frenzied dispute that followed would only be overshadowed by the Synod's somewhat unified horror at the results of the initial patriarchal election: Fr Matta el-Meskeen, Fr Makary el-Syriany, and Fr Antonios el-Syriany had received the highest votes.[10] All three were monks and, we should note, were disciples of Fr Mina. But this was hardly the concern. They were the infamous university-educated "Sunday School" monks. Neither the *maglis* nor the Synod would tolerate one of these young reforming monks as patriarch.[11] On December 9, 1956, the Synod decreed that the patriarch-elect must be over forty years old, with at least fifteen years of monastic experience. All three were unsurprisingly excluded: Matta and Makary were thirty-six years old, while Antonios was thirty-two.[12] Nevertheless, the Synod members were still terribly determined that they wanted a monk—just not a "Sunday School" monk. Over the next month, the names of some twenty-one monks and one bishop (Mikhail of Asyut) emerged from the tumultuous infighting. Among them, apparently, was Fr Mina; though, as far one can tell from his letters, he was hardly concerned and was casually planning his departure to the desert just outside Alexandria, where he dreamed of rebuilding St Menas' Monastery.[13] It would matter little in the end. The government could no longer tolerate the turmoil and took the atypical step of intervening for the *sake* of the Church. "The Ministry," declared the government on February 1, 1957,

... found that there is a great deal of conflict between the Coptic community and the various religious circles around the office of patriarch. ... Since the government is eager to preserve the dignity and holiness of the patriarchal Church, to avoid bitter election campaigning and to ensure the selection of a candidate who will be a father and shepherd for all Christians, and since the country is facing certain circumstances, the Minister of the Interior issued an order to *stop* the elections for patriarch.[14]

Few—clergy or lay—could seriously argue with the decision.

* * *

The forced delay of the election saw the community grow increasingly anxious. "Nasser," it was commonly said at the time, "is waiting for one of his army officers to grow a beard that is long enough for a patriarch."[15] A year later, in January 1958, the government finally allowed the elections to proceed.[16] Time had allowed wounds to heal, and reason unexpectedly prevailed. Some even tried to persuade Fr Mina to accept his own nomination, but he would not hear a word of it. Almost a year would pass before the nominations were finalized.

The day before the close of the nominations period, there were four candidates, all of whom were monks.[17] But Metropolitan Athanasius, as locum tenens, had yet to put forward his nomination.[18] Fr Mina, at his small church in Old Cairo, was told that Athanasius was on the phone. The conversation was recorded and thankfully preserved by his brother Hanna.[19]

"Fr Mina, why are you not part of this election? ... You should not have missed this duty," abruptly questioned the Metropolitan. "Who am I, but a little worm, to even consider this glorious and serious responsibility," Mina replied. "[It] should be given to a divinely chosen person, and not to whoever wants it." "But I still did not hear your answer"—Athanasius now grew slightly frustrated—"as to why you didn't allow yourself to be nominated and allow the Lord to choose according to his will?" "Your Holiness," he answered, "all my fathers the monks who were nominated are suitable for this critical position, but as for me, I am content with the Lord's grace that is with me." "Fr Mina," declared the Metropolitan, "I have already submitted a nomination for you!"[20]

There was not much Fr Mina could do; the nominations were effectively closed. Athanasius took the discerning step of nominating the confession father of the three young "Sunday School" monks who were rejected because of their age. Fr Mina reluctantly accepted, his brother Hanna recalls, but sternly warned those around him "not to campaign for him, either by flyers, or through meetings"—and, "everyone respected his wishes."[21] We should be careful to note that this was at a time before widespread media. Consequently, a quiet monk in a small church in Old Cairo (albeit an apparent miracle-worker) would have been barely known to the populace in greater Egypt and, therefore, had little chance of success. And further, this was entirely disparate from the past patriarchal elections, which were rife with campaigning, newspaper electioneering, and public defamation of competing candidates.

Fr Mina would be one of the five final nominees, including Frs Demian el-Muharraqi, Timotheos el-Muharraqi, Angelos el-Muharraqi, and Mina el-Antony.[22] If anything, Fr Mina seemed to be intent on sabotaging his own chances. When journalists attempted to take his photo for the newspaper announcements of the candidates, Fr Mina hid his face in his customary shawl. Many ridiculed: "And what will this man of the shawl do for the Church?"[23] Others, numbering not a few bishops, were far more explicit in defaming and denouncing Fr Mina. Rumors and accusations began to circle that he was an "eccentric figure" practicing sorcery in Old Cairo—an explanation for the miracles—or, more commonly, that he was a fraud.[24] But those who knew the quiet monk could sense something at work beyond the whispers, allegations, and election agitations; they had long known that he was different. He was also, importantly, the favorite of the Sunday School Movement. Even though he was not properly "part" of the movement, he had long guided and enabled them; and, most significantly, he was the confessor and spiritual father of the three previous (rejected) patriarchal candidates—the three famous Sunday School monks.[25] Fr Mina was, above all, for many a hermit with no allegiances to clergy or the prerevolution Coptic elite; his allegiance was to God alone.

* * *

On April 8, 1959, Doctor Kamal Ramzy Stino, minister of supply, announced the voting regulations to select the final three candidates. Nine days later, on April 17, eligible voters gathered in Cairo and were given election cards with five names, with either two or four names to be struck off. Four hundred and sixty-eight electors representative of the entire community participated. Twenty-two of the *maglis*, as well as five bishops, refused to vote—suggesting they were unhappy with *all* the candidates.[26] Damian el-Muharraqi received 323 votes, Angelos el-Muharraqi 316, and Mina el-Baramousy 280 votes. In a return to one of the earlier traditions, it was decided that the final decision should fall to an "altar ballot."[27] Two days later, on April 19, at the cathedral, the names of the candidates were written on three pieces of paper in "India ink." The papers were placed in a sealed envelope on the altar in the presence of all gathered, including government officials.[28] At 10:20 a.m., a five-year-old boy from regional Tanta reached into the envelope, selected a paper, and passed it to Metropolitan Athanasius. The entire Church waited with breath held. Athanasius read out the name: "Hegumen Mina el-Baramousy the Recluse."[29]

The congregation exploded in deafening cheers. The cathedral bells announced a decision had been made. After some four years, there would be a patriarch once more. The name "Hegumen Mina" was spread throughout Cairo within an hour, broadcast on radio, and shouted from the streets. Hearing the news, a servant began wildly ringing the bells at St Menas' Church in Old Cairo. Still celebrating the Liturgy, Fr Mina begged him, tears in eyes, to stop until he had completed the service.[30] A photograph of Fr Mina taken on that morning as he emerged from the altar in his liturgical vestments, cross in one hand, leaning on the sanctuary door with the other, can only faintly reveal his emotion; fifty-six years of age, his eyes tired, glazed with tears, his face without expression, without any degree of shock nor elation, almost as though he had long ago resigned himself to the burden he would now carry.[31] "This is a new test, a new task that God has given me," he is recorded as saying to those around him as he emerged, though it seemed he was not talking to them but rather to God:

> I have always lived as a solitary, my God, and I would have continued to live and die solitary. But you have not wanted it. My God, may your will be done, for your will is impenetrable and you are mysterious, Lord.[32]

Few could perceive what this would mean for the monk. Many have spoken of the enormity of the burden; that he was walking "into the valley of Coptic confusion and discontent," a community deeply fractured, exhausted, and broken.[33] But this still misses the meaning of his words. Becoming patriarch would mean for Fr Mina—and this alone—the loss of solitude. This was his one true burden. One can almost see it in his face and hear it in his words. When asked by a journalist a few days later, "Have you ever thought that you would be a patriarch?" his words betray his agony: "Of course not."[34]

* * *

As an ancient custom, on May 9, 1959, the day before his ordination, Fr Mina traveled to Baramous, his original monastery.[35] It would be the first time since his dismissal for defending the expelled elderly monks two decades earlier in

1936. During the Liturgy, Fr Mina saw Hegumen Basilious—who had played a part in the exile—and knelt before him begging for absolution.[36] It would be characteristic of his life as patriarch. Before leaving, he visited the other monasteries of the Wadi al-Natrun, seeing many of his beloved disciples who were now monks. "When he came to the Syrian Monastery," recalled Fr Antonios el-Syriany (the future Shenouda III), "they asked me to address the patriarch-elect. I talked a little, then he held his handkerchief and wiped tears from his eyes . . . I was so touched that he wept in front of everyone."[37]

Around sunset, the convoy of vehicles returned to Cairo where thousands escorted him to the cathedral. Fr Mina made his way through the crowds, knelt before the altar, and arose to pray Vespers before retiring to his room. At half-past two in the morning, the guard of the papal residence noticed an unfamiliar man walking through the courtyard and began shouting at him, only to find it was the patriarch-elect. Fr Mina kindly asked him to open the doors of the church, and he began praying the psalmody, to the surprise of the deacons, who arrived a few hours later. Although he would pray the later Liturgy during his ordination, he stayed quietly in the corner while another priest celebrated in the early hours. As Fr Raphael notes, "He regarded it as his source of consolations."[38] He spent that night as he had spent every night for the previous three decades.

A few hours later he was escorted by several bishops—a liturgical remnant of the past, when monks would be brought bound in iron fetters—to the cathedral, where he was handed a key, opening the door with the words: "Open the door of righteousness to me, so I can thank the Lord . . ."[39] He entered and prostrated himself before the sanctuary, remaining there until finally Metropolitan Athanasius said to him gently, "Rise up, Fr Mina, let us start." He arose with copious tears falling from his eyes. "The Lord who chose you will assist you," reassured Athanasius. "Do not be troubled."[40] Metropolitan Youannis of Giza read out the letter of nomination, and then, one by one, by seniority, the bishops laid their hands on him. The moment had come. Athanasius placed his hands on the head of Fr Mina. He declared three times, "We ordain you Pope Kyrillos VI, Pope of Alexandria and Patriarch of the See of St Mark."[41] Each time the people responded, shouting, "Amen, Lord have mercy."[42]

It took a few moments for the resounding words to settle in the cathedral. *Kyrillos?* All had expected that he would be Mina III, after his beloved St Menas. When asked on a later occasion as to the reason for the name "Kyrillos," he mentioned in passing that during the elections he had visited the windmill. There he had a vision of Cyril V (1831–1927) holding a baby, saying, "Fr Mina hold this baby, you will nurse grace as you are nursing this baby in your hands; moreover, grace will nurse you just as you are nursing this baby."[43]

Kyrillos (Cyril) VI—Fr Mina was no more—was dressed in the patriarchal vestments and knelt before the sanctuary. Metropolitan Athanasius took the papal staff and handed it to Kyrillos, saying, "Receive the shepherd's staff from the Shepherd of Shepherds, Jesus Christ . . . to shepherd the flock and feed them. . . . He entrusts to you the souls of his flock and will ask for their blood from your hands."[44] Hearing these words, Kyrillos became tearful. When he stood a few moments later to chant the Gospel, considering what he had just heard, he dared not read what was written, "I am the good shepherd . . . ," but instead spontaneously added, "*Christ said*, 'I am the good shepherd.' "[45] At that point in the Gospel, Kyrillos wept profusely and uncontrollably and would do so, with handkerchief in hand, for the rest of the Liturgy. Perhaps this was why he asked Bishop Lukas of Manafalout (1930–1965) to read aloud his address, but I suspect, in fact, that this choice prefigured his unusual silence as patriarch.

"My beloved," read out the bishop, as Kyrillos stood by,

> . . . in the depth of my heart, I feel the weight of the responsibility that has been laid upon me and the holy gift that has been tied to my neck . . . but who am I? It is the grace of God that will work in us and with us. . . . I have great trust in the mercies of our Lord, who says to his Church: "For a mere moment I have forsaken you."[46]

Kyrillos knew well that the Church had felt forsaken in the previous decades—a burden that was now fastened around his neck. But, intriguingly, he made no mention of reforms or projects, nor did he criticize the actions of those in the past. Kyrillos' only concern, in his words, was to bring comfort to "tired souls" and for humanity to "smell Christ's aroma in us."[47] These words were in continuity with his prepatriarchal ministry. Never being one to talk, his only self-understanding was to bring peace to the affliction of those around him, quietly, humbly, ever aware of the need for his own transformation as a precondition of the transformation of the Church. "I wish"—declared Kyrillos, hinting at what Isaac the Syrian called "luminous love"—"I could open my heart to you, so that you could see the deep love I have towards all, which is *flowing from the heart* of our Savior who loved us and redeemed us with his blood." "If our mission is so great and important," he continued,

> . . . it also requires us to gather and unify all our efforts. . . . I am confident that our brethren, the metropolitans and the bishops, our blessed children

the priests and deacons, and all the members of the *maglis al-melli*, general and subdivisional, different organizations and working associations, and all the servants in the vineyard of the Lord will cooperate with us in love, faithfulness, self-sacrifice, and self-denial, under the leadership and grace of the great head of shepherds. *As for us, let us disappear so that [Christ] might be manifest with his blessed glory.* I ask the Lord to grant us one spirit, one heart, and one mind, to work in one opinion and one counsel, which is that of the Holy Spirit who has led the Church during its long glorious history, having one holy objective, which is the glory of God.[48]

Acutely aware of the need of unity for healing, Kyrillos was utterly convinced that this unity must in a very real sense be *kenotic*, that is, self-emptying. Each competing voice of reform—the bishops, *maglis*, clergy, laymen, and above all the patriarch—must, without compromise, "disappear" that Christ might appear and heal his despondent Church. In these words, with their Pauline allusions to the Christological hymn of Philippians ("one heart" and "one mind") Kyrillos prophetically announced what may be termed his "kenotic ecclesiology."

* * *

After the Liturgy Kyrillos stood patiently as thousands took his blessing. Many of his bishops, seeing him sweat in the bulky patriarchal vestments in the oppressive heat of May, begged him to sit down and rest, but he refused.[49] Without any premeditation, in a hint of his later "open-door policy," he graciously did away with the tense divide that had for too long separated the patriarch from the people. And so Kyrillos would remain there, standing for hours until he had greeted each person, clergy or lay, wealthy or poor, prominent or peasant.

While the crowds thronged around the new patriarch, Fr Salib Suryal recalls that he noticed Metropolitan Athanasius, then in his mid-seventies, exhausted by the last few years of turmoil, wearily enter the sanctuary and sit at the first step of the altar.[50] Breathing heavily, the aged metropolitan looked out at the people with speechless contentment. "Now let your servant depart in peace," he suddenly cried out. "I have passed on the Church to the monks; to the one who will lead the Church to peace. . . . I am filled with joy, let your servant depart in peace."[51] Few could have suspected that Athanasius' unlikely nomination of a relatively unknown and unusual monk would change anything. But after some thirty-seven years of his episcopate, spanning the entire melancholic period of darkness that had engulfed the Church, Athanasius knew with surreal certainty that he could finally rest—and so he did a few years later, no doubt with a quiet gleam of satisfaction.

The Patriarch Remained a Monk

> "I have often repented of having spoken, but never of having been silent."
> —*St Arsenius the Great*

S OME DAYS AFTER his consecration and enthronement as Kyrillos VI, a function was held in his honor at the prestigious and exclusive Mohamed Ali Club in downtown Cairo. As he entered to the cheers and ovation of all, he could not have felt more a stranger. When asked to bless the lavish and opulent banquet set before him, he struggled to hide his distress and whispered to one of his disciples, "My son . . . is that the food of monks?"[52] Without causing a scene, he quietly dispatched the same disciple to source some falafel and salad, to the awe and confusion of onlookers. It is little wonder that his brother, Hanna, ended his memoirs with the words: "Becoming pope did not change him."[53]

* * *

Though only six of the forty-four years of his monasticism were spent in a monastery, he had in fact never "left" the monastery.[54] "In personal contact," wrote Wakin, a Western journalist, after meeting Kyrillos in the early 1960s, "the patriarch confirms what his gestures and words indicate. He is impregnable in his piety . . . you talk and he hears, but he does not seem to listen or to belong to the present moment. . . . Impervious, his expression still seems to be filled with the undistracted stare of the desert dweller."[55] Until his very last breath, he would not forget that he was the poor monk Mina.

Rather than relaxing his ascetical endeavors—as might certainly be expected, if not demanded, by his age and patriarchal commitments—Kyrillos intensified his asceticism, believing, as Fr Raphael once noted, that "he was passing through a bitter tribulation, and, therefore, *more* fasting and prayers with tears were required."[56] "He never changed his daily canon," continued his disciple,

> . . . he shut all the doors of the world within himself—the desires and the needs—he gave up everything . . . he neglected the bodily needs so that they

no longer had any authority over him. After he had tasted, participated, and lived with Christ . . . what need did he have for anything else?[57]

The sources are here unanimous; as patriarch, he was extremely severe with himself. As for his canon, it was largely unchanged from his very first days as a monk.

According to his closest disciple who served him while patriarch, Fr Raphael Ava Mina, Kyrillos' diet was meager and austere.[58] When he broke his fast around midday—having started the day with psalmody at three in the morning—it would inevitably be with a piece of bread (qorban) and dukkah.[59] With much pleading, he could occasionally be convinced to add a few small spoons of beans. Often Kyrillos would be delayed by meetings, and then he would have his breakfast only after three in the afternoon. For lunch, he would usually have some dried bread with a small number of cooked vegetables—but, Fr Raphael recalls, he would never actually eat the vegetables but only dip his bread in their sauce. Before he slept, he would usually be satisfied with some fruit or bread at most. "I never saw him touch a piece of chicken or meat, or even have a sip of milk."[60] That was during the non-fasting days. In fasting times, especially that of Lent and the Theotokos fast, even though he had been awake since the earliest hours of the morning, he would eat only once, late in the evening.

At one point during the fifty days of the Resurrection, Kyrillos gave his regular cook a few days of leave, upon which Fr Raphael, who in his own words "did not know how to cook," thought to take care of the kitchen.[61] Each evening he would lay out roasted chicken, a few small pieces of meat, rice, bread and cheese; only to find the chicken and meat untouched, with the bread and cheese eaten. Given the poor refrigeration of the day, each evening would see a new meal largely wasted. "I need to tell you something . . . I don't think he likes chicken," the disciple recalls telling the cook when he returned. Confused, the cook rebuked Fr Raphael, saying, "He would never eat it like that. . . . You need to cut the chicken so fine and mix it with the rice so that he cannot see it!"[62] A man of sixty, physically large and athletic, and yet they had to trick him, lest he eat only bread and cumin.

Becoming patriarch had likewise done little to improve his clothes.[63] Kyrillos' inner garments, made of coarse and cheap fabrics, basted not sewn, resembling sackcloth—as witnessed after his death by many—were girded by a leather belt and the great monastic habit (eskim).[64] Over this, he wore a light inner cassock of marginally more value, covered with another outer cassock or "faragia" (exorason), with his uncut hair being wrapped in a characteristic black shawl.

On only a few early occasions did he wear the patriarchal vestments during the Liturgy, generally preferring his simple white monastic vestments, with a long white shawl wrapped around him. Even at the inauguration of the new cathedral, he refused to wear the exorbitant garments gifted to him by the Emperor of Ethiopia.[65] One could easily be forgiven for mistaking him for a simple priest or monk. Never once in the five years that Fr Raphael served him did he even think to change his shoes; and when after the Liturgy deacons would rush to tie the shoelaces of the aged patriarch, he would refuse, saying, "Leave them, my son, and let this evening end in peace."[66]

This exceedingly simple outer life reflected a far more severe inner life. It was well known that Kyrillos slept little. But just how little is for the most part unknown. Each day he would awake at three in the morning for psalmody and Liturgy that would finish some five hours later.[67] The entire day, until late, would be spent in meetings and visits, only to be interrupted by "his work" of Vespers at six in the evening. Most nights he would retire to his patriarchal cell just before midnight. This would allow for three to four hours of sleep at most. Yet even this is called into question. An examination of his letters (unpublished and thus unknown until now) reveals that if a time of writing was specified, then it was consistently between the hours of one to two in the morning.[68] Even the few hours of sleep, it appears, would be regularly sacrificed.

When he did sleep, it would be upon a single bed (which was unusual given the size of the man) made from brass, with a thin blanket whether winter or summer. On one occasion an official from the Vatican visited Kyrillos during an illness. He became rather distressed on seeing Kyrillos' modest cell and immediately offered to furnish it at his own expense. "I like this simple place," was all Kyrillos offered in reply.[69] On occasion, Fr Raphael recalls, he would go into the cell for some errand at night to find the patriarch asleep. "It wasn't like a human sleeping; you feared him asleep even more than in his patriarchal vestments . . . by more than a thousand times."[70] Whenever he entered during those five years, the disciple observed, Kyrillos would always, without exception, be found sleeping on his side with his legs stretched perfectly straight. Evidently, the years in the windmill and at St Menas' in Old Cairo must have been spent sleeping on a hard, narrow pew to give this unusual posture without bent knee.[71]

It is nearly impossible, though, to speak of his sleep without speaking of the prayer that for half a century perpetually disturbed that sleep. We cannot understand his personality otherwise. Kyrillos' experience—incarnated from his beloved *Sixty-Fourth Homily* of Isaac the Syrian—exchanged sleep for vigil.[72] Though his interior prayer life was hidden in his cell, it shines through in glimpses observed at the highest point of his prayer, in the Eucharist. "He used to pray [in the Liturgy]," remembers Fr Raphael,

> . . . with a deep voice, bowed head, and closed eyes with almost no hymns nor chant, but with fear and respect. He never allowed himself to lean against the altar nor to talk with anyone during the Liturgy. While praying, he used to shed many tears. . . . His Holiness enjoyed celebrating the prayers of the Divine Liturgy *by himself* because it gave him the greatest spiritual comfort. . . .[73]

This explains one of the curiosities of his time as patriarch. During the festal Liturgies of Nativity and Resurrection, he would often be seen standing at the side of the altar without celebrating—only to celebrate a later, far quieter, Liturgy.[74] A brief glance at newspaper clippings reveals the same, with many of these major feasts being celebrated at a monastery, after which he would return to Cairo for an exchange of greetings and official undertakings. The altar was his comfort. The only time, his disciples observed, that they saw him genuinely upset was when in the early hours of the morning he had to "share" the altar and concelebrate, often stubbornly telling bishops or priests who came to pray with him to celebrate on one of the many other altars at the cathedral.[75] "If you want to select the most quintessential photograph of Pope Kyrillos VI," declared his successor and disciple, Shenouda III,

> . . . it would surely be the picture where he is surrounded by a cloud of incense or that picture where he is before the altar; for he was never far from the altar of incense. . . . He did not talk a lot to people during tribulation, but he always talked to God while praying the Liturgy.[76]

There is one such photograph that is, to my mind, more revealing than any other.[77] Standing before the eucharistic altar in what appears to be the early hours, Kyrillos remains silent, absorbed in ceaseless prayer; his tired eyes closed, his hands clasped on his chest, with a white shawl overflowing and obscuring much of his face. He stands as he had for half a century—perhaps some fourteen thousand Liturgies—before his God, knowing no other source of comfort, no other hope, no other helper. Words fail to describe those moments. Speaking in the third person, in a rare disclosure, Kyrillos told a Western journalist that "as a hermit, he has had very deep experience with prayer" and that his only ambition was to see his Church "develop this experience with prayer."[78] And when interviewed by the press after his enthronement as to his strategy of reform, he answered, "It is better not to speak, rather to pray."[79]

* * *

These observations of his ascetic life are just that—"observations." As significant as they certainly are, they remain external perceptions of his person nonetheless. As patriarch, Kyrillos never delivered a homily, he wrote only a few of the earliest festal letters and delegated the rest, and other than the odd spiritual canon here and there that he gave to his disciples (which we may assume was secondary to his personal experience), he rarely, if ever, spoke of his own interior life. When pressured by the *al-Watani* newspaper just before his enthronement to discuss his program of reform, he answered unpretentiously: "We prefer to carry out our mission in *silence*."[80] True to his word, he became inexplicably silent—the highest of ascetic endeavors—a most curious contradiction of terms, a *silent patriarch*.

How well, then, can one who is silent be known? Those who knew him well claim they knew him not at all.[81] And yet strangely, no one, scholar or lay, has thought to ask: why was he silent; and most significantly: why did he, unexpectedly, become increasingly silent as patriarch? "The pope himself told me," Fr Raphael recalls, "that what he gained from silence greatly exceeded what he would have achieved by any other means."[82] What is it, then, that he gained?

As we have seen throughout his prepatriarchal life, in what may be called his "patristic discipleship," Kyrillos was mesmerized by the *Sixty-Fourth Homily* of Isaac the Syrian.[83] It is, therefore, unsurprising that one of its principal concerns is silence. Within this homily, I suggest, lies the primary explanation for his unusual silence, as well two other intimately related secondary rationales.

"Love silence above all things," begins Isaac, "because it brings you near to fruit that the tongue cannot express. First let us force ourselves to be silent, then from out of this silence something is born that leads us into silence itself."[84] One Syriac scholar suggests that this "something" is *inner silence*.[85] Should a solitary practice this silence, Isaac discloses, "I know not how much light will dawn on you from it."[86] "When a man draws near to silence," he continues, "the keeping of [other ascetic labors] is superfluous for him . . . he is found to have gone beyond them, for he has approached perfection."[87] Beyond this, for Isaac, silence leads to stillness, which he defines in a circular fashion as the "silence to all things."[88] At this point in the homily, I would suggest, Kyrillos became ever more attentive. "It is impossible," counsels Isaac, "when we dwell in a place *inhabited by many*, that we should not be met by other men." Here he gives the paradigmatic example of Abba Arsenius the Great (350–450) who "loved still-ness more than all other men." "When, therefore, that man [Arsenius]," Isaac continues,

> . . . beheld all these things, and saw that it would not be possible to avoid them as long as he was near the habitation of men; and when he found that it was often impossible, because of the place of his abode, to be far with-drawn from the proximity of men and from the monks who settled in those parts—then from grace he learned this way of life: *unbroken silence*. And if out of necessity he ever opened his door to some of them, they were glad-dened only by the *mere sight* of him. . . .[89]

For Kyrillos, even more than Arsenius in the fifth century, solitude was an impossibility given his office. As a monk in Old Cairo he had painstakingly forged the "desert as a state of mind;" but now as patriarch, surrounded by innumerable crowds, he would need to be more tenacious, more radical. He embraced what was an "unbroken silence"—the only means of maintaining stillness and solitude in the face of the world. Given that Kyrillos quoted the *Sixty-Fourth Homily* most frequently and consistently, these words by inher-ent necessity articulate the lens through which we must interpret his unusual silence. It was not from ineptitude, deficiency, or lack of confidence as many at the time mocked, nor was it merely for the sake of delegation to those more able. Silence was—and this is no mild claim—Kyrillos' means of maintaining *solitude in the world*.

Isaac, here, also hints at a second related "fruit" of silence. When "out of necessity" the solitary "opened his door . . . they were gladdened by the mere *sight* of him." Just beholding a solitary in silence was words enough. "It is enough for me to see you, Abba," said one monk to Antony the Great.[90] Silence was, therefore, Kyrillos' unconventional method of reform, a most uncanny incar-nation of that maxim; one that would be made especially disturbing in that he was the leader of millions and yet, to the confusion of many, simply chose not to speak.

A third tantalizing rationale for silence and stillness, and one that speaks ever so true to the life of Kyrillos, is found towards the end of the homily. "Even if," Isaac declares,

> . . . you are wronged or cheated or mocked and so forth, you will not be moved, because of your love of stillness. . . . Whoever enters into stillness

without this continual rumination will not be able to bear those things that we are obliged to undergo and to endure from all sides.[91]

When we consider—although its extent is unknown to most—that Kyrillos was acutely mocked and persecuted from the very beginning of his monastic life until his death, we begin to appreciate and fathom these words of St Isaac; words that Kyrillos had scribed, memorized, lived, and breathed for the last four decades; words that had been given to him by one he cherished as spiritual father. No matter the accusation, attack, or abuse, those closest to him insist, "he never lost his inner peace."[92] Silence forged within him, as we shall see, an inner stillness in the face of relentless tribulation. For over a decade as patriarch, his was the "undistracted stare of a desert dweller," for Kyrillos had never actually left his *internalized desert*.

* * *

Kyrillos, here, was in good company. Many in the early years of Christianity had already perceived the inherent dangers of the episcopacy. In the mid-fourth century, Athanasius had to practically beg Dracontius to return to his episcopate after he had escaped for fear that the "bishop's office is an occasion for sin."[93] For many of these early monk-bishops, there was but one solution—to "intensify one's asceticism."[94]

When Abba Netras left his cell on Mount Sinai in the fifth century to become the bishop of Pharan, his disciples asked why he had now as a bishop subjected himself to far stricter ascetic austerities than when he was in the desert. "I do this in order not to destroy the monk in me," replied Abba Netras.[95] John Chrysostom, similarly, as the patriarch of Constantinople, was remembered as always eating alone, shunning any invitation to the mansions of the rich, and absolutely refusing to entertain.[96] As a bishop—though he was a former provincial governor—Ambrose became a man of "much abstinence, and many vigils and toils, whose body was wasted by daily fasts."[97] A few early bishops even set about quietly transforming their residences into quasi-monastic communities, gathering monks or unmarried clergy around them, in effect re-creating their monastic settlements in the world.[98] This was certainly the case with Kyrillos. Beyond his own severe ascesis, Kyrillos chose very early on in his patriarchate to turn away from the practice of his predecessors—the *fellah* Melek at worst, married clergy at best—and instead ordained deacons as servants, and had monks as secretaries. It is a practice reminiscent of Martin of Tours, who, although a bishop, lived in a monastic community just outside his city. "There was," writes Martin's biographer,

> ... the same humility in his heart, and the same holiness in his garments. Full alike of dignity and courtesy, he kept up the position of a bishop properly, yet in such a way as not to lay aside the objects and virtues of a monk.[99]

But would this not be a cause of tension? How could one be a "world-rejecting" monk and at once serve as an administering bishop? Rousseau, for one, notes that in the lives of the holy "monk-bishops" during the first centuries, there was in fact little display of the "tension and frustration which the term [monk-bishop] implies."[100] Though we may expect some discontinuity or disjuncture, what we find is a remarkably "consistent pattern of behavior, always springing from the same singleness of purpose, the same charismatic personality."[101] "Ascetical authority," in other words, was called to nourish, safeguard, align, and ultimately transform "pragmatic authority."[102] "Not all bishops are bishops," teases Jerome.[103] And it appears—or so history suggests—that ascetical authority is the authentic and transparent means of becoming such a "true bishop."[104]

* * *

"Not only has a monk become Patriarch," wrote Edward Wakin in the early 1960s, "but the patriarch has remained a monk."[105] Wakin—writing in disappointment (albeit sympathetically) at Kyrillos' "absorption" in prayer and apparent inaction—failed to perceive even dimly the significance of his words. Though intended as a criticism, Wakin unknowingly articulated the truth of the man: there was absolutely no disjuncture in the life of Kyrillos, he was a monk-patriarch. Though a leader of millions, Kyrillos was, for the most part, a silent and solitary patriarch. Living as a recluse, he retreated with the concerns of this world into another world, and only there, in his internalized desert, in an inner world of stillness, gazing at his God, would this world make sense and have meaning for him. For this reason, it may be less than gently suggested (to borrow from St Jerome and to dispute Wakin) that unless the patriarch had remained a monk, he would have ceased to be a "true patriarch." But few, at least at the beginning of his reign, would agree. "Many Copts were disappointed," wrote one scholar; and, ironically, most vocal among them were the monks and bishops themselves.[106]

Confronting an Expected Dissension (1959–1963)

"Naturally speaking, people are filled with repulsion at the idea of holiness. . . ."
—*Dorothy Day*

A MONG THE MEMOIRS of those who knew Kyrillos VI lies the record of a little-known and most curious episode. A certain Fr Benjamin (1944–1987), a hermit of the Wadi al-Natrun desert, recalls an encounter with the patriarch (who was unknown to him) in the early 1960s. Benjamin, then a young man of twenty, had for many years been infatuated with the idea of monasticism and promised to depart to a monastery the very moment his compulsory military training was complete—that is, until the day he was on leave and happened to meet a pretty girl wandering the streets of Alexandria. He was immediately enamored by the young girl, and they promised to meet the next day again. "I went to one of the hotels to spend the night there," recalls the future hermit,

> . . . and in the morning I went out looking for her in different churches. But I couldn't find her anywhere, so I went into one of the churches feeling hurt. I saw Pope Kyrillos VI censing the church, so I stood in my place in the aisle where he was coming through. When he was right in front of me, he suddenly took the censer in his other hand, and slapped me on the face and continued his way without uttering a word as if nothing had happened!. . . . I stood . . . I regretted . . . and went out immediately to my military unit. I was very upset with myself, how could I be concerned with such a thing? And what is even stranger . . . how did the pope know?[107]

The bizarre encounter is suggestive of Kyrillos' early years as patriarch; often accused of being "heavy-handed"—in this case, literally. But would the Church, like Fr Benjamin (who eventually became a saintly hermit), in time, see the workings of an enigmatic and mysterious plan at play?

* * *

From the very first days of his enthronement, and even nomination, Kyrillos was attacked and defamed. Intriguingly, though, most Western sources, perhaps in part from brevity, ignore the almost incessant tribulations through which he passed. Their Arabic counterparts are only marginally (if at all) more accurate. And yet, tribulation, humiliation, defamation, and accusation were the uninterrupted and persistent hallmarks of his patriarchate, as they had been from his early years as a monk—mocked and exiled from the Baramous Monastery, later evicted from the windmill, and perpetually persecuted by the hierarchy during his years at St Menas' in Old Cairo.

Much of this has been forgotten, if not ignored, both by scholars and the everyday believer. Is this, we might ask, due to a lack of access to historical sources? Certainly, this is part of the story. But I suggest, even more, that later piety has laudably preferred not to condemn nor even remember those who opposed Kyrillos. In an attempt to "preserve" his sanctity, history has for many been reimagined, whereby, if he really was a saint, then surely *all* should have accepted and recognized him as such during his life. Could it be that the derision and hostility to which Kyrillos was subjected—despite its actually attesting to his sanctity—was something that most Copts (and scholars, too) sought to forget in an attempt to "whitewash" and "unwrinkle" the sheets of history? Whatever the reason may actually be, Kyrillos suffered unceasingly for the greater part of his clerical life; and, for the most part, at the hands of those in the Church. "Saints by their natures," an Orthodox scholar notes, "are as disturbing as they are inspiring."[108] Kyrillos, it appears, was not what the people wanted but what they needed.

The reasons for his relentless "persecution," especially in the earlier years of his patriarchate, are many. Historically speaking, it was perhaps to be expected; the previous half-century had seen a deeply divided Church become increasingly fractured. By the time Kyrillos became patriarch there were numerous competing voices of reform, with often conflicting agendas, and, most importantly, in various states of agitation (let us not forget the kidnapping of Yusab II). Even then, no matter the "voice," and no matter whether it was right or not, reform and change are rarely well received. We should also remember that his most hostile critics were in fact bishops, many of whom were guilty of simony, and therefore exceedingly unlikely to favor a patriarch who made it his initial concern to condemn that same simony. But it was, oddly, two other matters that most irritated and vexed his adversaries: the abundant and diverse *miracles* (with subsequent accusations of witchcraft), and even more than this, Kyrillos' singular obsession with *prayer*.

"The greatest thing that caused difficulty for Kyrillos at the beginning of his patriarchate," claims a priest who was close to him, Fr Louka Sidarous,

> ... that provoked criticism, from elders, bishops, priests, and foreigners ...
> [was that they said], "we wanted a patriarch, and not a chanter.... What is

this, all day and night in psalmody, prayers, Matins, Vespers, Liturgy . . . and you just leave the Church the way it is? . . . the Church needs reform, healing, it needs one to go on its behalf to the government and President, one who can understand these issues and bring results for the Copts. . . ." So arose the tide of criticism against him because of this one thing: *prayer*.[109]

So severe was the criticism at one early point that a movement in the Synod sought to stand him down because of this same obsession with prayer—which, they alleged, was at the expense of patriarchal duties.[110] "The pope's behavior was unusual for the people at that time," remarked one elderly monk. "The monks could not put up with it. . . . The pope's methods were also a surprise for us—us elders. We had never seen anything like it."[111] Even those closest to him became frustrated—whenever they approached him with a concern, they were inevitably told to simply *pray*. On one occasion a group of priests from Alexandria visited Kyrillos with a "major" problem. On their way, still some distance off, one "who talked a lot but had a pure heart," moaned, "What's the point? . . . He will just tell us to pray." After they arrived and exchanged greetings, Kyrillos turned to that same priest, looked him carefully in the eyes, and asked him as a matter of fact, "You don't like prayer, my brother?" To which the priest mumbled incoherent words of sincere remorse, while Kyrillos continued, "Can you do anything without prayer?" Needless to say, the man hid his face, became red, and went awfully silent.[112] "The patriarch is a very holy man," complained another priest interviewed by Wakin in the early 1960s. "He is a saint. . . . There is much praying every day at the patriarchate, but we need more than prayer. Prayer is not enough." Kyrillos, had he had the chance, likely would have replied, "Prayer is everything."[113]

* * *

In the face of this persistent abuse and slander, Kyrillos remained, as far as one can tell, ever gracious and gentle, always staunchly immediate in his forgiveness. In late 1959, twelve eminent Cairo-based priests initiated a movement against Kyrillos—apparently on account of his absorption in prayer. They began furiously writing and circulating defamatory pamphlets, often staying up into the early hours of the morning. For the better part of a year and a half, they persisted in their efforts until suddenly their printing press malfunctioned. Undeterred, they hurriedly had it fixed and resumed their efforts. Almost immediately the machine halted once more. This time, however, they were told another component had become damaged, rendering the press irreparable. At this point, one of the leading priests became frightened and rushed to the patriarch, kneeling down and crying, "I have sinned; absolve me, Your Holiness."

"What is the matter, my son?" replied Kyrillos. "I insulted you too much," the priest started, but before he could finish, Kyrillos interrupted, "Yes, staying up until 1:30 a.m. each day, printing pamphlets and distributing them from Alexandria to Aswan until the printing press broke." "But"—the priest asks, now extremely uncomfortable—"how do you know all this? . . . Why didn't you talk to us?" "I was *praying* for you," replied Kyrillos (which, we should note, was likely their very accusation). Terrified, the priest begged for absolution, to which Kyrillos gently assured, "With all my heart I absolve you, my son." The rest of the priests were likewise immediately forgiven, becoming, according to the account, some of his most faithful clergy.[114]

The episode is characteristic of the period: relentless persecution, penetrating clairvoyance, and inevitably immediate forgiveness.[115] More curious, though, were the confused accusations leveled at Kyrillos on account of the endless and bewildering miracles. Meinardus, a German Coptologist who shared the disappointment of many with this "praying patriarch," was at least able to concede: "There is no doubt that he is a genuine *thaumaturges* . . . with extraordinary spiritual gifts."[116] Others were far less charitable—denouncing Kyrillos as a fraud at best, and guilty of witchcraft at worst. Many present bishops (among other numerous accounts) recall as young novices entering their respective monasteries in the early 1960s only to be warned to "stay well away" from Kyrillos who, so they were told, was dabbling in witchcraft.[117] How else, it was alleged, could the copious and surreal miracles be explained?

An especially poignant case is that of Nazmy Boutros.[118] A solicitor and leading figure of the *maglis al-melli* in Alexandria, who was also well known to many of the most eminent priests of the time, Boutros had little patience with the miracles of the new patriarch, though he admits, "I did not know him well, but heard conflicting stories about him." He began writing *anonymously*, even during the nomination process, in several newspapers ("the three papers") against the patriarch, vehemently accusing him of being a "con man" and a "sorcerer." When Kyrillos arrived in Alexandria for the first time in mid-1959, he had never met Boutros or the rest of the *maglis*. As Boutros came near to greet the patriarch, Kyrillos looked at him carefully: "Oh, you are the man of the three papers." Boutros fell to the ground. Kyrillos, he recalls, immediately grabbed him and said, "Don't worry, these are just words. . . . I am joking with you." Boutros was unsure how to respond. After a few minutes, Kyrillos asked him if he had any children. "I have a ten-year-old daughter. . . . God did not grant any other children." "Next year," Kyrillos declared, "you will have a boy, and I will baptize him." And so it happened.

Not only was the cheek turned, so to speak, but the very accusation was returned to the accuser. To those who accused him of miracles, he replied with miracles. Time and time again, the sources speak of this selfless forgiveness and reconciliation. In one remarkable case, Kyrillos went so far as to reconcile the infamous (and reposed) Hegumen Sergius—during the hegumen's funeral, of all times—posthumously lifting the excommunication of his predecessor.[119]

* * *

This brings us to Fr Samuel Tawadros el-Syriany (1911–1983), a monk and historian. In his Arabic *History of the Patriarchs of Alexandria* (an incredibly difficult book to come by), we find one of the few extant scholarly criticisms of Kyrillos—one that is, admittedly, an account marred by a deeply personal slight.[120]

On August 20, 1960, Kyrillos issued a ruling commanding all monks to return to their monasteries by September 30, with the threat of "defrocking" for disobedience.[121] Fr Samuel, then a monk serving outside his monastery in a parish of Mansoura, took no actual issue to the decree itself—knowing well the problems of monks living within cities—but was offended at the spirit of "defamation and confrontation" in the decree, and that exception was not made for those "distinguished monks" (including himself) who had success-fully served in their parishes.[122] What was worse, Fr Samuel complains, was that Kyrillos himself had been in a similar situation when he too was a monk in Old Cairo.[123] That being said, Samuel continues, "He was among the first to obey" and returned to his monastery. But three months later, on December 31, 1960, Fr Samuel returned once more to Alexandria and met Kyrillos, saying: "I remain attached to this parish that I labored to build, similar to your attachment to St Menas' at Old Cairo; if you do not allow to me to serve there, at least allow me to pray there for the Feast of the Nativity?" Kyrillos was not moved and refused the request. Dejected and inconsolable, Fr Samuel spent the next seven days in Alexandria and on Christmas Eve visited a quiet church to pray Vespers. There, by unfortunate chance, was the patriarch, who happened to be visiting—and it was now some three months after the deadline for the monks to return to their monasteries. Kyrillos, on seeing the disobedient monk, rebuked him publicly and humiliated him, commanding his immediate return to the monastery.[124]

As time passed, Kyrillos could not ignore his heavy heart. A few months later, he visited the monasteries of Wadi al-Natrun. All the monks greeted him, but he could not see Fr Samuel. Kyrillos kept asking about him, and on hearing he had remained in his cell, sent for him repeatedly throughout the day. Samuel, in his own words, "totally refused to meet [Kyrillos]."[125] After much insistence, with intervention from the abbot and threats that Kyrillos would walk all the way to his cell, Fr Samuel made his way to the church. Kyrillos was waiting there, gently smiling, and he begged Fr Samuel for forgiveness and absolution. One of the patriarch's companions tried to object, to which Kyrillos thundered, "Keep quiet, this is none of your business!" Overcome, Fr Samuel absolved and also besought the patriarch for absolution.[126] Despite Fr Samuel's interpretation of the event, it would appear that he was in fact in the wrong, and yet it was Kyrillos who "emptied himself" in seeking reconciliation. It would be the model of his kenotic ecclesiology.

Fr Samuel's criticism of Kyrillos, written in 1977, must be read within this context of personal slight and pain (that he himself records). Nonetheless, Samuel's is an important—albeit lone—voice. "He was not without errors but a human like any other," begins Fr Samuel's account.[127] Kyrillos, he claims, failed to distinguish between those who honored him and those who deceived him; was often affected by hearsay slander; would measure faithfulness by how much one prostrated in front of him; and, at least in Fr Samuel's estimation, enjoyed the praise of people. But it was his dealing with clergy that most affected Fr Samuel, and especially so the bishops, who found his measures of reform to be "unfamiliar." Later, he concedes, Kyrillos' "sharpness diminshed and he became more amicable with the clergy."[128] Samuel also readily admits that the patriarch forgave all who had hurt him when he was a monk—except that is, he claims, for Hegumen Barnaba el-Bakhouri (1874–1963).

For decades the name of this monk has been carefully forgotten.[129] In April 1936, Kyrillos VI (then Fr Mina el-Baramousy) left the Baramous Monastery in defense of the expelled seven elderly monks. We must recall, however, that he did not question the judgement of the abbot, only that they should not be evicted on Palm Sunday Eve. A recently discovered letter that was written two decades after the expulsion sheds light on the incident: Bishop Macarius, then bishop of the Baramous Monastery, makes mention that the seven monks had challenged Hegumen Basilious (the superintendent), and that this challenge then developed into a "rebellion" against Hegumen Barnaba (the abbot).[130] It was this same Hegumen Barnaba who was responsible for Kyrillos' exile as a monk. Fr Samuel states in his own account that on March 9, 1948, Barnaba was "forced to abdicate" as abbot of the monastery (the reason is not given), and served in various capacities, before eventually becoming the patriarchal vicar in Alexandria. Here, Fr Samuel makes his final accusation. In 1960, when Kyrillos VI visited Alexandria, he ordered Barnaba's "immediate dismissal."[131] At eighty-six years of age, Hegumen Barnaba was forced to leave and "unable to find a place in any of the monasteries" lived with his sister in Kafr al-Dawar in northern Egypt, where he would die on March 13, 1963.[132]

Though certainly negative, we need to keep in mind that Fr Samuel's account was shaded by personal experience. But even were it not, are his comments on the whole really so troubling? If this is the worst that can be said of a man's life, sanctity is near. Fr Samuel, for completeness, accepts without question that Kyrillos was a miracle worker and that he was incredibly honorable in his service. As to the above criticisms themselves, in the first place, it needs to be noted, that by January 1961 Fr Samuel had returned to his monastery and, therefore, had very few dealings with Kyrillos for the greater part of the patriarchate. This suggests that Samuel's criticisms were consequently founded upon hearsay. Second, the various primary accounts suggest overwhelmingly that Kyrillos inevitably ignored hearsay complaints (contra Samuel), for the most part investigating matters personally. Third, Kyrillos (as we shall see) was in the habit of keeping company with those who frequently disagreed and challenged him. And fourth, virtually all accounts are unanimous (other than Samuel's) that Kyrillos treated praise with disdain.[133] As for the complaint that Kyrillos acted in a vindictive manner toward the elderly Hegumen Barnaba, it may be reasonably suggested that his dismissal was not a punishment, but rather distrust (especially if we consider his "forced abdication" from Baramous); not revenge, rather a matter of suitability. This becomes all the more likely when we consider Kyrillos' treatment of other clergy who opposed him.

* * *

During the difficult years of the elections after the death of Yusab II, Fr Aghabious el-Muharraqi was campaigning for one of the monks from his monastery. In doing so he actively defamed Fr Mina (now Kyrillos VI), attempting to "discredit his character," at times even in front of Mina's own family. On hearing of this, Fr Mina replied: "It is out of zeal, my sons."[134] After his enthronement as patriarch, he called for Fr Aghabious and appointed him as the priest of his former St Menas' Church in Old Cairo. Aghabious, fearing the worst, thought it was a ploy to observe him carefully and eventually seek retribution. Instead, three years later Kyrillos ordained Aghabious as the metropolitan of the largest diocese in Sudan. Aghabious (later Metropolitan Stephanos) would tell this story frequently, always in tears.[135]

The same kenotic attitude comes across time after time in the few extant minutes of the Synod's meetings. One remarkable account is an episode concerning Bishop Gabriel of St Antony's Monastery (1951–1965)—the same bishop who played a vital role in dismissing Pope Yusab II. Gabriel had, for undisclosed reasons, been disseminating insulting and derogatory letters against Kyrillos VI, hoping perhaps he would suffer the same fate as his predecessor. In reaction, on June 22, 1961, the Synod assembled to investigate and discuss this, as well as a number of no less significant accusations (of a theological nature) against Gabriel.[136] "I am so sad at the beginning of my patriarchate," Kyrillos is recorded as saying in the minutes, "to stand in a trial of a bishop; in any event, do not mention any accusations against Bishop Gabriel that are related to me. I forgive him and am *giving up my rights*."[137] Echoing once more Philippians 2, Kyrillos was, with great personal loss, affirming his kenotic ecclesiology. It would be his patriarchal stance and method of reform.

At the same Synod meeting in 1961, Kyrillos had intended to deal with another far more serious matter that had caused him great agony and that, I suggest, may explain the harsh dealings with his fellow bishops. Metropolitan Youannis of Giza—who was himself ordained, as we have seen, in painful circumstances of alleged simony at the time of Yusab—recalled, shortly before his death, the little-known happenings of that fateful 1961 Synod.[138] Kyrillos, Youannis recollects, had summoned him (as secretary of the Synod) and requested him, without any further details, to include in the agenda the "ordinations that took place during the time of Anba Yusab II." "I agreed," stated Youannis,

> . . . when the Synod assembled I kept listing the various agenda items and deliberately ignored the subject of bishops ordained by Yusab, which he [Kyrillos] requested more than once. At the conclusion of the session I asked the pope to pray the final prayers; after which he left with a somber face.[139]

Late that night Youannis was awakened by a servant requesting his immediate presence at a meeting with Kyrillos and Metropolitan Athanasius of Beni Suef. "You know that I pray a daily Liturgy," started Kyrillos, his voice deep and melancholic, "but tonight I felt something toward you inside me, and I wanted to clear the matter before I celebrate the Eucharist in the morning. . . . I asked you to raise a certain matter to the Holy Synod which you knew about and either ignored or forgot, I do not know."

"I did not forget," Metropolitan Youannis recalls saying,

> but ignored it deliberately in sympathy to you and to keep *you* and *us* in a holy unity; as the ordinations of bishops at the time of Yusab were mostly conducted in the same way. So if now you reject these ordinations, it will mean that you will be forced to strip the Synod of all its credibility. . . .[140]

Kyrillos, perhaps realizing how widespread the practice had been and how scandalous it would be to bring into question the majority of the Synod, "looked at the floor and after a period of silence stood up and said, 'Then give me absolution, my father'. . . . We absolved each other," concludes Youannis, "and left on good terms."[141] Though Kyrillos had intended to face the Synod directly—at least partially explaining his initial dealings with the bishops on account of their simony—he once more wisely saw that the forgiveness of even so great an evil was to be preferred over dragging the Church into another tragic trial. From here on it appears that Kyrillos' demeanor towards his bishops dramatically changed.

As for Youannis, we can only imagine that he would not have taken lightly to the (albeit aborted) suggestion. He knew well that Kyrillos was aware of his alleged simony, especially since Kyrillos' Sunday School disciples (two of whom became bishops in 1962) had openly opposed Youannis' ordination. Later history would suggest that Youannis did not leave on such "good terms" as he supposed and claimed.

* * *

"None of those who opposed him had any success," once commented the late Pope Shenouda III.[142] The consequences for those who dared conspire against Kyrillos were often severe; as a "holy man," it was as though, many claimed, God himself were protecting him.[143] Their unfortunate accounts are littered throughout the sources.

In 1960, for instance, Kyrillos deprived a leading and powerful Coptic family of their "usual prerogative" of selecting the bishop for their diocese of Girga (Yusab's former diocese). The stubborn head of the family proceeded to hold a "miniature election," selecting the name of one of the three monks out of a box—all of whom were "local clergy under the family's thumb."[144] Shortly afterward that same man suddenly died. The rest of the family, somehow undeterred by the death, traveled to Cairo to notify Kyrillos of their selection. He refused, to which they threatened, "We will convert to Catholicism unless you take our man." "No, no, no . . ." thundered Kyrillos.[145] Their fates are unknown.

One other unfortunate man, Fr Raphael Ava Mina recalls, pretended to be the spokesman of a diocese, and voiced disapproval of a monk who was to be ordained bishop. "If you ordain him for us, we will send him back to you!" In reply, Kyrillos declared, "I leave you to God, I leave you to God . . ." The poor man did not make it home, having been struck by a car and killed.[146] Another heard the same words and suffered a massive stroke;[147] and one well-known priest who was unrepentant in his fierce verbal abuse of the patriarch did not see evening before dying of a sudden heart attack.[148]

But it was the death of one of his metropolitans that most disturbed Kyrillos. Towards the end of 1962—triggered perhaps by Kyrillos' attempted investigation into the matter of simony in the 1961 Synod—Metropolitan Youannis of Giza sought to appoint a committee to depose the patriarch.[149] Some, such as Fr Raphael, suggest Youannis' motive was that Kyrillos was "an uneducated man . . . who had no priorities other than prayer."[150] But the timing is suggestive of the former. Youannis traveled throughout Egypt gathering signatures, turning not a few bishops against the patriarch, before eventually returning to his diocese. Kyrillos had just begun Vespers at the cathedral in Alexandria when he was notified of the plot. As he raised incense near the icon of St Mark, he was heard to say, "St Mark, this will be the last time I come in here to you . . . I will go to the desert and never come back if this man's project succeeds."[151] The next day, some 250 kilometers (155 miles) away, Metropolitan Youannis of Giza was found dead at his residence. The *Ahram Newspaper* reported on February 12, 1963,

Anba Youannis, Metropolitan of Giza and Qalobeya, died yesterday in his bed at the cathedral building in Giza. The Metropolitan took one spoon of medicine from the bottle next to his bed. He immediately felt sharp pain . . . one of the doctors tried to revive him, but he left this life. The doctor was originally treating him for bronchitis, but the metropolitan mistakenly took the medicine that caused his death. A police investigation requested that a coroner examine his body and extract the liquid to determine what was in this bottle.[152]

Stories abound as to the contents of the bottle, with consensus suggesting a pesticide that had been inadvertently left in the room by a servant.[153] At the funeral, as he prayed over the body, Kyrillos was heard by many loudly weeping: "... all of this ... for what? A few pieces of paper with signatures. ..."[154]

Classically, this account has been repeated in the literature, especially in collective and popular memory, with the specific mention of two other bishops. They, along with Youannis, allegedly conspired against Kyrillos; and both, so the accounts state, were killed in a train accident while collecting signatures. This is problematic for several reasons: first, ecclesial records make no mention of any bishops in the reign of Kyrillos VI who were killed in train accidents; second, no two bishops died on the same day during his reign; and third, the exact same thing was reported in 1956 (and historically occurred) when two bishops sought signatures against (ironically) Yusab II.[155] This is likely, then, a reflection of "hagiographic synthesis" with the transposition of events, and, therefore, a necessary correction must be made: Youannis, so far as the evidence indicates, acted alone.[156]

But in spite of the conspiracy, at each Liturgy for forty consecutive days, his disciples recall Kyrillos commemorated Youannis at the altar. There was no joy nor triumph. This was not the death of his enemy but of his *son*. No matter who it was that opposed him, Fr Mikhail Dawood comments, Kyrillos "considered himself responsible to heal those souls as a shepherd searching out his lost sheep."[157] And though he may have initially been harsh with these same bishops, at a very early point Kyrillos changed in his demeanor; these bishops—irrespective of simony or worse—were his *sons*. When the Synod a few years later punished Anba Abraam of Luxor (1949–1974), it was Kyrillos who greatly reduced the punishment. On another occasion Fr Salib Suryal recalls that he implored Kyrillos to discipline a group of unruly bishops: "What is it to you my brother [*ya akhi*]?" replied the patriarch. "These are my sons ... I am here to teach them ... It's my choice how I teach them!"[158]

This teaching, almost invariably, was that of *silence*. One present bishop's recollection is characteristic. As Kyrillos sat with Metropolitan Daniel of Khartoum (1922–2000) on a balcony at the cathedral, a number of bishops and clergy (unaware that Kyrillos was above them) began cursing him—"curses that you could never even hear on the street"—but Kyrillos, so the metropolitan recalls, was entirely unperturbed.[159] It was as though he simply could not hear them. "Knowing their plans," writes Fr Raphael of these and other bishops,

> ... he would still meet them in humbleness and speak to them with love. All he did was pray with tears, so the Church might walk in peace and safety, but they were the tears of painful, unjust treatment. It was but a short time that

they *all* departed from our world, one after the other. The pope was mourning them for years, he would say when any of them died: "It was as if *a part of my spirit* was taken from me."[160]

* * *

"I once walked into a room," reminisces a disciple of Kyrillos, "where Fr Marcos Dawood and Pope Kyrillos were talking."[161] This is perhaps the only extant record, albeit brief, of an exquisitely private moment—Kyrillos with his confessor—of which only a few words were overhead. We have no way of determining their immediate context but can only speculate that it was in connection with these incredibly difficult years. Fr Marcos was overheard to speak into the patriarch's ear quietly, "Did you teach us this? You never taught us this. . . ." "So what did I teach you?" whispered Kyrillos in reply. "You taught us to be patient and long-suffering. . . ."[162] The confession, or at least what was overheard of it, ended there.

For several decades Kyrillos had lived a personal kenotic asceticism—a method of loss—but it seems that as patriarch he initially grappled with how this should or could be translated into the episcopal milieu. To suffer personal loss was one thing; but how would "episcopal loss" be perceived, especially with the almost intractable difficulties of the period, in a Church ravaged by simony, and ruled for decades by untouchable and inaccessible patriarchs? It appears that at this early point of his patriarchate he experienced a concrete and *cumulative* appropriation of his earlier kenotic ascesis into the episcopal dimension—one that would alter the fundamental meaning structures in not only his life but far more importantly in the life of the Church.[163] This may also explain his early softening toward his fellow (and often hostile) bishops.

And yet it would be a struggle of great agony, one of tears. A letter to a dear friend in late August 1962 speaks not only of this "grief" but also of the enduring mystical "comfort" he was receiving in its midst. "You may notice," writes Kyrillos,

> . . . that the date of this letter is fifteen days ago, I wanted to write to you daily, but God knows it is because of too much grief and difficulties . . . I could not write even one line, but the Almighty Lord, who comforts us at all times with the Comforter, his Holy Spirit, has comforted us during these days. We thank him from all our hearts, asking him to provide for the needs of our life according to his good will.[164]

Beauty from Ashes: Throwing Money in the Desert

> "Not every quiet man is humble, but every humble man is quiet."
> —*St Isaac the Syrian*

> "True humility is not thinking less of yourself; it is thinking of yourself less . . ."
> —*C. S. Lewis*

K YRILLOS, WE ARE TOLD, had from his earliest days an intense dislike for praise. On a visit to a monastery in Alexandria, he sat during the Liturgy—customarily refusing to preach—to hear the homily of a local priest. A miracle, the priest began to relay, had just the other day occurred by the prayers of the patriarch. Kyrillos immediately stood up and left. When he eventually returned, a disciple notes, "One could see that he had been weeping."[165]

Those closest to him recall Kyrillos' genuine discomfort when some supernatural happening was manifest. When, for instance, a young girl screamed that there was unnatural light surrounding Kyrillos, he turned his face in anguish and was heard to pray, "Protect me, O God . . . protect me!"[166] At the patriarchate among his disciples, it was no different. He always felt a stranger. Whenever they fussed over him, he would gently shake his head mumbling, "The boy became a patriarch."[167]

* * *

To come close to Kyrillos' understanding of humility, we must once more return to his adopted spiritual father, Isaac the Syrian. Being quiet, gentle, or meek by *nature* is not true humility, Isaac begins, for there is a difference between "natural" and "supernatural" humility.[168] True humility, rather, is a union with Christ's own humility—and this entails above all embracing *stillness* in the face of temptation and tribulation, as Christ did.[169] "Even if," Isaac declares, "heaven were to fall and cleave to the earth, the humble man would not be dismayed."[170] One of the most striking manifestations of this true humility is, therefore, *silent endurance of humiliation.*[171] "The man who endures accusations against himself with humility has arrived at perfection."[172] "This," teaches Isaac,

> will be a sign for you: the strength of the temptations you encounter. . . .
> The nearer you draw nigh and progress, the more temptations will multiply
> against you . . . know that at that time your soul has in fact secretly entered a

new and higher level . . . for God leads the soul into the afflictions of trials in exact proportion to the magnificence of the grace he bestows.[173]

This may explain in part the peculiar increase in Kyrillos' tribulation as his miracles became increasingly manifest—and, as for his spiritual progress, we can only dare to assume the same.[174] Humility for the sake of God, Isaac concludes, makes one like a child—"and the defenselessness of small children *forces* God to take particular care of them."[175] In the face of humiliation, it is God alone who defends the humble; and the beginning of humility is, therefore, humiliation.

* * *

Around Kyrillos' patriarchal cell and scattered throughout his letters is frequently found one particular maxim of St Isaac: "Honor flees away from before the man that runs after it; but he who flees from it, the same will it hunt down, and will become to all men a herald of his humility."[176] In the periodical, *Harbor of Salvation*, that he wrote in his first few years as a monk, no theme is as prevalent throughout the volumes as humility. In a rare letter to Fr Makary el-Syriany (the future Bishop Samuel), Kyrillos wrote of his love of humility. "Truly, my son," he writes, "I am very sad because I cannot achieve humility up until now. . . ."[177] No matter his spiritual progress and ascetic endeavors, Kyrillos would painstakingly seek after humility.

When pressed as to Kyrillos' greatest strength, Fr Raphael (his closest disciple), after a few moments of thought, answered, "He surrounded himself with those who did not flatter but rather opposed him."[178] They, in Kyrillos' mind, would safeguard his humility. When Kyrillos was a young monk—as we saw in the heated correspondence with his outspoken brother—Hanna had rebuked Fr Mina for his desire for solitude. Now, though a patriarch, Kyrillos kept his brother close for the very same reason. "I was serving the patriarch for five years," recalls Fr Raphael Ava Mina,

> . . . there was not a single time that [Hanna] told him you are good, you are a saint. . . . Instead each time he would ask him why did you do this or that . . . and precisely because of this, Kyrillos respected him greatly. . . . If [Hanna] had flattered him, he would have had nothing to do with him.[179]

Those who attempted to flatter Kyrillos, on the contrary, were met with inevitable disinterest. On the day that he was elected patriarch, April 19, 1959, a most unexpected (or perhaps expected) guest arrived. After being expelled from the patriarchate a few years earlier, Yusab II's valet, the infamous and corrupt Melek, had become a source of embarrassment to his hometown of Girga. He took up residence in Clot Bey (and was rumored to own the building) opposite the Old Cathedral.

"I would like to meet Fr Mina the Recluse," declared Melek to the monk-disciples at St Menas' in Old Cairo. "He isn't free at the moment," they replied. "I need to meet him," repeated the agitated Melek, "I need to be his right-hand man and servant . . . the people in the patriarchate are all wicked . . . I fear for him and can protect him; I don't even want a cent from him!" The monks relayed the happenings to Fr Mina, who told them to give Melek a glass of cordial and send him on his way with the express instruction: "He is not to stay here."[180] Though after his ordination Kyrillos would allow the aging Melek to attend liturgical services at the patriarchate, he would always keep the sly man at arm's length. But even then, so Kyrillos' disciples attest, he treated Melek with fatherly love, and on one occasion went so far as to apparently heal him from an abdominal complaint.[181]

Whether with his confessor, his brother Hanna, or the numerous outspoken bishops (and former disciples) that he ordained, Kyrillos surrounded himself with truth. "Why did he love these people?" Fr Raphael questions. "Because they *opposed* him!"[182] They kept him humble. On one occasion Kyrillos, exhausted by the day's proceedings, gave his disciple a stack of incoming letters and asked him to open and read them to him. Unable to read the derogatory and insulting words, the disciple informed Kyrillos that they were improper and sought permission to destroy them immediately. "But the pope insisted," the disciple recalls,

> . . . that I should read them to him. After I did, he smiled and said, "Don't worry about this, my son, nor become disturbed; may the Lord look at me and have pity on me. Worse than that has often been said, but thanks to the Lord he has saved and watched over me."[183]

The same would occur on several occasions—with Kyrillos invariably insisting on reading or hearing those painful letters. After Kyrillos' death, when his private drawers were examined, they were for the most part empty, except that is, for these and similar letters laden with words of derision, mockery, and ridicule. They were, evidently, the only letters Kyrillos thought worth keeping.[184]

* * *

Barely a month after his enthronement as patriarch, on June 22, 1959, Kyrillos journeyed into the desert at Mariout, forty-five kilometers (28 miles) southwest of Alexandria. It would be his first move at reform; one that would turn the *maglis* decidedly against him and provoke an outcry from both Copts and foreigners. For decades Kyrillos (then a monk) had been infatuated with St Menas, consumed by an irrepressible dream to rebuild the monastery at Mariout. And now, ordained a patriarch only some weeks earlier, it became an urgent priority. As an acute point of contention—and consequently, a severe test of humility—this action as a culmination of a history of infatuation must be examined to make sense of both Kyrillos and his unexpected sense of reform.

In July 1905, a German expedition discovered the Abu Mena shrine and monastery complex after almost one thousand years, only for it to be abandoned once more in 1920.[185] Sensing an opportunity, Kyrillos (then Fr Mina) in early 1937 requested permission from Youannis XIX to rebuild St Menas' Monastery at Mariout. "Have we," mocked Youannis, "finished rebuilding the cities to begin rebuilding the desert?"[186] With the eruption of World War II in 1939, Fr Mina's eviction from the windmill in 1941, and the death of Youannis in 1942, there would be little progress. But strangely St Menas had not abandoned the site. In October 1942, various newspapers recorded an alleged apparition of the Saint at the pivotal Battle of al-Alamein, protecting, so they claim, the Allies from the onslaught of Rommel.[187]

Displaced after his eviction from the windmill, Fr Mina traveled to Alexandria in mid–1943 to meet Prince Omar Toson (1872–1944) who "encouraged" the prospect, should the patriarchate agree.[188] In the absence of a patriarch on the throne, the director of the Ministry of Arabic Antiquities permitted Fr Mina to "practice religious rituals" at the site pending formal approval. "Please help me to carry out this venerable and sublime idea," wrote Mina on June 28, 1943, begging Habib el-Masri for the *maglis'* permission, "before someone else precedes us and does it; especially as the martyr is an Egyptian, and his monuments should be under our hands and not anyone else's."[189] During the stay in Alexandria he was also able to meet with Banoub Habashy, with whom he cofounded the St Menas' Association.[190] But with the death of the prince and chaotic feuding in the wake of Macarius III's enthronement, the dream again faded.[191] A few years later, undeterred by the turmoil of Yusab II's election (and just before Yusab's enthronement), he tried once more. "During these circumstances," wrote Fr Mina to his brother on May 14, 1946,

... we are very calm and quiet, thanking the Lord for every condition, asking his help and support, and to grant us St Menas' Monastery at Mariout so that we can start refurbishing it and start offering the oblations there. Please, Hanna, do your best concerning this issue because it is very, very, very important![192]

Fr Mina heard little in reply. In a small consolation, the Ministry of Arabic Antiquities granted him formal permission in 1948 to celebrate liturgical services on feasts at Mariout. The next decade would be spent in a similar fashion. Every few years a request was made to the patriarch and appropriate ministers to permanently inhabit the site—always with the reassurance: "I promise to rebuild [the monastery] at my own cost."[193]

On March 5, 1958, amid the feuding—and his own nomination—after the death of Yusab II, Fr Mina suddenly received word that the *maglis* had decided to rebuild St Menas' Monastery. "I am writing to you this letter at midnight," frantically wrote Fr Mina to Mounir Shoukry (then president of the St Menas' Association),

... I was so happy and glad for this news to the extent that I could not go to sleep before writing this letter to you. You might be astonished, but if you know the reason, you will not be astonished. You have to know, my dear son, that in 1943 I came to Alexandria and met the late Mr Banoub Habashy, I presented to him the idea of praying the Holy Liturgy and living in St Menas' Monastery ... but God's will did not permit it to happen at that time until the fixed time was due, and God wanted to fulfil the hopes. During these days....[194]

With those words the letter abruptly ends. An hour later Fr Mina, reconsidering his approach, wrote a letter instead to his brother Hanna. It seems there were sensitive issues at play, and he hoped his brother could discuss these issues with Mounir in person. "I am writing you," started Fr Mina,

... this letter in a late hour of the night, one-thirty AM, I do not know why but perhaps it is from God ... you know my longing and desire for around twenty years to reconstruct St Menas' Monastery in Mariout.... Now, all that I hope for, is to meet Doctor Mounir Shoukry in Alexandria and discuss with him if St Menas' Association is registered and if he had informed them of the decision of overhauling the altar, because I wish to participate in this project; but my intention is even to register everything in the name of St

Menas' Monastery, because the *ambitious greed* of other directions has been
so clear. . . . I cannot wait for the quick reply. . . . I plead to the almighty Lord
Jesus, to declare his will and grant me the desire of my heart, to see with my
eyes the renovation of this Monastery.[195]

Things finally seemed to progress. "As for St Menas," reads a curious letter
from Fr Mina to his brother on June 23, "he is always insisting on renovating
the Monastery at Mariout."[196] Despite the relative popularity and stability that
he had secured (albeit with occasional hierarchical persecution) over the last
two decades in his church in Old Cairo, he was ready to relinquish it all, in a
moment, to depart for St Menas' at Mariout—a place inaccessible by road, without water or bare necessities, a desert of desolation. Comfort, stability, popularity meant nothing to him. It is precisely for this reason that we depict this
history of infatuation. Nothing so consumed him over the years as this. But just
as suddenly, the dream began to fade once more. This letter would be the last we
would hear of the monastery, for it was cast aside by the more pressing concerns
of communal dissension in late 1958, and, ultimately, by his own nomination
and enthronement as patriarch.

* * *

We can only imagine his elation, as Kyrillos set out to Mariout on June 22, 1959,
to consecrate the site.[197] Some months later he would return. On November
27, two convoys of vehicles, one from Cairo and the other from Alexandria,
converged at the deserted site. An altar was erected over the tomb of St Menas,
and an open-air Liturgy was celebrated. When some present besought him to
rest on an exquisite chair especially prepared for him, Kyrillos curiously refused:
"This chair is for St Mark [the founder of the Coptic Church]."[198] Few could possibly understand what he meant. Afterward, Kyrillos drove to a nearby site and
laid the foundation stone for what would eventually become the monumental
Monastery of St Menas.[199] After more than a millennium, "Life was breathed
into the shrine."[200] Surrounding Bedouins claimed the patriarch was a "good
omen"—rainfall had marked his arrival, ending a lingering drought.[201]

Others were not so convinced. Kyrillos' first move toward reform was exceedingly unwelcome for most. "In some ways, the incident symbolizes the reign of
the new Patriarch," wrote Wakin critically in the early 1960s,

> . . . religious grandeur demonstrated by a charismatic leader suffering what
> the politically-oriented regard as *withdrawal symptoms*. The community was

besieged, the minority anxious, the hierarchy, clergy and monks in disarray, the Church wounded by turmoil, and the Patriarch lays a foundation stone in a deserted place for *another* monastery.[202]

Another British observer was similarly frustrated. "One of the monasteries struck me in particular as typifying the decline of the Egyptian Church," commented James Wellard in his study:

This project, I was told, was dear to the heart of the present Patriarch . . . It will certainly be an enormous cenotaph [empty tomb], but who, one wonders, will visit it, who needs it? . . . Who, then, is to fill the cells . . . when the ancient sites are almost empty and would be empty if it were not for a few old men who regard them as places for retirement.[203]

It was, however, the Coptic reformers (especially the *maglis,* as we shall soon see) who were most vocal in decrying the wasted expenditure and efforts on an "unnecessary" monastery. Even Kyrillos' closest disciples began to murmur. "All of us used to say," recalls Fr Salib Suryal, "'what is this man? . . . taking the money of the Copts and throwing it in the sand!'"[204] Many were simply dismayed and perplexed by what they perceived to be a politically and socially ineffective gesture.[205] But "Kyrillos saw," comments Fr Raphael, "what we could not see, and knew what we did not know. . . ."[206] Conceivably this is what Kyrillos alluded to when he enigmatically wrote to his brother that St Menas was "always insisting" that he rebuild the monastery.

But Wakin was at least in some sense right. Kyrillos' move to establish St Menas' Monastery was indeed "symbolic," and he most certainly was in "withdrawal." It was symbolic both of his person and of his method of reform, in that it was a rediscovery of the necessity of prayer and holiness. As for Kyrillos' "withdrawal symptoms" in departing solitude, it was representative of the symptoms of the Church at large. It was precisely because the Church was "besieged," "anxious," "in disarray," and "wounded by turmoil"—in *withdrawal*—that Kyrillos by necessity laid the foundation stone for "another" monastery.

Few at the time could perceive the "brilliance of Kyrillos' move."[207] At St Menas', which would eventually become one of the largest and most visited monasteries of Egypt, Kyrillos revived the notion of the *maulid,* that is, the notion of pilgrimage. In the earlier centuries of the Church, the *maulid* acted to unite and revive bonds that crossed social, economic, and class divisions. They were profoundly communal in nature, and, therefore, potent in their capacity to heal the communal and ecclesial factionalism that had marked the previous half-century.[208] Kyrillos was tapping into a rich and powerful current and at once making it visible, present, and contemporary for his people. We do well to remember that as a young boy, Kyrillos had, as far as we can tell, first developed his love of St Menas at one such *maulid*. To my knowledge, though, only one scholar, Nelly van Doorn-Harder, has perceived and explicitly articulated the sheer gravity of Kyrillos' move.[209]

She argues convincingly that raising the memory of a popular yet "somewhat inactive saint" acted to re-route pilgrimage to the heart of the Coptic faith; to a location near Alexandria—"not too far and not too near"—one that was geographically well-placed and thus easily accessible. There the monks, under the express direction of Kyrillos, would embody the radical self-denial and ideals of St Menas that would heal, and be witnessed and, one hoped, emulated by visiting laymen and women in their daily lives.[210] The restoration of St Menas' Monastery therefore, revived the most central of institutions, and in doing so, rehabilitated Coptic identity.[211] Similar in quality to Kyrillos' patterning of holiness and subsequent formation of "white habits" in Old Cairo (when a monk), it would now be amplified on a far wider, perhaps even national level.[212] Since then numerous dilapidated monastic sites have been rediscovered and restored, serving as "crucial centers" for the continual reform and revival of the Church.[213]

Wakin, and numerous others in his wake, were woefully mistaken. In reviving monasticism, and at once making it visible, palpable, and accessible, Kyrillos was, in fact, laying the foundation stone of reform, a stone that would in a few short years—and this is no mild nor modest claim—resurrect the Church. Could this be what Kyrillos meant when he said that the exquisite chair at the ceremony was "for St Mark"? To witness, in some mysterious sense, the revival of his Church?

* * *

It is true, to be fair, that Kyrillos was in withdrawal. Though he had for many decades inhabited an "internalized desert" amid an ever bustling and deafening Cairo, as patriarch he felt the heightened need for frequent retreats into desert solitude. There he would be revived by the fruits of solitude, of silence and insight, and there he would find comfort in the midst of the multitudes of his tribulations.[214]

Many monks observed that he ate little while at the monastery, and to his disciples' utter dismay, he invariably refused to take medication. "With St Menas," he would say, "the medications of the world are not needed."[215] On one occasion

Fr Raphael Ava Mina recalls seeing Kyrillos downcast on his arrival, having dealt with several painful matters at the patriarchate. "My son," Kyrillos said, "we do not need to go back to the world . . . won't we find here one loaf of bread for each day with a small amount of the mountain salt?" But within a few days, his disciple observed, his joy had returned, and he hastened back to the "world" to comfort his people.[216] This may in part explain Kyrillos' occasional and unusual practice of celebrating the major Feasts of Resurrection and Nativity at the monastery alone before quickly hurrying back to Cairo or Alexandria to undertake "official" duties.[217]

Unsurprisingly, abundant miracles are said to have taken place at the monastery.[218] One, however, was burned deep into the desert memory and was witnessed by numerous monks. In April 1966, a few hours after Kyrillos arrived from Alexandria, there was a blinding and suffocating sandstorm that struck the monastery and the surrounding desert.[219] Such sandstorms (*khamseen*) would ordinarily last up to some fifty days.[220] But Kyrillos was due back in Alexandria for scheduled appointments that evening. The monks watched as Kyrillos quietly entered the Church and prostrated before the icon of St Menas. "Are you upset because we are leaving you?"—asked Kyrillos while looking carefully at the icon—"we will be back as soon as we can." With those words, the patriarch raised his cross, and at that moment, to the shock of the onlooking monks, the sandstorm suddenly dissipated.[221]

St Menas, both personally and through his monastery, was a source of power and comfort for Kyrillos. At the monastery he received insight and inspiration for his method of reform, and, invariably, it was there that he would "solve" the problems of the Church—often in the most remarkable ways.[222] One of Kyrillos' closest deacons, a friend from his days at Old Cairo by the name of Professor Hanna Youssef Hanna, recollects attending Vespers at St Menas' Monastery. During the doxologies, Kyrillos stood silently in the sanctuary. Suddenly he smiled widely and laughed. "A sight that shocked me," reminisces Hanna, "for knowing him for so many years, I knew firsthand how strict he was on himself and others inside the sanctuary."[223] After the service, Hanna asked him for the reason, but the patriarch evaded. Finally, upon being pressed, Kyrillos promised to tell him on the strict condition that the incident be concealed until his death:

> "When I entered the sanctuary," Kyrillos said, "I was deeply troubled by an issue related to the Copts. Suddenly, St Menas appeared to me and asked why I was distressed. When I explained the reason, he responded, 'Do you think

you are alone? We are all here supporting you.' Then, he lightly pushed me, and so I laughed. . . ."²²⁴

Notes

¹Wakin, *A Lonely Minority*, 103.

²Until the ninth century, it was often the case that a dying patriarch would select his own successor, but for the most part candidates were nominated by consultation and elected by "the people" (both clerical and lay). The following centuries would see much of the same, occasionally in conjunction with the government or by the casting of lots, and rarely, should a dispute arise, the elect would be revealed in vision to a holy monk or bishop. The various methods and their history are detailed in Meinardus, *Christian Egypt: Faith and Life*, 90–113.

³The principal concern, stemming from the earliest centuries of the Church, was that a bishop was in fact "wed" to his diocese, and so for a bishop to become patriarch (the bishop of Alexandria), would mean to leave one "bride" for another. At each successive dispute concerning this "rule," two opposing arguments are generally made: bishops are experienced and proven administrators and, therefore, are most suitable for elevation to patriarch; whereas others suggest that monks, though inexperienced, are holy, ascetic, and ideally "untouched" by the world and are, accordingly, ideally suited to be molded by God and the Church. The latter have, in the Coptic Church, much of history and the canons in their support, while the former lack historical precedent.

⁴O. H. E. Burmester, *The Egyptian or Coptic Church: A Detailed Description of Her Liturgical Services* (Cairo: Printing Office of the French Institute of Oriental Archaeology, 1967), 177–87.

⁵Meinardus, *Christian Egypt: Faith and Life*, 117. Confirming this liturgical practice, until the early twentieth century most of the patriarchs-elect were monks, four were laymen, one was a priest, and another a deacon.

⁶Ibid., 117, n. 4.

⁷Here, I should be clear, I am not engaging in any of the rhetoric that continues up until the present day as to whether a bishop can be elevated to patriarch; rather, I am simply presenting the context of the constant communal feuding as to Yusab's successor. The last two patriarchs, Shenouda III (1971–2012) and Tawadros II (2012–), were "general bishops" (a practice begun by Kyrillos VI) before becoming patriarchs, whereby they were never consecrated to any specific diocese but rather were charged with tasks such as education in the case of the former, and assistance to a metropolitan in the latter.

⁸Meinardus, *Christian Egypt: Faith and Life*, 139.

⁹The very senior bishop interviewed sought anonymity. Anonymous Bishop, "Interview about the Life of Pope Kyrillos." Zaklama claims that Athanasius, at one point during the election, was overheard praying before a portrait of Pope Cyril V, saying, "I received priesthood from your hands and hope that God grants me my wish and I will give the papal chair to a monk." See Nashaat Zaklama, *The Spiritual Life and Pastoral Message of Pope Kyrillos VI* [in Arabic], vol. 2 (Cairo: Sons of the Evangelist, 2007), 218.

¹⁰I. H. al-Masri suggests that there were 5,500 voters who could each cast several votes: Fr Matta el-Meskeen received 5,400 votes; Fr Makary (future Bishop Samuel), 5,300; and Fr Antonios (future Pope Shenouda III), 5,200. See al-Masri, *Story of the Coptic Church*, 7:15.

¹¹Hasan, *Christians versus Muslims*, 85. Hasan quotes her interview with Bishop Bemen: "We felt that if the Pope was chosen from among the members of the SSM, he would be younger, more energetic, more dynamic, and more moral."

¹²Matta and Makary had been monks for eight years, and Antonios, only two years. I. H. al-Masri notes that this ignored historical precedence, where St Athanasius was twenty-seven and St Cyril was thirty-six; see al-Masri, *Story of the Coptic Church*, 7:15.

¹³It is exceedingly difficult to come across any primary evidence of this, but it is claimed by Wakin, *A Lonely Minority*, 106; and al-Masri, *Story of the Coptic Church*, 7:26. I. H. al-Masri is somewhat ambiguous in her claim. Certainly, judging by Fr Mina's letters in 1958 (which we shall see), he was hardly concerned.

[14]Cited by Wakin, *A Lonely Minority*, 105. The "certain circumstances" were the Anglo-French-Israeli invasion of Suez, and in such circumstances it would appear the government could afford no further embarrassment.

[15]Ibid., 107.

[16]On November 3, 1957, the government finally ratified the Synod's earlier decision, which decidedly excluded the "Sunday School monks," and specified that nominations would be compiled by a committee of nine bishops and nine *maglis* members, as well as limiting the pool of eligible voters to the well-educated and established. Voters had to be of good reputation, churchgoers, educated at a university level, or at least pay over LE 100 of taxes a year. See Mariz Tadros, "Vicissitudes in the Entente between the Coptic Orthodox Church and the State in Egypt (1952–2007)," *International Journal of Middle East Studies* 41, no. 2 (2009): 271. For the regulations concerning the election and voting see Meinardus, *Christian Egypt: Faith and Life*, 130–39. Needless to say, the Sunday School Movement members were outraged, and denounced in their periodical the Synod's right to nominate candidates—a "right of the people." Reiss, *Erneuerung in der Koptisch-Orthodoxen Kirche*, 198–200; anonymous, "The Patriarchal Elections" [in Arabic], *Sunday School Magazine* 11, no. 7 (1957). The right of the bishops, so they argued, was to lay hands on the people's elect.

[17]Fawzi, *Kyrillos and Abdel Nasser*, 20. Fawzi states there were overall eleven nominations, and six were excluded. Hanna and Nasr suggest Fr Mina's nomination was put in after all others had been submitted. Atta and Raphael Ava Mina, *Life of Pope Kyrillos*, 17; Nasr, *Readings in the Life of Abouna Mina*, 20.

[18]Athanasius was born on December 4, 1883; entered Baramous Monastery on July 10, 1903; became the vicar of the Patriarchate in 1917; and was ordained a bishop by Cyril V on December 27, 1925. He was known for his sense of reform, and was locum tenens after the repose of Macarius III and Yusab II. Athanasius died on July 22, 1962.

[19]The conversation is recorded by Hanna Youssef Atta (Fr Mina's brother); Atta and Raphael Ava Mina, *Life of Pope Kyrillos*, 17.

[20]Ibid.

[21]Ibid.; Raphael Ava Mina, *Spiritual Leadership*, 14.

[22]Nasr, *Readings in the Life of Abouna Mina*, 22; Atta and Raphael Ava Mina, *Life of Pope Kyrillos*, 17.

[23]Raphael Ava Mina, *Service and Humility*, 32.

[24]Hasan, *Christians versus Muslims*, 86. The same was repeated to me in various interviews as will be seen in later chapters.

[25]Reiss, *Erneuerung in der Koptisch-Orthodoxen Kirche*, 202; Hasan, *Christians versus Muslims*, 86; van Doorn-Harder, *Modern Coptic Papacy*, 127.

[26]Meinardus, *Christian Egypt: Faith and Life*, 139. The bishops of Qena, Akhmim, Khartoum, Atbara, and Asyut.

[27]While it may appear to many as "archaic and absurd" to decide the destiny of millions by chance, there is, as Wakin notes, "on reflection . . . intuitive wisdom." Wakin, *A Lonely Minority*, 109. A vote for a single winner in an environment of dissension and opposing ambition—as we have already seen—invites manipulation, whereas a ballot at least forces candidates to consider the possibility that one of the other candidates may one day become their patriarch. Moreover, more radically, it makes clear that though man thinks, it is God who decides.

[28]Samuel Tawadros el-Syriany, *The History of the Popes*, 176–77.

[29]Meinardus, *Christian Egypt: Faith and Life*, 140. The decision was ratified by President Nasser on April 23, 1959.

[30]Anonymous, "Mina el-Baramousy: The New Patriarch of the Copts" [in Arabic], *al-Ahram*, April 20, 1959; Atta and Raphael Ava Mina, *Life of Pope Kyrillos*, 17.

[31]See Figure 12.

[32]Wakin, *A Lonely Minority*, 104; Anonymous, "The Deserted Windmill." Hanna states that Fr Mina said to his followers, after walking out of the altar, "Glory be to God. The Lord has chosen to demonstrate his power and glory through my weakness. I tremble with fear in the glory of your power. You are just and

right. You do not forget your beloved. From you we receive power and help, O our Lord and Redeemer." Atta and Raphael Ava Mina, *Life of Pope Kyrillos*, 17. Also see anonymous, "Mina el-Baramousy."

[33]For instance, see Wakin, *A Lonely Minority*, 104.

[34]El-Gowaily, "Interview with the Monk." His full reply was: "Of course not, monastic life is built on steering away from public office."

[35]Atta and Raphael Ava Mina, *Life of Pope Kyrillos*, 18.

[36]Samuel Tawadros el-Syriany, *The History of the Popes*, 178.

[37]Shenouda III, "Speech at the First Year Commemoration of Kyrillos VI."

[38]Raphael Ava Mina, *Spiritual Leadership*, 15.

[39]Ps 118.19.

[40]Raphael Ava Mina, *Spiritual Leadership*, 15.

[41]The appellation of pope (Gk. *papas*, "father") has been the title of the Coptic bishop of Alexandria since the time of Heraclas (232–248), the thirteenth patriarch. It was a title used for centuries, before being assumed also by the Roman pontiff. Ecclesiologically, however, it differs somewhat from the Roman usage, and simply denotes the patriarch.

[42]Raphael Ava Mina, *Spiritual Leadership*, 17; Atta and Raphael Ava Mina, *Life of Pope Kyrillos*, 18.

[43]Raphael suggests that the patriarch had told his brother Hanna of the vision, and that it occurred at the windmill; see Fr Raphael Ava Mina, *The Miracles of Pope Kyrillos VI*, vol. 2 (Sydney: Coptic Orthodox Publication and Translation, 1990), 64–65; al-Masri, *Story of the Coptic Church*, 7:28. The fullest account of the occurrence suggests that the vision occurred after the results of the patriarchal election but before the ordination; see Raphael Ava Mina, *Spiritual Leadership*, 27. This would suggest that Kyrillos visited the windmill just before his ordination.

[44]Zaklama, *Pope Kyrillos VI*, 1:159.

[45]Atta and Raphael Ava Mina, *Life of Pope Kyrillos*, 18.

[46]Zaklama, *Pope Kyrillos VI*, 1:159.

[47]Ibid.; Meinardus, *Christian Egypt: Faith and Life*, 149.

[48]Zaklama, *Pope Kyrillos VI*, 1:159; Meinardus, *Christian Egypt: Faith and Life*, 149.

[49]Photographs of the consecration indicate he took off the patriarchal vestments after the chanting of the Gospel and wore his simple vestments until the end of the Liturgy, after which he once more returned to the patriarchal attire. It would prefigure Kyrillos' simplicity throughout his patriarchate.

[50]Suryal, "Pope Kyrillos VI."

[51]Ibid. Cf. Lk 2.29.

[52]Adly, *Fr Mikhail Dawood's Memoirs*, 21–22.

[53]Atta and Raphael Ava Mina, *Life of Pope Kyrillos*, 18.

[54]He had lived at his monastery only from 1927 to 1933. From early 1934 to 1936, he had been at the cave in Baramous Monastery; from 1936 to 1941, at the windmill in Cairo; from 1941 to 1947, between St Samuel's Monastery and Old Cairo; from 1947 to 1959, at St Menas' Church in Old Cairo; and from 1959 to 1971, at the patriarchate.

[55]Wakin, *A Lonely Minority*, 113.

[56]Atta and Raphael Ava Mina, *Life of Pope Kyrillos*, 19.

[57]Atta and Raphael Ava Mina, *Memories about the Life of Pope Kyrillos*, 39. This is missed in the English translation.

[58]Atta and Raphael Ava Mina, *Life of Pope Kyrillos*, 19.

[59]A mixture of finely ground cumin, nuts, salt, sesame seeds; this can be added to food, or dipped into with a piece of bread.

[60]Atta and Raphael Ava Mina, *Life of Pope Kyrillos*, 19.

[61]Raphael Ava Mina, "Lecture on the Virtues of Pope Kyrillos."

[62]Ibid.

[63]Watson notes, "It is often the case that those who establish a reputation for lives of inner depth and strength have quite simple outer lives"; see Watson, *Among the Copts*, 48.

[64]Fr Louka Sidarous, "Lectures on Pope Kyrillos," audio recording (Alexandria, undated), Lecture 1.

[65]Raphael Ava Mina, "Some Misconceptions"; Raphael Ava Mina, "My Memories," audio recording. Raphael states that he kept offering the garments throughout the Liturgy, with Kyrillos adamant in his refusal.

[66]Atta and Raphael Ava Mina, *Life of Pope Kyrillos*, 20. The archdeacon of the patriarchate, Youssef Mansour, recalls that when he accompanied Kyrillos on his trip to Ethiopia, he took the liberty of packing the patriarch's bags. He noticed that the socks, handkerchiefs, and undergarments were old, worn, and hardly befitting for the patriarch, and sourced new garments. "I will never forget," Youssef recalls, "how His Holiness blamed me when he discovered all the new clothes. . . . 'Why aren't we satisfied with what God gave us,' said Kyrillos. 'Many need what we think is unsuitable for us. We must be satisfied with what we have of food and clothes, without asking for more.'" See Raphael Ava Mina, *Miracles of Pope Kyrillos VI*, 1:115.

[67]For instance, see Zaklama, *Pope Kyrillos VI*, 1:190. He records a "day in the life of the patriarch" on May 17, 1959; also see Atta and Raphael Ava Mina, *Life of Pope Kyrillos*, 20.

[68]The same is to be found in prepatriarchal letters.

[69]Atta and Raphael Ava Mina, *Life of Pope Kyrillos*, 20. In another work, Fr Raphael comments as to Kyrillos' inevitable answer when people saw his cell: "No matter what it is [referring to his cell], it is still better than the manger." See Anonymous, *School of Virtue*, 12–13.

[70]Raphael Ava Mina, "My Memories," audio recording.

[71]Raphael Ava Mina, "Interview about the Life of Pope Kyrillos VI."

[72]Isaac the Syrian, *Ascetical Homilies* 64.450.

[73]Atta and Raphael Ava Mina, *Life of Pope Kyrillos*, 22. By this is meant to celebrate without other clergy. But according to the Coptic canons, there must still be at least three people present: the celebrant, a deacon, and a member of the congregation.

[74]Ibid. Fr Raphael states he would also often pray the *kiahk* (Nativity) psalmody by himself, alone in his cell.

[75]Anonymous, *School of Virtue*, 26; Raphael Ava Mina, "Interview about the Life of Pope Kyrillos VI."

[76]Shenouda III, "Speech at the Tenth Year Commemoration of Kyrillos VI."

[77]See Figure 23.

[78]Wakin, *A Lonely Minority*, 116.

[79]Ibid., 115.

[80]Anonymous, "Speech of the New Patriarch-Elect" [in Arabic], *al-Watani*, April 26, 1959. Also cited in Raphael Ava Mina, *Memories: Part II*, 15.

[81]Fr Tadros Malaty, "Interview about the Life of Pope Kyrillos: Part I," ed. Daniel Fanous (2015); Sidarous, "Lectures on Pope Kyrillos," Lecture 2. Fr Tadros comments, "I believe that even those who were considered close to him, did not know all the facets of his character or life. For his efforts were spent in hiding his heavenly gifts." Whereas Fr Louka adds, "No one in the world knows the life of Kyrillos. . . . The people could only see what was from the outside; but no one could see what mystery he was living with God."

[82]Raphael Ava Mina, *Spiritual Leadership*, 22.

[83]As we have seen, of all the homilies, it is the one he most often cites (by far) and, fascinatingly, most of his maxims are to be found there.

[84]Isaac the Syrian, *Ascetical Homilies* 64.452.

[85]Ibid.

[86]Ibid. Isaac suggests that though at the beginning it requires voluntary effort, after some time "a certain sweetness is born in the heart" and a "multitude of tears is born"; see ibid., 64.453.

[87]Ibid.

[88]Ibid., 21.235.

[89]Ibid., 64.453.

[90]Ward, *Sayings of the Desert Fathers*, 7.

[91]Isaac the Syrian, *Ascetical Homilies* 64.460.

[92]Alfeyev, *World of Isaac the Syrian*, 25.

[93] Athanasius, *Letter to Dracontius* 4.9.560.

[94] Rapp, *Holy Bishops*, 143.

[95] Ward, *Sayings of the Desert Fathers*, 157.

[96] Palladius, *Dialogue on the Life of St. John Chrysostom* 12.7–29, cited in Rapp, *Holy Bishops*, 149.

[97] Paulinus, *Life of Ambrose* 38.1, cited in Rapp, *Holy Bishops*, 149.

[98] Cf. Philip Rousseau, "The Spiritual Authority of the 'Monk Bishop': Eastern Elements in Some Western Hagiography of the Fourth and Fifth Centuries," *Journal of Theological Studies* 23, no. 2 (1971): 415–16.

[99] Sulpicius Severus, *On the Life of St. Martin* 10 (NPNF² 11:9).

[100] Rousseau, "Spiritual Authority," 407.

[101] Ibid., 415.

[102] Rapp, *Holy Bishops*, 149.

[103] Jerome, *Letter 14, to Heliodorus*, 9 (NPNF² 6:17).

[104] In the life of St Basil the Great, for instance, though he "encountered a Church beset by heresy, internecine rivalry, and inadequate and incompetent leadership"—a situation to which Kyrillos VI could relate, at least in part—ascetical authority, Sterk suggests, had a singular purpose: the reform of the bishop's office. See Andrea Sterk, *Renouncing the World Yet Leading the Church: The Monk-Bishop in Late Antiquity* (Cambridge, MA: Harvard University Press, 2004), 63–64. This, for Basil, and later Kyrillos, was not in the strict etymological sense of a return to an original condition as opposed to a present state of deformity, but rather in an ontological sense, whereby the episcopal office is transformed and transfigured into that of the one true Shepherd.

[105] Wakin, *A Lonely Minority*, 118.

[106] Watson, *Among the Copts*, 54.

[107] Anonymous, *Life of Fr Benjamin the Hermit* [in Arabic] (Cairo: publisher and date unknown).

[108] Susan Ashbrook Harvey, "Holy Women, Silent Lives: A Review Essay," *St Vladimir's Theological Quarterly* 42, no. 3/4 (1998): 403.

[109] Sidarous, "Lectures on Pope Kyrillos," Lecture 1.

[110] Ibid.; Ibrahim, *The Copts of Egypt*, 175; anonymous, *School of Virtue*, 27. The latter account notes, "Some of the clergy were against him. They complained to the Egyptian government, asking them to form a patriarchal Council to manage the Church affairs. They believed that Pope Kyrillos VI was an uneducated person who knew nothing except prayer. Therefore, they concluded, the Pope purposely intensified his prayers in order to cover his ignorance and his failure at solving the difficult and accumulated Church problems."

[111] Anonymous, *School of Virtue*, 27.

[112] Sidarous, "Lectures on Pope Kyrillos," Lecture 1. The account is relayed by Fr Louka, who was traveling with the priests.

[113] Mina el-Baramousy [Kyrillos VI], *HS*, 4:2.

[114] Fr Raphael Ava Mina, *The Fruits of Love* (Cairo: St Mina Monastery Press, 1999), 13–14.

[115] For instance, for another typical account, see the story of Albert Girgis in Atta and Raphael Ava Mina, *Life of Pope Kyrillos*, 28.

[116] Meinardus, *Christian Egypt: Faith and Life*, 45.

[117] This was repeated by several bishops and clergy; Bishop Yostos, "Interview about the Life of Pope Kyrillos VI," audio recording, ed. Daniel Fanous (2016); anonymous bishop, "Interview about the Life of Pope Kyrillos"; Fr Jacob Magdy, "Interview about the Life of Pope Kyrillos," ed. Daniel Fanous (2015).

[118] The account was told by Nazmy Boutros himself to Fr Tadros Malaty and Fr Louka Sidarous; Malaty, "Interview about the Life of Pope Kyrillos: Part I"; Sidarous, "Lectures on Pope Kyrillos," Lectures 1, 3.

[119] Ibrahim Hilal, "Malati Sarjiyus," in *CE*, 2097.

[120] Samuel Tawadros el-Syriany, *The History of the Popes*, 171–200.

[121] The decree was in a bid to correct four "problems" in the Church: (1) a revival of monastic life necessitated monastic discipline, best applied within a monastery; (2) monks outside their monasteries prevented the ordination of new graduates from the Theological College, as many parishes were being

served by monk-priests instead; (3) it was contemporary with another decree, namely, that all new priests be graduates of the seminary; and (4) monks outside of their monasteries had caused a number of issues for the Church at that time (and judging by the decree some financial misappropriation). We should also note that Kyrillos was not the first patriarch to release such a decree; as we have seen, Yusab II did the same in May 26, 1946 (though, admittedly, that was evidently to silence the contention around Yusab's enthronement, namely his opponent Fr Dawood el-Macary). Some also suggest Kyrillos sought to deal with Fr Matta el-Meskeen (which we shall see). For a discussion see ibid., 180–82; Meinardus, *Christian Egypt: Faith and Life*, 44–45. I. H. al-Masri quotes the entire decree, which warns the congregation not to support or raise funds for any monks disobeying the decree, as well as warning monks that no fund-raising for any area of the Church would be allowed without prior written approval. See al-Masri, *Story of the Coptic Church*, 7:35.

[122]Samuel Tawadros el-Syriany, *The History of the Popes*, 181.

[123]See Chapter 5: "Habib Girgis and the Sunday School 'Movement' "; Yusab had seemingly tried to return Fr Mina back to his monastery in 1949 in a move to punish his disciples. See ibid., 180.

[124]Ibid., 182.

[125]Ibid., 183.

[126]Ibid., 183–84.

[127]Interestingly, Fr Samuel's account contains the subheading "Perfection Belongs to God Alone" when discussing Kyrillos' miracles. The agenda is evident.

[128]Samuel Tawadros el-Syriany, *The History of the Popes*, 184. Also see van Doorn-Harder, "Planner, Patriarch and Saint," 240. Fr Raphael notes that Kyrillos was occasionally quick to judge in matters concerning the clergy, but would just as quickly forgive. Raphael also states that this was exceedingly mild relative to his predecessors, and whatever harshness there may have been was "necessary for the role." Raphael Ava Mina, "Interview about the Life of Pope Kyrillos VI."

[129]As mentioned previously, during my research, the monks of the Baramous Monastery stated that they had only heard rumors and therefore would refuse to discuss the reason of the 1936 incident, nor would they confirm the name of the abbot at the time.

[130]Macarius, "Letter to Hegumen Youssef el-Baramousy, August 20, 1956." The reasons for the challenge are not given.

[131]Samuel Tawadros el-Syriany, *The History of the Popes*, 199. That he was evicted was confirmed by the monks at Baramous.

[132]Ibid. For a biography that does not include these details, but confirms others, see Augustinos el-Baramousy, *The Baramous Monastery*, 225–26.

[133]For instance, see Shenouda III, "Speech at the First Year Commemoration of Kyrillos VI." Shenouda said, "He was the first Pope in our era to open his doors. . . . Everyone could give him first-hand information directly to his ears and so he knew the facts of any matter and not through other channels." Also see Raphael Ava Mina, "Interview about the Life of Pope Kyrillos VI."

[134]Raphael Ava Mina, *Service and Humility*, 5.

[135]Ibid.

[136]This concerned a book he had written about "Prophecies from Heaven"; see Samuel Tawadros el-Syriany, *The History of the Popes*, 198.

[137]Pope Kyrillos VI, "Synod Minutes" [in Arabic] (Cairo: Unpublished, 1961); Fr Raphael Ava Mina, *A Stream of Comfort* (Cairo: Sons of Pope Kyrillos VI, 1989), 70.

[138]Fr Samuel, a historian, preserves the words that were told to him by Youannis in his historical survey; see Samuel Tawadros el-Syriany, *The History of the Popes*, 198.

[139]Ibid.

[140]Ibid. The sentence is completed by: ". . . if you discuss this matter you may find that some members of the Holy Synod, perhaps your children, will say 'tonight is very similar to last night.' " It seems Youannis was insinuating in a very ambiguous away that some may turn around and threaten Kyrillos with the same accusation. It should be noted that the editor of the second edition of *The History of the Popes* (published in 2002) deletes these sentences, as well as several other of the author's criticisms of Kyrillos. The editor of the second edition—apparently without consulting the author, who died in 1983—gives no

reason for the deletions, nor does he mark the place of the deletions. Future readers should, accordingly, consult the first edition published in 1977.

[141]Ibid.

[142]Shenouda III, "Speech at the First Year Commemoration of Kyrillos VI."

[143]Brown has made several fascinating comments as to the phenomenon of "cursing" in the life of the "holy man." For instance, a representative comment: "The exercise of the curse points backwards to the position of the holy man as an arbitrator and mediator. The vengeance of God falls only on the man whose case the holy man has rejected." Brown, "The Rise and Function of the Holy Man," 88. With Kyrillos it would appear this is less as a result of rejection and more as something of divine defense of the humble "defenseless one" as described by Isaac the Syrian. See Alfeyev, World of Isaac the Syrian, 121; Isaac the Syrian, Ascetical Homilies 72.499.

[144]Wakin, A Lonely Minority, 114.

[145]Only some months later he would ordain one of the monks of unsullied reputation, Bishop Mina (1919–2003), who was one of his trusted secretaries.

[146]Raphael Ava Mina, Spiritual Leadership, 26.

[147]Atta and Raphael Ava Mina, Life of Pope Kyrillos, 41.

[148]Fawzi, Kyrillos and Abdel Nasser, 48–49.

[149]We should note that, almost universally, Youannis' name is not given.

[150]Atta and Raphael Ava Mina, Life of Pope Kyrillos, 41. Fawzi suggests that Youannis attempted to form a custodian committee claiming that Kyrillos was illiterate (which he obviously was not); and that it was not enough for a pope to be a man of prayer. Fawzi, Kyrillos and Abdel Nasser, 48.

[151]Atta and Raphael Ava Mina, Life of Pope Kyrillos, 41.

[152]Anonymous, "Death of the Metropolitan of Giza after Taking Medicine" [in Arabic], al-Ahram, February 16, 1963.

[153]Some popular sources at the time rumored that the servant confessed to the "murder," but this was eventually retracted when it emerged he confessed under duress during torture by the authorities.

[154]Magdy, "Interview about the Life of Pope Kyrillos."

[155]The episcopal records are tabulated in Nasr, Readings in the Life of Abouna Mina, 220–22.

[156]Bishop Yacobos of Jerusalem (1946–1956) and Bishop Thomas of Gharbeya (1930–1956) both died on March 24, 1956, in a tragic train accident, reportedly en route to collect signatures against Yusab II.

[157]Adly, Fr Mikhail Dawood's Memoirs, 28.

[158]Suryal, "Pope Kyrillos VI." Also for a related account of Kyrillos' rescuing from prison one of his "children"—a man who had written profusely against him—see Atta and Raphael Ava Mina, Life of Pope Kyrillos, 42. A similar account is that of a metropolitan (whose name was not disclosed) who ignored Kyrillos and ordained a priest in disobedience. Later it was Kyrillos who emptied himself in forgiving his "son." Raphael Ava Mina, "Interview about the Life of Pope Kyrillos VI."

[159]Yostos, "Interview about the Life of Pope Kyrillos VI."

[160]Atta and Raphael Ava Mina, Life of Pope Kyrillos, 41.

[161]Raphael Ava Mina, "Interview about the Life of Pope Kyrillos VI."

[162]Ibid.

[163]Turning points pivot around epiphanies—"often, in moments of crisis." Though Kyrillos had numerous epiphanies (often of a kenotic nature) during his monastic life, many of which were of "major event" type, what we find here is of the quality, in Denzin's words, of a "cumulative epiphany." See Denzin, Interpretive Biography.

[164]Pope Kyrillos VI, "Letter to Salama Rizq, August 29, 1962" [in Arabic], in FRC-1: Letter 48 (Alexandria, 1962). The parallels to Isaac are intriguing. God's hand is discerned, Isaac notes, when in these trials "are mingled both consolation and griefs, light and darkness, wars and aid." Isaac the Syrian, Ascetical Homilies 42.343.

[165]Atta and Raphael Ava Mina, Life of Pope Kyrillos, 20.

[166]Ibid.

[167]If Kyrillos simply asked for a cup of tea, they would all frantically hurry off to meet his request; Kyrillos in disbelief would shake his head, saying, "His shirt is at his knees and ten are at his service." Ibid.

[168]Part II/18, cited in Alfeyev, *World of Isaac the Syrian*, 116.

[169]Part II/18, ibid. "Lowly thoughts, discerning, and painstaking reflection," writes Isaac, "the insignificance in which a person regards himself, his heart broken, and the flow of tears stemming from the suffering of mind and discernment of the will . . . you will find that they have none of these. . . . They do not meditate and recollect the *lowliness of our Lord*; they are not pierced by the sharp pain that comes from the knowledge of their sins."

[170]Isaac the Syrian, *Ascetical Homilies* 71.497. Also see Part II/37, cited in Alfeyev, *World of Isaac the Syrian*, 119.

[171]Kyrillos (then Fr Mina) echoes these sentiments to Fr Makary; see Hegumen Mina the Recluse [Kyrillos VI], "Letter to Fr Makary el-Syriany, undated" [in Arabic], in FRC-1: Letter 497 (Cairo: date unknown).

[172]Isaac the Syrian, *Ascetical Homilies* 5.157.

[173]Ibid., 42.341.

[174]One perceptive priest has gone so far to suggest that the "gift of miracles" can, accordingly, be given only to those who undergo one of two excruciating forms of suffering: agonizing physical disease or perpetual humiliation; Magdy, "Interview about the Life of Pope Kyrillos."

[175]Alfeyev, *World of Isaac the Syrian*, 121; Isaac the Syrian, *Ascetical Homilies* 72.499.

[176]Isaac the Syrian, *Ascetical Homilies* 5.166. Fr Raphael's account has a first part to the maxim as: "*Renounce the world, God will love you; renounce what the people have, they will love you too. Whoever runs after dignity . . .*" Raphael Ava Mina, *Service and Humility*, 27. The first part (in italics) is not actually from Isaac the Syrian and appears to be Talmudic in origin, a rabbinic aphorism. Interestingly, though, when Kyrillos himself cites the maxim, he only mentions the second part of the saying, which is actually from Isaac. For an example, see Mina the Recluse [Kyrillos VI], "Letter to the Monks at the Monastery of St Samuel, January 7, 1950."

[177]Mina the Recluse [Kyrillos VI], "Letter to Fr Makary el-Samuely, October 27, 1950." Kyrillos (then Fr Mina) spoke of the fear of demons in the presence of humility, and how fierce animals were made tame by the scent of humility—evidently his personal experience while a monk at the windmill.

[178]Raphael Ava Mina, "Interview about the Life of Pope Kyrillos VI."

[179]Ibid.

[180]Raphael Ava Mina, "My Memories," audio recording.

[181]Ibid. In 1967 Kyrillos would prepare the Holy Chrism (*myron*), only to find that the large vessels consecrated for this purpose were missing. Melek—who happened to be present at the event—had sold them (though he denied it), enraging the patriarchal deacons. That night, Fr Raphael claims, the family of Melek came to Kyrillos screaming that Melek was dying of a severe abdominal complaint. "Don't worry," reassured Kyrillos, "about the vessels . . . I forgive him; tell him to come and see me." The next day Melek recovered. As for Melek's end: "He lost all his money and lived his last days in poverty while begging in the streets . . . until he died on May 15, 1973." See Serapion, "Choosing the Patriarch: Lessons from the History of Our Glorious Church," 25–27.

[182]Raphael Ava Mina, "Interview about the Life of Pope Kyrillos VI."

[183]Atta and Raphael Ava Mina, *Life of Pope Kyrillos*, 22.

[184]Raphael Ava Mina, "Interview about the Life of Pope Kyrillos VI." Fr Raphael stated during the interview that he destroyed the painful letters in 2010—he had preserved them until then—as he could no longer (after some four decades) bear to have them in his cell any longer.

[185]For a history of the Menas Shrine (which at one point was internationally renowned) and the site, see Meinardus, *Monks and Monasteries (1989)*, 168–78.

[186]Atta and Raphael Ava Mina, *Memories about the Life of Pope Kyrillos*, 42.

[187]*Egyptian Gazette* November 10, 1942, cited in Meinardus, *Monks and Monasteries (1961)*, 354. Winston Churchill said of the battle: "Before Alamein we never had a victory. After Alamein we never had a defeat"; Winston S. Churchill, *The Hinge of Fate* (Boston: Houghton Mifflin Harcourt, 1985), 541.

For a discussion of witnesses and sources, see Bishop Kyrillos Ava Mina, *The Great Egyptian and Coptic Martyr: The Miraculous Saint Mina* (Mariout: St Mina Monastery Press, 2005), 52–57.

[188]Mina the Recluse [Kyrillos VI], "Letter to Habib Pasha el-Masri, June 28, 1943." Prince Omar Toson, known as the "scholarly prince," was the great grandson of Mohamed Ali, and had a deep interest in archaeology—even becoming the head of the Coptic Archaeological Society.

[189]Ibid.

[190]Hanna mentions that he met with Banoub in 1943 in Alexandria; see Mina the Recluse [Kyrillos VI], "Letter to Hanna Youssef Atta, March 5, 1958." Banoub Habashy was an archaeologist and the first president of the St Menas' Association; he died in 1955.

[191]Mina the Recluse [Kyrillos VI], "Letter to Mounir Shoukry, March 5, 1958." The letter is cited in Raphael Ava Mina, *Memories: Part II*, 44–45.

[192]Hegumen Mina the Recluse [Kyrillos VI], "Letter to Hanna Youssef Atta, May 14, 1946" [in Arabic], in RC-2: Letter 29 (St Samuel's Monastery: 1946).

[193]For instance, see Kyrillos' letter begging Yusab's secretary; Hegumen Mina the Recluse [Kyrillos VI], "Letter to Hanna Youssef Atta, 1950" [in Arabic], in RC-2: Letter 35 (St Samuel's Monastery: 1950). Also see Kyrillos' letter to the general manager of the Ministry of Antiquities in the 1950s (date given as 195_), Hegumen Mina the Recluse [Kyrillos VI], "Letter to General Manager of the Ministry of Antiquities, 195_" [in Arabic], in FRC-1: Letter 37 (Old Cairo, 195_).

[194]Mina the Recluse [Kyrillos VI], "Letter to Mounir Shoukry, March 5, 1958." The letter is cited in Raphael Ava Mina, *Memories: Part II*, 44–45.

[195]Mina the Recluse [Kyrillos VI], "Letter to Hanna Youssef Atta, March 5, 1958." The letter is cited in Raphael Ava Mina, *Memories: Part II*, 48.

[196]Hegumen Mina the Recluse [Kyrillos VI], "Letter to Hanna Youssef Atta, June 23, 1958" [in Arabic] (Old Cairo, 1958). The letter continues, "Cooperate with Dr Mounir Shoukry. . . . First, we will build a hermitage or two outside the rest house which is there. Then we will start overhauling the altar through the manager of the Coptic Museum, because he is responsible for this operation. Once we put our feet there, be sure that the Lord will work with us. It is very important to care and meet Dr. Mounir Shoukry, and whoever has anything to do with this matter. In the Patriarchate in Alexandria, there is a letter from the Archaeology Department with a permission to perform religious rites at St Menas' Monastery."

[197]Mounir Shoukry, "Letter to Pope Kyrillos VI, June 24, 1959" [in Arabic], in FRC-2: Letter 65 (Alexandria, 1959).

[198]Atta and Raphael Ava Mina, *Life of Pope Kyrillos*, 39.

[199]Wakin, *A Lonely Minority*, 112.

[200]Meinardus, *Monks and Monasteries (1989)*, 178.

[201]Atta and Raphael Ava Mina, *Memories about the Life of Pope Kyrillos*, 105. This is missed in Atta and Raphael Ava Mina, *Life of Pope Kyrillos*.

[202]Wakin, *A Lonely Minority*, 112.

[203]James Wellard, *Desert Pilgrimage: A Journey into Christian Egypt* (London: Hutchinson & Co, 1970), 198.

[204]Suryal, "Pope Kyrillos VI." The lecture continues, "But we didn't understand history. . . . For this reason we need to read the history of our country and Church."

[205]Van Doorn-Harder, "Planner, Patriarch and Saint," 236.

[206]Raphael Ava Mina, *Service and Humility*, 36.

[207]Van Doorn-Harder, "Practical and Mystical," 230.

[208]Meinardus, *Christian Egypt: Faith and Life*, 214–19; Hasan, *Christians versus Muslims*, 217.

[209]Gruber, "Sacrifice in the Desert," 154. Gruber attributes the success of the St Menas' Monastery to Kyrillos' careful "cultural posturing"—a term he uses to explore the unusually evolved dysfunctional "divisiveness and collective incompetence" of much Coptic ecclesial bureaucracy as a means of "exhibiting harmlessness to an ever leery [i.e., Muslim] majority"—that is, the move appears dysfunctional and ineffective to external eyes and yet subtly and carefully begins an action that could not have otherwise been taken directly. I have several concerns with this suggestion: it is philosophical at the cost

of historical; Kyrillos' action was primarily criticized from within the community (not by the Muslim majority); and finally, it presupposes that Kyrillos was deliberate in his posturing.

[210]Van Doorn-Harder, "Practical and Mystical," 230; Nelly van Doorn-Harder, *Contemporary Coptic Nuns* (Columbia, SC: University of South Carolina Press, 1995), 274; van Doorn-Harder, *Modern Coptic Papacy*, 142.

[211]Van Doorn-Harder, *Modern Coptic Papacy*, 142.

[212]Gruber, for instance, argues that monasteries are the "cultural nexus of Coptic social and cultural life, a vital link of ethnic aspiration and spiritual revival." See Mark Francis Gruber, "The Monastery as the Nexus of Coptic Cosmology," in *BDC*, 81.

[213]Van Doorn-Harder, *Modern Coptic Papacy*, 143.

[214]Shenouda III, "Speech at the First Year Commemoration of Kyrillos VI." He states, "When he became Pope . . . the life of solitude did not escape him; he often went to St Menas' Monastery in the Mariout desert. . . . He wanted to be filled with the fruits of solitude."

[215]Atta and Raphael Ava Mina, *Memories about the Life of Pope Kyrillos*, 105. This is missed in the English translation.

[216]Ibid. This is missed in the English translation.

[217]For instance the comment, "as for him, he prays alone"; see Anonymous, "Kyrillos on the Meaning of the Feast" [in Arabic], *al-Ahram*, January 1, 1967.

[218]For a remarkable account, see Salib's account of a young man stranded at a train station; Suryal, "Pope Kyrillos VI."

[219]We may assume it was in April, as this is the month of spring in which these characteristic sandstorms occur.

[220]The name *khamseen* means "fifty," though many accounts suggest these sandstorms often resolve within one week.

[221]Atta and Raphael Ava Mina, *Life of Pope Kyrillos*, 30. Also note another similar miracle mentioned by Fr Raphael: "In 1964, the Pope was at St. Mina's Monastery when there was a severe storm. The monks came to him asking for his prayers that the storm would end. He then raised his cross and said, 'Put the air of the heavens in a good mood.' The storm became so calm that there wasn't even a breeze. The Pope then said, 'St Menas, when we asked you to calm the storm, did you have to stop the breeze as well?' Then a gentle breeze surrounded the area, and all were astonished." A similar account is recorded in Raphael Ava Mina, *Miracles of Pope Kyrillos VI*, 1:79.

[222]Fr Raphael catalogues the intersections between Kyrillos' visits to St Menas' Monastery and the achievements of his patriarchate; see Atta and Raphael Ava Mina, *Memories about the Life of Pope Kyrillos*, 105. This is missed in Atta and Raphael Ava Mina, *Life of Pope Kyrillos*.

[223]The account was personally relayed to Fr Tadros; see Malaty, "Interview about the Life of Pope Kyrillos: Part I."

[224]Ibid.

8

The Healing of Enmity: Within and Without

An Abrupt Solution:
The Ethiopian Church and the Emperor, 1959

"What attracts me is a *vocation of loss*—a life which would give itself freely . . .
known to God alone; in brief, to lose oneself in order to find oneself."
—*Fr Lev Gillet*

IN THE EARLY 1960s an American journalist put a series of written questions
to the patriarch hoping to hear something of his ambitions for the Church.[1]
Kyrillos wrote in reply that his only ambition was to see his people develop a
"deep experience of prayer"; he then added that prayer had already, within a few
years, solved the three major problems of the Coptic Church. First among the
three—even before the *unity* of the fractured community and the precarious
waqf endowments—was, surprisingly, the "Ethiopian problem."

* * *

The roots of this "Ethiopian problem"—though few today have recognized its
significance in the life of Kyrillos—date to the fourth century. According to
Rufinus of Aquileia (340–410), a Syrian merchant by the name of Meropius set
sail for India, and en route he was shipwrecked on the coast of Ethiopia. Though
Meropius and his crew were put to the sword by overly inquisitive natives, his
two young sons, Frumentius and Aedesius, were spared and sent to the palace where they rose to positions of prominence. Some years later Frumentius
(now chancellor) was sent to Athanasius (298–373), patriarch of Alexandria,
to request a suitable bishop for his people. Thereupon Athanasius—seeing no
other man more worthy—ordained Frumentius as the first bishop, later known

as *abune*, for Ethiopia. Frumentius returned, baptized King Ezana, and converted the kingdom of Aksum (modern-day Ethiopia).[2]

The episode established a precedent seemingly set in stone: Coptic patriarchs would nominate and consecrate the head of the Ethiopian Church, who would inevitably be a *Copt*. And so it remained for the next millennium and a half, more or less uninterrupted—other than during the brief intrusions of the Catholic "missions" in the sixteenth and seventeenth centuries.[3] But by the early twentieth century, the situation became increasingly untenable. The Ethiopian Church, something of a state religion, was numerically superior to the Coptic Church in Egypt, which, we might add, was decidedly under the thumb of a Muslim majority.[4]

When *Abune* Mettaos, metropolitan of Ethiopia, died in 1926, a modest gain was made. After a series of negotiations, the Coptic Synod ordained an Egyptian metropolitan, Kyrillos (1926–1936, 1945–1950), to be assisted by four Ethiopian bishops (Abraam, Boutros, Isaac, and Mikhail). The success would, however, be short-lived. The violent Italian invasion of Ethiopia in 1935—what one scholar called "Mussolini's imperialist aggression against a seemingly defenseless people"—both complicated and at once advanced the movement towards ecclesial autonomy.[5] The Italians sought to destabilize the Church and rupture any relationship with the Copts. Kyrillos, *abune* of Ethiopia, was able to make his way back to Egypt, but his assistant bishops were not so fortunate. Boutros resisted the occupation and was shot dead by the Italians in a public square; Mikhail and Isaac simply "disappeared"; while Abraam instead chose to play to the invaders, who in return "made him" patriarch of Ethiopia.[6]

With the Italians distracted by World War II toward the end of 1940, the Ethiopians reasserted their independence, with assistance from British and French forces. Though the Italians had ultimately failed in directly severing the bonds between the Ethiopian and Coptic Churches, indirectly and ironically (given Ethiopian independence from the Italians), there came an increasingly agitated call for ecclesial independence from Alexandria.[7] Haile Selassie (1892–1975), emperor of Ethiopia, made it an urgent and personal priority.[8] By 1942, Ethiopian priests were being ordained by the Ethiopian *echege* (a figure second in authority to the *abune*).[9] Thus, Meinardus concludes, "for all practical purposes the function of the Coptic *abune* became obsolete."[10] Despite this, in 1942 and 1945, the Coptic Synod rejected Ethiopian calls for autocephaly. Veiled threats were made in return by the emperor, who hinted that Ethiopia might sever ties with the Coptic Church.[11] In June 1947, Selassie made his position explicit. He would no longer negotiate. On the death of the current Egyptian *abune*, Selassie declared, an Ethiopian should be consecrated with full authority to ordain other Ethiopian bishops. When Kyrillos (the last Coptic *abune*) died in October 1950, Yusab II felt he had no other choice but to comply with Selassie's demands. On January 13, 1951, Yusab consecrated the first Ethiopian *abune*, Basilious (1951–1970), who in turn set about ordaining his own bishops.[12] But, we should be clear, this was not yet autocephaly, but more so delegated authority with the Coptic patriarch still directing the Ethiopian Church through an Ethiopian *abune*. There was still an ever-present fear within the Coptic Synod that autocephaly would mean certain ecclesial schism and loss of patriarchal status.

Chaos and darkness, however, would soon descend upon the Coptic Church during the unfortunate years of Yusab II. Would the newfound authority of the Ethiopian *abune* persist now that Yusab was deposed?

It was a fair concern. The Ethiopian *abune*, Basilious, was consecrated at Yusab's hands, and thus the very credibility of his elevated status was called into question. Beyond this, the Ethiopians were enraged that they were not given a vote, or even consulted, regarding the deposition of Yusab.[13] Over the next few years, the heated and somewhat oblivious Ethiopian insistence in petitioning Yusab's return to the throne—attempting numerous interventions, beseeching the Egyptian ambassador, and even holding their own "synod" to negotiate his return—betrayed dilating insecurity among the Ethiopian hierarchy.[14] While it is unwise, and perhaps unwarranted, to claim that anything more sinister was at play (endemic simony during Yusab's reign, for instance), the Ethiopian demands in the face of a resolute Coptic Synod confirm that they felt their increasing autonomy was on exceptionally uncertain ground. And with anxiety came profound resentment. This quickly evolved into explicit threats to the already fraying and fragile bonds between Ethiopia and Egypt.[15] The union of more than a millennium and a half was at a critical breaking point. This was, in short, the "Ethiopian problem."

* * *

Six days after his name was selected from the altar ballot, on April 19, 1959, Fr Mina was writing from his church in Old Cairo. While preparations were underway for his ordination and enthronement, he was busy with another plan. A delegation was sent to Emperor Haile Selassie, with a letter in hand from the recluse and patriarch-elect. "I send you this letter," wrote Fr Mina on April 25,

... after the grace of God chose my weakness for this immense rank. . . . As I realize the call of God and the enormity of this responsibility to shepherd souls, I am confident that he who called me is also capable of aiding me to steer the ship of this Church to its harbor of salvation. . . . I am pleased to express to your Majesty what I hold in my heart; abundant love and great appreciation for our beloved Ethiopian people. . . . There is no doubt that once there is the spirit of true Christian love, harmony, and mutual understanding, then all difficulties can be mitigated, and we can reach acceptable solutions and begin a new era in strengthening the holy bond that you have protected, labored in maintaining, and supported all your life . . . love can do everything, and overcome all obstructions in peace. The *first thing* that we will undertake after ordination, God willing, in the Holy Synod, will be the needs of the dear Ethiopian Church. . . . What will make me most joyful is the participation of my brethren, the bishops of Ethiopia, in *putting their hands on the head* of the pope of Alexandria for the first time in the history of our Church during the ordination. This will multiply my feelings of the depth and spirit of this bond. I look forward with joyful eyes to the day I meet Your Majesty in Ethiopia and in Egypt.[16]

There is little political banter in the letter. Fr Mina is adamant that his most urgent priority is the "Ethiopian problem." He not only requests the presence of the Ethiopian Church at his ordination but is yearning, for the first time in history, that they "place their hands on [his] head" and thus share in his consecration. The suggestion, a mere six days after his election, was nothing less than historically subversive. President Nasser—who held a rather complicated stance toward Ethiopia—had evidently perceived the significance of the move and went so far as to forcibly prevent any Ethiopian representative from attending the consecration.[17] But Fr Mina was not dissuaded. Six days after his enthronement as Patriarch Kyrillos VI, on May 16, 1959, he wrote once more to Emperor Haile Selassie:

We have been greatly affected by the feelings of pain that your Majesty has expressed in your verbal message, that you could not participate in the ordination. We beseech God that the grace of his Holy Spirit work to restore the Church's peace and comfort with the spirit of sincere love and forgiveness that we expressed in our previous letter. . . . Because of our feelings of the increased needs of the Church of St Mark in Ethiopia, in its current revival, through Your Excellency's encouragement and attention, we are pleased to *elevate the rank* of the head of St Mark's Church in Ethiopia. . . .[18]

On June 29, 1959, shortly after his enthronement, Kyrillos declared the autocephaly of the Ethiopian Church and elevated *Abune* Basilious to "Patriarch-Catholicos."[19] One scholar commented that it would be Kyrillos' "greatest act of healing."[20] While many have made a note of the "great speed" (barely six weeks) with which Kyrillos acted to heal the fractures that were threatening separation, the decision was in fact made days after his enthronement—if not earlier, as we have seen.[21]

It is difficult to explain Kyrillos' immediate and decisive resolve; especially when one considers the heated contention and resistance of the previous centuries, and that Kyrillos was replacing the "sorely" missed (at least for the Ethiopians) Yusab in the face of an evidently disapproving Egyptian president. Watson, with whom many agree, has suggested that Kyrillos must have discussed the situation from his early days as a hermit at the Baramous Monastery living near the saintly Fr Abdel Messih el-Habashy ("the *Ethiopian*"). This, as we have seen previously, is exceedingly unlikely given that the relationship is overstated in the extreme. They had limited contact, and the Ethiopian saint entered the surrounding desert only *after* Kyrillos (then Fr Mina) had already been expelled from the monastery.[22] It may be far more reasonably suggested that Kyrillos' determination was secondary to *another* relationship: that of his closest disciple and confidant, Fr Makary el-Syriany. In the mid-1940s, Makary had served in Ethiopia and had labored in educating, building, and establishing the theological seminary.[23] This may, conceivably, explain the urgency that Kyrillos brought to the "Ethiopian problem." But I would suggest that he also had another motive.

It is important to see that until his election as patriarch, it had been the Ethiopians who had demanded ecclesial independence. And yet, here, it is Kyrillos who writes, initiates, compromises, and makes their struggle his own. What had caused such a radical shift? Could it be that Kyrillos saw through the complicated and tragic history; saw beyond the distorted lens of pride and politics—both personal and ecclesial; and acted determinedly, as he had so many times before, in what can only be termed "ecclesial kenosis." That is to say, an appropriation of his own *personal kenosis* into a *kenotic ecclesiology*. What was imperative and vital for the Kingdom was done—and done immediately. It was a lucid moment of national and ethnic kenosis and self-emptying. It was the loss of ecclesial and patriarchal status, influence, and authority; indeed, the loss of Ethiopia at the cost of his own Alexandria. The loss of *a* church for *the* Church.

* * *

Kyrillos would be the first patriarch in history to visit Ethiopia twice—indeed, there were only three other recorded patriarchal visits in the previous fifteen hundred years.[24] On October 26, 1960, he traveled to Ethiopia for a two-week pastoral tour, with the final two days in Eritrea.[25] For the duration he was accommodated at the Menelik Palace (the personal residence of the emperor). Selassie kept on the property several lions, which were secured by chains. Kyrillos on one occasion casually approached the lions. Both he and the lions gently accepted the presence of the other. "Why be astonished?" the emperor is remembered as commenting to shocked onlookers, "He is a holy man."[26]

Five years later, on January 13, 1965, Kyrillos returned once more, this time to preside over the Inaugural Oriental Orthodox Conference in Addis Ababa. On disembarking from his flight, he was greeted by a twenty-one-gun salute and thousands cheering. As the emperor made to kiss his hand, Kyrillos' first words were: "I want to go to the church to celebrate the Liturgy."[27] Indeed, he had come prepared, had been fasting, and even brought the *prosphora* (bread to be offered in the Eucharist) with him from Egypt. He had one thing on his mind. "If the priest is present, flour is handy, and the altar is available," he was fond of saying, "[then] if we don't pray, what shall we say to God?"[28] Though there were few palpable resolutions from the proceedings of the conference, the "convergence of needs and expressions of solidarity" would be far-reaching.[29]

* * *

Shenouda III recalls a conversation with Haile Selassie where he talked of his love for Kyrillos. "Whenever I used to sit with Pope Kyrillos," fondly reminisced the emperor, "I always had the feeling I was a young child with my father."[30] Photographs of the period suggest the same, with the emperor invariably holding his hand and looking up at Kyrillos with admiration, awe, and perhaps not a little fear. But it would be a relationship that would be tested more than once.

Almost immediately another age-old conflict erupted—an incredibly complex and dark dispute (well beyond our scope) between the Coptic and Ethiopian monks concerning ownership of Deir al-Sultan Monastery on the rooftop of the Church of the Holy Sepulcher.[31] The dispute was marked by confusion and convolution, since it was enmeshed in all matters of underhand politics between Egypt, Ethiopia, Jordan, and Israel. But within that chaotic correspondence emerges the unique stance and attitude of Kyrillos. While the various bishops on both sides were clamoring and appealing to civil courts and higher government authorities, Kyrillos' letters during the period warn that such appeals would simply "inflame the situation and disturb the quiet atmosphere required to reach a solution."[32] And though, for instance, Emperor Selassie would regularly feign innocence and plead ignorance despite his explicit involvement and machinations, Kyrillos remained ever humble, delicately traversing the awkward and precarious ground between the two Churches, without escalating the situation or making any threat. The matter would become far more complicated by the later history of the Ethiopian Church, both within and without—it was a story marked by revolution, famine, and genocide. The dispute over Deir al-Sultan, unsurprisingly, and perhaps in consequence, still burns in the present day. It can only be hoped that the spirit of love and forgiveness that Kyrillos tenderly brought to the fractured Churches in 1959 may one day heal again.

The Rise and Fall of the Muslim Brotherhood

> "I have been a conspirator for so long that I mistrust all around me."
> —*Gamal Abdel Nasser*

IN THE MID-1960s Kyrillos visited the Coptic Hospital in Cairo and, according to the accounts, healed an elderly metropolitan who happened to be an old friend.[33] As he left the ward, Kyrillos, without any explanation, turned to his secretary and said, "Let us go visit Sheikh Hassan Mamoun, the sheikh of al-Azhar." Mamoun (1894–1973) was the grand imam of al-Azhar Mosque and University—the highest Islamic authority in Egypt. After several phone calls, the secretary replied that the sheikh was occupied in meetings and that it would be best to schedule an appointment (especially since it would be the first time a Coptic patriarch would visit al-Azhar). "We will go now," insisted Kyrillos. "God will make all things work to the good."[34]

Arriving at al-Azhar, Kyrillos, careful not to cause any offense, left his patriarchal staff in the vehicle and placed his cross in a pocket of his cassock. Though the visit was unannounced, the sheikh immediately left his meeting to greet the patriarch. On entering the office, Kyrillos noticed a tremor in the elderly sheikh's hands, for he was some eighty years old and suffered from Parkinson's disease. Without a word, Kyrillos took and stilled the sheikh's hands between his own hands. Touched by the love and gentleness of Kyrillos, Sheikh Mamoun's heart was opened before his mind.

"We should have met long ago," began Kyrillos. "Permit me to ask you a question—the Crusades," Kyrillos continued, "was it a war between the Christians and Muslims of Egypt, or between Western foreigners and Muslims?" (The newspapers and radio stations during the early 1960s were teeming with defamatory and dangerous slander that Copts had led the Crusades against the Muslims.)

"It was undoubtedly," replied Mamoun, "between foreigners and Muslims!"

"May I ask Your Excellency in that case," Kyrillos followed, "to issue a declaration to be published in newspapers and broadcast on the radio so that the matter is made clear to the whole nation of Egypt . . . for many are speaking contrary to your words, and perhaps will cause a Muslim to kill his Christian brother."[35] The very next day, the secretary of the al-Azhar arrived at the patriarchate with a copy of the declaration in hand.[36]

Some have suggested that this was a turning point in the sectarian conflicts of the 1960s.[37] While that may in part be true, there were several other complex factors. At the center of this interplay of factors stood Kyrillos, tenderly taking into his own hands the trembling and agitated hands of an indifferent and unpredictable Muslim president who was at the head of an increasingly hostile Muslim nation.

* * *

The story of the Muslim president and the Coptic patriarch had begun a decade earlier. On July 23, 1952, the Free Officers—in a calculated response to the Palestinian events of 1948, systemic corruption, increasing peasant revolts, and the burning of Cairo in early 1952—seized control of government buildings, police stations, the army headquarters, and, importantly, radio stations. Within hours the monarchy was overthrown, King Farouk was forced to abdicate, and declarations of a new government were broadcast over the radio. But these second-rank officers "had no programs, almost no ideology, and barely any 'philosophy.'"[38] Though the Free Officers were the armed dimension of the revolutionary movement, its militant base was organically linked to society by two *other* forces: the Marxist left and, most especially, the Muslim Brotherhood. And the two of these "could not be reconciled."[39]

With Gamal Abdel Nasser's assumption of the presidency—which was in effect the arrest of his rival, Prime Minister Naguib (1901–1984) and the "return of the military to their barracks"—the first semblance of a government emerged in early 1954.[40] Almost immediately it became obvious that the stabilization of government necessitated the suppression of those two irreconcilable forces: the Communists, who had already severed ties with the Revolutionary Command Council (RCC) and the Muslim Brotherhood, which had dared to support Naguib against Nasser.[41] Though "officially" pursuing the goals of its founder— namely aid, spirituality, and solidarity, albeit with the occasional assassination and violent outburst—the Brotherhood sought to impose on the policies of the RCC, especially those concerning education, sexuality, and culture. It was very much a "sociological opposition."[42] By July 1954, Nasser ordered the dissolution of the Brotherhood on grounds that they opposed agrarian reform; attempted to infiltrate and subvert the military; maintained a clandestine "paramilitary" organization; and, finally, persistently sought to impose upon and influence the RCC.[43] It would take a few months for the reaction. On October 26, 1954, while Nasser was delivering a speech in Alexandria, Mohammed Abdel Latif, a member of the Brotherhood, fired nine shots from seven meters (23 feet), all of which inexplicably missed Nasser. Panic erupted, but Nasser stood his ground on the podium and shouted for calm. "My countrymen," he screamed overcome with emotion in words so compelling that some have claimed the entire episode was orchestrated,

> my blood spills for you and for Egypt. I will live for your sake and die for the sake of your freedom and honor. Let them kill me; it does not concern me so long as I have instilled pride, honor, and freedom in you. If Gamal Abdel Nasser should die, each of you shall be Gamal Abdel Nasser . . . Gamal Abdel Nasser is of you and from you and he is willing to sacrifice his life for the nation![44]

The speech was live-broadcast on the radio. Egypt and the Arab world erupted in a roar. In that moment, Nasser was given a pretext for the final suppression of the Brotherhood, but more importantly, in that same moment, the masses fell helplessly in love with him.[45] Nasser had transcended the office of president; he had become *al-raïs*, the undisputed leader of Egypt. A severe and violent repression of the Brotherhood followed. Six were hanged, hundreds were put on trial, and tens of thousands were arrested. "This was the *first time* we were hard with them," recalls Zakaria Mohieddin.[46] Within weeks all opposing

political parties were abolished, opposing voices imprisoned, and any dissenting press closed.[47]

The Brotherhood went underground. There, hidden from the eyes of the government, the outlook of the Brotherhood became decidedly violent, in part, no
doubt, because of its violent repression. But soon Nasser changed and employed
relative tolerance toward the Brotherhood. "One wonders," writes Roussillon,
"whether the opening given the Brotherhood between 1959 and 1965, reflected
a temptation within Nasserist circles to retrieve not so much the Brotherhood's
ideology, but their capacity to *manage politically* those values associated with
religion."[48] Only when it became undeniable some years later that the Brotherhood was secretly reorganizing (with the underhanded support of "oil-rich
Saudi Wahhabism") to conspire against the state, did brutal repression become
irrepressible. Thousands were arrested, and the Brotherhood's most powerful
ideologue, Sayyid Qutb, was hanged on August 29, 1966.[49] The relationship
of Nasser and the Brotherhood was complicated. Few, then, could expect the
Church to fare any better.

* * *

Though Nasser's father was born in Beni Murr, a village whose population
was 40 percent Coptic Christian, he was brought up in Alexandria and, to all
accounts, seemed to have had "no strong views on [Copts]."[50] Nor did he, at
least personally, hold Islam as a central tenet of his ideology. Religion was for
Nasser a means of consolidating his leadership—so far as it served his policy.[51]
Citizenship, for instance, was not dependent nor determined by religion; it was,
rather, a right. "The freedom of religious belief," dictated Nasser in the 1962
National Charter,

> must be regarded as sacred in our new free life. . . . The essence of religion
> does not conflict with the facts of our life. . . . All religions contain a message
> of progress. . . . The essence of all religions is to assert man's right to life and
> freedom.[52]

Religion could be regarded as a positive element, Nasser's ideology suggests, as
long as it did not impose upon the freedom of others nor obstruct the progress
of the nation. When asked about his policy on religion, Nasser replied, "I have
no religious policy, but rather a national policy."[53] In other words, Nasser seems
to have been very much uninterested in the Copts.[54] That said, support of the
Church was nonetheless vital for Nasser's image in the Middle East as the leader

of pan-Arabism; and so, some have insinuated that Nasser's only concern was that he be photographed alongside the Coptic patriarch.[55]

But despite the propaganda, the reality (at least at the beginning) was the opposite. Though appearing secular, we should not miss, as one scholar notes, that "at the same time the foundation was being laid for the cultural supremacy of Islam."[56] Whatever security and assurances may have been promised to religious minorities were soon eclipsed by Nasser's national policies. These years, whether intentional or not, were the breeding grounds of the violent Islamic movements in the 1970s: both directly, because of the state's complicated attitudes toward the Muslim Brotherhood, which arbitrarily shifted between quiet tolerance and violent repression; and indirectly, in consequence of Nasser's policies that betrayed an implicit "Islamisation of public life."[57]

The little political representation and influence Copts once had was swiftly replaced. In the new regime, they had token parliamentary seats (at most 1 percent)—what Nisan described as a "political crumb with no concomitant power"—in a government founded upon a pan-Arab ideology arising from Islamic culture.[58] Under Nasser's education policies of 1955, the teaching and memorization of the Quran became compulsory in Egyptian schools, numerous Coptic schools were closed (in part because of economic policies), and university scholarships for overseas study excluded Copts for the most part.[59] With the nationalization of schools also came a rarely noticed, and perhaps unexpected, consequence. Coptic schools had once served both Christians and Muslims, reportedly including Nasser (and his father). Their closure meant Muslim children would have fewer opportunities to become familiar with the Christian minority.[60]

But it was Nasser's economic policies that most hurt the Church. Agrarian (land) reform, in September 1952, limited family holdings to a maximum of two hundred acres, in the great socialist hope of redistributing wealth away from landowners to peasants.[61] Despite Nasser's hopeful dreams, the effects were for the most part overexaggerated, as many have noted; the reform affected barely ten percent of arable land and benefited only a relatively small proportion of the landless peasants.[62] But this does not take into account one matter: the Copts formed a disproportionate majority of that landowning class.[63] Land reform effectively disintegrated the large Coptic estates of the Wissa, Khayyat, and Andraos families, while the nationalization of businesses crippled powerful Coptic companies such as the Magar and Morgan Bus Company and the

Banque du Caire, which was dominated by Copts. In a few short years, wealth was effectively redistributed away from Copts to their Muslim neighbors.[64]

And though originally the regime sought to displace influence and pedigree with merit as the criterion for advancement—initially benefiting Copts, who generally had more higher education—it was eventually checked by the decreased recruitment of Copts in government ministries and university faculties.[65] The private sector, previously a disproportionate stronghold of Copts, was suppressed, while the public sector became exceedingly difficult to enter and perhaps impossible to scale. With the increasingly anti-Western rhetoric and Nasser's forced deportation of smaller non-Muslim communities (mostly Greeks, Jews, and West-Europeans), the Copts were left exposed as a seemingly alien population within their own land.[66] Permits for churches were delayed (most indefinitely), while many churches were seized by the Ministry of Islamic Affairs. Coptic religious courts were closed, wealth was redistributed, and the once-influential Coptic laity became powerless. "The break in continuity was severe—economically, politically, and socially."[67]

Nasser's nationalization and economic policies would eventually fail, with short-run gains paling in the face of long-term losses of productivity and efficiency. But culturally these changes spelled impending doom for the Coptic population, that is, at least for those who remained. The 1960s saw a mass exodus of Copts to the Western world, further weakening the domestic Church.[68] Nasser seemingly, against much of popular memory, and in at least the estimation of several historians, "oppressed the Copts in an abusive fashion."[69]

* * *

"There was little confessional tension, or trouble between Church and state, under Nasser," declares Pennington.[70] This is somewhat understating the case. There were, in fact, several churches that were attacked (by both mobs and government).[71] But it is true when compared to the years before and after Nasser. There are two preeminent reasons for this: Nasser's mistrust and Kyrillos' ascetic transcendence.

"Suspicion was Nasser's besetting sin and principal weakness," comments Anthony Nutting, a British Deputy Foreign Secretary. "Not only did his distrust of his colleagues cause disharmony . . . it also made him interfere continually in their work. . . . Worse still, he pried into the private lives of his ministers, whose telephones were tapped."[72] Nasser's secular ideology, fierce security measures, and legendary secrecy could never tolerate the existence of the Muslim

Brotherhood—not even when their ideological visions converged. And so, in the aftermath of the violent dissolution of the brotherhood, with the exceedingly tight grip of the regime, there was little room for the chaos that so often engenders sectarian conflict (other than from government sources). This ensured that Nasser's reign would not be "entirely negative" for the Copts.[73]

There may not have been explicit persecution, but Copts, having suffered (in varying degrees) persecution and exclusion for one and a half millennia, could read the signs, and many emigrated accordingly. Agrarian reform had economically crippled the Church, while political marginalization, educational indoctrination, and public discrimination struck deeply at its future. Land was lost, private industry was destroyed, and Coptic education sabotaged. Fr Tadros Malaty, perhaps the most prolific Coptic scholar of his generation, expresses the sentiments of many: "In that first period of Nasser's reign, he and his government had a very serious and hidden plan against the Church. . . ."[74]

Though Nasser, as far as one can tell, did not harbor any personal animosity towards the Christians, he was evidently suspicious of all and feared what he could not control. What he had not realized (at least in those early years) was that unlike the other unruly and turbulent elements of his day, Kyrillos and his Church did *not* need to be controlled. That realization would take some years. Until then, whatever Nasser's exact intentions may have been, the Church in the late 1950s stood on perilous and fragile ground. Nasser in a moment could have prohibited or literally "deported" Christianity—if not worse—on even the slightest suggestion that it was incompatible with his policies; had it not been, that is, for Kyrillos' ascetic transcendence.[75]

The Patriarch and the President, 1959–1965

> "A doubtful friend is worse than a certain enemy. Let a man be
> one thing or the other, and we then know how to meet him."
> —*Aesop's Fables*

IN EARLY OCTOBER 1959, a Muslim man, a prominent member of the National Council and close friend of Gamal Abdel Nasser, entered the patriarchate. A few months earlier Kyrillos had healed that same man's son of some ailment. It was evidently a rather dramatic miracle, for the man—his name was concealed given the sensitivities of his government position—converted to Christianity soon after.[76] He found Kyrillos sitting, distracted, and unusually downcast. "What is bothering you, *sayedna* [my master]?" he gently asked.

"That man [Nasser]," grumbled Kyrillos, ". . . I have asked him more than ten times for an appointment—all in vain!"

"Is that all?"—he interrupted—"I myself will get the appointment, and we shall go together." Nasser, so the man later reported, was entirely uninterested when told that Kyrillos had hoped to discuss the troubles of the community.

"Problems with what and whom?" dismissed the President, "the Copts have everything good. . . . What's wrong with them, they have it good now!"[77] But the man pressed once more, and a meeting was eventually scheduled for a few days later.

Several suggestions have been made as to why Nasser refused to meet Kyrillos for some five months after his ordination. It was likely a coalescence of factors: indifference at best, undisclosed machinations at worst. Fr Mikhail Dawood, the son of Kyrillos' confessor, claims it was due to the patriarch's stance toward the Personal Status Laws that governed marriage and divorce, and his call for a fast in defiance of the government.[78] Another historian, on the other hand, brings attention to the election period that preceded Kyrillos' ordination.[79] The final years of Yusab's reign—recall his painful abduction and abdication—in the mid-1950s had left Nasser with the impression that the Copts were a source of problems. This was exacerbated by defamatory reports Nasser had received during the patriarchal elections, suggesting that Kyrillos (then Fr Mina) was practicing sorcery. "Sort it out! I don't want to interfere," Nasser is said to have told a Coptic politician at that time.[80] And others suggest that Nasser was simply uninterested in the Copts and had little time for them.[81] But perhaps the most feasible explanation, though certainly in the context of the others, is that Kyrillos was himself responsible.

Wakin and Meinardus, supported by several prominent Arabic sources, claim that the tension dated back to Kyrillos' ordination (which, we should note, Nasser failed to attend).[82] Immediately after the enthronement, Nasser sent a message that Kyrillos should pay him a "ceremonial visit"—no doubt for the sake of propaganda. "The patriarch is visited," Kyrillos is reported to have replied, "but does not visit."[83]

A short while later, Nasser sent a delegate to greet the new patriarch; Kyrillos sent two bishops in return for good measure. The president was unimpressed, commenting in frustration: "Is this a country within a country?"[84] Ramzy Stino, the future deputy prime minister, tried to intervene at Nasser's command to persuade Kyrillos. "Nasser sent one delegate, I sent two," Kyrillos told the politician, "He didn't elect me; God and providence did." As Stino made to leave, Kyrillos added firmly, "Please don't try to take care of the Church. It is *my* problem."[85] It was a tenacious message to Nasser that Kyrillos owed him no favors; and to Stino and the other lay Coptic notables, that he was not a puppet for hire.

* * *

It seems that after some five months of tension Kyrillos sought, for reasons unknown, to finally meet Nasser.[86] When they did meet—through the pleading of the aforementioned man who was a close friend of the president—it hardly went according to plan. Other than the official summary declarations recorded in the press, there is only one detailed account of that visit, recorded by Fr Salib Suryal.[87] "This episode," Salib, a close confidant, relative, and disciple, claims, "Pope Kyrillos told me himself—though it is not well known and could not have been told previously."[88] As will soon become clear, the account could not have possibly been made public during the years of Nasser's presidency because of its personal and potentially divisive disclosures in a time of deep sectarian sensitivity, under a president, we should recall, whose secrecy was legendary.

On October 12, 1959, Kyrillos traveled to meet Nasser. After exchanging the usual greetings, they walked down the corridor to the library of the president. As they were still walking, Salib narrates, Nasser turned to Kyrillos and said, "Well . . . what do you Copts want? What is it exactly that you are lacking?" Nasser, it appears, could not contain the months of tension.

"What is this?" Kyrillos dismissed, "We are still walking and have not even sat down." By the time they reached the library, Kyrillos, too, had become frustrated. "Is this," the patriarch said, "the hospitality with which you receive me?" (Salib interjects in his account and repeats—"these words are from the mouth of Kyrillos himself.")

"Yes . . . ," Nasser hastily replied, "I tell you the Copts lack nothing for you to come and tell me their requests!"

Kyrillos could bear no more. "Enough!" he said, now rising with unusual intensity in his eyes. "I leave you to God, I leave you to God . . . enough; I don't want anything from you!" With those words, Kyrillos left in a hurry.

The Muslim man who had organized the meeting ran after him. "Thank you for your efforts," Kyrillos told him when he finally caught up, "but that man did not show the faintest hospitality . . . at the very least we could have sat over coffee; then he could have heard my words and thrown them away." Arriving back at the patriarchate in the evening, Kyrillos immediately prayed Vespers, finding comfort, as he always had, in prayer, before retiring to his patriarchal cell at midnight.

Two hours later that same Muslim man frantically knocked on the door of the patriarchate. "Gamal Abdel Nasser," he exclaimed to the attendant, "wants the pope immediately!"

"I can't just wake him up," the attendant hushed, knowing well that Kyrillos was an elderly man who would have to arise in an hour for psalmody. After some muffled argument, the Muslim man finally made it to the door of the patriarch. But before he had the chance to knock—Salib recalls—Kyrillos promptly opened the door in patriarchal attire and said, "Come, let us go quickly." Kyrillos, it would seem, had not slept and had been awaiting that moment. They returned to Nasser, but this time they would meet at his family home.

As they arrived and exited the vehicle, Kyrillos said only a few words: "Where is *she*?" Nasser's daughter had apparently become severely ill; Salib suggests that she "seemed to be possessed by an evil spirit." Several medical specialists who were called upon that evening concurred that no organic illness could be identified. Recalling the cryptic words of Kyrillos earlier in the day—"I leave you to God"—Nasser could not help thinking that the two events were related. Kyrillos went into the home (without his secretary or any clergy) and quietly prayed for the girl for some fifteen minutes. When he had finished, the girl was restored to perfect health.

Nasser was quite reasonably in shock. "From this moment," the president mumbled to the patriarch, "I will call you *my father*, and in the future, do not go to the presidential palace, but rather when you meet me, you meet in my own house. And these children," Nasser said, presenting his family before Kyrillos, "are like your children . . . pray for us in the same way exactly as you do for your family."[89] So ends the remarkable episode.

* * *

Whatever one may think of Salib's account, it cannot be denied that *something* happened. Examining the history of the period there can be no argument that a period of deep animosity was abruptly and powerfully aborted by that meeting in October 1959. Not simply in that the tension was resolved or that a constructive relationship had finally begun—that could, of course, be naturally expected after any meeting—but rather that a deep, palpable, and authentic friendship ensued suddenly that evening. Over the next decade, many would express their shock in hearing the Muslim president refer to the Coptic patriarch as "my father" and in seeing Nasser's children contribute to the building of St Menas' Monastery at Mariout.[90] Nasser and Kyrillos would be regularly seen in public holding hands (an Arabic symbol of deep friendship), with Nasser calling the patriarch from his hospital bed in the Soviet Union, and Kyrillos personally begging the president to revoke his resignation in the wake of the tragic events of 1967. All sources, as we shall see, agree: the relationship turned remarkably, almost instantly.

Even members of Nasser's family seem to have been confused by the strength of the friendship. Mona Gamal Abdel Nasser, his daughter, once asked a barrister (and future dean of the Coptic Institute) with whom she worked, Zaki Shenouda, "What's with your pope?"

"What do you mean?" he asked in reply.

"Whenever a president visits, my father [Nasser] farewells them at the guests' rooms door; but with Kyrillos, he farewells him at the car door and remains there standing until the car leaves."[91] Should it be authentic, this is remarkable on three counts: in the first, Mona seems (albeit within the brevity of the anecdote) to have been unaware as to the reason for their friendship; second, she at the same time makes note that the relationship was atypical for her father; and third, the account is recorded by a prominent Coptic barrister, Zaki Shenouda, who in the same breath, despite Mona's apparently being unaware of the miracle, makes mention of the healing of one of Nasser's children. These observations may not, however, be entirely unexpected. Mona at the time was only twelve years old, and Nasser was extremely secretive even with his own family—concealing, for instance, his heart attacks from his wife.[92]

On several occasions I attempted to corroborate the healing account with the children of Gamal Abdel Nasser. Most declined any contact. The exception was Abdel Hakim Nasser, who was kind enough to allow a lengthy interview. Abdel Hakim claimed that he had never heard of such a healing, but qualified that he was only four years old at the time and thus had no recollection of the meeting. Admittedly, he later added, one of his siblings was possibly unwell at that time and there was some suggestion that Kyrillos may have prayed for the child—though, he makes clear, he was unaware of any miraculous healing.[93]

Since this episode was revealed—in the late 1970s or early 1980s—a few minor variations have appeared that for the most part question whether it was Nasser's son or daughter that was healed.[94] Fr Salib claims, rather specifically, that it was Nasser's daughter—in all likelihood, the thirteen-year-old Hoda Gamal Abdel Nasser (b. 1946).[95] But other than that particular detail, no other Coptic source has ever questioned or disputed Salib's account—that is, with the exception of Kyrillos' other disciple, Fr Raphael Ava Mina.[96] Raphael admits that a healing miracle in Nasser's household must have occurred; he simply disagrees that it occurred in those circumstances and on that fated night in October 1959.[97] As further evidence of the healing, Raphael claims that Kyrillos indirectly disclosed the happenings to the renowned and saintly nun, Mother Irini (1936–2006), the former abbess of Abu Sefein Monastery in Old Cairo. On one occasion, she overheard a phone conversation between Nasser and Kyrillos. After Kyrillos hung up the phone, she asked, "What were these incredible and loving words from Nasser?"

"What words?" Kyrillos said without much thought. "Has God not shown him *miracles*?"

"So, the admission," Fr Raphael remarks, "escaped from Kyrillos without his realising . . . something definitely happened."[98]

Yet, perhaps just as remarkable as the miracle itself, scholars (both Arabic and Western) have missed the parallels of the episode with an event in the life of Anba Sarabamoun in the early nineteenth century.[99] The parallels are striking; and though they are suggestive of hagiographic imaginings, the very fact that all Coptic and Arabic scholars (with their Western counterparts) have missed the parallels argues otherwise.

Sarabamoun (d. 1853), whose "hidden life, known only to God, came to an end" when he was forcibly ordained, was made bishop of Menoufia in the early years of the nineteenth century.[100] Interestingly, his episcopacy—like Kyrillos'— saw an intensifying of asceticism; and, in a few short years, he became known throughout Egypt for his gifts of exorcism, healing, and clairvoyance.[101] In the very first years of his episcopate, Sarabamoun was called upon by Mohammed Ali, the khedive of Egypt, to heal his daughter Zohra (b. 1795).[102] After numerous protests of humility, Sarabamoun healed the young girl to the disbelief of the royal court. Mohammed Ali tried to bestow upon the holy man a small fortune but was instead met with the words: "I have no right to gain, through the gifts of God, what he does not make me in need of. My dress, as you see, is a coat of red wool, and my meals consist of bread and cool lentils."[103] After being pressed, Sarabamoun's only request was that "we may build churches as we please" and that Ali should "treat our sons equally."[104] Immediately afterward, the fate of the Copts is said to have changed: the following decades being remembered as a period of stability for the Copts, with, most fascinatingly, Ali—like Nasser— preferring to deal solely with the patriarch as the single representative of the community.[105]

Looking back to late antiquity, we likewise find significant precedent for healing miracles of the imperial family by holy bishops that, in most cases, resulted in the baptism of the imperial household.[106] Though we have no evidence that the alleged healing of Nasser's daughter (nor Mohammed Ali's) culminated in baptism, in a very real sense, we may still talk of conversion—that is, from animosity (or at the least, indifference) to profound friendship.

Ultimately, as Fr Tadros Malaty comments, whether Kyrillos healed Nasser's daughter or not, one thing is inescapable: their relationship and the standing of Copts in Egypt suddenly changed.[107] It was not simply a change of circumstance or fortune; Nasser went from an uninterested (and largely negative) critic of Christians to calling and indeed treating the patriarch as though he were his own father. Something dramatic must have taken place. But how precisely that transformation suddenly happened is, like much of Kyrillos' interior life, hidden from history.

* * *

"Nasser and Kyrillos VI got on well together," writes Mohammed Heikal:

> They admired each other, and it is well known that the Patriarch could come and see Nasser whenever he liked. Kyrillos, always anxious to avoid a confrontation, made use of this friendship to resolve any problems facing the community.[108]

Heikal should know. He was Nasser's "alter ego," one of his closest advisers and mouthpiece as the editor-in-chief of *al-Ahram* newspaper. But that not withstanding, the story is told clearly enough in the photographs of the period with Nasser invariably looking at Kyrillos in admiration (if not wonder).[109] "What then," a French scholar asks, quite reasonably, "Do a young Muslim officer, clean-shaven and an international symbol of anti-colonialism and pan-Arabism, and an old Coptic monk with an unkempt beard and austere black cassock have in common?"[110] Quite a lot, in fact. Both were products of the rural exodus, led frugal lives, dwelt in relatively humble dwellings, and wore simple clothing—Nasser often preferring simple shirts and trousers, and Kyrillos rarely, if ever, wearing the extravagant patriarchal vestments. But more importantly, I would add, both confessed a rare and determined obsession with their "work."[111]

For the first few years, their relationship saw the healing of sectarian tensions.[112] But then, oddly, a strange silence slowly took hold. By early 1964, contrary to the accounts of some Western historians, the tide once more moved against the Church. Building permits were revoked, renovations were forcibly halted, bishops held Liturgies on the road after their people had been kicked out of their parishes by the authorities, the church in Helwan Gardens was seized (for no other reason than it happened to be adjacent to the home of a government minister), while a Muslim mob literally took apart the Church of St Mary piece by piece.[113] Kyrillos wrote furiously to Nasser. There was no response. No matter the destruction, and no matter the protest, Nasser remained silent.

In March 1965, the Holy Synod convened in Alexandria and advised Kyrillos to go to Nasser directly. But Kyrillos had not spoken to Nasser in several years, and so the "situation was very unpredictable."[114] Kyrillos spent the entirety of Lent in Alexandria that year. At the beginning of Pascha, he left for St Menas' Monastery in Mariout. "The whole week," Fr Raphael, his disciple, recalls, "he was praying, and no one knew what he was doing."[115] On the eve of the Resurrection, April 24, 1965, Kyrillos unexpectedly asked all visitors to leave the monastery (even his own relatives) and told the monks to turn off the generators. When asked why, he answered, "There is no need for light tonight, the holy men don't want them. . . ." The monks did not understand him and thought he must have been joking but complied out of obedience. That night Kyrillos refused to celebrate the communal Festal Liturgy and instead prayed a later Liturgy with only a few monks. At one-thirty a.m., having just started the prayers, Kyrillos turned to his disciple and asked the time before saying, "[*Yalla yabni:*] Quick, my son, we are late, hurry." But then, to their surprise, Kyrillos began to celebrate in an unusual manner. "He began to weep," Fr Raphael recalls,

> . . . tears falling onto the paten, wiping his cheeks from right and left. . . . We only awoke from sleep when we had to respond with a chant. We prayed from one-thirty to three-thirty a.m., not understanding a single word . . . as if he were praying entirely by himself. . . . The church was pitch dark except for a candle. As we had communion, we were unsure as to what was happening.[116]

After the Liturgy Kyrillos said to Fr Raphael, "Son, shouldn't you go and feed the visitors?"

"What visitors? You sent them all home," replied his disciple.

"My son, shouldn't you ask [them first]?" repeated Kyrillos, "The church is filled to the last space, there wasn't a single spot empty. . . . We couldn't turn a single light on. . . . May their blessings be with us." And then, turning around to the nave of the church, he added, "Go in peace, go in peace, remember us in your prayers."[117] Kyrillos then did the sign of the cross on the church and left.

"I was confused," Fr Raphael comments rather understandably. "Later we put food in front of *sayedna*, but he wouldn't touch anything."[118] Kyrillos had apparently been visited by those who are known—as well as they can be known—as the "spirit-borne" anchorites often described in the monastic literature, hermits that exhibit indescribable spiritual gifts.[119]

Their prayers were evidently heard immediately. The next day the vicar of the patriarchate arrived with news that Nasser had requested a meeting. Two weeks later, on May 9, 1965, Kyrillos traveled to Cairo to meet the president. "I haven't heard anything of you at all," said the president after hearty greetings. An unnamed government minister had, so Nasser protested, "hidden everything from me . . . I saw the dossier filled with requests and issues of which he had shown me nothing."[120] Nasser promptly removed the minister from his office and saw to personally investigating each of the issues. Matters were resolved and the church of Helwan, which had been closed for over a year, was finally reopened.[121] Nasser then asked Kyrillos to visit his home, as his children—who may not have seen Kyrillos since the apparent healing—wanted to meet the patriarch.[122] In turn, Kyrillos requested Nasser to visit him at the patriarchate. But the "old cathedral" in Azbakeya was hardly fit for the occasion. It was tired, in need of renovation, and was surrounded by food markets bustling with the chaos of live produce, known as the "street of chickens and pigeons." And so, Nasser gently suggested, Kyrillos should consider building another.[123] But that would be problematic in and of itself.

* * *

Under the 1856 Ottoman rescript, "religions other than Islam might be permitted to exist but not to expand."[124] Permission was required from the "head of state" to renovate old churches and to build new, with applicants (essentially only the Copts) encountering, in Mohammed Heikal's words, "perhaps *more* than the usual bureaucratic delays."[125] Practically and historically, the permission was rarely, if ever granted. Instead, congregations would often purchase land and then slowly and quietly erect shops on its perimeter, before setting up a clandestine altar in hopes that the authorities would not notice. But when they did—and they always did—all manner of tumult ensued.

"It was understandably humiliating," Heikal comments, "for the Patriarch to find that any applications for building permits he made got lost in the labyrinth of the Ministry of the Interior."[126] It appears that during this meeting of May 1965, Kyrillos seized the opportunity, especially now that Nasser had suggested building a new cathedral. "Nasser was sympathetic," Heikal recalls, "and asked how many new churches the Patriarch thought he needed. The answer was between twenty and thirty a year. Right, said Nasser, and immediately gave him permission to build twenty-five churches per year."[127] As for the building of the cathedral, Heikal goes on to suggest that he personally intervened, and "spoke to Nasser" on behalf of the Copts, securing not only permission but a great deal of financial aid. While Heikal's account is, to put it kindly, at times conceited, the recollection is reliable. Many, including Fr Salib Suryal, affirm the details—albeit with one significant correction.[128] Bishop Samuel, a disciple of Kyrillos, had in fact met with Heikal prior and suggested, given the recent sectarian tensions, the idea of the cathedral as "point of unity" between the government and the Church.[129] "Those outside [Egypt] would recognize there was peace," Samuel explained, "and those inside would be certain the government was not against the Church."[130]

A few months later, on July 24, 1965, at the laying of the foundation stone of the new cathedral, Nasser took the credit himself. "I opened up the subject," the president declared in his official address, "that the government was not only willing to financially contribute but also morally, since the revolution was principled upon love and unity, not on hatred and discrimination."[131] Nasser donated one hundred thousand pounds, in addition to the significant costs of labor. He no doubt realized the benefits, one scholar claims, for it would be a "national" project that would establish Egypt's place as a leader in the Middle East.[132] On August 24, 1967, excavation began, and within ten remarkable months the momentous cathedral was complete. The consecration on June 25, 1968, was something of a triple celebration: commemorating the nineteen hundred years since the martyrdom of St Mark, the long-awaited translation of the saint's relics from Venice to Cairo, and the opening of the cathedral.[133]

Representatives from ecclesial communities around the world were present, with both government and Church coming together in national unity.[134] Emperor Haile Selaisse sent exorbitant patriarchal vestments—which, of course, Kyrillos refused to wear, instead preferring his simple garments with a white shawl.[135] Only a few short years earlier, the Church had stood at the edge of certain sectarian bloodshed in the face of an unpredictable president. But now Kyrillos looked out at the thousands gathered in the cathedral; gazed at Nasser, who could hardly contain his delight (though he was apparently battling the effects of peripheral artery disease on the day); and saw the gathering of the global Church in his cathedral.[136]

At the end of the proceedings, Kyrillos traveled back to the patriarchate with his disciple, Fr Raphael, next to him in the vehicle. "My son," Kyrillos said after some silence, "did you see the glory of today?"

"I did," replied the young deacon.

"And did you see the patriarchs?"

"I did," he replied again.

"And the President and Emperor Haile Selassie?"

"Yes, *sayedna*, I did," he replied once more.

"My son," Kyrillos said with heaviness, ". . . all of this, everything, is not worth even *one* day in the windmill [*tahuna*]. . . ."

All the glory, all the ecclesial and national triumph, meant nothing next to a decrepit, austere, and desolate windmill that he had inhabited as an unknown monk on the outskirts of Cairo some three decades earlier. "I was too young and too fearful to ask him what he meant," Fr Raphael comments, "what could have possibly been there . . . *what* did he see in the windmill?"[137]

The Maglis and the "Mummy's Curse," 1964–1967

> "Slander is worse than cannibalism."
> —*St John Chrysostom*

H EGUMEN SERGIUS—a most interesting and controversial priest—once called the *waqf* (monastic endowments managed by the *maglis*) the "mummy's curse."[138] Every patriarch who had dared to "touch" the issue found himself seemingly cursed. Winning over a seemingly hostile Muslim president was one thing; the *maglis* and the *waqf* were altogether another. Even then, Kyrillos' relationship with Nasser would for the next decade be enmeshed in this "mummy's curse."

The beginning for Kyrillos was quite promising. He made clear at his enthrone-ment that he was determined to work in "self-sacrifice and self-denial" with the (predominantly lay) *maglis* or "Community Council."[139] At an early meeting in July 1959, this evidently was the case, with the secretary of the *maglis* stating, "It was a historic meeting in the life of the Council," one of love, appreciation, and cooperation.[140] "For seventy years," Kyrillos told a journalist a year later,

> . . . the *waqf* (religious endowments) were a stumbling block in the life of the Church, and now they have been reorganized. Prayer did all this, without the necessity of speaking about it. The rest of our problems will be solved this way.[141]

But though the precarious *waqf* dispute may have been initially settled, the scent of its curse would linger for nearly a decade.

* * *

Under Nasser's government, the *maglis* "was reduced to a shadow of its for-mer self."[142] Governance of "Personal Status Laws" was transferred to the civil courts, and later with nationalization policies, their remaining dominion over schools was transferred to the Ministry of Education, and the benevolent soci-eties to the Ministry of Social Affairs. With the agrarian reforms of 1952 and the subsequent expropriation of monastic lands, the *maglis* was left with only the *waqf* endowments—making the *waqf* all the more valuable.[143] It was effec-tively a systematic disabling and demotion of the *maglis* (and any other private organization for that matter). But Nasser had not finished. On July 19, 1960, a presidential decree excluded patriarchal lands from the *maglis'* legislation and limited each *waqf* holding to two hundred acres of cultivatable land and two hundred acres of barren land. The rest were essentially "nationalized."[144] The "Agrarian Reform Authority" was authorized to expropriate excess holdings of any *waqf* and compensate the Church in exchange.[145] The decree was not without Kyrillos' knowledge; he was apparently its architect.[146] Nor was it "in the least autocratic in implementation"; he had consulted the *maglis* at every stage.[147] The remaining and still very considerable *waqf* holdings were now to be managed by the "Coptic Orthodox Waqf Organization," which brought together six bishops and six laymen (mainly former *maglis* members).[148] The prized *waqf* were no longer to be managed by the *maglis*. "This little administration sleight of hand," an English scholar comments, "was, in fact, typical of the religious insight of Kyrillos."[149]

Many leading Copts rushed to write the "epitaph" of the *maglis*. "We want the government," wrote the founder of the *al-Watani* newspaper, Anton Sidhom,

> ... to cancel the Community Council [*maglis*]. It is has done nothing during the troubles of recent years. During all its existence the Council has only caused trouble; it has spent the past eight years quarrelling with the patriarch. We want to abolish it. It has lost its function.[150]

In contrast, others, such as Judge Farid Pharaony, a leading member of the Alexandrian *maglis*, continued to insist, as many had before him, that "the only thing a priest can handle is spiritual. . . ."[151] For the most part, the greater community was simply pleased to hear nothing of the contention that had plagued the Church for too long. On July 11, 1961, Kyrillos seized the opportunity of the expiration of the five-year term of the current *maglis* to inform the government that "he did not favor holding a new election," thus ensuring the extension of the council elected in 1956 for the time being.[152] Growing stagnant, and with little to do, the once formidable "Community Council [had] been reduced to a loyal whimper."[153] A few years later that increasingly ignored "whimper" grew into barely restrained indignation.

For some fifty years, the details of Kyrillos' clash with the *maglis* have only been hinted at, as hearsay and conjecture—that is, until now with the discovery of numerous official letters concerning the period.[154] Such correspondence represents direct documentary evidence (not sensationalized newspaper slander) of accusations leveled against Kyrillos in the mid-1960s, as well as, importantly, his response. These claims should, of course, be read within the context of almost a century of heated contention and are rather mild in that regard.

On April 25, 1964, the *maglis* wrote to Kyrillos of its members' loyalty to him and went on to suggest that advisers within the patriarchate had sabotaged their relationship. The lengthy letter specifies seven "concerns": Kyrillos, so the *maglis* claimed, had performed his episcopal ordinations in an autocratic manner—specifically those of bishops Isaac of Tanta and Mina of Girga (though the *maglis* acknowledged their "good qualities")—without the consultation of the *maglis* or community; had ordained priests who were not graduates of the Theological College; had transferred priests between parishes, causing instability; had allegedly prevented the union of parish budgets; had interfered in the financial management of the *maglis*, namely in requesting the "allocations to the patriarch"; had harbored negative intentions toward the *maglis* by obstructing their election process in 1961; and finally, had "limited" the authority of the *maglis*.[155]

A few weeks later, on May 13, Kyrillos replied.[156] Before refuting the seven "sharp accusations," Kyrillos explains why he had avoided chairing the *maglis* meetings. As the only clergy among twenty-four laymen, he was helplessly outnumbered on previous occasions—a matter made acutely painful by the *maglis'* involvement in the press. "It was truly sad," the patriarch writes,

> to read daily this reckless campaign against His Holiness in *Misr* newspaper, and the *maglis* is silent, and silence is acceptance. At the same time, the *maglis* is providing this newspaper with money from the endowment's income, a matter which encouraged its persistence.... The *maglis* knows very well that degrading the dignity of the religious head is not limited to the person only, but also degrades the *maglis* which he heads....[157]

Kyrillos, it would appear, was aware of the *maglis'* involvement with the contentious newspaper. As for their seven accusations: Kyrillos discloses his reasons for the episcopal ordinations, gives evidence of the candidates' worthiness, and explains the dynamics of their dioceses and nominations; he defends his ordination of priests, who, he claims, were in fact Theological College graduates except for a handful to be sent to rural areas with little income; and explains that many of the issues of transferred priests concerned "matters of confession" and clerical "wisdom" for the sake of peace that had nothing to do with the *maglis'* authority.[158] Kyrillos is, however, adamant that he neither interfered in the *maglis'* financial management—rather, they had mismanaged themselves into near bankruptcy—nor did he harbor any negative intent or limit their authority. Nasser, the patriarch reminded them, had, in fact, limited their authority with his civil, education, and agrarian policies years before Kyrillos was even ordained.[159] If anything, Kyrillos argues, their "limited" role suggests "there is no need to elect twenty-four members without work for them"—hence the 1961 obstruction to the *maglis'* election.[160] But even then, Kyrillos continues, he "actually tried to form a subcommittee of the *maglis* in Beni Suef and Giza ... and thus his intentions are clear."[161] As for the accusation that he had requested the "patriarchal allocations" from the *waqf*, this would be a long-running issue that would cause great contention with the new Coptic Orthodox Waqf Organization. They, too, would turn against the patriarch.

On September 18, 1965, Hanna Girguis Saad and Ragheb Hanna, chairmen of the Waqf Organization, presented their letter of resignation to Kyrillos.[162]

The letter suggests some degree of confusion as to their role—perhaps they mistook the scope of their authority given the value of the *waqf*—with many of their grievances having little to do with the *waqf* and more to do with Kyrillos' treatment of the *maglis*. For instance, the last straw that provoked their resignation was Kyrillos' rejection of an episcopal candidate proposed by two of the organization's members—quite clearly a non-*waqf* issue.[163] (Their resignation was in fact in reaction to news Kyrillos was to ordain Dioscorus of Menoufia [1965–1976] instead of their candidate the following day.[164]) As for their other grievances (those which did relate to the *waqf*), they centered around Kyrillos' insistence on receiving his "patriarchal allocation" from the endowments.[165] There were some two hundred acres of "patriarchal *waqf*" from which, Kyrillos argued, he was entitled to receive income.[166] "[The request] shocks those," delicately accused the chairmen of the Waqf organization, "who know about your asceticism in your *previous* life."[167]

Despite their insinuations, the patriarch insisted that this was well within his rights. But it was not for personal expenditure as was clear to anyone who saw his patriarchal cell. Whether or not Kyrillos had initially made clear his intention to use these funds for rebuilding St Menas' Monastery (as he would eventually) is unclear, though it is certainly explicit in later documents and his personal letters.[168] "If we are asking for money to be allocated," Kyrillos wrote to his brother, Fr Mikhail, "we have the full freedom to spend it on rebuilding St Menas' Monastery for instance, or any other project."[169] "Let us be patient," Kyrillos wrote on December 16, 1964, to his older brother, Hanna,

> with those people who are hurting us although we did good deeds to them. . . . Rest assured, we travel only according to God's will, whether to Alexandria or Cairo, because we exist and move through him; moving or settling is between God's hands. We cannot move one step without his order. . . . I wanted to write a lot more, but the pen is annoying; anyway, be comforted and do not think about it too much.[170]

* * *

In many respects, most distressing of all was the public and sensationalist "airing" of the 1964 conflict in the *Misr* newspaper. It was hardly a secret that the *maglis*, or at least certain members, were morally behind the reports, if not financially. *Misr* was the oldest newspaper of the Coptic community and was founded in 1895 by Tadros Shenouda. Originally a pro-British paper, it later aligned itself with a lay-reformist agenda, especially regarding the long-running *maglis*-patriarch conflicts.[171] By the time of Kyrillos, it had become increasingly anticlerical, and it began to mock and ridicule the patriarch. "Its only objective was to hurt his image."[172] Unsurprisingly, its most vocal defamation of Kyrillos coincides with the *maglis* conflict of 1964 and parallels it.

"The wheel of reform has completely stopped nowadays," reported *Misr* on March 7, 1964:

> The Coptic congregation is behind and is not progressing. . . . The pope is supposed to be the leader, but the wheel is paralyzed, he has prevented it from moving and developing; he is not looking after the wheel of reform. . . . Chaos is everywhere. . . . He does not care nor does he show any interest, neither he himself nor those surrounding him. People are starting to worry and become unhappy; murmuring, they have started wondering: when will these processions and ceremonies end, so that His Holiness the Pope would turn to serious business and compensate us for the wasted time.[173]

Kyrillos, so the *Misr* declared, "has no plan for reform."[174] Accusations of "many disgraceful things" were made, including the old rumors of sorcery to explain the ever-increasing reports of miracles.[175] When the first articles began to appear, and sales evidently doubled, Kyrillos joked, "Send them some money, they have no doubt run out of paper and ink."[176] Not even his missionary efforts in Africa were free from ridicule:

> As for . . . the incursions and raids of Kyrillos in Africa, Asia, Latin America, the western and the eastern countries, which have stretched to Mars and Saturn, and the rest of the solar system . . . a very funny report, which only smokers would enjoy. We have nothing to do with smoking, so we will leave it to them to feel happy with the rising fog of its smoke, and fly in its smell, meditations, imaginations. . . . [177]

Evangelism was, so the editors of *Misr* suggested, of little use to the Church in Egypt—history would of course disagree. Nor, evidently, was prayer of any use. "We cannot understand the wisdom of His Holiness the Pope," wrote the editors on April 18, 1964,

> . . . in going to the churches in an early hour—four or five o'clock in the morning—knocking on its doors and waking up its servants; at this time most of the congregation would still be asleep. . . . is it a prepared plan to exhaust the priest and the service of the church or just a morning stroll to breathe the early morning fresh air?[178]

These were only a few of the troubling articles that appeared almost daily from 1964 to 1965 at the alleged bidding of the *maglis*. But Kyrillos, now in his early sixties, never responded to the accusations, nor did he defend himself against them. Despite the protests of his closest bishops and advisors, he remained silent—even firmly preventing Bishop Athanasius of Beni Suef from writing a defense on his behalf.[179] "His Holiness was never troubled," recalls Fr Raphael:

> He never published a report of denial or a memo of defense. . . . They stabbed him several times; they defamed him for many years; they thought that they would one day draw him into the conflict, they became harsher and harsher, exaggerating in hurting and attacking him, hoping he would say one word and thus fall into their trap. . . . [180]

Letters to his brother reveal Kyrillos' silent prayers. "I am pleading to the Lord of the Church," wrote the patriarch to his younger brother, Fr Mikhail on December 18, 1964, "to avenge his justice from those who wish to spread false rumors, and through the intercessions of St Menas—we just need the truth to be revealed."[181] Kyrillos would remain silent until 1966. It was only when one of his disciples congratulated him on the government's forced closure of the *Misr* newspaper that he finally broke his silence. "What are you saying?" the patriarch cried out. "The newspaper was shut down? My son, it has two hundred workers who all have families, from where will they feed them?"[182] He hastened to make phone calls to the government officials responsible who informed him that nothing could be done despite his pleas that the poor workers should not suffer because of those in charge.[183] Kyrillos, so his shocked disciples claim, did not rest until he had secured employment for those who had lost jobs.[184] Silence was only broken to proclaim solidarity and show mercy to his enemies.

Officially, *Misr* was declared bankrupt, and it had allegedly failed to secure a necessary license from the government for operation.[185] Most scholars and observers—depending upon popular memory and not evidence—have suggested that *Misr* was closed by Nasser at the request of Kyrillos, which, so they suggest, argues for the strength of their friendship.[186] But this directly contradicts the accounts of those closest to Kyrillos that he was grieved on hearing of the closure. It would appear, rather, that *Misr* simply faced the same fate as many other dissenting Egyptians newspapers of the mid-1960s, that is, nationalism. Nasser had restricted the radio and the press to those few outlets he felt to be in line with his nationalist purposes.[187] *Misr* seems to have fallen foul for this reason—especially that it was outspoken—independently of any manipulation of Kyrillos.

* * *

With the closure of *Misr* in 1966, the public mouthpiece of the *maglis* was silenced, but they themselves were not. One of the few remaining responsibilities of the *maglis* was the financial management of the patriarchate, which included the care of the priests in Cairo and Alexandria, as well as other workers. By April 1967, the *maglis* had run into severe financial deficit. The crisis was precipitated by poor weather corrupting the cotton crops, thereby severely decreasing the *waqf* income of the *maglis*, and it was made all the worse by the economic downturn of 1967.[188] Some five hundred priests went unpaid, with the *maglis* in need of thirty-one thousand pounds. This would spark the *maglis* crisis of 1967. Blame was squarely placed on Kyrillos. The patriarch, so the *maglis* accused publicly in the state-owned *al-Ahram* newspaper on April 21, 1967, had spent over fifty thousand pounds on St Menas' Monastery; had sequestered almost twenty thousand pounds of inheritance from metropolitans who had reposed; had interfered in the *maglis'* management of local parishes and renovations at the old cathedral; and had once more requested the "patriarchal allocation" of the *waqf* and other income.[189] Kyrillos' "frivolity," especially the expenditure on another "unnecessary monastery," was the cause, so they alleged, of the dire financial crisis.

A few days later, on April 25, Kyrillos replied through the vicar of the patriarchate in the *al-Ahram* newspaper. He would *not* be silent on this occasion. Kyrillos was very much surprised by the accusations, especially because the funds used for St Menas' were not taken from the *maglis* but rather from his own income and "donations were given specifically for the monastery," nor did it reach fifty-thousand pounds as they alleged; and whatever funds were left by previous metropolitans were inherited by their successors. Kyrillos did not, however, deny that he had interfered in the renovation of the old cathedral—he was forced to rectify works done by an incompetent contractor—but he was confused how that could have caused the deficit when it was undertaken at his own cost (and not at that of the *maglis*); nor does he deny that he requested the "patriarchal allocation" from the *waqf* for the construction at St Menas', but this was rejected, to his dismay, by the *maglis* in any event. The letter concludes with the words: "That is enough, and thanks to God on every occasion."[190]

Al-Ahram reported (which the patriarchate did not deny in its corrections in a later article) Kyrillos' final comments:

> According to its constitution, the *maglis* is the governing body of the patriarchate's management, therefore, the financial situation has deteriorated because of its poor decisions. I will not extend my hand to them after their attitude towards me . . . the only final solution is for the Council to resign.[191]

On the same day, the *maglis* published a panicked rejoinder. Pleas were made that it was "not a disagreement as such, but difference in opinion" and that "we are keen on cooperating with His Holiness."[192] Perhaps they had expected Kyrillos to remain silent, as he always had. But now they were exposed. The pledged support was too little too late; the *maglis* had taken the Church into a dire monetary crisis with hundreds of priests (the lifeblood of the parishes) unpaid for months.[193] It was little wonder, Fr Raphael recalls, that Kyrillos, who evidently liked to play on words, termed the *maglis al-melli*, the "*maglis al-mefalis* [the bankrupt]."[194]

On May 10, 1967, Kyrillos met with the president. Nasser was sympathetic; a presidential decree was issued. Patriarchal assets were guaranteed; a donation of ten thousand pounds was made to assist in resuming operations; the *waqf* would be placed under the authority of a twelve-member committee; and, in light of the severe deficit and obvious financial mismanagement, the *maglis* was, in effect, suspended before eventually being dismantled a few months later.[195] The few remaining responsibilities of the *maglis*, patriarchal financial management and theological institutions, were now placed under the charge of the patriarch directly. It was to good effect. Two years later the patriarchate would have a financial surplus.[196]

Kyrillos brought to an end the *maglis*-patriarch saga that had raged for nearly a century.[197] Ibrahim has suggested that the move would "establish a hierarchical structure within the Coptic Church; total religious guidance and authority would be through the figure of the patriarch."[198] While this overstates the case, in light of the decline in socio-economic influence of lay Copts under Nasser, as well as the many charisms of Kyrillos, it would lay the foundation for the centrality of patriarchal authority vis-à-vis the government, or at least reaffirm it.[199]

* * *

At two points during that meeting with Nasser on May 10, Kyrillos, conscious of the time, sought to conclude the proceedings. "It is not yet time," the president pleaded. "I add my voice"—Nasser now stood up—"to all those congratulating you on your eighth-year anniversary of the papacy" (it was eight years to the day).[200]

Kyrillos then stood and, strangely, placed his hand on Nasser's chest. "I put my hand," said the patriarch, *partially* quoting from Proverbs, "on the hands of God, as it is written: 'The king's heart is in the hand of the Lord.'"[201] Nasser was overcome by the gesture. That night, many accounts attest that a government official notified Kyrillos that the president was overjoyed by the meeting and that, curiously, his angina (chest pain) had resolved the moment Kyrillos touched his chest.[202] Nasser's "secret" heart attacks, two documented in 1969 and 1970, and one suspected in 1965, were hidden from the public, and even his wife was not told until 1969.[203] And yet, so the accounts claim, Kyrillos was aware in 1967.

It is exceedingly unlikely, though, that Nasser knew how that verse ended: "The king's heart is in the hand of the Lord, like the rivers of water; *He turns it wherever He wishes.*"[204] One can only imagine the gleam in Kyrillos' eyes when he silently passed over those last few words as he touched (and healed) the heart of the president.

Notes

[1]Wakin, *A Lonely Minority*, 116.

[2]Meinardus, *Two Thousand Years*, 132; Bengt Sundkler and Christopher Steed, *A History of the Church in Africa* (Cambridge: Cambridge University Press, 2004), 34–41. Meinardus elsewhere gives three different traditions as to how Christianity came to Ethiopia; see Meinardus, *Christian Egypt: Faith and Life*, 369–71.

[3]Meinardus, *Two Thousand Years*, 133.

[4]Meinardus, *Christian Egypt: Faith and Life*, 382. Meinardus suggests the sensitivity between the two Churches was due to "reciprocal minority problems."

[5]Sundkler and Steed, *A History of the Church in Africa*, 695.

[6]Zaklama, *Pope Kyrillos VI*, 1:220–21.

[7]Meinardus, *Two Thousand Years*, 133.

[8]Sundkler and Steed, *A History of the Church in Africa*, 695.

[9]The *echege* was a celibate monk from Ethiopia's most powerful monastery but apparently not a bishop.

[10]Meinardus, *Two Thousand Years*, 133.

[11]Watson, "Abba Kyrillos," 23.

[12]Donald Crummey, "Church and Nation: The Ethiopian Orthodox Täwahedo Church," in *The Cambridge History of Christianity: Eastern Christianity*, ed. Michael Angold (Cambridge: Cambridge University Press, 2006), 485; Meinardus, *Two Thousand Years*, 134.

[13]Meinardus, *Christian Egypt: Faith and Life*, 394.

[14]For instance see al-Masri, *Story of the Coptic Church*, 6:81, 95–96. This is also suggested by Selassie's letter to the ambassador in which he expresses solidarity with Yusab, as well as not so subtly requesting the ordination of another local bishop (implicitly, in return for his support).

[15]Meinardus, *Christian Egypt: Faith and Life*, 394.

[16]Fr Mina el-Baramousy, "Letter to Emperor Haile Selassie, April 19, 1959," cited in Zaklama, *Pope Kyrillos VI*, 1:222–24; Nasr, *Readings in the Life of Abouna Mina*, 123–24.

[17]Van Doorn-Harder, *Modern Coptic Papacy*, 138. This claim is supported by the fact that no Ethiopian bishops are seen in the photographs of the ordination. On the other hand, Zaklama suggests it actually had to do with the Ethiopian bishops protesting about Deir el-Sultan monastery; see Zaklama, *Pope Kyrillos VI*, 1:376.

[18]Fr Mina el-Baramousy, "Letter to Emperor Haile Selassie, May 16, 1959," cited in Zaklama, *Pope Kyrillos VI*, 1:125; Nasr, *Readings in the Life of Abouna Mina*, 123–24.

[19]On June 1, 1959, Kyrillos sent a delegation to Ethiopia in preparation of the June 29 declaration. The declaration is reproduced in Meinardus, *Christian Egypt: Faith and Life*, 395–96. It specified that the pope of Alexandria is the "supreme spiritual head of the Church of Ethiopia"; the archbishop of Ethiopia will be elevated to Patriarch-Catholicos who can consecrate bishops and metropolitans, and shall be invited to all Coptic Synod gatherings; the Ethiopians would participate in Coptic patriarchal elections; and that all previous agreements not consistent with this declaration would be annulled.

[20]Watson, "Abba Kyrillos," 21.

[21]For instance, see ibid., 23.

[22]See Chapter 3, "St Isaac the Syrian: Patristic Discipleship and an Urgent Corrective."

[23]For a brief discussion, see Reiss, *Erneuerung in der Koptisch-Orthodoxen Kirche*, 175. Also, in support of this, we should note that Fr Makary was the only monk present at the important delegation in early 1959 that negotiated the terms of the autocephaly declaration; see Zaklama, *Pope Kyrillos VI*, 1:227.

[24]Fawzi, *Kyrillos and Abdel Nasser*, 37.

[25]Al-Masri, *True Story of Christianity in Egypt*, 2:438.

[26]Al-Masri, *Story of the Coptic Church*, 7:137; Fawzi, *Kyrillos and Abdel Nasser*, 40–41.

[27]These words are recorded by his successor; see Shenouda III, "Speech at the Tenth Year Commemoration of Kyrillos VI."

[28]Raphael Ava Mina, *Spiritual Leadership*, 11.

[29]Watson, "Abba Kyrillos," 25. Also see al-Masri, *Story of the Coptic Church*, 7:44–46. These resolutions called all Churches to hold fast to Scripture; encourage youth participation; renew focus on the place of families; foster a deeper sacramental understanding; prioritize theological education, scholarship, and publishing; and the revival of monasticism. The next conference was held in January 1966, and there a pan-Oriental Orthodox Liturgy was celebrated, with each Church celebrating according to its rites and language.

[30]Shenouda III, "Speech at the Tenth Year Commemoration of Kyrillos VI." Also see Nasr, *Readings in the Life of Abouna Mina*, 305–6; Fawzi, *Kyrillos and Abdel Nasser*, 42.

[31]For a fair study, see Otto Meinardus, *The Copts in Jerusalem* (Cairo: Commission on Ecumenical Affairs, 1960). He later updated his study in Meinardus, *Christian Egypt: Faith and Life*, 436–37.

[32]Zaklama, *Pope Kyrillos VI*, 1:378.

[33]The healed metropolitan was Kyrillos of Beliana (1948–1970), a dear friend of the patriarch from their days as young monks in Helwan Theological College; the metropolitan would repose the year before his friend. The account is recorded by Fr Raphael Ava Mina, who attended on that day; see Raphael Ava Mina, "My Memories," audio recording.

[34]Ibid.

[35]Ibid.

[36]This may have been the declaration of May 7, 1967. For the declaration see Zaklama, *Pope Kyrillos VI*, 1:96–97.

[37]For a discussion of the relationship of Kyrillos and the Sheikh, see Sandrine Keriakos, "Saint Marc: Enjeux communautaires et dynamiques politiques," *Conserveries Mémorielles* 14 (2013): 43–47.

[38]Alain Roussillon, "Republican Egypt Interpreted: Revolution and Beyond," in *The Cambridge History of Egypt: Modern Egypt, from 1517 to the End of the Twentieth Century*, ed. M. W. Daly (Cambridge: Cambridge University Press, 1998), 338.

[39]Ibid. The Marxist movement will not be discussed given its early "self-dissolution" in January 1956.

[40]Naguib was forced to step down and remained under house arrest until Nasser's death; see ibid., 340; Jason Thompson, *A History of Egypt: From Earliest Times to the Present* (Cairo: The American University in Cairo Press, 2008), 294. For a discussion of Nasser's consolidation of power from Naguib, see P. J. Vatikiotis, *Nasser and His Generation* (London: Croom Helm, 1978), 138–51; Vatikiotis, *The History of Egypt*, 383–85.

[41]Vatikiotis, *Nasser and His Generation*, 135. For some two years, the Brotherhood and the RCC were able to coexist in a state of codependence.

[42]Roussillon, "Republican Egypt Interpreted," 341. For a discussion of the evolution of the Brotherhood in relation to Nasser, see Vatikiotis, *Nasser and His Generation*, 85–96; Joel Gordon, *Nasser's Blessed Movement: Egypt's Free Officers and the July Revolution* (New York: Oxford University Press, 1992), 92–108.

[43]Vatikiotis, *Nasser and His Generation*, 135.

[44]Gordon, *Nasser's Blessed Movement*, 179; see also 179–83.

[45]Vatikiotis, *Nasser and His Generation*, 144–45.

[46]Cited in Gordon, *Nasser's Blessed Movement*, 184.

[47]Thompson, *A History of Egypt*, 294.

[48]Roussillon, "Republican Egypt Interpreted," 349.

[49]Ibid. For a discussion of the 1964 plot, see Gilles Kepel, *Muslim Extremism in Egypt: The Prophet and Pharaoh* (Berkeley: University of California Press, 1985), 31–35.

[50]Pennington, "The Copts in Modern Egypt," 163. For a biographical sketch of Nasser see Vatikiotis, *Nasser and His Generation*, 23–42.

[51]See Peter E. Makari, "Christianity and Islam in Twentieth Century Egypt: Conflict and Cooperation," *International Review of Mission* 89, no. 352 (2000): 94.

[52]National Charter June 20, 1962; ibid., 95.

[53]Cited in Keriakos, "Saint Marc," 53.

[54]See for instance Tadros, *Motherland Lost*, 169. Tadros claims, "Nasser did not hold any personal animosity towards Christians. He was simply not interested in the Church . . . for him forging a good relationship with the Church leadership was enough."

[55]Voile, *Les Coptes d'Égypte*, 210.

[56]Van Doorn-Harder, *Modern Coptic Papacy*, 134.

[57]Voile, *Les Coptes d'Égypte*, 56.

[58]Mordechai Nisan, *Minorities in the Middle East: A History of Struggle and Self-Expression* (Jefferson, NC: McFarland, 2002), 144.

[59]Voile, *Les Coptes d'Égypte*, 56. Also see Nisan, *Minorities in the Middle East*, 144.

[60]Nelly van Doorn-Harder, "Copts: Fully Egyptian, but for a Tattoo?" in *Nationalism and Minority: Identities in Islamic Societies*, ed. Maya Shatzmiller (Montreal: McGill-Queen's University Press, 2005), 26.

[61]The reform specified two to three hundred feddans; one feddan is equal to 1.038 acres.

[62]Thompson, *A History of Egypt*, 297.

[63]Van Doorn-Harder, *Modern Coptic Papacy*, 129; David Zeidan, "The Copts—Equal, Protected or Persecuted? The Impact of Islamization on Muslim–Christian Relations in Modern Egypt," *Islam And Christian-Muslim Relations* 10, no. 1 (1999): 57.

[64]Pennington, "The Copts in Modern Egypt," 164.

[65]Ibid., 164–65.

[66]Ibid., 165.

[67]Thompson, *A History of Egypt*, 307.

[68]This, of course, would change the fate of the Church from the late 1980s. With the increased influence and wealth of the diaspora came increased support for the Church at home.

[69]Nisan, *Minorities in the Middle East*, 144.

[70]Pennington, "The Copts in Modern Egypt," 165.

[71]Maura Heardon, "Lessons from Zeitoun: A Marian Proposal for Christian-Muslim Dialogue," *Journal of Ecumenical Studies* 47, no. 3 (2012): 414.

[72]Anthony Nutting, *Nasser* (London: Constable & Robinson Limited, 1972), 304.

[73]Anthony McDermott, *Egypt from Nasser to Mubarak: A Flawed Revolution* (Abingdon, UK: Routledge, 2013), 186.

[74]Malaty, "Interview about the Life of Pope Kyrillos: Part I." He lists three main factors: media were given a green light to attack the Church, agrarian reform, and Nasser initially refused to meet Kyrillos.

[75]For instance, consider Nasser's deportation of non-Muslim communities.

[76]Suryal, "Pope Kyrillos VI." For the details of that man's position in the government; see Fawzi, *Kyrillos and Abdel Nasser*, 55.

[77]Suryal, "Pope Kyrillos VI," 10; Atta and Raphael Ava Mina, *Life of Pope Kyrillos.*

[78]Adly, *Fr Mikhail Dawood's Memoirs*, 31. The premise was that unified Personal Status Laws (PSL) would create equilibrium in curbing Muslim divorces but also in increasing Coptic divorces. Mikhail suggests Kyrillos reacted with a "three day fast" in defiance. Nasser sent his "Coptic liaison," Ramzy Stino, to whom Kyrillos reportedly said, "Come Ramzy, my beloved, tell the President, Kyrillos fasts for you and your country. He is not against you, he is one of your sheep; tell him this, we are submitting to the country."

[79]Nasr, *Readings in the Life of Abouna Mina*, 149.

[80]Ibid.

[81]Tadros, *Motherland Lost*, 169.

[82]Otto Meinardus, *Patriarchen unter Nasser und Sadat* (Hamburg: Deutsche Orient-Institut, 1998), 34; Wakin, *A Lonely Minority*, 113; Zaki Shenouda, *My Memories of Pope Kyrillos VI* [in Arabic] (Cairo: Egyptian Brothers Press, 1992), 17.

[83]Wakin, *A Lonely Minority*, 113. Some, such as Girgis Helmy Azer, a former member of the *maglis*, suggest that some of his illustrious disciples advised Kyrillos not to visit; see anonymous, "Pope Kyrillos: A Miracle Worker for Copts" [in Arabic], *Rose al-Yusuf*, November 11, 1996.

[84]Shenouda, *My Memories*, 17.

[85]Wakin, *A Lonely Minority*, 113–14; Meinardus, *Patriarchen unter Nasser und Sadat*, 34. Wakin suggests that when Kyrillos did eventually visit at some early point, he did not meet with Nasser but wrote in the guestbook only.

[86]From what can be made of the accounts, it appears that (1) Kyrillos initially refused to visit Nasser without first being visited as a sign of the dignity of the patriarchal office; (2) months later, because of circumstances facing the Coptic community, Kyrillos then sought to meet Nasser; and (3) that Nasser at that point refused Kyrillos' visit.

[87]Kyrillos met with the editor of *Misr* newspaper the following evening and asked him to publish the following: "Pope Kyrillos is most keen on national unity and thanks President Nasser for what he perceived of love and appreciation at the friendly meeting that took place yesterday; which highlighted the essence of the meaning of national unity." Cited in Zaklama, *Pope Kyrillos VI*, 2: 79. This, of course, was the official statement and cannot be expected to detail any of the previous night's happenings.

[88]Suryal, "Pope Kyrillos VI."

[89]Ibid. Also see Nasr, *Readings in the Life of Abouna Mina*, 150. Most sources record a single other discussion at the "second stage" of that first meeting in 1959, during which Kyrillos expressed his sentiments that faith would secure productivity for the nation. For the dialogue see Zaklama, *Pope Kyrillos VI*, 2:79.

[90]This was confirmed by Nasser's son; Abdel Hakim Nasser, "Interview About Nasser and Kyrillos VI," ed. Daniel Fanous (2017).

[91]Shenouda, *My Memories*, 18.

[92]Tahia Gamal Abdel Nasser Nasser, *Nasser: My Husband* (Cairo: The American University in Cairo Press, 2013), 103–5.

[93]Nasser, "Interview About Nasser and Kyrillos VI." Importantly, Abdel Hakim confirmed that Nasser was endeared to Kyrillos and treated him with greater respect than any other figure, though he

was unaware of any animosity in their early relationship. At the time of this meeting in 1959, Hoda was thirteen years old; Mona, twelve years old; Khaled, nine years old; Abdel Hamid, seven years old; and Abdel Hakim, four years old.

[94]These can feasibly can be traced to I. H. al-Masri's mistaken assertion (evidently following Salib's account until that point) that it was in fact Nasser's son, the four-year-old Abdel-Hakim (b. 1955) who was healed. See al-Masri, *Story of the Coptic Church*, 7:48; Fawzi, *Kyrillos and Abdel Nasser*, 18.

[95]This may be suggested since Mona seems to have been unaware of the miracle, according to Zaki Shenouda's account, leaving only Hoda.

[96]Though Fr Raphael admitted during an interview with the author that there was some contention in the relationship (which he claims was due to Kyrillos' refusing to meet Nasser) in 1959, he objects to the details of Salib's account of the relationship's being healed in one night: "I do not like that story [repeats twice more]. . . . There, I said it three times." But he does claim that a miracle occurred sometime in 1960 (not that night); qualifying that its details were never known, as Kyrillos refused to speak of it: "He entered the depth of the house alone, but when he went in, we don't know what he did. . . . It emerged that he healed someone, that someone was sick . . . but neither Nasser nor Kyrillos opened their mouths about the matter. Kyrillos entered the house; how could he then say what he did or what he saw there?" See Raphael Ava Mina, "Interview about the Life of Pope Kyrillos VI." We should, of course, remember that Fr Raphael was a relatively young seventeen-year-old in 1959, and would not become Kyrillos' deacon and disciple until five years later, and so we must not necessarily dispute Salib's account on this basis—not to mention Raphael's own admission that Kyrillos never spoke to him, nor to anyone else, about his knowledge of that episode.

[97]Though we must accept this as a possibility, unlike Fr Raphael's suggestion of sometime in 1960, an alternate possibility is that the miracle occurred during the 1965 meeting. There was relative silence between 1959 and 1965 (though there are reasons for this as we shall see), and so this is a logical alternative. But given the detailed description from Salib, a close confidant of Kyrillos (and who happened to be a professor of canon law), it is exceedingly unlikely that he had this detail wrong. We are, of course, not necessitating that a miracle occurred, but simply that we either take the account as false (i.e., it was not actually told to him by Kyrillos) or else we accept a central detail such as the date, especially in that it is essential to the greater narrative.

[98]Raphael Ava Mina, "Interview about the Life of Pope Kyrillos VI."

[99]The singular exception is Voile—that being said, it is a fleeting mention with no further elaboration other than noticing that *both* had healed the child of the national leader; see Voile, *Les Coptes d'Égypte*, 167.

[100]For a biography, see Rudolph Yanney, "Saint Sarabamon: Bishop of Menoufia," *Coptic Church Review* 8, no. 4 (1987).

[101]Ibid., 110–11.

[102]She was also known as Princess Khadija Nazli Khanum. Genealogical records are difficult to come by, but she is said either to have been poisoned or to have committed suicide decades later.

[103]Yanney, "Saint Sarabamon: Bishop of Menoufia," 111.

[104]Meinardus, *Christian Egypt: Faith and Life*, 18.

[105]Magdi Guirguis, *The Emergence of the Modern Coptic Papacy: The Egyptian Church and Its Leadership from the Ottoman Period to the Present* (Cairo: The American University Press in Cairo, 2011), 65.

[106]For instance, see Polybius and John, *Life of Epiphanius of Cyprus* (PG 41:84–89); and the account concerning the household of Theodosius, reported in the *Life of Donatus of Euroia* (223–319), cited in Rapp, *Holy Bishops*, 299.

[107]Fr Tadros notes, "Regardless of what is said concerning the healing of the son and daughter [he seems to be aware of both traditions] of Gamal Abdel Nasser, we were in touch with the *difference* of the President's dealing in the first period of his reign and the second." Fr Tadros Malaty, "Interview about the Life of Pope Kyrillos: Part II," ed. Daniel Fanous (2016).

[108]Heikal, *Autumn of Fury*, 166.

[109]Fr Salib Suryal reports that Zakaria Mohieddin (1918–2012), a former prime minister of Egypt, was heard to loudly exclaim at Kyrillos' funeral: "Whatever Pope Kyrillos asks for, it happens. . . . Gamal

Abdel Nasser granted it immediately." See Suryal, "Pope Kyrillos VI." Also, Pope Shenouda III said at the first anniversary of Kyrillos' repose: "The president Gamal Abdel Nasser loved him especially and honored him exceedingly"; Shenouda III, "Speech at the First Year Commemoration of Kyrillos VI."

[110]Voile, *Les Coptes d'Égypte*, 208.

[111]Meinardus, *Patriarchen unter Nasser und Sadat*, 35; Vatikiotis, *Nasser and His Generation*, 309–11. Vatikiotis has detailed Nasser's relative simplicity and scorn of luxury.

[112]Wakin recorded Kyrillos' answer to his question as to his dealing with the government: "We are always in touch with the government whenever necessary. Stino is the government's liaison officer on Coptic matters. We send him most of our petitions and he sends them to the president. Sometimes we contact Nasser directly or the government ministers concerned. Most of the time we receive favourable responses and good will." See Wakin, *A Lonely Minority*, 117. The comment suggests frequent contact, at times indirect and at others direct. We should note, however, that though the book was published in 1963, the interview took place, evidently, between 1960 and 1961.

[113]This is against Pennington's assertion that there was "little confessional tension" under Nasser; see Pennington, "The Copts in Modern Egypt," 165. For instance see Suryal, "Pope Kyrillos VI," 80–81; Raphael Ava Mina, "Interview about the Life of Pope Kyrillos VI"; Fr Antonios Henein, "Lecture on Pope Kyrillos VI," audio recording (Cairo, unknown); Zaklama, *Pope Kyrillos VI*, 2. Henein recalls that in reaction to the government minister who closed Helwan Gardens, Kyrillos sent Bishop Benjamin of Menoufia to take a makeshift altar and pray on the land—thereby consecrating the land according to an early *fatwa*—but he was obstructed and proceeded to pray a Liturgy on the street, which subsequently swelled with multitudes of Copts.

[114]Raphael Ava Mina, *My Memories*, audio recording.

[115]Ibid.

[116]Ibid.

[117]Ibid. Cf. Atta and Raphael Ava Mina, *Life of Pope Kyrillos*, 40.

[118]On a later occasion, Fr Raphael asked Kyrillos concerning whether he had seen the "Spirit-borne" anchorites, and he did not deny it; see Raphael Ava Mina, "My Memories," audio recording.

[119]The notion of the "Spirit-borne" anchorites perhaps dates back to St Antony the Great (251–356): "Some say . . . he was 'Spirit-borne,' that is, carried along by the Holy Spirit, but he would never speak of this to men. Such men see what is happening in the world, as well as knowing what is going to happen." See Ward, *Sayings of the Desert Fathers*, 7. Also for a discussion, see Fr Samaan el-Syriany, *The Hermit Fathers*, trans. Lisa Agaiby and Mary Girgis (Sydney: St Shenouda Monastery Press, 1993).

[120]Raphael Ava Mina, "My Memories," audio recording; Raphael Ava Mina, "Interview about the Life of Pope Kyrillos VI"; Zaklama, *Pope Kyrillos VI*, 2:80–81.

[121]Zaklama, *Pope Kyrillos VI*, 2:80–81; Fawzi, *Kyrillos and Abdel Nasser*, 68.

[122]Fr Salib Suryal records the account that Nasser asked his children to donate their pocket money to the Church as they would to the mosque; on that occasion their donation, Salib claims, equalled the exact amount remaining for the deposit on additional land purchased for St Menas' Monastery; see Suryal, "Pope Kyrillos VI"; Nasr, *Readings in the Life of Abouna Mina*, 156.

[123]Raphael Ava Mina, "Some Misconceptions"; Zaklama, *Pope Kyrillos VI*, 2:81.

[124]Heikal, *Autumn of Fury*, 165; van Doorn-Harder, *Modern Coptic Papacy*, 137.

[125]Heikal, *Autumn of Fury*, 165; van Doorn-Harder, *Modern Coptic Papacy*, 137.

[126]Heikal, *Autumn of Fury*, 166.

[127]Ibid. Most scholars have followed Heikal here as it is the only source as to that particular negotiation. Some sixty-eight permits, according to Ansari, were given in the 1960s—which even if we allow for this directive to be placed in 1965, still falls short by at least half. But, of course, we have no knowledge as to how many permits were actually applied for. See Hamied Ansari, "Sectarian Conflict in Egypt and the Political Expediency of Religion," *Middle East Journal* 38, no. 3 (1984): 399.

[128]Many have commented that Heikal was not the most impartial of observers—having spent years ghost writing Nasser's speeches—and, for instance, he inaccurately claims, in another place, that Fr Matta el-Meskeen was a bishop; see Heikal, *Autumn of Fury*, 168.

[129]Suryal, "Pope Kyrillos VI"; Nasr, *Readings in the Life of Abouna Mina*, 152. Salib suggests Kyrillos sent two bishops (including Bishop Samuel) to pray a Liturgy at Heikal's home in thanks—without questioning, we might add, how a Liturgy could be prayed at the Muslim Heikal's house.

[130]Suryal, "Pope Kyrillos VI."

[131]For the entire address, see Zaklama, *Pope Kyrillos VI*, 1:490. For the addresses at the laying of the Foundation Stone, see Nasr, *Readings in the Life of Abouna Mina*, 269–74.

[132]Van Doorn-Harder, *Modern Coptic Papacy*, 137.

[133]For Nasser's address at the Consecration, see Nasr, *Readings in the Life of Abouna Mina*, 284.

[134]Samuel Tawadros el-Syriany, *The History of the Popes*, 181.

[135]Raphael Ava Mina, "Some Misconceptions"; Raphael Ava Mina, "My Memories," audio recording. Fr Raphael states that he kept offering the garments throughout the Liturgy, with Kyrillos adamant in his refusal.

[136]Nasr, *Readings in the Life of Abouna Mina*, 155. Nasr claims Nasser was in pain that day due to his chronic peripheral vascular disease. For a description of Nasser's medical conditions (for which he underwent treatment in the Soviet Union), see Vatikiotis, *Nasser and His Generation*, 304.

[137]Raphael Ava Mina, "Some Misconceptions"; Raphael Ava Mina, "My Memories," audio recording.

[138]Sergius, *al-Manarah al-Misriyyah*, March 14, 1944; cited in Ibrahim, *The Copts of Egypt*, 150.

[139]In a fascinating letter written to the *maglis* (when he was still a monk in Old Cairo) in the 1950s—one may suggest 1956, with the election of the new members of the Council—Kyrillos tells them that he was praying for their success well before their election, that they had his full support, and encouraged the *maglis* to immediately begin their work of reform, stating among other suggestions, "instead of sending one monk on a scholarship to Athens, send seven who could edify the [Church]." See Hegumen Mina the Recluse [Kyrillos VI], "Letter to *Maglis al-Melli*" [in Arabic], in FRC-1: Letter 320 (Old Cairo, 195_).

[140]Anonymous, "His Holiness Chairs the *Maglis* Meeting in Alexandria" [in Arabic], *al-Ahram*, July 19, 1959.

[141]Wakin, *A Lonely Minority*, 116.

[142]Hasan, *Christians versus Muslims, 103*; van Doorn-Harder, *Modern Coptic Papacy*, 139.

[143]Van Doorn-Harder, "Planner, Patriarch and Saint," 235. They were also entrusted with the financial administration of the patriarchate and theological institutions.

[144]Samuel Tawadros el-Syriany, *The History of the Popes*, 195.

[145]Wakin, *A Lonely Minority*, 151.

[146]Kyrillos said of the decree: "It will lead to the proper organization of the Coptic *waqf* which previously always caused dissension among the Coptic people. . . . It will also enable the value of the exchanged land to be used in industrial and reconstruction projects being carried out by the Revolution"; ibid.

[147]Watson, *Among the Copts*, 59.

[148]Zaklama, *Pope Kyrillos VI*, 1:404–06; Watson, *Among the Copts*, 59; Adel Azer Bestawros, "Coptic Community Council," in *CE*, 582.

[149]Watson, *Among the Copts*, 59.

[150]Cited in Wakin, *A Lonely Minority*, 152.

[151]Ibid.

[152]Bestawros, "Coptic Community Council," 582. For the reasoning behind this, see the *maglis'* accusation and Kyrillos' reply; Deputy of *maglis al-melli*, "Letter to Pope Kyrillos VI, April 25, 1964" [in Arabic], in FRC-1: Letter 372 (Cairo: 1964); Pope Kyrillos VI, "A Reply to the Memorandum of the *Maglis al-melli*, May 13, 1964" [in Arabic] (Cairo, 1964).

[153]Wakin, *A Lonely Minority*, 153.

[154]These were found by the author wedged among the letters of Pope Kyrillos preserved by Fr Raphael Ava Mina.

[155]Deputy of *maglis al-melli*, "Letter to Pope Kyrillos VI, April 25, 1964." The letter ends with a request that Kyrillos chair the meetings of the *maglis*, that he address their concerns, and a plea for his prayers: "Your Holiness, we are still your faithful sons, hoping you remember us in your prayers, before the throne of grace."

[156]It is unclear whether the letter was written by Kyrillos, or by a secretary.

[157]Kyrillos VI, "A Reply to the Memorandum of the *Maglis al-Melli.*"

[158]Ibid.

[159]Ibid.

[160]Ibid.

[161]Ibid.

[162]Ragheb Hanna and Hanna Girgis Saad, "Letter to Pope Kyrillos VI, September 18, 1965" [in Arabic], in FRC-1: Letter 368 (Cairo: 1965). We do not have Kyrillos' reply to this letter. But Kyrillos' objections to those particular accusations may be fairly accurately reconstructed by consulting the later correspondence (as we shall see) when the same accusations are leveled once more by the *maglis* in 1967 in the wake of their bankruptcy.

[163]They also accuse Kyrillos of ignoring their report on clerical reform—again well beyond the scope of the Waqf Organization.

[164]Hanna and Girgis Saad, "Letter to Pope Kyrillos VI, September 18, 1965."

[165]The *maglis'* letter of April 15, 1964, suggests that Kyrillos first requested this in Autumn 1962, and the request is detailed in Ragheb and Hanna's resignation letter of 1965; see Deputy of *maglis al-melli*, "Letter to Pope Kyrillos VI, April 25, 1964"; Hanna and Girgis Saad, "Letter to Pope Kyrillos VI, September 18, 1965."

[166]A letter Kyrillos wrote months earlier to his younger brother, Fr Mikhail, details his knowledge of the endowments that were legally allocated to several bishops, as well as indicating that Kyrillos knew of the *maglis'* collusion and repeated letters to Ragheb Hanna (the chairman of the Waqf organization). Kyrillos begins: "I also received a letter from Mr Ragheb Hanna, including a copy of the letter of the *maglis*, which is void of courtesy, politeness, and religion. . . . Discuss the issue with Mr Ragheb and make it clear to him my question is: whether or not I have credits and benefits from the income from the endowments under the name of the Patriarch?" See Pope Kyrillos VI, "Letter to Fr Mikhail, December 18, 1964" [in Arabic], in FRC-1: Letter 47 (Cairo, 1964).

[167]Hanna and Girgis Saad, "Letter to Pope Kyrillos VI, September 18, 1965."

[168]One may speculate that given the *maglis* had reacted negatively to his desire to rebuild St Menas' Monastery in the early 1960s, Kyrillos may have sought to secure funds indirectly through his patriarchal endowments rather than ask for financial support directly.

[169]Pope Kyrillos VI, "Letter to Fr Mikhail undated, 196_" [in Arabic], in FRC-1: Letter 148 (Cairo: 196_). The letter is only dated as "196_" but the content suggests late 1964 to early 1965.

[170]Pope Kyrillos VI, "Letter to Hanna Youssef Atta, December 16, 1964" [in Arabic], in RC-2: Letter 32 (1964).

[171]Ibrahim, *The Copts of Egypt*, 51; B. L. Carter and Mirrit Boutros Ghali, "Coptic Press," in *CE*, 2011; Elizabeth Iskander, *Sectarian Conflict in Egypt: Coptic Media, Identity and Representation* (New York: Routledge, 2012), 26.

[172]Atta and Raphael Ava Mina, *Life of Pope Kyrillos*, 41.

[173]*Misr*, March 7, 1964, cited in Raphael Ava Mina, *A Stream of Comfort*, 59–60.

[174]*Misr*, April 17, 1965, ibid., 60.

[175]*Misr*, April 18, 1964, cited in Fawzi, *Kyrillos and Abdel Nasser*, 47–48.

[176]Adly, *Fr Mikhail Dawood's Memoirs*, 29.

[177]*Misr*, April 11, 1964, cited in Raphael Ava Mina, *A Stream of Comfort*, 65. The report referred to here was issued by the Coptic Organizations in Alexandria on the fifth anniversary of Kyrillos' ordination.

[178]*Misr*, April 18, 1964, cited in Fawzi, *Kyrillos and Abdel Nasser*, 47–48.

[179]Adly, *Fr Mikhail Dawood's Memoirs*, 29. Similarly see the same attitude in another account, Raphael Ava Mina, *Miracles of Pope Kyrillos VI*, 2:44.

[180]Raphael Ava Mina, *A Stream of Comfort*, 66.

[181]Kyrillos VI, "Letter to Fr Mikhail, December 18, 1964."

[182]Atta and Raphael Ava Mina, *Life of Pope Kyrillos*, 41.

[183]Adly, *Fr Mikhail Dawood's Memoirs*, 29.

[184]Atta and Raphael Ava Mina, *Life of Pope Kyrillos*, 41; Adly, *Fr Mikhail Dawood's Memoirs*, 29.

[185]Mary Massad, "The Story of the *Misr* Newspaper," *Watani International*, May 3, 2015; Carter and Ghali, "Coptic Press," 2011; Voile, *Les Coptes d'Égypte*, 88.

[186]Voile, *Les Coptes d'Égypte*, 88. Voile gives as a reference an interview with a prominent layman.

[187]Iskander, *Sectarian Conflict in Egypt*, 28–35.

[188]Anonymous, "Serious Rift between Pope Kyrillos VI and the *Maglis*" [in Arabic], *al-Ahram*, April 21, 1967.

[189]Hasan, *Christians versus Muslims*, 86.

[190]Pope Kyrillos VI, "Statement from the Coptic Orthodox Patriarchate, April 24, 1967" [in Arabic], in FRC-1: Letter 393 (Cairo, 1967). The statement was published in *al-Ahram* on April 25, 1967. Kyrillos in the statement also details the degree of the financial mismanagement by the *maglis,* including the misappropriation of funds for uses other than those which were specified in their constitution.

[191]Anonymous, "Serious Rift."

[192]Anonymous, "The *Maglis* Issues a Statement about Its Disagreements with Pope Kyrillos" [in Arabic], *al-Ahram*, April 24, 1967.

[193]Fawzi, *Kyrillos and Abdel Nasser*, 46. The *maglis* had gone so far as to borrow 2000 LE from *al-Tawfiq* Organization to pay the poorest of the workers of the patriarchate.

[194]Raphael Ava Mina, "My Memories," audio recording.

[195]Nasr, *Readings in the Life of Abouna Mina*, 157; Samuel Tawadros el-Syriany, *The History of the Popes*, 196; Zaklama, *Pope Kyrillos VI*, 2:81. On December 6, 1967, the President decreed (in response to Kyrillos' request) that the minister of the interior would select twelve new members who would administer the *waqf* for three years; and that the patriarch would take charge of all financial affairs and theological institutions of the Church. See ibid., 1:408–9.

[196]Fawzi, *Kyrillos and Abdel Nasser*, 46; Raphael Ava Mina, "My Memories," audio recording.

[197]The *maglis* would eventually reconvene under Pope Shenouda III in 1971, albeit in a much-modulated capacity that would ensure a relatively peaceful and stable relationship with future patriarchs. Nor would the *waqf* always be managed without interference. Fr Mikhail Dawood recalls an event in 1968 when the Agrarian Reform Authority claimed payments of 150,000 LE from the patriarchate. The matter was resolved after three days of prayer, when, so Mikhail claims, St Menas had assisted and the government was found to owe some 250,000 LE to the Church. Cited in Raphael Ava Mina, *Service and Humility*, 20–21. Mahoney also claims that in 1968 some 150–200 *waqf* were expropriated by the government on the grounds that they might have some Muslim beneficiaries. This would remain a sensitive issue between state and government for decades; see O'Mahony, "Coptic Christianity," 500.

[198]Ibrahim, *The Copts of Egypt*, 177.

[199]Pennington, "The Copts in Modern Egypt," 166; Tadros, "Vicissitudes in the Entente," 271–72.

[200]Zaklama, *Pope Kyrillos VI*, 2:82.

[201]Proverbs 21.1. Fascinatingly, no scholars have noticed the parallel with Demetrius II (1861–1870)—but I suspect Kyrillos would have been aware of it. On the celebration for the opening of the Suez Canal, Demetrius kissed the sultan on his chest. The sultan was troubled, and the guards asked the pope as to why. The pope said, "The book of God says: 'The king's heart is in the hand of the Lord' (Proverbs 21.1), when I kissed his heart, I have kissed the hand of God." The sultan was pleased and gave him abundant land to help the poor and the schools. For a brief discussion of Demetrius II, see Meinardus, *Two Thousand Years*, 71; van Doorn-Harder, *Modern Coptic Papacy*, 85.

[202]Nasr, *Readings in the Life of Abouna Mina*, 157.

[203]Vatikiotis, *Nasser and His Generation*, 304–5. Nasser's wife claims she was unaware of any heart attacks until 1969, and even then she was not told but only realized when she saw doctors rushing around and an elevator being installed in the family home; see Nasser, *Nasser: My Husband*, 103–5.

[204]Once more, strangely, no commentators have noticed this in reference to Kyrillos VI. Though, we should note, Nelly van Doorn-Harder came to the same conclusion when discussing the episode of Demetrius II and the Sultan. See van Doorn-Harder, *Modern Coptic Papacy*, 85.

9

Three Bishops and a Monk:
A Kenotic Ecclesiology

The Idea of Reform: Personal Ascetic Influence

> "To live is to change; and to be perfect is to have changed often."
> —*Cardinal Newman*

"WHO IS POPE KYRILLOS? The one who works miracles? Who casts out demons?" quietly asked Fr Raphael, shaking his head. "That is not all there is to Kyrillos; but if you want to know who he really is, I will tell you":

In 1968, there was a much-loved priest whom Kyrillos relocated to the patriarchate for six months to serve closely with him. . . . The whole parish [unaware of the reason] rose in something of a revolution; Sunday School, youth groups, the church committee . . . all of them . . . asking, "How could you remove this beloved priest?" . . . The people began cursing, buses arrived at the patriarchate overflowing with people. "We want our priest back," they screamed. Then after the six months, Kyrillos moved him to another [far more thriving] parish . . . but once more the revolution arose; cursing and criticism began once more. And yet Kyrillos remained silent. This went on for some time until an old friend from Kyrillos' time in Old Cairo rebuked him: "You are causing trouble, everyone is disturbed and angry; just return the priest to his parish—do we need more troubles?" Kyrillos calmly confided to his dear friend, "If you only knew the reality . . . this priest is not worthy of priesthood."[1]

At this point Fr Raphael became visibly moved with emotion:

Not worthy of priesthood? . . . and yet he stayed silent for six months, being
mocked, criticized, sworn at . . . and not once did Kyrillos open his mouth to
explain. Not merely a mistake, the man was not worthy of priesthood at all,
and yet he puts him in his bosom, in the patriarchate, and then returns him,
healed. . . . This is Pope Kyrillos. . . . This is Pope Kyrillos![2]

The corrupt priest—allegedly guilty of financial swindling—was very much
a product of his time. He was deserving of punishment and public humiliation, even defrocking. But, despite the personal cost of six months of criticism,
Kyrillos loved and healed him. Considering the Western ecclesial controversies
in the late twentieth and early twenty-first centuries, this move may, of course,
have been less than ideal, perhaps even questionable—placing in some sense
the reputation of the priest above the rights of the faithful. But this is to miss
that Kyrillos had little concern for reputation, personal or otherwise. It was not
the reputation of the priest that concerned him, but rather healing him. Kyrillos refused to turn a blind eye to the corruption, but neither was he willing to
forsake the corrupt priest.

This episode was paradigmatic of Kyrillos' method of reform: always at a
cost to himself; through his personal holiness and ascetic influence; and, above
all, quietly, without judgment, seeking only healing. There can be no doubt that
Kyrillos was a thaumaturge ("miracle worker"), but this was foremost in the
healing of his Church. Just as he healed the priest, Kyrillos took into his bosom
a broken, fractured, and impoverished Church, silently bearing all manner
of ridicule, gently healing with his person. This would be characteristic of his
"method" of reform.

* * *

The idea of reform is an ancient one. And yet, at least for the Orthodox Christian
world, it remains a rather undesirable term. Centuries of subjection to Turkish
Ottoman rule—in Egypt, even more, under the repressive thumb of Islam—
caught between Roman antagonism and Protestant missionary zeal, "meant
that terms like reformation, revision, evolution, and innovation have become
taboo."[3] Orthodoxy, to some degree, "barricaded itself in," fighting for historical
continuity by "ossifying" an emphasis on tradition.[4] Not to mention the increasing divisions (and theological estrangement) in the post-"*Reform*ation" Western
world, which would foster deep suspicions of the very word "reform." "Such
terms . . . if not quite forbidden," one scholar comments, "then [are] at least seen

as problematic and foreign to Orthodox tradition and spirituality."[5] The urgent priority was not renewal or reform, but simple survival.

But though there is certainly an emphasis on "tradition," the Orthodox Church has always been characterized by a deep pneumatology—the renewing breath of the Holy Spirit—and, consequently, within the Church's history there are numerous moments of "critical appropriation of the original message, a deep intuitive understanding . . . a dynamic, creative process."[6] And so while the idea of "reformation" is usually found in Protestantism, it can be applied within Orthodoxy, Meyendorff claims, "to those elements which are only human and there are many of them in the historical Church."[7]

* * *

"Reform" here, we should note, is not strictly speaking that of organizational or institutional renewal, or adjustment to the spirit of the times, nor is it the reestablishment of doctrine—though these certainly are related. Rather, by "reform," at least for our purposes, is meant the correction, healing, and transformation of distortion, dysfunction, and corruption—a return, that is, to the created intention.

The study of the idea of reform began in a tangible way with Gerhart Ladner (1905–1993). What he found in examining the New Testament and patristic literature was quite unexpected. Whereas renewal may have had pre-Christian origins, reform was "essentially Christian in its origin and early development."[8] Reform was undeniably an ideal from the very beginning—but the earliest Christian idea was not that of the reform of the *Church*. It was the reform of the *person*.

Earliest Christianity related the idea of reform to the Pauline doctrine of the human person, "the experience of newness in Christ."[9] Scriptural language of *metamorphōsis-reformatio* and *anakainōsis-renovatio* (e.g., Rom 12.2; 2 Cor 3.18; Phil 3.21), suggests an "individual process," specifically "personal reformation" towards that "image-likeness of man to God."[10] When Ladner looked to the early patristic literature, he found the same.[11] Reform always pivoted around an *individual's* repentance and transformation. Gregory of Nyssa, for instance, described man's "reformation" as a "re-assimilation" through purification, to the image of God.[12] A favorite description was that of a painting's restoration, "spoiled but not completely ruined by the application of wrong colors and especially by the accumulation of dirt and dust."[13] But, Athanasius adds, the image can only be renewed, "if the one after whom it has been made—Christ in the case of the divine image in man—is *present* again."[14] Reform at the earliest was, therefore, neither a response to institutional stagnation nor a sterile return to an archaic past. Reform had to do with the transformation of the human person *into* the image of God—who is Christ. Reform for the Fathers, in short, meant *personal reform.*[15]

Over the centuries, the idea gradually assumed a *supra*-individual and communal character.[16] Early monasticism, especially in the thought of Basil the Great and Eustathius of Sebaste, represented a "movement of more general radical reform which demanded of all Christians fullest adherence to the evangelical apostolic way of life."[17] There, in the radical nature of monasticism, personal reform that was also communal found its deepest expression. Chrysostom would later attempt to reform the Christian societies of Antioch and Constantinople from that very same basis. But, Ladner comments, "he failed, probably because he attempted to reach out too far beyond the *ascetic sphere of influence.*"[18] Reform, from *above*, however well intentioned, would from then on be similarly fated. The Western Carolingian and Gregorian reforms of the ninth and eleventh centuries, which were essentially legislated inner reform, could not but fail. Their capacity to "reform," Bellitto argues, was limited, for it was not a reform of hearts.[19] It was from outside, not from within.

* * *

Two vital conclusions emerge from this all-too-brief study of reform. The first is that true, authentic, and thoroughly Christian reform is, above all, existentially *personal*—the exquisitely personal transformation into the image of God.[20] And if reform is ultimately personal, then any elucidation of reform in the Coptic Church in the mid-twentieth century must also be intensely *personal*. The second draws from Ladner's and Bellitto's observations that supra-individual (or institutional) attempts at reform have inevitably failed. In the case of Chrysostom in the fourth century, Ladner suggests, this was a consequence of reaching out beyond his *"sphere of ascetic influence"*: beyond his disciples and, consequently, beyond his capacity to transform hearts. Whether Ladner perceived the fuller meaning of these words is unclear (he made no further comment). But his fleeting words invite the question: if inner reform was fated to be limited to the "reach" of personal ascetic influence, was there any way to *extend* that reach?

What if, for instance, reform could move through "ascetic influence," though a revolution of hearts, from individual to individual—something of a discipleship of reform? What if a handful of disciples went on to become reformers, having first undertaken their own personal reform? What if they, too, reached out within their ascetic influence? And, what if beneath them, as in the case of modern Egypt, there was a *network of discipleship* forged by a unique Sunday School system that had the capacity to extend that sphere of ascetic influence well beyond their individual reach?

I suggest this is precisely what Kyrillos put in place. He reached out through his unique ascetic influence and brought about an extraordinary revolution of hearts that went well beyond him. Kyrillos' life of personal *ascesis*, followed by the discipling and dissemination of that ascesis, saw the transformation of an entire Church in twelve short years—the history of which is nothing less than miraculous. Perhaps this is what Ladner envisioned when he spoke of the patristic idea of reform: "It can under certain circumstances quicken the heartbeat of a whole civilization."[21]

Kyrillos took into himself a weeping and broken Church—as he did that corrupt and unworthy priest—and healed through his own personal ascetic reform at a precious personal cost. For this reason, the following accounts of his disciples—Saad Aziz (Bishop Samuel), Waheeb Atallah (Bishop Gregorious), Nazir Gayed (Pope Shenouda III), and Youssef Iskander (Fr Matta el-Meskeen)—will be intensely personal in tracing Kyrillos' ascetic influence, an influence that brought about one of the most profound transformations in the history of Christianity.

The "General Bishops": Episcopal Innovation and Samuel, 1962–1966

> "In whatever place you live, do not easily leave it."
> —*St Antony the Great*

U NKNOWN TO ALL but a few, one of Kyrillos' first moves of reform—if not the very first—was a deliberate innovation. The details of the episode have rarely surfaced, and even then, only in fleeting allusions. Within weeks of his patriarchal consecration, in May 1959, Kyrillos approached one of his former disciples, Professor Waheeb Atallah (then dean of the Theological College), with a novel idea. "I was asked," Waheeb recalls, "to suggest a plan for the see of St Mark, so I proposed to His Holiness a detailed written suggestion ... to ordain several 'general bishops' with Cairo as their headquarters."[22]

The plan—unassuming and ostensibly ordinary—was nothing less than a reform of the episcopacy. Waheeb suggested the consecration of four "general bishops," ordained not for a specific geographical diocese but rather for functional needs: seminary education; public and social affairs; the diaspora; and liturgical rites.[23] Putting aside for a moment the freedom with which such "general bishops" could move unrestrained by diocesan and congregational needs, Kyrillos had other motives. A bishop, to put it politely, could only be ordained for a diocese when another reposed. To await their repose, and therefore a "vacancy," would be to delay urgent reform for years, if not decades. The innovative idea, coming after two thousand years of uniform practice, gave Kyrillos the immediate means to infuse reform—in the persons of his disciples—into the hierarchy of the Church. This makes clear that the dramatic reforms of the next decade were not simply fortuitous or haphazard in nature; they were in fact designed to some extent within the first weeks of Kyrillos' becoming patriarch.

For some of his closest disciples, the novel suggestion proceeded directly from Kyrillos' personality. "The awareness of his weaknesses," wrote Waheeb some decades later, "was truly authentic and remained with him all his days; he remained utterly humble ... this gave rise to an additional gift, which was the capacity to delegate...."[24] "[Kyrillos] never worked alone," claims Fr Youssef Asaad,

> but always let others participate with him. ... If someone was celebrating the
> Liturgy in a way which people liked, he rejoiced greatly saying, 'bring him
> to pray with me;' if someone was talented in preaching ... he would sit and
> listen to the homily like any other individual in the congregation. ... [25]

Kyrillos had said as much at his ordination: "As for us, let us *disappear* so that [Christ] might be manifest." Never did Kyrillos feel threatened by another metropolitan, bishop, or by anyone more able than he; instead he embraced, delegated, and empowered with little concern for himself, ordaining over the next decade three of the four suggested "general bishops." They would, however, take convincing—and perhaps a little force.

* * *

In mid-1962, a little over three years after the episcopal innovation was suggested, Kyrillos took issue with (of all things) Waheeb's attire.[26] Having been made a celibate archdeacon a few years earlier, Waheeb had taken to wearing his cassock *too* frequently.[27] He was told, in no uncertain terms, to either cease wearing the cassock or be tonsured a monk. And so, he became a monk.

It was by no means a pressured or impetuous decision. Waheeb had always contemplated monasticism and for this reason, refused marriage and the call to the priesthood on several occasions.[28] Kyrillos, on the other hand, had been encouraging his tonsure for at least three years.[29] The matter of the cassock simply brought things to a head. "I accepted your call as the voice of God," wrote Waheeb (now Monk Pakhoum) from the Muharraq Monastery to Kyrillos in mid-September 1962, "feeling that God had spoken through your mouth."[30]

Another of Kyrillos' disciples, Fr Antonious el-Syriany (formerly Nazir Gayed), who had entered the Syrian Monastery eight years earlier, had been a student of Waheeb. On hearing that his professor had been tonsured, he wrote to Monk Pakhoum in joy, but *also* with a warning. "Peace to your pure soul, blessed father," Antonious wrote on September 22, 1962, from his desert cave,

> I congratulate you because you chose monasticism over professorship, may the Lord strengthen you, I congratulate you from all my heart. I want to tell you some words, but embarrassment is preventing me, and your honor as my great teacher is obstructing me. I am your young student, I am not worthy to talk in your presence, but because of the great love between us, I will tell your reverence a frank word: My blessed father, *beware from going back to the Theological College*, at least in the early years of your monasticism. I know from all my heart and mind that you have discerned the reality of monasticism; its depth, its original philosophy which the fathers lived. I am certain that you comprehend that monasticism is giving everything and being united to the only One. I have heard many things from people . . . that is why I am repeating myself another time: My blessed father, *beware of going back to the Theological College*. I am aware how curious it is for me to tell you this. . . .[31]

Antonious had evidently written after hearing rumors—some perhaps quite sinister—that his former professor's monasticism would be short-lived.[32] Antonious also spoke from his own experience. Some years earlier, many (including Waheeb) had tried to entice Fr Antonious to leave the desert to accept a scholarship for doctoral studies in Strasburg, but he refused adamantly, preferring the "sublime and beautiful" path of solitude.[33] Fearing the same for his dear friend, Antonious felt he had no choice but to warn against any return to the Theological College. The timing was, however, terrifically unfortunate.

At 4:00 a.m. the next day—in reaction to an entirely unrelated matter—
Antonious was awakened by Bishop Theophilus, head of the Syrian Monastery.
"Kyrillos is extremely upset . . . ," said Theophilus, breathless, having just tra-
versed the desert to Antonious' cave. "He refused even to greet me until I bring
you with me."[34] "But I don't even have any shoes," mumbled Antonious, looking down at his somewhat inappropriate sandals.[35] The sudden summons was,
however, hardly unexpected. A few weeks earlier, when he was acting-abbot
in place of an absent superior, Antonious decided to close the monastery in
a "blanket ban" to all visitors. During this brief period a group of forty German tourists, bearing a letter of exception from the hand of Kyrillos himself,
attempted to enter the monastery. But—and this would have immediately come
to mind as Theophilus awoke Antonious—the visitors were summarily refused
by Antonious.[36] He had, therefore, little choice but to accompany Theophilus
to see Kyrillos.

"When I arrived," reminisces Antonious,

> [Kyrillos] looked at my *galabeya* [cassock] that was covered in dirt and said,
> "What is this?" "It's the best one I have," I replied. ". . . And where is your
> *emma* [priest hat]?" "Bishop Athanasius took it from me when he became a
> bishop." "Why?" sternly asked Kyrillos, "was it the *emma* of a bishop?" Paus-
> ing for a moment, he then asked: "And why didn't you receive the [German]
> guests?" "I did . . . but outside the monastery," I answered. [Kyrillos] then
> gave me some water and told me to relax, before asking: "Why do you refuse
> to work with me?" "*Sayedna* [master]," I managed, "I love monasticism. . . ."
> "How about we make you a bishop abroad?" Kyrillos nimbly inquired. "The
> monastery is better . . ." I quickly replied. "How about we make you a Bishop
> for the Theological College?" he tried once more. "For whom? The teachers
> are more than the students?" I cheekily answered. . . . There was no result;
> the conversation ended there.[37]

Sensing that Kyrillos was displeased, Antonious made ready to depart. As
custom would have it, a monk-priest would bow before the patriarch on departure, while the latter prayed for him. "So," an unsuspecting Antonious recalls,

> he put his hand on my head and said, "Shenouda, *Bishop of Education!*". . . . I
> cried out, "What's this!?" The hands of Pope Kyrillos were not like my hands,
> he had somehow quickly grasped my head, and I couldn't move at all . . .
> and then Bishop Theophilus also laid his hand on my head. "You have no

absolution to move from this place," added Kyrillos.[38] . . . I went by a trick and was ordained a bishop.[39]

Bishop Theophilus—forever a trickster—had been in on it the entire time. They both knew Antonious would stubbornly refuse to leave his desert cave regardless of the circumstance, nor would he ever accept becoming a bishop. The ordination was, by all accounts, unexpected; at that time, there were no vacant dioceses, nor was there any concept of a "general bishop."[40] Antonious was forbidden—under threat of excommunication—to leave the patriarchate before the consecration.[41] But—and this is vital to see—just a few days earlier he had written to Monk Pakhoum, imploring him to remain in the desert, warning against any return to the Theological College; and yet now Antonious was to be ordained a bishop for that *same* Theological College. The timing could not have been worse.

* * *

Almost immediately, rumors began to circulate. Monk Pakhoum received an anonymous letter detailing the "secret" ordination of Antonious. "I am sorry," wrote the unnamed informant on September 25,

> . . . to let you know that your tonsure as a monk was a reason for stirring the hatred of some of your colleagues who envy you . . . they wanted to cut the path for your promotion in the tasks chosen by God . . . so they rushed in making conspiracies and meetings. . . . Fr Antonious el-Syriany was chosen, it is all set up, and he will be ordained next Sunday as a Bishop for the Theological College. . . . This, we are telling you before it happens, and it is surrounded with top secrecy at the patriarchate.[42]

The unfortunate timing provided ripe ground for speculation—namely, that Pakhoum was removed to make way for Antonious. Later scholars have even mistakenly suggested that Pakhoum left in defiance *after* Antonious was ordained bishop over the Theological College.[43] But the primary sources make quite clear that Pakhoum was tonsured when Antonious was still living in his cave. While the timing and the anonymous letter may be suggestive of malice and conspiracy, the reality, as is borne out in the associated letters of the period, was, in fact, the opposite.

"A few days ago," lamented Antonious within hours of his meeting with Kyrillos,

I wrote a letter congratulating you for your monasticism and advising you not to go back to the Theological College . . . then a few days later His Holiness the pope sent me a telegram and Bishop Theophilus came and took me. . . . While leaving, he extended his arm to bless me as usual, but instead, he ordained me a Bishop for the Clerical Colleges. It was a shock! I begged him, but he said: "This is the will of God, you have no absolution to leave the patriarchate". . . . I have advised you to live the life of renunciation . . . but I myself could not complete that path. I am extremely ashamed while writing this letter to you.[44]

Three days later Antonious would write once more to Pakhoum, "I am so embarrassed . . . how could I tell you to delay returning to the Theological College, and then I become the Bishop of the Theological College!"[45] In the same letter, Antonious states he was also aware of the malicious rumors, but could only repeat his embarrassment as to the timing and that it was very much against his will.[46] There was little he could do. On September 30, 1962, Kyrillos consecrated Antonious—by force—Shenouda, "Bishop of the Theological College and Clerical Institutes." In reply to a letter of congratulations from a German scholar, Shenouda wrote,

I thank you for your gentle words of congratulation. . . .as a matter of fact, however, a letter of *consolation*—not of congratulation—was fit for the occasion. How may a monk be congratulated on leaving the calmness of the wilderness and abiding again amid the disturbance of the city? . . . for me, it is, indeed, a matter of shame. I remember that day of my consecration to the episcopacy in tears and lamentation.[47]

Though Shenouda was distraught, and despite the fermenting gossip, Monk Pakhoum was, on the contrary, genuinely thrilled at the consecration of his former student, dispatching two congratulatory telegrams and a more detailed letter. How could he not be overjoyed, Pakhoum wrote, when he had been the architect of the "General Bishops" suggestion some three years earlier?[48] He also had other reasons for never doubting the pure intentions of the newly ordained Shenouda (and for that matter, Kyrillos). In the revealing letter, Pakhoum disclosed an earlier private conversation with Kyrillos concerning the leadup to his tonsure. "I am going to tell you," wrote Pakhoum to Shenouda on October 5, 1962, the details of a conversation which took place between the pope and me, on the same Monday, September 10, 1962 [a few days prior to leaving the College and becoming a monk]. I said to His Holiness the Pope: "I will leave everything; I will hand back my papers and work." "Why?" questioned the pope. "Because I perceive that monasticism is all about calmness, serenity, silence, isolation, and spiritual discipline, and all of that necessitates that I leave everything." But His Holiness did not approve that I leave my work at the College and said: "*What if I call you* to do something at the College?" I replied: "That would be considered as an order, and orders must be obeyed; in my mind, I have to submit the idea of monasticism to the idea of obedience." "Very well let it be so," Kyrillos concluded, "after around a month, *I will call you*. . . . Go early, even tonight if possible, the earlier you go, the earlier you will come back. . . ." These are the details of the story, without frills or additions, I have told it to you as it is. . . .[49]

Kyrillos had no intention of ever removing Pakhoum from the Theological College. Even before his tonsure, he had made clear his plans; his decision was not haphazard nor underhanded. Almost to the day, one month later, on October 25, Monk Pakhoum was suddenly "called" to leave his monastery and return to the Theological College. There he would become associate dean under Shenouda's leadership—and, we might note, Kyrillos' chief secretary for good measure.

One thing, however, was clear. From then on, no matter the intent, Kyrillos' reforms through the persons of his disciples would always be marked by rumors, accusations, and lies, spread by contentious agitators. Discerning what is truth in the accounts is therefore urgently necessary, not merely as a historical corrective (as vital as that is), but also to reveal the quarrelsome world into which these men sought to breathe life, while at the same time clutching at some semblance of unity.

* * *

The importance of that little-known episode cannot be too deeply underscored. In it, the fates of all three "general bishops"—Kyrillos' choice of reforming disciples—would be intertwined. Two of the three, Bishop Shenouda and Monk Pakhoum (the future Bishop Gregorious), have been our subjects thus far. The third was just as unsuspecting.

On the morning of the fateful day of Shenouda's consecration, September 30, 1962, Kyrillos was descending the staircase as he made his way to the cathedral.[50] Suddenly, without explanation, he stopped. There he stood for a few minutes, surrounded by his perplexed entourage, still and silent, absorbed in deep thought (or perhaps prayer). "Go and get his brother," commanded Kyrillos, "quickly go and get his brother!" By "brother" he meant the patriarchal secretary, Fr Makary el-Syriany, who, one western journalist noted in the early 1960s, was "usually referred to as 'the intelligent one' at the patriarchate."[51] Makary, one of Kyrillos' closest disciples dating back to the years at St Menas' in Old Cairo, unquestioningly came down as requested. "Go stand," Kyrillos motioned, "next to your brother."[52] Little did Makary know that he would, that day, be consecrated as Bishop Samuel, standing alongside his "brother" Bishop Shenouda.[53]

Bishop Samuel (1920–1981), born Saad Aziz, lost his father at an early age.[54] The loss had a remarkable effect on his mother. She opened her house to the poor and destitute, as well as, importantly, to the members of the Sunday School Movement, who at the time were rejected by the local parish in Giza.[55] These years would become the paradigm for Saad's life. From then on, he would live for others. He was remembered as always seeking out the most difficult villages for his rural service.[56] While attaining his law degree from Cairo University, he filled the edges of his notebooks with one scrawling question: "Lord, what do you want me to do?"[57] Under the eminent Habib Girgis—the founder of the Sunday School Movement—he studied theology, as well as completing further bachelor's degrees in Education and Psychology at the American University in Cairo, as a "consecrated [*takrees*] servant." Girgis then sent him to Ethiopia in 1944 for two years where he assisted in founding a Theological College, opened his heart to the local youth, taught Scripture, and developed a Sunday School curriculum.[58] On his return, and much to the displeasure of his friends and family, he was tonsured Monk Makary under the discipleship of Fr Mina (the future Pope Kyrillos) in early 1948.[59] As the first of the "Sunday School monks," he eventually settled at the Syrian Monastery in Wadi al-Natrun.

The talents of the young monk did not go unnoticed. Yusab, the patriarch at the time, delegated him in 1954 to be the official ecclesial representative at the second assembly of the World Council of Churches in Evanston, Illinois.[60] It was a historically significant event for the Coptic Church, effectively ending more than a millennium of isolation under Islam.[61] The conveners were so taken by Makary that, as a result, he was offered a scholarship at Princeton, where he completed a master's degree in education.[62] As he began preparing to undertake doctoral studies, he was called back to Egypt to serve at the Theological College in 1955.[63] Though his education may have been cut short, in this brief period, he sowed the seeds for the diaspora in the United States.

But it was his first love that would forever consume him—the poor, destitute, uneducated, and illiterate. In 1959, Makary reignited the "rural *diakonia*." It was an organized system to serve those beyond the traditional reach of the Church in the rural villages—many of which had no church, let alone a priest. Though there is some suggestion that this may have begun in 1957 in close cooperation with Fr Boulos Boulos of Damanhur, Arabic sources accurately note that it only began to flourish when Kyrillos was ordained patriarch.[64] One of Kyrillos' earliest moves was to empower his former disciple, Fr Makary, as his chief secretary via the Department of Social Services of the Higher Institute of Coptic Studies.[65] The project reached well beyond its original purpose. In line with the integrative approach of the Sunday School center of Giza, socioeconomic development, infrastructure, adult education and literacy programs, medical aid, vaccination drives, and agronomic services were set up in parallel with religious education projects.[66] Makary's only publications—"Family Planning from a Christian Point of View" and "With the Youth"—confirm his preoccupation with the social outworking of his faith.[67] The central concern was to reach out to those unable to "access" the Church and to "help them meet their concrete needs in a holistic way."[68]

At first, some twenty villages of Beheira were singled out for the "*diakonia* experiment."[69] A handful of servants would travel via bus, or more often by bicycle, visiting four to five villages per day, five days per week.[70] Unsurprisingly—though very much to the shock of the servants—many in the villages were not even baptized.[71] Not content with simply dispatching priests to perform baptisms, Fr Makary took the innovative step of regularly sending clergy with newly created "portable altars."[72] The Church literally, in all its capacity, went to the people.

After Kyrillos ordained Makary as Bishop Samuel in 1962—fittingly, as the "general bishop for ecumenical, public, and social affairs"—this "experiment" would grow rapidly, almost furiously; from some 3,275 families in 1961 in the one diocese of Beheira, to twelve dioceses by 1966, serving 71,914 families in 2,154 villages of Lower and Upper Egypt.[73] It was a movement in and of itself. Samuel's "diocese" was, therefore, the "episcopizing" of his life's work. Beyond meeting the concrete needs of these villages, the importance of the "rural *diakonia*" in *connecting* these distant villages to the Sunday School network cannot be overstated. Rural Egypt, once inaccessible, was now very much within reach of Kyrillos' "sphere of ascetic influence."

But there were also other groups of disconnected Copts, and they too were close to the heart of both Kyrillos and Samuel.[74] President Nasser's economic and agrarian reforms, and later the rise of Islamism, did much to hurt land-owning Copts and provoked a mass emigration, especially of the educated and upper class, to Europe, the Gulf States, the United States, Canada, and Austra-lia.[75] Kyrillos quickly took notice and delegated Bishop Samuel to establish and organize these new communities. By 1965 parishes were established and priests ordained in Toronto, New Jersey, Los Angeles, Kuwait, and, shortly after, Sydney and Melbourne.[76] The financial, political, and social implications of these young and vulnerable communities in the Western world would eventually "prove vital for the Church in Egypt."[77] For instance, the highly educated emigrants, mostly middle and upper class, began almost immediately organizing desper-ately needed donations for their kinsmen in an economically faltering Egypt.[78] Samuel, in his capacity as bishop of "ecumenical affairs," was also able to draw upon his many contacts in the Western world to secure aid, grants, and funds for these migrant communities, as well as his now rapidly diversified and growing domestic projects within Egypt.[79]

From here the story of Bishop Samuel would take numerous twists and turns over the next decade and a half, beyond the life of Kyrillos. Most of that story is filled with ceaseless self-sacrifice for his Church, some is shrouded in mystery, and some is painful. But there can be no doubt that this man, one of Kyrillos' closest reforming disciples, gave his life for the Church. And so, it was somewhat tragically fitting that his end would ultimately be that of a martyr. On October 6, 1981, standing alongside President Sadat, he was assassinated by Islamic jihad-ists at the untimely age of sixty. An obituary in the *Times of London* a few days later remembered him as a "major figure in the Coptic revival" and as a "small bustling man, with a big heart. . . ."[80]

* * *

Though space does not allow a full detailing of them, Kyrillos' episcopal reforms were by no means limited to the "general bishops."[81] In June 1959, Kyrillos con-secrated as the first bishop of his patriarchate, Metropolitan Basilious of Jeru-salem (1923–1991)—a former student of Habib Girgis who held a Ph.D. from Thessalonica.[82] And a few weeks before the ordinations of Bishops Shenouda and Samuel, on September 9, 1962, Kyrillos consecrated one of his disciples, Fr Macarius el-Syriany, as Athanasius, bishop of Beni Suef and Bahnasa. Atha-nasius (1923–2000) would be the first "Sunday School monk" to be ordained a bishop.[83] To this day he is remembered as the "model and epitome of a diocesan bishop," having worked closely with Bishop Samuel in transforming the infrastructure and society of his diocese, as well as healing much animosity through dialogue with Islamic scholars and elders.[84] Through him and with him, Kyrillos would exhibit an extraordinary attitude toward women, considering the time and context.[85] The Sisters of St Mary, a consecrated female movement of community service, was established; and the renowned Mother Irini was made abbess of the Monastery of Abu Sefein in 1962, inaugurating her remarkable and miraculous mission in reviving the contemplative life for women.[86]

But perhaps no ordination so symbolized the power of Kyrillos' reform as that of yet another disciple, Fr Mathias el-Syriany, as Bishop Domadius of Giza (1925–2011). He was consecrated on March 31, 1963, after the repose of a controversial predecessor, Metropolitan Youannis of Giza. Youannis, we should recall, had long resisted the Sunday School Movement (SSM) and, importantly, died suddenly after unknowingly ingesting poison while plotting against Kyrillos. The diocese was both the home of the Giza center of the SSM, as well as, strangely, the last stronghold against reform.[87] Reform in the person of a disciple of Kyrillos had, therefore, conquered a decisive frontier.

These moves, foremost that of the "general bishops," were unprecedented. With them, Kyrillos penetrated the Holy Synod "without completely alienating the old guard"—and without awaiting their repose.[88] The "Sunday School monks," all disciples of Kyrillos from his days at that small and unassuming Church of St Menas in Old Cairo, had entered the Synod. "It is impossible," one Western scholar has commented, "to know if Kyrillos knew what forces he was unleashing."[89] I would suggest that he most certainly did. The ordinations were neither impulsive nor impetuous. They were calculated, intentional, and profoundly inspired. Each one of those young bishops had taken Kyrillos as a confessor in the late 1940s and early 1950s; lived with him, prayed with him, and been discipled by him. They were not, so to speak, "unknowns." Kyrillos had deliberately encouraged and empowered these young reformers, and many young reformers, especially these, were impassioned. I might also add—rather explicitly—that the tensions of these disciples are too often examined (only) through the lens of the ensuing history, which postdates the life of Kyrillos (though one cannot deny the later increasingly personal nature to the conflicts). My concern here, however, is to examine their contentions during the years of his patriarchate, that is to say, looking forwards rather than backwards. Kyrillos, I would suggest once more, must have expected contention to some degree. For at the front line and coalface of reform, tempers inevitably flare.

At the Heated Coalface of Reform:
Gregorious and Shenouda, 1967

> "There are no bad days and good days,
> but there are days of prayer and days without prayer."
> —*Pope Kyrillos VI*

NINETEEN SIXTY-SEVEN was not a good year. But for Kyrillos, there was evidently no such thing—there were only years *with* prayer, and years *without* prayer. Despite the numerous contentions and struggles of his disciples, the distasteful *maglis* financial crisis, and even the agonizing Six-Day War, Kyrillos seemingly remained immovable. A year of diverse conflict it may have been, but with prayer, it could not be said to be a "bad year." As to the tensions among his disciples, they were to be expected.

* * *

Monk Pakhoum may have been the architect of the "general bishops" innovation—two of them, Shenouda and Samuel, were already ordained—but he could never have imagined how such plans would play out in this year.

Pakhoum (1919–2001), born Waheeb Atallah, was a "quiet man, a scholar by disposition."[90] In his late teens he had climbed the rugged hills to Fr Mina's windmill to "sit at his feet."[91] Though Waheeb had "exceptional grades," he shocked his family by refusing to enter into the study of medicine, and instead choosing to study under Habib Girgis, completing a bachelor's of theology with distinction in 1939.[92] Despite being heavily involved with the Sunday School Movement during these years, he was never considered a "typical representative of any particular center."[93] But like many of these young men, he was formed at the hands of both Fr Mina (Kyrillos) and Habib Girgis—a peculiarity that should not escape us.

Forever drawn to monasticism, he pushed those sentiments aside and went on to complete a bachelor of philosophy in 1944 from Cairo University while simultaneously lecturing at the Seminary.[94] Eventually, he would be appointed dean and professor of theology after the death of Habib Girgis in 1951.[95] After studying for a diploma in Egyptian antiquities, he completed—the first of any of the SSM—a Ph.D. in biblical and Coptic studies at the University of Manchester in 1955, under the great orientalist Walter Till (1894–1963).[96] While there, at Manchester, he developed something of an "international reputation," even lecturing before the distinguished Fellowship of St Alban and St Sergius.[97] On his return to Cairo, he continued to do research and to teach, and to mentor many other consecrated servants.[98] Finally, in 1962, under the "persuasion" of Kyrillos (as we have seen) he was tonsured Monk Pakhoum at the Muharraq Monastery, eventually becoming the patriarchal secretary for religious affairs.[99]

Pakhoum has been remembered by one scholar as "slightly aloof from the rough and tumble of Church politics."[100] This was most certainly the case in later life, but under Kyrillos—though few may be aware of it—Pakhoum was intimately and fiercely involved in laying the foundations of reform. In an interview with Wakin in the early 1960s, for instance, Pakhoum placed the number of "good" priests at two hundred, of some seven hundred in total. "He made it clear," Wakin reported, "that the rest are either incompetent or indifferent."[101] It would be this matter of "incompetent" clergy that would bring Pakhoum into dispute with Bishop Shenouda in early 1967—one that was not too dissimilar to that of the Apostles Paul and Peter.

At a 1959 Synod meeting, early in Kyrillos' patriarchate, it was decreed that no candidate was to be ordained to the priesthood unless he was a graduate of the Theological College—"no matter the personal or academic qualifications."[102] Within a few years, this was the case. The effect on the story of reform was pervasive. And so, when Fr Pakhoum picked up a fateful copy of the *al-Ahram* newspaper, he could barely contain himself. "I have read this morning in *al-Ahram*," wrote Pakhoum to Bishop Shenouda on March 18, 1967,

> an invitation to ordain Mr Zakareya Mahrous as a priest on Sunday. Believe me, my heart is heavy, and about to explode, I want to cry but cannot. . . . A non–Theological [College] graduate is being ordained in the presence of the director and bishop of the Theological College! Bishop Shenouda, who stayed at the Monastery for five months protesting against the pope for ordaining non–Theological College graduates is attending the ordination of a non–Theological College graduate. He might as well perform the ordination. . . . My head is about to explode. . . .[103]

Such an ordination was nothing new. Kyrillos, despite being the author of the decree, had—if we recall the *maglis* conflict—occasionally ordained non–Theological College graduates for rural areas. The concern here, however, was that the bishop of the Theological College, Shenouda, was involved—the same Shenouda who spent five months protesting in a self-imposed exile (or perhaps suspension) when Kyrillos acted similarly.[104]

"My peace and love to a person so dear to my heart," replied Bishop Shenouda in a lengthy letter on March 22:

> I did not participate in his ordination; Bishop Makarios wished that I would
> conduct the whole ordination, but I apologized and explained my opinion to
> him. He knows quite well that this is a *special* situation. . . .[105]

The ordination was an exception. In the first place, Shenouda continued, the
congregation adored Zakareya, with some four thousand people attending the
ordination. Zakareya had served within the Sunday School Movement for sixteen years, was Superintendent of the service at Nag Hammadi, was "beloved and
trusted by everyone," and was, therefore, "from our flesh and bones." Though,
Shenouda concedes, theological education is "without doubt a basic element"
of the formation for priesthood, some candidates may be geographically limited—"Zakareya . . . is married with children, and has family responsibilities; he
cannot resign, come to Cairo [to study theology], and become a burden together
with his family, so what could he do?" Qena was, after all, 590 kilometers (367
miles) south of Cairo in Upper Egypt. Knowing this, Shenouda reveals, he had
in fact spent the last year searching for a theological graduate to fill the vacancy
but found no one suitable. The reality was that some rural areas and villages
were unsuitable for educated priests; they needed someone who could relate to
them (and live with them). "This is a good occasion," Shenouda concludes,

> my beloved teacher, to discuss this matter together because this could hap-
> pen *again* at any time. . . . Blessed father, you know how much I love the
> Theological College and my faith in it. You know that I stayed in the monas-
> tery for five months for its sake, and I came back also for its sake, and for its
> sake—with the grace of God—I am ready to do whatever I can. . . . Thus, I
> hope all my words in this letter are taken within this context . . . ordinations
> such as that of Zakareya are an *abnormal situation*. . . . Please forgive me; I
> wish that my love to you and to the Theological College would melt any error
> that you might find in me, be safe in the Lord. . . .[106]

The conflict gave birth to contention and, therefore, a principle of reform—
namely, an ideal may at times require economy. Pakhoum's reply a few days
later, on March 26, likewise makes clear his only concern was to discern the
principle.[107] "Permit it, temporarily," wrote Pakhoum, "to let me forget that I am
talking to you as a bishop, for here, I wish to talk to you as a dear friend." "Do I
err, Bishop Shenouda," questions Pakhoum,

if I say that you have forgotten yourself and your principles. . . . What has happened, Bishop Shenouda? . . . Zakareya might be very appropriate for that ordination, he might even be a saint, he might be better than all the priests on earth in the present, past, and future, I don't know, he might be the best person on earth, I don't judge, he might be suitable not only to be a priest but a bishop, a patriarch. . . . I am not talking about this, but I am talking about the *status* of Bishop Shenouda as the director and bishop at the Theological College. . . .[108]

Pakhoum repeats that his primary concern is that it was done at the hands of Shenouda.[109] These were only early days in the story of reform; it was not yet the time of flexibility and economy. "We are still at the stage of establishing the rule," Pakhoum continued. It was not the time for exceptions—most certainly not at the hands of the one "responsible for establishing the rule." Without firmness and an unwavering stance in this early stage, Pakhoum cautions, Shenouda would have no grounds to oppose other metropolitans or bishops who still feared theologically trained clergy. "Let us cooperate together," concludes Pakhoum, "in the narrow, hard path, full of rocks and dust; we have a long journey ahead, a heavy mission upon our shoulders. Forgive and absolve me for the pain which I have caused you, because of my situation, and the harshness of my letter."[110]

Fittingly, Pakhoum makes clear that they were both heavily burdened with reforming the Church. It is within this context—and it cannot be reiterated sufficiently—that the contentions of Kyrillos' disciples must be understood; here, at the heated coalface of reform.

* * *

A few months later, on May 9, 1967, once things had settled, Pakhoum received word that the patriarch wished to speak with him. The detailed account of that little-known conversation is preserved in Pakhoum's memoirs. "I entered [the office of] His Holiness the Pope," recalls Pakhoum. Then:

. . . he closed the door, and it was only the two of us. The pope said, "We called you to be a bishop for Dairut and you refused, a bishop for Manfalout and you refused, a bishop for Menoufia and you refused, and yet we were not angry." I said, "Your Holiness, I did not refuse, but I apologized. . . ." The pope was relieved and smiled . . . [saying,] "You apologized, as you have said, to stay at the Theological College? . . . then you will stay at the Theological

College, and we will ordain you a Bishop for the Coptic Studies Institute." I panicked: "What? Your Holiness? Does the Coptic Studies Institute need a bishop? It is *under the authority of Bishop Shenouda*."[111]

Despite the intense debate, as well as the pleading of Professor Aziz Attia (the founder of the Coptic Studies Institute), Bishop Athanasius of Beni Suef, and Bishop Samuel, Pakhoum could not be persuaded. Kyrillos felt the matter could go no further. While leaving to his private quarters, he turned and said, "Will you come this evening?"

"Of course," replied Pakhoum. "I must come, it is the celebration of your ordination as patriarch." "I did not pay any attention," he later recalled.[112] Nor did he have any reason to. A few years earlier, when Kyrillos had tried to ordain Pakhoum for the diocese of Dairut, fearing the same fate as Shenouda, Pakhoum went into hiding for four months until Kyrillos reassured him, "Would I ordain you *against your will*? I only did that for Bishop Shenouda . . . thank God that I did not ordain you, if I had done so, you would have given me a tough time!"[113]

"I entered late into the church," recalls Pakhoum of the anniversary celebration that evening,

> the prayers were at the end . . . the pope came out of the Sanctuary heading towards me, but I still did not understand, and I thought the pope would ask me to preach the Vespers homily or a word for the celebration. He came to me smiling, held me with his left hand, and held my other hand with his right hand and pulled me into the sanctuary. Then, and only then, I became alarmed. . . . The pope did not give me a chance to think, and while I was going backward trying to escape and leave the church, and while trying in vain to let go of his grasp, politely as much as I could, objecting and saying words which I cannot remember . . . "Not like this," "This is not appropriate," "Why," . . . But the pope did not give an ear to my pleas; his left hand was still strongly grasping my hand. . . . Then he strongly held my forehead with his right hand while saying, "Gregorious, *Bishop of the Coptic Studies Institute*. . . ." I was in incredible shock, and I didn't know what to do . . . should I leave the church . . . I kept praying inaudibly, my heart was heavy, I was perplexed, and some priests told me that my face went pale. . . .[114]

Several bishops came near to congratulate him. Bishop Gregorious—as he would soon be known—could only reply, "If there is a must for this ordination, *do not* let it be for the Coptic Studies Institute." As much as he did not want to be ordained a bishop, he had well discerned the problem of his "diocese." And his concern was not misplaced. By morning, his fears had proved true. A number of those around Bishop Shenouda arrived to "talk." Suggestions were made that Pakhoum should escape from the patriarchate before the consecration. The phone rang relentlessly. And by 12:00 a.m., Shenouda sent a telegram to Kyrillos: "The ordination of two bishops for the same diocese contradicts the Church canons; *God exists!*"[115]

Whenever this episode has been reported in the past—albeit very rarely—it is invariably narrated negatively. The actual letters and correspondence show otherwise. Again, we must carefully note that it was the *principle* that was of utmost concern.

Gregorious thankfully preserved his phone call to Shenouda immediately after the telegram:

> "The Church canons," Shenouda began, "forbid ordaining two bishops for the same diocese. . . . You know, personally, I don't mind leaving everything for you, actually, I was leaving everything for you, but I am talking about the canonical situation. . . ." I replied, "Bishop Shenouda, be totally assured that I could never take over your speciality. I was forced to that ordination; this matter never came to my mind . . . I tried to escape the church . . . but now, he has ordained me and uttered the ecclesial Apostolic blessing. . . . I spoke much to the pope about it and informed him that this is an impossible situation and that the *Coptic Studies Institute* is the competence of Bishop Shenouda. The pope agreed to change the 'uttering' to *Higher Studies and Coptic Culture* . . . be assured; I cannot accept intruding on your specializations . . . I am not saying this out of courtesy to you, but for the sake of my eternity."[116]

"I did not sleep for one minute that night," recalls Gregorious.[117] The next day Kyrillos accepted his suggestion. Gregorious would be ordained that day, May 10, 1967, as "General Bishop for Higher Studies, Coptic Culture, and Scientific Research."[118] Gregorious had also asked that Shenouda attend the ordination, but he never arrived. Instead, two days later, Shenouda wrote a letter of congratulations:

> I am ready—in an official or friendly status—to give up everything to Your Grace, and I will be in total happiness, satisfaction, and conviction before God, myself, and people, feeling that you are better than I in everything. . . .
> It is not a matter of specializations between you and me; our long deep love

is higher than that, all that is mine is also yours, ignoring the officialities and formalities. You are a part of me, and I am a part of you, we are one, before our conscience, before God and before people. But what about the canonical situation of the case? . . . I am ready to officially, in writing, give up to you any specific specialization that will be written in your rite . . . I can give up Sunday School, and your name will be the Bishop of Sunday School Services, I can give up the Coptic Studies Institute or the Theological College if you wish. . . . I am ready for any other solution that Your Grace may suggest; I am even ready to sacrifice myself for you to make your status comfortable.[119]

Shenouda was concerned with the principle. He was happy to give up his own "specializations" for its sake.[120] And though he did not attend the ordination—which, as we shall see, had more to do with brewing issues with the patriarchate—he attended and gave the speech at the ceremony of the "bestowing of the rite" to Bishop Gregorious on May 18.[121] The eloquent speech was replete with genuine love, admiration, and esteem. Shenouda refused, however, to shy away from discussing the matter of their overlapping diocese:

Some of you might have asked an important and dangerous question: what are the specializations of Bishop Gregorious and what are the specializations of Bishop Shenouda? . . . Everything which is his speciality is of my speciality, and everything which is of my speciality is his speciality . . . I am not even exaggerating if I say that I *personally* belong to the specialities of Bishop Gregorious.[122]

Once more, there was more than meets the eye when it came to Shenouda and Gregorious. The above account is not only a historical and fascinating corrective—more importantly, it allows us to see that superficial mentions of a "furious telegram" and a heated personal conflict distort in some sense the reality and significance of their contention. Though their relationship would be tested again and again over the following decades, with no doubt increasing animosity, their correspondence (at least at this early point) reveals that they were both struggling to discern truth in treading the path of reform.[123] Kyrillos was all the while watching, guiding, and praying. He could see the potential of personal conflict, but for him, the invaluable gifts that each one of these disciples would impart to the Church were far more important. Just as remarkable, all three of Kyrillos' "general bishops"—his delegates and agents of reform—were literally *forced* to become bishops in identical circumstances.[124]

* * *

The year, however, was not yet spent. Perhaps most painful and difficult—other than the Six-Day War a few months earlier—were the events of October 1967. At its center was one of Kyrillos' most illustrious disciples, Bishop Shenouda (1923–2012).

Shenouda began life as Nazir Gayed on August 3, 1923, in the humble agricultural town of Abnub, Upper Egypt.[125] "It may have been," he later reminisced, "that my childhood years were short."[126] This was on two counts. Shortly after giving birth, his mother died, leaving him with five sisters and two brothers, one of whom, Raphael, would raise him. The family moved throughout Egypt, before eventually settling in Shoubra, Cairo.[127] The second was that Nazir was exceptionally gifted and, having far surpassed his peers, gave himself at an early stage to academic pursuits. At the age of sixteen, he entered the Sunday School Movement at St Antony's in Shoubra, quickly becoming a teacher, and later its leader.[128] In 1947 he received the degree of bachelor of arts, majoring in English and history, from Cairo University. While in his final year, he was permitted to enroll at the postgraduate Theological College—an exception made by the dean, Habib Girgis. By day he worked as a high school teacher, studied towards a diploma in archaeology and classics, and even served as an infantry officer in the 1948 Palestinian war, while in the evening he completed a bachelor of divinity degree.[129] On graduating in 1949, Nazir was appointed a lecturer in biblical studies, and in the same year he founded the Sunday School magazine and became its editor-in-chief. After resigning from secular employment and taking up a full-time lecturing position at the Theological College, he lived from 1950 to 1951 with Kyrillos (then Fr Mina) at St Menas' in Old Cairo.[130] Once more, the dual formation under Habib Girgis and Fr Mina is readily, and intriguingly, apparent.

On July 18, 1954, under Fr Mina's direction, he was tonsured Monk Antonious at the Syrian Monastery. There he was tasked with the care of the library, before eventually inhabiting a cave three kilometers (1.9 miles) from the monastery and coming under the discipleship of Fr Matta el-Meskeen.[131] In mid–1956, Fr Matta would leave the monastery after a deep-set contention with the abbot, and he was followed by Antonious (and some twenty others).[132] "All that I wish," wrote Antonious shortly after, ". . . is that people might forget all about it, and about us, so that we can live in the calmness that we aimed at by that action."[133] The monks returned to their original confessor in Old Cairo, Fr

Mina, who directed them to St Samuel's Monastery.[134] Antonious would stay there less than a year.

Though the exact circumstances remain unknown, his letters—in which he alludes to that difficult year with tears—suggest severe misgivings and a distressing dispute with Fr Matta.[135] Little known to most—despite their publicized conflicts a few decades later—Antonious would, from these early years, take issue with many of Matta's writings.[136] But at the same time, Matta's creative influence on Antonious cannot be denied. Their conversations in the desert may have formed the foundations of Antonious' mesmerizing work, *The Release of the Spirit*, in which he calls Matta, "my father-monk."[137] In May 1957, Antonious left Fr Matta and returned to the Syrian Monastery. Soon after, Matta effectively disappeared into the desert for a decade, ensuring that his conflict with Antonious would largely be suspended and, therefore, postdate the life of Kyrillos.[138]

Shortly after becoming patriarch, in early 1959, Kyrillos appointed Antonious as his personal secretary.[139] "I stayed for only three months," Antonious later recalled, "but then I escaped again to my cave in the mountain . . . I felt I was doing nothing, so I left."[140] In that time a Western journalist observed that Antonious "never left his room except to perform his duties."[141] But he did not escape for long (as we have seen) and was ordained by force as Bishop Shenouda on September 30, 1962. Empowered by Kyrillos, he fulfilled the vision of Habib Girgis and transformed all facets of education—"from kindergarten Sunday School classes to graduate-level seminary education."[142] Under Shenouda, women were encouraged to study theology for the first time, the "day" students at the Theological College tripled and the "evening" students increased ten-fold.[143] Each Coptic child, lay leader, priest, bishop, and even patriarch, from here on, would be fed from the spirit of reform. The effects of Shenouda's episcopacy are immeasurable. The synergistic revival of theological education and Sunday schools, in the words of an English scholar, "create[d] what amounts to a cultural and intellectual renaissance among the Copts."[144]

* * *

"Among Arabic speakers," writes John H. Watson, "Shenouda became known for his captivating use of language . . . he is something of a demagogue, in the better, classical sense. He is a dangerous mover of crowds. . . ."[145] Unsurprisingly, then, most scholars, if not all, have traced the events of October 1967 to Shenouda's weekly lectures.

Attended by thousands, these incredible Friday evening lectures were She-nouda's conduit of reform. They were marked by an unpretentious spirit of humor, at once uncompromising and charismatic, scholarly yet delivered in the language of the people. Mohamed Heikal (1923–2016), the editor in chief of *al-Ahram* and Nasser's trusted Minister of Information, claimed these "lessons of Friday" were intentionally provocative as an answer to Hassan Banna's "lessons of Tuesday" for the Muslim Brotherhood.[146] "The activist tenor," another scholar suggests, "of Shenouda's lessons hinted at a criticism of the regime."[147] It was this "aggressive" and "apparent politicisation of the Sunday School Movement" that, many suggest, began to "alarm" Kyrillos and provoked the dramatic suspension of Shenouda.[148] These comments, and the greater part of scholarship in their wake, have not only dramatically overstated the political differences of Kyrillos and Shenouda, but they have also unfairly and inaccurately politicized the conflict. The reality—pieced together by an analysis of the historical correspondence and interviews—is entirely otherwise. For the last half-century, the entire episode has been misdated, misinterpreted, and misrepresented. The title "lesson of Friday," in the first place, was not even Shenouda's—it was an invention of Heikal's.[149] The lectures were, in fact, of a spiritual, practical, and ascetical nature.[150] The contention, intriguingly, was in fact precipitated by a matter of reform two years earlier, in 1965.

After the death of Metropolitan Kyrillos of Qena, in August 1965, discussions were held as to his successor. Shenouda wrote publicly in *al-Keraza*, "It is the congregation's *right to choose* their shepherd."[151] The issue was not Kyrillos' suggested candidate (who was very much worthy and considered by many to be a saint); it was the principle. "It is a beautiful chance," carefully wrote Shenouda,

> . . . for His Holiness the Pope to win the entire congregation . . . by ordaining for them the person whom they choose. It is very easy to let people submit to our authority and then lose them, but it is better and acceptable to God, to win their love, and the good shepherd gives his life for the sheep.[152]

It had been Shenouda's mantra ever since, as a young university student, he had opposed Yusab's controversial ordination of Youannis of Giza.[153] But, now, it was a public challenge to Kyrillos.[154] Though seemingly mild, Shenouda, in an interview a few decades later, as well as in correspondence from the period, suggests that it was one of their most important points of disagreement.[155] It was, again, the principle that was of concern. Similarly, in the mid-1960s, Shenouda

spent five months protesting in a self-imposed exile—possibly suspension—
after Kyrillos ordained a non–Theological College candidate to the priesthood
(though Shenouda, as we have seen, later did the same in 1967).[156] Shenouda's
relationship with Kyrillos was strained further in May 1967, when Gregorious
was ordained for an overlapping "diocese" (more accurately a portfolio) too
close to home; and yet again when Bishop Samuel was delegated to head a committee on "evangelism education," a task that Shenouda considered to belong to
his "diocese."[157] The following events were simply the last straw.

On July 27, Fr Girgis Asham, the manager of the patriarchate, wrote to
Bishop Shenouda. "We would like to inform you," the letter began, "that the
patriarchate is overloaded with expenses for the Theological College, at a time
when its financial resources have decreased dramatically because of agricultural
pests that have destroyed the crops, resulting in a great deficit in rent."[158] Consequently, the letter continued, tuition fees were to be increased, students would
no longer be allowed to board, and meals would no longer be provided.[159] Similar letters, that same day, were also sent to the closely related Didymus Institute
as well as the Higher Institute of Education, both under Bishop Gregorious.[160] It
was nothing less than a financial decapitation. But the hands of the patriarchate,
though Shenouda could not see it, really were tied.[161]

Earlier that year the *maglis*—which had been managing the finances of the
patriarchate until April—had run into a severe financial deficit precipitated
by the disastrous cotton crops that diminished the *waqf* endowment income.
Simultaneously, an economic downturn, compounded by the severe losses of
the Six-Day War, brought about the financial crisis that (as we have seen) would
force Kyrillos to seek Nasser's hand in dismantling the *maglis*, with the financial
management of the patriarchate and theological institutes transferred to the
patriarchate.[162] This is vital to appreciate. Scholarship has not, to any degree,
properly situated Shenouda's suspension within this context.

At the same time, Shenouda had become exceedingly popular. His weekly
lectures began in a small lecture theater, before rapidly filling St Mark's hall, then
a small corner of the cathedral, until eventually, people were overflowing from
every entryway and passage.[163] The incredible growth did not go unnoticed.
"The world rose against me," reminisced Shenouda in an interview, "evil advisers began to provoke the Pope against me, as if I, as bishop, were taking over
the entire Church."[164] At one point, Shenouda began speaking at several confer-
ences in various dioceses in succession with each bishop following him to the
next conference, until eventually, a group of bishops began traveling to hear his

lectures. "They began to say to the Pope," Shenouda continued, "that I was polarizing the bishops . . . and the whole world began to turn upside down. . . ."[165] Rumors began circulating.

One Friday morning Shenouda was summoned to the police station. An engineer produced a letter detailing that the roof of the Theological College was unsafe and could at any moment collapse. Shenouda knew there was little he could do; Kyrillos could not be reached by phone. The lecture was moved at the last moment to the courtyard. Then the electricity was disconnected; Shenouda ordered kerosene lights. Then the water was disconnected. "In the end," he lamented, "I found the situation untenable, and so I wrote an article in *al-Keraza*. . . ."[166] Shenouda had thus far remained silent. But the constant "random" obstructions and financial withdrawal had left him no choice. "We have been silent for a long time," he wrote in *al-Keraza*, October 1967,

> trying to reach a solution through negotiations so that we might not disturb the congregation with upsetting news. . . . Then the new school year scheduled to begin on September 26 was at hand . . . the budget is on halt, the debts have accumulated to a shameful extent, there is no water supply in the building, electricity will soon be cut off, there are decisions to cancel the boarding department and forbidding students from sleeping over, forbidding meals, in addition to the fact of insufficient teachers and ancillary staff. . . . It is an indirect closure of the College, as we know quite well the students' capabilities. . . .[167]

Shenouda then proceeded to reproduce in full the July letters written to him by Fr Girgis, as well as his response to each one; he detailed the water, electricity, telephone, and food invoices that went unpaid; he lamented over the aforementioned closure of the lecture theater but refrained from "disclosing details;" and, finally, he expressed his dismay and embarrassment that theological education was deemed to be worth so little.[168] It was a very public and traumatic airing of his conflict with the patriarchate, and therefore with Kyrillos himself. "After a long silence, my brethren," concluded Shenouda at the end of the article,

> I was forced, painfully, to speak frankly; to find a solution for the fate of your Theological College. . . . As for you, my brethren the students . . . if I am the reason for this great storm, I am ready to withdraw until things calm down. I am ready to go back to the monastery, to my beloved cave in the mountain, to spend the rest of the days of my sojourn, to live in peace and let others have rest, "sufficient for the day is its own trouble."[169]

As a final protest, Shenouda closed the Theological College and withdrew to his monastery.[170] The students revolted at the patriarchate.[171] Kyrillos swiftly dispatched a telegram to Shenouda on October 8: "Your stubbornness, traveling, and insistence on not sending letters to the students requesting their return to the college judges you; you have no absolution to return to Cairo except through our permission."[172] This suggests that it was Shenouda who *first* left to the monastery, and, in consequence of his closing the Theological College, Kyrillos refused to allow his return. The rationale for the suspension was therefore multifaceted; it was a reaction to a constellation of factors, most of which had to do with the matter of reform.

Shenouda sent a telegram a few weeks later requesting a trial before the Holy Synod.[173] It was, as far as one can tell, ignored. "What happened was expected," wrote Shenouda to a dear friend on November 15, 1967,

> . . . thus I wasn't surprised, but rather anticipated it, it is a struggle which whoever defends the truth should face. . . . But I am sure that the Lord will work . . . I am not ready at any time to live in peace and ignore defending the truth; or to gain more privileges and special services and stop announcing the word of God. . . . I am trying now to make use—as much as possible—of my solitude, feeling that it is a blessing from the Lord to have some retreat to do something for the glory of his name.[174]

Shenouda would be suspended for eight and a half months. After "numerous negotiations to resolve the problem," Kyrillos permitted him to return to Cairo for the opening of the new cathedral on June 25, 1968.[175] There he was greeted with Kyrillos' characteristic wide smile. "[The] contention," Shenouda commented, "was not about the person, but about the *principle* . . . it never contradicted the sentiments of love."[176] Once more, the concern was the "way" of reform. "So," Shenouda concludes, "a period of disagreement was passed, but the old love had its effect: I used to sit with Pope Kyrillos to talk and laugh in the same manner as old, but"—now laughing—"we used to disagree if we entered into a discussion of the Church canons."[177] The disciples of both Kyrillos and Shenouda make clear that the animosity ended there and then, with the two returning to their friendship of old.[178]

* * *

As to Kyrillos' purposes in the whole affair, it is difficult to say with any certainty. But there is a certain though faint glimmer that hauntingly dances throughout the letters, interviews, and articles of the period. Almost as though—impossible as it is to verify or even imagine—the entire episode was intentional, conscious, even calculated. One can only suspect ever so vaguely that Kyrillos was still "forming" his earlier disciple—forming him, that is, for the years to come.

The Leaven of Monastic Revival: Matta el-Meskeen, 1969

> "Abba Poemen also said about Abba Isidore that wherever
> he addressed the brothers in church he said only one thing,
> 'Forgive your brother, so that you *also* may be forgiven.'"
>
> —*Abba Isidore*

T HE FOURTH DISCIPLE was decidedly the least obedient. He was never to become a bishop. And yet, at the hands of Kyrillos, as a most unusual fruit of *disobedience*, that same disciple would share in an improbable and unrivaled monastic revival.

* * *

The last we saw of that young man, a pharmacist by the name of Youssef Iskander (1919–2006), he had sold his business, properties, and vehicles, to come under the discipleship of Fr Mina (the future Pope Kyrillos) at St Menas' in Old Cairo.[179] The young man had begged Fr Mina, in mid-1948, to be tonsured at the monastery and not in Old Cairo. Eventually, Fr Mina conceded. And so, on August 10, he was tonsured Monk Matta el-Samuely at St Samuel's Monastery, where Fr Mina was a "remote" abbot.[180] When Fr Mina called Matta to return a few months later, the latter refused. "We found," wrote Monk Makary (the future Bishop Samuel) to Matta on December 14, 1948, after arriving in Cairo,

> our father Hegumen Mina waiting for us for a long time. As soon as we entered, he asked us about you, so I gave him your letter. . . . He was so upset and in pain because you did not come. Fr Mina asked me to write this letter especially for you, to inform you that he is upset as you did not respond to his request; he told me, "Write that obedience is more important than sacrifice." I asked his reverence to write to you, but it looks as though he is quite upset. . . .[181]

Matta admitted the same disobedience in his autobiography.[182] A year later Fr Mina requested that Makary and Matta both return to Old Cairo to "finish their education."[183] Mina knew, only too well, that their monastic formation would (at that time in history) be paradoxically hindered by their stay in a monastery. It seems, even in these early days, he had a program of reform. But Matta evidently disobeyed once more. Still, Fr Mina saw something in his headstrong disciple.

In March 1951, Matta developed an eye infection and was forced to leave the harsh conditions of the desert.[184] Once more, by Matta's own admission, it was Fr Mina who reconciled with him, and sent him to the Syrian Monastery in Wadi al-Natrun to join Mina's other disciples—the growing number of "Sunday School monks."[185] There, on March 19, Matta was ordained a priest by the name with which he would become internationally renowned: Fr Matta el-Meskeen (Matthew the Poor).

Soon he would grow restless. "I could not," writes Matta in his autobiography,

> bear the life of the community at the Syrian Monastery because it was an artificial life impossible for the man who wanted the freedom to worship in spirit and truth. . . . I left the monastery and dug a cave with my hands. . . . I saw to my own provisions never going to the monastery except for the Eucharist approximately every two months.[186]

Deep in the desert, the years would be spent in contemplation, vigilance, and severe asceticism. There he would meet Fr Abdel Messih el-Habashy (the Ethiopian hermit and saint); there, Fr Antonious (the future Bishop Shenouda) would come under his discipleship; and there, many of the Sunday School monks would take him as a confessor.[187] In March 1954, he was called by the patriarch of the time, Yusab II, to become the vicar of Alexandria, but after bitter dissension with the *maglis*, he disappeared a year later to his cave.[188] Soon after, in July 1956, he would, unfortunately, also contend with Theophilus, the bishop of the monastery.[189] Having no other recourse, he left the desert and returned to Fr Mina in Old Cairo. "After two hours," Matta continues,

> the door opened, and I found twenty-one monks [including Fr Antonious] of my children coming to me, which greatly annoyed me. I tried to make them go back to the monastery where they had been tonsured, telling them I wanted to live alone. . . . My persuasions were useless in front of the monks' enthusiasm . . . who said that they would live and die with me.[190]

From there the group of "Sunday School monks" traveled, with Fr Mina's blessing, to the Monastery of St Samuel. Shortly afterward, Fr Mina would be consecrated patriarch.

* * *

Three years after their arrival, the monks received an urgent message from the patriarchate. "We were surprised," recalled Fr Matta in his autobiography,

> by a telegram sent to the person responsible for the Anba Samuel Monastery requiring our immediate departure from there. All of us left immediately on January 27, 1960; leaving everything behind us as if we were to become monks all over again. It was a new exodus. I met the patriarch [Kyrillos VI] respectfully asking him the reason for such a procedure. He answered that it was for us to live in the Monastery of el-Syrian. . . .[191]

No further explanation was given by the newly consecrated patriarch. It was very much, as one historian comments, for "reasons unknown."[192] This and the events that follow have, for the last half-century, been shrouded in mystery and, consequently, have become murky water in scholarship, with many assumptions and mischaracterizations. But buried within a dusty, forgotten, and decaying collection of documents in a monastery of the Western Desert, I discovered a letter—unknown until now—that may explain Kyrillos' actions.[193] The letter was written by the abbot of the Monastery of St Samuel only months before the abovementioned telegram.

Less than three months after his consecration, in August 1959, Kyrillos had sent two monks, Fr Abdulsayed anba-Paula and Fr Youannis el-Syriany, to the Monastery of St Samuel, where Matta was then residing with his monks. Each carried a letter of recommendation from Kyrillos. But on their arrival, a feud erupted. Fr Mina el-Samuely (the new abbot of the monastery) wrote anxiously to Kyrillos on August 18, 1959:

> As soon as [the two monks] arrived at the Monastery, all the "*university-graduate monks*" met them at the monastery's gate and refused to accept them. After reading the recommendation letter, they informed them that they must go back in the same convoy; and actually, that was what had happened, they carried out their aim and let the fathers go back in the same convoy.[194]

The abbot was beside himself. "Then," he continued,

I headed to the monastery concerning this issue on Wednesday evening . . . to discuss with them their attitude toward the two fathers. But I found that they had agreed that Monk Sidarous [who was also recently sent by Kyrillos] should *also* leave the Monastery like the other two fathers. I discussed it for a long time with the "university-graduate monks," *headed by* Hegumen Matta el-Meskeen, concerning their attitude. . . . I asked them what the two fathers had done, and why they had sent them back? They answered, "The fathers have done nothing at all, but we have all decided—our university-graduate group—not to accept any monk from any other monastery because it does not cohere with our ideas and work and, so that we may live in a calm environment." I tried to convince them by any means, but they totally refused to let him stay with them in the monastery.[195]

Fearing a "revolution," the abbot took Monk Sidarous with him. "I do not accept this situation," concluded the abbot in his letter to Kyrillos, "and cannot live in the midst of it!"[196]

St Samuel's was, we should recall, made up of generally illiterate and rural monks. Whereas the "university-graduate monks," as they called themselves, were originally disciples of Kyrillos from his days in Old Cairo: the same group of disciples that he had sent to the Syrian Monastery, and the same group who had followed Matta to St Samuel's.[197] "Headed" now by Fr Matta, they felt the divide between them and the noneducated monks to be a source of friction. No longer would they accept any other monks to join them, and, in defiance of Kyrillos' letters and instructions, they even evicted the poor Monk Sidarous.

This fascinating letter is revealing on two counts. It indicates once more Fr Matta's somewhat dependable disobedience, but more importantly, it also suggests the (almost) commendable reason for his disobedience: these "university-graduate monks" had already clashed with the old noneducated monks and so now sought separation. Was this, then, Kyrillos' rationale for his telegram instructing Matta and the "university-graduate monks" to return to the Syrian Monastery? Did he hope there would be less conflict among the relatively higher educated monks? Or was it simply to deal, once and for all, with Matta's near perpetual disobedience? I suspect it had more to do with the former. Especially since—as we shall see—Kyrillos would eventually confide in a dear friend that he hoped these "university" monks would be the "leaven" by which the monasteries in Egypt would one day rise.[198]

* * *

In any event, the monks returned as requested to the Syrian Monastery on January 28, 1960. But they did not feel welcome. And so, only seventy days later, on April 9, Matta and his monks departed for a "consecrated house [*bet al-takrees*]" that Matta had established a few years earlier in Helwan, just south of Cairo.[199] Living there was apparently Kyrillos' own idea; he had hoped to shortly send them out throughout the monasteries, given that they were unwilling to live at the Syrian Monastery.[200]

But by mid-August, Kyrillos decided otherwise and issued a decree throughout Egypt commanding *all* monks to return to their original monasteries by September 30, with the threat of "defrocking" for disobedience.[201] It is somewhat unclear whether that decree was directed at Fr Matta's monks specifically.[202] At that time, some one hundred fifty out of three hundred monks were "outside" their monasteries and serving in parishes.[203] These "cheaper monk-priests" effectively obstructed the ordination of much-needed (though more expensive) theologically trained married priests—not to mention that monasteries could hardly be reformed when the monks were not even there.[204] And so when, for instance, Fr Salib Suryal questioned Kyrillos as to whether this decree excluded Fr Matta, he was told, unequivocally, it applied to "all."[205] Evidently, Kyrillos had larger concerns than Matta. But that does not mean Kyrillos had not expected a reaction from Matta.

At 2:00 a.m. on August 11, Fr Matta recalls in his autobiography—simultaneous with the decree—Kyrillos sent Bishop Benjamin of Menoufia and Bishop Mina of Girga to Matta's monks with a "letter *threatening* excommunication" should they not leave Cairo within twenty-four hours.[206] A few hours later, Bishop Benjamin returned alone to Matta. He had not agreed with Kyrillos' letter.

"I am a bishop of the Church," declared Benjamin, "and know its canons. All of you have *absolution* and are blessed. Build an altar, pray and celebrate Liturgies. I am he who is responsible before God."[207] That same day Benjamin told Kyrillos what he had done. It was not received well.[208] Matta and a handful of monks—some had already left him—boarded two jeeps and disappeared to an uninhabited stretch of desert 150 kilometers (93 miles) southwest of Cairo, the mythic Wadi al-Rayan.[209]

There was silence and no reaction for two months. Then, on October 17, 1960, the anticipated excommunication was duly published in *al-Ahram*:

> In accordance, and to apply the decree of His Holiness the Pope of Alexandria and Patriarch of the See of St Mark, a declaration has been made by the

Bishop of al-Syrian Monastery that Fr Mina, Hegumen Matta el-Meskeen, and monks Stephanos, Kyrillos, Ashia, and Dionysius . . . who *did not comply* with the papal decree, although it was declared in the newspapers multiple times, are now barred from their clerical ranks, and monastic order; they are now laymen as they were before, and the Church no longer recognizes their monastic life.[210]

This declaration has been the cause of much confusion. Matta's disciples claim it was not a true excommunication but rather a "paid declaration" by Bishop Theophilus, the head of the Syrian Monastery.[211] Matta's own autobiography is curiously silent. Sources are divided as to what exactly it was, with some suggesting a mere declaration that was independent of Kyrillos; others, an "ambiguous suspension"; and others still, a formal excommunication. The latter is most likely. In the first, Matta's disciples append to his autobiography an account of Fr Salib Suryal's conversation with Kyrillos, which clearly states that it was an excommunication from the Synod; second, Kyrillos never corrected Bishop Theophilus' statement; third, Bishop Benjamin felt the need to absolve the monks; and finally, Fr Matta himself seems to have taken the "excommunication"—at least personally—in all seriousness. "Out of honesty and truth," recalls Fr Salib, "Matta never celebrated the Liturgy during the period of his excommunication."[212] When a famed German Coptologist, Otto Meinardus, visited him during these years, he likewise stated that Matta did not celebrate.[213] Though disobedient to the decree, Matta was, at least personally, obedient to the consequence.

Excommunicated or not, Wadi al-Rayan was hardly a place of respite. "It is an uninhabited valley," Matta wrote,

of seven kilometers wide and thirty kilometers long [4 miles by 19 miles]; with springs of salt water, but from which one can drink, and far distanced palm trees. We dug out for ourselves separate caves with approximately half a kilometer between each. Each of us lived a life of solitude and prayer. Through friends in Cairo every two months, God sent us food with camel caravans. A difficult life of nine whole years. To me, physically, it was the most difficult period of my life.[214]

The valley was entirely desolate and, like the monks, cut off from civilization. The desert was mostly parched and infertile, ensuring that malnutrition was an ever-present concern, and that "salty but drinkable water" would nearly poison them. Besides that, they were attacked by drug smugglers at least three times.[215] But they survived. The original six monks would eventually become ten by 1966, and then twenty-two by 1969.[216] There, the monks, despite brutal conditions, would emulate and recreate ancient monasticism.[217] It was a "monastic experiment" that, in the words of one scholar, has "taken on mythical proportions."[218]

Other than Matta's autobiography, the only glimpse we have of these precious years is Meinardus' interview with the monks.[219] In January 1966, he flew by a small plane and landed, to their shock, just meters away from one of the monk's caves. Meinardus noted that the hermits spent their time in contemplation, manual work, and scribing ancient texts: "The writings of Isaac of Nineveh served as a *spiritual guide* to Abouna Matta el-Meskeen. Subsequently, all of his disciples copied his writings."[220] That manuscript was in fact from the hand of Kyrillos—a gift to Fr Matta many decades prior. Once more the notion of "patristic discipleship" would repeat itself, with Isaac the Syrian becoming a "spiritual guide" for this unique "monastic experiment." These nine years, lived by handfuls of hermits, would never be forgotten by the Church and would impart something intangible to monastic reform.

When Meinardus asked upon his departure whether Matta hoped one day to visit Jerusalem, he responded:

> Jerusalem the holy is right here, in and around these caves, for what else is my cave, but the place where my Savior Christ was born, what else is my cave, but the place where my Savior Christ was taken to rest, what else is my cave, but the place from where he most gloriously rose again from the dead. Jerusalem is *here*, right *here*. . . .[221]

But though Fr Matta may have found the holy city in his desolate desert, there was still the matter of his excommunication.

* * *

Kyrillos had never forgotten Matta. "As for our children whom you mentioned," he wrote to Fr Salib Suryal on February 4, 1967,

> they . . . were the subject of our attention and care from the very beginning, we still care. . . . Many times we opened our hearts and extended our hands happily to them. . . . We do not have anything toward anyone except love in our hearts. . . . What we really care about is obedience. . . . The obedience that we asked them for, is the same obedience which they will ask from others because they are an *ideal* example for others. . . . Be sure, my son, that our door is open. . . .[222]

Over these nine years, Kyrillos had extended his hand more than once.[223] But Fr Matta was unwilling. On Easter Monday, April 14, 1969, a mutual friend—in fact, the one who introduced them decades prior—thought he would try one final time. Fr Salib Suryal, a disciple and distant relative of Kyrillos, and one of the first Sunday School priests, a man beyond reproach, had the ear of all. Earlier that day Kyrillos heard that Matta happened to be visiting Helwan, near Cairo, and swiftly sent a priest to persuade Matta to reconsider the Synod's request that he send his monks two by two to different monasteries. Hearing this, Salib sensed the door had opened once more. As Kyrillos' ten-year anniversary was only a few weeks away, Fr Salib approached the now-sixty-six-year-old patriarch.

Their conversation has been preserved by Salib in every detail—and, importantly, is attested to by Matta's own disciples.[224] Though lengthy, the account is vital in discerning the history of monastic revival in Egypt, and even more vital to understanding the very person of Kyrillos.

"All of them should go back to *one* monastery," Salib counselled Kyrillos, "there is no other option . . . they understand that what you are doing is *scattering* them." Kyrillos had insisted from the very beginning and had repeated for the previous nine years that he had a specific purpose for these monks. "No, my son," he replied in his deep voice, "before God, that was never the case, what I am saying is that they are a good *leaven*, and when each pair of them go to a monastery, they will be like the old wine when added to the new wine, it tastes far better." But Kyrillos also knew the monks had suffered deeply for these last years.

"It is time to solve this problem," gently repeated Salib. "You have solved the problem of Ethiopia and many other difficult problems; only this problem remains, standing there all the time."

Kyrillos stayed silent for some time. "So be it," conceded the aged patriarch. "Let them all go to *one* monastery . . . let them go to Muharraq Monastery."

Fr Salib bowed before him and said, "You are now a *father*."

"What was I before?" Kyrillos countered.

"You were a pope, a patriarch. . . ."

As Fr Salib traveled to Helwan the next day, he fell asleep. He awoke, in his account, to a voice repeating the words: "St Macarius' Monastery [*abu maqqar*] . . . St Macarius [*abu maqqar*]. . . ." Salib knew little of that monastery, nor had he ever visited—which was not surprising. It had only a few monks, was terribly poor, and was in a state of imminent collapse.

When he arrived, Salib immediately rebuked Fr Matta for dividing the Church. Through his prolific writing, Matta had since become internationally renowned, and his excommunication was hardly edifying. But, Salib added, he had some incredible news: Kyrillos had finally agreed for the monks to all go to *one* monastery. "Of course, I did not"—aware that he was changing Kyrillos' plans—"mention *Muharraq* Monastery at all." The Monastery of St *Macarius* was ideal, he told Matta, it was ripe for rebuilding; there were elderly monks that needed to be served; it was close to Cairo; and most importantly, its bishop, Mikhail of Asyut, lived almost five hundred kilometers (311 miles) away—for, he reminded Matta, "you are intolerable to management."[225]

In his autobiography Matta states that he initially refused to meet the patriarch and only agreed after "Fr Salib insisted, telling me [Kyrillos] was sick and in pain and had spent three sleepless nights with his conscience pricking him."[226] But there was a minor problem of which Matta was unaware. In an already tenuous and fragile negotiation, Salib had led Matta to believe that he was going to the Monastery of St Macarius, whereas Kyrillos only agreed to Muharraq. "O Lord, help me," Salib recalls of his later meeting with Kyrillos:

> I said to him, "It is better that they go to St Macarius." "What!?" Kyrillos thundered. I have never seen him so angry, and his face was fuming, he was about to slap me in the face! "Did I tell you St *Macarius'* Monastery? I told you *Muharraq* Monastery; you are taking your own decision, thinking you know everything, I am sending you with specific words, and you are saying your own?" I decided to keep quiet totally. . . . Then he had to take a phone call. . . .

Once Kyrillos calmed slightly, Salib reminded him that Fr Kozman—the abbot of Muharraq Monastery—had a "mighty personality," and that, knowing Fr Matta, such an assignment would inevitably end in more division. He then quietly told Kyrillos about hearing the voice on the train that whispered, "St Macarius."

"So, you had an inspiration?" Kyrillos said in disbelief.

"The inspiration comes not only to patriarchs," Salib replied, "it may occasionally come upon a worthless priest." But, by this stage, Kyrillos needed little convincing. On deeper consideration, he realized Muharraq would have caused him more pain.

Some days later, in the late evening, Matta, Salib, and Bishop Mikhail visited the patriarchate. Salib recalls:

I sat next to Fr Matta intentionally. The conversation at the beginning was very harsh. His Holiness said to Fr Matta, "You have grayed." [Matta] answered, "Because of you, Your Holiness." I kicked his leg, saying, "Be wise, don't start." His Holiness said, "No, I just want to tell you that you have had so many experiences during those days; they will benefit you for the rest of your life and will benefit the people who are going through hardships . . . you will never regret those days that were like a teacher for you."

In Fr Matta's autobiography, he is unusually brief: "Kyrillos apologized and asked me to forgive him and give him absolution for what had happened, and he also gave me absolution and forgiveness."[227] Matta immediately called and sent jeeps to collect his twenty-one monks deep from within the desert. Early in the morning, Friday, May 9, 1969, Kyrillos celebrated a Liturgy to "change the form" (a liturgical service whereby a monk is "changed" from one monastery to another) of Matta's monks. Salib recalls the historic event (and near hiccup):

I found monks coming. . . . [Kyrillos] finished with all of them until it was Fr Matta's turn. He said, "*Mettaous*, a monk . . ."—so Fr Matta, while lowering his head, interrupted, "Your Holiness, *Matta el-Meskeen*, please—Matta el-Meskeen, Your Holiness." Kyrillos continued, "Mettaous, a monk at the Monastery of . . ."—Matta interrupted again, "Please, Your Holiness, Matta el-Meskeen." So Kyrillos said, "Matta el-Meskeen, a monk at the Monastery of St Macarius."[228]

Matta remained headstrong as always, even with his insistence on a name. But regardless, Kyrillos saw something in him—something seemingly worthy of perpetual forgiveness.[229]

Late that evening, Salib was contacted by the patriarchate. Kyrillos wanted him urgently. "I panicked," he recalls, "thinking that something bad had happened."[230]

"Listen, my son," Kyrillos told Salib, "I haven't slept all night." Salib, thinking the worst, reassured him that it was a "historical deed" of reconciliation. "No, no," the patriarch corrected, "I mean, how could twenty-two monks live in such a debilitated monastery . . . so I thought to call for an urgent meeting of the *waqf* [endowments] committee to fix a monthly stipend for these monks. . . . This matter is bothering me, my son; I haven't slept all night." Salib could only smile.[231] Such was the heart of Kyrillos. It was not enough to forgive; his eyes could not rest until he knew those monks were also able to rest.

* * *

When Matta el-Meskeen arrived at the Monastery of St Macarius in Wadi al-Natrun, he found it, in his words, to be in a "deplorable state." Only four monks remained: one blind, and another bedridden. "Not one liveable cell existed," he recalls.[232] How things would change!

Less than a decade later, there were eighty monks, counting among their number surgeons, ophthalmologists, dentists, engineers, and professors in agricultural development. The ancient sites were restored, one hundred and fifty cells were constructed, and desert lands were reclaimed in an incredible agricultural feat.[233] "The administrative, agricultural, and institutional revolution at the Monastery of Saint Macarius was very great. The spiritual revolution was greater," writes one Western scholar.[234] So rapid, inconceivable, and profound were Matta's spiritual and agricultural endeavors that Kyrillos reportedly nicknamed him: "Matta el-*Maskoon* [the possessed]."[235]

For Kyrillos—despite Matta's characteristic disobedience—these extraordinary monks were the "leaven" by which monastic life would once more rise. Matta disagreed and thought it best to create an insular, isolated, and wholly separate community that would remain free from external influence. In the end, both of their visions would meet in a synergy of methods—that is, the *dissemination* of Kyrillos, and the *concentration* of Matta—with many of Matta's earlier monks dispersing to other monasteries and bringing about an unprecedented revival. And though in later years few of Matta's monks would leave their desert sanctuary, Matta's prolific writings most certainly did.[236] The spiritual concentration would, therefore, be disseminated with almost limitless reach. For instance, Matta's seminal work, *Orthodox Prayer Life*, an immersive commentary on an anthology of patristic sayings concerning prayer, almost single-handedly attracted hundreds (if not thousands) to the monastic life.[237] A deeply experiential work, developed over decades of ascetical struggle, it transformed the monastic landscape. "It was a seed," Watson comments, "planted in the wasteland of the Wadi al-Rayan in the fifties but in our time it has become a forest—an ecumenical forest."[238] And that it was, except that the seed was planted long before the years of Wadi al-Rayan.

Matta, in fact, had in hand two manuscripts in 1948, both of which would lead to that magisterial work. The first was the abovementioned anthology of sayings on prayer; the second was Kyrillos' (then Fr Mina's) own handwritten manuscript of Isaac the Syrian's *Ascetical Homilies*.[239] In the monastic experiment of the '60s at Wadi al-Rayan, Matta himself noted that Isaac was a "spiritual guide" for the community. Just as fascinating is the observation that Kyrillos, along with Bishop Shenouda and Fr Matta el-Meskeen (two of his most illustrious disciples), were all *hermits* taken by force out of their solitude to share in one of the greatest ecclesial reforms in history. Both Shenouda and Matta were formed by Kyrillos, following his own experience, under a "patristic discipleship" to Isaac the Syrian, who lived some thirteen hundred years earlier. All three had been enraptured by solitude. And all three would, reluctantly, take that solitude *into* the world. From then on, the desert monasteries would be delicately "woven into the fabric of the parish churches of the cities, towns and villages."[240] Ecclesial reform, once more, was secondary to *personal* ascetic reform through the vital sphere of *ascetic influence*. One can only ask, therefore, how many of those ascetic threads bore the imprint of Isaac the Syrian?

Many scholars have placed this monastic revolution at the feet of Matta el-Meskeen, with a few others suggesting Bishop Theophilus, or even Fr Abdel Messih el-Habashy.[241] But it was Kyrillos who was, in fact, the father of this revolution (albeit with the help others); it was he who bore the inheritance of Isaac the Syrian from his own spiritual father, Masudi.[242] Arguably, then, though Matta had an undeniably vital role, Coptic monasticism was rebirthed in the spirit of Isaac, as lived through the heart and mind of Kyrillos VI.

Perhaps there is no more fitting witness of this monastic revival than that of an entry, less than a decade later, in the journals of Fr Alexander Schmemann (1921–1983), dean of St Vladimir's Orthodox Theological Seminary. He never expected his words—raw, authentic, and unpretentious—to be read by anyone but himself. "Today I had an extraordinary day," Fr Alexander wrote on February 11, 1978, during his trip to Egypt:

> A visit in the desert to three monasteries with an uninterrupted tradition from Antony the Great, Makarios, etc. . . . And the most amazing, of course, is how *very much alive* it all is: *Real monks!* In my whole life, I have seen only imitations, only playing at monastic life, false, stylized; and mostly unrestrained idle talk about monasticism and spirituality. And here are they, in a real desert. A real, heroic feat. So many young monks. No advertisements, no brochures about spirituality. Nobody knows anything about them, and they do not mind it. I am simply stunned. I have a thousand questions, and I will have to gradually start sorting it all out. . . .[243]

Postscript on Reform: The Sphere of Ascetic Influence

> "One of the brothers asked me: 'Tell us what you have seen in vision?' . . .
> *When you see a man pure and humble that is vision enough!*
> What can be greater than such a vision: to see the invisible God
> in a visible man, the temple of God?"
>
> —St Pachomious

I T IS ONE OF THE curiosities in the life of Kyrillos that he had the extraordinary capacity not only to heal disease—he apparently worked an immense number of miracles, into the tens of thousands—but also to exorcise demons. This was well attested to and was witnessed by two of the most credible figures in the last half-century, Fr Matta el-Meskeen and Fr Salib Suryal, among many others. But equally remarkable was the manner of the exorcisms.

In his later years, Kyrillos became increasingly unwell. At one point he developed pneumonia and was unable to celebrate the Liturgy. As something of a consolation, he continued to celebrate Vespers each Saturday evening. One such evening celebration happened to coincide with the eve of the final school examinations, and so young men and women gathered at the cathedral to take the blessing of Kyrillos. He would often suggest a random page from a textbook that would invariably be found in their diverse examinations. On this particular evening, as the crowds were too large, and he was weak with pneumonia, Kyrillos sat in the sanctuary while young men went, one by one, to greet him. "Kyrillos was sitting awake for some thirty minutes greeting them," Fr Raphael Ava Mina recalls,

> but it dragged on, and he was overcome by sleep. . . . The people in the queue, undeterred, kept kneeling before him, kissing his hand, and if one had a pen or some notes, they would touch it to his hand and then leave. . . . It happened that one man came before him and suddenly threw himself on the ground. . . . [Kyrillos] was asleep, he did not pray or do anything, but nonetheless, the young man began hysterically screaming [he was apparently possessed]. . . . Kyrillos awoke and stood, looked at the young man, and lifted his cross. . . . The boy rose and kissed the cross. "What is wrong, my son?" Kyrillos asked. "It is over now; you are well."[244]

"This possessed young man," Raphael recalls in disbelief, "simply went before him, nothing else; [Kyrillos] was asleep. . . . *Even in his sleep*, from his body, he could exorcise demons!"[245] Healing proceeded from his person, not through any charm, prayer, or act; and so too, it would appear, reform proceeded from the holy patriarch. For what can be greater, Abba Pachomius noted in the fourth-century, than to behold one pure and humble, "the invisible God in a visible man"?[246] There was in Kyrillos an unmistakable gift—something that spoke more powerfully than words, something that healed and transformed hearts.

* * *

The earliest Christian idea of reform, as revealed in both the New Testament and patristic writings, was that of *personal ascetic reform*. But, as we have seen, the reach of that reform was always limited by the sphere of one's "ascetic influence," that is, the reach of one's capacity to *disciple*. This explains the peculiar failure of top-down legislated ecclesial reforms in the past two millennia, for hearts can never be transformed from above. Programs of reform, one scholar writes, may give an appearance of efficacy, and dynamic clergy may even bring people to the altar, but none of these produces lasting change when compared to even one "encounter with genuine holiness."[247] "Holiness," in the words of Bishop Meletios of Preveza, "will beget more holiness."[248]

It is for this reason that this account has been intensely personal and has sought to trace the *personal* ascesis of Kyrillos that was *imparted* to his disciples, and *through* them, to the entire Church. It is for this same reason that the accounts of these disciples are personal narratives of their discipleship, delegation, and contentions. For each—among many others—in his own way— would be transformed by that encounter with genuine holiness. And, in what Meinardus has called "one of the great events in world Christianity," each one would, with Kyrillos, reach far beyond his own personal ascetic influence.[249]

Their ordinations (or delegation in the case of Fr Matta) would be among the most pragmatic of Kyrillos' decisions and the essence of his reform.[250] It was an "episcopizing" of the different centers, and therefore visions, of the Sunday School Movement. "Each embodied a certain line and direction," comments Reiss, "*now* with episcopal authority."[251] In Bishop Samuel, the vision of Giza was "episcopized" as an outworking of social reform; in Shenouda, the spirituality, and asceticism of St Antony's in Shoubra was "episcopized" through educational reform; in Gregorious, the cultural orientation of the center of Geziret Bedran was "episcopized" in transforming the arts, higher research, and Coptic culture; and finally, in Matta el-Meskeen (though he remained a monk), these Sunday School centers would converge in an unprecedented monastic revival.[252] The different "competing visions" of the centers were "ordained."

And though they would certainly contend with one another, Kyrillos discerned that *each* of his disciples was vital for reform.[253] Ordaining and empowering his disciples over functional areas, rather than territorial dioceses, meant overlapping spheres of contention—contention that at times would be directed against Kyrillos himself. But it mattered little to him. Kyrillos had, after all, at his consecration made emphatically clear that his was a vocation of loss, that his only concern was to "disappear" that Christ might appear once more—a *kenotic ecclesiology*. It was the Church that was of concern, not himself.

* * *

Kyrillos' method of reform, as Nelly van Doorn-Harder aptly suggests, "even in the Coptic framework," was sublimely "unusual."[254] What began with Kyrillos and his young disciples in that small, quiet, and unassuming Church of St Menas in Old Cairo would, in the twelve years of his patriarchate, transform the Church. To deconstruct, or reverse-engineer his method of reform—as artificial as that may be—we must look to those disciples.

Bishop Samuel's role in the story of reform is often limited to his program of meeting the concrete needs of the inaccessible, and therefore disconnected, rural villages. But, as hinted previously, this is to miss the importance of those "rural *diakonia*" projects in *connecting* these villages (as well as the diaspora) to the Sunday School network. Rural Egypt, once languishing without parishes, clergy, or religious education, was now brought within reach of Sunday School servants (male and female) as well as priests, and, consequently, within the sphere of Kyrillos' "ascetic influence." Without these basic needs met, without a Sunday School system and parish life—the very transmission of discipleship—they would have remained well beyond his ascetic reach.

At the same time, without a like-minded hierarchy, ascetic reform would be perpetually obstructed. And the hierarchy could not be reformed until its "birthplace" was transformed—that is, the monasteries.[255] Kyrillos, as far as one can tell, took a twofold approach. It would be futile to create a monastic revival—and therefore able, holy monks—if their ordination as bishops was to be hindered by an uncooperative Synod. To find a way around this, and without waiting for a vacant diocese, Kyrillos ordained "general bishops" (Shenouda, Samuel, and Gregorious) who would be charged with functional areas rather than geographical territories. Within a few years, the Synod could ordain new "revived" monks for future dioceses, and it was here that Fr Matta el-Meskeen was indispensable.

Though Matta had contended with most (if not all) of his superiors over the years, Kyrillos saw something in his disciple. Had he not forgiven Matta in 1969 and relocated those monks to the Monastery of St Macarius, they would have languished excommunicated in Wadi al-Rayan. Kyrillos' radical reconciliation, an act of kenotic self-humbling, triggered that monastic experiment at St Macarius, and then permitted it to flourish.[256] It, therefore, becomes exceedingly difficult to separate Kyrillos' *kenotic ecclesiology* from his program—if we may speak of a program—of reform. Reform springs, again and again, from his self-emptying.

Taken together with Kyrillos' use of these monks as "leaven" throughout the monasteries, as well as his vision in tonsuring tens of his earlier disciples at the Syrian Monastery under Bishop Theophilus, the seeds were sown for a monastic transformation. The monasteries once more became the true training grounds for the episcopacy. But more importantly, the monasteries would be reconnected with the parishes as icons of holiness. The rapid monastic transformation would weave the threads of revival and holiness—threads that bore the imprint of Isaac the Syrian—throughout the fabric of the Church in the twentieth century. And there, these "monastic threads" would brush against the Sunday School Movement.

Many have sought to situate the story of reform in the hands of various figures in the nineteenth and twentieth centuries, for the most part, Habib Girgis *or* Kyrillos VI. But no model or suggestion has been able to explain the exquisite transformation of the Church in the space of twelve short years. I suggest that the elucidation of this story of reform is best approached by asking one question: what if Kyrillos and his remarkable disciples had beneath them a unique network of discipleship that had the capacity to extend their sphere of ascetic influence?

Half a century before, Habib Girgis founded the Sunday School Movement on two principles: *education* of the young and *discipleship*. Both, I suggest, explain the rapid dissemination of reform. In its most basic form, each class was discipled under a Sunday School servant. And, therefore, each child, youth, and adult within the Church was already—and this is crucial to see—within the network, and discipled under a servant, teacher, lecturer, or priest. And that entire "movement" was fathered in its most prominent persons by the "confessor of Sunday School" himself, Kyrillos VI. It created a catalytic network of dissemination for Kyrillos' ascetic influence that would spread throughout the entire Sunday School network (including those disconnected but vital rural areas under Samuel). Kyrillos' personal ascetic reform, which transformed his disciples, was imparted onto that network of education and discipleship forged by Habib Girgis—permitting the sphere of Kyrillos' ascetic influence to go well beyond his inner circle of disciples. Through Shenouda, Gregorious, and Samuel's work, each child, youth, and adult, lay and clergy, was in a sense a disciple—as incredible as that may seem—of Kyrillos. We may then speak of a method of reform (albeit an unusual one) that was exquisitely *personal* and at once able to spread like wildfire within a decade throughout the hearts of Christian Egypt.

Undoubtedly, therefore, this story of reform was carried upon the backs of countless (and nameless) other men and women, clergy and lay alike. This study has looked to Kyrillos' closest disciples in elucidating the method of reform. But for each of these, there were mothers, fathers, siblings, with all, in their own way, forging a sacred space within their homes, creating in these disciples hearts receptive for reform. This narrative has looked to those figures who disseminated Kyrillos' ascesis throughout the Sunday School network. But for each of these renowned disciples, there was a myriad of unseen and largely forgotten laity (both male and female) receiving that reform and discipling their own small Sunday School classes—changing the mindset of the next generation, one child at a time. Though they may have been forgotten by history, their legacy remains vivid and unmistakable.[257]

* * *

What began in the Church of St Menas in Old Cairo would end, a few decades later, in the transformation of an entire Church. Few could have suspected the influence of a mostly silent urban recluse and his handful of restless disciples. Within a matter of years, Kyrillos resolved the "Ethiopian problem" that threatened further ecclesial division, brought peace to the *maglis*-clergy conflicts of the previous century, and saw the end of the precarious *waqf* that tore almost irreparably into the life of the Church. That same method of kenotic and ascetic personal reform was imparted to his disciples, and through them it discipled the next generation of clergy *and* laity. To my knowledge it is one of the most profoundly tenacious, diffuse, and transformative spiritual revolutions in the history of Christianity since the Apostolic Age.

Notes

[1]Raphael Ava Mina, "Interview about the Life of Pope Kyrillos VI."
[2]Ibid.

[3]Pandelis Kalaitzidis, "Challenges of Renewal and Reformation Facing the Orthodox Church," *The Ecumenical Review* 61, no. 2 (2009): 137. It should be noted, however, that Pandelis is primarily discussing applied "doctrine" rather than reform from "distortion/corruption." That said, he does not always maintain this distinction in his discussion; even so, many of his comments are still pertinent.

[4]Ibid., 151.

[5]Ibid., 137.

[6]Ibid., 145. Pandelis gives several examples of "reform" within Eastern Orthodoxy as evidence that the Church has no issue in principle with the idea of reform; see ibid., 140–44.

[7]John Meyendorff, *Orthodoxy and Catholicity* (Lanham: Sheed and Ward, 1966), 133.

[8]Gerhart B. Ladner, *The Idea of Reform: Its Impact on Christian Thought and Action in the Age of the Fathers* (Eugene, OR: Wipf & Stock, 2004), 9. Ladner notes that the "idea of reform is a variant of the more general idea of renewal." For a summary of the four interlocking aspects of Ladner's perception of renewal, see ibid., 9–34. For a discussion of the terms "renewal" versus "reform," see Christopher M. Bellitto, *Renewing Christianity: A History of Church Reform from Day One to Vatican II* (New York: Paulist Press, 2001), 6.

[9]Ladner, *The Idea of Reform*, 2.

[10]Ibid.

[11]For the three aspects of reform in Eastern patristic thought—namely, the return to paradise, the recovery of the lost image-likeness, the representation on earth of the heavenly *basileia*—see ibid., 63–132.

[12]Ibid., 91.

[13]Ibid.

[14]Ibid., 92. Ladner is paraphrasing St Athanasius, *On the Incarnation*, Popular Patristics Series 3 (Crestwood, NY: St Vladimir's Seminary Press, 1996), 41–43.

[15]Bellitto, *Renewing Christianity*, 23. Ladner also makes note of the role that baptism and the Eucharist play in this "re-assimilation," whereby the Eucharist stands at the center of postbaptismal reform. Needless to say, the implications in the life of Kyrillos are fascinating; see Ladner, *The Idea of Reform*, 319. For a profound discussion of Ladner's connection of the Eucharist to the idea of reform see Ann W. Astell, "'Memoriam Fecit': The Eucharist, Memory, Reform, and Regeneration in Hildegard of Bingen's *Scivias* and Nicholas of Cusa's Sermons," in *Reassessing Reform: A Historical Investigation into Church Renewal*, ed. Christopher M. Bellitto and David Zachariah Flanagin (Washington, DC: The Catholic University of America Press, 2012), 191–213.

[16]It should be noted, in the words of Bocken, that all attempts "to realise institutional or cultural reforms since early Christianity are in one way or another related to the personal search for the reparation of the original bond between the human soul and its divine source. . . ." See Inigo Bocken, "Visions of Reform: Lay Piety as a Form of Thinking in Nicholas of Cusa," ibid., 215.

[17]Ladner, *The Idea of Reform*, 342.

[18]Ibid., 343. For what Ladner meant by "failed," see pp. 125–30.

[19]Bellitto, *Renewing Christianity*, 42.

[20]We could add to Ladner's voice that of Congar. Interestingly, though Congar's monumental study of reform was a theological exploration, it frequently looks beyond "reform" to the "reformer." Most intriguing is Congar's *conclusion*. There he makes mention of the fascinating case of Lamennais and Lacordaire. Both were French clergy in the early nineteenth century. Lamennais was an impatient reformer who was eventually self-defrocked and died an isolated schismatic, whereas his disciple, Lacordaire, remained a reformer within the Church. Congar laboriously details the theological method of reform, but his conclusion, ultimately, is that reform is seen most powerfully and clearly in the *personal* life of Lacordaire. Given that Congar himself walked on a similar path in his own quest for reform, I would suggest Lacordaire (or at least what he represents) was the essence, therefore, of Congar's own theology of reform. See Yves Congar, *True and False Reform in the Church* (Collegeville, MN: Liturgical Press, 2011), 331–35. Also see Yves Congar, "Attitudes Towards Reform in the Church," *CrossCurrents* 1, no. 4 (1951): 98. Lacordaire and Kyrillos, we might incidentally note, had much in common. We might even ask: If reform is a transformation into the image of God (who is Christ himself), then is this perhaps

why Kyrillos and Lacordaire—as well as a few other precious souls over the centuries—all look so similar, in a word, "christified"? Is this why in Peter Brown's seminal works, the "holy man" inevitably transforms into an image of "Christ the exemplar"?

[21] Ladner, *The Idea of Reform*, 82.

[22] Monk Pakhoum el-Muharraqi, "Letter to Bishop Shenouda, October 2, 1962" [in Arabic], in *BBG* 1:217–18. It is unclear to what degree Kyrillos suggested the idea and Waheeb constructed it. Waheeb also made clear in the same letter: "I always saw that the Theological College and Sunday School should have a bishop, this was my wish for the Theological College since around twenty years ago, I wrote it in my private memoirs probably when I was a student at the Theological College."

[23] Reiss details this in a small footnote in which he cites from the document in Gregorious' possession; Reiss, *Erneuerung in der Koptisch-Orthodoxen Kirche*, 221, n. 79. Interestingly, Waheeb also details this "hand-written document" in one of his letters; see Pakhoum el-Muharraqi, "Letter to Bishop Shenouda, October 2, 1962." See also van Doorn-Harder, *Modern Coptic Papacy*, 147–48. It should be noted that the notion of bishops without dioceses ("titular bishops") surfaced to some degree—though not in the same functional capacity—in, for instance, other Eastern Orthodox Churches.

[24] Bishop Gregorious, "Pope Kyrillos the Sixth" [in Arabic], *al-Watani*, March 18, 1990. He is also recorded to have said, "The pope liked to concede sermons for his brethren the bishops and his children the priests, giving them a chance to serve with him as partners in the Apostolic service, and an announcement from him that he is their father and pastor, and as the head, he cannot do without them and without their services and efforts, together with him, for building the Holy Church." Cited in Raphael Ava Mina, *Memories: Part II*, 17.

[25] Fr Youssef Asaad, *Commemoration of Pope Kyrillos VI*, March 1984; cited in Raphael Ava Mina, *Memories: Part II*, 17.

[26] *BBG* 1:177.

[27] Generally, the members of the diaconate in the Coptic Church wear their cassocks only for formal services or liturgical celebration.

[28] Pakhoum el-Muharraqi, "Letter to Pope Kyrillos VI, September 16, 1962."

[29] See Gregorious' description in Pakhoum el-Muharraqi, "Letter to Bishop Shenouda, October 5, 1962."

[30] Pakhoum el-Muharraqi, "Letter to Pope Kyrillos VI, September 16, 1962."

[31] Fr Antonious el-Syriany, "Letter to Monk Pakhoum el-Muharraqi, September 22, 1962" [in Arabic], ibid.

[32] Antonious gives a brief and vague mention of these rumors in the same letter. He also details them a few days later in his explanation as to why he wrote that letter: "Suddenly, I heard about the monasticism of Archdeacon Waheeb Atallah. Lots of talk was spread about it; some of this was that it was just a solution for the problem of the [clothes]; or that he was pushed to it by the pope; or that he would come back after one week to work as usual at the Theological College. . . . My love towards you pushed me to defend you, so I said that it is impossible for Dr Waheeb Atallah to be pushed or obliged to join monasticism . . . it is not only a change of [clothes], but it is a change of life. I felt that people would misunderstand your monasticism. . . . During these circumstances, I sent my first letter to you, warning or talking out of love not to go back to the Theological College quickly, caring for your reputation . . . as a person who loves you, who would be greatly hurt to hear about his teacher, the teacher of the entire generation, that he was pushed to monasticism, or that his monasticism was just a formal status." See Antonious el-Syriany, "Letter to Monk Pakhoum el-Muharraqi, September 28, 1962."

[33] Fr Antonious el-Syriany, "Letter to Waheeb Attallah, September 15, 1956" [in Arabic], in *BBG* 1.

[34] "A Whisper of Love: Interview with Shenouda III," video recording (CTV, undated).

[35] Fr Antonious Younan, "On Pope Kyrillos VI," audio recording (Cairo, unknown).

[36] "A Whisper of Love."

[37] Ibid.

[38] Ibid.

[39] Kamal, "An Interview with Pope Shenouda III," Part 2.

[40] Shenouda said as much in an interview: "My ordination was unexpected, when I was ordained a bishop, there wasn't any diocese without a bishop." See Fawzi, *Kyrillos and Abdel Nasser*, 133.

[41]This was a very stern threat; see Antonious el-Syriany, "Letter to Monk Pakhoum el-Muharraqi, September 25, 1962."

[42]Anonymous, "Letter to Monk Pakhoum el-Muharraqi, September 25, 1962" [in Arabic], *BBG* 1:207. The letter ends: "Do not try to know who I am, because you will know it later through this signing, 'brother, friend and beloved.'" The letter was published by Bishop Gregorious, but he does not disclose whether he later discovered the identity of the author.

[43]Reiss, *Erneuerung in der Koptisch-Orthodoxen Kirche*, 233.

[44]Antonious el-Syriany, "Letter to Monk Pakhoum el-Muharraqi, September 25, 1962."

[45]Antonious el-Syriany, "Letter to Monk Pakhoum el-Muharraqi, September 28, 1962."

[46]Ibid.

[47]Meinardus, *Two Thousand Years*, 5.

[48]Pakhoum el-Muharraqi, "Letter to Bishop Shenouda, October 2, 1962."

[49]Pakhoum el-Muharraqi, "Letter to Bishop Shenouda, October 5, 1962." He, like Shenouda, was undeniably committed to monasticism. In a lecture in 1988, he spoke words that were personally reflective: "The sacrifice of the burnt offering [of a monk] is special. It is burnt, entirely, on the altar of God. No one else has a share in it, not the poor, the priest, nor him who offered it. All is for God"; see Gruber, "Sacrifice in the Desert," xiv.

[50]Younan, "On Pope Kyrillos VI."

[51]Wakin, *A Lonely Minority*, 123. Wakin notes, incidentally, that three monks were already making a "particular impact" at the time of his writing in 1960: Makary (future Bishop Samuel), Antonios (future Pope Shenouda III), and Matta el-Meskeen. Fascinatingly, these monks were somewhat destined to be reformers. Waheeb Atallah, unsurprisingly, features sparingly in Wakin's study as he was still to be tonsured a monk.

[52]Younan, "On Pope Kyrillos VI."

[53]Though Shenouda and Samuel would take different approaches to their theology and ministry, their biographical parallels are remarkable. Both lost parents at an early age; both were from the SSM; both were disciples of Fr Mina; both were SSM monks at the Syrian Monastery; ordained on same day as general bishops; previously nominated patriarch in 1956 and in 1971; and both, I might add, were uncompromising in their incarnation of the gospel. See, for instance, Reiss, *Erneuerung in der Koptisch-Orthodoxen Kirche*, 225–26.

[54]Anonymous, *Bishop Samuel: Pages from His Life, Service, and Thought* [in Arabic] (Cairo: Antoun Yacoub Michael, 1981), 14. Samuel first began with the SSM at St Mark's in Giza in 1937 after his family relocated there for his study, but his father would pass away in early 1938; anonymous, *Early Life of Anba Samuel* [in Arabic] (Giza: Friends of Anba Samuel, 1991), 11, 32. There Zareef Abdullah, the future Fr Boulos Bolous, would—though a layman, and only three years his senior—become his first spiritual guide. For a collection of their spiritual correspondence, see ibid., 12–23.

[55]Anonymous, *Life, Service, and Thought*, 14.

[56]Suryal, "On the 'Takrees' Movement: Part 1"; Reiss, *Erneuerung in der Koptisch-Orthodoxen Kirche*, 103. Cf. Anonymous, *Life, Service, and Thought*, 15; anonymous, *Early Life of Anba Samuel*, 40–44. It was a most difficult endeavor, but it would prepare him for the discomfort and obstructions that the SSM would face in Giza from a fairly hostile leadership. Eventually, though he certainly struggled with it, he would learn to say, "When one door of service is shut, our Lord wants us to find another door. . . ." Ibid., 44.

[57]Anonymous, *Life, Service, and Thought*, 17.

[58]Anonymous, *Early Life of Anba Samuel*, 46–61; Anonymous, *Life, Service, and Thought*, 18–20.

[59]His journal entries suggest he had sought monasticism from at least 1944. For varied reasons it was obstructed until Fr Mina (Kyrillos) tonsured him; see Anonymous, *Early Life of Anba Samuel*, 62–69.

[60]Anonymous, *Life, Service, and Thought*, 24.

[61]Reiss, *Erneuerung in der Koptisch-Orthodoxen Kirche*, 229.

[62]Al-Masri, *True Story of Christianity in Egypt*, 2:420; Anonymous, *Life, Service, and Thought*, 24–25. The thesis was "The Religious Education in the Coptic Church."

[63]Anonymous, *Life, Service, and Thought*, 28.

[64]Reiss and Meinardus suggest it began in 1957, whereas all early Arabic sources—including the earliest biographies of Bishop Samuel—place it in 1959; see Reiss, *Erneuerung in der Koptisch-Orthodoxen Kirche*, 226–27; Meinardus, *Christian Egypt: Faith and Life*, 46. See also Maurice M. Assad, "The Coptic Church and Social Change," *International Review of Mission* 61, no. 242 (1972): 127; Anonymous, *Early Life of Anba Samuel*, 30–31.

[65]Reiss, *Erneuerung in der Koptisch-Orthodoxen Kirche*, 226–27.

[66]Ibid., 227–28; Anonymous, *Life, Service, and Thought*, 31.

[67]Hasan, *Christians versus Muslims*, 96. Hasan's comments here concerning Bishop Samuel are, at the least, sensational, at worst fabrication—and as such she remains, here, very much a peripheral, a tertiary source.

[68]Reiss, *Erneuerung in der Koptisch-Orthodoxen Kirche*, 227–28.

[69]Anonymous, *Life, Service, and Thought*, 30–31.

[70]Assad, "The Coptic Church and Social Change," 127.

[71]Interestingly, as Meinardus notes, the project's purpose was "to strengthen the Coptic identity throughout Egypt, and especially in those parts, where the Copts constitute a distinct minority." Meinardus, *Christian Egypt: Faith and Life*, 45.

[72]Anonymous, *Life, Service, and Thought*, 30–31; Assad, "The Coptic Church and Social Change," 128.

[73]Meinardus, *Christian Egypt: Faith and Life*, 46. In 1966 eighty-four were employed by the "rural diakonia," 60 percent of whom were graduates of the Theological College in Cairo.

[74]Interestingly, Wakin wrote in 1961, while the patriarchal secretary, before being ordained a bishop, "Makary is intimately involved in policy making for the patriarch, any merging of the viewpoints of the two men reinforces the validity of the answers." Wakin, *A Lonely Minority*, 116.

[75]Van Doorn-Harder, *Modern Coptic Papacy*, 141; Tadros, *Motherland Lost*, 197–98.

[76]For a more detailed discussion of these diaspora parishes, see al-Masri, *Story of the Coptic Church*, 7:42–51; Nasr, *Readings in the Life of Abouna Mina*, 86–91.

[77]Van Doorn-Harder, *Modern Coptic Papacy*, 141. Also see, Reiss, *Erneuerung in der Koptisch-Orthodoxen Kirche*, 231–32.

[78]Van Doorn-Harder, *Modern Coptic Papacy*, 141. To give some sense of the aid he was able to secure, on his death, Heikal claims, the sum of some eleven million pounds sterling was to be found in his Swiss bank account—though his will stated this was not to be touched by his family and was solely for the use of the Church; see Heikal, *Autumn of Fury*, 167.

[79]For a discussion of his ecumenical work, see the anonymous, *Life, Service, and Thought*, 46–52; van Doorn-Harder, *Modern Coptic Papacy*, 139–40, 48.

[80]"Obituary of Bishop Samuel," *Times of London*, October 12, 1981.

[81]For a catalogue of "Sunday School" bishops, see Nasr, *Readings in the Life of Abouna Mina*, 83.

[82]Zaklama, *Pope Kyrillos VI*, 2:182. Basilious, too, was unwilling to accept ordination: "[Kyrillos] insisted on burdening me with this responsibility, in spite of my pleading with him in tears to excuse me."

[83]For a brief biography see ibid., 195–96; van Doorn-Harder, *Modern Coptic Papacy*, 149.

[84]Reiss, *Erneuerung in der Koptisch-Orthodoxen Kirche*, 222.

[85]Van Doorn-Harder, "Practical and Mystical," 231.

[86]Ibid.; van Doorn-Harder, *Contemporary Coptic Nuns*, 37–38, 62.

[87]Reiss, *Erneuerung in der Koptisch-Orthodoxen Kirche*, 223.

[88]Tadros, *Motherland Lost*, 175.

[89]Watson, "Abba Kyrillos," 43.

[90]Tadros, *Motherland Lost*, 178.

[91]Hasan, *Christians versus Muslims*, 86.

[92]Zaklama, *Pope Kyrillos VI*, 2:204; Tadros, *Motherland Lost*, 177.

[93]Reiss, *Erneuerung in der Koptisch-Orthodoxen Kirche*, 232–33.

[94]Watson, *Among the Copts*, 99; Tadros, *Motherland Lost*, 177.

[95]Reiss, *Erneuerung in der Koptisch-Orthodoxen Kirche*, 233.

[96]Watson, *Among the Copts*, 99. His 538-page dissertation was titled: "The Etymology of Greek words in the Coptic Language"; Hasan, *Christians versus Muslims*, 205.

[97]Watson, "Abba Kyrillos," 36.

[98]Van Doorn-Harder, *Modern Coptic Papacy*, 149.

[99]Zaklama, *Pope Kyrillos VI*, 2:204.

[100]Watson, "Abba Kyrillos," 44.

[101]Wakin, *A Lonely Minority*, 131.

[102]Monir Atteya Shehata, *Religious Education and the Clerical College and the Church's Sunday School* [in Arabic] (Cairo: Association of Anba Gregorious, 2005), 256–57. Gregorious notes that by January 31, 1961, when he gave this speech at the inauguration of the new Theological College, all eleven newly ordained priests of Cairo and Alexandria were theological school graduates—including Fr Mikhail Dawood and Fr Bishoy Kamel. See also Bishop Gregorious' (then Fr Pakhoum) memoirs on January 29, 1965, which note his discussion with Kyrillos VI in reference to these ordinations; *BBG* 1:358–59.

[103]Monk Pakhoum el-Muharraqi, "Letter to Bishop Shenouda, March 18, 1967" [in Arabic], in *BBG* 1:383–84. Zakareya would eventually be ordained as Fr Timatheous Mahrous.

[104]Bishop Shenouda, "Letter to Monk Pakhoum el-Muharraqi, March 22, 1967" [in Arabic], ibid. It is unclear when this first suspension occurred, but it may be suggested in the period of 1965–1966.

[105]Ibid.

[106]Ibid.

[107]Monk Pakhoum el-Muharraqi, "Letter to Bishop Shenouda, March 26, 1967" [in Arabic], ibid.

[108]Ibid.

[109]Though Shenouda did not actually perform the ordination, he attended and accepted the nomination. The same letter makes clear that the bishop of Qena in fact sought Shenouda's opinion, who gave his wholehearted recommendation.

[110]Pakhoum el-Muharraqi, "Letter to Bishop Shenouda, March 26, 1967."

[111]*BBG* 1:401–2.

[112]Ibid., 403.

[113]Ibid., 358. Also see his earlier letter: Monk Pakhoum el-Muharraqi, "Letter to Pope Kyrillos VI, May 16, 1964" [in Arabic], in *BBG* 1:318–19. Pakhoum escaped an attempted earlier ordination for the congregation of Dairut. He went into hiding on May 17, 1964, until September 27, 1964.

[114]*BBG* 1:404–5. I. H. al-Masri states that Kyrillos surprised the congregation, but it was in fact Pakhoum (Gregorious) who was surprised; see al-Masri, *Story of the Coptic Church*, 7:52. In his account Gregorious notes that everyone in attendance seemed to know except him. Three months earlier, for instance, the faculty of the Institute had written to Kyrillos requesting that Monk Pakhoum be ordained as the "dedicated" bishop for the "Coptic Studies Institute" given that Bishop Shenouda was distracted "with other matters"; see, Teaching Staff of the Coptic Studies Institute, "Letter to Kyrillos VI, February 10, 1967" [in Arabic], in *BBG* 1:398–99.

[115]*BBG* 1:408; Tadros, *Motherland Lost*, 127. As a bishop of a functional area and not a diocese in the strict sense, the scope for overlapping authority, duties, and egos, was ever present, given the blurred jurisdictional borders.

[116]*BBG* 1:408–09.

[117]*BBG* 1:409.

[118]Also see the decree cited in Pope Kyrillos VI, "Ordination of the Bishop of Higher Education and Scientific Research" [in Arabic], *Keraza* (June 1967).

[119]Shenouda, "Letter to Bishop Gregorious, May 12, 1967." Shenouda was ordained a bishop for the "Theological College, Coptic Studies Institute, Religious Institutes, Charitable Organizations and Sunday School throughout the regions of the Republic."

[120]Shenouda would repeat this in his letters over the next few days; see Shenouda, "Letter to Bishop Gregorious, May 14, 1967"; Shenouda, "Letter to Bishop Gregorious, May 15, 1967."

[121]The reasons for not attending are in Shenouda, "Letter to Bishop Gregorious, May 14, 1967."

[122]Shenouda's speech of May 18, 1967, is cited in *BBG* 1:424–26.

[123]Though their relationship would be healed in this moment, their later relationship after the death

of Kyrillos was tested many times. As this conflict would postdate the life of Kyrillos, it is beyond our scope.

[124]These were the only three bishops to be forced in this manner—though others required a good deal of convincing. Another of Kyrillos' secretaries, Fr Metias, escaped in 1969, knowing well Kyrillos' methods. In 1977, he was ordained by Shenouda III.

[125]For a brief biography, see Meinardus, *Two Thousand Years*, 79–80; van Doorn-Harder, *Modern Coptic Papacy*, 157–58; Matthias Gillé, *Der Koptische Papst Schenuda III: Beobachtungen zu Theologie und Biografie* (Marburg: Tectum Verlag, 2017), 39–49.

[126]Kamal, "An Interview with Pope Shenouda III," Part 1.

[127]Gillé, *Der Koptische Papst Schenuda*, 39; Watson, *Among the Copts*, 64.

[128]Meinardus, *Two Thousand Years*, 3; Gillé, *Der koptische Papst Schenuda*, 42–43.

[129]O'Mahony, "Coptic Christianity," 507.

[130]Shenouda III, "Speech at the Tenth Year Commemoration of Kyrillos VI."

[131]Meinardus, *Two Thousand Years*, 4.

[132]Reiss seems to suggest that Fr Antonious influenced the entire group to follow after Matta; Reiss, *Erneuerung in der Koptisch-Orthodoxen Kirche*, 188–89.

[133]Antonious el-Syriany, "Letter to Waheeb Attallah, September 15, 1956."

[134]Reiss, *Erneuerung in der Koptisch-Orthodoxen Kirche*, 188.

[135]Fr Antonious el-Syriany, "Letter to Waheeb Attallah, June 1960" [in Arabic], in *BBG* 1:163–64, and his "Letter to Waheeb Attallah, July 13, 1960" [in Arabic], in *BBG* 1:164–65.

[136]Antonious el-Syriany, "Letter to Waheeb Attallah, June, 1960" and "Letter to Waheeb Attallah, July 13, 1960," just cited. In these letters Antonious warned Waheeb not to edit any of the writings of Matta, given that they were, for him at least, to some degree suspect.

[137]Pope Shenouda III, *The Release of the Spirit*, trans. Wedad Abbas (Cairo: COEPA, 1997). Also see Maged S. A. Mikhail, "Matta al-Maskin," in *The Orthodox Christian World*, ed. Augustine Casiday (Abingdon, UK: Routledge, 2012), 362. It should be noted that Shenouda (then Nazir Gayed) first became close with Fr Matta in the early 1950s even before his tonsure—accounting for Nazir's writing the original "foreword" to the book in its first printing.

[138]For a brief discussion see Mikhail, "Matta al-Maskin," 363; Cornelis Hulsman, "Reviving an Ancient Faith," *Christianity Today* 45, no. 15 (2001): 38; Pennington, "The Copts in Modern Egypt," 168. Mikhail's balanced comments are discerning: "By the time both were nominated for the patriarchate in 1971 . . . relations were already tense. Always indirect or through proxy, their disputes were an open secret in general, Fr Matta never defended himself, and the patriarch [Shenouda III] refrained from identifying the abbot by name in his criticism. . . . Doubtless, a component of their personal feuds will never be grasped by outside observers." Mikhail, "Matta al-Maskin," 362–63.

[139]Antonious was ordained a priest on August 31, 1958.

[140]Kamal, "An Interview with Pope Shenouda III," Part 2.

[141]Wakin, *A Lonely Minority*, 124.

[142]Van Doorn-Harder, *Modern Coptic Papacy*, 158.

[143]Reiss, *Erneuerung in der Koptisch-Orthodoxen Kirche*, 224.

[144]Watson, *Among the Copts*, 66.

[145]Watson, "Abba Kyrillos," 40; Pennington, "The Copts in Modern Egypt," 167–68.

[146]Heikal, *Autumn of Fury*, 168.

[147]Sedra, "Class Cleavages and Ethnic Conflict," 225.

[148]Heikal's comments here are representative of the *mis*-representation: "The pace of developments began to alarm [Kyrillos]. He felt the Sunday schools and theological colleges were becoming increasingly political and so told Shenouda to stop his Friday lessons and go back to the monastery in Wadi Natrun"; Heikal, *Autumn of Fury*, 168. Similarly, see Sedra, "Class Cleavages and Ethnic Conflict," 225; Vatikiotis, *The History of Egypt*, 418. Ibrahim and McCallum both follow Hasan in making this same claim; see Ibrahim, *The Copts of Egypt*, 176; Fiona McCallum, "The Political Role of the Patriarch in the Contemporary Middle East" (St Andrews, Scotland: University of St Andrews, 2006), 138; Hasan, *Christians versus Muslims*, 87–88. It should be noted that care should be taken when considering Hasan's study. As

previously noted, the work is rather sensationalist. For instance, her comments: "Kyrillos VI, who had at first welcomed these two reform-minded monks [Shenouda and Samuel] in his administration, began to tire of them"; or, again, "The pope was coming under pressure from Nasser's authoritarian regime to rein in his now outspoken bishop." The attitude is overly familiar. It is wise for future generations of scholars to be wary of several of her claims. For fair reviews of her study, see Paul Sedra, "Review of *Christians versus Muslims in Modern Egypt: The Century-Long Struggle for Coptic Equality*," *Middle East Journal* 58, no. 3 (2004); Ralph M. Coury, "Review of *Christians versus Muslims in Modern Egypt: The Century-Long Struggle for Coptic Equality*," *The American Historical Review* 110, no. 2 (2005).

[149]Watson, "Abba Kyrillos," 40.

[150]I suspect Shenouda's later lectures in the context of rising Islamic extremism and Sadat's actions in the late 1970s have been transposed in the minds of many onto his lectures in the mid-1960s.

[151]Bishop Shenouda, "Editorial" [in Arabic], *al-Keraza* (August 1965): 2.

[152]Ibid.

[153]The candidate would eventually be ordained. Shenouda would discover later as patriarch that occasionally the principle was not always possible, practical, or beneficial; an ideal perhaps, but one that in certain circumstances was an impossibility.

[154]The candidate was Bishop Makarios of Qena (1923–1991). His biographer notes that it was, in fact, not a simple ordination: "After the Late Metropolitan Kyrillos of Qena departed to the heavens, His Holiness Pope Kyrillos VI performed an altar draw, where he wrote the names of Fr Ekladios el-Antony, Fr Antonios el-Baramousy, and another blank piece of paper. Following the Divine Liturgy, His Holiness invited one of the deacons to draw one of the three pieces of paper in the presence of the entire congregation. The deacon picked the blank paper, which meant that God wanted someone else for this diocese. So, Pope Kyrillos chose Fr Boles el-Baramousy for this task." See Bishop Cherubim, *Blessed Servant: Life and Miracles of Bishop Makarios of Qena* (Qena: Coptic Diocese of Qena, date unknown), 11.

[155]Kamal, "An Interview with Pope Shenouda III," Part 2. Also see Fawzi's interview with Shenouda: "I was following the Church's rules, that is the right of the people to choose their pastor; Kyrillos considered this as within his authority as he knew the monks deeply. . . . That is what we do now . . ."; Fawzi, *Kyrillos and Abdel Nasser*, 143. It is important to note that Shenouda on occasion would also ordain bishops in this manner—as always the principle (as he would later discover) requires *economy*. He also states in the former interview that the second crucial point of disagreement, which he wrote about publicly, was that of the "inheritance of the bishoprics," which he believed should be solely for the diocese.

[156]Pakhoum el-Muharraqi, "Letter to Bishop Shenouda, March 18, 1967." We should also note, Kyrillos had for the most part—more than any patriarch before or after him—ordained candidates from the Theological College; see al-Masri, *Story of the Coptic Church*, 7:100.

[157]Bishop Pachomious states that Samuel was tasked with specifically theological teaching in "evangelism," for a number of Ethiopian groups; Bishop Pachomious, "Interview about the Life of Pope Kyrillos VI," audio recording, ed. Daniel Fanous (2016).

[158]The entire letter is reproduced in Bishop Shenouda, "An Open Word about the Theological College and Religous Institutes" [in Arabic], *al-Keraza* (October, 1967): 4.

[159]Ibid.

[160]The letters are cited in the same work, 7:10. The Higher Coptic Institute was mainly concerned with Coptic heritage and culture and therefore was vital in translation, archaeological studies, museums, restoration of monasteries, recording of ancient Liturgies and chant, revival of Coptic iconography, art, and architecture; see Zaklama, *Pope Kyrillos VI*, 1:414–42.

[161]Shenouda mentions in the October issue of *al-Keraza* that he was aware of the financial crisis, but disagreed as to its extent; see Shenouda, "An Open Word," 6. As seen in the previous chapters, it was far more severe than he admits. Shenouda goes on to suggest that just as the Egyptian government maintained its commitment to the universities despite the Six-Day War, the Church should likewise prioritize the theological institutions.

[162]See previous discussion, Chapter 8: "The Maglis and the 'Mummy's Curse': 1964–1967."

[163]"A Whisper of Love."

[164]Ibid.

[165]Ibid. This is likely what Shenouda meant when he wrote in *al-Keraza*: "The story started a long

while ago, I feel ashamed to mentions its details"; Shenouda, "An Open Word," 2. A bishop who wished to remain anonymous recalls that there were false rumors at the time that Shenouda was attempting to oust Kyrillos; anonymous bishop, "Interview about the Life of Pope Kyrillos."

[166]"A Whisper of Love."

[167]Shenouda, "An Open Word," 2, 5.

[168]Ibid., 9.

[169]Ibid., 13.

[170]Anonymous, "A Miracle Worker for Copts." A later letter tells of Shenouda's concern for his students; Bishop Shenouda, "Letter to Bishop Gregorious, October 8, 1967" [in Arabic], in *BBG* 2:16–17.

[171]An anonymous bishop states it was this specifically that provoked the suspension; Anonymous Bishop, "Interview about the Life of Pope Kyrillos." cf. Raphael Ava Mina, "Interview about the Life of Pope Kyrillos VI." Sedra and Heikal both state that the revolution and outcry "forced the Pope to retract the decision"—in fact it was the *opposite*; the revolution provoked the suspension—which would take some eight months for Kyrillos to resolve. See Sedra, "Class Cleavages and Ethnic Conflict," 225; Heikal, *Autumn of Fury*, 168. Shenouda himself in an interview with Fawzi, claims Kyrillos had little care for the objections of the youth—and that when Shenouda returned it was Kyrillos' "full will"; see Fawzi, *Kyrillos and Abdel Nasser*, 149.

[172]Shenouda reproduced the telegram in his letter; Shenouda, "Letter to Bishop Gregorious, October 8, 1967."

[173]Shenouda, "Letter to Bishop Gregorious, October 23, 1967."

[174]Bishop Shenouda, "Letter to Soliman Nessim, November 15, 1967" [in Arabic] (Desert of Scetis: 1967). In that letter Shenouda states the reason why he had expected it, namely, that he had "defended the right of the congregation to choose their pastor."

[175]"A Whisper of Love." Also see Hanna Youssef Atta, "Letter to Pope Kyrillos VI, June 17, 1968" [in Arabic], in FRC-1: Letter 407 (Alexandria: 1968). Hanna wrote to his brother, Kyrillos VI, a week before the opening of the cathedral, requesting that he forgive Bishop Shenouda. According to those close to Shenouda, he arrived late that evening and therefore was not present at the consecration.

[176]Fawzi, *Kyrillos and Abdel Nasser*, 144. When asked later in that interview, "But the Pope was angry with you that day?" Shenouda replied: "People insist on their opinions; then, if there is a mistake, they fix it with reconciliation and openness, [and] the matter then ends with the previous mood; they are just temporary emotions and they end."

[177]Kamal, "An Interview with Pope Shenouda III," Part 2. Also see Fawzi, *Kyrillos and Abdel Nasser*, 144, 49–50.

[178]Raphael Ava Mina, "Interview about the Life of Pope Kyrillos VI"; Yostos, "Interview about the Life of Pope Kyrillos VI"; anonymous bishop, "Interview about the Life of Pope Kyrillos"; Pachomious, "Interview about the Life of Pope Kyrillos VI." Shenouda himself states that some restrictions were, however, placed on his future preaching—perhaps to prevent a recurrence; see "A Whisper of Love."

[179]For other biographical details, see John H. Watson, "Abouna Matta el-Meskeen: Contemporary Desert Mystic," *Coptic Church Review* 27, nos. 3 and 4 (2006); Mikhail, "Matta al-Maskin."

[180]Mina el-Samuely [the Younger], "Letter to Hegumen Mina the Recluse, August 10, 1948." It was written on the day of the tonsure.

[181]Makary el-Samuely, "Letter to Fr Matta, December 14, 1948."

[182]Matta el-Meskeen, *Autobiography of Fr Matta el-Meskeen*, 20. Matta also writes, " 'Monasticism is obedience.' This saying is correct and an undisputed truth, but the origin of obedience in monasticism was that it belonged to the spiritual father who was experienced, and obeyed God based on the principle that obedience will lead him to freedom. Thus, *obedience with me was limited* to the gospel and truth, without bruising my freedom in prayer and worship"; ibid., 19.

[183]Hegumen Mina the Recluse [Kyrillos VI], "Letter to Monks at the Monastery of St Samuel, November 11, 1949" [in Arabic], in SSC, Letter 49.

[184]Matta el-Meskeen, *Autobiography of Fr Matta el-Meskeen*, 21.

[185]Ibid.

[186]Ibid.

[187]Ibid., 22–23.

[188]Ibid., 27–30. Also see William Soliman, "Hegumen Matta el-Meskeen" [in Arabic], *Sunday School Magazine* 8/9 (1955). Interestingly, Matta states his best work on reform was his "personal influence" among Coptic intellectuals; see Matta el-Meskeen, *Autobiography of Fr Matta el-Meskeen*, 28.

[189]Matta el-Meskeen, *Autobiography of Fr Matta el-Meskeen*, 31.

[190]Ibid., 32. This was on July 20, 1956.

[191]Ibid., 33.

[192]Mikhail, "Matta al-Maskin," 361.

[193]The letter was found among a buried collection in the possession of Fr Raphael Ava Mina.

[194]Fr Mina el-Samuely [the Younger], "Letter to Pope Kyrillos VI, August 18, 1959" [in Arabic], in FRC-1: Letter 195 (Qalamoun Mountain, 1959).

[195]Ibid.

[196]Ibid.

[197]Interestingly, in his autobiography, Matta gives the same name "university-graduate monks" to his group. Matta el-Meskeen, *Autobiography of Fr Matta el-Meskeen*, 33.

[198]Suryal, "The Theological College."

[199]Matta el-Meskeen, *Autobiography of Fr Matta el-Meskeen*, 33.

[200]Ibid., 34, n. 4. The editor of Matta's autobiography (one of his disciples) adds the following note: "Living there was the idea of the Patriarch, who approved it until their problem was solved. But the patriarch had decided to break up this cohesive group, disseminate the monks among all the monasteries, and appoint them to the various services in the Church. He actually began to implement his idea and chose two of them in his Secretariat but found that their adherence to their father confessor [Matta] was not affected, but instead they showed a disinterest for anything."

[201]See discussion and footnotes concerning the decree in Chapter 7: "Confronting an Expected Dissension: 1959–63." The decree was cited in al-Masri, *Story of the Coptic Church*, 7:35.

[202]For varying perspectives on whether the decree had anything to do with Matta, see Raphael Ava Mina, "Interview about the Life of Pope Kyrillos VI"; Rubenson, "Matta el-Meskeen," 417; Reiss, *Erneuerung in der Koptisch-Orthodoxen Kirche*, 237, n. 4; Wakin, *A Lonely Minority*, 128; Samuel Tawadros el-Syriany, *The History of the Popes*, 181; Suryal, "The Theological College." Symbolic is Fr Salib's claim that the decree had nothing to do with Matta; whereas, on the other hand, Fr Samuel Tawadros—who suffered under that decree—thought it had everything to do with Matta. Maged Mikhail gives voice to some of these possibilities and concludes it either had to do directly with Matta, or Kyrillos at least knew that Matta's group would resist; see Mikhail, "Matta al-Maskin," 361.

[203]Reiss, *Erneuerung in der Koptisch-Orthodoxen Kirche*, 237, n. 143.

[204]Wakin quotes Kyrillos' words concerning the decree: "The monasteries will become once more the religious schools where monks will devote time to study and writing." See Wakin, *A Lonely Minority*, 128.

[205]Suryal, "The Theological College." Salib at this point reminded Kyrillos that he too had spent most of his monasticism outside the monastery.

[206]Fr Samuel Tawadros claims the date of the decree was August 20; Samuel Tawadros el-Syriany, *The History of the Popes*, 181.

[207]Matta el-Meskeen, *Autobiography of Fr Matta el-Meskeen*, 34.

[208]Ibid.

[209]Matta had visited Wadi Rayan in 1958. Sleeping under a palm tree, he reportedly had a vision of a man declaring to him, "I have waited for you for many years." See Otto Meinardus, "The Hermits of Wadi Rayan," *Studia Orientalia Christiana* 11 (1966): 301.

[210]Anonymous, "Excommunication of Priests and Monks" [in Arabic], *al-Ahram*, October 17, 1960. The same was declared in *Misr*, October 12, 1960; cited in Meinardus, "The Hermits of Wadi Rayan," 301.

[211]To substantiate this claim, the monks note that Kyrillos had written a letter in 1966 to Fr Matta in which he requested three monks to be moved to a monastery and referred to Matta (without any reference to the excommunication) as: "Reverend and pious Fr Hegumen Matta el-Meskeen." "This letter," the editor of the autobiography writes, "was preserved by the late Anba Andrawos, bishop of Damietta, who introduced it in 1971 to the patriarchal elections as evidence that there was no ecclesiastical sanction."

But this invites the question of why the Synod was under the impression that Fr Matta was excommunicated in the first place. See Matta el-Meskeen, *Autobiography of Fr Matta el-Meskeen*, 41; Mikhail, "Matta al-Maskin," 361.

[212]Suryal, "The Theological College."

[213]Meinardus, "The Hermits of Wadi Rayan," 303, n. 1. Meinardus notes that there were in 1966 only three priests: Matta, Mousa, and Mina. The Liturgy, he notes, was mostly celebrated by Fr Mousa, though occasionally by Mina. He makes no mention of Fr Matta celebrating the Liturgy, even though he was a priest—and, importantly from a liturgical perspective, Matta was the senior priest and spiritual father of the community.

[214]Matta el-Meskeen, *Autobiography of Fr Matta el-Meskeen*, 35.

[215]In April 1961, the monks left the Wadi Rayan in search of a more liveable habitation, but eventually returned in November 1961, after a plot of Arab nomads to poison them with arsenic; see Meinardus, "The Hermits of Wadi Rayan," 302; Matta el-Meskeen, *Autobiography of Fr Matta el-Meskeen*, 38–40.

[216]Meinardus, "The Hermits of Wadi Rayan," 302–3. They began as six monks, but Fr Daoud and Fr Dionysius eventually departed for the Syrian Monastery, with other monks joining Fr Matta between 1962 and 1965.

[217]Watson, "Fr Matta el-Maskeen," 69.

[218]Van Doorn-Harder, *Modern Coptic Papacy*, 158.

[219]Meinardus, "The Hermits of Wadi Rayan."

[220]Ibid., 304, n. 2.

[221]Ibid., 308.

[222]Pope Kyrillos VI, "Letter to Fr Salib Suryal, February 4, 1967" [in Arabic] (Cairo, 1967). The letter is cited in Suryal, "The Theological College."

[223]For instance, see Fawzi's interview with Shenouda III; Fawzi, *Kyrillos and Abdel Nasser*, 148.

[224]Suryal, "The Theological College." The lecture is transcribed by the disciples in Matta el-Meskeen, *Autobiography of Fr Matta el-Meskeen*, 43–50. Interestingly, many have suggested that Matta was returned because of pressure from (oddly) the Vatican or from the insistence of Bishop Mikhail of Asyut. In the first place, Bishop Mikhail did not personally know Matta until the moment of their reconciliation; and in the second, Pope Shenouda's interview with Fawzi claims both rumors were inaccurate. See Fawzi, *Kyrillos and Abdel Nasser*, 147–48.

[225]Suryal, "The Theological College."

[226]Ibid.

[227]Matta el-Meskeen, *Autobiography of Fr Matta el-Meskeen*, 42.

[228]Suryal, "The Theological College."

[229]There can be no arguing that Matta could not have anyone above him—not even the patriarch. That said, perhaps Kyrillos saw something else, namely, that placed in a monastery with absolute authority, Matta could create a monastic revival that thrived on his almost obsessive vision of a pure monastic renaissance. Kyrillos discerned that Matta, irrespective of the disobedience, had a vital role to play in the history of revival.

[230]Suryal, "The Theological College."

[231]Salib replied, "No, have a good rest, sleep and relax, money is pouring over Fr Matta from everywhere. There is no need for the Endowments Committee or fixing a monthly amount of money, you will see this Monastery after a year or two. . . ." Matta had an international following by that stage.

[232]Matta el-Meskeen, *Autobiography of Fr Matta el-Meskeen*, 51.

[233]For a summary of the restoration of the Monastery of St Macarius, see Meinardus, *Two Thousand Years*, 163–64; Watson, "Contemporary Desert Mystic," 70; Voile, *Les Coptes d'Égypte*, 52–53; Reiss, *Erneuerung in der Koptisch-Orthodoxen Kirche*, 239–41.

[234]Watson, "Contemporary Desert Mystic."

[235]Heikal, *Autumn of Fury*, 168; Raphael Ava Mina, "Interview about the Life of Pope Kyrillos VI." Though, of note, Heikal incorrectly described Matta as a "bishop."

[236]Rubenson has accurately noticed that Matta was "not an academically trained systematic theologian, but a spiritual writer who read deeply both patristic and modern theological literature." See Rubenson, "Matta el-Meskeen," 415.

[237]Matta el-Meskeen, *Orthodox Prayer Life*. For its evolution and impact see Rubenson, "Matta el-Meskeen," 417.

[238]Watson, "Contemporary Desert Mystic," 71.

[239]Matta el-Meskeen, *Orthodox Prayer Life*, 10, 292.

[240]O'Mahony, "Coptic Christianity," 502.

[241]Reiss, *Erneuerung in der Koptisch-Orthodoxen Kirche*, 179. For instance, Reiss suggests that the revival found roots with Matta in the 1960s. Meinardus, however, claims the revival did not begin when Kyrillos VI delegated Matta in 1969, but rather in the 1950s under Theophilus; see ibid., 212, n. 40; Otto Meinardus, "Review of Albert Gerhards and Heinzgerd Brakmann, *Die Koptische Kirche. Einführung in das Ägyptische Christentum*," *Ostkirchliche Studien* 44, nos. 2/3 (1995): 212–13. Reiss correctly notes that while Bishop Theophilus opened the doors for the "Sunday School" monks, he was not, properly speaking, their spiritual father. But even this misses that Fr Mina was the confessor, father, and instigator of their monasticism.

[242]This is rarely noticed in scholarship, other than a fleeting mention in Meinardus' study of Coptic monasticism: "As a reviver of an ancient school of monasticism, Anba Kyrillos VI belongs to the illustrious company of reformers." For a few brief exceptions, see Samuel Rubenson, "Tradition and Renewal in Coptic Theology," in *BDC*, 189.

[243]Schmemann, *Journals of Alexander Schmemann*, 188–89. Rubenson notes with great insight: "Egypt is not only the land of Christian monastic origins, but *also* of modern monastic revival." See Rubenson, "Tradition and Renewal," 35.

[244]Raphael Ava Mina, "Lecture on the Virtues of Pope Kyrillos."

[245]Ibid.

[246]Veilleux, *Pachomian Koinonia*, 1:330. The middle sentence is omitted in that translation without explanation.

[247]Stephen R. Lloyd-Moffett, *Beauty for Ashes: The Spiritual Transformation of a Modern Greek Community* (Crestwood, NY: St Vladimir's Seminary Press, 2009), 114.

[248]Ibid. These comments are in the context of a similarly profound—albeit on a far smaller scale—transformation of one of the most scandalized and divided dioceses of Greece, the Metropolis of Preveza. Though Bishop Meletios (like Kyrillos) had no formal program of reform, and similarly disappointed many in his first years by a lack of strategic planning, he gathered around him several holy monks to provide the diocese with frequent and pervasive encounters with genuine personal holiness, and the result was a remarkable transformation of that diocese within only a few years. Once more, it was through his sphere of "ascetic influence."

[249]Meinardus, *Two Thousand Years*, 3.

[250]Watson, "Abba Kyrillos," 44.

[251]Reiss, *Erneuerung in der Koptisch-Orthodoxen Kirche*, 236.

[252]Ibid. Reiss mentions only the three bishops in this regard. Interestingly, Reiss also notes that in later decades these distinctives would eventually blur.

[253]Tadros writes, "The founding fathers of the Coptic Church's revival differed in their approaches and often clashed . . . but together they achieved a complete revolution . . . they had brought down the old order and built a new one. . . . But ultimately their success was due to a giant who loomed large above them: Kyrillos VI." Tadros, *Motherland Lost*, 180–81.

[254]Van Doorn-Harder, "Planner, Patriarch and Saint," 240.

[255]Van Doorn-Harder, *Modern Coptic Papacy*, 149.

[256]We should, however, note that *after* the death of Kyrillos, only a handful of the monks from St Macarius' Monastery would be ordained bishops—in part explained by Fr Matta's philosophy of monasticism, and in part explained by the deepening of his conflict with Kyrillos' successor, Shenouda III. Nevertheless, this does not discount Matta's role in the monastic revival, nor his impact on other monastics (in other monasteries) who would eventually become bishops.

[257]Though it is to some degree beyond the scope of the present work, it is my deep hope that the fascinating histories of these countless men and women—especially those lay Sunday School servants—who shared in the movement of reform in the mid-twentieth century, may one day be taken up by future scholars to further deepen our understanding of the remarkable events of this period.

10

A Hidden Life Made Manifest (1968–1971)

Apparitions at Zeitoun, 1968

> "The man who sighs over his soul for but one hour is greater than
> he who raises the dead by his prayer . . . the man who is deemed worthy
> to see himself is greater than he who is deemed worthy to see angels. . . ."
> —*St Isaac the Syrian*

W HEN THE SIX-DAY WAR erupted on June 5, 1967, Fr Raphael Ava
Mina stormed into Kyrillos' office. News of the Egyptian Army's success had just been broadcast. "The war has begun," Raphael exclaimed, "our
army is advancing and winning!"

"What are you saying . . . are you insane!?"—Kyrillos shouted while raising
his hands to heaven—". . . My sons! My sons! My sons are at war . . . God protect them! God protect them!" That evening the elderly patriarch paced up and
down repeating those words.

"I kept thinking," Fr Raphael reminisces,

> about what he said, in spite of the frequent news reports of the great advance-
> ment of the Egyptian Army. . . . I tried to let him see how well our army was
> doing, and that he need not worry about his people, but Kyrillos answered
> saying, "You do not understand, my son; God protect them. . . ." Indeed, I did
> not understand. After four days, we discovered the news was *incorrect*. . . .[1]

Kyrillos, despite the propaganda, saw something that no one else could. The
Church had suffered several contentious episodes in 1967, and now this tragic
war would leave the nation in mourning.

* * *

In response to Egypt secretly mobilizing forces along the border, Israel launched a preemptive strike against the Egyptian airfields. Within moments, the greater part of the Egyptian Air Force was destroyed. Simultaneously, an Israeli ground offensive at the Gaza Strip and the Sinai Peninsula caught the Egyptian Army by surprise, inflicting heavy losses and mass confusion. Fewer than a thousand Israeli soldiers were killed, compared to over twenty thousand of the Arab forces. In just five days, the air force was decimated, tens of thousands killed, the Sinai Peninsula seized, intangible assets obliterated, and national pride and regional credibility abrogated.[2] Nasser's regime was discredited, and his policies devalued.[3] Unable to bear the seismic failure and embarrassment, the president, in a public broadcast on June 9, stepped down.[4] But the magnitude of the defeat was still unknown.[5] Frenzied demonstrations erupted. Eric Rouleau, *Le Monde's* foreign correspondent, described the reaction:

> And then [after the statement], from the twelfth story of the house in which we were . . . we heard a swelling tumult, muffled and menacing—like an approaching storm, yet the weather was perfect. . . . From all sides we saw people coming out of their houses like ants, and heads leaning out of windows. We went down. It was dusk and the city was half immersed in the darkness of the blackout. It was an extraordinary spectacle to see all those people hurrying from all sides, shouting, weeping, some wearing pyjamas, some barefoot, women in nightdresses, children, all tormented by a suffering beyond endurance and imploring, "Nasser, do not leave us, we need you. . . ." Women fell to the ground, like the weeping women of antiquity. . . . Men burst into tears.[6]

As soon as Kyrillos heard the broadcast, he too rushed to the Presidential Palace. The roads were blocked by hundreds of thousands of grief-stricken men and women. Nasser immediately dispatched an army convoy to escort the papal vehicles to his home. But even there, Nasser would not receive any visitors. After some time, a phone was brought to Kyrillos; Nasser was on the line. "I have never refused to meet you in my house," he apologized, "but I am sick and am surrounded by doctors."

"I wish to hear one promise from you only," Kyrillos answered.

"Say it, my father."

"The people," Kyrillos replied, "demand that you remain in power."

"And I," Nasser said, "am at their command and your command."

When Kyrillos returned to the patriarchate early the next morning, he had the cathedral bells rung in celebration.[7] Minutes later there was another broadcast: Nasser would remain president. Not even Nasser's wife had expected the retraction.[8]

When the Egyptian people finally realized the extent of the nation's losses in the war, they asked for the heads of several high-ranking officers. Abdel Hakim Amer, the commander-in-chief of the armed forces, was arrested for alleged conspiracy and subsequently committed suicide. The army was depoliticized, and loyalists to Amer were removed. Nasser effectively distanced himself from the entirety of the failed war, as well as its aftermath.[9] "When the masses love," a famed Egyptian playwright, Tawfiq el-Hakim, comments, "they do not question or discuss. . . . When [Nasser] would forcefully tell a nuclear power that if she did not like what we did, she should drink the Nile, we felt proud . . . confidence in our leader paralyzed our thoughts."[10] But though the catastrophic war had somehow left the President intact, the Church was left vulnerable once more.

* * *

The Copts suffered on two fronts in the fallout of the war. Standing alongside their Muslim brethren, they, too, had lost fathers, husbands, and sons. But that did little to silence the accusations of "Christian" espionage; the Coptic Church was, after all, a member of the World Council of Churches which happened to support the founding of Israel.[11] At the same time, religious sentiments were slowly resurrected from the ashes. Many felt the war was a "punishment" for a "lack of faith," and in Egypt, the reemergence of "faith" could in an instant radicalize and spark sectarian violence.[12] Tensions swiftly intensified. Nasser was compelled to publicly praise the bravery and patriotism of Coptic soldiers to soften somewhat the increasing accusations from the Muslim Brotherhood.[13] But as Christians braced themselves for a new wave of tribulation, Egypt suddenly witnessed a turn of events from a most unexpected source.[14] The painful year of 1967—marked by the Six-Day War, rising religious tensions, the *maglis'* financial crisis, contentions between disciples, and Shenouda's suspension—was in a moment forgotten.

On the evening of April 2, 1968, three Muslim mechanics, Farouk Mohammed Atwa, Hussein Awad, and Yacout Ali Mocamoun, were working at a municipal garage located opposite the Church of St Mary in Zeitoun, a suburb of Cairo.[15] At around eight-thirty that night, Atwa noticed a young girl walking on the dome of the Church and, fearing she would jump, he began shouting. One of these mechanics described the sight:

> A figure dressed in white on top of the dome of the church. I thought she was going to commit suicide and shouted to her to be careful. My friend called the police, and I woke up the doorkeeper. He comes out and looks and cries, "It is the Virgin," and runs to call the priest.[16]

The priest was just as shocked. "I was at home," recalls Fr Constantine Moussa (d. 1982),

> only steps from the church when Ibrahim [the doorkeeper] came in very distressed, saying, "St Mary has appeared on the dome". . . . I went myself and saw an illuminated half body of St Mary . . . some of the bus depot workers directed spotlights in her direction, but she illuminated more. . . .[17]

A crowd began to gather. The police arrived and attempted to disperse them, stating that the so-called apparition was merely an illusion caused by the reflection of the adjacent streetlights. They duly proceeded to break the offending lights, but the apparition only became more intense. "The *ma'amur* [police chief]," one witness reported, "became frightened and said that he wanted nothing more to do with this; while others came closer to be sure of what they saw."[18] A week later the vision recurred, as it would for some seventy nights over the next fourteen months. City officials—for the most part, Muslim—first suspected an elaborate hoax and disconnected all lights and electricity in the surrounding areas. The apparitions persisted unchanged.[19]

Over these fourteen months, the nightly attendees averaged from ten to one hundred thousand people. Witness accounts and recorded testimonies were taken from doctors, engineers, press, government officials—and President Nasser himself. Cynthia Nelson (1933–2006), a professor of anthropology at the American University in Cairo, was one such eyewitness. She visited on several occasions and had expected a mass delusion of the uneducated (and therefore suggestible) lower class. Instead, she found that most of those present were from the middle and upper classes, including numerous Europeans from the embassies.

"I could trace the outline of a figure," Nelson recalls,

> there was no doubt in my mind that there was a light and that if I looked for the image, it would come into focus. I immediately "explained" this perceptual experience as an illusion caused by reflected light. But the source of the

light was a mystery, for the streetlights had been disconnected all around the church for several days. And within another week all the trees around the church would be cut. . . .[20]

Interestingly, Nelson felt the need to "explain" the apparition away—and yet she found no such explanation. At times the Virgin was still; others reported she would move from side to side blessing the masses, and on occasion, she would have an olive branch in hand, surrounded by white doves. Investigative committees were established by Kyrillos VI, by Stephanos I of the Coptic Catholics, and by the government. Each independently, lacking any alternate explanation, affirmed the apparitions.[21] "Official investigations have been carried out," stated the government report. "It has been considered an undeniable fact that the blessed Virgin Mary has appeared at the Coptic Orthodox Church of Zeitoun in a clear and bright luminous body, seen by all present . . . whether Christian or Muslim."[22] Kyrillos had sent some of his most trusted bishops, doctors, and scientists to investigate the apparition—though he himself had strangely avoided any visit. On May 4, 1968, the patriarchate declared the apparition to be genuine; a day later it was published in *al-Ahram*:

> This committee stationed itself at Zeitoun for days without interruption. . . . The extraordinary visions of the past weeks have been attested to by thousands of people from all walks of life, Egyptians and foreigners of various nationalities; and groups of them have agreed on time and place of the apparition. With the facts collected, we have concluded that the apparitions are not false individual visions or mass hallucinations but are real.[23]

Multiple accounts suggest that President Nasser traveled with Hussein el-Shafei (the secretary of the Higher Islamic Council at the time) to Zeitoun. There he would watch from the balcony of a fruit merchant opposite the church until 5:00 a.m.[24] Shenouda III would later note that Nasser was in desperate need of comfort after the humiliating defeat of 1967. More than a million of his people had witnessed the apparitions and sought that same comfort. In the minds of most Egyptians, therefore, it was impossible to separate the apparitions from the failed war.[25] The wife of Anwar Sadat (Nasser's eventual successor) once remarked, "Faith was the only resort for most Egyptians."[26] Nasser reportedly declared the apparition to be a consolation, that the defeat was indeed God's will.[27] Some discerned an omen that God would aid the Arabs in their war against Israel; for others, it was a vindication of Christian Egypt, soothing, in part, the sectarian tensions; while others still remarked that it was a testament to the sanctity of Kyrillos himself.[28] Whatever the interpretation, the apparitions gave hope.[29] "It is a sign from heaven," Bishop Gregorious declared at the May 4 press conference, "that God is with us, and will be with us."[30]

Within the history of the Coptic Church—and greater Christendom at that—the apparitions were altogether unusual. Never had an apparition been so frequent, nor witnessed by so many. Not once did the Theotokos speak; there was no utterance, no oracle.[31] It was as though she spoke silence to the anxieties of a broken nation. Just as one may receive indescribable comfort from the gentle silence of one's mother, likewise, for fourteen months the Theotokos comforted the nation.

Whatever one may make of these unusual apparitions, Nelson, an anthropologist, is at pains to make clear that this was not the "overactive imagination" of superstitious, lower class, and easily fooled peasants, but rather, the witnesses were overwhelmingly middle and upper class.[32] A Marxist (and Muslim) sociologist remarked to Nelson that it was *this* that most disturbed him—that the apparitions were witnessed and testified to by the "intellectual elite" of Egypt:

> It would be more understandable if such a thing had occurred in Upper Egypt, where it is known that the peasants are great believers in supernatural phenomena like this—but physicians, scientists, professors—these people are *more* rational! They must have to compartmentalize their thinking, or else they are schizophrenic.[33]

It may only be suggested that to believe a million or so "rational" men and women (many of whom were intellectuals), over several months, were all "schizophrenic" when most had never exhibited any signs of mental illness either before or after the events is, at the very least, suggestive of prejudiced imperception. The account of a prominent Cairo surgeon is, in this sense, symbolic:

> A patient of mine upon whom I had operated two years ago for cancer returned to my office three weeks ago for a check-up. Upon examination, I discovered that the man had another tumor. I actually felt the tumor during the internal examination and removed a piece of tissue for biopsy. When the test showed it was malignant I recommended an immediate operation, but the man refused, saying he did not have enough money. . . . Two weeks later he returned and asked for another examination. To my astonishment I could not find the tumor, but only some white scar tissue. The man told me he had gone to Zeitoun and prayed to the Virgin for help. I do not believe in

such miracles, but I *cannot* explain the disappearance of the tumor and *it is driving me mad. . . .*[34]

Miracle after miracle was reported—most without any medical explanation. As the apparitions recurred, month after month, it became something of an existential dilemma. No one, try as they might, could explain the apparitions. Ultimately, one had to choose either to believe or not. But all—believers and unbelievers alike—began to ask what Kyrillos, the famed miracle-worker, thought of the apparitions? And, why had he never visited Zeitoun?

* * *

In a fascinating, little-known interview with Michael Khalil, published by *al-Akhbar* newspaper on May 11, 1968, we find a most precious disclosure from the silent patriarch.[35] Why, Khalil asked, had Kyrillos not headed the press conference declaring the apparitions genuine? And, most importantly, why hadn't he seen the apparitions personally? "All these," Kyrillos said while smiling, "are usual accusations spoken during such holy phenomena—because the apparition of the Mother of the Light is something which surpasses the human mind."[36] Kyrillos had not attended the press conference as he had already delegated three bishops to investigate and attend on his behalf—but, he makes clear, they "expressed my personal point of view, beliefs, and opinion." "As for my visitation to the church," Kyrillos corrects,

> I will go at the appropriate time chosen by God to pray following the *same routine* I do in all churches. . . . I will go to this holy place after everyone is convinced of the apparition. I did not want it to be said that I influence the people to do as I do. Thus, I left them to reach their *own* conclusions on the matter. . . .[37]

But he also had other reasons for not visiting. "The truth is," he continued,

> I see the Mother of the Light, the peaceful dove, the pure lady Virgin Mary, mother of Jesus Christ; I have seen her since my young age, and I see her with faith. I have experienced the marks of her wonders in the house where I was brought up, in al-Nile Street in Alexandria. That was in 1910, the Virgin appeared in the house of my parents with her luminous attire, and her glittering crown. . . . On that day, she healed a sick person in that house. This incident deeply touched all the members of my family including me. Her

icon remained a source of blessings in my parents' house, so we all grew up in her love. This blessed and holy incident has never departed my mind. . . .[38]

This is an exceedingly rare disclosure. Kyrillos, rarely, if ever, spoke of himself—and never publicly. But here he reveals an apparition of the Theotokos and healing in his family home when he was some eight years of age. We can only assume that he spoke of his mother, who died a few years later. For this reason, he felt little need to visit Zeitoun to witness the apparition of St Mary, for he had, in some mysterious sense, always seen her.

"Take Care of the Church": Last Moments of a Saint, 1971

> "Abba Moses asked Abba Zacharias, who was at the *point of death*, 'What do you see?' He said, 'Is it not *better* to hold my peace, Father?'"
> —*Abba Zacharias*

O N SEPTEMBER 28, 1970, only hours after an emergency Arab League Summit, President Nasser died from a heart attack. Though he was a heavy smoker with a strong family history of heart disease—two of his brothers had met similar fates in their fifties—Nasser's death came as a shock to the public (and even Nasser's own family).[39] Kyrillos' statement that evening expressed the pain of all: "Sadness heavily engulfs our nation. . . . We did not believe that this man, who held within him the hopes of all Egyptians and Arabs, could die."[40] The cathedral bells were rung, and, strangely, a commemoration Liturgy was celebrated for the Muslim president. Nasser, we should carefully recall, had always called Kyrillos "my father"—and so the patriarch prayed for his son.[41]

Whatever Egyptians may have felt for the president, an eminent historian notes, the "fifteen years of Nasser's revolutionary regime did not resolve any of the perennial concerns of their country."[42] Despite his commendable efforts, population growth increased uncontrollably, a new and extravagant upper class emerged untouched by his socialist policies, illiteracy barely moved, unemployment rose steadily, foreign policy was shattered by the 1967 war, and corruption remained rife.[43] But though Egypt had hardly improved in Nasser's reign, the same cannot be said of the Church under Kyrillos.

* * *

Some years earlier, in 1966, one of Kyrillos' disciples delivered a speech in which he praised the work of the patriarch and wished that God would prolong his life. "My son," Kyrillos replied with his characteristic enigmatic brevity, "it's all a matter of *five* years."[44]

Throughout the ascetical literature, there are numerous instances of holy men declaring premonitions of their deaths.[45] Few, if any at all, have noticed just how much of that ascetical literature pivots around the "point of death." The phrase is found, for instance, in sixteen accounts of the *Apophthegmata Patrum*. In the life of many, Christian or otherwise, the last words are considered a profound summation of one's life. But for the desert fathers, they not only reveal who someone really is in the face of death—where there can be no pretense—but such words reveal what is absolutely and positively needful—an exquisitely personal utterance of their "way" to Christ. For Abba Zacharias, for instance, it was silence; for Arsenius, the transformation of his life sacrificed; for Bessarion, that a monk should be "all eye," that is, forever watchful; for Abba Isaac, that his disciples follow in his path, as he followed that of his father; and, quite mesmerizingly, for Abba Joseph of Panephysis:

> . . . when he was at the *point of death*, while some old men were seated around him, he looked towards the window and saw the devil sitting close to it. Then calling his disciple he said to him, "Bring my stick, for there is one there who thinks I am getting old and have no more strength against him."[46]

For Kyrillos, the silent patriarch, the last years would be marked by similar utterances—especially that of "traveling" and his "care for the Church." The "point of death" for Kyrillos was not a few hours, nor even a few days or weeks. Looking through the extant literature of accounts, memoirs, and letters, it appears the "point of death" for Kyrillos lasted some five years—perhaps from the moment of his premonition in 1966, which also coincided with his first episodes of angina.[47] From that moment he had, like Isaac the Syrian before him, lived with the "remembrance of death."[48] But that translation of an ancient injunction—*memento mori*—somewhat misses the literal meaning of the injunction, that is, "*remember to die*."[49] The last years were lived at the "point of death," with Kyrillos each day remembering to die. In late 1968, for instance, Kyrillos would insist on praying early Liturgies at the newly constructed cathedral. The windows were still to be fitted, and coupled with the soaring ceilings, in the middle of winter, the conditions were severe. "On such nights," Fr Raphael recalls, "very few would attend."[50] Kyrillos, however, remained immovable, energetically rushing to the cathedral in the early hours of the morning. At times he would celebrate even though he had fevers higher than forty degrees Celsius (104°F). No matter how his bishops protested, Kyrillos persistently "remembered to die."

* * *

On May 5, 1970, Fr Marcos Dawood—the dear friend and confessor of Kyrillos—spoke to his son, Fr Mikhail Dawood, to organize a trip to the Monastery of St Menas. Knowing that Kyrillos was at the monastery, Fr Marcos insisted on going along, despite being extremely unwell at the time. "I tried to stop him," his son recollects,

> but he answered, "If you refuse, you will regret it forever." There, Fr Marcos stayed alone with the pope. At our departure, Fr Marcos said, "Your Holiness, I am *traveling*; do you want anything?" Kyrillos answered, "Thank you, I am traveling after you." The next day my father asked me to visit one of his relatives, but I apologized, so he replied, "Tomorrow you will be busy. . . ."[51]

The next day he was indeed busy. Fr Marcos passed away on May 7. Many had heard those words of Kyrillos, but few understood them. When another dear priest, Fr Pemen, reposed, Kyrillos seemed to be aware of this before any communication had arrived. One of Kyrillos' disciples recalls his confusion. "Fr Pemen," Kyrillos suddenly said, "has traveled, my son."

"He has traveled with your blessing," the disciple responded.

"I am telling you," Kyrillos repeated, "he has *traveled*, my son."

Still unsure as to what he meant, the disciple added, "In your love, *sayedna* [my master]."

"I meant, my son," Kyrillos explained, "he has *traveled* to heaven."

On that same visit to the Monastery of St Menas, the monks were just as perplexed. Fr Raphael Ava Mina, his disciple from the patriarchate who had since been tonsured, recalls Kyrillos' odd departure:

> In May 1970, the pope said his good-bye in a completely different manner [than usual]. He called upon Hegumen Mina Ava Mina, the monastery's abbot, and spoke to him very briefly while fighting back his tears, which eventually conquered him. He gave him *kalanswas* [the monastic head covering] for each of the monks in the monastery, he then [chanted] praises for St Mark and St Mina in both churches of the monastery. He was holding an icon of St Mark that he had since he was in solitude in the desert, and he

tried to smile at us, but his tears kept coming down vigorously. He did not sit down with any of us but instead got into his car with his tears falling from his face. We saw that and then asked ourselves: Where is the pope's smile? Where are his long meetings with each of us? . . . What is the secret behind those tears? Why was he holding St Mark's icon in his hand? These questions remained unanswered. . . .[52]

It would be his last visit to the Monastery of St Menas. It was nearly impossible for him to contain his emotions, for he evidently knew what they could not. Over the next months, Kyrillos began delegating tasks, entrusting odd jobs to certain disciples, priests, and bishops. Envelopes were arranged for widows and the destitute, souls that he had secretly supported for decades.[53] He knew the end was near.

The years of severe asceticism would eventually take their toll. Kyrillos developed a crippling deep-vein thrombosis, but even then, his canon remained unchanged. The doctors attempted to treat Kyrillos with medications and rest, but he was noncompliant.[54] The thrombosis propagated some ten centimeters (almost four inches) in consequence. At this point, Kyrillos reluctantly accepted their orders of two months' bedrest.[55] A brief time later, on October 24, 1970, the patriarchate released a statement in *al-Ahram* stating that Kyrillos was confined once more to bedrest and that the minister of health had organized a team of cardiologists to provide around-the-clock care.[56] Though the announcement had not stated the words explicitly, Kyrillos, now sixty-eight years of age, had suffered a heart attack. "You can imagine," Fr Raphael reminisces in his memoirs,

> the sorrow that His Holiness went through when the doctors ordered him to stay in bed after suffering several heart attacks. Being separated from the altar affected him greatly, especially after forty years of praying the daily psalmody and Liturgy. Upon the pope's request, I set up speakers in his cell, so that he would be able to follow the prayers at the cathedral. . . .[57]

The agony of the heart attacks could never compare to being forced away from the altar—the place of his daily comfort for some forty years. Each morning he would rise early, turn on his speakers, and share in the liturgical life of the cathedral. "[Kyrillos] would listen," Raphael notes, "so carefully as to later correct the priests, saying do not rush in the prayers, or would even correct their pronunciation of the Coptic language."[58] As he lay bedridden for these few months, Kyrillos would also have to contend with an old enmity. At one point a movement apparently arose to precociously "retire" Kyrillos and discuss the matter of his successor.[59] Even to the end, he would sit on his balcony and hear old hierarchs cursing his name, but never once would he react, to the dismay of those around him.[60] It would matter little in any case. They were too late. Though he may have become increasingly ill and enfeebled, the Church had already been healed from within.

After recovering and briefly returning to his duties for a few months, Kyrillos became unwell with influenza in the first week of March 1971.[61] "I want . . . ," Kyrillos croaked in his ever-deep voice to one of his visiting relatives at that time. "I want. . . ."

"What would you like, Your Holiness? We will bring it," the visitor responded.

"I want . . . I want to *travel*."

The visitor thought he meant the Monastery of St Menas and so replied, "But the weather is still too cold. . . ."[62]

Kyrillos had sufficiently recovered on March 7 so that, against the orders of his doctors, he celebrated the Liturgy.[63] We have no record of that Liturgy but can only dare to imagine the sentiments of the elderly patriarch. The next day he called his secretary, Hegumen Benjamin Kamel, into his room and asked him to take a seat.[64] "That's it, Father," Kyrillos managed.

"What do you mean, *Sayedna*?" Benjamin replied.

"That's it, everything is over. . . ."

"Don't say that!" Benjamin interrupted. "May God grant you health and prolong your life."

"Health is gone. . . . Life . . . has ended," Kyrillos quietly said before pausing and adding, "*Take care of the Church*, Father, attend to its needs. . . . May God be with you and look after your affairs." Before Hegumen Benjamin could understand the words, Kyrillos extended his hands and blessed him, handed him some important files that he had never entrusted to anyone, and gave him the cross to kiss, as a sign their meeting was over. Benjamin left the room speechless.

On Tuesday, March 9, Kyrillos awoke at 5:30 a.m., switched on his speakers and prayed with the fathers in the cathedral from his cell.[65] Doctor Michel Girgis—a cardiologist who had been living at the patriarchate since Kyrillos' heart attack a few months earlier—examined the frail patriarch before allowing any visitors in. One by one Kyrillos comforted them, repeating, "May God take care of your affairs." After a few hours, Kyrillos came to the door and asked "as to whether there remained any of his children who wanted to see him."[66] He then raised his cross and looked at all those who were around him and said one final time, "God take care of your affairs."[67]

As the door closed, Kyrillos suddenly became light-headed and fell. A disciple managed to assist him to his bed and called out for the doctor. By the time he arrived only minutes later, Kyrillos VI, the silent patriarch, at 10:30 a.m., had breathed his last.[68] Kyrillos had, in his own words, *traveled*.

* * *

Those closest to the reposed patriarch were permitted to enter his room. They found him wearing an inner garment of a coarse fabric resembling sackcloth.[69] In tears, they changed his clothes to those rarely worn white-and-gold patriarchal vestments. They had not yet read Kyrillos' will, which threatened excommunication for anyone who dared to ignore his wish to be "buried with the clothes I am wearing at that time, with no need for any other."[70] "This was the will of God," one of his closest disciples noted, "that he would be honored in his death even though he had not honored himself during his life."[71] On his desk they found envelopes with various names: some for widows, others for parishes and monasteries, suggesting, one disciple commented, "a person who knew the exact day of his departure."[72] When his private drawers were examined, letters addressed to Kyrillos were found—letters teeming with mockery, ridicule, insult, and derision. They were, evidently, the only letters Kyrillos thought worth keeping.[73]

The news spread rapidly; bells began ringing throughout Cairo, Alexandria, and the entire nation. A delegation arrived from the Monastery of St Menas, with a copy of Kyrillos' will in hand.[74] The next day, March 10, the body was seated upon the patriarchal throne in the cathedral, on which he rarely sat in life. Hundreds of thousands took the blessing of the patriarch who had desired to remain hidden and unknown.[75] Seven thousand people refused to leave and remained at the cathedral in a vigil that night until 5:00 a.m. on March 11, when the body was prepared for the funeral.[76] Once his will was discovered, the attire was returned to his simple black cassock; the patriarchal staff was placed in his left hand and the cross in his right.[77]

Standing over the coffin, Bishop Antonious of Souhag, the locum tenens, delivered the eulogy:

> It is extremely hard for us to stand and grieve him, but this is the will of
> God. . . . It is hard for us to see for the final time his pure body among us in
> this great cathedral that he built. . . . The heart of Pope Kyrillos was open to

all, his door was open to the poor before the rich, the young before the old . . .
welcoming them, patiently and lovingly listening to them with a smile that
never left his lips. . . . A true man . . . and they are all too rare. . . . History will
record his virtues that are seldom granted to others, especially his incredible
humility that accompanied him as a solitary hermit. . . . He is immortal, he
will not be forgotten. We shall not forget him; the nation will not forget him.
He departed in the hope of the Resurrection. . . .[78]

And then, in words directed to Kyrillos and not the congregation, Bishop
Antonious looked to the reposed holy man:

Sleep, my master, and rest, your deeds will follow you. . . . I, my master, if I
speak, my tongue may betray me, my feelings regardless of what I say cannot
convey nor embrace all that you are due, for you were a great saint in the very
depth of that word. . . .[79]

The metropolitans, bishops, priests, and deacons carried the body in a procession around the altar three times, before laying the coffin to rest beneath the
cathedral. It would be a temporary burial place. Kyrillos' will had also stipulated
that he was to be buried at the Monastery of St Menas. It took almost two years
to prepare an appropriate site.[80] In that time, one of Kyrillos' disciples, Bishop
Shenouda, was consecrated patriarch on November 14, 1971. Though Shenouda
III was counseled by many—including some of Kyrillos' own family—to leave
the body at peace, he knew otherwise than to ignore the will of his former spiritual father.[81] On the timely eve of the Feast of St Menas, November 22, 1972, the
coffin was exhumed. Bishop Gregorious was unsurprised to find that the corpse
had not decomposed in the slightest.[82] The next day the coffin was moved to the
Monastery of St Menas. The press was alight with news of unusual meteorologi-
cal events that day: unprecedented lightning and heavy rains in Cairo (a rarity
for that time of year), and the opposite on their arrival in Mariout.[83] "I don't
know," remarked Shenouda, "how the spirit of Kyrillos VI will greet the spirit
of St Menas, in what manner will they greet each other?"—before adding with
gentle delight—"He never loved anyone in his life like he did St Menas. . . ."[84]

After Vespers, the body of the solitary patriarch was finally laid to rest in that
place for which he had yearned since 1936, a place of solitude where he could be
hidden in God. But try as he might, that life hidden in God was now manifest.

What began in a cave of the Baramous Monastery, took root in the windmill,
and radiated in the modest Church of St Menas' in Old Cairo would eventually,
only a few decades later, end in the transformation of an entire Church. The

previous patriarch was kidnapped and dethroned, leaving the Church without a leader for almost four years. Now the very opposite: monasteries once decrepit and on the brink of closure were revived as icons of holiness; clergy once illiterate, corrupt, and ineffective were theologically educated, creating parishes as centers of revival and healing; the episcopate, once the humiliating home of simony, became the light of the Church as prophetic overseers. Holiness had begotten holiness. At the funeral, Bishop Antonious of Souhag had said as much: Kyrillos was "a saint in the very depth of that word." Well before his canonization, the Church had declared him a saint. And, for many, that was the case even before his death.

* * *

In mid-1981, a mere decade after Kyrillos' repose, the Church was in the grips of tragedy once more. Anwar Sadat, the new president of Egypt, had turned to Islam in a bid to consolidate his authority. Many of the Muslim Brotherhood were released, Islamic societies were funded, pulpits amplified, and radical ideologies tolerated. Portraying himself as the "devout president," Sadat unleashed unpredictable forces upon the always-fragile sectarian current. Churches were bombed, businesses destroyed, Christians massacred, and the constitution amended to something close to *Sharia* law. Shenouda could not (and did not) remain silent. Egypt was in upheaval. Sadat, on September 3, 1981, reacted by imprisoning—along with a large contingent of Islamic and political figures— some eight bishops, twenty-four priests, and dozens of prominent Copts. Two days later he placed Pope Shenouda III under "house arrest" at the Monastery of St Bishoy, where he would remain for more than three years, and appointed a committee of five bishops in his place.

The priests were imprisoned in twelve cells, two by two. A little-known account by one of those priests, Fr Ibrahim Abdo, preserves a most curious occurrence during their imprisonment. Having no other recourse except God's mercy, they each agreed to prostrate themselves, chanting *Kyrie eleison* ("Lord, have mercy") four hundred times every day. "This is history," Fr Ibrahim recalls,

> that I am recording for our children and our children's children so that you will know the power of your Church and what the spirituality of your Church can do. . . . On that thirty-second day [of imprisonment], the fifth of October, we were standing at three in the afternoon praying the ninth hour canonical prayers. . . . We looked and saw Pope Kyrillos [VI] entering our cell, and I was with another priest. . . . He was floating above the ground a bit,

in his hand a cross. . . . [We saw him] just as you see me now. Not a dream-vision. We were not sleeping. I told you, we were standing at three in the afternoon praying the ninth hour prayers. With a wide smile [Pope Kyrillos] said, "Don't be afraid. The matter has been resolved," and he disappeared. In the midst of the prayers, I stuck my mouth in the [cell] opening and shouted, "You Copts! Shall I tell you some joyous news?" They responded, "What? What is it, Abouna?" I told them, "We are leaving [prison] today!" "How do you know?!" I said, "Pope Kyrillos was just here and said, 'Don't be afraid. The matter has been resolved.' So, we are getting out today!" I then found Fr Tadros Yacoub—I was in cell sixteen he was in cell seventeen with another father . . . —saying: "Okay, since Fr Ibrahim has said this, then [Pope Kyril-los] wants me to say as well; he was truly just [in our cell] as well and said the same words, 'Do not be afraid. The matter has been resolved' and many other things that I will not reveal. . . ."[85]

The day after, October 6, 1981, Sadat was assassinated by an Islamist while, ironically, at an annual victory parade. When the warden broke the news to the imprisoned priests, they were not in the least surprised.

This account may, naturally, seem incredible to some. I asked that priest, Fr Tadros Yacoub Malaty—a priest well known to me—who was, according to the account, in the next cell, whether these events did, in fact, take place. His reply was initially guarded.[86] Fr Tadros, a man of unquestionable integrity and honesty (and perhaps the most prolific Coptic scholar of his generation), has for some six decades refused to speak of himself. "For me," Fr Tadros hesitat-ingly added, "I do not remember the details, but I remember that Pope Kyrillos revealed to us that we would be free from the jail and nothing would hurt us." I pressed for further details. "I do not remember the details," he replied, "because I am not interested in these matters." When I urged once more that I preferred not to reproduce Fr Ibrahim's account if it was an embellishment or inaccu-rate, he finally conceded, "It is true and should be written."[87] As for Fr Tadros' final comment in the above account—"and many other things that I will not reveal"—I had not the audacity to ask.

Even after death, Kyrillos lived his last words: "Take care of the Church." In the Coptic Church's most vulnerable moment in 1981, with Islamic radical-ism unleashed, the patriarch exiled, and deep factions developing, once more Kyrillos mystically interceded. This account—one that I consider to be beyond reproach—reveals not only that Kyrillos was indeed a saint, but that even after his death, his only concern was to fulfill his own words. And for tens of millions around the world, he continues to do the same even now, with volumes of post-death miracles appearing every few years. One cannot, therefore, but recall Kyrillos' vision in 1942 of receiving a "broken" patriarchal staff from the reposed Youannis XIX. That broken staff, symbolic of a broken Church, fractured and profusely bleeding, was placed in Kyrillos' hands; and there, in twelve short years, it was mended and healed in ways that we will never truly comprehend. Kyrillos passed on that staff—the Church—healed and so full of light and life, to his successors. For tens of millions of Copts (and Muslims), however, his hand has never—not for an instant—left that same staff.

Kyrillos' was a most remarkable life—a life that lives well beyond death. In the long, rich, and profound history of Christianity, there have only been a few stories of ecclesial reform and healing that are as genuinely beautiful, revolutionary, and irresistibly transformative as this one.

Notes

[1]Raphael Ava Mina, *Fruits of Love*, 7–8; also his audio recording, "My Memories."

[2]Laura M. James, *Nasser at War: Arab Images of the Enemy* (New York: Palgrave Macmillan, 2006), 102.

[3]Vatikiotis, *The History of Egypt*, 406.

[4]McDermott, *Egypt from Nasser to Mubarak*, 10.

[5]Vatikiotis, *The History of Egypt*, 406–7.

[6]Eric Rouleau, *Middle East Record*, 1967, 554; cited in McDermott, *Egypt from Nasser to Mubarak*, 34–35.

[7]For the accounts of Kyrillos visiting Nasser see Zaklama, *Pope Kyrillos VI*, 2:82–83; Nasr, *Readings in the Life of Abouna Mina*, 158; Fawzi, *Kyrillos and Abdel Nasser*, 74–75.

[8]Nasser, *Nasser: My Husband*, 96–97. Nasser's wife recalls that he was feeling unwell and so took a sedative before sleeping. By the next morning he had changed his mind. Some have suggested it was simply a "tactical move"; see McDermott, *Egypt from Nasser to Mubarak*, 10.

[9]For a discussion of Nasser's role and responsibility in the failure of the war see Vatikiotis, *Nasser and His Generation*, 255–60.

[10]Cited in ibid., 319–20.

[11]On one hand the Copts were accused of espionage and of being sympathetic to the state of Israel—they were, after all, a member of the World Council of Churches, which supported the founding of Israel—and on the other, Kyrillos publicly stood alongside Nasser, in line with other Middle Eastern Churches, in rejecting the occupation of Jerusalem—perceived to be ongoing Western Zionist imperialism that served only to divide the region—as well as clearly opposing the Vatican's *Nostra aetate*. In August 1967, Kyrillos cancelled the annual pilgrimage during the Feast of St Mary in protest of the latter; he also sent Bishop Samuel to explain the Arab-Christian perspective throughout all Egypt; see Fawzi, *Kyrillos and Abdel Nasser*, 75. The Vatican's exoneration of the Jewish nation in the crucifixion of Christ came at an exquisitely sensitive time for the Coptic Church—rising pan-Arabism, displaced Arab Christians in Palestine, the transfer of holy sites to Israel, and the ever-so-divisive Deir al-Sultan—and so, one needs to read all declarations from the patriarchate in these years within this context of a nation at war. We also need to bear in mind—as was reiterated by the likes of Fr Tadros Yacoub Malaty—that we cannot tell what to trust out of these declarations concerning Israel in newspapers and media controlled by Nasser. For various perspectives, see Meinardus, *Two Thousand Years*, 84; van Doorn-Harder, *Modern Coptic Papacy*, 136; Watson, *Among the Copts*, 131. For a discussion of Christian (including

non-Orthodox) attitudes after the Six-Day War, see Paul Charles Merkley, *Christian Attitudes to the State of Israel* (Montreal: McGill-Queen's University Press, 2001), 37–43. Also in this vein for the sensitivities of the period, see the account of a disgraced monk, Armanious, who published in 1960 a forged letter from Kyrillos to Ben Gurion, Prime Minister of Israel, attempting to drive a wedge between Nasser and Kyrillos; see Fawzi, *Kyrillos and Abdel Nasser*, 94–125.

[12]Makari, "Conflict and Cooperation," 95.

[13]For instance, see Cynthia Nelson, "The Virgin of Zeitoun," *Worldview* 16, no. 9 (1973): 10.

[14]Heardon, "Lessons from Zeitoun," 410.

[15]The Church was built in 1925 by Khalil Ibrahim Pasha for his family; Meinardus, *Two Thousand Years*, 201.

[16]Cited from his testimony in major newspapers by Cynthia Nelson, "The Virgin of Zeitoun," 5; For another account see Atta and Raphael Ava Mina, *Life of Pope Kyrillos*, 36; Fayek Ishak, "Apparation of the Virgin Mary," in *CE*, 2308b–2310a; I. H. al-Masri, a Coptic historian, witnessed the apparitions herself, see al-Masri, *True Story of Christianity in Egypt*, 2:447–48.

[17]Zaklama, *Pope Kyrillos VI*, 2:22–23.

[18]Nelson, "The Virgin of Zeitoun," 5.

[19]Heardon, "Lessons from Zeitoun," 415.

[20]Nelson, "The Virgin of Zeitoun," 6.

[21]See Heardon, "Lessons from Zeitoun," 415.

[22]Ibid.; van Doorn-Harder, *Modern Coptic Papacy*, 153.

[23]Cited in Nelson, "The Virgin of Zeitoun," 6. For the entire decree (which is missed in the English translation), see Atta and Raphael Ava Mina, *Memories about the Life of Pope Kyrillos*, 76; Fawzi, *Kyrillos and Abdel Nasser*, 80–82.

[24]Fawzi, *Kyrillos and Abdel Nasser*, 78; Sundkler and Steed, *A History of the Church in Africa*, 924–25; al-Masri, *Story of the Coptic Church*, 7:53; Nasr, *Readings in the Life of Abouna Mina*, 101. Nasr, for instance, states that Bishop Shenouda claimed Nasser stayed all night to see it as he too, like Egypt, needed comfort after the war. Interestingly, Voile states she searched through *al-Ahram* archives looking for a mention that Nasser visited Zeitoun but found nothing—but she does concede that it was confirmed to her (though she does not state the details) while she was examining the microfilm; it was well known, albeit not documented; see Voile, *Les Coptes d'Égypte*, 229.

[25]Nelson, "The Virgin of Zeitoun," 8; van Doorn-Harder, "Practical and Mystical," 232.

[26]Watson, *Among the Copts*, 62.

[27]McDermott, *Egypt from Nasser to Mubarak*, 183.

[28]Nelson claims Bishop Samuel said the former after the May 4 press conference, see Nelson, "The Virgin of Zeitoun," 6. For the other interpretations, see Sundkler and Steed, *A History of the Church in Africa*, 925; Atta and Raphael Ava Mina, *Life of Pope Kyrillos*, 36; Raphael Ava Mina, *Memories: Part II*, 25; van Doorn-Harder, *Modern Coptic Papacy*, 153; van Doorn-Harder, "Practical and Mystical," 153. One interesting and symbolic account is that of a Muslim *hadji* who lived along the road that many Christian pilgrims took to the church; he would shout and scream at them, even throwing rocks—until, that is, St Mary reportedly appeared to him, at which point he painted his home in white crosses—albeit, apparently, remaining a Muslim. See Ronald Bullivant, "The Visions of the Mother of God at Zeitun," *Eastern Churches Review* 3 (1970–1971): 76.

[29]Later, Nelson notes the apparitions would take on other meanings and purposes—like the "conversion" of Muslims to Christianity; Nelson, "The Virgin of Zeitoun," 10.

[30]Voile, *Les Coptes d'Égypte*, 221–23.

[31]Heardon, "Lessons from Zeitoun," 416; Voile, *Les Coptes d'Égypte*, 220; Meinardus, *Christian Egypt: Faith and Life*, 264–69.

[32]Nelson, "The Virgin of Zeitoun," 10–11.

[33]Ibid., 11.

[34]Ibid.

[35]Khalil, "Interview with Pope Kyrillos." The interview is also cited, importantly, by Fr Raphael Ava Mina; see Raphael Ava Mina, *Memories: Part II*, 22–25.

[36]Khalil, "Interview with Pope Kyrillos."

[37]Ibid.

[38]Ibid. Also of interest is an account of the reception of the relics of St Mark from the Vatican when a vision of doves (which rarely fly at night) appeared. This caused a metropolitan and Fr Raphael to rush out of their vehicle and view the vision; they turned around and found Kyrillos in the car, entirely undisturbed, uninterested, and not the least inclined to "see the vision." See Raphael Ava Mina, "My Memories," audio recording.

[39]Vatikiotis, *Nasser and His Generation*, 303–4.

[40]Cited in Zaklama, *Pope Kyrillos VI*, 2:85.

[41]This was of course not a funeral, but rather simply an obedience to the litanies of the liturgy, which command one to pray for the leader of the nation.

[42]Vatikiotis, *Nasser and His Generation*, 361.

[43]For a fair assessment of Nasser's presidency see ibid., 348–64.

[44]Atta and Raphael Ava Mina, *Life of Pope Kyrillos*, 43.

[45]Rapp, *Holy Bishops*, 296.

[46]Ward, *Sayings of the Desert Fathers*, 68, 18, 42, 101–4.

[47]For the dating of his angina see al-Masri, *Story of the Coptic Church*, 7:71.

[48]Interestingly, it is one of the final themes in Kyrillos' favorite homily of Isaac; Isaac the Syrian, *Ascetical Homilies* 64.458; Alfeyev, *World of Isaac the Syrian*, 74.

[49]For a fascinating discussion of this notion see David Bentley Hart, *The Hidden and the Manifest: Essays in Theology and Metaphysics* (Grand Rapids, MI: Eerdmans, 2017), 253. For instance, "the ancient injunction *memento mori*—whispered by a slave into the ear of a victorious general in his triumphant chariot or by a monk to his own heart in the solitude of his own cell—has frequently been translated as 'Remember that thou art mortal,' which may be faithful to the phrase's special horatory force; but of course, the literal meaning of the injunction is 'remember to die.'"

[50]Atta and Raphael Ava Mina, *Life of Pope Kyrillos*, 21; Atta and Raphael Ava Mina, *Memories about the Life of Pope Kyrillos*, 45. The Arabic original states that there were "very few" attendees, while the English states there were "none."

[51]Adly, *Fr Mikhail Dawood's Memoirs*, 36. Also see al-Masri, *Story of the Coptic Church*, 7:71.

[52]Atta and Raphael Ava Mina, *Life of Pope Kyrillos*, 43.

[53]Ibid.

[54]Ibid., 42.

[55]On another occasion, Kyrillos was very obedient to his medical team, even when it was to his physical detriment; for instance, see the account of special diet that led to severe muscle loss, in Raphael Ava Mina, "My Memories," audio recording.

[56]Anonymous, "Pope Kyrillos' Illness: A Statement from the Patriarchate" [in Arabic], *al-Ahram*, October 24, 1970.

[57]Atta and Raphael Ava Mina, *Life of Pope Kyrillos*, 23.

[58]Atta and Raphael Ava Mina, *Memories about the Life of Pope Kyrillos*, 51. This is missed in the English translation.

[59]Anonymous Bishop, "Interview about the Life of Pope Kyrillos."

[60]Yostos, "Interview about the Life of Pope Kyrillos VI."

[61]Zaklama, *Pope Kyrillos VI*, 2:397.

[62]Atta and Raphael Ava Mina, *Life of Pope Kyrillos*, 43.

[63]Zaklama, *Pope Kyrillos VI*, 2:397.

[64]Nasr, *Readings in the Life of Abouna Mina*, 177; Atta and Raphael Ava Mina, *Life of Pope Kyrillos*, 43.

[65]Zaklama, *Pope Kyrillos VI*, 2:397.

[66]Atta and Raphael Ava Mina, *Life of Pope Kyrillos*, 44–45.

[67]Ibid.

[68]Fawzi, *Kyrillos and Abdel Nasser*, 156–57; Nasr, *Readings in the Life of Abouna Mina*, 178; Habib, *Among the Fathers*, 8; Zaklama, *Pope Kyrillos VI*, 2:398.

[69]Sidarous, "Lectures on Pope Kyrillos," Lecture 1.

[70]"Will of Pope Kyrillos VI," cited in Zaklama, *Pope Kyrillos VI*, 2:478.

[71]Atta and Raphael Ava Mina, *Life of Pope Kyrillos*, 45.

[72]Ibid., 43.

[73]Raphael Ava Mina, "Interview about the Life of Pope Kyrillos VI."

[74]The will: "I, the undersigned, with my signature, stamp, and handwriting, called by the grace of God, Kyrillos VI, request the following: 1. The fifty acres at the desert of Mariout and all dwellings on it belong to the Monastery of St Menas the Miracle Worker; 2. The piece of land at Saiouf in Alexandria; 3. The property at King Mariout; 4. The property at Moharem Bek; 5. All the property, land, and church in Old Cairo; All of these are the property of the Monastery of St Menas. I also request that after my departure and death, my body be buried in the tomb under the church of the monastery at Mariout. And that I be buried with the clothes I am wearing at that time with no need for any other. Whoever sees this will and does not execute it will be excommunicated. . . . Signed Pope Kyrillos." Cited in in Zaklama, *Pope Kyrillos VI*, 2:478.

[75]Atta and Raphael Ava Mina, *Life of Pope Kyrillos*, 45.

[76]Zaklama, *Pope Kyrillos VI*, 2:399.

[77]Ibid.; Atta and Raphael Ava Mina, *Life of Pope Kyrillos*, 45.

[78]Zaklama, *Pope Kyrillos VI*, 2:401–2.

[79]Ibid., 403.

[80]Atta and Raphael Ava Mina, *Life of Pope Kyrillos*, 46.

[81]Zaklama, *Pope Kyrillos VI*, 2:478.

[82]Bishop Gregorious, "Interview About the Relics of Pope Kyrillos VI," audio recording (undated).

[83]Nasr, *Readings in the Life of Abouna Mina*, 201; Raphael Ava Mina, *Spiritual Leadership*, 26; Atta and Raphael Ava Mina, *Life of Pope Kyrillos*, 46; Zaklama, *Pope Kyrillos VI*, 2:473.

[84]Shenouda III, "Speech at the Tenth Year Commemoration of Kyrillos VI." Also see al-Masri, *True Story of Christianity in Egypt*, 2:452.

[85]Fr Ibrahim Abdo, "My Memoirs of 1981," audio recording (date unknown). Based on a translation provided in Shenoda, "Cultivating a Mystery," 254–55.

[86]Malaty, "Interview about the Life of Pope Kyrillos: Part II."

[87]Ibid.

Timeline

1902	August 2	Birth of Azer Youssef Atta (future Pope Kyrillos VI) in Damanhur
1906	Before August	Fr Tadros el-Baramousy's prophecy: "he is one of us"
	June 13	Denshawai Incident
1910		Family moves to Alexandria
1912		Death of Esther, Azer's mother
1919	March 9	Revolution of 1919
	October 13	Birth of Waheeb Attalah (future Bishop Gregorious)
	December 19	Birth of Youssef Iskander (future Fr Matta el-Meskeen)
1920	July	Azer finishes high school and joins Thomas Cook & Son
	December 8	Birth of Saad Aziz (future Bishop Samuel)
1922	February 22	Declaration of Egyptian Independence from British
1923	August 3	Birth of Nazir Gayed (future Pope Shenouda III)
1927	July 27	Azer enters Baramous Monastery
	August 7	Death of Pope Cyril V
1928	February 9	First issue of *Harbor of Salvation* periodical
	February 25	Azer tonsured Monk Mina el-Baramousy
	March	Hassan el-Banna forms Muslim Brotherhood
	December 16	Youannis XIX consecrated patriarch
1931	July 18	Monk Mina ordained a priest
		Begins his studies at Helwan Theological College
1933	Early	Youannis XIX attempts to ordain Fr Mina as Bishop
		Mina flees to Monastery of St Shenouda
	Before August	Returns to Baramous Monastery
1934	January	Begins solitude and inhabits a desert cave at Baramous Monastery
1935	March 15	Fr Abdel Messih el-Masudi dies
1936	April 4	Leaves solitude and accompanies seven expelled monks to Cairo
	June 23	Inhabits windmill at Moqattam on outskirts of Cairo

	Late	First recorded "healing miracle"
1937	February	First rejected request to relocate to Monastery of St Menas, Mariout
1941	October 28	Evicted from windmill for first time by Arabic Antiquities
		Lives between Old Cairo churches
		Death of Youssef Atta, Fr Mina's father
1942	February 4	King Farouk's "Great Humiliation"
	June 21	Pope Youannis XIX dies
	July 31	Fr Mina has vision of "patriarchal staff"
1943	June 28	Earliest mention identifying as "the Recluse"
	December	Appointed abbot of Monastery of St Samuel
1944	February 19	Macarius III consecrated patriarch
1945	February 25	Fr Mina appointed Confessor of Abu Sefein Convent
	March 16	Elevated to hegumen by Bishop Athanasius
	Mid	Leaves Monastery of St Samuel
		Returns to windmill; evicted by British a few months later
		Fr Mina lives once more between Old Cairo churches
	August 31	Death of Pope Macarius III
	September 2	World War II ends
1946	June 12	Yusab II consecrated patriarch
1947	September	Fr Mina establishes St Menas' Church in Old Cairo
1948		Builds hostel adjacent to St Menas' Church for university students
	April 14	Saad Aziz tonsured Monk Makary el-Samuely
	May 30	Waheeb Zaky ordained Fr Salib Suryal
	August 10	Youssef Iskander tonsured Monk Matta el-Samuely
1949	January 23	Yusab II consecrates Bishop Youannis of Giza
	January 26	Yusab II attempts to remove Fr Mina from Cairo
	February 12	Hassan el-Banna (founder of Muslim Brotherhood) killed
1951	August 21	Death of Habib Girgis
1952	July 23	Free Officers Revolution
1954	July 18	Nazir Gayed tonsured Monk Antonios el-Syriany
	July 24	Yusab II is kidnapped
1955	September 27	Yusab is dethroned and exiled to Muharraq Monastery

1956	January 23	Gamal Abdel Nasser becomes President of Egypt
	July 20	Fr Matta el-Meskeen leaves Syrian Monastery
	November 13	Death of Yusab II
1959	May 10	Fr Mina (Kyrillos VI) consecrated patriarch
	June 22	Consecrates Monastery of St Menas in Mariout
	June 29	Ethiopian Church granted autocephaly
	October 12	Visits President Nasser for first time
	November 27	Lays foundation stone of Monastery of St Menas
1960	January 27	Requests Matta el-Meskeen to return to Syrian Monastery
	August 20	Issues decree for monks to return to their monasteries
	October 17	Matta el-Meskeen (and his monks) "excommunicated"
	October 26	Kyrillos' first pastoral tour of Ethiopia
1962	September 9	Ordains Macarius el-Syriany as Bishop Athanasius of Beni Suef
	September 16	Waheeb Atallah tonsured Monk Pakhoum el-Muharraqi
	September 30	Ordains Bishops Shenouda and Samuel as "general bishops"
	October 25	Monk Pakhoum returns to Theological College
1963	February 11	Death of Metropolitan Youannis of Giza
	March 31	Ordains Mathias el-Syriany as Bishop Domadius of Giza
1964	March	*Maglis al-melli* controversy with Kyrillos
1965	January 13	Presides over inaugural Oriental Orthodox conference in Ethiopia
	April 25	Celebrates Liturgy with "anchorites" at St Menas
	May 9	Visits President Nasser
	July 24	Lays foundation stone of new St Mark's Cathedral
1966	January 7	Celebrates Liturgy with Oriental Orthodox Churches in Cairo
	April	Kyrillos "halts" sandstorm at St Menas' Monastery
1967	April 21	*Maglis* runs patriarchate into severe financial deficit
	May 10	Kyrillos meets with Nasser; *maglis* suspended and dissolved
	May 10	Ordains Monk Pakhoum as Bishop Gregorious
	June 5	Six-Day War with Israel

	October 8	Kyrillos suspends Bishop Shenouda
1968	April 2	Apparitions of St Mary at Zeitoun
	June 23	Reception of St Mark's relics from Vatican
	June 25	Kyrillos returns Bishop Shenouda from the monastery
		Consecration of St Mark's Cathedral
1969	May 9	Kyrillos reconciles with Fr Matta el-Meskeen
1970	May 5	Last visit to Monastery of St Menas
	September 28	Death of President Nasser
	October 24	Kyrillos suffers a heart attack and is confined to bedrest
1971	March 7	Kyrillos celebrates his last Liturgy
	March 9	Death of Kyrillos VI
	November 14	Shenouda III consecrated patriarch
1972	November 22	Kyrillos' body relocated to Monastery of St Menas in Mariout

A Note on Sources

DURING MY RESEARCH, I discovered a wealth of primary sources. This material came predominantly from the Monastery of St Menas in the Western Desert, the Monastery of St Samuel at the Qalamoun Mountain, the Patriarchal Archives in Cairo, and Kyrillos VI's family; I also obtained materials in the possession of friends and disciples of Kyrillos. Occasionally duplicates of these materials were found at various sites. The documents include autobiographical memoirs, letters, decrees, statements, prayers, and brief diary entries. These materials were appraised through established methodologies of historical methods of inquiry/source criticism as well as modern biographical analysis. Below is a selected description of the discovered primary sources, which I have limited here (for the sake of space) to memoirs, letters, decrees, and statements that were found as major collections. I hope to publish an edited collection of some of the letters and documents as a second volume in the future, at which point the catalogue of all discovered primary sources will appear in its entirety. For the sake of brevity, the following classification was used to group the major collections depending on where they were discovered.

The first of the major collections, comprised of close to one hundred letters, was found at Kyrillos' family home in Alexandria, preserved by Marcos Hanna Youssef Atta. Also known as "Reda," he is the nephew of Kyrillos VI and the son of his primary biographer, Hanna Youssef Atta (1895–1976). This collection was discovered in two parts: the first in 2015, Reda Collection, Part 1; and the second in 2016, Reda Collection, Part 2. These letters, mostly of a personal nature, were passed on directly from Reda's father, Hanna, who was the recipient of these letters from Kyrillos. The letters date from January 1929 to January 1965—including the earliest-known letter from Kyrillos' hand. Reda also mentioned that his father destroyed a few letters that were of a sensitive nature. It should be noted that the family requested that the content of some of these letters (mostly to do with unrelated family matters) be confidential, a request that I have duly respected. The apartment building of Kyrillos' family home, in which these letters were found, was due to be demolished only a month or so after I visited in 2016, and so one can only express thanks that the letters were discovered before this happened.

A second collection—St Samuel Collection—was preserved at the Monastery of St Samuel at Qalamoun Mountain, where Kyrillos was once abbot. Some fifty letters, dating mainly to the 1940s and 1950s, were found buried within hundreds of other documents in Kyrillos' (then Fr Mina's) original cell at the monastery, and all this documentation was left exposed to the elements in the corner of a locked adjacent room. This collection also included several historical documents that describe the state of the monastery and its affairs before Kyrillos became abbot in the mid-1940s, as well as the movements of the young monks that he sent to the monastery (including Fr Matta el-Meskeen and Fr Makary el-Syriany).

The third, and perhaps most significant, collection was preserved by Fr Raphael Ava Mina (b. 1942). He served as Kyrillos' deacon for five years (January 1964 to August 1969) before becoming a monk at the Monastery of St Menas in the Western Desert, and later he was even a patriarchal nominee. Like the other collections, these sources were effectively hidden—for varying reasons—for almost half a century. Fr Raphael stated that shortly after the death of Kyrillos, he visited several monasteries, as well as those figures close to the patriarch, and gathered these documents over several years. Unfortunately, there is little within the collections to indicate where these documents were found, though an examination of the addressee and recipient is often suggestive. This also explains the duplicates that were found in the various collections. The collection was found in two parts: Fr Raphael Collection Part 1 and Fr Raphael Collection Part 2. Both include hundreds of letters of correspondence between Kyrillos and several important figures, dating from April 1933 to June 1970, including letters throughout his reign as patriarch, official decrees and patriarchal correspondence, written prayers, and occasional diary entries. Fascinatingly, the collection also includes the original copy of Kyrillos' autobiography, which until now has only been published in small, incomplete, and disconnected fragments. Separate from these materials, Fr Raphael also preserved seventeen volumes of Kyrillos' handwritten periodical from the late 1920s, the *Harbor of Salvation*. Again, it should be noted, Fr Raphael requested these collections remain confidential, other than through selective publication and with context given.

As to the question posed in the preface: how do these primary sources relate to the known earliest biographies? Ever so briefly, let me answer: Both Kyrillos' brother, Hanna (the father of "Reda" Marcos), and Fr Raphael had access to many of these letters. It appears that each wrote his respective biography after examining some of the letters at his disposal. Many of those primary sources are described here—two of the above collections are directly from the hands of Fr Raphael and Hanna (via his son Reda). But, we should note, each held diverse groups of letters independent of the other. We can only assume that Hanna Youssef Atta, who is the only credible biographer of Kyrillos' prepatriarchal life, relied upon these letters, his memory, and other unnamed sources when he wrote the first section (the prepatriachal biography) of *My Memories about the Life of Pope Kyrillos VI*, which he coauthored with Fr Raphael Ava Mina in the early 1970s.[1] In the preface of that biography, he states that he agreed to write the first section also to give assurance that Fr Raphael's postpatriarchal life in the second section was accurate and reliable in his opinion—further confirming that each source was in agreement with the other's account.

Notes

[1] Though it was published with Fr Raphael's postpatriarchal life appended in 1981, it was in fact written before Hanna died in 1976.

Bibliography

Note on Arabic Sources

I have chosen for the most part in the text to provide English translations of quotations from Arabic sources, without any transliteration. This was secondary to both the biographical nature of the book and to its primary audience. When a transliteration is provided in a quotation of an Arabic source, it is represented in colloquial form without diacritical marks, for the same reason—that is, as it would be pronounced in contemporary, everyday conversation. Similarly, in bibliographic citations, English translations of Arabic titles are given, without additional transliterations, with the expression "[in Arabic]" appended to the title.

Primary Sources

Abdel-Messih, Yassa. "Letter to Mr. Kamel, August 20, 1942" [in Arabic]. In FRC-1: Letter 357. 1942.

Abdo, Fr Ibrahim. "My Memoirs of 1981." Audio recording. Date unknown.

Adly, Nabil. *Fr Mikhail Dawood's Memoirs with Pope Kyrillos VI* [in Arabic]. Cairo: Egyptian Brothers Press, 1993.

Anonymous. *Archdeacon Iskander Hanna (1880–1944)* [in Arabic]. Nasr, Cairo: Sons of Pope Kyrillos VI, date unknown.

_____. "Confrontation with the Man Who Deposed the Pope Fifty Years Ago" [in Arabic]. *Al-Musawwar*, July 4, 2003, 52–54.

_____. "Death of the Metropolitan of Giza after Taking Medicine" [in Arabic]. *Al-Ahram*, February 16, 1963.

_____. "Excommunication of Priests and Monks" [in Arabic]. *Al-Ahram*, October 17, 1960.

_____. "Kyrillos on the Meaning of the Feast" [in Arabic]. *Al-Ahram*, January 1, 1967.

_____. "Letter to Monk Pakhoum el-Muharraqi, September 25, 1962" [in Arabic]. In *BBG*, 1:207.

_____. "The *Maglis* Issues a Statement About Its Disagreements with Pope Kyrillos" [in Arabic]. *Al-Ahram*, April 24, 1967.

_____. "The Patriarchal Elections" [in Arabic]. *Sunday School Magazine* 11, no. 7 (1957): 13–17.

_____. "Pope Kyrillos' Illness: A Statement from the Patriarchate" [in Arabic]. *Al-Ahram*, October 24, 1970.

_____. "Serious Rift between Pope Kyrillos VI and the *Maglis*" [in Arabic]. *Al-Ahram*, April 21, 1967.

_____. "Speech of the New Patriarch-Elect" [in Arabic]. *Al-Watani*, April 26, 1959.

Anonymous bishop. "Interview about the Life of Pope Kyrillos." Audio recording. Edited by Daniel Fanous, 2016.

Antonious el-Syriany, Fr. "Letter to Monk Pakhoum el-Muharraqi, September 22, 1962" [in Arabic]. In *BBG*, 1:203.

_____. "Letter to Monk Pakhoum el-Muharraqi, September 25, 1962" [in Arabic]. In *BBG*, 1:207–8.

_____. "Letter to Monk Pakhoum el-Muharraqi, September 28, 1962" [in Arabic]. In *BBG*, 1:208–9.

_____. "Letter to Waheeb Attallah, July 13, 1960" [in Arabic]. In *BBG*, 1:164–65.

_____. "Letter to Waheeb Attallah, June, 1960" [in Arabic]. In *BBG*, 1:163–64.

_____. "Letter to Waheeb Attallah, September 15, 1956" [in Arabic]. In *BBG*, 1:144–47.

Athanasius, Bishop. "Interview about Pope Kyrillos VI." Audio recording. 1990.

Athanasius, Metropolitan. "Letter to Fr Mina el-Baramousy, December 29, 1943" [in Arabic]. 1943.

_____. "Letter to Fr Mina el-Baramousy, March 12, 1945" [in Arabic]. In SSC: Letter 7. Beni Suef, 1945.

_____. "Letter to Hanna Youssef Atta, December 17, 1943" [in Arabic]. In RC-2: Letter 1. 1943.

Athanasius, Saint. *Letter to Draconitus*. In NPNF² 4:558–560.

_____. *Life of Antony*. In NPNF² 4:194–221.

_____. *On the Incarnation*. Translated by a Religious of C.S.M.V. Popular Patristics Series No. 3. Crestwood, NY: St Vladimir's Seminary Press, 1996.

Atta, Hanna Youssef. "Letter to Pope Kyrillos VI, June 17, 1968" [in Arabic]. In FRC-1: Letter 407. Alexandria, 1968.

Atta, Marcos Hanna Youssef. "Personal Correspondence, January 28, 2015." Edited by Daniel Fanous, 2015.

_____. "Personal Correspondence, March 5, 2015." Edited by Daniel Fanous, 2015.

Basil the Great. *Letter to Gregory* 2. In NPNF² 8:110–112.

Budge, E. A. Wallis. *Texts Relating to St Mena of Egypt and Canons of Nicaea: In a Nubian Dialect*. London: Trustees of the British Museum, 1909.

Burmester, O. H. E. *The Egyptian or Coptic Church: A Detailed Description of Her Liturgical Services*. Cairo: Printing Office of the French Institute of Oriental Archaeology, 1967.

Clarke, W. K. Lowther. *The Lausiac History of Palladius*. New York: Macmillan Company, 1918.

Clement of Alexandria. *Stromata*. In Ante-Nicene Fathers, ed. Philip Schaff, vol. 2:299–567. Reprint. Peabody, MA: Hendrickson Publishers, 1999.

Deputy of *maglis al-melli*. "Letter to Pope Kyrillos VI, April 25, 1964" [in Arabic]. In FRC-1: Letter 372. Cairo, 1964.

Drescher, James. *Apa Mena: A Selection of Coptic Texts Relating to St. Menas.* Cairo: Publications de la Société d'Archéologie Copte, 1946.

El-Gowaily, Galal. "Interview with the Monk That Will Become Patriarch" [in Arabic]. *Al-Ahram*, April 25, 1959.

Gayed, Nazir. "Why We Interfered" [in Arabic]. *Sunday School Magazine* 2, no. 9 (1949): 1–10.

Gregorious, Bishop. "Interview About the Relics of Pope Kyrillos VI." Audio recording. Undated.

Hanna, Ragheb, and Hanna Girgis Saad. "Letter to Pope Kyrillos VI, September 18, 1965" [in Arabic]. In FRC-1: Letter 368. Cairo, 1965.

Henein, Fr Antonios. "Lecture on Pope Kyrillos VI." Audio recording. Cairo, date unknown.

Hopko, Fr Thomas. "Fifty-Five Maxims for Christian Living." Unpublished, 2008.

Isaac the Syrian, St. *The Ascetical Homilies of St Isaac the Syrian.* Translated by Holy Transfiguration Monastery. Boston: Holy Transfiguration Monastery, 2011.

Jerome. *Letter 14, to Heliodorus.* In NPNF² 6:13–18.

Kamal, Atef. "An Interview with Pope Shenouda III." Video recording. CYC, undated.

Khalil, Michael. "Interview with Pope Kyrillos" [in Arabic]. *Al-Akhbar*, May 11, 1968.

Kyrillos VI, Pope. "Article Twenty-Nine on Prayer" [in Arabic]. Unpublished, undated.

_____. "Letter to Fr Mikhail Undated, 196_" [in Arabic]. In FRC-1: Letter 148. Cairo, 196_.

_____. "Letter to Fr Mikhail, December 18, 1964" [in Arabic]. In FRC-1: Letter 47. Cairo, 1964.

_____. "Letter to Fr Salib Suryal, February 4, 1967" [in Arabic]. Cairo, 1967.

_____. "Letter to Hanna Youssef Atta, December 16, 1964" [in Arabic]. In RC-2: Letter 32. 1964.

_____. "Letter to Hanna Youssef Atta, Undated ?1959–1962" [in Arabic]. In FRC-1: Letter 280. Old Cairo, undated.

_____. "Letter to Salama Rizq, August 29, 1962" [in Arabic]. In FRC-1: Letter 48. Alexandria, 1962.

_____. "Ordination of the Bishop of Higher Education and Scientific Research" [in Arabic]. *Keraza* (June 1967): 34–35.

_____. "A Reply to the Memorandum of the *Maglis Al-Melli*, May 13, 1964" [in Arabic]. Cairo, 1964.

_____. "Statement from the Coptic Orthodox Patriarchate, April 24, 1967" [in Arabic]. In FRC-1: Letter 393. Cairo, 1967.

_____. "Synod Minutes" [in Arabic]. Cairo: unpublished, 1961.

Macarius, Bishop. "Letter to Hegumen Youssef el-Baramousy, August 20, 1956" [in Arabic]. In SSC: Letter 14. Baramous Monastery, 1956.

Magdy, Fr Jacob. "Interview about the Life of Pope Kyrillos." Edited by Daniel Fanous, 2015.

Makary el-Samuely, Fr. "Letter to Fr Matta, December 14, 1948" [in Arabic]. In FRC-1: Letter 213. Qalamoun Mountain, 1948.

Malaty, Fr Tadros. "Interview about the Life of Pope Kyrillos: Part I." Edited by Daniel Fanous, 2015.

_____. "Interview about the Life of Pope Kyrillos: Part II." Edited by Daniel Fanous, 2016.

Mark the Deacon. *The Life of Porphyry, Bishop of Gaza.* Translated by G. F. Hill. Oxford: Clarendon Press, 1913.

Matta el-Meskeen, Fr. *Autobiography of Fr Matta el-Meskeen* [in English]. Wadi al-Natrun: St Macarius Monastery, forthcoming.

_____. "On Pope Kyrillos: Part I." Audio recording. In *Recollections.* Wadi al-Natrun, undated.

_____. "On Pope Kyrillos: Part II." Audio recording. In *Recollections.* Wadi al-Natrun, undated.

Matta el-Samuely, Fr. "Letter to Hegumen Mina el-Baramousy, Undated ?1950" [in Arabic]. In SSC: Letter 17. St Samuel Monastery, 1950.

Mina el-Baramousy [Kyrillos VI], Fr. "Letter to Attia Labib, March 1933" [in Arabic]. In FRC-2: Letter 19. Cairo, 1933.

_____. "Letter to Hanna Youssef Atta, December 3, 1933" [in Arabic]. In RC-2: Letter 8. Baramous Monastery, 1933.

_____. "Letter to Hanna Youssef Atta, December 24, 1933" [in Arabic]. In RC-2: Letter 10. Baramous Monastery, 1933.

_____. "Letter to Hanna Youssef Atta, Undated ?1936" [in Arabic]. In FRC-1: Letter 529. Baramous Monastery, Undated.

Mina el-Baramousy [Kyrillos VI], Monk. *Harbor of Salvation* [in Arabic], vol. 1. Wadi al-Natrun: Baramous Monastery, Amsheer 1644; February 1928.

_____. *Harbor of Salvation* [in Arabic], vol. 2. Wadi al-Natrun: Baramous Monastery, Baramhat 1644; March 1928.

_____. *Harbor of Salvation* [in Arabic], vol. 4. Wadi al-Natrun: Baramous Monastery, Pashans 1644; May 1928.

_____. *Harbor of Salvation* [in Arabic], vol. 7. Wadi al-Natrun: Baramous Monastery, Misra 1644; August 1928.

_____. *Harbor of Salvation* [in Arabic], vol. 16. Wadi al-Natrun: Baramous Monastery, Kiahk 1646; December 1929.

_____. "Letter to Hanna Youssef Atta, January 17, 1929" [in Arabic]. In RC-2: Letter 57. Baramous Monastery, 1929.

_____. "Letter to Hanna Youssef Atta, November 21, 1930" [in Arabic]. In RC-1: Letter 11. Baramous Monastery, 1930.

_____. "Letter to Hanna Youssef Atta, Undated; ?1930" [in Arabic]. In FRC-1: Letter 489. Cairo, undated (1930?).

Mina el-Samuely [the Younger], Fr. "Letter to Hegumen Mina the Recluse, August 10, 1948" [in Arabic]. In FRC-1: Letter 256. Qalamoun Mountain, 1948.

_____. "Letter to Pope Kyrillos VI, August 18, 1959" [in Arabic]. In FRC-1: Letter 195. Qalamoun Mountain, 1959.

Mina the Recluse [Kyrillos VI], Fr. "Letter to Fr Mina el-Samuely [the Younger], February 5, 1944" [in Arabic]. In FRC-2: Letter 13. Qalamoun Mountain, 1944.

_____. "Letter to Habib Pasha el-Masri, June 28, 1943" [in Arabic]. In FRC-1: Letter 327. Alexandria, 1943.

_____. "Letter to Hanna Youssef Atta, December 24, 1943" [in Arabic]. In RC-2: Letter 70. Old Cairo, 1943.

_____. "Letter to Hanna Youssef Atta, February 25, 1945" [in Arabic]. In RC-2: Letter 61. Old Cairo, 1945.

_____. "Letter to Hanna Youssef Atta, January 20, 1944" [in Arabic]. In RC-2: Letter 42, 1944.

_____. "Letter to Hanna Youssef Atta, March 2, 1945" [in Arabic]. In RC-2: Letter 68. Old Cairo, 1945.

Mina the Recluse [Kyrillos VI], Hegumen. "Autobiographical Fragments" [in Arabic]. In FRC-1: Letter 1. Old Cairo, undated (1945–1949?).

_____. "Letter to Fr Antonious el-Syriany, September 6, 1958" [in Arabic]. In FRC-1: Letter 443. Old Cairo, 1958.

_____. "Letter to Fr Makary el-Samuely, October 27, 1950" [in Arabic]. In FRC-1: Letter 246/210. Old Cairo, 1950.

_____. "Letter to Fr Makary el-Syriany, 1951" [in Arabic]. In FRC-1: Letter 522. Old Cairo, 1951.

_____. "Letter to Fr Makary el-Syriany, Undated ?1948–1951" [in Arabic]. In FRC-1: Letter 427. Old Cairo, undated.

_____. "Letter to Fr Makary el-Syriany, Undated" [in Arabic]. In FRC-1: Letter 497. Cairo, unknown.

_____. "Letter to General Manager of the Ministry of Antiquities, 195_" [in Arabic]. In FRC-1: Letter 37. Old Cairo, 195_.

_____. "Letter to Hanna Youssef Atta, 1950" [in Arabic]. In RC-2: Letter 35. St Samuel's Monastery, 1950.

_____. "Letter to Hanna Youssef Atta, August 7, 1945" [in Arabic]. In RC-2: Letter 69, 1945.

_____. "Letter to Hanna Youssef Atta, December, 1946" [in Arabic]. In RC-2: Letter 11. Old Cairo, 1946.

_____. "Letter to Hanna Youssef Atta, July 6, 1946" [in Arabic]. In RC-2: Letter 4. St Samuel's Monastery, 1946.

_____. "Letter to Hanna Youssef Atta, June 18, 1945" [in Arabic]. In RC-2: Letter 54, 1945.

_____. "Letter to Hanna Youssef Atta, June 23, 1958" [in Arabic]. Old Cairo, 1958.

_____. "Letter to Hanna Youssef Atta, March 5, 1958" [in Arabic]. In FRC-1: Letter 511. Old Cairo, 1958.

_____. "Letter to Hanna Youssef Atta, May 14, 1946" [in Arabic]. In RC-2: Letter 29. St Samuel's Monastery, 1946.

_____. "Letter to Hanna Youssef Atta, November 1, 1945" [in Arabic]. In RC-2: Letter 55. Old Cairo, 1945.

_____. "Letter to Hanna Youssef Atta, October 11, 1949" [in Arabic]. In RC-2: Letter 14. Old Cairo, 1949.

_____. "Letter to Hanna Youssef Atta, September, 1947" [in Arabic]. In RC-2: Letter 12. Old Cairo, 1947.

_____. "Letter to Hanna Youssef Atta, Undated March ?1945" [in Arabic]. In RC-2: Letter 30. St Samuel's Monastery, Undated.

_____. "Letter to *Maglis al-Melli*" [in Arabic]. In FRC-1: Letter 320. Old Cairo, 195_.

_____. "Letter to Monk Makary el-Samuely, January 11, 1950" [in Arabic]. In FRC-1: Letter 438. Old Cairo, 1950.

_____. "Letter to Monks at the Monastery of St Samuel, November 11, 1949" [in Arabic]. In SSC: Letter 49. Old Cairo, 1949.

_____. "Letter to Monks at the Monastery of St Samuel, Undated" [in Arabic]. Old Cairo, Undated.

_____. "Letter to Mounir Shoukry, March 5, 1958" [in Arabic]. Old Cairo, 1958.

_____. "Letter to Pope Yusab II, 195_" [in Arabic]. Old Cairo, 195_.

_____. "Letter to Syrian Monastery Superintendent, October 7, 1950" [in Arabic]. In FRC-1: Letter 89. Old Cairo, 1950.

_____. "Letter to the Monks at the Monastery of St Samuel, January 7, 1950" [in Arabic]. In FRC-1: Letter 429. Old Cairo, 1950.

Nasser, Abdel Hakim. "Interview About Nasser and Kyrillos VI." Edited by Daniel Fanous, 2017.

"Obituary of Bishop Samuel." *Times of London*, October 12, 1981, 10.

Pachomious, Bishop. "Interview about the Life of Pope Kyrillos VI." Audio recording. Edited by Daniel Fanous, 2016.

Pakhoum el-Muharraqi, Monk. "Letter to Bishop Shenouda, March 18, 1967" [in Arabic]. In *BBG*, 1:383–84.

_____. "Letter to Bishop Shenouda, March 26, 1967" [in Arabic]. In *BBG*, 1:388–93.

_____. "Letter to Bishop Shenouda, October 2, 1962" [in Arabic]. In *BBG*, 1:217–18.

_____. "Letter to Bishop Shenouda, October 5, 1962" [in Arabic]. In *BBG*, 1:219–22.

_____. "Letter to Pope Kyrillos VI, May 16, 1964" [in Arabic]. In *BBG*, 1:318–19.

_____. "Letter to Pope Kyrillos VI, September 16, 1962" [in Arabic]. In *BBG*, 1:192–93.

Paulinus. *Life of St Ambrose, Bishop of Milan*. Translated by R. J. Deferrari. Pages 33–68 in *Early Christian Biography*, Fathers of the Church Series, vol. 15. Washington, DC: Catholic University of America Press, 1952.

Raphael Ava Mina, Fr. "Interview about the Life of Pope Kyrillos VI." Audio recording. Edited by Daniel Fanous, 2016.

_____. "Lecture on the Virtues of Pope Kyrillos." Audio recording. Alexandria: St Menas' Monastery, undated.

_____. "My Memories of the Life of Pope Kyrillos VI." Audio recording. St Menas' Monastery, Mareotis: St Menas' Monastery, undated.

_____. "Pope Kyrillos VI—Some Misconceptions." Audio recording. In *Liturgy in the Coptic Orthodox Church*. Alexandria, 2015.

Rufinus of Aquileia. *The Church History of Rufinus of Aquileia: Books 10 and 11*. Translated by Philip R. Amidon. Oxford: Oxford University Press, 1997.

Rufus, John. *The Lives of Peter the Iberian, Theodosius of Jerusalem, and the Monk Romanus*. Translated by Cornelia B. Horn and Robert R. Phenix. Atlanta: Society of Biblical Literature, 2008.

Schmemann, Fr Alexander. *The Journals of Fr Alexander Schmemann 1973–1983*. Crestwood, NY: St Vladimir's Seminary Press, 2000.

Shehata, Monir Atteya. *BBG* [in Arabic]. Vol. 1 of 3. Cairo: Association of Anba Gregorious, 2005.

Shenouda, Bishop. "Editorial" [in Arabic]. *Keraza* (August 1965): 2.

———. "Letter to Bishop Gregorious, May 12, 1967" [in Arabic]. In *BBG*, 1:413–15.

———. "Letter to Bishop Gregorious, May 14, 1967" [in Arabic]. In *BBG*, 1:415–416.

———. "Letter to Bishop Gregorious, May 15, 1967" [in Arabic]. In *BBG*, 1:417.

———. "Letter to Bishop Gregorious, October 8, 1967" [in Arabic]. In *BBG*, 2:16–17.

———. "Letter to Bishop Gregorious, October 23, 1967" [in Arabic]. In *BBG*, 2:18–19.

———. "Letter to Monk Pakhoum el-Muharraqi, March 22, 1967" [in Arabic]. In *BBG*, 1:384–86.

———. "Letter to Soliman Nessim, November 15, 1967" [in Arabic]. Desert of Scetis, 1967.

———. "An Open Word About the Theological College and Religous Institutes" [in Arabic]. *Keraza* (October 1967): 1–13.

Shenouda III, Pope. *The Release of the Spirit*. Translated by Wedad Abbas. Cairo: COEPA, 1997.

———. "Speech at the First Year Commemoration of Kyrillos VI" [in Arabic]. Cairo, 1972.

———. "Speech at the Funeral of Kyrillos VI" [in Arabic]. Cairo, 1971.

———. "Speech at the Tenth Year Commemoration of Kyrillos VI" [in Arabic]. Cairo, 1981.

Shenouda, Zaki. *My Memories of Pope Kyrillos VI* [in Arabic]. Cairo: Egyptian Brothers Press, 1992.

Shoukry, Mounir. "Letter to Pope Kyrillos VI, June 24, 1959" [in Arabic]. In FRC-2: Letter 65. Alexandria, 1959.

Sidarous, Fr Louka. "Lectures on Pope Kyrillos." Audio recording. Alexandria, undated.

Sulpicius Severus. *On the Life of St. Martin*. In NPNF² 11:1–17.

Suryal, Fr Salib. "On the 'Takrees' Movement: Part 1." Audio recording. In *Lectures on the History of the Modern Church*. Cairo, 1988.

———. "On the 'Takrees' Movement: Part 2." Audio recording. In *Lectures on the History of the Modern Church*. Cairo, 1988.

———. "Pope Kyrillos VI." Audio recording. In *Lectures on the History of the Modern Church*. Cairo, 1988.

———. "The Theological College." Audio recording. In *Lectures on the History of the Modern Church*. Cairo, 1988.

Teaching Staff of the Coptic Studies Institute. "Letter to Kyrillos VI, February 10, 1967" [in Arabic]. In *BBG*, 1:398–99.

Veilleux, Armand. *Pachomian Koinonia*. Vol. 1 of *The Life of St Pachomius and His Disciples*. Kalamazoo, MI: Cistercian Publications, 1980.

Ward, Bendicta. *The Sayings of the Desert Fathers: The Alphabetical Collection*. Kalamazoo, MI: Cistercian Publications, 1984.

"A Whisper of Love: Interview with Shenouda III [Video Recording]." CTV, undated.

Yostos, Bishop. "Interview about the Life of Pope Kyrillos VI." Audio recording. Edited by Daniel Fanous, 2016.

Younan, Fr Antonious. "On Pope Kyrillos VI." Audio recording. Cairo, date unknown.

Yusab II, Pope. "Letter to Bishop Athanasius and Bishop Macarius, January 26, 1949" [in Arabic]. In FRC-1: Letter 259. Patriarchate, Cairo, 1949.

_____. "Letter to Hegumen Mina el-Baramousy, October 18, 1946" [in Arabic]. In FRC-1: Letter 199. Cairo, 1946.

Secondary Sources

Al-Masri, I. H. *The Story of the Coptic Church: 1870–1927* [in Arabic]. Vol. 5. Cairo: Maktabat al-Mahabba, 1986.

_____. *The Story of the Coptic Church: 1928–1946* [in Arabic]. Vol. 6. Cairo: Maktabat al-Mahabba, 1988.

_____. *The Story of the Coptic Church: 1956–1971* [in Arabic]. Vol. 7. Cairo: Maktabat al-Mahabba, 1988.

_____. *The Story of the Copts: The True Story of Christianity in Egypt*. Vol. 2. Newbery Springs, CA: St Anthony Coptic Orthodox Monastery, 1982.

Alfeyev, Hilarion. *The Spiritual World of Isaac the Syrian*. Kalamazoo, MI: Cistercian Publications, 2000.

Anonymous. *Bishop Samuel: Pages from His Life, Service, and Thought* [in Arabic]. Cairo: Antoun Yacoub Michael, 1981.

_____. *Early Life of Anba Samuel* [in Arabic]. Giza: Friends of Anba Samuel, 1991.

_____. "From the Deserted Windmill of Bonaparte to the Throne of St Mark" [in Arabic]. *Al-Watani*, May 10, 1959.

_____. "His Holiness Chairs the *Maglis* Meeting in Alexandria" [in Arabic]. *Al-Ahram*, July 19, 1959.

_____. *Life of Fr Benjamin the Hermit* [in Arabic]. Cairo: Publisher and date unknown.

_____. "Mina el-Baramousy: The New Patriarch of the Copts" [in Arabic]. *Al-Ahram*, April 20, 1959, 1–3.

_____. *The Path of Virtue* [in Arabic]. Cairo: Sons of Pope Kyrillos VI, Undated.

_____. *Pope Kyrillos VI: School of Virtue*. Cairo: Sons of Pope Kyrillos VI, Undated.

_____. "Pope Kyrillos: A Miracle Worker for Copts" [in Arabic]. *Rose al-Yusuf*, November 11, 1996.

Ansari, Hamied. "Sectarian Conflict in Egypt and the Political Expediency of Religion." *Middle East Journal* 38, no. 3 (1984): 397–418.

Assad, Maurice M. "The Coptic Church and Social Change." *International Review of Mission* 61, no. 242 (1972): 117–29.

Astell, Ann W. "'Memoriam Fecit': The Eucharist, Memory, Reform, and Regeneration in Hildegard of Bingen's *Scivias* and Nicholas of Cusa's Sermons." In *Reassessing Reform: A Historical Investigation into Church Renewal*, edited by Christopher M. Bellitto and David Zachariah Flanagin, 190–213. Washington, DC: Catholic University of America Press, 2012.

Atiya, Aziz Suryal. "'Abd al-Masih Salib al-Masu'di." In *CE*, 7b.

Atta, Hanna Youssef, and Fr Raphael Ava Mina. *The Life of Pope Kyrillos the Sixth*. Cairo: Sons of Pope Kyrillos VI, 2002.

———. *My Memories about the Life of Pope Kyrillos VI* [in Arabic]. Cairo: Sons of Pope Kyrillos VI, 1981.

Augustinos el-Baramousy, Fr. *The Baramous Monastery: Past to Present* [in Arabic]. Cairo: Baramous Monastery, 1993.

Ayad, Boulos. "Fr Ibrahim Luka: His Deeds, Program, Struggle for the Renaissance of the Coptic Church and the Christian Unity." *Coptic Church Review* 27, nos. 3 & 4 (2006): 113–18.

Ayalon, Ami. *The Press in the Arab Middle East: A History*. Oxford: Oxford University Press, 1995.

Beadnell, H. J. L. *The Topography and Geology of the Fayum Province of Egypt*. Cairo: National Printing Department, 1905.

Behr-Sigel, Elisabeth. *Lev Gillet: A Monk of the Eastern Church*. Translated by Helen Wright. Oxford: Fellowship of St Alban and St Sergius, 1999.

Bellitto, Christopher M. *Renewing Christianity: A History of Church Reform from Day One to Vatican II*. New York: Paulist Press, 2001.

Bestawros, Adel Azer. "Community Council, Coptic." In *CE*, 580b–82b.

Bocken, Inigo. "Visions of Reform: Lay Piety as a Form of Thinking in Nicholas of Cusa." In *Reassessing Reform: A Historical Investigation into Church Renewal* 214–31. Edited by Christopher M. Bellitto and David Zachariah Flanagin. Washington, DC: Catholic University of America Press, 2012.

Botman, Selma. "The Liberal Age, 1923–1952." In *The Cambridge History of Egypt: Modern Egypt, from 1517 to the End of the Twentieth Century*, edited by M. W. Daly, 285–308. Cambridge: Cambridge University Press, 1998.

Brock, S. P. "Early Syrian Asceticism." *Numen* 20, no. 1 (1973): 1–19.

Brown, Peter. "The Rise and Function of the Holy Man in Late Antiquity." *Journal of Roman Studies* 61 (1971): 80–101.

———. "The Saint as Exemplar in Late Antiquity." *Representations* 1, no. 2 (1983): 1–25.

Browning, Robert. "The 'Low Level' Saint's Life in the Early Byzantine World." In *The Byzantine Saint*, edited by Sergei Hackel, 117–27. Crestwood, NY: St Vladimir's Seminary Press, 2001.

Bullivant, Ronald. "The Visions of the Mother of God at Zeitun." *Eastern Churches Review* 3 (1970–1971): 74–76.

Carter, B. L. *The Copts in Egyptian Politics*. London: Croom Helm, 1986.

Carter, B. L., and Mirrit Boutros Ghali. "Coptic Press." In *CE*, 2010a–13b.

Cherubim, Bishop. *Blessed Servant: Life and Miracles of Bishop Makarios of Qena.* Qena: Coptic Diocese of Qena, Date unknown.

Chesterton, G. K. *St. Thomas Aquinas and St. Francis of Assisi.* San Francisco: Ignatius Press, 2002.

Chiala, Sabino. "The Arabic Version of St Isaac the Syrian: A Channel of Transmission of Syriac Literature." In *St Isaac the Syrian and His Spiritual Legacy.* Edited by Hilarion Alfeyev, 59–68. Yonkers, NY: St Vladimir's Seminary Press, 2015.

Churchill, Winston S. *The Hinge of Fate.* Boston: Houghton Mifflin Harcourt, 1985.

Congar, Yves. "Attitudes Towards Reform in the Church." *CrossCurrents* 1, no. 4 (1951): 80–102.

_____. *True and False Reform in the Church.* Minnesota: Liturgical Press, 2011.

Coquin, René-Georges, Maurice Martin, and Peter Grossmann. "Dayr Anba Samu'il of Qalamun." In *CE*, 758a–60b.

Coury, Ralph M. "Review of *Christians versus Muslims in Modern Egypt: The Century-Long Struggle for Coptic Equality.*" *American Historical Review* 110, no. 2 (2005): 591.

Cromer, Evelyn Baring, Earl of. *Modern Egypt.* Vol. 2. New York: Macmillan, 1908.

Crummey, Donald. "Church and Nation: The Ethiopian Orthodox Täwahedo Church." In *The Cambridge History of Christianity: Eastern Christianity*, edited by Michael Angold, 457–87. Cambridge: Cambridge University Press, 2006.

Daly, M. W. "The British Occupation, 1882–1922." In *The Cambridge History of Egypt: Modern Egypt, from 1517 to the End of the Twentieth Century*, edited by M. W. Daly, 239–51. Cambridge: Cambridge University Press, 1998.

de Certeau, Michel. *The Mystic Fable.* Vol. 1, *The Sixteenth and Seventeenth Centuries.* Chicago: University of Chicago Press, 1992.

Den Heijer, Johannes. "History of the Patriarchs of Alexandria." In *CE*, 1239b–42b.

Denzin, Norman K. *Interpretive Biography.* London: Sage Publications, 1989.

Drijvers, Han J. W. "Hellenistic and Oriental Origins." In *The Byzantine Saint*, edited by Sergei Hackel, 25–33. Crestwood, NY: St Vladimir's Seminary Press, 2001.

El-Khawaga, Dina. "The Laity at the Heart of the Coptic Clerical Reform." In *BDC*, 143–67.

Evdokimov, Paul. *The Struggle with God.* Mahwah, NJ: Paulist Press, 1966.

Fakhry, Ahmed. "The Monastery of Kalamoun." *Annales du Service des Antiquités de l'Egypte* 46 (1947): 63–83.

Fanus, N. "Man of Prayer and Goodness" [in Arabic]. *Nahdat al-Kanais* 3 (1966): 85–99.

Fawzi, Mahmud. *Pope Kyrillos and Abdel Nasser* [in Arabic]. Cairo: Al Watan Publishing, 1993.

Gillé, Matthias. *Der koptische Papst Schenuda III: Beobachtungen zu Theologie und Biografie.* Marburg: Tectum Verlag, 2017.

Girguis, Ramzy Wadie. *Pope Kyrillos: The Heavenly Harp.* Translated by Safwat Youssef. Cairo: Sons of Pope Kyrillos VI, 2003.

Gordon, Joel. *Nasser's Blessed Movement: Egypt's Free Officers and the July Revolution.* New York: Oxford University Press, 1992.

Gorman, Anthony. *Historians, State, and Politics in Twentieth Century Egypt: Contesting the Nation.* New York: RoutledgeCurzon, 2003.

Gorman, Michael J. *Inhabiting the Cruciform God: Kenosis, Justification, and Theosis in Paul's Narrative Soteriology.* Grand Rapids, MI: Eerdmans, 2009.

Gorodetzky, Nadejda. *Saint Tikhon of Zadonsk: Inspirer of Dostoevsky.* Crestwood, NY: St Vladimir's Seminary Press, 1976.

Gregorious, Bishop. *Muharraq Monastery: History, Description, Content* [in Arabic]. Al-Qusiya: Muharraq Monastery, 1992.

_____. "Pope Kyrillos the Sixth" [in Arabic]. *Al-Watani,* March 18, 1990.

Gruber, Mark Francis. "The Monastery as the Nexus of Coptic Cosmology." In *BDC,* 67–81.

_____. "Sacrifice in the Desert: An Ethnography of the Coptic Monastery." Ph.D. dissertation, State University of New York at Stony Brook, 1990.

Guirguis, Magdi. *The Emergence of the Modern Coptic Papacy: The Egyptian Church and Its Leadership from the Ottoman Period to the Present.* Cairo: The American University Press in Cairo, 2011.

Habib, Youssef. *Goodbye Pope Kyrillos: Among the Fathers and Leaders* [in Arabic]. 1971.

Hart, David Bentley. *Atheist Delusions: The Christian Revolution and Its Fashionable Enemies.* New Haven: Yale University Press, 2009.

_____. *The Hidden and the Manifest: Essays in Theology and Metaphysics.* Grand Rapids, MI: Eerdmans, 2017.

Harvey, Susan Ashbrook. "Holy Women, Silent Lives: A Review Essay." *St Vladimir's Theological Quarterly* 42, no. 3/4 (1998): 397–403.

Hasan, S. S. *Christians versus Muslims in Modern Egypt: The Century-Long Struggle for Coptic Equality.* New York: Oxford University Press, 2003.

Hatch, William Henry. "A Visit to the Coptic Convents in Nitria." *American School of Oriental Research Annual,* no. 6 (1924): 93–107.

Heardon, Maura. "Lessons from Zeitoun: A Marian Proposal for Christian-Muslim Dialogue." *Journal of Ecumenical Studies* 47, no. 3 (2012): 409–26.

Heikal, Mohamed. *Autumn of Fury: The Assassination of Sadat.* London: Corgi, 1984.

Hilal, Ibrahim. "Malati Sarjiyus." In *CE,* 2096b–97b.

Hulsman, Cornelis. "Reviving an Ancient Faith." *Christianity Today* 45, no. 15 (2001): 38–40.

Ibrahim, Vivian. *The Copts of Egypt: Challenges of Modernization and Identity.* New York: Tauris Academic Studies, 2011.

Ishak, Fayek. "Apparition of the Virgin Mary." In *CE,* 2308b–10a.

Iskander, Elizabeth. *Sectarian Conflict in Egypt: Coptic Media, Identity and Representation.* New York: Routledge, 2012.

James, Laura M. *Nasser at War: Arab Images of the Enemy.* New York: Palgrave Macmillan, 2006.

Kalaitzidis, Pandelis. "Challenges of Renewal and Reformation Facing the Orthodox Church." *The Ecumenical Review* 61, no. 2 (2009): 136–64.

Kepel, Gilles. *Muslim Extremism in Egypt: The Prophet and Pharaoh*. Berkeley, CA: University of California Press, 1985.

Keriakos, Sandrine. "St Marc: Enjeux communautaires et dynamiques politiques." *Conserveries Mémorielles* 14 (2013): 1–58.

Khalil, John. "A Brief History of Coptic Personal Status Law." *Berkeley Journal of Middle Eastern & Islamic Law* 3, no. 1/2 (2010): 81–139.

Kyrillos Ava Mina, Bishop. *The Great Egyptian and Coptic Martyr: The Miraculous St Mina*. Mariout: St Mina Monastery Press, 2005.

Ladner, Gerhart B. *The Idea of Reform: Its Impact on Christian Thought and Action in the Age of the Fathers*. Eugene, OR: Wipf & Stock, 2004.

Leeder, S. H. *Modern Sons of the Pharaohs*. London: Hodder and Stoughton, 1918.

Lloyd-Moffett, Stephen R. *Beauty for Ashes: The Spiritual Transformation of a Modern Greek Community*. Crestwood, NY: St Vladimir's Seminary Press, 2009.

Macarius, Bishop. *The Ethiopian Servant of Christ: The Life of Fr Abdel Mesih el-Habashy*. Translated by Michael Cosman. Sydney: St Shenouda's Monastery Press, 2009. First published by Baramous Monastery, 1996.

Makari, Peter E. "Christianity and Islam in Twentieth Century Egypt: Conflict and Cooperation." *International Review of Mission* 89, no. 352 (2000): 88–98.

Massad, Mary. "The Story of the *Misr* Newspaper." *Watani International*, May 3, 2015.

Matta el-Meskeen, Fr. *Orthodox Prayer Life: The Interior Way*. Crestwood, NY: St Vladimir's Seminary Press, 2003.

McCallum, Fiona. "The Political Role of the Patriarch in the Contemporary Middle East." St Andrews, Scotland: University of St Andrews, 2006.

McDermott, Anthony. *Egypt from Nasser to Mubarak: A Flawed Revolution*. Abingdon, UK: Routledge, 2013.

McDonald, Matthew. "The Nature of Epiphanic Experience." *Journal of Humanistic Psychology* 48, no. 1 (2008): 89–115.

Meinardus, Otto. *Christian Egypt: Faith and Life*. Cairo: The American University in Cairo Press, 1970.

———. *Coptic Saints and Pilgrimages*. Cairo: The American University in Cairo Press, 2002.

———. *The Copts in Jerusalem*. Cairo: Commission on Ecumenical Affairs, 1960.

———. "The Hermits of Wadi Rayan." *Studia Orientalia Christiana* 11 (1966): 295–317.

———. *Monks and Monasteries of the Egyptian Deserts (1961)*. Cairo: The American University Press in Cairo, 1961.

———. *Monks and Monasteries of the Egyptian Deserts (1989)*. Revised ed. Cairo: The American University Press in Cairo, 1999.

———. *Patriarchen unter Nasser und Sadat*. Hamburg: Deutsche Orient-Institut, 1998.

———. "Review of Albert Gerhards, and Heinzgerd Brakmann, *Die Koptische Kirche. Einführung in das Ägyptische Christentum*." *Ostkirchliche Studien* 44, no. 2/3 (1995): 212–14.

_____. *Two Thousand Years of Coptic Christianity*. Cairo: American University Press in Cairo, 1999.

Merkley, Paul Charles. *Christian Attitudes to the State of Israel*. Montreal: McGill-Queen's University Press, 2001.

Mettaous, Bishop. *The Sublime Life of Monasticism*. Putty, Australia: Saint Shenouda Monastery Press, 2005.

Meyendorff, John. *Orthodoxy and Catholicity*. Lanham: Sheed and Ward, 1966.

Mikhail, Maged S. A. "Matta al-Maskin." In *The Orthodox Christian World*, edited by Augustine Casiday, 359–65. Abingdon, UK: Routledge, 2012.

Mitchell, Richard P. *The Society of the Muslim Brothers*. Oxford: Oxford University Press, 1993.

Morton, H. V. *Through Lands of the Bible*. London: Dodd, Mead & Company, 1938.

Nasim, Sulayman. "Habib Jirjis." In *CE*, 1189a–89b.

Nasr, Amir. *Readings in the Life of Abouna Mina el-Baramousy the Recluse* [in Arabic]. Cairo: Al-Nesr Press, 1996.

Nasser, Tahia Gamal Abdel Nasser. *Nasser: My Husband*. Cairo: The American University in Cairo Press, 2013.

Nelson, Cynthia. "The Virgin of Zeitoun." *Worldview* 16, no. 9 (September 1973): 5–11.

Nisan, Mordechai. *Minorities in the Middle East: A History of Struggle and Self-Expression*. Jefferson, NC: McFarland, 2002.

Nutting, Anthony. *Nasser*. London: Constable & Robinson Limited, 1972.

O'Leary, De Lacy. *The Saints of Egypt*. New York: Macmillan, 1937.

O'Mahony, Anthony. "Coptic Christianity in Modern Egypt." In *The Cambridge History of Christianity: Eastern Christianity*, edited by Michael Angold, 488–510. Cambridge: Cambridge University Press, 2006.

Pennington, J. D. "The Copts in Modern Egypt." *Middle Eastern Studies* 18, no. 2 (April 1982): 158–79.

Plekon, Michael. *Hidden Holiness*. Notre Dame, IN: Notre Dame University Press, 2009.

Raphael Ava Mina, Fr. *Christian Behaviour: According to the St Pope Kyrillos the Sixth*. Cairo: Sons of Pope Kyrillos VI, 2000.

_____. *The Fruits of Love*. Cairo: Saint Mina Monastery Press, 1999.

_____. *The Miracles of Pope Kyrillos VI*. Volume 1. Cairo: Sons of Pope Kyrillos VI, 1983.

_____. *The Miracles of Pope Kyrillos VI*. Volume 2. Sydney: Coptic Orthodox Publication and Translation, 1990.

_____. *The Miracles of Pope Kyrillos VI*. Volume 3. Sydney: Coptic Orthodox Publication and Translation, 1992.

_____. *The Miracles of Pope Kyrillos VI* [in Arabic]. Vol. 9. Cairo: Sons of Pope Kyrillos VI, 1989.

_____. *My Memories about the Life of Pope Kyrillos VI: Part 2* [in Arabic]. Shoubra: Sons of Pope Kyrillos, 1985.

————. *Pope Kyrillos VI and the Spiritual Leadership.* Cairo: Sons of Pope Kyrillos VI, 1977.

————. *Service and Humility in the Life of Pope Kyrillos VI.* Cairo: Sons of Pope Kyrillos VI, 1999.

————. *A Stream of Comfort.* Cairo: Sons of Pope Kyrillos VI, 1989.

Rapp, Claudia. "'For Next to God, You Are My Salvation': Reflections on the Rise of the Holy Man in Late Antiquity." In *The Cult of Saints in Late Antiquity and the Middle Ages: Essays on the Contribution of Peter Brown,* edited by James Howard-Johnston and Paul Antony Hayward, 63–82. New York: Oxford University Press, 1999.

————. *Holy Bishops in Late Antiquity.* Berkeley, CA: University of California Press, 2005.

Reid, Donald. *Whose Pharaohs? Archaeology, Museums, and Egyptian National Identity from Napoleon to World War I.* Berkeley, CA: University of California Press, 2002.

Reiss, Wolfram. *Erneuerung in der Koptisch-Orthodoxen Kirche: Die Geschichte der Koptisch-Orthodoxen Sonntagsschulbewegung und die Aufnahme ihrer Reformansätze in den Erneuerungsbewegunen der Koptisch-Orthodoxen Kirche der Gegenwart.* Hamburg: Lit Verlag, 1998.

Rousseau, Philip. "The Spiritual Authority of the 'Monk Bishop': Eastern Elements in Some Western Hagiography of the Fourth and Fifth Centuries." *Journal of Theological Studies* 23, no. 2 (1971): 380–419.

Roussillon, Alain. "Republican Egypt Interpreted: Revolution and Beyond." In *The Cambridge History of Egypt: Modern Egypt, from 1517 to the End of the Twentieth Century.* Edited by M. W. Daly, 334–93. Cambridge: Cambridge University Press, 1998.

Rubenson, Samuel. "Matta el-Meskeen." In *Key Theological Thinkers: From Modern to Postmodern,* edited by Staale Johannes Kristiansen and Svein Rise, 415–25. Surrey: Ashgate, 2013.

————. "Tradition and Renewal in Coptic Theology." In *BDC,* 35–51.

Samaan el-Syriany, Fr. *The Hermit Fathers.* Translated by Lisa Agaiby and Mary Girgis. Sydney: St Shenouda Monastery Press, 1993.

Samuel Tawadros el-Syriany, Fr. *The History of the Popes of the Chair of Alexandria, 1809–1971* [in Arabic]. Cairo: Hijazi Press, 1977.

Schmemann, Fr Alexander. *The Eucharist: Sacrament of the Kingdom.* Crestwood, NY: St Vladimir's Seminary Press, 1988.

Sedra, Paul. "Review of *Christians versus Muslims in Modern Egypt: The Century-Long Struggle for Coptic Equality.*" *Middle East Journal* 58, no. 3 (2004): 510–11.

————. "Class Cleavages and Ethnic Conflict: Coptic Christian Communities in Modern Egyptian Politics." *Islam and Christian-Muslim Relations* 10, no. 2 (July 1999): 219–35.

Seikaly, Samir. "Coptic Communal Reform: 1860–1914." *Middle Eastern Studies* 6, no. 3 (1970): 247–75.

Serapion, Bishop. "Choosing the Patriarch: Lessons from the History of Our Glorious Church." Los Angeles, 2012.

Shehata, Monir Atteya. *Religious Education and the Clerical College and the Church's Sunday School* [in Arabic]. Cairo: Association of Anba Gregorious, 2005.

Sheldrake, Philip. "Christian Spirituality as a Way of Living Publicly: A Dialectic of Mystical and Prophetic." *Spiritus* 3, no. 1 (2003): 19–37.

Shenoda, Anthony. "Cultivating a Mystery: Miracles and a Coptic Moral Imaginary." Dissertation, Harvard University, 2010.

Shenouda III, Pope. *A Model of Service: The Life of Hegumen Mikhail Ibrahim* [in Arabic]. Cairo: Patriarchate, 1977.

———. "Our Teacher Archdeacon Habib Girgis: Pioneer of Religious Education in Modern Times" [in Arabic]. *Al-Watani*, August 18, 1991.

Shoukry, Mounir. "John XIX." In *CE*, 1351a–51b.

———. "Yusab II." In *CE*, 2363b–64a.

Sisters of Abu Sefein. *Abu Sefein: Biography and History of the Convent* [in Arabic]. Old Cairo: Abu Sefein Convent, 1989.

Skedros, James. "Hagiography and Devotion to the Saints." In *The Orthodox Christian World*, edited by Augustine Casiday, 442–52. Abingdon, UK: Routledge, 2012.

Sladen, Douglas. *Egypt and the English*. London: Hurst and Blacket Limited, 1908.

Soliman, William. "Hegumen Matta el-Meskeen" [in Arabic]. *Sunday School Magazine* 8/9 (1955): 27–42.

Sozomen. *Ecclesiastical History*. In NPNF² 2:179–427.

Sterk, Andrea. *Renouncing the World Yet Leading the Church: The Monk-Bishop in Late Antiquity*. Cambridge, MA: Harvard University Press, 2004.

Strauss, Anselm *Mirrors and Masks: The Search for Identity*. Cambridge: Cambridge University Press, 1959.

Sundkler, Bengt, and Christopher Steed. *A History of the Church in Africa*. Cambridge: Cambridge University Press, 2004.

Suriel, Bishop. *Habib Girgis: Coptic Orthodox Educator and a Light in the Darkness*. Yonkers, NY: St Vladimir's Seminary Press, 2017.

———. "Habib Girgis: Coptic Orthodox Educator and a Light in the Darkness." Dissertation, Fordham University, 2010.

Swanson, Mark N. *The Coptic Papacy in Islamic Egypt*. Cairo: American University Press in Cairo, 2010.

Tadros, Mariz. "Vicissitudes in the Entente between the Coptic Orthodox Church and the State in Egypt (1952–2007)." *International Journal of Middle East Studies* 41, no. 2 (2009): 269–87.

Tadros, Samuel. *Motherland Lost: The Egyptian and Coptic Quest for Modernity*. Stanford, CA: Hoover Institution Press, 2013.

Thompson, Jason. *A History of Egypt: From Earliest Times to the Present*. Cairo: American University in Cairo Press, 2008.

Tignor, Robert L. *Egypt: A Short History*. Princeton, NJ: Princeton University Press, 2010.

Tischendorf, Constantin von. *Travels in the East*. Cambridge: Cambridge University Press, 2010.

Vatikiotis, P. J. *The History of Egypt: From Muhammad Ali to Mubarak*. 3rd ed. Baltimore: The Johns Hopkins University Press, 1985.

_____. *Nasser and His Generation*. London: Croom Helm, 1978.

Vlachos, Hierotheos. *Orthodox Psychotherapy: The Science of the Fathers*. Translated by Esther Williams. Levadia, Greece: Birth of the Theotokos Monastery, 1994.

Van Doorn-Harder, Nelly. *Contemporary Coptic Nuns*. Columbia: University of South Carolina Press, 1995.

_____. "Copts: Fully Egyptian, but for a Tattoo?" In *Nationalism and Minority: Identities in Islamic Societies*, edited by Maya Shatzmiller, 22–57. Montreal: McGill-Queen's University Press, 2005.

_____. *The Emergence of the Modern Coptic Papacy: The Egyptian Church and Its Leadership from the Ottoman Period to the Present*. Cairo: The American University Press in Cairo, 2011.

_____. "Kyrillos VI (1902–1971): Planner, Patriarch and Saint." In *BDC*, 231–42.

_____. "Practical and Mystical: Patriarch Kyrillos VI (1959–1971)." *Currents in Theology and Mission* 33, no. 3 (2006): 223–32.

Van Doorn-Harder, Nelly, and Kari Vogt, editors. *Between Desert and City: The Coptic Orthodox Church Today*. Eugene, OR: Wipf & Stock, 2012.

Voile, Brigitte. *Les Coptes d'Égypte sous Nasser: Sainteté, Miracles, Apparitions*. Paris: CNRS Éditions, 2004.

Wakin, Edward. *A Lonely Minority: The Modern Story of Egypt's Copts*. New York: William Morrow & Company, 1963.

Ware, Kallistos. *The Orthodox Way*. Crestwood, NY: St Vladimir's Seminary Press, 2003.

Watson, John H. "Abba Kyrillos: Patriarch and Solitary." *Coptic Church Review* 17, no. 1 & 2 (1996): 4–48.

_____. "Abouna Matta el-Meskeen: Contemporary Desert Mystic." *Coptic Church Review* 27, no. 3 & 4 (2006): 66–92.

_____. *Among the Copts*. Brighton, UK: Sussex Academic Press, 2000.

_____. "The Ethiopian Servant of Christ: Abuna Abdel Mesih el-Habashy." *Coptic Church Review* 27, no. 2 (Summer 2006): 34–57.

_____. "Signposts to Biography—Pope Shenouda III." In *BDC*, 243–53.

Wellard, James. *Desert Pilgrimage: A Journey into Christian Egypt*. London: Hutchinson & Co., 1970.

Yanney, Rudolph. "Light in the Darkness: The Life of Habib Girgis (1876–1951)." *Coptic Church Review* 5, no. 2 (Summer 1984): 47–52.

_____. "Pope Cyril (Kyrillos) VI and the Liturgical Revival in the Coptic Church." *Coptic Church Review* 4, no. 1 (Spring 1983): 32–33.

_____. "Saint Sarabamon: Bishop of Menoufia." *Coptic Church Review* 8, no. 4 (1987): 109–13.

Zaklama, Nashaat. *The Spiritual Life and Pastoral Message of Pope Kyrillos VI* [in Arabic]. Two volumes. Cairo: Sons of the Evangelist, 2007.

Zeidan, David. "The Copts—Equal, Protected or Persecuted? The Impact of Islamization on Muslim-Christian Relations in Modern Egypt." *Islam and Christian-Muslim Relations* 10, no. 1 (1999): 53–67.

Index

Coptic community
  under Lord Cromer, 33–35
  negative effects of Nasser's policies on,
    277–78
  Six-Day War and aftermath, 365
  See also Muslim *vs* Copt relations
Coptic Orthodox Waqf Organization, 290,
  292–93, 305
Coptic Studies Institute, 326–28, 356
Copt *vs* Muslim relations. *See* Muslim *vs*
  Copt relations
Cromer, Lord (Evelyn Baring), 33–34, 49
Crusades, 274
cursing, 262
Cyril V, Pope (Hanna the Scribe)
  in Baramous before becoming patriarch,
    121
  exile of as patriarch, 58, 198
  Habib Girgis and, 161
  maglis and, 58, 196–99, 212
  passing of, 51–52
  reform and, 199, 212

Damanhur, Egypt, 22
Daniel of Khartoum, Metropolitan, 245
Dawood, Marcos, 109–10, 121, 126–27,
  144, 372
Dawood, Mikhail, 144, 280, 306, 356, 372
Dawood el-Makary, 184
Deir al-Sultan Monastery, 272–73, 299, 379
Demetrius II, Pope, 306
Demetrius of Menoufia, Bishop, 71
Demian el-Muharraqi, 222
Denshawai Incident, 34–35
"*diakonia* experiment." *See* "rural *diakonia*"
Didymus Institute, 332
Dioscorus of Menoufia, 293
Domadius of Giza, Bishop (Michael Khalil,
  Mathias el-Syriany), 174, 321, 369
Dracontius, 233

Ebeid, Makram, 184
echege, 268, 298
Ekladios Youssef, 152
El Alamein, battle of, 250, 263
Encomium (hagiography), 28–30, 48
epiphanies, types of, 117, 262

Esther (mother of Kyrillos VI), 22, 24–26,
  32, 46–48
Ethiopian Church
  autocephaly of, 271, 299
  "Ethiopian problem," 267–73
  Italian invasion of Ethiopia and, 268
  monks of, 118
  and Yusab II, 215
Eustathius of Sebaste, 310
Eutychius of Constantinople, 137
exorcisms, 170–71, 189, 347–48
Ezana, King, 268

Fadel, Alfred, 54
Fahmy, Marcos Bey, 110, 126–27, 144–45
Fakhry, Ahmed, 154, 182
Farouk, King, 152, 274
Fouad, Hassan, 96–97, 116, 124–26, 141
Free Officers Movement, 206, 274
Frumentius, 267–68

Gabriel of St Antony's Monastery, Bishop,
  209, 215, 242
el-Gawhary, Boutros, 163
Gawish, Sheikh Abdel Aziz, 35
Gayed, Nazir. *See* Shenouda III, Pope
general bishops, 312, 321, 328, 349, 353
Georg, Johan, 154
Georg, Johann, 56
Ghali, Boutros, Pasha, 35–36, 49, 196
Ghalloush, Ahmed, 25
Giamberardini, Gabriele, 183
Girgis, Azmi Farid, 131
Girgis, Habib
  nominated to be Metropolitan of Giza,
    205
  nominated to the *maglis* and papacy, 161,
    185
  reform and, 165–66, 187, 350–51,
    160–162
  Saad Aziz and, 318
  Salib Suryal and, 189
  Shenouda and, 329
  Sunday School Movement and, 161–62,
    165–66
  Waheeb Atallah and, 322
  the West and, 186

Endorsement by Pope Tawadros II

Pope Kyrillos VI, the 116th successor of the patriarchs of the Apostolic See of Alexandria, is a figure of great spiritual stature who was immersed in the depths of monastic life and a life of unceasing prayer. His patriarchate was characterized by authentic spiritual thought, faith, and manifest virtues. The history of his life grants him a well-attested place as both monk and patriarch. During his patriarchate the Virgin Mary appeared at her church in the suburb of Zeitoun in Cairo, appearing brilliantly for more than two years. He also brought back the relics of St Mark, the pure apostle and martyr, in addition to establishing in Cairo the largest cathedral in the Middle East.

I personally received a special blessing in that his sister, Mrs Shafia, was the principal of the Coptic school in Damanhur where I attended primary school (1960–1964). When I was sitting my final examinations (1969/1970), my mother received a special blessing from Kyrillos VI and a prayer for my future, and oh, how my family rejoiced! After I became patriarch in November of 2012, at the first meeting of the Holy Synod in 2013, we canonized Kyrillos VI as a saint forty-two years after his departure; I consider this a special grace in the first year of my service as patriarch.

We ask for his prayers and intercessions for our sakes, and I commend Rev. Dr Daniel Fanous for this important study, which I consider a scholarly and outstanding addition to the history of our Coptic Orthodox Church.

My sincere love and gratitude,

Pope Tawadros II
118th Pope of Alexandria and Patriarch of the See of St Mark

Cairo, 1st of June 2019
The Feast of the Lord Christ's Entry into Egypt